POWER PERSUASION

MOVING AN ANCIENT ART INTO THE MEDIA AGE

MARY ROSE WILLIAMS
CHRISTOPHER NEWPORT UNIVERSITY

MARTHA COOPER

Line Editor: Karen Gill
Content Editor: Lloyd Rohler
Text Design: Kevin Cook
Cover Design: Kevin Cook

For information about the videotapes designed to accompany this book, write or call:

The Educational Video Group
291 Southwind Way
Greenwood, Indiana 46142
Phone: (317) 888-6581
E-Mail: evg@iquest.net
Fax: (317) 888-5857

ISBN 1-889388-08-4

Printed in the United States of America

In Memorium:

This edition is dedicated to the

memory of Martha Cooper

whose original scholarship and skilled authorship

made this book possible.

PREFACE

As the title of the book suggests, we are concerned with the power of persuasion as this complex form of communication has evolved over time, especially as persuasion is practiced through various media. The book explains theories and reviews research about persuasion from a variety of sources. We attempt to integrate theories about persuasion that emerge from different disciplines (e.g., rhetoric, communication theory, media studies) and in different contexts (e.g., interpersonal, group, mass) to provide a coherent picture of how the practice of persuasion has evolved to its present state. The accompanying videotape includes a variety of messages illustrative of persuasion in the media age that exemplify those theories and research findings.

In producing the third edition, we have retained the central features of the first edition while improving the the content of the book and videotape by integrating contemporary examples to illustrate theoretical concepts. Hence, readers will find the overall organizational structure of the book familiar even as some of the material within is quite new and different. Readers familiar with the previous edition will find the most extensive changes in Chapters 1, 9, and 11.

The book continues to be organized in terms of three broad perspectives toward persuasion: the Classical Perspective, the Symbolist Perspective, and the Institutional Perspective. These perspectives are intended to capture both the classical roots of persuasion and more contemporary developments regarding its practice and study. Chapters 2 through 5 examine the Classical Perspective from its roots in Aristotle's theory of rhetoric to contemporary developments concerning evidence, reasoning, attitude-change, credibility and image-management. Chapters 6 through 9 investigate the Symbolist Perspective. Our explanations of theoretical concepts such as symbols, form, and identification are anchored in Kenneth Burke's theoretical and critical work, but we also integrate theories about language and nonverbal communication from aesthetics, semiotics and critical media studies with findings from social scientists about message designs and compliance-gaining behaviors. Chapters 10 through 14 are devoted to an Institutional Perspective that emphasizes the importance of institutions, communication technologies and the persuasion industries to the process of persuasion; they draw from theories about media and culture to investigate persuasive campaigns, social movements, ideology and propaganda.

As with the first edition, the book and videotape are designed to provide an integrated and multimedia approach to the study of persuasion. Each chapter begins with background information about a particular case of persuasion and ends with an extended analysis of that case that is based on theory and research about persuasion as it appears in the body of the chapter. The accompanying videotape provides sample messages on which these case studies are based. Some of the cases concern "classic" examples of persuasion, such as the famous "Daisy" political spot aired by the Johnson campaign during the 1964 presidential race between Lyndon Johnson and Barry Goldwater. Other videotaped examples concern important historical events: Franklin D. Roosevelt's famous "War Address" and excerpts of Leni Riefenstahl's classic propaganda film *Triumph of the Will* are illustrative. Others provide insight into more contemporary and ongoing cultural problems: public service announcements concerning AIDS and a film by the United Farmworkers of America advocating a grape boycott are of this type. Some messages on the videotape are typical public addresses delivered in political forums, such as the excerpt from former President Ronald Reagan's "Facts are Stubborn Things" speech. Others operate in the private sector, such as the commercial spots for Kentucky Fried Chicken. Some of the videotape examples illustrate the symbols and images of popular culture, such as the commercial for Oldsmobile that stars William Shatner and his daughter Melanie; others reflect both popular culture and the latest advances in communication technology, such as the excerpts from GOPTV. Readers familiar with the second edition will note the inclusion of three new cases and accompanying video segments: a biographical film of George W. Bush entitled, "President with a Purpose," Electronic Data Systems' "Herding Cats" commercial, and documentary film and television commercials from the Tourette Syndrome Association.

As with the first two editions, we are most concerned about the needs of people who participate in persuasion in the role of receivers rather than senders. Hence we emphasize the ways in which receivers can empower themselves by exercising skills of appreciation and criticism. While much of the information contained in the book is useful for those with practical concerns about crafting and presenting persuasive messages, the book is not a "how-to" manual. We have continued our interest, from the first edition, in examining persuasion as an instrument of power that entails ethical issues. Hence each chapter continues to provide discussion of both effects and ethics. However, an explicit and enlarged discussion of power and ethics now occurs in Chapter 1.

ACKNOWLEDGMENTS

All three editions of the book have benefited from the help and support of many individuals and institutions. Content Editor Richard L. Johannesen read and commented on the entirety of the first edition and the major revisions in the second edition. Lloyd Rohler served as content editor for this edition. Roger Cook of The Educational Video Group secured the footage and permissions for all of the videotaped examples. Northern Illinois University, Ball State University and the University of Oregon provided various support for the first edition. We are thankful to all of our colleagues who provided valuable input regarding the first two editions. Any errors or omissions remain the responsibility of the authors.

VIDEOTAPE CONTENTS

Chapter 1: The 2000 Bush Convention Film

Chapter 2: *The Truth About Semi-automatic Weapons*, an NRA documentary

Chapter 3: "Facts Are Stubborn Things," excerpts from Ronald Reagan's address to the 1988 Republican Convention

Chapter 4: "Minneapolis" and "New York City," two public service spots produced by the Centers for Disease Control

Chapter 5: Four KFC commercial spots

Chapter 6: Melanie and William Shatner "This Is Not Your Father's Oldsmobile" commercial

Chapter 7: "Declaration of War," Franklin D. Roosevelt's address to Congress

Chapter 8: The "Daisy" campaign spot, produced for the Lyndon Johnson campaign

Chapter 9: Electronic Data Systems, "Herding Cats" commercial

Chapter 10: Segments from GOPTV *Rising Tide*

Chapter 11: Tourette Syndrome Association documentary, *I'm a Person Too*, and national commercial.

Chapter 12: *No Grapes*, produced by United Farmworkers

Chapter 13: Gillette, " "The Best a Man Can Get"," a North Atlantic Shaving Group commercial

Chapter 14: *Triumph of the Will*, excerpts of the film produced by Leni Riefenstahl.

TABLE OF CONTENTS

PREFACE v
Acknowledgments vi
Video Tape Contents vii
TABLE OF CONTENTS .... **viii**

Chapter 1—Defining Persuasion: Key Issues **1**
FOCUS ON: *A President with a Purpose: The Sky's the Limit* 1
THEORETICAL FOCUS: Defining Persuasion 2
Persuasion in Contemporary Society 3
Defining Persuasion 4
The Range Of Persuasion 5
Perspectives Toward Persuasion 10
Persuasion And The "Myth Of Objectivity" 12
Assessing Persuasion 13
Persuasion and Ethics 16
CRITICAL FOCUS: *A President with a Purpose: The Sky's the Limit* 17
Critical Questions 17
NOTES 21

Chapter 2—The Classical Perspective **22**
FOCUS ON: NRA Defense Of Semiautomatic Weapons 22
THEORETICAL FOCUS: Persuasive Strategies Adapted To The Audience 23
Classical Theory 24
Contemporary Developments 29
CRITICAL FOCUS: National Rifle Association Documentary 35
Critical Questions 35
NOTES 40

Chapter 3—The Rational Human And Reasonable Argument **43**
FOCUS ON: Ronald Reagan's "Facts Are Stubborn Things" Address 43
THEORETICAL FOCUS: Arguments 43
Arguments Described By The Toulmin Model 44
Data—What Do We Accept As Evidence? 47
Familiar Patterns Of Thinking—Common Sense 48
Ethics And Tests Of Evidence And Reasoning 51
CRITICAL FOCUS: Reagan's Address To Republican Convention 55
Critical Questions 55
NOTES 60

Chapter 4—Motivation Theory And The Passions **62**
FOCUS ON: Motivating Americans To AIDS Awareness 62
THEORETICAL FOCUS: Emotions, Attitudes and Psychology 63
Foundations: Aristotle's Analysis Of The Emotions 64
Contemporary Developments In Motivation Theory 69
Ethical Issues In The Tactical Use Of Emotional Appeals 75
CRITICAL FOCUS: Public Service Announcements About AIDS 76
Critical Questions 77

NOTES ... 82

Chapter 5—Credibility And Image Management ... 85

FOCUS ON: KFC and "The Colonel's Way" ... 85
THEORETICAL FOCUS: Ethos And The Personal Influence Of Persuaders ... 86
Classical Foundations: Ethos ... 87
Contemporary Credibility Research ... 87
Charisma And Image Management ... 91
Ethos, Ethics And Image ... 97
CRITICAL FOCUS: KFC and "The Colonel's Way" ... 99
Critical Questions ... 100
NOTES ... 103

Chapter 6—The Symbolist Perspective ... 107

FOCUS ON: Finding A "New Generation" Of Oldsmobile Buyers ... 107
THEORETICAL FOCUS: Symbols And Identification ... 108
Symbolist Theory ... 109
The Process and Functions of Identification Through Symbols ... 114
The Two Realities: Empirical And Symbolic ... 120
The Problem Of Ethics From The Symbolist Perspective ... 121
CRITICAL FOCUS: Oldsmobile's "New Generation" Buyers ... 123
Critical Questions ... 123
NOTES ... 127

Chapter 7—Language And Persuasion ... 129

FOCUS ON: Language And Persuasion: FDR's 1941 "War Message" ... 129
THEORETICAL FOCUS: Language And Persuasion ... 130
Naming And Creating Reality ... 131
Figurative Uses Of Language ... 139
Ethics: Language And Persuasion ... 144
CRITICAL FOCUS: Roosevelt's War Message ... 148
Critical Questions ... 149
NOTES ... 152

Chapter 8—Nonverbal Symbols And Persuasion ... 157

FOCUS ON: The "Daisy" Political Ad ... 157
THEORETICAL FOCUS: The Power And Range Of Nonverbal Symbols ... 158
Conventionalized Nonverbal Symbols: Emblems And Icons ... 159
Delivery And Nonverbal Behaviors ... 162
Constructed Images And Persuasive Potency ... 166
Ethics of Nonverbal Symbolism and Reality-Fictions ... 171
CRITICAL FOCUS: The 1964 Johnson Campaign "Daisy" Spot ... 173
Critical Questions ... 173
NOTES ... 177

Chapter 9—Form And Structure ... 180

FOCUS ON: EDS—Herding Cats Commercial ... 180
THEORETICAL FOCUS: Form ... 181
Psychology Of Form ... 183
Message Structures ... 188
Compliance-Gaining ... 196
Ethics Of Form And Structure ... 199
CRITICAL FOCUS: Electronic Data Systems Herding Cats Commercial ... 201

Critical Questions 201
NOTES 204

Chapter 10—The Institutional Perspective 208
FOCUS ON: Political Institutions,The Media And GOPTV 208
THEORETICAL FOCUS: Defining The Institutional Perspective 210
Formal Communication Institutions 214
Redefining The Audience—Conformity 225
Flow Of Persuasive Messages 228
Ethical Concerns From An Institutional Perspective 230
CRITICAL FOCUS: GOPTV's *Rising Tide* 233
Critical Questions 233
NOTES 238

Chapter 11—Persuasive Campaigns 242
FOCUS ON: Tourette Syndrome Association 242
THEORETICAL FOCUS: Characteristics Of Persuasive Campaigns 243
Stages Of The Campaign Cycle 246
Persuasive Strategies And Tactics In Campaigns 251
Ethics In Persuasive Campaigns 256
CRITICAL FOCUS: Tourette Syndrome Association Awareness Campaign 259
Critical Questions 260
NOTES 263

Chapter 12—Persuasion And Social Movements 265
FOCUS ON: The Movement To Combat Pesticides In California Grapes 265
THEORETICAL FOCUS: Social Movements 266
Characteristics Of Social Movements 267
Stages Of Social Movements 274
Ethics And Social Movements 281
CRITICAL FOCUS: Organization and Tactics in the "*No Grapes*" Movement . 283
Critical Questions 283
NOTES 287

Chapter 13—Ideology 290
FOCUS ON: Advertising And The Ideology Of Masculinity 290
THEORETICAL FOCUS: Ideology, Worldview And Persuasion 292
Characteristics Of Ideology 292
The Building Blocks Of Ideology 294
Stages Of Ideology Formation 303
Ethical Concerns Regarding Ideology 310
CRITICAL FOCUS: "The Best a Man Can Get" 313
Critical Questions 314
NOTES 318

Chapter 14—Propaganda And Persuasion 322
FOCUS ON: Nazi Propaganda, *Triumph Of The Will* 322
THEORETICAL FOCUS: Propaganda 323
Characteristics Of Propaganda 324
Classical Analysis Of Propaganda 328
Propaganda In The Modern Institutional Society 335
Ethics And Propaganda 340
CRITICAL FOCUS: Triumph Of The Will 342
Critical Questions 342
NOTES 348

INDEX 351

I

DEFINING PERSUASION: KEY ISSUES

IN THIS CHAPTER:

Focus on:

A President with a Purpose: The Sky's the Limit **2000 Bush Campaign Film**

1. Theoretical Focus: Defining Persuasion
2. Persuasion in Contemporary Society
3. Defining Persuasion
4. The Range of Persuasion
   - The Intentional/Unintentional Dimension Of Persuasion
   - The Implicit/Explicit Dimension of Persuasion
   - The Sender/Receiver Dimension of Persuasion
   - The Public/Nonpublic Dimension of Persuasion
5. Perspectives Toward Persuasion
6. Persuasion and the "Myth Of Objectivity"
7. Assessing Persuasion
8. Persuasion and Ethics
9. Critical Focus: *A President With A Purpose: The Sky's The Limit.*

FOCUS ON: *A PRESIDENT WITH A PURPOSE: THE SKY'S THE LIMIT* 2000 BUSH CAMPAIGN FILM

Sometimes defining just what is and what is not a persuasive message can be a difficult problem. That was the case in 1984 when Ronald Reagan's campaign managers presented the major television networks with an unusual message.[1] At the Republican National Convention that year, the party told the networks that their candidate for president, Ronald Reagan, would be introduced by a film rather than by the more traditional introductory speech. The Republican campaign staff referred to the 18-minute film, titled *A New Beginning*, as a documentary about Reagan's first term of office. Journalists, on the other hand, described the film as "very creative advertising." And NBC's Tom Brokaw commented that "the Democrats and other commentators would probably call it propaganda."

The concern for whether *A New Beginning* was a documentary or was some form of persuasion stemmed from the perception of media executives that their coverage of the film depended on its classification as either a persuasive message or an informative message. If the film was a documentary, with the attendant implications that it was objective, factual and educational, then the media might broadcast it uninterrupted as part of their news programming. If, on the other hand, the film was simply a long campaign commercial, then shouldn't the Republican party purchase the airtime for its showing? Or, if the film was campaign propaganda, and if a network did show the film, didn't the broadcast journalists have a responsibility to warn the viewing public that what they were about to see was not news but an attempt at persuasion?

In 1984, all three networks decided that the Reagan film was a persuasive message. However, each of the networks chose a different strategy for dealing with this unique persuasive message. CBS showed only brief clips of the film while it was being viewed in the convention hall and aired an explanation by Bill Plante concerning why CBS was not showing the film in its entirety. ABC, meanwhile, called in media analyst Jeff Greenfield, who compared the Reagan film to a previously unbroadcast film about Walter Mondale, thereby treating the existence of the film as an object for political commentary rather than an instance of hard news. Only NBC showed the film in its entirety. Joseph Angotti, NBC's director of political coverage, explained: "I don't understand this business about not showing the film because it's 'Propaganda'. What's the difference between a film and a speech? We're here to cover an event." Still, decisions had to be made about just how to show this clearly persuasive message that some believed bordered on propaganda. NBC spent considerable time explaining to viewers just what persuasive tactics were used in the film and analyzing what was omitted from this story of the Reagan presidency.

In 1988, both George Bush, the Republican candidate, and Michael Dukakis, the Democratic candidate, offered the networks and their viewers introductory films. Similarly, in 1992, both incumbent George Bush and his Democratic challenger Bill Clinton offered films, as did Clinton and his rival Bob Dole in the 1996 election. By the 2000 campaign, videotaped biographies for the candidates were a convention tradition. The concern over whether or not to air the candidates' videos became moot as C-SPAN and the Fox News networks broadcast the conventions in their entirety.

Although the novelty of the videos has worn off and a media savvy audience has come to recognize them for the persuasive messages that they are, the initial case of the convention films points to the everyday importance of knowing what constitutes a persuasive message and deciding how to deal with such messages. Questions about what constitutes persuasion has implications for news management policies that affect what millions of viewers see on their television screens. If a biographical film is identified as persuasive, for example, media executives face difficult decisions about how to present such a film to a viewing public who might or might not be aware of its persuasive impact. At the conclusion of this chapter we turn our attention to *A President with a Purpose*, the biographical film of George W. Bush, that aired at the 2000 Republican National Convention.

THEORETICAL FOCUS: DEFINING PERSUASION

In this chapter, we are concerned with the problem of defining persuasion. There are several reasons for tackling this question. From a theoretical point of view, we want to understand what various means of influence exist among people and how we can explain their workings. From an ethical point of view, we want to understand the limits on our attempts to influence one another. And from a practical point of view, we want to understand what it means when we are or are not being subject to influence.

We will first consider the range of persuasive messages that confront people daily. Following this, we will consider both a general definition of persuasion and key issues which allow the entire range of persuasion theories to be grouped into three broad theoretical perspectives for studying persuasion. These three perspectives provide the basis for the remainder of this book. Later in the chapter we offer a set of critical questions that are useful in determining whether any particular message or communicative interaction is properly labeled "persuasive." This critical focus is applied to the case of the 1992 Clinton campaign film, *The Man From Hope*.

PERSUASION IN CONTEMPORARY SOCIETY

We live in a world in which persuasion and the power to persuade are of extraordinary importance. From the earliest theorists to the present, the art of persuasion has been connected to the democratic institutions that are the heart of our culture. When we list "freedom of speech" first among our rights as citizens guaranteed by the Constitution, we remind ourselves of the right to speak, to write, to express ourselves and to have access to the words and ideas of others as fundamental principles upon which our way of life is founded. The independent streak so much a part of the American character is based on our conviction that any of us has the right to "speak our minds." The concern we Americans have with civil rights and human rights comes in part from our belief that no distinctions of class, race, religion, gender or affiliation should prevent us from being able to influence the people and institutions around us. Even in our everyday lives persuasion occupies an important place. In the wide range of interpersonal influence taking place in relatively unstructured, face-to-face encounters everyday, we influence others' attitudes, beliefs, values and behaviors and are similarly influenced by others.

Not only is our culture fundamentally a culture built on persuasion, but persuasion also plays an important part in our personal lives, making each one of us "who we are": The image each of us has of ourselves as this or that sort of person—as a good or bad person, as likeable, honest, funny or talented—is influenced powerfully by our interactions with others. From early childhood, significant others, peer groups and authority figures play an important role in determining what we value, how we behave, what we believe—in short, who we are. This self-image is further shaped, modified and intensified by the multitude of persuasive messages we are exposed to in the media. Advertisers show us images of personal comfort, good grooming, high fashion, physical attractiveness, achievement and popularity. We are then encouraged by these persuaders to examine ourselves to see how we "measure up."

From the newspaper waiting on our doorstep when we wake up in the morning to the announcer on the nightstand radio as we fall asleep, we are immersed in a sea of persuasive messages. Some are obvious: the billboards we pass on the way to work or class, the television spot by the political candidate or the salesperson who phones us at home to sell some product. Others are less obvious: the feature film we see for entertainment, the news broadcast we watch for information or the professor whose lectures we attend. But all of these and more—indeed, just about all of the actions that humans perform around one another—are potentially persuasive, at least to some extent.

As some of these examples suggest, part of the reason our lives are saturated by persuasion is that we live in a culture dominated by the mass media. Not only are we a culture that places great importance on the ability to communicate with and influence others, but we have enabled ourselves to pursue that end as no other culture in history, through print, broadcast and cable television, radio, film, computer networks, video and audio recording, computer-generated mass mailings—and on and on. These communication technologies, both old and new, and the institutions that control them and work through them have tremendous power and presence in our lives, and they shape our attitudes, beliefs, values and actions in many obvious and subtle ways.

Defining Persuasion

In this section we arrive at the main purpose of this chapter. We begin the process of defining "persuasion," specifying what theoretical, ethical and practical matters it includes. Almost as important is a second term: "message." Careful thought about the definitions of these terms is all the more important because both are common words that we hear used rather carelessly in everyday conversation. Our aim in this book is to move beyond this careless, everyday attitude to a more precise understanding of the subject.

We begin with a definition deliberately formulated to be general and inclusive; after that, and in later chapters, we will turn to definitions that are narrower and more limited. In the broadest possible sense, *persuasion encompasses the processes by which language and actions influence the choice-making of ourselves and others.* Notice that this preliminary definition contains four important assumptions, about process, language and action, influence and choice-making. Later in this book we will look at three very broad and very different theoretical perspectives in the study of persuasion. Each of these traditions will, in turn, begin from different initial definitions of persuasion. All of these theoretical perspectives, however, share the assumptions contained in the broad definition offered here.

First, persuasion is a process. It is the result of a complex interaction of many factors working together, with the various elements and factors both influencing one another and shaping the final outcome.

Second, persuasion uses language and action. "Action" includes all of the behaviors we engage in that are meaningful—that is, that come to represent to others our attitudes, beliefs or intentions. Indeed, from one point of view, language is the most complex, sophisticated and the most essentially human kind of action; but there are other kinds of action as well. This category of action includes such group phenomena as rallies, demonstrations, moratoriums, boycotts or lawsuits; it also includes individual acts of nonverbal (literally: "without language") communication.

Third, persuasion is a process that leads to influence rather than to control. This distinction is important for both theoretical and ethical reasons. First, as Aristotle wrote about the art of persuasion over 2000 years ago, persuasion is an art rather than a science. It has principles that make it work, but those principles can never perfectly explain a particular case of persuasion because their object—how and why humans act and think the way they do—is never perfectly predictable. So even the best, most enduring theories of persuasion, including those we will examine at length in this book, will approach a full explanation of individual cases of persuasion but will never arrive there completely. No final theoretical word explains the meaning of human actions. The distinction between influence and control is also important in an ethical sense. If we want to have absolute, predictable control over the actions of others, persuasion is frankly an inefficient and unreliable way to go about it. Coercion or violence, history has repeatedly shown, are often more effective ways to control others' behavior, at least in the short run.[3] The decision to use persuasion to influence others, rather than these other means of control, represents an ethical decision to seek a humane way to achieve this influence, even if it means that one possible outcome is failure to persuade others to our position.

Finally, persuasion influences the choice-making capacity of ourselves and others. Persuasion is, at its very core, a practical area of study as well as a theoretical one. It is interested in effects and results. How do our actions, planned or unplanned, influence the decisions others make about how to behave, what to believe or value? Similarly, how is our choice-making influenced by the language and action of others? Persuasion is of theoretical interest to us because we want to understand this process by which others influence our choice-making and by which we influence others.

The substance of persuasion is messages. Persuasion takes place when people are exposed to messages with persuasive potential. However, this latter term must also be clarified beyond its "everyday" sense. A message is any behavior or action (including, but not limited to, speaking or writing) by a person or collection of persons which is selectively perceived and given meaning by others. There are two critical components in this definition. First, messages are behaviors or actions; they are things that can be seen, heard or felt. They may be verbal or nonverbal, occurring singly or as clusters of behaviors. Second, a behavior or action only becomes a message when someone else perceives it and attaches meaning or significance to it. Our interpretations of our own behavior are important, but equally important are others' interpretations of our behavior.

THE RANGE OF PERSUASION

If you compare other books and articles about persuasion, you will often notice that this central term, "persuasion," is defined in different ways by different authors. The reason for this is that different scholars are emphasizing different dimensions of this complex social phenomenon called persuasion. In this book, we will examine in detail three broad theoretical perspectives on persuasion, the Classical Perspective, the Symbolist Perspective and the Institutional Perspective. Although all three are perspectives on persuasion, as we described it earlier in this chapter, the three perspectives place very different limits on themselves and their area of study. Many of the key differences among these three perspectives can be explained as different positions with regard to four definitional issues. The terms of our general definition of persuasion, earlier in this chapter, were designed to reveal the similarities of the various theoretical perspectives reviewed throughout this book. By contrast, these four issues are designed to help us recognize the important differences among the various theories of persuasion in this book. These four fundamental dimensions of the persuasive process help to characterize how persuasion functions in our society and clarifies the roles played by the creators and audiences of persuasive messages.

Let us examine each more closely and then briefly note how they will help differentiate the Classical, Symbolist and Institutional perspectives on persuasion.

THE INTENTIONAL/UNINTENTIONAL DIMENSION OF PERSUASION

Is "persuasion" limited to intentional attempts to influence others, or does it include unintentional influence as well? Theories of persuasion draw the limits on this question differently, depending on what the theories were designed best to explain. For example, within the Classical Perspective, which we examine in Part II of this book, an important goal of theory is to help persuaders make good strategic choices in preparing messages, analyzing their audiences and presenting themselves. Thus, theories in this tradition (discussed in Chapters 2 through 5) tend to be interested only in intentional acts of persuasion; they typically have very little to say about unintentional instances of influence. Similarly, in the theoretical literature studying persuasive campaigns, including political and advertising campaigns (Chapter 11), and in many traditional forms of persuasive propaganda (Chapter 14), the focus is on a form of persuasion that is highly strategic and under centralized control. Here, too, theory tends to emphasize intention in persuasion and to pay little attention to unintended effects.

On the other hand, some theories of persuasion focus primarily on how audiences relate to and interpret messages, with very little regard for the question of the intention of the message-maker. Frequently, this perspective turns on the assumption that we cannot not communicate. That is, we cannot choose not to communicate in the presence of others, because even the attempt to avoid communicating may be viewed by others as meaningful and hence communicative.[4] So long as A and B are aware of one another, any of A's behaviors or actions that B perceives and finds meaningful becomes a message, regardless of A's intention in the matter. For example, if you notice another student on the first day of class, perhaps paying attention to how he is dressed and making some initial judgments about what he is like, you have made meaning of some behaviors and actions regardless of whether or not your new classmate intended for you to do so. Thus, from this point of view, persuasion sometimes can take place without deliberate intent by a persuader. The Symbolist Perspective, which we examine in Part III of this book, contains many theories which begin from this point of view. While the use of language, of nonverbal symbols and of message form and structure (discussed in Chapters 6 through 9) are elements which a persuader may strategically—that is, intentionally—try to control for persuasive effect, the main interest of the Symbolist Perspective is in understanding how audiences process and respond to messages. The question of the message-maker's intentions are often a minor part of the equation. Similarly, one of the main forms of institution-level persuasion, which we discuss in Part IV of this book, is ideology or ideological persuasion (Chapter 13). Essential to the power of this form of persuasion is that it perpetuates a world view and legitimates existing arrangements of social and political power often *without* the awareness of the persuaders involved. The purpose of advertisements for products such as toys and grooming aids is to sell merchandise, of course. And yet, as we will see in Chapter 13, such advertising—with or without the awareness or intent of the advertisers—also accomplishes another function: It socializes us into often unthinking acceptance of "proper" interpretations of masculinity and femininity in our culture.

THE IMPLICIT/EXPLICIT DIMENSION OF PERSUASION

Is "persuasion" limited to those forms of communication which are treated as explicitly persuasive, such as the campaign speech, the commercial advertisement or the editorial; or does it also include those genres of communication in which the persuasive dimension is at most implicit, such as entertainment, education, news reporting, artistic creation and so on? One of the most intriguing aspects of persuasion is that it often appears in a form that doesn't seem to be persuasion at all, yet under certain conditions the persuasive character of messages is made explicit for all to see. When teachers' union representatives sit down with school board members to discuss contract terms, the persuasive nature of their behavior is probably understood and accepted by all. Similarly, when a salesperson strikes up a conversation with us about the features of one of the products on the showroom floor, we all understand that this is persuasion, not a simple exchange of pleasantries. Often people who try to persuade us will say so up front, telling us that they are asking for money for charity or supporting a referendum on a local ballot. Many theories of persuasion are specifically directed to explaining such explicitly-persuasive phenomena. For example, the principles of ethics discussed in Chapters 2 through 5 specifically assume that both persuader and audience have acknowledged the persuasive purpose behind the persuader's words and actions.

However, other kinds of messages are implicitly persuasive, rather than explicitly persuasive, and as a result different theories may be better able to account for their persuasive potential. For example, the critically-acclaimed 1993 *Philadelphia* chronicled the plight and subsequent legal battle of a high-powered, young attorney in Philadelphia who contracted AIDS and, after notifying his employer of his health problem, was summarily dismissed from his job. Although this film was produced and viewed as "entertainment," it undoubtedly contributed to the ongoing public discussion about AIDS and provided a popular frame of reference for actual legal battles about discrimination against AIDS patients. It would be difficult to say with certainty that the film was explicitly persuasive, but it certainly was an instance of implicit persuasion. Indeed, many might argue that the film's persuasive potential was increased precisely *because* it was not explicitly persuasive. Audiences who might not even view a film on the subject of AIDS that was *explicitly* persuasive (perhaps a documentary) might very well attend and be influenced by a dramatic film on the subject.

Not only can entertainment be implicitly persuasive; news reporting can be as well. As we will discuss in Chapter 10, the simple fact that an event is covered by the news media typically causes audiences to believe that it is, therefore, significant or important. Similarly, the process by which 22 minutes of "news stories" for a one-half hour television news broadcast is selected out of the hours and hours of videotape available will inevitably shape and distort our perception of world events in predictable ways. Thus this selecting and editing process makes even news reporting persuasive, but implicitly so.

A third communicative arena in which persuasion is generally implicit is the classroom. Educators (and their textbooks!) are tacitly understood to have points of view on topics other than the course subject matter. Only genuinely unreasonable people imagine that educators would be much better at filtering out their own commitments than anyone else is. Doubtless, if you are reading this book as a part of a college course on persuasion, your instructor will have many opportunities to express his or her opinions on many inviting topics, including the many case study topics featured in the various chapters. No one really expects that such expression will not take place, only that it be done in accordance with tradition (and perhaps policies) that require that such attempted persuasion not draw attention to itself.

The reasoning behind these examples is clear: in our society we typically treat "entertainment," "education" and "news" as different kinds of messages than "persuasion," and we listen to them differently, interpret them differently and respond to them differently. Advertisers for children's shows must go out of their way to signal the difference because of parents' concern that children will not be able to understand the difference between these different communication modes otherwise. To five-year-olds, an animated commercial featuring their favorite cartoon characters may be no different from an animated cartoon featuring that same character. Thus government regulators, at parents' insistence, have intervened to protect these young viewers until they are experienced enough to be able to distinguish explicit and implicit persuasion on their own.

Conversely, other situations and social roles may require that all persuasion be kept implicit. Etiquette itself might even be defined as the art of persuading others in social situations without drawing attention to the fact that persuasion is going on. Most of us have experience with such social techniques as disguising a command as a question or a request. In a similar vein, certain situations or roles may require that negative feedback must be given in the most indirect manner possible, so that no attention is drawn to the attempt to influence the behavior or actions of others.

The Sender/Receiver Dimension of Persuasion

Is "persuasion" primarily the study of the strategic and ethical choices of persuaders/senders, or is it principally the study of the responses of audiences/receivers? Those theoretical approaches which are primarily interested in understanding persuasive strategies, in developing the skills of persuaders or in formulating ethical guidelines for persuaders will understandably focus primarily on the actions and choices of the persuader. From this point of view, the reactions and choices of the audience are of less importance, except insofar as they suggest directions for the persuader's strategic or ethical choices. The study of credibility and *ethos*, long one of the most important areas of persuasion theory and the subject of Chapter 4, has for obvious reasons been persuader-centered. Similarly, the characteristic issues of persuasive campaigns tend to focus on strategic and ethical choices made by candidates, campaign managers or advertising agency specialists. The goal-driven character of such persuasion makes the emphasis on persuader, rather than audience, a natural one.

However, some theoretical perspectives find it useful to place the emphasis on receivers and audiences, not senders, writers and speakers. Even in intentional acts, wherein persuaders may decide what tactics they will employ, it is audiences who are the final arbiters of persuasion. In Chapters 6 through 9, the Symbolist Perspective, we will examine in detail how the motives and values of an audience set the limits on persuasion. Furthermore, in our study of ideological persuasion (Chapter 13) we will discover that there are certain forms of persuasion for which the task of identifying a *specific source* (perhaps in order to assign legal or ethical responsibility) is all but impossible, facing us with the possibility of a persuasive discourse for which no one is "in charge." But there is also a practical reason why the study of persuasion should be audience-centered. Persuaders require the support, understanding or action of an audience. If their objectives could be reached without persuading anyone, presumably they would do so. So whether we consider examples of intentional persuasion or unintentional persuasion, the critical factor in understanding its outcome becomes the audience.

The Public/Nonpublic Dimension of Persuasion

Is "persuasion" limited to influence through public communication or does it include nonpublic or interpersonal communication as well? "Public" and "private" are very important terms in the understanding of persuasion, and any definition of persuasion will usually be shaped in some way by the distinction between "public" and its alternatives, which for now we lump together for the sake of convenience as "nonpublic." For our purposes, the two terms refer to different roles within which persuaders cast themselves and their audience. A role is defined by a set of often unspoken rules telling us how to act appropriately for a particular social position. Each of us plays many roles in the course of a day—student, neighbor, son or daughter, husband or wife, voter, customer, dinner guest and so on. And, of course, we may play more than one role at the same time, depending on whom we are with and what we are doing.

Certain people, such as political figures, play a special role in our society as "public figures." The rest of us, even though we are not public figures, are nevertheless at certain times "the public." Many of the persuasive messages we encounter in our lives—speeches, pamphlets or advertisements for political campaigns—specifically address us as voters and as members of political communities, in short, as members of the public. When we say that such a role should be taken seriously, we mean that its special character as an audience for persuasion should be respected. When an audience member approaches a persuasive message from the standpoint of her role as a citizen empowered to participate in the democratic process, she may expect campaigns to respect her ability to weigh issues, to evaluate the competing candidates' claims fairly and soberly and to balance our society's celebration of individual freedom with her sense of "the public good." When political campaigns do not do so—when they pander to selfish, private interests or treat her as if she lacks the common sense and judgment necessary to be a good citizen—she may become angered, disillusioned, cynical or alienated by the entire campaign process. To call an audience "a public," then, is to conceive of them as a collective of responsible, thoughtful people; it means we give them credit for using standards of judgment and acting on motives and interests that we value highly in our society. Theories of public persuasion have a long and distinguished history and are discussed in detail in our investigation of the Classical Perspective and elsewhere.

Nonpublic, as the counterpart to public, refers to different kinds of role relationships between audience and persuader. When we relate to a persuader as the public to public figure, we are understood (at least in theory) as making choices based on reasonableness, careful judgement and a sense of public good. However, there are other persuasive roles for persuader and audience. Two that we will consider in Chapters 10 through 14 we call consumers and the masses. Consumers are the audiences for commercial persuasion: persuasion designed to sell products and services. As an audience, consumers are typically assumed to be capable of becoming very informed on a subject (think about the knowledge you may carry around in your head about cars, clothes, home electronics or your favorite television series). Like the public audience, the consumer audience is understood as making careful and often reflective choices. Unlike the public audience, however, the members of the consumer audience are understood to make their decisions based on private gain or personal tastes rather than public good. Moreover, the typical approach of consumer persuasion to its audience is to stratify the audience—dividing it according to income, age, life-style, education or other demographic variables—and to address itself only to those segments of the audience most crucial to persuasive success. We typically differentiate between public audiences and consumer audiences on both theoretical and ethical grounds. For example, First Amendment law typically accords less protection to commercial speech than to political speech .

A second type of nonpublic audience for persuasion is typically referred to as the masses or the mass audience. As we will see in our examinations of ideology and propaganda (Chapters 13 and 14), the principle of conformity generally disregards individual demographic characteristics such as age, sex, income or life-style, instead conceiving of the audiences in terms of the famous "lowest common denominator," a gross measure of what the masses seem capable of digesting. Mass persuaders commonly pretend that their audience is a collectivity, with no individual preferences or distinguishing characteristics, and are interested in them primarily for their ability to act, not to judge, decide or learn. The chief pressure in mass persuasion is the pressure to conform—to avoid being different, to forego any claim to individuality, to blend seamlessly into the mass. The concept of audience as a mass is most relevant to persuasion that occurs in social movements and propaganda (Chapters 12 and 14). However, the pressure on people to conform to mass thinking (or, perhaps more appropriately, mass action) underlies any concept of the audience as "mass."

Perspectives Toward Persuasion

Throughout this book we will draw on various theories regarding persuasion, all roughly grouped under the general definition we proposed earlier in this chapter. Each is made distinct, however, by its different answers to the four issues we discussed in the previous section. Although different theories were developed to illuminate different aspects of the all-encompassing phenomenon of persuasion, we will see that the ability to compare theories and apply them by analogy to new areas for which they were not originally intended can lead to important insights. Sometimes a theory of persuasion designed to explain a unique type of persuasion, such as a public oration, is equally helpful for explaining another type of persuasion, such as a 30-second television spot, even though the original theorist never dreamed of the forms that contemporary persuasion might take. In other cases, new techniques and forms of persuasion simply cannot be explained by earlier theories, requiring the development of new theories.

We believe that the most productive way to obtain the benefit of a multiplicity of theories about persuasion while retaining a focus on persuasion as we broadly define it is to place diverse theories in an organizing context we term a perspective. A perspective is a way of viewing, a stance for observing something, giving a clear view of some parts of the object (while causing other parts of it to recede or disappear). By focusing on different dimensions of the persuasive process and reviewing theories that sometimes start from very different definitions and assumptions, we can gain different perspectives on the persuasive process. But by continually returning to the definitions and assumptions laid out in this chapter, those perspectives can each provide a coherent understanding of the process.

In the chapters that follow we will examine three major perspectives on persuasion: the Classical Perspective, the Symbolist Perspective and the Institutional Perspective. Each of these perspectives is useful in studying persuasion; each includes theoretical principles that arose from the unique persuasive activities going on at the time.

The Classical Perspective began with the writings of Aristotle, some four centuries before the common era, and contemporary developments from this perspective continue to shape and guide much of the research in persuasion today. The Classical Perspective is most typically characterized by a concern for explicit and intentional persuasion in the public realm. The Classical writers were concerned with how persuaders make choices among different strategies, depending upon the audience and situation, in order to be successful in influencing their audience. Contemporary theorists, also interested in particular strategic choices and their adaptation to an audience and situation, often are concerned with implicit and private persuasion as well as the more traditional explicit and public persuasion. The Classical Perspective on persuasion and its contemporary developments will be covered in Chapters 2 through 5.

The Symbolist Perspective is a more distinctively 21st Century approach to understanding persuasion. The Symbolist Perspective and its contemporary developments investigate the ways in which all persuasion is really "self-persuasion"—that is, how persuasion involves the active (even if unseen) participation of audiences in order to be effective. This natural tendency to participate in our own persuasion is called "identification." Central to the Symbolist Perspective is the recognition that human beings are creatures of symbols just as surely as fish are creatures of the water. We are creatures who, by our nature, understand and respond to symbols. While the Symbolist Perspective generally applies equally well to either public or nonpublic persuasion, it is generally audience-centered, emphasizing how audiences interpret and respond to messages and the implicit and often unintentional dimension of persuasion. However, like the Classical Perspective, the Symbolist Perspective also provides insight into explicit persuasion. The various kinds of symbols and the various ways in which symbols and symbolic form can promote identification will be examined in Chapters 6 through 9.

The third section of this book examines the Institutional Perspective on persuasion, a division of a different sort than the first two. While the Classical and

Symbolist perspectives are major *theoretical* distinctions in understanding how persuasion works, our discussion of institutional persuasion is organized around four important varieties of persuasive *practices* that arise in society, particularly contemporary society. Classical treatments of persuasion tend to be best at giving insight into speaking before public audiences, because that was the dominant form of persuasion at the time of its beginnings. For us today, "live" public speaking is comparatively rare, while mediated, mass persuasion by the government, by religious and educational institutions and by corporations is far more commonplace. Therefore, in this section of the book we examine persuasion taking place at the institutional level, in which institutions may act as the persuaders, the audience or the context within which persuasion takes place. Some of these institutions are public, while others are not. The persuasion emanating from these institutions, taking place within them or directed toward them is sometimes explicit and at other times implicit; at times it is intentional and other times unintentional. In Chapters 10 through 14 we will use these dimensions of persuasion to examine four kinds of institutional persuasion: persuasive campaigns, social movements, propaganda and ideology.

Persuasion And The "Myth Of Objectivity"

Our general discussion of persuasion and message and the more specific theoretical issues which followed it lead to one other issue deserving special mention here. While we stress that it is at times theoretically or ethically useful to draw a distinction between messages that are "persuasive" and those that are "simply informative" and this distinction is a popular and familiar one, we seriously question whether that distinction can usefully be made in most cases of actual practice. As we noted above, any message is at least theoretically capable of influencing the choice-making capacity of those who are exposed to it; all messages are, therefore, at least potentially persuasive.

Political anthropologist F. G. Bailey has linked the popular belief that we can produce messages that are "factual" and "informative" without being persuasive to a cultural myth—it may be called the "myth of objectivity."[5] Our culture places great value on the ability to "be objective." When someone tells us to be objective, they usually mean something like the following: be neutral rather than taking sides; be descriptive rather than evaluative; be detached and dispassionate rather than taking sides; be informative rather than persuasive. In Chapter 2 we will discuss the history of these assumptions and the philosophy behind them. Now, it is enough to simply note that most people assume not only that "being objective" is possible, but it is often the more effective and ethically superior way to influence others.

Yet, this ideal of "objectivity" is unreachable. Everything we say and do reflects our motives, desires, attitudes and preferences. What could be important enough to us to be worth communicating, yet still be something about which we are neutral and disinterested? Even if there could be something from which we were "objectively" detached and yet motivated to communicate, once we attempt to put our ideas into language we immediately enter the realm of persuasion. We have frequently tried to demonstrate this idea to our students by asking them to write paragraphs about men and women. One paragraph should be positive, a second negative and a third neutral. Students find it fairly easy to write positive and negative paragraphs. However, the neutral paragraphs tend to be much shorter; some are only a sentence. Even seemingly neutral sentences like, "Women are the opposite sex of men," tend to carry a value loading. For example, to be opposite is usually perceived as less valuable than being the same in our culture. In addition, the phrasing of this seemingly neutral sentence seems to make men the standard to which women are compared, thereby indicating a higher value to men than to women. Many students simply cannot produce any sentences they can comfortably describe as purely neutral. The lesson of this exercise is clear. Anything which is important to us is almost impossible to express in purely objective terms. As we will elaborate further in Chapter 7, language is inherently persuasive. Anything we try to express through language becomes filtered and influenced by our attitudes and values, our world-view, whether we mean for this to happen or not.

Nevertheless, as a society we cling to the ideal of objectivity, and it is important to reflect upon why this is so. We do so because, imperfect and troublesome as it is, the ideal of objectivity has been a useful one. We know that responsible and effective persuaders have thought clearly about their own motives and recognize what their commitments and values are. We know that it is usually better to avoid inflammatory or chauvinistic language when attempting to persuade others. We know that groups are more likely to make better decisions in an atmosphere where as many points of view as possible can be considered, rather than a single point of view.

The "myth of objectivity" has three implications for students of persuasion. First, any human social act has the potential to be persuasive in some degree. Objectivity is not the natural human state: concern, care and involvement with our world are included in the natural human state. Our actions toward others will inevitably reflect this commitment and involvement. Second, the "forms and mannerisms" of objectivity are still very important to understanding persuasion and practicing it successfully. Journalists who do not know how to separate expressions of their opinions from the prose they write cannot hope to understand why their editors or readers respond to them as they do, because such unawareness inhibits their ability to meet audience expectations. Conversely, editorial writers who never move beyond a dry recitation of "the facts" to a call for action rarely succeed, because when they abdicate their responsibilities as persuaders they also forfeit many resources available to their craft. Third and most important, that unworkable and certainly unreachable ideal of objectivity serves to remind us that persuasion involves a decision to appeal to others in ways that empower and dignify all those who take part. We do not persuade our furniture; we simply place it where we want it. That call, "be objective," is at least a reminder that we are dealing with human beings here, creatures of judgment, integrity and passion, who should be treated as such and thereby be allowed a fair chance to decide how to respond to our persuasive attempts.

ASSESSING PERSUASION

Twenty-five centuries ago, Aristotle explained that rhetoric, or persuasion, was the offshoot of ethics and politics.[6] Ever since, students of persuasion have been concerned with the relationship of persuasion, power and ethics. The fundamental structure of this relationship is well understood. *Politics*, the art of establishing and maintaining power, is grounded in *ethics*, individual moral choices and in *rhetoric*, the ability to recognize and use the persuasive resources around us. Moving the ancient art of rhetoric into the media age only amplifies the importance of this connection. Consequently, two themes that must be considered when assessing persuasion in contemporary society are power and ethics.

A persistent issue regarding persuasion is the nature of the relationship between persuasion and power. Ancient theorists, such as Aristotle, treated persuasion as a skill that could be used strategically to exert power. Instead of physical force, the skilled orator could wield verbal force. A citizen could become powerful as an adept persuader, rather than by virtue of birthright, money or physical resources. Numerous examples in this book provide contemporary confirmation for this classical approach to persuasion and power. Moreover, the classical notion suggested that effective persuasion can compete with even physical violence as a motivating force for change in human attitudes and behavior. The persuasive efforts of charismatic leaders like Gandhi or groups of ordinary people, such as members of the Civil Rights Movement, testify to the possibility of confronting physical force with persuasion. Thus, persuasive speaking is frequently treated as an instrument of power, a means by which to influence others. This approach has persisted through the centuries as new communication technologies replaced the old.

The Classical Perspective, however, assumed that because anyone could speak at a public gathering anyone could take on the role of persuader and thereby wield the power of persuasion. Because contemporary persuasion frequently occurs through the mass media, not everyone has easy access to the channels of persuasion. In countries such as mainland China, where governments control tightly the channels for communication, opposing points of view are unlikely to find their way into the media. Even in liberal democracies, many ideas, events and perspectives are absent from the mosaic of messages because of the cost of buying media time or the preferences of those who control the media. Dissident and minority voices can be silenced because a particular world view prevails and labels such voices as foolish, ignorant or out-of-step with the times, even in societies where formal protections for free speech and press exist. Constraints on the free exercise of persuasion by a diversity of people are further complicated by the tactics of campaigns and social movements that alter our perception of what is news, what is worthy of media coverage and even what our values and myths and world views should be. Within a fairly open communication system, potential persuaders may need to do more than produce messages; they may need to develop new channels of communication as well. The proliferation of chat rooms and personal web sites, or the production of independent documentary films on social issues testifies to this need. Thus from an Institutional Perspective, the struggle for power involves a struggle for control over the means of communication and persuasion as surely as it entails the preparation and presentation of persuasive messages. However, the struggle for control over the means of communication that is inherent within the Institutional Perspective retains the classical notion that the ability to persuade is the route to power.

Another aspect of the classical notion is that the power of persuasion resides with persuaders, those skilled in the craft of making and presenting messages. This view appears to neglect the power of audiences as either receivers or co-creators of meaning. The Symbolist Perspective provides an alternative view of the relationship between persuasion and power by recognizing that people confer meanings on messages that often fall outside the explicit intentions of persuasion. Thus, much persuasion is self-persuasion. From this perspective, it may seem as if messages hold the key to power because of the words, images or forms they embody. Almost instinctively, human beings endow such language and nonverbal cues with persuasive force. But because—as the Symbolist Perspective suggests—receivers give those messages meaning, we can use the Symbolist Perspective as a basis for locating power in the hands of receivers.

The primary way that receivers exert power during the process of persuasion is by choosing to attend to some messages rather than others. We all construct a mosaic of meaning from the message fragments that confront us daily.[7] As we piece together a snippet from the morning news, an image from a familiar advertisement, a conversation with a friend, an article that we read and countless other communicative exchanges, we develop our attitudes and beliefs about everything from consumer products to social issues. Our construction of such a mosaic offers an area for claiming our power as receivers of persuasion. We may choose when, by whom and for what reasons we are willing to be persuaded. Such choice, however, is dependent on our ability to make our way through the maze of competing messages by analyzing carefully those to which we direct our attention. Only by uncovering the structural pattern of a message, investigating the connotative meaning of a particular linguistic construction or determining the likely effect of a particular visual image can receivers consciously choose to allow themselves to be persuaded. Otherwise, receivers abdicate their power to those who design and present messages. By critically evaluating messages, then, receivers are in a better position to exercise choice in persuasion.

Traditional approaches to persuasion—whether Classical, Symbolist or Institutional—suggest that critical analysis is primarily beneficial for its contribution to our resistance of persuasion. For example, by uncovering the errors in a political speaker's presentation of the facts or by noting the sexual exploitation common to the depiction of women in contemporary advertising, receivers are better able to reject those messages and resist persuasion. Another possibility, less frequently suggested, is that such critical analysis will allow receivers to choose their preferred means of persuasion. Uncovering the persuasive potential of messages can just as easily assist a receiver in furthering the process of persuasion. By becoming aware of how we are being persuaded, we can take more responsibility in those situations where we want to persuade ourselves. For example, many people desire personal growth of the type envisioned by psychologist Abraham Maslow, as we discuss in Chapter 4. Knowing the grounds for self-persuasion can provide a key to individuals seeking self actualization. Similarly, some people may want to persuade themselves about issues such as social justice, racial equality or environmental protection. They may want to identify with a particular community of shared interests. Again, critical analysis of the messages around them may enhance such individual attempts to build and identify with the community of their choice. Instead of allowing marketers to define who they are by their demographic characteristics, individuals can create who they are by consciously choosing the messages to which they attend. But doing so requires critical analysis. Once we are aware that a certain type of advertisement or television show or film entails a world view with which we identify, we may choose to attend to that type of message and, as a result, define a new market. In ways such as these, receivers can turn the power of persuasion to their own advantage, thus empowering themselves.

Persuasion and Ethics

Making choices about whether to persuade or to be persuaded and how to engage in the process of persuasion necessarily entails moral judgments. Hence, it is not surprising that the relationship between persuasion and ethics is of continuing concern. From the Classical Perspective, ethical questions concern the means of persuasion and are typically directed toward persuaders. From the Symbolist Perspective, ethical concerns center on the outcomes of persuasion and the world view or sources of identification that are promoted, placing receivers in a position of responsibility. The Institutional Perspective—with its concern for large audiences and complex organizations as sources for persuasive messages—blurs the lines of ethical accountability for sources and audiences alike.

It is tempting to bypass the whole subject of ethics when confronted with persuasion in the media age, because persuasion seems somewhat removed from individual responsibility and accountability. Yet, it is within the Institutional Perspective that some of the most pressing moral problems emerge most clearly. Propaganda, for example, is frequently associated directly with immoral or amoral persuasion. Few could deny that the effectiveness of many propaganda campaigns—Hitler's Nazi campaigns, for example—is far overshadowed by the immorality and ethical problems of such campaigns. Similarly, the study of ideology alerts us to subtle forms of persuasion that easily escape ethical investigation. The sexual exploitation that characterizes depictions of women in contemporary advertising and the relentless competitiveness that permeates some depictions of masculinity in advertising are notable more for their moral implications than for what they imply about effective persuasion. Numerous decisions about campaigns and social movements and their attendant persuasive tactics are similarly bound to ethical concerns. The result is that ethical considerations appear to be even more important as we move to an Institutional Perspective toward persuasion.

As with the relationship between power and persuasion, the relationship between ethics and persuasion seems easier to untangle if we are able to analyze persuasive messages critically. Approached only from a technical perspective within a complex organizational structure that depends on the division of labor, many artists, media writers, film producers or legislative aides may not consider themselves to be persuaders. Yet, each individual who contributes to the production of even a fragment of a message within our culture holds the potential for persuading others. If there are no formal lines of ethical responsibility regarding the end-product, ethical concern must rest with those individuals who contribute to the production of a message. Ethical questions about strategy, tactics and effects are provided throughout this book and should provide a starting point for all who have potential for persuading others. But ethical responsibility does not lie solely with persuaders. As audience members as well as persuaders, we must take responsibility for the messages that circulate within our culture. Especially from the Symbolist Perspective, the importance of receivers determining what world view they are affirming when they attach particular meanings to particular words, nonverbal cues or message structures is clear. From an Institutional Perspective, such choices by receivers take on even greater significance as those choices influence the distribution of power. Critical analysis thus provides a way to exercise ethical responsibility by exposing ideologies that are morally problematic or propagandistic messages that define some human beings out of existence. When ethical concerns are a part of such critical analysis, the impact of that analysis goes beyond merely claiming one's power as a receiver to empowering both self and other for the greater good.

CRITICAL FOCUS: *A PRESIDENT WITH A PURPOSE: THE SKY'S THE LIMIT*

In this chapter, our primary interest has been simply defining the territory covered by the term "persuasion." To help you apply this discussion of the characteristics of persuasion, consider the following list of questions. The questions are not really designed to help you determine whether or not some message is actually persuasive. They investigate neither the effectiveness nor the ethics of particular persuasive tactics. Instead, as befits this early stage of the book, these questions simply investigate the potential of a message to be persuasive.

CRITICAL QUESTIONS

1. Is the message in a **context** we would ordinarily call a persuasive context?
2. Is the message **similar to other messages** that have appeared to be persuasive or have been called persuasive?
3. Does the creator of the message **acknowledge persuasive intentions**?
4. Does the **principal audience for the message** seem to indicate that the message is persuasive in intent?
5. Does the message seem **capable of producing some change** in the attitudes, values, beliefs or behaviors or of **reinforcing** an already existent behavior or attitude in its likely audience?
6. How are the concepts of **power** and **ethics** relevant to the message?

Following the controversy about Reagan's convention film in 1984, George Bush's media consultants advised shortening the 1988 Bush film from 16 to 7 minutes in the hope that networks would be more willing to air it.[8] However, as Lane Venardos, Vice President of Special Events for CBS news and executive producer of the network's convention coverage, explained: "Length is not the issue; it never has been. The issue is content."[9] As our critical questions suggest, we believe the issue is more than just content. When in doubt about whether or not a message is persuasive, these questions provide a more comprehensive method for deciding. We will consider each question in regard to the George W. Bush film of 2000, *A President with a Purpose.*

Certain situations or contexts—such as law courts or commercial breaks during a television program—are so closely linked to persuasion that any message occurring in them may be treated as potentially persuasive. To determine whether or not the Bush film is persuasive, then, we can examine the context, asking what kind of persuasion is expected in such a context and why such persuasion is expected. Shown at the 2000 Republican National Convention, the film was part of a media extravaganza to showcase the Republican Party. While in years past candidates were actually chosen at political conventions, contemporary procedures typically insure that a party's candidate will have been selected by the time the convention takes place. As a result, the convention functions more as a public relations event, providing a forum whereby the party can obtain free media coverage that will show the public the unity and virtues of the party. So, even though a political convention is covered by a broadcast news team, the convention itself functions like a rally, a persuasive event designed to rally the faithful and find new converts. Because the nature of the event is persuasive, it is likely that a film that constitutes part of that event will also be persuasive.

Another way to analyze the persuasive potential of the film is by determining whether or not it is similar to other messages that have been deemed persuasive. This is a particularly useful method if the message is novel or unique. If a message resembles more familiar messages that we would treat as persuasive, then perhaps this message deserves to be treated in the same way. Finding specific similarities is particularly helpful in making such determinations. The introductory film for George W. Bush, of course, followed the pattern established by films for Reagan, Bush the senior, Dukakis, Dole and Clinton. Perhaps more important than this direct comparison, however, is a comparison of the film to other persuasive messages. In 1984, some journalists had referred to Reagan's film as a campaign advertisement. Certainly the same could be said of Bush's film. In appearance and style, the film resembles many campaign spots as it takes advantage of music, direct address by the candidate, testimony of family and members of his Texas constituency and nostalgic pictures to present an image of Bush. Furthermore, as with his father's in 1988, George W.'s film focuses heavily on his family to present a message about the candidate's values and life style.

A more obvious way to recognize messages as persuasive is by determining whether or not the message-makers themselves acknowledge that they mean to influence us in some way. The fact that the 2000 campaign was tightly controlled and strictly scripted in advance suggests convention managers recognized the potential persuasive power of all messages of the convention and thus might be considered an acknowledgement of the persuasive intentions of the film. Furthermore, with only a change in lighting and the in-person appearance on stage of the candidate to separate the film from the speech, the film seems to be part of the speech itself—a speech in which, Bush told *The New York Times*, he would make a low-key appeal to Democrats and Republicans alike, to accept him. Finally, the music used in the film is the same music used in Bush's campaign commercials, which clearly are intended by the message-makers to be persuasive.

One may also determine if a message is persuasive by asking if the principal audience for the message is likely to be in a decision-making role. By asking what choices the audience can make and why the message-maker would find such choices important we can determine if the message has persuasive potential. The immediate audience for the Bush film was the assembly of delegates at the convention. However, perhaps more important were the viewing audience who watched any number of television channels that carried part or all of the convention, and the virtual audience who experienced the event via Internet chat rooms, streaming video, and on-line magazines. All of these audiences were important to Bush because of the choices they could make. The American citizenry ultimately would choose or not choose Bush as their executive leader. The convention delegates would more immediately decide how much of their time and money to contribute to the campaign effort.

Certain messages—such as warning signs or heavy metal rock lyrics—are sometimes treated as if they are potentially persuasive, simply on their own merits or as though they would be capable of influencing anyone who was exposed to them. However, in more ambiguous cases, it is helpful to ask if the given message is capable of producing or reinforcing some change in the audience. Doing so requires identification of the content of the message that seems capable of producing change and specifying the sort of change that it seems capable of producing.There is little question that the film is capable of producing some change in the attitudes, values, beliefs or behaviors of the persons who were exposed to it. The delegates in the convention hall were being primed for Bush's acceptance speech. The film was a vivid reminder to them of who their candidate was, his roots, his family and his personal qualities. Similarly, the film introduced George W. to the viewing public who may have been less familiar with his personal accomplishments and qualities that with his family heritage.

The film carried through the conventions' theme of 'purpose' largely through implication. First, the film begins with Bush implying that purpose means having a vision of where he wants to lead. Bush's vision is one of inclusion; he looks toward "a day that everybody in this country feels that the great American dream belongs to them as much as anybody else." How he pictures that dream comes out of his perception that Americans feel a sense of loss. "There's a kind of life I think that a lot of Americans feel is slipping away: safe for kids everywhere, baseball, barbecues, football games after church." Picturesque images of the Texas landscape, a flag raising at a boy scout camp and children playing baseball reinforce the Norman Rockwell-like wholesome qualities of the American dream that Bush envisions.

Second, the man with purpose takes responsibility for making life better for everyone. Testifying to her son's sense of duty, for example, Barbara Bush relates how at age seven, George W. assumed the responsibility of helping his parents through the death of his sister. Perhaps in an effort to assure anti-abortion Republicans without alienating the more moderate pro-choice Republicans and Democrats, Bush implies that responsibility means giving birth and being a parent. Describing how he felt at the birth of his twin daughters, Bush explains, "there was an incredible feeling of life and the preciousness of life, and I realized I was responsible for loving them with all my heart and all my soul, and I was going to be responsible for helping get them a good education." That sense of responsibility extends to helping to improve society as a mentor and, as Governor, supporting education programs.

The film implies that Bush's purpose is different from that of the administration of his opponent. His direct references to family values along with the testimony by knowledgeable others of his ethical nature suggest that he will not bring scandal to the White House as did Clinton. His appearance with school children and his work as a mentor also imply that he will make the Office of the President respectable and one to which children once more will want to aspire.

A purpose of unity and unity of purpose also are implied in the film and reflect the overall theme of the 2000 Republican National Convention. All non-family members appearing in the film are either black adult professionals or black, smartly dressed, well-mannered school children. Gone is the rascism that underpinned the Willie Horton ads of George Bush, Sr.'s campaign against Dukakis. Further, unity of purpose is promoted in the subjects to which Bush attends in the film. Such topics as educational opportunity for all children; family and American values; and honesty, character and trustworthiness, are ones with which no one inside or out of the party are likely to take offense or oppose.

Finally, to have purpose also means being patriotic. Bush's lack of war experience obviated the type of battle images that appeared in the senior Bush's and Bob Dole's films of the two previous conventions. To convey George W.'s sense of patriotism the film presents a montage of images of great people and moments in America's history. Included are the statue of Lincoln, Martin Luther King, Jr. at the March on Washington, astronaut Neil Armstrong speaking from the moon, John F. Kennedy at his inaugural and Ronald Reagan at Nuremberg. Quoting other famous people, Bush's voice is interspersed with those of Armstrong, Kennedy and Reagan; thus audiences are encouraged to view Bush as patriotic by association. The film concludes with a profession of his pride and his love of America and of being an American.

By using the critical questions provided in this chapter, it is fairly easy to conclude that the Bush film was a persuasive message. Just what to do about airing the film once it was determined to be persuasive was a thornier question for the major networks when the first introductory video was produced in 1984. As new forms of messages continue to be developed, however, the question remains relevant. When messages present audiences with choices that have consequences, is it reasonable to consider what guidelines should be followed in presenting them. One possbility would be to surround the message with commentary that makes its persuasive content readily apparent to the viewer.

Is such forewarning helpful? A study of the earlier case of Reagan's 1984 film suggests that such commentary, or forewarning, does not particularly affect how an audience views such persuasive messages.[10] When subjects were exposed to the film with commentary, they tended to like the film more than when they were exposed to only the film, without commentary. The investigators were particularly suprised by this finding, especially given the popularity of inoculation theories that suggest that if an audience were forewarned it would be more able to resist persuasion. Consequently, the investigators formulated several explanations for why NBC's appeared to be so ineffective in assisting audiences in resisting the persuasion of the Reagan film. First, they argued that perhaps the audience responded to the film as a film, rather than as a persuasive message. Second, they observed that maybe the discursive logic of the commentary was simply an inappropriate weapon with which to combat the narrative logic of the film. Finally, they explained that the audience might just be receiving the film as entertainment rather than as a potentially persuasive message.

All of the explanations for why audiences were not affected by NBC's commentary about Reagan's film are grounded in the notion that audiences didn't really watch the film as a persuasive message. Our analysis of Bush's film suggests that it too is a persuasive message, but would forewarning about its persuasive potential be helpful for a viewing audience?

This book is grounded in the belief that you will find it helpful to be able to analyze persuasive messages. But analysis requires more than just noticing that a message is persuasive; analysis requires an ability to adapt critical skills to different kinds of messages. In the chapters that follow, we will be surveying a variety of theoretical perspectives and their accompanying critical tools for analyzing persuasion.

NOTES

1. For a summary of the controversy surrounding the Reagan film, see Herbert W. Simons, Don J. Stewart and David Harvey, "Effects of Network Treatments on Perceptions of Political Campaign Film: Can Rhetorical Criticism Make a Difference?" *Communication Quarterly* 37 (1989): 184-189.
2. "Webs Undecided Over Airing Convention's Biopic on Bush," *Variety*, 10 August 1989, 37.
3. Some scholars argue that even coercion is a type of persuasion and on occasion may be ethical. For such a discussion, see Chapter 12; see also Richard L. Johannesen, *Ethics in Human Communication* , 3rd ed. (Prospect Heights: Waveland, 1990), p. 86. We do not include physical force and coercive violence as a symbolic action in our general definition of persuasion.
4. This concept was first elaborated by Paul Watzlawick, Janet Helmick Beavin and Don D. Jackson, *Pragmatics of Human Communication* (New York: W. W. Norton, 1967), pp. 48-51.
5. F. G. Bailey, *The Tactical Uses of Passion* (Ithaca: Cornell UP, 1983), pp. 29-41.
6. Aristotle, *On Rhetoric: A Theory of Civic Discourse*, trans. George A. Kennedy (New York: Oxford UP), p. 53.
7. For an explanation of the mosaic-model of communication that emphasizes the role of receivers in constructing coherent meaning from message fragments provided by the media, see Samuel L. Becker, "Rhetorical Studies for the Contemporary World," in *The Prospect of Rhetoric*, eds. Lloyd F. Bitzer and Edwin Black (Englewood Cliffs: Prentice-Hall, 1971), 33.
8. "Pieces of Reagan Film Aired: Length, Content Reasons for Cuts," *Variety* 17 August 1989, 35.
9. "Pieces of Reagan Film Aired," 35.
10. Simons, et. al., "Effects," 84-198.

2
THE CLASSICAL PERSPECTIVE

IN THIS CHAPTER:
Focus on:
National Rifle Association Documentary

1. Theoretical Focus: Persuasive Strategies Adapted to the Audience
2. Classical Theory
3. Contemporary Developments
    - Philosophy and the Emphasis on Formal Logic
    - Psychology and Emphasis on Motivational Factors
    - Social Research and Credibility Factors
4. Ethics in the Classical Perspective
5. Critical Focus: National Rifle Association Documentary

FOCUS ON: NRA DEFENSE OF SEMI-AUTOMATIC WEAPONS

For many years concerned citizens in the United States have argued about the appropriate interpretation of the Second Amendment to the constitution that guarantees a citizen's right to keep and bear arms. For some, the part of the amendment referring to the necessity of a "well regulated Militia" leads them to conclude that this right is significantly restricted and not a blank check for just anyone to own and use any sort of weapon. Others have interpreted the amendment broadly to protect nearly anyone's right to own and use practically any weapon. The pervasiveness of gun related crimes in our society, reflected by the fact that we lead the world in violent crime statistics, has led to numerous debates concerning gun control.

An incident which fueled this debate occurred in 1989. On January 17 of that year, Patrick Purdy opened fire on a schoolyard of children in Stockton, California. He was armed with an AK-47 rifle. Beyond the children that he killed and wounded, Purdy psychologically wounded many terrified witnesses to this crime as the tragic event was relayed through the media to a general public shocked by the senseless and brutal violence of his act.

Purdy's assault provided impetus for those who had long advocated stricter regulations concerning the sale and ownership of guns. Shortly after the incident, more than 30 state legislatures considered resolutions or bills to prohibit the manufacture, sale or possession of semiautomatic weapons like the one used by Purdy in his deadly attack on the school playground. On March 13, 1989, the California legislature became the first to pass such a bill. Similar measures were introduced at the national level; the most prominent of these was Senator Metzenbaum's proposal to prohibit the manufacture and importation of assault firearms and to strengthen gun registration laws. President George Bush, who less than a month before had stated his support for a less restricted right to bear arms, including semiautomatic weapons, reversed his decision and banned all imports of semiautomatic assault rifles.[1]

In the midst of the movement to prohibit or severely restrict the availability of weapons like those used by Purdy, the National Rifle Association reacted by producing a multiplicity of persuasive messages designed to halt quick passage of more restrictive gun control laws. With approximately 2.8 million members and a $70 million annual budget, the National Rifle Association has been a vocal and often effective opponent of any attempt to strengthen gun control in the United States.[2] The Association's $12 million annual budget for lobbying has allowed it to influence national and state policies concerning gun control for many years.[3] During the controversy in 1989, the association placed full-page advertisements in numerous magazines and newspapers, deluged their membership with pamphlets and materials to aid them in contacting their political representatives about the issue, contracted and ran several television spots concerning the issue, arranged for lobbyists to speak directly to legislative and Congressional committees who were attempting to fashion restrictive legislative proposals, and produced a short documentary entitled "The Truth About Semi-Automatic Weapons." The documentary was sent to members of the U.S. Senate and House of Representatives as well as to various state legislative representatives and was made available to numerous members of the National Rifle Association and the general public. We examine this documentary later in this chapter to illustrate how the Classical Perspective toward persuasion can be used to understand explicit attempts to persuade an audience. However, before we move to an analysis of this instance of persuasion, a review of the Classical Perspective is in order.

THEORETICAL FOCUS: PERSUASIVE STRATEGIES ADAPTED TO THE AUDIENCE

For most people, persuasion is a method of influence. In Chapter 1, we define persuasion as a process by which people influence the choice-making of others. The earliest treatments of persuasion as a field of study began with a similar assumption. These early treatments emerged during the ancient world of the Greek and Roman democracies. Consequently, some features of the theory of persuasion developed by classical thinkers were influenced by ideas common to public citizenship of that time and the instances of persuasion they commonly observed in their culture. In this chapter, we introduce the theoretical perspective toward persuasion initiated by the classical theorists and preview contemporary investigations of persuasion that follow the Classical Perspective.

During the classical period, most persuasion involved a single speaker who presented his case to an audience of fellow citizens. Such persuasion tended to be explicit—the audience was aware that they were being asked by the speaker to make a choice. The classical theories of persuasion provided advice to persuasive speakers about what to say and how to say it such that these ancient orators could influence their audience by taking into account their predispositions. In addition, these early theorists of persuasion were concerned that their advice be used for good rather than evil objectives and, as a consequence, considered the ethical boundaries that should govern a speaker's use of persuasive strategies.

The contemporary developments that we preview in this chapter exhibit similar concerns. While the types of messages concerned have shifted from just public addresses to include contemporary commercial advertisements or other modern forms of persuasive action, many theorists continue to study the strategies available to persuaders and the ethical implications of those strategies. Thus, even though some of the theoretical concepts to be discussed in this and the following three chapters do not draw on classical theory explicitly, they can be characterized as "classical" because they approach persuasion from the same general perspective as initiated by classical thinkers. Fundamental to this perspective is the notion that *persuasion involves strategies that take into account audience predispositions*. The Classical Perspective orients us toward an instrumental view of persuasion in which persuaders are seen as strategists who choose among the persuasive tactics available in order to most effectively persuade their audiences. This perspective orients us toward intentional persuasion, toward instances in which both audience and source are aware that persuasion is the goal, and it directs our attention to the tactics that either assist or inhibit the realization of that goal.

Classical Theory

In the oldest systematic textbook on persuasion, *Rhetoric*, Aristotle began by saying that persuasion is an art because it has principles that make it work. Three of the most important principles are the modes of proof: the means by which a message can influence its audience in intended ways. Aristotle sharply criticized earlier teachers of rhetoric for only teaching how to incite an audience's emotions. He said that is artistically wrong because there is more to the art of rhetoric than pandering to the audience's emotions. He also said that it is ethically wrong because to ignore our capacity to reason is to treat us as if we were animals unworthy of human respect. People are better than that, thought Aristotle, and as persuaders we owe it to them and to ourselves to appeal to what is best (reason and rationality) rather than what is less than the best (emotional responses).

The proper way to influence one another (this was the central value of Athenian culture, a value we still share today in Western culture) was by formulating and delivering arguments. For the Athenians, the public forum provided a place where those arguments could be presented. Today a variety of public forums serve a similar function. According to the Athenians, the best decisions are those in which we reason together to arrive at our conclusions.

Following his mentor Plato, Aristotle called the art of reasoning together to reach conclusions *dialectic*. Dialectic is a kind of scientific or philosophical way of communicating. Within a dialectical conversation people assume an attitude of inquiry, formulate precise definitions through a process of examining like instances and reason carefully and rigorously. Dialectic demands that the people taking part remain open-minded in their search for the truth. Today we don't use the term "dialectic" much, but the idea that people can reason together to arrive at conclusions has remained. Trial by jury, in which a just decision is expected to emerge from a clash between prosecution and defense, illustrates this kind of communication in modern culture. Scientists talking to other scientists about hypotheses is another, perhaps the best, example from our culture.

Aristotle said the goal of rhetoric wasn't so much finding the truth of a matter as convincing an audience to make the best decision about that matter. Rhetoric *assumes* a process of inquiry—you need to have engaged in inquiry about a subject to be an effective and ethical persuader—but it can't help you find the truth if you don't already know it. What rhetoric does, according to Aristotle, is to make the truth or the results of your inquiry effective in the everyday world, the world outside of professional or scientific communication. Rhetoric deals with opinions, with our best educated guesses about what is true, not with absolute certainty. In other words, in the realm of persuasion lies everything in our world where we make decisions about what to feel, think or do *without* the kind of absolute certainty that many suppose science can give us. While dialectic may approach the true and the necessary, rhetoric deals with the probable and the contingent. After all, asked Aristotle, who bothers to argue about things that are already scientifically true? We only argue about those things that might go one way or the other.

Because rhetoric, or persuasion, operates in the realm of the probable and the contingent, ethical questions moved to the forefront of concern for classical rhetoricians. For Aristotle, the problem centered around whether the same persuasive techniques could be used for either good or ill. Simply put, how could one avoid the use of persuasion in the service of falsity? It is unsettling to wonder if all the communicators around us "have an angle," "are conning us" or are to be distrusted. It's disturbing to think that "truth" and "necessity" get to play only small roles in the choices we make while "opinion," or "good reasons" play a very large part. Various answers to the ethical question were offered by ancient thinkers. While Aristotle claimed that "good" positions were easier to defend than "bad" ones, other thinkers such as Cicero and Quintilian maintained that a complete theory of rhetoric or persuasion must include the concept of the "good man."[4] In other words, the ethical question could be settled if orators were trained to be virtuous so that they would strive to argue for morally right positions rather than morally bankrupt ones.

Keeping in mind that the classical rhetoricians viewed oratory, or public address, as the prime example of persuasion in action, we can turn to Aristotle's treatment of rhetoric, or the art of oratory, in order to uncover the major tenets of the Classical Perspective toward persuasion. Aristotle defined rhetoric as "the faculty of observing in any given case the available means of persuasion."[5] Three elements in this definition are important. First, by noting that rhetoric is a "faculty of observing," Aristotle emphasized that rhetoric is an art—a method that can be approached systematically. Put another way, persuasion is the product of that art. This position implies that persuasion is not merely the result of chance or luck, but can be the product of a systematic process or method initiated by a would-be advocate or persuader. Second, by noting that this art or method applies "in the given case," Aristotle's definition implies that persuasion may vary from circumstance to circumstance. In other words, what is persuasive in one situation may differ from what is persuasive in another situation. Finally, Aristotle's definition makes clear that the emphasis of his theory of rhetoric concerns "the available means of persuasion" or the techniques by which persuasion may be accomplished.

Given Aristotle's suggestion that persuasion may vary from case to case, it is not surprising that in the *Rhetoric* he distinguished among the various cases of the practice of persuasion dominant in Athenian culture. He observed that "there are three divisions of oratory—(1) political, (2) forensic, and (3) the ceremonial oratory of display."[6] But more important than the categories of persuasive speaking themselves was Aristotle's basis for distinguishing among them. He explained that the "three divisions [were] determined by the three classes of listeners to speeches. For of the three elements in speech-making—speaker, subject and person addressed—it is the last one, the hearer, that determines the speech's end and object."[7] Aristotle argued that the three types of oratory could be divided according to the type judgment that the audience made as a result of a public address. In political oratory, hearers make judgments about future actions by considering the advantages and disadvantages of particular policies. In forensic oratory, hearers make judgments about past actions by considering the justice or injustice of those actions. In ceremonial oratory, hearers make judgments about present events and people by considering the value and importance of those events and people. By casting the judgment of the audience as the definitive factor for the types of persuasive speaking, Aristotle emphasized the importance of the audience to the process of persuasion.

The audience also emerges as important in Aristotle's discussion of the means of persuasion. Aristotle identified three means of persuasion—*ethos*, *pathos* and *logos*.[8] *Ethos referred to the personal character of the speaker.* Aristotle's notion was that audiences could be persuaded if they perceived a speaker as credible because "we believe good men more fully and more readily than others." *Pathos*, on the other hand, *referred to the psychological state of the audience*. He argued that the emotional state of a hearer could affect persuasion because "our judgments when we are pleased and friendly are not the same as when we are pained and hostile." *Logos referred to the substance of a message, to the arguments presented that provided appropriate proof in the given case.*

With *ethos* and *pathos*, we can readily understand why the audience is important. *Pathos*, after all, is the audience's emotional mind set. *Ethos* depends on the audience's perception of who is credible and what constitutes a "good man." However, the link between the audience and *logos* is not so apparent. For it is tempting to think of *logos* in terms of the subject matter rather than the audience. If a speaker wanted to prove through argument that waging war against another city-state would be advantageous, it would seem reasonable for that speaker to assemble evidence that would suggest the possible benefits of such an action. The need for arguments and supporting evidence to prove the case appear to lead the speaker toward investigation of the subject matter of war rather than toward an investigation of the audience. However, Aristotle noted that along with understanding human character and the emotions as a way of effecting persuasion, an orator must also be able to reason logically. Once again Aristotle argued that our ability to reason logically rests on our acceptance that the audience is the focus of all persuasion. Aristotle believed that humans were fundamentally reasonable people who made decisions on the basis of what made sense. Thus, even *logos* as a means of persuasion rested upon one's concept of the audience; in the case of *logos*, the audience was conceived as reasonable people. This assumption becomes more apparent if we examine Aristotle's discussion of the primary form of argument that he advised using to effect persuasion.

Aristotle argued that *enthymemes* were "the substance of rhetorical persuasion."[9] The enthymeme was the preferred form of argument for Aristotle. Exactly what an enthymeme is has been the subject of much discussion by philosophers and rhetoricians. Aristotle referred to the enthymeme as a "rhetorical syllogism."[10] He had developed the notion of a syllogism in his work concerning dialectic where he described the process of logical reasoning. *A syllogism is a deductive form of argument that consists of a major premise, a minor premise and a conclusion*. Probably the most familiar example of a syllogism is the following: All men are mortal (major premise). Socrates is a man (minor premise). Therefore, Socrates is mortal (conclusion). Within this configuration, three terms (men, mortal and Socrates) are related to one another in order to draw a conclusion about Socrates. Rhetoricians who have studied Aristotle's work point out that a rhetorical syllogism is one in which the audience helps to construct the syllogism by supplying some part of the argument.[11] The rhetorical syllogism, or enthymeme, may be incomplete. For example, in everyday talk a speaker might simply say, "Socrates is mortal." The major and minor premises can be omitted because the audience will likely supply those missing parts. By supplying the common sense idea that men are mortal and the social knowledge that Socrates is a man, the audience participates in the construction of the argument. Put another way, when *logos* takes the form of an enthymeme, the audience provides the materials of the proof as easily as the speaker can.

Furthermore, as an audience participates in the construction of such arguments, those arguments tend to be based on probabilities rather than necessities. Because most common sense ideas and even everyday examples are based on observation and beliefs, they are *usually* true rather than *necessarily* true. The conclusions drawn from such materials are, therefore, only *probably* true rather than *always, necessarily* true. Aristotle and his commentators have pointed out that by encouraging the audience to participate in the construction of an argument, enthymemes depend on beliefs and values already held by hearers. By omitting those premises likely to be supplied by an audience, persuaders reduce the risk of either boring their audiences by explicitly recounting each step of an argument or alienating their audiences by including some premise with which they might disagree. For some conclusions there may exist a variety of premises that could lead the audience to agreement. Allowing the audience to fill in the needed premise increases the likelihood that each hearer will supply the appropriate premise. Such audience participation, in addition, provides the audience a sense of satisfaction with their own ability to reason appropriately. This characteristic of enthymemes is probably most apparent when the enthymeme supplies one or more of the premises but lets the audience draw the conclusion. An audience's adherence to the conclusion can be stronger if they drew that conclusion themselves as a result of the "facts" presented by a speaker. For example, the Clinton campaign film described in the previous chapter provides viewers with a variety of facts about Bill Clinton's life, but leaves the conclusion that Clinton would make a good president to the viewer. The makers of the film counted on the American public to supply their own common sense to reason that the man from Hope was Presidential material. Viewers very likely supplied differing premises about what makes for a good president, but the film provided enough variety about Clinton's background to allow audience members a variety of ways for completing the argument.

Although Aristotle clearly identified the enthymeme as the preferred form of argument within a persuasive message, he also noted a second form of proof—the example. By explaining that the example was the counterpart to induction and could be thought of as "a rhetorical induction," Aristotle underscored his concern for the reasoning powers of an audience in his discussion of *logos*.[12] Logical induction requires a series of instances that are shown to be comparable, from which the advocate may draw a conclusion regarding the class of instances. However, when the induction becomes "rhetorical," the conclusion may not apply to an entire class so much as to another comparable instance.[13] That reasoning process entails only probabilities rather than certainties; examples may reason from one case to another without necessarily implying that the conclusion will hold in every similar instance. Like enthymemes, in which parts of the argument may be omitted for convenience, rhetorical inductions may not include an exhaustive series of examples but may focus on a single instance, relying on the audience to supply other instances from their own experience. Again the audience is expected to help construct the proof furnished by examples during the production of *logos*. Many contemporary television commercials operate with this sort of reasoning. Whether they are advertising pain killers or laxatives, commercials often dramatically portray the ability of their over-the-counter medications to relieve a suffering person's ailments. Most viewers can recall similar instances from their own experience to add to the induction. Yet, most viewers are also aware that the power of these drugs is only usually, not always, effective. Sore throats and headaches sometimes require a visit to the doctor and a prescription drug.

Much of Aristotle's treatise concerning rhetoric is devoted to an exploration of the ideas just discussed. His work considers each type of oratory in turn, revealing the types of enthymemes, the various emotions and the aspects of personal character most relevant to each type. He catalogued an array of arguments typical to Greek oratory during his time and included brief explanations of the subject matter of these arguments (e.g., war and peace, ways and means, etc.). Similarly, he reviewed the nature and causes of various human emotions, from anger to happiness, and suggested the states of mind an orator must understand in order to affect *pathos* in an audience. He provided a discussion of virtue, especially those qualities perceived as virtuous by the ancient Greeks, and other components of personal character of which a speaker who depended on *ethos* would need to be aware. Toward the end of the *Rhetoric*, Aristotle discussed other aspects of public address, such as organization, choice of language, and delivery, that could bear on the persuasiveness of the message. However, his emphasis remained with the three modes of persuasion and how each applied to the ancient Greek audience as he understood that group and how each varied given the type of decision the audience was asked to render.

Later classical writers canonized the various components of the art of oratory into five categories: invention, arrangement, style, delivery and memory. Like Aristotle, Cicero, Quintilian and others emphasized *invention (the discovery and selection of the means of persuasion)*. In doing so, they added details concerning how an orator might find suitable arguments, furnished additional examples of arguments that were deemed reasonable by their respective Greek and Roman audiences, elaborated on the virtues and habits of personal character relevant to their contemporary audiences, and generally tried to provide helpful advice to aspiring persuaders during their times. Hence, their body of work provides the basis for what may be termed a Classical Perspective toward persuasion.

Using Aristotle's work as a guide, then, we can characterize the Classical Perspective. Five characteristics emerge as fundamental to this perspective. First, persuasion is assumed to be episodic, consisting of single events in which a single message is presented by a speaker to an audience. As mentioned earlier, the activity that gave rise to the study of persuasion in the ancient world was public address, the primary means of influence and decision-making in everyday public life. The orations studied were assumed to be presented orally; but often, particularly during the later Greek and Roman times, were written as well. Advice concerning these orations was advice assumed to apply in the given case—advice subject to modification when circumstances change. A second characteristic of this perspective also arises from the nature of the persuasive phenomena they observed. Persuasion is assumed to be overt and intentional. In other words, Aristotle and others assumed that those orators who stood in the public forum did so purposively, with an intent to persuade their audiences regarding public matters. Moreover, the advice provided by works like the *Rhetoric* addressed how to construct persuasive messages in situations that called for persuasion explicitly. The classical emphasis on the method, or art, of rhetoric reveals a third characteristic of persuasion from this perspective—strategic tactics. In other words, the Classical Perspective embodies a concern for instruments, for the tools by which persuasion is accomplished. Fundamental to the effectiveness of any of those tools is the nature of the audience. Consequently, a fourth characteristic of the Classical Perspective is a concern for the nature of the audience. Without a thorough understanding of the audience, the likelihood of successful persuasion was deemed very small. Finally, because of the recognition that these tools could be used for good or ill, the Classical Perspective entails a concern for ethics. Aristotle and others worried about the boundaries that should govern the strategic choices and instrumental uses of persuasion.

CONTEMPORARY DEVELOPMENTS

The approaches toward and concerns about persuasion manifested by the Classical Perspective find allies in much contemporary thought regarding persuasion. Many scholars and researchers still examine single messages and how those single messages may be crafted to elicit the desired response from an audience.[14] Similarly, there still exists much explicit, intentional effort at persuasion. In arguments between husbands and wives and in contemporary marketing efforts alike, persuaders purposely attempt to influence their audiences to behave or believe in particular ways. Frequently such attempts are approached episodically. What can a wife say right now in this situation to persuade her husband to help with the housecleaning? What can a corporation say to consumers today to get them to switch from MCI to AT&T for their long-distance service? As these questions suggest, persuaders are still concerned with the means of persuasion, with the tools or instruments by which such influence is accomplished. These practical concerns have been accompanied by considerable contemporary research on the nature of today's audience and means of persuasion as well as philosophical and legal concern for the ethics of contemporary persuasion.

All three of the means of persuasion first identified by Aristotle serve as the foundation for similar lines of inquiry by contemporary thinkers concerned with persuasion. Concepts similar to *logos, pathos* and *ethos* provide the theoretical constructs for a variety of research and theory from diverse academic disciplines. For convenience, we can review some of these contemporary developments according to the divisions first recognized by Aristotle.

Philosophy and the Emphasis on Formal Logic

The study of arguments as forms of logical reasoning has been investigated at length by analytic philosophers. Often beginning with Aristotle's original formulations concerning the syllogism, these philosophers have developed theory and methods for ascertaining the *validity* of arguments. *Validity refers to the soundness of arguments or the confidence with which one may accept the conclusion of an argument as true.* In general, analytical philosophers have suggested that arguments must meet two criteria in order to be deemed valid. First, the premises for the argument must be true. Second, the argument must use correct reasoning to reach its conclusion. Often the first requirement, that the premises be true, is referred to as *material validity.* Similarly, the second requirement, that the reasoning be correct, is termed *formal validity*. An example may assist in illustrating the concept of validity. Consider the argument that "The window is broken because I threw a rock through it." For this argument to be valid, the premise, "I threw a rock through it," would need to be true and the reasoing, that if I throw a rock through the window it will break, would need to be correct. The reasoning pattern just described would be correct if throwing a rock through a window was a sufficient condition for the window to break. If we change our example slightly, we can see how an argument might be deemed invalid. Suppose I said instead: "The window is broken. Someone must have thrown a rock through it." In this case the premise that must be true is that "the window is broken." The reasoning that must be correct is "if a window is broken it must be because a rock was thrown through it." We can see the problem immediately. A thrown rock may be a sufficient cause for a broken window but it is not a necessary cause for a broken window. Throwing a chair could also break a window. Sometimes windows simply crack and break as the result of airplanes breaking the sound barrier overhead or as a consequence of violent weather. In this case, then, the reasoning is faulty, and the argument is invalid.

With the example just described, ascertaining the truth of the premises is relatively simple. We can verify the premises empirically, through observation, by simply looking to see if the window is broken or asking if I really did throw a rock through the window. However, with many arguments the truth of the premises is more difficult to determine. If an advocate argues that abortion should be illegal because such an act is murder, how can we tell if an abortion is "murder?" Such a premise depends for its "truth" on whether or not removal of the fetus is the same as criminally taking a life. Is the fetus a living human? As you know there are various opinions regarding the answer to this question. The controversy concerning the "true" answer to this question presents a thorny problem for evaluating the validity of the argument above. Consequently, the first criterion for validity provided by formal logicians, observation, is difficult to apply to everyday argument.

Similar difficulties arise when people attempt to apply the second criterion of valid argument. Although there are various rules of formal logic other than that of necessary and sufficient cause, that rule provides a convenient basis for illustrating the difficulty of applying the rules of formal logic. For years, the lobby for tobacco companies in the United States claimed that the causal link between smoking tobacco and problems such as lung cancer and heart disease was tenuous. Lobbyists admitted that there might be a high correlation between smoking and contracting lung disease but that smoking had not been shown to be a necessary and sufficient cause of the lung disease. At the time that argument was accepted as true since scientific evidence to dispute it did not exist. Despite the lack of contradictory evidence, however, popular opinion and common sense alike suggested that smoking did cause lung disease. The argument may have been invalid, but it was nonetheless persuasive and convincing. To complicate matters even further, sometimes valid arguments are not apparently persuasive. To return to the subject of smoking, tobacco companies now admit there has been long-time evidence establishing the causal link between tobacco and cancer. Many people believe that they would decrease their chances of developing cancer, yet, they continue to smoke. Likewise, many smokers admit that they would save money if they quit smoking (i.e., they would no longer spend hundreds of dollars each year buying tobacco products) and agree that they want to save money, but still they smoke. The premises are true. The reasoning looks good, but nothing changes—persuasion doesn't take place.

Problems such as those just described have led a number of analytic philosophers to question the wisdom of emphasizing formal logic as a way of investigating how people reason and explaining what persuades people. Consequently, many have turned to the development of "informal logic," a study that applies the formal rules of logic loosely in order to account for real arguments and their real consequences. Notable among such attempts are the works of Stephen Toulmin, Chaim Perelman and L. Olbrechts-Tyteca. These philosophers have returned to the concept suggested by Aristotle, that humans may be reasonable but may not necessarily follow the rules of formal logic when they exercise their power of reasoning. In place of the rules of formal logic, these theorists describe the ways that people appear to reason in real circumstances (particularly in the legal field) in order to describe how *logos* operates in contemporary societies. Other informal logicians have developed less formal rules by which to identify fallacious or weak arguments, rules that can be applied to everyday arguments rather than to the symbolic configurations more familiar to formal logicians. These ideas provide the basis for Chapter 3 of this book.

PSYCHOLOGY AND EMPHASIS ON MOTIVATIONAL FACTORS

Just as logicians have explored the implications of *logos* and attempted to add insight to what Aristotle said about reasoning, so others have approached persuasion by investigating concepts akin to *pathos*. Contemporary psychological and sociological research, particularly after World War II, has investigated motivational factors related to persuasion.

During the first half of the twentieth century in the United States, many psychologists followed a line of inquiry initiated by John Watson, termed *behaviorism*.

Among various assumptions of behaviorism, one of particular note to those interested in persuasion is the notion that people behave in ways that maximize their rewards and minimize their punishments. Psychologists, concerned with how people learn, developed behavioral learning theory based on the same assumption. They termed the process that used the assumption *operant conditioning*. Operant conditioning occurs when a response is deemed more or less likely because of its positive or negative consequences.

A host of experimental studies were conducted to assess the promise of behavioral learning theory. For example, in one study students were asked to write essays that defended a position contradictory to their own attitudes. The researchers then randomly awarded the essays grades of "A" or "D." In later surveys, the researchers found that students who received an "A" for their essays tended to change their attitudes toward the position they had advocated while students who received a "D" did not.[15] Hence the idea that positive reinforcement could cause people to change their minds, could persuade people, seemed to be validated.

Confident in their belief that rewards and punishments could be powerful motivators, various psychologists and sociologists explored just what factors could serve as rewards or punishments. Carl Hovland and his colleagues at Yale University, for example, investigated the impact of source credibility, message comprehensibility, order of arguments, style, fear appeals, repetition and the intelligence and personalities of audience members on an audience's perception of rewards or punishments which are likely to result from a particular persuasive appeal.[16]

Others followed the path marked out in the Yale studies. As a consequence, there exists a huge number of sometimes contradictory studies of the effects of particular source, message, receiver and channel factors on persuasion. For example, early research indicated that understanding a message increases the likelihood that an individual will be persuaded by that message. Subsequently, investigators inquired as to whether increasing the number of understandable arguments in a message would or would not enhance persuasiveness. In one study, subjects serving as "jurors" were presented with either one or seven arguments favoring either the defense or the prosecution in a simulated bigamy trial. Results of the study indicated that messages containing more arguments were more effective.[17] However, in other studies the results indicated that more arguments could result in boredom and irritation by an audience member rather than in persuasion.[18]

The problem of what is rewarding and what is not becomes clearer if we consider the development of a particular theory of attitude change proposed by Leon Festinger. Based on the assumption that people respond positively to reward, one could expect that the greater the reward the greater the persuasive effect of a particular interaction. In a series of studies, Festinger tested this hypothesis.[19] He arranged for students to participate in a boring and tedious task—turning pegs in holes over and over again. Then, a collaborator asked those students to convince other students to participate in the same task. Some of the subjects were offered a small amount of money for their persuasive efforts; others were offered a substantial monetary reward. To the surprise of many, when students were interviewed later, those who had received substantial reward for convincing another student to engage in the boring task reported that the task was tedious, while those who had received minimal compensation tended to report that the task was really "quite fun and interesting." The results led Festinger to speculate that students who had received minimal monetary reward were uncomfortable trying to persuade another student to participate in a miserable task for only a small reward. To rationalize their behavior, they convinced themselves that the task really wasn't that bad after all. Meanwhile, those students who had been paid well could reason that the task was boring, but the generous payment legitimized convincing someone else to participate. This explanation led to Festinger's development of the theory of cognitive dissonance. This theory holds that inconsistency is uncomfortable for people, and when confronted with such inconsistency in attitude and/or behavior, people will adjust their attitudes in order to regain consistency. One implication of this theory is that the internal reward of cognitive consistency may be far stronger than external rewards such as monetary gain.

In general, researchers have found rewards to be more powerful motivators than punishments (although just what constitutes a "reward" has been studied widely), but Aristotle's suggestion that persuasion occurs "in the given case" appears to hold. In other words, a reward in one situation may act as a punishment in another situation. Throughout this text, we introduce the results of various studies that assist in explaining the persuasive power of a particular interaction. Still, some general ideas regarding what constitutes a reward and, therefore, what motivates potential "persuadees" is worthy of investigation.

Social scientists such as Abraham Maslow have investigated what motivates people. Maslow developed a theory of human motivation based on his clinical observations that identified the needs of successful, happy people. In addition to these works, other authors have revitalized the study of *pathos* without recourse to behavioral learning theory. These works are discussed in Chapter 4.

SOCIAL RESEARCH AND CREDIBILITY FACTORS

Aristotle argued that among the means of persuasion, *ethos* was the most powerful. As mentioned in the prior section, Hovland and his colleagues at Yale included among the motivational factors studied the credibility of the source of a persuasive message. Numerous contemporary scholars have been similarly intrigued by the seeming power of individuals, especially "authorities," to affect persuasion. Much of the study of this subject grows out of the same social science perspective reviewed earlier.

For instance, in 1951 Hovland and Weiss found that when students were exposed to identical messages attributed to either high or low credibility sources, opinion change in the direction advocated by the source was much greater when the source had high credibility than when the source had low credibility.[20] Two years later, Hovland and Kelman conducted a follow-up study which asked students to evaluate a radio program. The program included a speech advocating lenient treatment of juvenile delinquents. Some students listened to the speech where the speaker was introduced as a judge in juvenile court. Others heard the same speech with an introduction that identified the speaker as a member of the studio audience. Still others were presented with an introduction that included an interview with the speaker that revealed his criminal record including his juvenile delinquency. When asked to rate the speaker on fairness and impartiality, those who heard the "judge" rated him as "fair" twice as often as those who heard the "criminal" rated him as "fair." In addition, those students who heard the "judge" testified to more opinion change than those who heard the "criminal."[21]

That the *ethos* of a source is related to the persuasive impact of a message is generally accepted.[22] However, just what constitutes *ethos*, or credibility, has been the subject of much inquiry. Aristotle argued that a man would be perceived as having high *ethos* if he displayed good sense, good character and good will.[23] Numerous contemporary scholars have similarly attempted to identify the constituents of *ethos*. Recent reviews of the plethora of studies concerning source credibility suggest that nearly all studies "agree on the existence of both a safety or trustworthiness factor and a competence or expertise factor."[24] In addition, many researchers argue that dynamism, a dynamic or charismatic personality, is a third dimension of *ethos*.[25]

The constituents of *ethos* identified by scholars all depend on perceptions by an audience. In other words, if an audience does not perceive a source as trustworthy or an expert, then it matters little if the source is in fact trustworthy or an expert. The importance of audience perceptions led Aristotle to suggest that speakers might demonstrate their *ethos* by displaying habits of excellence in their life and communicative actions. Contemporary students of leadership follow a similar path. Hence, those studies that examine how particular people emerge as leaders, especially opinion leaders, provide helpful, additional information regarding *ethos*.[26] Similarly, contemporary concerns regarding charisma and credibility have led many to speculate about how leaders can enhance their charisma or repair damaged credibility. These subjects hold particular importance for students of political science who have attempted to explain the rise and fall of particular elected officials. Among public relations experts are those who concentrate solely on "image building." One of the earliest and most penetrating studies of this contemporary concern with image was provided by Daniel Boorstin who investigated the creation of images by the mass media and postulated that a person might obtain celebrity status just by obtaining media coverage. Much like the old parable about the emperor's new clothes, a person could become famous simply because people said he or she was famous. The work of those concerned with leadership and image management is discussed in more detail in Chapter 5 of this text.

Ethics in the Classical Perspective

As mentioned earlier, classical thinkers like Aristotle were concerned with the problem that persuasion could be used for either good or evil ends. In a classic statement on the subject, Cicero, a Roman rhetorician, noted that while "no little part of disasters was brought about by men of eloquence, …I find that many cities have been founded, that the flames of a multitude of wars have been extinguished, and that the strongest alliances and most sacred friendships have been formed not only by the use of the reason but also more easily by the help of eloquence."[27] Cicero, thus, was optimistic about the use of persuasion for good ends. Aristotle put his faith in the general ability of good to triumph over evil. He argued that "rhetoric is useful because things that are true and things that are just have a natural tendency to prevail over their opposites" and explained that if falsity or injustice prevailed the fault lay with ineffective persuaders.[28] However, ample instances of persuasive power gone awry exist in the form of tyrannies, exploitations and simple con-jobs. For thinkers like Aristotle and Cicero, one way of avoiding the evil uses of persuasion was to train potential persuaders in philosophy and ethics. If only "good" men engaged in persuasion, then the results of persuasion were also likely to be good.

Contemporary thinkers also wrestle with this problem. Like their classical counterparts, however, contemporary persuasion theorists and practitioners often separate their concerns with effectiveness from their concerns with ethics. When ethics are considered alongside effectiveness, questions are raised concerning various means of persuasion and whether those means are or are not ethical. Some argue that only *logos* is ethical, while *pathos* and *ethos* are inherently unethical means of persuasion.[29] The position of these thinkers seems to be that the power of reason is a uniquely human characteristic. As a consequence, to employ persuasive tactics that subvert or bypass that power of reason is to treat an audience as less than human, to engage in unethical persuasion. Others suggest that there are standards for judging the ethical use of all three means of persuasion.[30]

More often, contemporary communication scholars suggest a variety of perspectives to judge the ethics of communication generally, including the ethics of both persuaders and "persuadees."[31] In addition to scholarly treatments of ethics, both professional organizations and governmental bodies have attempted to deal with ethical questions by providing rules and guidelines for those engaged in persuasion. For example, both the Federal Trade Commission and the Federal Communications Commission have issued rules concerning what types of messages are legally acceptable in advertising. Similarly, professional organizations such as the American Bar Association have designed ethical codes for those who practice persuasion within their fields. We draw on sources such as these throughout this book as questions of ethics arise.

CRITICAL FOCUS: NATIONAL RIFLE ASSOCIATION DOCUMENTARY

From the Classical Perspective, then, we are concerned with explicit persuasion in which a source purposefully attempts to influence an audience to make particular choices or take particular actions. The strategies of a persuader concerning what is included in the message as well as how the message is constructed are of particular interest. Those strategies should be examined to determine how effectively they take the particular audience into account as well as for their ethical implications. The accompanying questions should be used to guide your general analysis of persuasion from a Classical Perspective.

CRITICAL QUESTIONS

1. In what direct and/or indirect ways does the sender acknowledge an **intention to persuade** the audience?
2. What **specific choices** is the audience asked to make?
3. What **persuasive tactics** does the persuader use in the message?
4. What **characteristics of the audience** seem to be assumed by the persuader?

5. What **ethical parameters** seem to bound the persuasive message?

The documentary produced by the National Rifle Association during the controversy about restrictions on semiautomatic weapons provides fertile ground for exploring the Classical Perspective toward studying persuasion. First, we can examine the ways in which the message illustrates an intention to persuade. Identifying both the persuader and the audience to whom the persuasive message is directed is a good starting point for such analysis. The documentary was produced by the National Rifle Association, a known lobbying group whose mission is to advocate less restrictive policies governing the manufacture, sale and ownership of firearms. As mentioned earlier, the audience for this film ranged from Congressional and state legislative representatives to members of the Association and the general public. Moreover, the situation in which the message appears—a time when various restrictive policies were being debated and many were concerned with the disastrous consequences of such weapons falling into the hands of the wrong people—makes clear that the documentary was probably produced and received by people who were aware that decisions needed to be made.

Further investigation of the message itself clarifies the NRA's intention to persuade. The documentary begins with scenes from a Senate hearing in which Senator Metzenbaum asks why something like a machine gun should not be prohibited, and NRA spokesman, James Jay Baker, argues that the real question should be how to keep such weapons out of the hands of criminals. Such a vivid portrayal of the legislative process in action alerts the viewer to a situation of public controversy, a situation that calls for persuasion. The film returns to similar scenes from the hearings throughout, reinforcing a viewer's perception that they are dealing with a situation in which people will purposefully attempt to influence one another. Near the end of the film, the primary narrator, policeman Leroy Pyle, intones that "it would be a shame to vote a particular way just because of a misunderstanding." That statement indicates his, and the NRA's, desire to influence how the legislative audience will vote on the proposals concerning semiautomatics. The film ends with a plea for viewers to write their elected representatives, again underscoring the intention for persuasion of the producers of the film.

In situations where persuasion is explicit, it is usually easier to identify particular persuasive strategies and to determine the ethical stance a persuader is taking toward an audience. Knowing the particular choices an audience is being asked to make is equally important. Is the audience asked to think differently, or are they asked to actually change their behavior in some way? The NRA documentary explicitly asks viewers to think diffrently. Early in the film, NRA lobbyist Baker says we should think about how to keep dangerous weapons out of the hands of criminals. He even corrected Senator Metzenbaum about what the purpose of the hearing was supposed to be, suggesting to the viewer that he or she not be sidetracked from the fundamental question of how to keep guns from criminals by focusing on how to get rid of the guns entirely. Later, Leroy Pyle tells viewers he wants to give them some facts to help them use their power of reason rather than being carried away by their emotions. He is asking the audience to think in a particular way. As he talks, Pyle explains that the media has confused many viewers, indicating that he wants them to understand the truth about semiautomatic weapons, to think about these weapons in a different way. As just mentioned, the film is also explicit about the behavior that is desired from the viewer. The call to write one's elected representatives is exemplary. But even Pyle's lamentation about voting the wrong way because of a basic misunderstanding implies an action desired of the legislative audience. He wants members of Congress and state legislatures to vote the "right" way.

Investigating the choices asked of an audience clarifies the intentions of a persuader and provides a basis for comparing one persuasive message to another. Such comparisons may eventually result in generalizations about the strategies that are used most often or most effectively when particular types of choices are asked of the audience. Furthermore, knowing the type of persuasion with which you are dealing by determining the type of choice the audience is asked to make helps an analyst determine which ethical standard or standards should be applied. In the case of the NRA documentary, because we know that the audience is asked to think about a public controversy in new terms and to act on that thinking by voting or otherwise influencing the democratic process, we may decide that standards for ethical persuasion common to democratic politics are most appropriate. Because we know the audience is being asked to make a choice about a public policy, we can expect the persuasive strategies to be those common to deliberative debate and political communication.

We can use Aristotle's three means of persuasion as an initial basis for characterizing persuasive strategies in a message. Does the message include arguments, appeals to the passions or reliance on the *ethos* of the source? Are all three means of persuasion used, or does the message seem to rely more heavily on one means as opposed to the others? We explore what makes each of these tactics effective in subsequent chapters; for now it is enough to just describe the tactics that seem to be used. In the case of the NRA documentary, all three means of persuasion are in evidence, but reasonable arguments seem to be emphasized. For example, early in the film Pyle explains that he is a police officer with considerable experience with firearms. His experience as a training and safety instructor enhances the *ethos* of the message by letting us know he is trustworthy; he is not a criminal or a fanatic gun collector. The film reveals that his job requires him to work with firearms and that he knows about such weapons. Furthermore, the film reveals that he is in a position to sympathize with the audience's emotional state of mind. He explains that he understands how viewers may feel about the recent event in Stockton because he lives nearby, and he has had friends on the force who have fallen victim to the misuse of semiautomatic weapons. Could such a person mislead the audience? The film hopes viewers will answer in the negative by focusing on the professional and personal integrity of the narrator.

Not only do Pyle's statements about where he lives and his friends who have died enhance his *ethos*, but such statements also engage the emotions of viewers. By explicitly recognizing the distraught frame of mind with which many may come to the controversy, Pyle is in a position to try to calm such viewers. He asks us to "cut through those emotions" in order to make a rational decision based on the facts. His personal manner of presentation and the accompanying visuals that show firearms in a pastoral setting of a rifle range rather than on a city street seem designed to calm the audience. His references to the mistakes made by the media in discussing the issue similarly assist in defusing an audience's fearful reaction to an image of machine guns in the street and schoolyard. His comparisons of guns with wooden stocks to those with plastic stocks and his appearance in a sportsman's vest present a calming scene in which to view the issue. Defusing fear and replacing it with calm seems a wise strategic choice by the NRA in their effort to have their arguments heard. So, even though Pyle suggests that he wants viewers to decide based on the facts rather than on their emotions, he probably really wants viewers to decide based on the facts combined with a calm emotional state rather than based on the facts combined with a fearful emotional state.

While both *ethos* and *pathos* are evident in the film, there can be little doubt that the emphasis in this persuasive message is on *logos*, the arguments themselves. The central argument seems to be that semiautomatic weapons are not the same as fully automatic weapons and therefore should not be subject to the same restrictive gun regulations as fully automatic weapons. Pyle demonstrates the difference by firing the weapons and dismantling them to show their working parts. After demonstrating this point, Pyle turns to the question of whether or not semiautomatic weapons are the same as assault rifles. He argues they are not because they work differently, but says it's confusing because semiautomatic weapons can be made to look like their fully automatic assault counterparts. The film reinforces this point by showing us testimony from an official of the Bureau of Alcohol, Tobacco and Firearms that indicates the difficulty of determining what is an assault weapon. Pyle then explains that semiautomatic weapons cannot be easily converted into fully automatic weapons, a point reinforced by other testimony at the Senate hearing. By explaining and demonstrating that semiautomatic weapons work differently from fully automatic weapons, Pyle and the NRA hope that viewers will decide that semiautomatics should not be prohibited as fully automatic weapons are. If, as Pyle asserts, semiautomatics are popular among hunters and sportsmen, then why should they be banned? Thus goes the logic of the NRA's argument, an argument whose elaboration comprises most of the film. The argument is an enthymeme in that it calls on viewers to supply the general principle that if a gun is dissimilar to those guns now banned, it should not be banned. If a gun is not fully automatic and not an assault rifle, it must be less dangerous and, therefore, less in need of restrictive policies. If a gun is popular with sportsmen and hunters it is not often the source of criminal behavior. The logic is not unassailable as we will explain in the following chapter, but it is fairly clear as we examine the message for the persuasive strategies employed.

Given the persuasive strategies we have identified, we can now explore what the persuader seems to be assuming about the audience? Does the persuasive message presume a receptive or hostile or neutral audience? Does the message suggest an audience composed of people who share particular demographic features (e.g., particular age group, educational level, socioeconomic status)? How does this picture of the audience compare with the actual audience that we identified earlier?

The NRA documentary seems to assume that much of its audience is hostile toward their point of view initially. The beginning scenes show Baker recasting the controversy from Metzenbaum's definition of "why *not* ban semiautomatic weapons" to the NRA's concern for how to keep dangerous weapons out of the hands of criminals.

Given the legislative initiatives and public attitudes following the Stockton schoolyard massacre, the mood of many audience members conformed to that of Metzenbaum: why *not* ban these dangerous weapons? Instead of addressing that question head on, the NRA documentary poses a different question: how to keep dangerous criminals from obtaining these weapons. Then the film tries to defuse the fear and anger of viewers about the tragic episode in Stockton, again suggesting that the NRA viewed much of its audience as hostile.

This hostile audience was probably also viewed as relatively ignorant of firearms. The lengthy demonstrations of various firearms during the film's presentation seems well designed for an audience unfamiliar with the internal workings of such weapons. The emphasis on *logos*, however, also suggests an audience viewed as essentially fair and reasonable. In other words, freed of unpleasant emotions and confusing terminology, the audience is assumed capable of making a rational decision. Pyle's statement that it would be a "shame" to vote the wrong way because of a misunderstanding is illustrative. A persuader making such a statement assumes his audience is reasonable and that they value their reasoning over the passions they may associate with gun control.

In addition to these assumptions, the film also addresses a somewhat receptive audience. Pyle speaks of the popularity of semiautomatics, "as many of you know," and the film makes a direct plea for viewers to contact their representatives. Furthermore, some elements of the film actually suggest it is also directed toward those sympathetic to the NRA's position. The lack of elaboration by Baker about his recasting of the issue at least suggests that the film is aimed toward those already familiar with the general position of the NRA concerning gun control, but perhaps undecided about just where semiautomatic weapons fit into that general position. News reports at the time suggest that many members of the NRA did experience ambivalent feelings following the Stockton incident.[32]

Finally, the Classical Perspective orients us toward asking about the ethical boundaries of the message under consideration. Generally, we may ask if the purpose of the persuasive message seems to fall into the category of "good" or "evil." In other words, if the persuader is successful would we classify the resultant effects as good or bad for society? More specifically, we can ask if the persuader employs "anything goes" tactics, or if the persuader limits his or her strategies to content that is based on truth or the best opinions available? Are there some tactics that just seem "wrong?" Given the type of decision being asked of the audience, are there likely to be specific ethical codes that would govern this message?

When we consider the NRA documentary, several conclusions emerge. If the NRA is successful, then semiautomatic weapons will not be further prohibited. Is that good or bad for society? The film provides us little reason for deciding that such a policy would be good; however, other messages from the NRA point out that such a policy does uphold the right to bear arms. Opposing advocates seem to make a relevant claim when they explain that if semiautomatic weapons remain legal, they will at least eventually and occasionally fall into the wrong hands and result in tragedy. A representative argument of this type appeared in *The New Republic*:

> ...all assault rifles are semiautomatic weapons. But not all semiautomatic weapons are assault rifles. Only those semi-autos that can shoot large numbers of bullets without reloading—and are therefore ideal for playground massacres—are the objects of concern.[33]

What the writer of this editorial seems to be saying is that following the NRA's advice will only lead to other tragedies.

Clearly, there are well meaning advocates on either side. Perhaps a better test of ethical boundaries lies in an examination of the tactics used in the message. Generally the documentary seems to argue for a reasonable approach to the issue and collects testimony and demonstrations from knowledgeable sources. However, by focusing on reasoning to the exclusion of emotion, the documentary probably presents the illusion of being devoid of emotional appeals while our investigation suggests that it is really subtly manipulating the emotions of the audience. This may be an area in which ethical questions arise. By focusing so explicitly on the "facts" and even by using the documentary form for their message, a form that many associate with factual and educational information, the NRA may be masking the reality that there are informed experts on either side of this issue. By showing us the similarities and differences among weapons, the documentary may confuse more than it clarifies, leading to further ethical considerations. However, none of the information presented is blatantly false or fabricated, and generally the message seems within the bounds of what is considered ethical regarding persuasion devoid of influence from the passions.

By identifying the message as a part of a controversy about an issue of public importance, we may be able to better evaluate the ethical boundaries of the message by consulting general ethical standards for democratic discussion and debate. Such standards would include concern for the truth of the message and the ability of opponents and audience members alike to challenge the arguments presented in a spirit of fair play and with a commitment to the public good.[34] While we do not really doubt the truth of the message, we must wonder if the documentary form of the message is sufficiently open to allow the arguments to be challenged. Direct communication in face-to-face situations is generally more conducive to actualizing the spirit of fair play. Few opponents of the NRA have sufficient funds to make similar documentary films that tell the other side of the story. Regarding the public good, we once again find ourselves with conflicting interpretations regarding what is more important—an unrestrained right to bear arms or a restrictive policy that might prevent some criminal behavior.

The critical questions presented here are typical of the initial analysis of persuasive messages that is fostered by the Classical Perspective. To more fully analyze any persuasive message requires application of questions from subsequent chapters. However, these questions can be used to begin the critical process.

Notes

1. Richard W. Bruner and Josh Sugarmann, "Taking Aim at the NRA," *The Nation* 248 (3 April 1989): 5.
2. Bruner and Sugarmann, "Taking," 5.
3. Hedrick Smith, *The Power Game: How Washington Works* (New York: Ballantine Books, 1989), 235,238,250.

4. Cicero, *On Oratory and Orators*, trans. and ed. J. S. Watson (Carbondale: Southern Illinois University Press, 1970), 23-28; see also, Quintilian, *On the Teaching of Speaking and Writing*, trans. and ed. James J. Murphy (Carbondale: SIU P, 1987).
5. Aristotle, *Rhetoric*, trans. W. Rhys Roberts (New York: Modern Library, 1954), 1355b.
6. Aristotle, *Rhetoric*, 1358b.
7. Aristotle, *Rhetoric*, 1358a-1358b.
8. Aristotle, *Rhetoric*, 1356a.
9. Aristotle, *Rhetoric*, 1354a.
10. Aristotle, *Rhetoric*, 1356b.
11. Lloyd Bitzer, "The Enthymeme Revisited," *Quarterly Journal of Speech* 45 (1959): 399-408.
12. Aristotle, *Rhetoric*, 1356b.
13. See Gerard A. Hauser, "Aristotle's Example Revisited," *Philosophy and Rhetoric* 18 (1985): 171-180.
14. For a sampling of research that applies the Classical Perspective to modern media, see Ronald Primeau, *The Rhetoric of Television* (New York: Longman, 1979); see also, John Harrington, *The Rhetoric of Film* (New York: Holt, Rinehart and Winston, 1973).
15. Robert N. Bostrum, J. W. Vlandis and M. E. Rosenbaum, "Grades as Reinforcing Contingencies and Attitude Change," *Journal of Educational Psychology* 52 (1961): 112-115.
16. See, for example, Carl I. Hovland, Irving L. Janis and J. J. Kelley, *Communication and Persuasion* (New Haven: Yale University Press, 1953).
17. B. J. Calder, C. A. Insko and B. Yandell, "The Relation of Cognitive and Memorial Processes to Persuasion in a Simulated Jury Trial," *Journal of Applied Social Psychology* 4 (1974): 62-93.
18. B. J. Calder, "Cognitive Response, Imagery, and Scripts: What is the Cognitive Basis of Attitude," *Advances in Consumer Research* 5 (1978): 630-634.
19. Leon Festinger, *A Theory of Cognitive Dissonance* (Evanston: Row, Peterson, 1957). See also, Festinger, *Conflict, Decision, and Dissonance* (Stanford: Stanford University Press, 1964).
20. C. Hovland and W. Weiss, "The Influence of Source Credibility on Communication Effectiveness," *Public Opinion Quarterly* 15 (1951): 635-650.
21. H. Kelman and C. Hovland, "'Reinstatement' of the Communicator in Delayed Measurement of Opinion Change," *Journal of Abnormal and Social Psychology* 48 (1953): 327-335.
22. Kenneth Andersen and Theodore Clevenger, Jr., "A Summary of Experimental Research in *Ethos*," *Speech Monographs* 30 (1963): 77.
23. Aristotle, *Rhetoric*, 1378a.
24. Erwin P. Bettinghaus and Michael J. Cody, *Persuasive Communication*, 4th Ed. (New York: Holt, Rinehart and Winston, 1987), 85.

25. See, for example, David Markham, "The Dimensions of Source Credibility of Television Newscasters," *Journal of Communication* 18 (1968): 57-64; Jack Whitehead, Jr., "Factors of Source Credibility," *Quarterly Journal of Speech* 54 (1968): 59-63; and J. C. McCroskey, T. Jensen and C. Valencia, "Measurement of the Credibility of Peers and Spouses," paper presented at the International Communication Association Convention, Montreal, 1973.
26. See, for example, E. Katz and P. F. Lazarsfield, *Personal Influence* (New York: Free Press, 1955).
27. Cicero, *De Inventione*, trans. H. M. Hubbell (Cambridge: Harvard University Press, 1949), 3.
28. Aristotle, *Rhetoric*, 1355a.
29. See, for example, Arthur N. Kruger, "The Ethics of Persuasion: A Re-Examination," *Speech Teacher* 16 (1967): 304-305.
30. See, for example, Fanklyn Haiman, "Democratic Ethics and the Hidden Persuaders," *Quarterly Journal of Speech* 44 (1958): 387-392.
31. See, Richard L. Johannesen, *Ethics in Human Communication*, 3rd Ed. (Prospect Heights: Waveland, 1990).
32. Bruner and Sugarmann, 5.
33. "Lies, Damn Lies, and NRA Ads," *The New Republic* 200 (8 May 1989): 6.
34. For a summary of ethical perspectives based on democratic debate, see Martha Cooper *Analyzing Public Discourse* (Prospect Heights: Waveland, 1989), 135-152.

3

The Rational Human And Reasonable Argument

IN THIS CHAPTER:

Focus on:

Ronald Reagan's "Facts Are Stubborn Things" Address

1. Theoretical Focus: Arguments
2. Arguments Described by the Toulmin Model
3. Data—What Do We Expect as Evidence?
4. Familiar Patterns of Thinking—Common Sense
5. Ethics and Tests of Evidence and Reasoning
6. Critical Focus: Reagan's Address to Republican Convention

Focus On: Ronald Reagan's "Facts Are Stubborn Things" Address

Known as "the great communicator," former President Ronald Reagan was famous for presenting persuasive addresses that relied less on reasoned arguments and more on stories and anecdotes that touched the hearts of many Americans.[1] However, in one of the final addresses of his term of office, Reagan appealed directly to his audience's common sense by reminding them of the "facts." In his 1988 address to the Republican National Convention, he offered a variety of evidence and arguments to attempt to prove that electing a Republican for four more years would be superior to electing a Democrat. His speech was informally titled "Facts Are Stubborn Things" and is typical of an approach to persuasion that emphasizes reasonable argument. Later in this chapter, we examine an excerpt from Reagan's speech in light of what we know about reasonable argument as a means of persuasion.

Theoretical Focus: Arguments

Perhaps you've heard someone say, "I'm not going to try to persuade you; I just want to give you the facts." Or maybe you've said at sometime, "I don't believe that! It just doesn't make any sense." In both cases, the persuasion that is or isn't happening is grounded in our sense of ourselves as reasonable people who take the facts into account. In the first instance, the speaker probably is trying to persuade you through an appeal to your reason rather than by some other means. In the second instance, you are resisting persuasion according to what makes sense, according to what is reasonable.

Just what "thinking rationally" or "being reasonable" means has been the subject of study for a long time. As we pointed out in the last chapter, the ancient Greeks understood at least two processes in which people were reasonable: *dialectic* and *rhetoric*. In dialectic participants followed rather strict and formal rules concerning what made sense. Dialecticians approached their subjects systematically, making certain not to skip any of the steps in the reasoning process. Aristotle himself wrote several volumes that explained the essential components of logical reasoning and provided advice for those who intended to engage in dialectic.[2] Yet, Aristotle also observed that persuasion was different from dialectic and wrote about persuasion under the heading of "rhetoric."

But Aristotle's separation of rhetoric from dialectic did not imply that persuasion somehow bypassed the rationality of human beings. Instead, Aristotle argued at the beginning of the *Rhetoric* that rhetoric was the counterpart of dialectic. In other words, persuasion should be grounded in the good sense generated through the process of dialectic. Instead of requiring trained advocates and worrying about philosophical questions—what constitutes justice or happiness as in dialectic—in rhetoric persuaders talk with ordinary people, untrained advocates, about how to reach goals such as justice or happiness. Moreover, Aristotle explained that one of the three essential means of persuasion in such cases was *logos*, or the arguments themselves. Thus he suggested that arguments, or appeals to an audience's reason, are an important part of the process of persuasion.

In this chapter we investigate how arguments contribute to persuasion. We will begin by discussing what an argument is and then move to a consideration of what contemporary audiences understand to be reasonable. Because persuasion that appeals to reason is generally assumed to depend on the "truth," we explore a variety of ways that people test arguments to make sure that they are truthful.

Arguments Described By The Toulmin Model

From the time of Aristotle, logicians typically have described an argument as one or more premises that lead to a conclusion. In more ordinary language, we often talk about people making arguments that function as reasons for their actions. One of the most clear descriptions of an argument is provided by the British philosopher Stephen Toulmin.[3]

Toulmin was trained as an analytic philosopher and, therefore, was familiar with traditional descriptions of an argument as a configuration of premises and conclusion. However, Toulmin noted that in everyday speech, what everyone recognized as an argument often did not meet the philosopher's formal definition of an argument. Consequently, he developed his own model for an argument. The Toulmin model describes six functional parts of an argument. They are: *claim*, *data*, *warrant*, *backing*, *qualifier* and *rebuttal*. The model is diagrammed in Figure 3.1.

The claim is the point that an advocate, or persuader, is trying to make. It is the conclusion that the persuader hopes the audience will reach. For example, a familiar television commercial makes the claim that Total is more nutritious than other breakfast cereals. That is the conclusion the advertiser wants the audience to accept. Similarly, as you shop for a new car, the dealer is likely to make several claims regarding the car he shows you. He may claim that the car you're looking at is economical or powerful or just an all-around good buy. Each of these would be a claim in Toulmin's scheme.

Figure 3.1

Toulmin Model of an Argument

Toulmin points out that when confronted with claims in everyday life we frequently ask the person making the claim for support. The support, or grounds, for the claim is what Toulmin calls *data*. Ordinarily we associate the term data with scientific facts. We think of data as raw information, something to be gathered and interpreted. In arguments, data can be raw information of the scientific variety, but that is not necessary. According to Toulmin, data is anything that an audience accepts as support for a claim. So, if an auto dealer claims that the car he is selling is economical, he might support that claim with the sticker price, with a reference to *Consumer Report's* evaluation of the cost of maintenance for that model, or with an explanation that his nephew owns a car just like this one and is really satisfied with how economical it is. Similarly, if a television spot shows a picture of one bowl of Total next to four bowls of another brand of cereal, while a voice-over tells viewers that you must eat four bowls of the other brand to get all the minerals and vitamins in one bowl of Total, then that visual acts as data for the claim.

The *warrant* explains why the claim is true if the data is accepted as true. For example, if someone believes that a particular car is economical because the sticker price is under $15,000, then that belief must rest on a warrant that any automobile under $15,000 is economical. Put another way, the warrant entails a definition of what is economical. If one's concept of economy doesn't take into account the purchase price, then the claim wouldn't seem to follow from this data. To be a bridge between data and claim, a warrant must supply the necessary definitions, values or other connectives to make the argument sensible. In the case of the Total commercial, if you think vitamins and minerals are important to nutrition, then the claim is warranted by the data. If not, then the claim is unwarranted or the data is irrelevant to the claim.

Sometimes a warrant requires support just as a claim can require support. When support for a warrant is supplied, that support is called *backing*. If you happened to see the Total commercial just described, you might ask: "How important are minerals and vitamins to nutrition?" This question calls for support of the warrant that there is such a relationship. Support for the warrant might come in the form of reference to the amount of various vitamins that experts recommend for a healthy diet. If the commercial spot included this sort of information, then the commercial would be including backing as part of its argument.

Not only do warrants sometimes require backing, but sometimes there are exceptions to a warrant. A car may be economical because its sticker price is $15,000, unless your definition of economical is only those cars under $10,000. In this case the warrant that any automobile under $16,000 is economical is denied by a different definition. Such a denial is the *rebuttal* of an argument. We could also rebut the claim about the car's economy if we considered factors other than the sticker price as relevant to the economy of the car. Then the argument would follow a pattern diagrammed in Figure 3.2. So rebuttals are exceptions or conditions under which the claim would not be true even if the data were true.

Figure 3.2

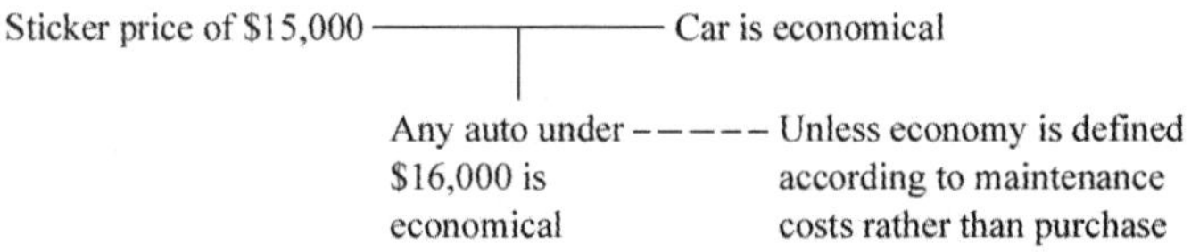

Claims may not always be absolutely true for all possible circumstances, even for perfectly reasonable arguments. A *qualifier* is a term that indicates the strength of a claim, like "probably," "generally," "usually," "sometimes," etc. If our data for a car's economy is the judgment of *Consumer Reports*, we might qualify the claim by saying that "*most likely* the car will be economical." By inserting the qualifier we recognize a possible rebuttal, unless the car you buy happens to be the one lemon out of a million cars. Or we might qualify the claim that Total is nutritious with the phrase, "probably is more nutritious," thereby, recognizing that some competitors might also fortify their cereals with vitamins and minerals.

As you may have guessed by now, in any given persuasive message some or all of the parts of an argument identified by Toulmin may appear. Sometimes, especially in messages like televised advertisements, the message just presents data. The viewer is asked to fill in the claim and everything else. At other times, a persuasive message may be filled with claims, and the listener is expected to supply the data and other parts. Toulmin recognized that some of the parts of an argument might remain implicit, awaiting the help of receivers for their completion. In this sense, Toulmin's model accommodates the thinking of Aristotle regarding the enthymeme. In other words, audience members may participate in the construction of an argument, adding what they think makes sense to what the persuader provides in order to construct a reasonable argument.

For the critic of persuasion, a valuable analytical tool from the Classical Perspective is the ability to identify the arguments in a persuasive message. Identifying the arguments means at the very least being able to identify the claims, whatever data is presented in their support, and to determine the warrants necessary to make the claims sensible on the basis of the data presented. Once we identify these features, it is much more likely that we can determine backing, rebuttals and necessary qualifiers.

As the reader is probably aware, much contemporary persuasion—whether in politics, advertising or interpersonal interaction—fails to qualify claims, ignores the need for backing of warrants and neglects to mention rebuttals. We explore the ethical implications of such practices later in the chapter. Before doing that, however, we should discuss just what counts as good data and reasonable warrants.

DATA–WHAT DO WE ACCEPT AS EVIDENCE?

To identify data for an argument it is helpful to know what typically serves as data in an argument. In general, data falls into one of three categories: *examples*, *quantitative* and *statistical information* and *testimony*. In a public address the speaker may present data verbally or visually with charts, graphs and the like. The same is true with print messages. When television or film is used as the medium of transmission, the sight and sound scripts provide the data. Hence, we may see action occurring in scenes that acts as data for a claim presented from an on or offscreen narrator. But whether it emerges as a picture or a story, in print or in a sophisticated computer graphic display, data usually appears as one of the three types just listed.

Examples can be real or hypothetical. An advocate for the National Rifle Association shows an automatic weapon and a semiautomatic weapon to demonstrate the difference between the two in order to support the claim that semiautomatics should not be subject to gun control laws. When persuaders support claims about the future, they often have no real examples and therefore must construct hypothetical ones. This technique has been used in the recent discussion about health care reform. Persuaders opposing managed care conjure up images of socialized medicine in which people have few choices about which doctors to see and what care they will receive, finally eventuating in less effective care. Because the proposed plans are yet to be tried, these scenarios are not factual but only hypothetical. Examples can be short or extended. When a politician presents a brief anecdote on the campaign trail, the example may be as simple as pointing out how a competitor voted on a particular piece of legislation. Extended examples, on the other hand, are usually crafted into stories that are either told or enacted. The moral of the story may be blatant or subtle. In a recent half-hour cartoon to fight drug abuse, an elaborate animated story was constructed to support the notion that drugs are dangerous.

Statistics are numerical collections of examples. We usually do not think of statistics as aggregates of examples because statistics in the form of numbers seem so sterile, stipped of the concrete details of a good example. Yet, if we break down any complex statistic, we find at its base a large number of concrete and probably colorful examples. When we observe that nearly 80 percent of those in poverty in the United States are women and children, for example, that statistic depersonalizes thousands of examples of real people whose lives are often shattered by their economic circumstances. Statistical data may be as simple as the number of unemployed appearing in a speech advocating that we should change our economic policies or as complex as a graph or chart that compares the relative effectiveness of two methods of treating alcoholism. Graphs and charts are often used in print and visual media to make statistics more memorable and have more impact on an audience. Persuasive speakers often present raw numbers to impress an audience with the factual and scientific basis for a claim.

Testimony is, of course, the judgment or opinions of other people. Testimony may appear in the form of a quotation used by a public speaker or may be delivered live in front of a camera in the form of an interview. Sometimes testimony is simply implied by the existence of Oprah Winfrey's signature on a diet drink or Michael Jordan's picture on a box of Wheaties. The point of testimony is that someone other than the persuader, someone we probably like or trust, is endorsing the claim through their words or other symbolic actions.

Communication researchers have conducted a number of social scientific studies to investigate the persuasive effects of evidence or data. Most researchers believe that information, by itself, is not necessarily persuasive.[4] In his review of such studies, for example, Thompson concluded that "evidence is of doubtful value unless used for specific ends and in particular situations."[5] However, research does indicate that evidence can be persuasive in a number of particular circumstances. Those circumstances and the findings of the studies are summarized as follows.[6]

1. Saying that an item of evidence is a "fact" increases persuasiveness.
2. Evidence that is verifiable is more persuasive than that which is not.
3. Evidence that is specific is more persuasive than evidence which is general.
4. Reluctant and unbiased testimony is more persuasive than biased testimony.
5. Personal experience is more persuasive than evidence that is not self-referenced.
6. Persuaders with low credibility benefit more from using evidence than those with high credibility.
7. Evidence is more important when the audience lacks familiarity with the topic than when the audience is well informed.
8. Factual evidence is of particular persuasive value when the audience is composed of people of high intelligence.
9. Evidence is more persuasive when the source of the evidence is given and his or her qualifications are provided.
10. Evidence is particularly persuasive when confirming an audience's beliefs or actions, helping them to resist counter-persuasion.

Familiar Patterns Of Thinking–Common Sense

While data is frequently explicit within arguments, warrants are more often implicit. The audience often participates in constructing the argument by supplying a connection between the persuader's data and claim. Of course, sometimes audience members supply additional data from their own experience as well. The reason that persuaders can count on an audience to make connections between data and claims is that audience members are socialized into particular patterns of thinking that are familiar, that we would ordinarily recognize as common sense. In western culture, there are four such patterns of thinking that are generally recognized as common sense.[7] These patterns are studied by logicians as patterns of reasoning. They have been identified by cognitive psychologists as patterns of understanding that people intuitively grasp as they develop and mature. The patterns include *analogical*, *categorical*, *disjunctive* and *causal thinking*.

Analogical thinking occurs when we recognize similarity among things, cases, events and so forth. Examples work as proof for a claim because they are perceived by an audience as similar. In other words, if something was true in a particular case, then it is likely to be true in other similar cases. If the life of a cartoon character is devastated by his flirtation with drugs, then the same could happen to anyone else who uses drugs. Sometimes the thread of similarity is stretched by the use of examples that don't fit precisely. In these cases, examples operate as comparisons or analogies. For instance, a public service announcement showed an egg frying in a pan to suggest what happens to the brain when someone uses drugs. The image of the fried egg works if the audience perceives the similarity.

Analogical thinking is often cued by the use of language that includes comparative terms such as "like," "as in the case of," "similar to" and so forth. Words like these cue an audience to turn on their pattern of analogical thinking and search for similarities. Visually we may be cued to perceive similarity by the placement of an image within the frame or context of the action or person about whom the claim is being made. Television commercials that show monkeys getting a Diet Pepsi from a machine ask us to perceive the similarity between humans and monkeys by placing the monkeys in a setting more commonly associated with humans. Or, in more traditional commercials, "typical" housewives may be shown trying to get a nasty stain out of their children's clothes so that viewers will recall their own similar problems with getting clothes clean.

Categorical thinking occurs when we recognize that some thing or action belongs to a particular category. If we have a positive judgment about the category or class, then we may transfer that positive assessment to the particular case under discussion on the grounds that it belongs to that category. For example, a persuader associates her position on the environment with the Democratic agenda, hoping that if the audience has positive attitudes toward the category of Democratic policies then those attitudes will be transferred to the particular policy in question when the audience realizes that this policy belongs to the larger category of Democratic programs.

While examples may sometimes be persuasive because they appear to represent a particular class, more often statistics and testimony find their force within categorical thinking. Statistics, particularly those expressed as percentages, often characterize the attributes or opinions of a particular class. For example, census bureau statistics tell us what is typical of various demographic and geographic classes—the average income, the average number of family members, etc. When statistics such as these are put in the service of persuasion, such as when we are told that a high percentage of dentists recommend a particular brand of toothpaste or a huge percentage of doctors eat oat bran, we may put our categorical thinking to work. The class, dentists, knows what's good for your teeth; so if this class recommends Crest, maybe we should use it ourselves. The same sort of thinking occurs with testimony. If a well-known sports figure endorses a particular brand of basketball shoes, we may attribute the characteristics associated with the class of famous basketball players to our decision about which pair of shoes to buy. "If Michael Jordan says Nikes are good they must be good, because he's a superstar and he wears them."

We usually think of categories as exclusive. In other words, we perceive things as belonging to one category as opposed to a multiplicity of others. If something like a Maple could belong to a variety of classes instead of just the category "trees," there wouldn't be much sense in having categories in the first place. For most of us, categories, like perceived similarities, help us make sense and order out of an otherwise chaotic world. As a result of this exclusivity, we are often cued to implement our categorical thinking with terms such as *all* or *none*. Stereotypes of people or places are probably the most blatant examples of categorical thinking. When a landlord expresses frustration at his tenants for not reporting a leaky faucet until major plumbing is needed, he may say, "Well it's the renter mentality." Or when a woman expresses her frustration with an insensitive male colleague by exclaiming, "Men, they're all alike," she is defining the situation by placing a particular person within a category. Anytime we understand something to be true because it would be true by definition, we are probably invoking categorical thinking. This type of thinking can operate persuasively as we attribute the characteristics of the class to a particular instance.

A third type of familiar thinking is disjunctive thinking. Similar to categorical thinking, disjunctive thinking depends on our ability to place instances within classes. However, disjunctive thinking goes beyond assigning something to a category by constructing an order that allows the instance in question to belong to only one of two categories. Either the case is X, or it is Y. The familiar saying, "Either you're part of the solution or you're part of the problem," is illustrative of this type of thinking. Another example is the dictum "Either you're a winner or you're a loser." Such either/or thinking serves the same function as categorical thinking—it helps us simplify an otherwise complex world.

Persuaders often invoke disjunctive thinking when they provide data that shows that some instance does *not* fit a particular category, thereby implying that it fits into the opposite of that category. A popular Pepsi commercial that claimed Pepsi was the preferred drink of "a new generation" by juxtaposing a fraternity party where college students were drinking Diet Coke and playing bingo with a retirement home where senior citizens were drinking Diet Pepsi, dancing and doing lip-sync to rock and roll music set up opposing categories to suggest that either you drink Diet Pepsi or you are old fashioned.

Finally, we may think causally. Causal thinking occurs when we search for cause-effect relationships. Looking for blame, trying to place responsibility, holding people accountable and so on all embody causal thinking. Anytime a persuader tries to envision the consequences or results of taking a particular action, buying a particular product or voting a particular way, he or she is probably engaging in causal thinking.

Frequently, statistics find their persuasive force by encouraging an audience to apply causal thinking. If in a number of cases people who ate a high-fat, low-fiber diet contracted cancer, then we are asked to see the cause of cancer as dietary and to make changes accordingly. Examples can be used to stimulate causal thinking as well. If in a particular example a certain symptom was associated with a particular result, then we are asked to conclude that the symptom was a cause of the eventual result.

Sometimes causal thinking is invoked when there really exists a causal relationship. The results of numerous scientific studies actually do suggest that smoking is the cause of much heart and lung disease. Antismoking campaigns have long relied on such evidence to make their claim that smoking is hazardous to your health. However, more often persuaders encourage an audience to apply causal thinking when a cause has not been established, when only a correlation exists. For example, political candidates may point out various economic problems that occurred during an incumbent's administration to prove that the incumbent is unworthy of re-election. High unemployment or high inflation may correlate with the time in office of the incumbent but may not be the direct result of the official's policies. If, however, audience members initiate a pattern of causal thinking, they may attribute the poor state of the economy to those policies because of the correlation.

At other times, persuaders suggest that symptoms or signs of a problem are the cause of a problem simply because those symptoms are generally present when the problem occurs. For example, many advertisements for weight reduction programs show "before" and "after" pictures of successful clients. In the "before" pictures, clients frequently appear disheveled and poorly dressed in addition to being overweight. In the "after" pictures, they are usually well groomed and smiling as well as slimmer. The copy for such persuasive messages typically reinforces the notion that getting rid of the fat caused the change. However, both the weight and the personal appearances of these clients may be symptoms of physical or psychological characteristics that are actually the cause of one's outward appearance. Hence, we easily confuse a symptom for a cause when we plug in our tendency to think causally. Causal thinking patterns may provoke an audience to think that the symptom is the cause.

As with the other familiar patterns of thinking, causal thinking is encouraged by particular linguistic and visual cues. Statements that include "if/then" clauses encourage us to think causally. Visual texts that follow one scene with another may encourage us to attribute cause because of proximity in time. Simply placing two objects or people in the same scene may establish a correlation that encourages us to attribute cause. For example, if a film follows an interview with a public housing official concerning governmental policy with scenes of the homeless living on the streets, viewers may attribute the problem of homelessness to current policies and blame the housing official for that problem.

Ethics And Tests Of Evidence And Reasoning

Because persuaders can always select the evidence that they use to support a particular claim and invoke familiar patterns of thinking that may or may not make sense, there is always potential for a persuader to make connections that really aren't there and to tell only part of the story. As a result, persuasion frequently has a negative connotation, leaving the impression that persuaders manipulate their audiences by telling half-truths or invoking faulty reasoning. Aristotle pointed out that the best way to defend against such base uses of the art was to insure that each party to a controversy was trained in the art of rhetoric. If all parties involved in persuasion knew how to evaluate data and reasoning, then the truth—the best conclusion—was more likely to result. Such a position is common to the Classical Perspective toward persuasion and, thus necessitates a discussion of how to evaluate data and reasoning. Toulmin's model takes this idea into account by including the concepts of backing, qualifier and rebuttal. These parts of an argument are often missing from a persuader's argument, but may be essential components for audience members to search for as they attempt to evaluate the persuasive force of arguments. It may be reassuring to say that we are persuaded only by the facts, but we need to be able to evaluate the plausibility of those facts and the soundness of the patterns of thinking that cause us to interpret those facts in particular ways.

A variety of scholars, from those who study logic to those who teach argumentation, have provided lists of ways by which we can evaluate evidence and reasoning. Persuaders who consistently or knowingly violate these familiar tests of evidence and reasoning are usually judged unethical, while those who do not are typically perceived as ethical persuaders.

Among the tests of evidence, two stand out as particularly important. First, is there sufficient evidence for the claim? Second, is there evidence to the contrary? If no evidence is presented for a claim, then data or backing is needed. If some evidence is presented, but it doesn't seem sufficient, then the claim must be qualified. Similarly, if there is evidence to the contrary, then there is clearly a rebuttal, and at least the claim should be qualified and perhaps rejected.

A quick review of the message can expose whether any evidence is provided. A similar review of one's own knowledge about the topic under discussion may reveal whether or not there is evidence to the contrary. However, critical receivers may need to do some research themselves—consult library materials, seek out opposing views—in order to uncover whether or not there is evidence to the contrary. Within the context of the Classical Perspective toward persuasion, receivers are ethically obligated to seek out contrary evidence rather than merely assuming that a persuader is providing sufficient evidence.

A similarly difficult evaluative task occurs when some evidence is presented, but it is unclear whether or not that evidence is sufficient. The following questions can be used as tests of the sufficiency of the three types of evidence discussed earlier.

Are the examples representative? We all know that there are exceptions to every rule. If a persuader presents an example that is exceptional, rather than one that is typical, then the data may be insufficient to support the claim. Several years ago, the problem of missing children was dramatized by the story of the disappearance and brutal murder of Adam Walsh, who was snatched from a shopping center in Florida. Further study of the problem of missing children revealed that Adam's case was not typical, that most often missing children were taken by relatives engaged in custody battles who sincerely believed their children would be better off living with them than with their estranged spouses. Receivers should always expect that there exists more than a single example to support the argument. If there is only one example, then the chances that it is unrepresentative are very high. Representativeness of an example can also come into play with visual examples. Something as simple as a demonstration of a new knife that remains forever sharp on a late night commercial may be subject to questions of representativeness. Does the demonstration show a brand new knife or one that's been used for five years? Is it used to cut the types of things we typically cut or items for which we would never use such a knife? In short, is the example representative of the instances for which the claim is made?

Are statistics representative? Since statistics are collections of examples, it is not surprising that we would again be concerned with representativeness. However, with statistics we are less concerned with whether there is only one instance and more concerned with whether the collection of examples was gathered in a representative fashion. It is fine to say that the average American has blonde hair and blue eyes based on a survey that asked about the physical features of respondents; but if the survey was only distributed to ten people, it was not large enough to sample a cross-section of the population, therefore, the responses do not reflect the population as a whole. Even if the survey was mailed to thousands of people, the resulting statistics might not be representative if the respondents all lived in one geographic area, for example, in the upper Midwest where many people of Scandinavian origin live and where hair and eye coloring might be quite different from those living in the Southwest. Basically then, the test of how representative a statistic is, rests not so much on the size of the sampling from which it was drawn as on the adequacy of the cross-section the sampling addressed.

Are the people who provide testimony in a position to know what they are talking about? Most of us like to talk, and many people are willing to talk about almost anything if asked. A quotation about medical care from someone untrained and unschooled in this area may not provide sufficient evidence for claims about medicine. Just because Robert Young played the character of Dr. Marcus Welby on television does not mean that he knows the relative health advantages of caffeine-free coffee. He may be a good actor, but there are no grounds for considering him a qualified medical professional. Just as important as a source's credentials or background is the potential bias of that source. If the source has an interest in what he or she is discussing then we should assume that this self-interest clouds their judgment and places them in a less knowledgeable position. For example, Lena Horn might ordinarily be qualified to talk about how her diet has helped her to remain youthful; but if she is being paid to endorse a particular brand of breakfast cereal, as indeed she was paid to endorse bran flakes in recent television advertisements, that payment may cloud her judgment on the subject.

Just as types of data may be faulty, so may various patterns of thinking mentioned above be faulty. When a pattern of thinking is faulty or fallacious the claim is unwarranted without additional backing or data or qualifiers. Because warrants are sometimes merely implied in the message, evaluating a warrant involves checking our thinking as audience members as much as checking the reasoning of persuaders.

Among the various tests of reasoning proposed by logicians and rhetoricians, four correspond to the four patterns of thinking discussed earlier.

Questionable analogy. Are the two instances being compared sufficiently similar to justify the comparison? Shortly after the tragic bombing of the Alfred P. Murrah Federal Building in Oklahoma City in 1995, several news sources rushed to the conclusion that the tragedy was the work of Arab terrorists. These journalists based their conclusion on perceived similarities between the location and method of the bombing in Oklahoma City and similar tragedies in the Middle East, especially comparing it to the car bombing of U.S. Marine headquarters in Beirut, Lebanon. Probably their reasoning was also influenced by a second comparison with the bombing of the New York World Trade Towers; people with links to Arab terrorists were the defendants in a trial concerning that crime at the time of the Oklahoma City bombing. However, the FBI and other law enforcement agencies soon identified U.S. citizens with no apparent connections to the Arab world as the primary suspects for the Oklahoma City bombing.

Questionable classification. Whenever categorical thinking is used, it is possible that an inappropriate definition or category is being applied. If so, then the particular instance may not involve the characteristics of the class to which it is ascribed. For example, many conservative politicians have consistently opposed parental leave bills that would guarantee job security to parents who require time off to care for a new or ill child on the grounds that such legislation is "anti-family." Classifying the legislation in this way is designed to persuade others that the legislation violates a basic American value regarding the family. They frequently explain that such legislation would simply make it easier for mothers to work instead of encouraging them to stay home to care for their families, thereby further eroding the existence of the nuclear family in our culture. However, proponents of parental leave bills explain that the legislation is really pro-family in that it provides a means for caring for the family while taking into account the fact that most married couples include two wage earners rather than only one. They base their rebuttal on the test of reasoning that questions classifications.

False dilemma. When disjunctive thinking is invoked, one always runs the risk of oversimplifying the situation—of reducing the alternatives to two polar opposites rather than recognizing a complex range of alternatives. When more than two alternatives exist, such a reduction sets up a false dilemma. The Diet Pepsi commercial mentioned earlier portrays a world in which either you are young and raucous or old and boring; the type of soft drink you consume allegedly determines which of these life styles will predominate. Setting aside for a moment the problem with the causal thinking in that television spot, we can reflect on the validity of the two alternatives proposed. Surely some young people engage in quiet activities, and some older people do dance. Yet, the commercial seeks to reduce our alternatives unnecessarily.

Questionable cause. Causal connections raise questions on a variety of grounds. Just because two things correlate with one another does not mean that one causes the other. We all are mortal and breathe air, but we know that breathing does not cause death, the state of the environment not withstanding. Yet, sometimes persuaders ask us to make causal connections on the basis of just such correlations. For years some have suggested that smoking marijuana can lead the user to more dangerous drugs such as cocaine or heroine. As proof they offer statistics that a large percentage of cocaine and heroine addicts smoked marijuana at an earlier point in their lives. Such a statistic only points to a correlation, not to a causal link. All of those addicts probably drank water or Coca-Cola sometime in their lives, but no one would suggest that those substances led to their addiction. The important question to ask when examining a causal connection is whether or not a cause-effect relation exists or if the supposed cause is merely close in time or place to the effect and, therefore, existing only as a symptom of the problem which is the result of the same cause as the effect itself. In the case of drugs, an addictive personality, a genetic predisposition, or some other factor may be the cause for both smoking marijuana and becoming addicted to cocaine or heroine.

All four of the familiar tests of reasoning question the pattern of thinking that emerges so naturally and easily; they question our common sense. In the course of such questioning, breaks in similarity may appear; other categories may come to mind; and other factors that might act as causes may suggest themselves. Receivers are then in a position to assess the believability of the persuader's proof.

These familiar tests of evidence and reasoning apply to any persuasive message. If a message fails to pass these tests, then it may not be persuasive to an audience. Just because a persuader's argument doesn't pass all of these tests does not necessarily mean that he or she is unethical. Some persuasive messages focus less on presenting arguments than on appealing to the passions or authority. Even in those instances where a persuader explicitly claims to present arguments and facts, it is possible that the persuader simply made a mistake in preparing his or her message. However, if we encounter a pattern of insufficient evidence, irrelevant evidence or faulty reasoning in a case where the persuader explicitly claims to present us with reasonable arguments, we may judge a particular message or even the source of that message to be unethical. From the Classical Perspective and its contemporary development, the responsibility for applying these tests and making a judgment lies with the audience.

CRITICAL FOCUS: REAGAN'S ADDRESS TO REPUBLICAN CONVENTION

The ideas discussed in this chapter provide several means to analyze persuasive messages that appeal directly to our good sense and appreciation for factual data. When confronted by such messages we can and should ask a variety of questions.

CRITICAL QUESTIONS

1. What are the **claims** in the message?
2. What **evidence** or **data** is offered in support of those claims?
3. What **warrants** will need to be supplied to fill out the arguments?
4. Do the warrants follow **patterns of thinking** or **topics** familiar to the audience?

5. Do the evidence and reasoning meet the **tests for evidence and reasoning?**

If we apply these critical questions to the excerpt of Reagan's "Facts Are Stubborn Things" speech mentioned at the beginning of this chapter, the results are revealing.

In the videotaped excerpt Reagan makes his main claims explicit at the outset, asserting, "Eight years ago, we met at a time when America was in economic chaos, and today we meet in a time of economic promise. We met then in international distress and today with global hope." He then takes each claim in order and provides supporting data.

Beginning with the idea that eight years ago the country was in economic chaos, he provides a multiplicity of data that is punctuated by his repeated phrase, "facts are stubborn things." In order, Reagan enumerates the following "facts":

1. We had experienced the worst two years of back-to-back inflation in sixty years.
2. Interest rates were more than 21 percent.
3. Industrial production was down for two consecutive years.
4. The average weekly wage was down 9 percent.
5. Median family income was down 5.5 percent.
6. Democrats had passed the highest tax bill in 200 years.
7. Auto loans went up to 17 percent, causing factories to shut down.
8. Fuel costs had more than doubled.
9. People were waiting in gas lines and unemployment lines.
10. The misery index was almost 21 percent.

When familiar tests of evidence and reasoning are applied, Reagan's argument loses some of its strength. To be convinced that America was in economic chaos in 1980 on the basis of these "facts," the audience would need to supply a definitional warrant that defines economic chaos in terms similar to the facts enumerated. Consequently, it is appropriate to apply the test of reasoning known as "questionable classification." In other words, is an increase in inflation and interest rates and a decrease in employment (a misery index of 21 percent) equivalent to economic chaos? Certainly, such figures, if accurate, suggest economic trouble. However, "chaos" is probably an exaggerated term for a period of economic stagnation. The system was still functioning, just not as well as at some other times. Still, the audience likely granted Reagan his definitional warrant, realizing however that the chaos was milder than a complete breakdown of the system such as during the Great Depression.

In addition to applying a test of reason, it is appropriate to apply two of the tests of evidence. First, is the source of the evidence reliable? Since Reagan did not provide the sources of his statistical data, some audience members might initially question the validity of the data. Of course, many would probably believe that Reagan, as the chief executive for a government with extensive resources for collecting data, knew the facts. However, because Reagan also served as the top elected official for the Republican Party and his "facts" described conditions during the time of a Democratic administration, we could question whether or not his data was free of bias. Second, because nearly all of his data was statistical, we might be concerned with whether or not his statistics were representative? Were his figures representative of the entire four years of the Carter Administration or only representative of a particular period in 1980? Were people waiting in employment lines and gas lines all over the country or only in some areas? Questions such as these along with the recognition that Reagan's data might be biased lessen the impact of his argument slightly. Still the "facts" probably seem rather convincing. Consequently, research of the "facts" to determine whether they are consistent with other sources is in order.

Such research reveals larger problems with Reagan's argument. Although Reagan's facts concerning inflation were essentially correct, his statistics about interest rates were probably misleading. Economists at the time pointed out that the increase in interest rates was the result of inflation. When we adjust the interest rate to account for inflation, the rate was the same or less than in prior years.[8] So, while one might consider inflation a problem, interest rates were not a separate, additional problem. Similarly, while interest rates for auto loans were high, with inflation those interest rates were no higher than in previous years. Reagan's suggestion that automobile factories were being forced to close as a result of such high rates is unsupported by other data. Instead, foreign competition, consumer perceptions that foreign automobiles were more reliable and fuel efficient, and the decision by American auto makers to retool or sometimes move parts of their manufacturing overseas where the labor costs were less probably contributed more to the closing of domestic automobile manufacturing plants. A similar problem concerns Reagan's suggestion about taxes. Although he said that Democrats had passed the tax bill, that legislation was the result of a bipartisan effort in which many Republicans had also voted for the bill.

In addition to the problem that some of Reagan's "facts" were misleading, others were simply inaccurate. The *Economic Report* reveals that in current dollars, the average weekly wage *increased* 24 percent from 1977 to 1980, rather than decreasing as Reagan suggested.[9] Similarly, the *Statistical Abstract* showed that median family income had decreased only 3.4 percent between 1976 and 1980, rather than the 5.5 percent cited by Reagan.[10] And, according to the President's own economic report, industrial production was only down for one year, not two years; and between 1977 and 1980 as a whole, industrial production was up 8.6 points.[11]

Once we investigate the "facts," the situation appears much less threatening than suggested by Reagan. His use of misleading and inaccurate facts calls into question his objectivity in presenting data as well as his ethics as a persuader. These problems become even more apparent if we consider his support for the claim that his Republican administration changed the system to end the economic chaos of 1980. In support of the claim that his administration had significantly improved the economy, Reagan presented the following data:

1. We cut the tax rate for working folks.
2. We indexed taxes and stopped bracket creep.

3. The top 5 percent of earners now pay more taxes.
4. Low earners now pay nothing.
5. We created 17.5 million "good" jobs, 11 million in the past 4 years.
6. New home construction and new car sales are booming.
7. Exports are increasing.
8. Inflation is down to 3.5 percent and 4 percent.
9. Interest rates are less than half what they were before.

Again, careful examination of Reagan's argument reveals a variety of weaknesses. Two tests of reasoning especially apply. First, because his argument depends on a definitional warrant concerning what it means to "improve" economic conditions, we can ask about questionable classification. Are the types of economic changes that Reagan refers to equivalent to "improving" the economy? Most people would probably agree that decreasing inflation and interest rates and increasing sales of homes and autos is an improvement. Tax reform, on the other hand, might or might not signal an improvement in the economy. People paying less taxes would probably enjoy the use of additional disposable income, but those paying more would probably be less satisfied. If government revenues dropped as a result of tax reform causing some government workers to lose their jobs or others who benefited from government programs to lose their benefits, then those people would probably not view the economy as improved. On the other hand, if revenues increased and were put to use stimulating the economy, then tax reform might be viewed as an improvement.

A second test of reasoning that is important is "questionable cause." Reagan attributes the improvement to Republicans who "rolled up their sleeves and went to work in January of 1981." However, as we will see when we look at his data closely, many of the economic improvements may have resulted from factors other than the policies of the Republican administration.

In addition, the two tests of evidence applied earlier apply in this case as well. Is the source of the evidence trustworthy? Again, Reagan does not identify the source of his data, and there is some reason to believe that if he is the source he may be biased, wanting to take the credit for improved circumstances. Also, are the statistics representative? Do they reflect nationwide changes or improvements for only some sectors of the population? Do they reflect "real" improvements or only illusory ones? Again, additional research into the "facts" reveals a number of problems relevant to the tests of evidence and reasoning.

First, several of Reagan's facts appear to be inaccurate. His own economic report reveals only 15 million new jobs, rather than the 17.5 million that he cited. In addition, because some old jobs were lost, the "real" number of new jobs appeared to be only 12.1 million.[12] Moreover, when we compare the eight years of the Reagan Administration with the four years of the Carter Administration, improvements in employment appear to be particularly questionable. When we compute yearly averages, 1.8 million jobs were gained each year during the Carter Administration, while only 1.7 million jobs were gained each year during the Reagan Administration.[13] Moreover, one can dispute the notion that these jobs were "good." *Business Week* reported that during the Carter Administration (1976-1980) 45 percent of the jobless fell in the "prime employment" years (aged 24-55), while during the Reagan Administration (1980-1988) 55 percent of the jobless were in this category.[14] These facts imply that many of the jobs created during the Reagan years were not the sort of jobs likely to be filled by adult workers in their prime, jobs unlikely to be classified as "good." Instead, many of the jobs may have been for employees of fast food outlets and the like, jobs likely to be filled by teenagers or retirees.

Similarly, Reagan's data concerning tax reform may not have been wholly accurate. The President's own *Economic Report* revealed that the percent of personal income that people paid in taxes was the same in 1987 as it was in 1980, leading one to wonder what it means to say that the tax rate has been cut or that bracket creep has been stopped.[15] While some tax rates did decrease, the tax rates for the very rich decreased the most and tax rates for low income families on welfare actually increased.[16] Such revealing facts led Reagan's own former Budget Director, David Stockman, to call his tax reform a "Trojan horse" aimed at bringing the top rate down rather than encouraging all to work and save.[17]

Likewise, Reagan's statements about new home construction and new car sales were misleading. While these sectors of the economy may have improved, other sectors must have worsened, because his own Presidential report on the economy showed that the industrial production index was actually down slightly (2.1 percent per year) during the eight years of his administration as compared to the four years of Carter's administration (2.15 percent per year).[18] Moreover, although many new homes were being built, the rate of home ownership decreased from 65.5 percent in 1980 to 63.7 percent in 1988, suggesting that wealthy contractors were reaping rental profits, but average Americans were less able to purchase homes.[19]

In addition to the problems with Reagan's data verifying his claim that economic conditions had improved, there are problems with his causal connection that attributes improvements to his administration. For example, although inflation did decrease from 18 percent in 1980 to 3.5 percent to 4 percent in 1988, many attributed that decrease to a variety of factors unrelated to the Reagan administration. Economist Paul Samuelson suggested that the decrease was due in large part to the monetarist policies of Paul Volcker, Chairman of the Federal Reserve Board, who was a Carter appointee.[20] Others noted that oil price increases accounted for the high inflation during the Carter years and that Reagan benefited from an oil glut and a change in OPEC policies that drove oil prices down.[21] Finally, others explained that inflation went down because unemployment went up, noting that Reagan's policies had not solved our economic problems, but merely substituted one problem (unemployment) for the other (inflation).[22]

Finally, knowledge about the economy generally weakens Reagan's argument as it becomes apparent what data he omitted. You may recall that earlier in his speech he cited declining wages, increasing fuel costs, gas lines and unemployment as signs of economic chaos. Yet, his review of how the economy had improved makes no mention of these factors. This was probably so because of little improvement in many of these areas. For example, the average weekly adjusted wage during all the Reagan years except 1984 fell to an all-time low since 1961, according to his own *Economic Report*.[23] Additional factors that suggest a worsening of the economic picture were also omitted. The amount of poverty increased during the Reagan years as the gap between rich and poor expanded and the number of homeless mushroomed.[24] Even for many above the poverty line, conditions worsened. The income of young families, for example, fell from $17,068 in 1981 to $14,945 in 1987.[25] For the economy as a whole, some ominous signs were looming at the time Reagan made his optimistic address. Instead of increasing government revenues, tax reform had resulted in decreasing revenues. Meanwhile, government spending under the Reagan Administration had increased, resulting in an enormous budget deficit that many economic forecasters predicted would result in economic troubles that would make the problems of the Carter Administration look like a prosperous period.[26] So much data that Reagan did not mention calls into serious question his claim regarding improvement in the economy.

The other claims in Reagan's address can be similarly examined to determine the specific data and warrants necessary to support his arguments. By applying the tests of evidence and reasoning and consulting other data, we can assess the soundness of a persuader's arguments. Unfortunately, in the case of Reagan's address to the 1988 Republican Convention, his arguments appear to be less "factual" than the phrase by which the speech has become known would make it appear. Without critical examination, audiences may find it easy to accept Reagan's claims and applaud his use of "facts" in the process of persuasion. Careful examination of those "facts," however, reveals a variety of inaccuracies and some questionable reasoning. The result is serious concern for the ethics of Reagan as a speaker.[27]

NOTES

1. For a representative analysis of this type, see William F. Lewis, "Telling America's Story: Narrative Form and the Reagan Presidency," *Quarterly Journal of Speech* 73 (1987): 280-302.
2. Such works include *Categories, Prior Analytics, Topics,* available in various translations.
3. Stephen Toulmin, *The Uses of Argument* (London, Cambridge University Press, 1958), 94-145.
4. Marvin Karlins and Herbert I. Abelson, *Persuasion: How Opinions and Attitudes Are Changed*, 2nd Ed (New York: Springer, 1970), 34-37.
5. Wayne N. Thompson, *The Process of Persuasion: Principles and Readings* (New York: Harper & Row, 1975), 109-110.
6. This summary is based on the following sources: Thompson, *Process,* 110-112; James C. McCroskey, "A Summary of Experimental Research on the Effects of Evidence in Persuasive Communication," *Quarterly Journal of Speech* 55 (1969): 169-176.
7. While these patterns have been discussed by logicians and developmental psychologists alike, a succinct review of them may be found in Martha

Cooper, *Analyzing Public Discourse* (Prospect Heights: Waveland, 1989), 75-80.

8. Paul Samuelson, "The #1 Economic Problem is the Structural Budget Deficit," *Harvard Business Review* 66 (1988): 67.
9. *Economic Report of the President* transmitted to the Congress, February 1988 (Washington: U.S. Government Printing Office, 1988), Table B-45.
10. *U.S. Statistical Abstract, 1988*, Table 699.
11. *Economic Report*, Table B-48.
12. *Economic Report*, 58.
13. *Economic Report*, Table B-32.
14. "In Foreign Markets, Reaganomics Didn't Get Such High Marks," *Business Week* (6 Feb 1988): 26.
15. *Economic Report*, Table B-26.
16. Emma Rothschild, "The Real Reagan Economy," *New York Review of Books* (30 June 1988): 40; Isabel V. Sawhill, "Reaganomics in Retrospect: Lessons for a New Administration," *Challenge* (May/June 1989): 58.
17. Reported in Sawhill, "Reaganomics," 59.
18. *Economic Report*, Table B-48.
19. E. Jacoby and C. Anderson, "The Legacy of Reaganomics," *Builder* (October 1988): 54-58.
20. Samuelson, "#1," 68.
21. Jacoby and Anderson, "Legacy," 53.
22. Sawhill, "Reaganomics," 58.
23. *Economic Report*, Table B-45.
24. Louis Richman, "Who's Winning the Pocketbook Issue?," *Fortune* (29 August 1988): 44-46.
25. Richman, "Who's," 44.
26. See, for example, "Assessing Reaganomics: The Trouble with Theories," *The Economist* (21 Jan 1989): 74-76; see, also Samuelson, "#1."
27. On Reagan's habitual misuse of evidence, see Richard L. Johannesen, "An Ethical Assessment of the Reagan Rhetoric: 1981-1982," reprinted in Johannesen, *Ethics in Human Communication*, 3rd Ed (Prospect Heights: Waveland, 1990), 235-252.

4

Motivation Theory And The Passions

IN THIS CHAPTER:

Focus on:

Motivating Americans to AIDS Awareness

1. Theoretical Focus: Emotions, Attitudes and the Psychology of the Audience
2. Foundations: Aristotle's Analysis of the Emotions
   Anger and Patience
   Friendship and Enmity
   Fear and Confidence
3. Contemporary Developments in Motivation Theories
   Motivation and the Desire for Psychological Equilibrium
   Motivation and the Desire for Personal and Psychological Growth
4. Ethical Issues in the Tactical use of Emotional Appeals
5. Critical Focus: Public Service Announcements about AIDS

Focus On: Motivating Americans To AIDS Awareness

Beginning in the early 1980's, America witnessed both a steady increase in the incidence of Acquired Immune Deficiency Syndrome (AIDS) and a growing public awareness of the nature, extent and danger of this contagious and still incurable disease. By November 1988, over 78,000 cases of the disease, over 44,000 of which had already led to death, had been reported to the national Centers for Disease Control (CDC) in Atlanta.[1] As the initial outlines of a national health policy on AIDS began to emerge in the late 1980's, the CDC assumed its role in the effort to contain the spread of AIDS.[2] The mission of the CDC included coordinating the gathering of statistical information regarding the incidence of AIDS and researching and recommending measures for checking the progress of AIDS in the American population. Hence the CDC's mission soon came to include developing a plan of public persuasion, working in concert with other public health organizations. This required combining information about the disease with advice on its prevention. The CDC sought to raise public awareness and motivation, without which the task of preventing AIDS would be nearly impossible.

Several factors, both scientific and social, were shaping the persuasive situation the CDC was preparing to enter. The AIDS virus was known to be transmitted through unprotected sexual contact with someone who had already acquired the disease and through the sharing of hypodermic needles used by someone who was infected. A third means of transmission, through blood transfusions from a donor who had acquired AIDS, was virtually eliminated by the improved techniques for screening donated blood developed during the late 1980's.[3] The American public was at first largely unaware of the magnitude of the problem represented by AIDS. The gradually awakening understanding of the problem was accompanied by many popularly held misconceptions regarding the nature of the disease, such as how it was transmitted, who was at risk and what measures would reduce one's risk of acquiring AIDS. Further, popular belief held that AIDS was as a condition affecting only marginal groups—gay males, intravenous drug users, ghetto dwellers.[4] Not only was such stereotyping slowing the general public's recognition of AIDS as a risk to the entire American population, it was also triggering all-too-common outbursts of "gay-bashing" and harassment of homosexuals.[5] Each of these situational factors represented part of the challenge faced by the CDC's persuasive purposes.

As a part of its overall campaign to fight the spread of AIDS, the CDC produced a series of 60-second (and shorter) public awareness and education messages to be broadcast on television beginning in 1988. This series has several recurring features, including a consistent format, a quickly recognizable graphic slogan, "America Responds to AIDS," and recognizable music. The ads commonly feature identified individuals talking about the need to change our attitudes and behavior to control the spread of AIDS and are explicitly "set" in identifiable cities, including two ads we will examine more closely in this chapter, "Minneapolis" and "New York City."[6] The various ads center on different AIDS-related themes. "Minneapolis" discusses AIDS as a disease affecting "all of us," not just "others." "New York City" addresses the need for education and awareness, especially regarding safe sex practices.

The persuasive challenge faced by the CDC in its persuasive campaign to influence public awareness and attitudes regarding AIDS cannot be accounted for completely by the concepts discussed in Chapter 2. AIDS poses a danger that triggers some of our most fundamental attitudes, emotions, and motivations in complex ways. Reasonable argumentation alone is simply not enough to attempt such an important and wide-reaching change. In this chapter we will consider the ways in which emotions and motivations, constituting the psychology of the audience and of audience members, contribute to the persuasive process and constitute an area of important strategic choices for persuaders.

THEORETICAL FOCUS: EMOTIONS, ATTITUDES AND THE PSYCHOLOGY OF THE AUDIENCE

Both the classical approach to understanding motivation and the passions and its contemporary developments are shaped by two important assumptions: (1) the motivations and emotional state of audience members will influence their reaction to persuasive attempts; and (2) persuasive messages themselves can help create, intensify or suspend certain motivations and emotional states in their audiences. Thus the Classical Perspective draws our attention to the complex set of links between persuasive messages and audience motivations and passions and explores ways in which persuaders may use these links to design their persuasive strategies.

In the next part of this chapter we will review one of the first systematic discussions of the role of the emotions and audience predispositions in general as outlined in Aristotle's *Rhetoric*.[7] More contemporary theorists have tried to understand the fundamental psychological processes themselves. Following our review of Aristotle's theory, this chapter will examine several of these modern developments regarding motivations and attitudes. We will examine equilibrium theories and humanistic growth theories. While these contemporary developments often arrive at conclusions that depart significantly from Aristotle's original discussion of the passions, a common thread holds them together. They are all attempts to explain how audience predispositions and frame of mind can contribute to the outcome of attempted persuasion.

In the final portion of this chapter, we will examine three important issues raised by contemporary developments of the classical theories of audience motivation. What is the relation of so-called "subliminal perception" techniques to persuasion? How can persuaders tactically appeal to audiences' motivations and passions in a culture (such as our own) wherein reasoning or *logos* is traditionally held to be the superior form of influence? Finally, how can we respond to the many ethical questions raised by the use of appeals to emotions and psychological states?

Foundations: Aristotle's Analysis Of The Emotions

Aristotle, among the first theorists of persuasion, addressed the ethical and tactical problems associated with the presence of emotional appeals in persuasion. "The emotions," he wrote, "are all those feelings that so change men as to affect their judgments, and that are also attended by pain or pleasure."[8] Our judgments are influenced by these internal responses. These are internal responses centered in us rather than in the argumentation within a persuasive message or in the persuader. These internal responses influence our judgments as audience members.

Aristotle's systematic analysis of the emotions advises persuaders on three aspects of any emotion: the nature of the experience itself, those toward whom the emotion will most likely be directed, and the inclination the emotion creates in those who experience it. Figure 4.1 offers a brief summary of the 14 emotions whose persuasive potential Aristotle examined. Note that while some of the emotions are organized as pairs of opposites (anger and patience, friendship and enmity, etc.), others are grouped through some similarity or resemblance (pity and indignation, or envy and emulation).[9]

Aristotle's analysis of the emotions suggests a variety of strategies available to persuaders as they look for ways to influence their audiences. Equally important, Aristotle's theory suggests ways of understanding why some persuasive attempts fail to have the desired emotional effect on their audience. Consider the practical implications for persuaders of Aristotle's observations with regard to three pairs of emotions: anger and patience, fear and confidence and friendship and enmity.

Anger and Patience

What stirs an audience to anger? Persuaders can create or intensify anger in their audiences by showing how someone has treated them with contempt, spite or insolence. Audiences in such a frame of mind will feel gratified by persuaders who offer up images of "evening the score" with those who have angered them. They may be inclined to take action following a persuader's recommendations if those recommendations are perceived as leading to some kind of retribution.

Figure 4.1

A SUMMARY OF ARISTOTLE'S ANALYSIS OF THE EMOTIONS

Aristotle demonstrated that each of the various emotions, many of which he grouped as paired opposites, has recognizable causes and is accompanied by the experience of either pain or pleasure.

EMOTION	CAUSES AND CHARACTERISTICS	PAIN/PLEASURE
ANGER	The belief that we have been unjustifiably treated badly by some person. Anger is accompanied by an "impulse toward revenge."	**Pain** from being treated badly; **pleasure** from imagining revenge.
PATIENCE	(The opposite of anger) The belief that we have been treated well or at least not *intentionally* treated badly.	**Pleasure** at our good fortune or at being treated courteously.
FRIENDSHIP	The desire for good things to happen to others and the belief that they wish the same for us.	**Pleasure** when good things happen to them; **pain** when bad things happen to them.
ENMITY	(The opposite of friendship) The desire for bad things to happen to others because we are angry with them or because we have different likes or goals than they have.	**Pain** if good things happen to them; **pleasure** if bad things happen to them.
FEAR	Imagining something unpleasant or destructive awaiting us in the future.	**Pain** at the thought of bad things ahead.
CONFIDENCE	(The opposite of fear) The belief that we are safe from harm or that any danger is remote or unlikely.	**Pleasure** from belief that we are safe from danger.
SHAME	The prospect of events likely to bring disgrace or dishonor to ourselves or our friends.	**Pain** at the thought of the disgrace or dishonor itself.
SHAMELESSNESS	(The opposite of shame) The belief that we have not behaved dishonorably or any such dishonor is in the eyes of those who are unimportant to us.	**Pleasure** at having behaved without disgrace or dishonor.
EMULATION	The craving to have the good things that others have, things that we might have but do not.	**Pain**, not because someone else has the good thing, but because we do not.
CONTEMPT	(The opposite of emulation) The scorn we feel when bad things happen to those for whom we have little respect.	**Pleasure** at seeing evil befall those we find unworthy of emulation.
KINDNESS	The impulse to do good to others without selfish consideration for our actions.	**Pleasure** at seeing good come to others from our actions.
PITY	The distress of seeing undeserved harm or pain come to those we regard as our equals	**Pain** at imagining the undeserved harm to our equals.

	or allies.	
INDIGNATION	The resentment of good fortune coming to someone we believe does not deserve it.	**Pain** at the undeserved good fortune of another.
ENVY	The disturbance caused by the good fortune of an equal.	**Pain**, not because we desire the good thing ourselves, but because someone else has it.

Consider how the following passage from a speech by Black Muslim leader, Malcolm X, given a few hours after his home had been fire bombed, might create or intensify the feeling of anger in its principle audience, blacks in America during the mid-1960's:

> America is a society where there is no brotherhood. This society is controlled primarily by the racists and segregationists who are in Washington, D.C., in positions of power. And from Washington, D.C., they exercise the same forms of brutal oppression against dark-skinned people in South and North Vietnam, or in the Congo, or in Cuba, or any other place on this earth where they are trying to exploit and oppress. This is a society whose government doesn't hesitate to inflict the most brutal form of punishment and oppression upon dark-skinned people all over the world.[10]

While Malcolm X stops short of urging the audience to take direct action against the dominant white society who has angered them, his words certainly would strongly arouse such an audience to *imagine* such retribution.

Anger moves audiences to vengeance (or at least to an aroused state from *imagining* vengeance) against whomever they believe has deliberately wronged them. But they are commonly moved to patience when others have done them no wrong or harm or when an experienced harm was not the *intentional* result of another's actions. Further, in contrast to anger, patience does not need a specific person to be its object. We tend to feel patient rather than angry in any situation in which we are amused, hopeful or are treated with respect or courtesy. Moreover, says Aristotle, when we have acted on our feelings of anger or when time has passed since we were made angry, we tend to grow more patient.

Persuaders can encourage their audiences to be patient rather than angry, by arguing that they have not been harmed, or if harmed, it was not deliberate. Consider, for example, the case of CBS television commentator Andy Rooney, who was suspended from work for several weeks beginning February 8, 1990, following the publication of an interview in the Los Angeles newspaper, *The Advocate*. In that interview Rooney made comments offensive to many in the gay community. Rooney's comments, excerpted below, were broadcast on his return to the weekly series, *Sixty Minutes*, following his suspension:

> What do I say to defend myself? Do I say I am not a racist? Sounds like saying "I am not a crook." How do I apologize to homosexuals for hurting them with a remark I made that I didn't realize would hurt them? It's demeaning to have to sit here and defend myself. In the army in World

> War Two, I was infuriated to find that black soldiers had to sit in the back of the bus. I got on a bus in St. Augustine one day to go back to Camp Blanding, and I insisted on sitting in the back with the black guys. I was arrested. In 1970 I sat out with a camera crew to find out what happened to the man who was twice tried for the murder of that great civil rights leader Medgar Evers. I was arrested and dragged into court by two red-necked sheriffs who didn't like what we were doing.... My son says that one of the worst experiences of his young life was the night I asked a guest to leave our house because he kept using the word "nigger." I'd feel the same today if anyone used an insulting word about homosexuals.[11]

Rooney concedes at least the possibility of harm caused his audience by hearing racist and bigoted remarks. However, he attempts to defuse anger and promote patience by claiming that his remarks were not intended to offend. Indeed, Rooney mentions the special pain he feels because the interpretation of his action runs counter to his own dislike of bigotry.

FRIENDSHIP AND ENMITY

We might also interpret Rooney's defense of his actions as an attempt to establish friendship where there had been the potential for enmity. Who are our friends? They are those who share our likes as well as our dislikes, or perhaps those who have the same allies or enemies we have. We feel pleasure when good things happen to our friends and pain when unpleasant things happen to them. Thus, an audience might be moved to feel friendship toward some person or group when shown by a persuader that these others are working for the audience's best interests or that they share the same interests or even the same enemies. For example, the Illinois branch of the 1988 Bush-Quayle campaign organization distributed a pamphlet during the 1988 presidential campaign containing the following passage: "The Dukakis Record of Setting Murderers, Rapists, and Child Molesters Free...." The accompanying text depicted Bush as an advocate of law and order and a friend of police, while depicting Dukakis as an enemy of the police and a friend of heinous criminals. In the context of other Bush ads, the motivational intent of this ad is clear: to establish "friendship" or, more precisely, a relationship of voter support between Bush and white middle-class viewers and voters. The ad attempts to achieve this end by drawing attention to images of persons and actions both Bush and the audience presumably find offensive.

In much the same way, we may regard someone as our enemy because we are angry with them; but we also may feel enmity toward others for no reason other than that their likes and interests seem to be different than our own. Thus, it is possible for a persuader to induce audience members to regard some person or persons as their enemy by showing that these others have treated them with disrespect, frustrated their goals or deliberately attempted to humiliate them—all the causes Aristotle identified in his analysis of anger. Unfortunately, it is because of this same principle that persuaders may cause an audience to regard others as enemies simply because they belong to a particular type of group or have different goals and interests, to hate or oppose them simply because they are different. While such tactics are ethically abhorrent, they are unfortunately a familiar and persuasive part of the armory of the racist, the bigot, the hatemonger and the demagogue. In this regard, it is theoretically interesting—and ethically offensive—that the "Willie Horton" ads used by the Bush-

Quayle campaign in 1988 invariably featured a *picture* of Horton, who is black. As Roger Ailes, media advisor to the Bush/Quayle campaign, described the campaign's strategy: "The only question is whether we depict Willie Horton with a knife in his hand or without it."[12] The ads' strategy seems aimed not merely at middle-class voters but more specifically at *white* middle-class voters, exploiting complex negative racial stereotypes within this audience.

Fear and Confidence

According to Aristotle, fear is the pain we feel when we imagine something unpleasant or destructive awaiting us in the future. In order for such images to move us to fear, they must seem real and somehow close-at-hand. If unpleasant or destructive events seem unlikely or far-removed from our situation, they do little to stir fear in us. Hence persuaders who wish to move their audience to feel fear must not only create images of pain or destruction for their audience, but they must also make these dangers seem likely to happen. They must make their audience members feel that they are likely to be victims of these events. While the tales of violence and destruction we read about or see on television or in films may be upsetting to us, we do not feel fear until we believe that these things are *likely to happen to us*. Unless the audience is made to feel that these unpleasant images represent a very real and likely danger, the feelings of pain will quickly pass and with them the chance to lead the audience members to change their behavior in the desired way. Aristotle's analysis of fear suggests that such persuaders must find some way to make the danger not only unpleasant but also *imminent*.

This intensity must be created without leading audience members to see disaster as so certain and so devastating that they feel too numbed or helpless to respond. Contemporary research suggests that such "overkill" in the use of fear appeals may backfire and leave an audience less inclined to act or think differently than before.[13] Nor can a persuader ethically attempt to create fear in an audience by knowingly misrepresenting information or by dishonestly "stampeding" a frightened audience into a decision serving only the persuader's private ends.

Confidence, by comparison, could be created in an audience by a persuader who draws attention to the audience's power, prosperity or friends—all the things that make danger seem remote or unlikely. Such tactics are no doubt familiar to our readers in certain kinds of political persuasion, especially acceptance and nomination speeches at political conventions. These speeches are usually filled with reminders of the popularity of the candidate or the wide support that the party enjoys. When the candidate is an incumbent or of the same party as the incumbent, the speeches frequently remind the audience of the prosperity, successes and achievements brought about by the current administration. The presence of such efforts to bolster the confidence of the audience is not surprising. After all, political conventions are intended not only to nominate a candidate and establish a platform of issues and policies to define the candidacy, but also to create psychological momentum and optimism among the party members and audience.

Our examples above have only considered three pairs from the fourteen emotions covered in Aristotle's discussion of the passions, but they should serve to illustrate the general principles involved. Modern research into motivation and the passions has parted company with Aristotle's emphasis on the emotions themselves and looked much more closely at broader theories of human psychology. This research has nevertheless held to two important assumptions of Aristotle's original generalizations: How we react to persuasive phenomena is partly shaped by enduring aspects of our psychological makeup and by the experience of pleasure or pain which is at the heart of motivation.

CONTEMPORARY DEVELOPMENTS IN MOTIVATION THEORIES

Many contemporary theories of motivation and attitude change investigate basic psychological processes presumed to remain largely unchanged by context or personality type. The two best known areas of this theoretical research are equilibrium theories and personal growth theories.

MOTIVATION AND THE DESIRE FOR PSYCHOLOGICAL EQUILIBRIUM

Equilibrium theories of attitude and motivation are founded on several general assumptions. First, we hold within ourselves many different cognitions—thoughts, beliefs, memories, attitudes and values. Second, these cognitive elements can come into conflict with one another as we remember actions in conflict with our current values or when we must reconcile the knowledge that a friend holds a belief very different from our own. Finally, and most importantly, equilibrium theories hold that the experience of conflicting cognitions is unpleasant or uncomfortable and that we naturally move (consciously or unconsciously) to reduce this unpleasant experience of tension by changing our attitudes or our behaviors, thereby reestablishing equilibrium. The general strategic principle to guide persuaders, based on equilibrium theories, is as follows: Persuaders can influence their audiences by first creating cognitive imbalance. They can do so by showing audience members that there is inconsistency between their actions and their cognitive elements or between the consequences of various attitudes they hold. Then the persuaders can link their own proposals with the reduction of that inconsistency. Included among the foundational works in this line of research are Fritz Heider's "balance theory" of attitude change[14] and Leon Festinger's "cognitive dissonance" theory of attitude change.[15]

Cognitive Balance Theory Fritz Heider's model of cognitive balance is perhaps the most fundamental and representative of balance theories.[16] Cognitive balance theory bases its analysis on two concepts. The first is our tendency to experience certain phenomena as "belonging together," such as a persuader with her actions, a public interest group and its cause or the actions of a member of a group with the group itself. The basis of this" belonging together" can be our perceptions of "similarity, proximity, common fate, good continuation, set, and past experience."[17] The second central concept of the cognitive balance model is our reaction, either positive or negative, to the things or persons we perceive—liking or disliking them. Note that cognitive balance theory treats this liking/disliking as a dichotomy; there are no degrees of liking, no mixed feelings.[18] Note also the importance of "perception:" The relation is defined by the positive or negative relationship we *perceive* among our experiences, rather than any independent qualities those phenomena might possess.

The model is completed by considering the liking relation between P and O (a Perceiver and an Other, respectively) and between each of these two and some object X. In this model, X may represent anything (or anyone) toward which P and O might have either positive or negative sentiments, preferences or evaluations. Formally stated, P feels cognitive imbalance and pressure to change relevant attitudes, when P's attitudes toward O and X and P's perception of O's attitude toward X are not in agreement. Note that there are eight possible combinations of positive and negative liking in such three-part relations. Six of these three-part relationships are diagrammed in Table 4.2.

The three-part relationships—among a perceiver, a second person and some third element in a unit relation with the second person—must exist in one of two fundamental states, either balanced or unbalanced. In general, balance exists when the various elements and relations are in harmony from the point of view of the perceiver. More specifically, as shown in the sample cases described in Figure 4.2, cognitive balance exists from the perceiver's point of view when all three of the relations are positive or if two are negative. Balanced cognitive states are assumed to be relatively stable and resistant to psychological influence. Unbalanced states are assumed to be both unstable and uncomfortable, such that the perceiver is both susceptible to influences that might restore balance by creating psychological change.

Thus, in general terms, cognitive balance theory predicts that we will experience cognitive balance when we like people who like the same things we do (Case 1); or when we like people who dislike the same things we do or dislike the same things our friends do (Case 2); or when we like things that people we dislike don't like or dislike people who don't like the same things we do (Case 3). Conversely, we experience cognitive imbalance when someone we like feels positively about something we dislike (Case 4); or when someone we dislike appears to like the same thing we do (Case 5); or when we like something that a friend dislikes (Case 6). In these cases we experience pressure to restore balance by changing our attitude about the other person or the object in question.

The general model of cognitive balance makes intuitive sense, and research has confirmed its central theoretical predictions. However, as a contemporary development within the Classical Perspective, the general cognitive balance theory is only of limited use. Several problems arise when we attempt to use Heider's theory in specific situations to form persuasive strategy or to explain persuasive effects. The first of several pressing questions is: are the relationships among the various components of our attitudes as simple as the basic cognitive balance theory would have it? Heider's theory and its subsequent development simply reduces our evaluative response to either "liking" or intensity between some attitudes and others or the possibility that our attitudes might be mixed—both liking and disliking the same person or object in different ways. Second, can a *three-part* model of cognitive balance take into account the complex web of persons and objects involved in our attitudes and judgment? Third, can we predict how our attitudes might change without knowing the *importance* of the various elements making up our attitudinal relationships? Perhaps most important, while cognitive balance theory may assume that we will restore cognitive balance in the manner requiring the least effort, is the experience of cognitive imbalance alone enough to let us predict changes in our social behavior?[19]

Figure 4.2

Representative Schematics of Cognitively Balanced and Unbalanced States

Below are some illustrative cases of cognitive balance in which a perciever P considers person O and object X as "belonging together." Positive liking relations are indicated by a plus sign; negative linking relations are indicated by a minus sign. The relationship between O and X is P's *perception* of that relationship.

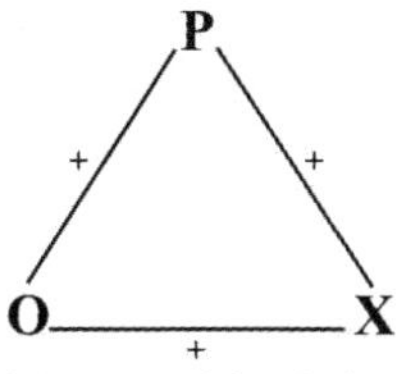

CASE 1: cognitive balance
P likes O
P likes X
O likes X

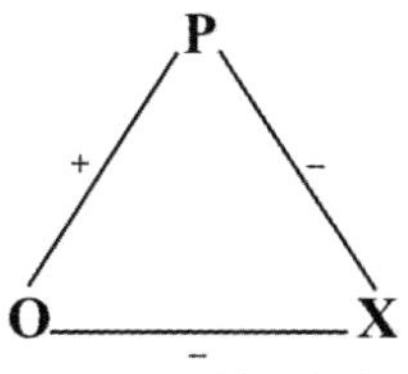

CASE 2: cognitive balance
P likes O
P dislikes X
O dislikes X

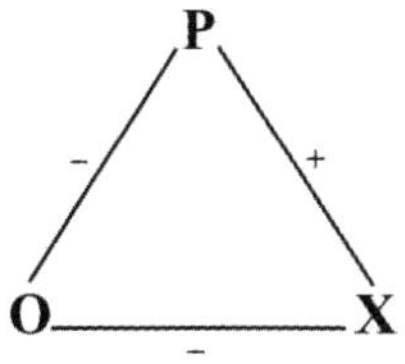

CASE 3: cognitive balance
P dislikes O
P likes X
O dislikes X

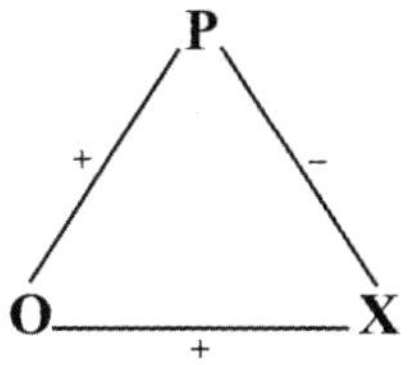

CASE 4: cognitive imbalance
P likes O
P dislikes X
O likes X

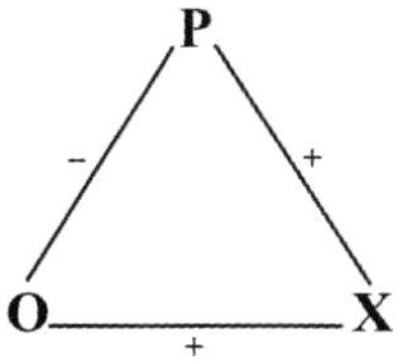

CASE 5: cognitive imbalance
P dislikes O
P likes X
O likes X

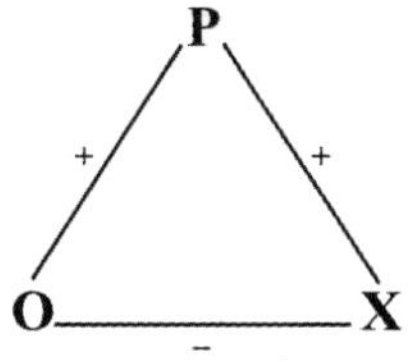

CASE 6: cognitive imbalance
P likes O
P likes X
O dislikes X

Adapted from: Charles A. Kiesler, Barry E. Collins and Norman Miller, Attitude Change: A Critical Analysis of Theoretical Approaches (New York: John Wiley & Sons, 1969), 159.

While the general model of cognitive balance as it stands seems convincing enough, its ability to answer more specific questions such as these is doubtful.

The descriptive breadth of the general cognitive balance model seems to be at the cost of its ability to help us make useful predictions in specific cases. While its general explanation of cognitive balance seems satisfying, it is difficult to form *precise* expectations about audience behavior using the general model.[20] Since such expectations are at the core of the Classical Perspective's emphasis on strategic choices by persuaders, the model itself is of only limited use to that perspective. A more recent approach, cognitive dissonance theory, attempts to include more of the richness of actual social, persuasive experience in its explanations.

Cognitive Dissonance Theory The equilibrium model which has offered most to contemporary theoretical and practical understanding of attitude change is certainly cognitive dissonance theory. Like the previous equilibrium models, cognitive dissonance theory is concerned with the consequences of tension or discomfort caused by cognitions which are inconsistent or in conflict with one another—or dissonant. Festinger's model defines its central term, "cognitions," with a great deal of flexibility, allowing it to include virtually any unit of our mental activity: any element of knowledge, opinion, attitude or preference we might have about anyone or anything. These cognitions can be related to other cognitive elements in one of three ways: as mutually irrelevant, mutually dissonant or mutually consonant.

Festinger's model, like the general balance model, does not always allow us to make precise quantified predictions of attitude change. Its overall description of our possible reactions to the tension of cognitive disequilibrium is, however, much closer to the complexity and nuance of actual audience responses. The image of tension and tension reduction in balance theory tends toward all-or-nothing explanations. Either our cognitions are in a state of equilibrium or they are not; if they are not, mechanisms engage to restore equilibrium. By contrast, cognitive dissonance theory suggests that pressure to reduce cognitive tension increases gradually, as the number and intensity of dissonant cognitions increase. Thus, not all cognitive dissonance will produce changes in behavior or attitude.

The most crucial departure of cognitive dissonance theory from other equilibrium theories we have considered is its recognition that restoring cognitive equilibrium and reduction of tension is not necessarily either automatic or internal. For example, Simons notes that if an attractive source advocates a position we dislike, we may engage in several alternative behaviors, only one of which is what persuaders normally desire. We may:

(1) discredit the source,

(2) decide that our disagreement is not very important or rationalize in some other way,

(3) seek social support or supportive evidence for our own viewpoint,

(4) misperceive the source's position,

(5) compartmentalize by ignoring or forgetting that the cognitions are discrepant,

(6) attempt to convince the source (if available) of his or her error, or

(7) modify our own attitudes.[21]

Hence, cognitive dissonance theory suggests the following strategic advice for persuaders: It is not enough to create the tension of cognitive dissonance in an audience, although this is a necessary first step to persuasion. In addition, cognitive dissonance theory advises the persuader to anticipate other possible means by which an audience could reduce dissonance—other than changing their attitude or behavior in accordance with the persuader's purposes—and to take steps to neutralize or eliminate these alternative means of tension reduction. For example, if a particular audience is apt to attempt to reduce dissonance by discrediting or derogating the source, the persuader must devote extra attention to shoring up her perceived credibility. If a particular audience might be likely to reduce dissonance by deliberately not perceiving the discrepant message (by misinterpreting it in a way that would not produce cognitive tension), then the persuader must take extra care to be clear and unambiguous in the presentation of his case. If a persuader anticipates that an audience might attempt to avoid the tension of cognitive dissonance by treating the course of tension as relatively unimportant, the persuader must take care to stress the importance of the issue, showing why it cannot be dismissed or ignored.

Despite the differences between these two equilibrium models, they share a common theme by which the classical view of motivation has been developed in contemporary research. Our motivations and our resultant behaviors are driven by the avoidance of the discomfort of imbalance among our cognitions. These contemporary theoretical developments have added significantly to our understanding of motivations.

MOTIVATION AND DESIRE FOR PERSONAL AND PSYCHOLOGICAL GROWTH

A different approach to the explanation motivation and its relation to pleasure is represented by the humanistic psychological theories of Abraham Maslow.[22] Maslow's psychology of motivation argues that we are motivated by growth, through the satisfaction of our needs, rather than by reduction of tension and preservation of equilibrium.

This growth tendency is directly related to Maslow's description of human needs as hierarchically ordered. These needs, listed in order from the lowest and most fundamental to the highest, together with the objects of the various needs, are:[23]

> *Physiological needs*: for food, rest and safety from the elements;
> *Safety needs*: for freedom from physical danger harm;
> *Social needs*: for affection, companionship and inclusion;
> *Ego needs*: for respect and status in our social world; and
> *Self-actualization needs*: for opportunities to realize one's own talents and potentials.

The power of these needs to motivate us is described by two general principles. First, individuals cannot be motivated by higher needs so long as lower or more fundamental needs remain unsatisfied. For example, we might risk physical danger if we believed it was the only way to prevent starvation; or we might give little consideration to our need for respect and status if we are in physical danger, and so on. Second, although various needs lose their ability to motivate us as they are satisfied and different individuals experience these motivations in different strengths at different times, the needs themselves remain as ongoing parts of our psychological makeup. Certain needs may be inoperative at a given moment in our experience, having no power to motivate us, but these needs may return to consciousness again to motivate us later.

Maslow defines *growth* as the process by which we are moved toward self-actualization: "not only as progressive gratification of basic needs to the point where they 'disappear,'" writes Maslow, "but also in the form of specific growth motivations over and above these basic needs, e.g., talents, capacities, creative tendencies, constitutional potentialities."[24] As a consequence of this emphasis on growth as a motivation, Maslow's view of human motivation differs from equilibrium theories in several important regards. Most important of these differences is that motivation, according to Maslow, is not explained simply by the avoidance of pain or tension. Humans have the capacity to be motivated by the various pleasant experiences of creativity and fulfillment, such as the exercise of one's talents. Maslow writes about such gratifying experience:

> It is simply inaccurate to speak in such instances of tension-reduction, implying thereby the getting rid of an annoying state. For these states are not annoying.... Almost always associated with negative attitudes toward the need is the conception that the primary aim of the organism is to get rid of the annoying need and thereby to achieve a cessation of tension, an equilibrium, a homeostasis, a quiescence, a state of rest, a lack of pain.[25]

Maslow differentiates among "rest" theories, equilibrium or "homeostasis" theories and "growth" theories. "Rest" theories limit motivation merely to the reduction of tension to zero. "Homeostasis" theories, including those of Festinger and Heider, explain motivation as the movement to an "optimum level" which may be neither too low nor too high, but not necessarily zero.[26] Maslow rejects both of these explanations of motivation, based as they are on the reduction of pain or tension, rather than seeking pleasure or satisfaction:

> The different basic needs are related to each other in a hierarchical order such that the gratification of one need and its consequent removal from the center of the stage brings about not a state of rest or Stoic apathy, but rather the emergence into consciousness of another 'higher' need; wanting and desiring continues but at a 'higher' level. Thus the coming-to-rest theory isn't adequate even for deficiency motivation."[27]

Moreover, Maslow argues that the time perspective of equilibrium theories may be inadequate to explain growth motivation. Equilibrium theories tend to focus on how we engage in fairly immediate action to reduce tension. However, hierarchically organized needs may motivate us to undertake long-term activities (education, careers, vocations, significant relationships) as opposed to the relatively short-term episodes equilibrium theories attempt to explain.[28]

We should use caution in generalizing from Maslow's theories for persuasive purposes. His purpose was not to formulate a handbook of persuasive advice but rather to describe the basis of psychological well-being. We can, nevertheless, draw some conclusions about human motivation relevant to our present discussion.[29] Maslow's humanistic psychology of growth suggests that effective persuasion will address the lowest order of unmet needs in an audience and then offer opportunities for the audience to meet these needs through the transaction with the persuader. Appeals to motivations that are already satisfied at the moment will be less likely to succeed, as will appeals to higher order motivations while lower order motivations remain unsatisfied. Maslow's theory, like others we have examined throughout this chapter, considers the quality of the experience of motivation itself. Unlike equilibrium theories, humanistic growth theory focuses on the pleasant and gratifying quality of this experience not on the painful or uncomfortable. This experience of growth is moreover a characteristic of our lives as a whole, rather than of particular situations or incidents. As a consequence, Maslow's theory urges us to consider the inappropriateness of expecting certain motivations to produce immediate change in an audience; these motivations are frequently associated with behaviors reaching across time and many situations. Our religious beliefs, our political convictions and our general sense of our own self-worth are connected to some of our highest order motivations. We are unlikely to revise these beliefs and convictions in a short time if they have taken a lifetime to establish. Finally, Maslow's theory suggests a clear ethical framework for persuasion. The process of persuasion which identifies the motivations of an audience and attempts to influence that audience by linking persuasive proposals to the satisfaction of these motivations is intimately concerned with the psychological growth and well-being of the audience. Thus persuasion—like all human interaction—is a process that should promote the well-being of all those involved, not merely the current purposes of the individual persuader.

ETHICAL ISSUES IN THE TACTICAL USE OF EMOTIONAL APPEALS

In some of the theories we have considered, such as Maslow's, ethical implications are explicitly featured as a part of the theories themselves. But the general study of motivation and attitude theory, as a whole, deserves close ethical inspection because of its history of ethical controversy.

In the opening pages of the *Rhetoric*, Aristotle takes to task the authors of previous texts on the art of persuasion, claiming that they dwelt on emotional appeals to the exclusion of other modes of persuasion (i.e., reasoning, argument and speaker credibility).[30] Certainly Aristotle believed that no truly ethical approach to persuasion could be carried on the strength of emotional appeals alone, and the classical tradition as a whole has held consistently to this position. However, contemporary understanding of emotions and motivations have developed from a scientific curiosity regarding the operation and structure of these psychological phenomena in and of themselves. Because these findings arose in a framework where ethical questions are strictly separated from theoretical questions, they represent potential persuasive approaches whose ethical status is not always clear.

For example, so-called "subliminal perception" or "subliminal advertising" is one such approach and is occasionally the object of ethical controversy. The idea underlying this approach to persuasion, developed out of psychophysical research in the 1950's. The human eye can detect visual images which escape *conscious* awareness and evoke individual reactions on a *subconscious* level. This occurs when visual messages are embedded in larger, unrelated pictures or messages or when they are only presented for a fraction of a second. Early researchers in this area, to cite an infamous example, claimed to have inserted single frames with the words "eat popcorn" into a theatrical film and found that the exposure to that subliminal message, lasting one twenty-fourth of a second, led the movie customers to buy much more popcorn.[31] Other well-known examples are more titillating. Accounts exist of advertisements for whiskey in which the images of nude women were air-brushed into the swirling pattern of ice cubes in a glass and ads in which the shapes of the letters "S-E-X" were hidden in the props and objects pictured.[32] Concerned parents worry that such "hidden" messages can exert undesirable persuasive influence over their adolescent children.

Certainly the possibility of such a precisely targeted means of influence, geared toward our basic motivations and operating without our conscious awareness as an audience, is at once both intriguing and frightening. What should we make of such claims from both a theoretical and an ethical point of view?

Regarding the persuasive value of this approach, we remain strongly skeptical about the success of this mechanical "subliminal perception" approach to persuasion. However, from the Classical Perspective the ethical status of an idea such as "subliminal persuasion" is clear; it represents an ethically-unacceptable approach to social influence. Ethical systems, after all, are founded upon certain social values, and the Classical Perspective provides a clear set of values—ideals about influence, language and public discussion.[33]

As we saw in Chapter 2, the Classical Perspective values perhaps most highly the capacity of humans to reason. Taken broadly this means our ability to weigh arguments and evidence together with our judgments about credibility and our own values and motives to arrive at a reasoned decision about matters of shared interest. Clearly, the *goal or ideal* of "subliminal persuasion" contradicts these values of the Classical Perspective. How could an audience reason to an independent decision about persuasive appeals of which they were unaware? Haiman's vigorous attack on "the hidden persuader" rejects such techniques as a violation of basic classical ethics:

> The hidden persuader, whether he is aware of it or not, is engaging in a nondemocratic practice. He takes advantage of the fact that although men may have the latent capacity for making rational, conscious choice, they are also part animal and as such can be exploited. They can, within limits, be made to respond reflexively. They can be moved to action by suggestions and pressure in the fringes of their consciousness. But because they can be so moved does not mean that they should be so moved, and anyone who moves them only intensifies their tendencies to respond immaturely and thwarts the more dignified humanity which democracy presumes.[34]

Four decades later, we are less alarmed than Haiman about the likelihood of subliminal persuaders undermining the democratic, classical impulse; but we share his ethical rejection of such techniques wherever they are contemplated.[35]

CRITICAL FOCUS: PUBLIC SERVICE ANNOUNCEMENTS ABOUT AIDS

From the Classical Perspective, all persuasion—even the most relentlessly logical approaches—must appeal to the psychology of the audience. The application of the principles of audience psychology discussed in this chapter invites you to recognize the operation of various motivational strategies in persuasive messages around us. As you examine persuasive messages for motivational strategies, the following questions should guide you.

CRITICAL QUESTIONS

1. What **frame of mind** does the persuader assume that the audience is in at the beginning of the message?
2. What kinds of **motivation** or frame of mind does the message appear to create within the audience?
3. What **pattern or sequence** is there in these motivational appeals, throughout the message?
4. What specific **elements** can you identify in the message that the persuader says or does to arouse these motivations in the audience?
5. Does the persuader's motivational **strategy**, perhaps in concert with other elements of the message, seem capable of accomplishing the intended purpose for the message? (Or, if the outcome of the persuasive attempt is known, how did the persuader's motivational strategy seem to contribute, to undermine or to have no influence on the intended outcome?)
6. Was the use of motivational strategies by the persuader **ethical**?

To demonstrate the application of these concepts, we can return to "Minneapolis" and "New York City," the public service announcements on AIDS prevention produced by the Centers for Disease Control discussed at the beginning of this chapter.[36]

The persuasive context faced by the CDC was completely understood by the public health officials. AIDS was unique in the modern history of medicine. As physician and historian Kenneth Ludmerer observed:

> AIDS was terrifying to the very core: a contagious disease without cure that was inevitably fatal. In this context it is not difficult to understand why the social response to AIDS has been so much deeper and more lasting than the response to the highly publicized epidemics of venereal disease, such as herpes, chlamydia, and penicillin-resistant cases of gonorrhea, in the early 1980's. Only in AIDS are the vital elements of dread and fear present.[37]

Public frustration and apprehension, confronted with the absence of any "quick fix" from medical science, began to produce a very predictable response: the search for stigmatized groups onto whom the blame for the problem could be placed. As Ludmerer observes:

> In most major epidemics there have been patients beyond the pale: what has differed from one epidemic to another is the matter of who has been deemed beyond the pale—and why. Because the forms scapegoating takes are culturally determined, they tell us much about the values, prejudices, and biases of a given society.[38]

Public concern with the disease was not coupled with much public understanding of AIDS or the threat it poses, however. Based on survey data reported at the 1989 Cornell Medical University Conference on Health Policy,

> Even though the public now sees AIDS as the most important health problem facing the country (68 percent), and 86 percent report having read or heard something about the disease in the past month, most people do not feel personally affected by the epidemic: The overwhelming majority (88 percent) say they do not know someone who has or has had the disease, nor have they seen its tragic impact on a friend or family member. Ninety-five percent say their chances of having or getting the AIDS virus are "low" or "none." Only 20 percent of Americans report they are very concerned about getting the disease.[39]

Thus, as we suggested at the beginning of this chapter, the CDC faced a general audience which found the prospect of AIDS frightening, but believed the disease was a problem banished to "other people"—strangers, impersonal statistics or members of stigmatized and "marginalized" groups toward whom the general public was not historically sympathetic.

The various theories of motivations and the passions discussed in this chapter combine to explain several important aspects of the CDC messages on AIDS. For the purpose of this Critical Focus we will draw primarily upon Aristotle's analysis of emotional appeals and its contemporary developments, examining the CDC's careful use of appeals to friendship, fear and confidence in the messages. More general implications of other theoretical perspectives in this chapter will be suggested later.

Appeals to Friendship, Fear and Confidence

Both "Minneapolis" and "New York City" seem designed to encourage feelings of friendship, based on a sense of common interest and common threat. Even the slogan featured prominently in both ads—"America Responds to AIDS"—suggests *community* actions. Both ads depict real, identified persons whose most noticeable characteristic appears to be their seeming "averageness" in every regard other than their association with AIDS. We are not shown drug addicts sharing needles in ghettos; no association of the disease with the gay community is ever made. Hence, mass audiences might find the cause that much easier to sympathize with.

By comparison, the CDC scrupulously avoided the darker emotions—anger and enmity—in these messages. Certainly the increase in incidence of AIDS during the 1980's coupled with the homophobic, anti-gay response to the disease's association with the gay community makes the topic a powerful potential inducement to enmity and hatred between the gay community and mainstream American society. Of course such enmity serves no practical purpose in checking the spread of the disease, but it has also been used as ammunition by anti-gay demagogues. As Jeffrey Levi of the National Gay Task Force observed, "Simply being identified as homosexual in the United States leaves one vulnerable to discrimination and rejection.... The vulnerability of gay people is intensified by the AIDS crisis."[40] For both practical and ethical reasons, then, the CDC attempted to create feelings of sympathy, like-feeling and allegiance, rather than hatred and enmity, through their messages, as shown in "Minneapolis." Elizabeth O'Brian, identified on-screen as an "AIDS volunteer," says:

> Personally, I learned about the disease and all the implications when my brother was diagnosed, and it was a harsh reality. I had to learn a lot really fast, even though I thought I knew a lot. The picture changed when it became a family issue.

A man identified by the on-screen words "Bill Travis has AIDS" says: "If I, son of a baptist minister and from a rural area, can acquire AIDS, anybody can." A woman identified by the on-screen words "Carole LaFavor has AIDS" says: "Obviously, women can get AIDS. I'm here to testify to that. It's not a 'we-they' disease. It's an 'us' disease." An off-camera voice says, "AIDS is not a problem that affects other people. AIDS affects us all."

The "Minneapolis" spot is similar in both format and overall strategy to a number of AIDS awareness messages produced by CDC. In particular, "Minneapolis" presents members of social groups not stereotypically associated with the disease: O'Brian, Travis and LaFavor are all Caucasian, appearing to range from mid-twenties to mid-forties and appear to be middle-class. Other ads in the campaign, including "New York City," seem even more explicit in this effort, including blacks and Asians among those who give testimony.

Most important for our present purposes, however, is the way in which differences among groups of Americans are portrayed within this message. Persons who have acquired AIDS are not shown as enemies or "outsiders;" rather, the disease itself is shown as the common enemy upon which feelings of friendship, sympathy and common cause are based. Both LaFavor's comment ("It's not a 'we-they' disease. It's an 'us' disease.") and the announcer's reminder ("AIDS is not a problem that affects other people. AIDS affects us all.") show recognition by the CDC of the factors which create hostility or friendship in persuasive messages.

Both Aristotle's discussion of fear and contemporary research on fear appeals remind us that any persuasion designed to arouse fear in order to prevent harm or danger must perform a careful balancing act. The object of fear must be made to seem realistic and imminent, but the portrayal must give some hope for the possibility of safety if correct action is taken. The CDC faced this dilemma in the series of messages of which "Minneapolis" and "New York City" were a part. The goal was to make the prospect of contracting AIDS, specifically through unsafe sexual practices, seem convincingly dangerous to their viewers so that the viewers would change their attitudes and behaviors. Thus, the CDC would have to emphasize to its audience that AIDS was spreading in the American population and that there exist preventative measures but no cure for AIDS. An appeal to the fear of AIDS could have the wrong effect on its audience if it inadvertently convinced viewers that nothing could be done to stop the inevitable spread of this lethal disease.

In "New York City," the AIDS public service announcements always tempered the danger of the disease with both the importance and effectiveness of prevention. Nancy DeVanter, an AIDS counselor, tells us:

> Deciding to have sex is potentially exposing yourself to the virus that causes AIDS. This is not like syphilis or gonorrhea, that can be treated with medication, and can go away.

Jolene Connor, a nurse, says, "Even if there is one encounter, one sexual encounter, that sexual encounter can be with someone who is already infected." A woman identified as a health care worker, Suki Port, tells viewers: "We've had a problem with young people not knowing how to protect themselves, but now that AIDS is here we have to be all the more careful, and we have an obligation to share with them the information we do know and to say that AIDS is a very serious disease." A male voice, off-camera, says:

> AIDS is a fatal disease. It's also preventable. Know the facts about AIDS. Protect yourself and your family. Tell others. For answers to your questions, call 1-800-342-AIDS.

The general motivational strategy in this message is one the reader will quickly recognize: fear appeals mixed with the opportunity to remove the source of the fear by education and behavior change. In all of these excerpts, the cause of fear is not AIDS itself, horrible though the disease is; rather, what is to be feared is lack of knowledge or of safe sexual practices—something that *is* "curable," and hence, a more strategically sound persuasive approach. Both ads also seem designed to motivate audiences through arousal of both fear and confidence. Both ads stress the harm AIDS can cause. In "New York City" we are told that no medication will make AIDS "go away," that infection can result from "even one sexual encounter," and that AIDS is "a very serious disease," in fact, "a fatal disease." AIDS is also called "a family issue;" "Minneapolis" emphasizes that AIDS is a danger not only to ourselves as individuals, but also to our loved ones, such as Elizabeth O'Brian's brother. Also, "New York City" draws attention to the danger of "young people not knowing how to protect themselves."

Both "New York City" and "Minneapolis" attempt to make the danger seem near in several ways. They present individuals who seem "typical" to many Americans, suggesting that the danger is not limited to "marginal" groups. They mention that "even one sexual encounter" can cause infection. They warn the audience that "anyone can" acquire AIDS. They remind us that women, as well as men, are at risk. Finally, they remind us that AIDS is found in rural environments as well as urban, conservative life styles as well as unconventional ones. Even the musical score for both ads is unsettling and anxious. Yet, at the same time, these ads attempt to instill a measure of confidence in their audience. "Minneapolis" offers its viewers a chance—"protect yourself and your family"—by helping them to "know the facts about AIDS" and encouraging them to "tell others." "New York City" reminds us that "AIDS is preventable." Both ads present people who are facing the challenge of AIDS calmly and with dignity. Both ads conclude with toll-free numbers for further information. The general structure of the messages is designed to underscore the general tension/ release pattern. The general theme of the message is repeated several times by different speakers in different languages, appealing to fear and friendship, after which the importance of knowledge and prevention is stressed, appealing to feelings of confidence.

"Minneapolis" and "New York City" both seem capable of motivating at least incremental changes in fundamental attitudes of the audience by appeal to particular emotions and motivations. The two ads carry off their delicate balancing act between fear and confidence. This balancing act is seen in the generally sober tone of the ads—neither frightening nor tragic, but seeming to reinforce the proper emotional state of concern and seriousness. The graphics for "America Responds to AIDS"—block letters, white on red against a black background—capture this balance between tension and control. Even the brief image of the family walking in the park, repeated in every ad in the series, seems to suggest seriousness. The family walks slowly *away* from us, dressed and behaving in a manner that seems not at all frivolous or playful. By linking these emotional states both to specific and immediate persuasive goals (getting viewers to call a toll-free number) and to long-range, less precise goals (changing attitudes and behaviors about AIDS) the ads demonstrate sound, classical persuasive strategy.

As significant as what these ads are capable of accomplishing, however, is what they *cannot* accomplish and in all probability were never intended to accomplish. Such persuasive messages, by themselves, are rarely able to accomplish immediate change in more deeply held beliefs or attitudes. Both Festinger's cognitive dissonance theory and Maslow's humanistic growth theory remind us that our motivations are embedded in a complex structure and context. True, the ads are capable of creating cognitive dissonance in at least two important ways. "New York City" creates tension between audience knowledge regarding the dangers of AIDS and audience behaviors—to the extent that audiences know that they are deliberately remaining uninformed about the disease or are not meeting their "obligation" to share what information they have. Both "Minneapolis" and "New York City" create tension between audience belief that AIDS "does not happen to us" and the ease with which the audience can identify with the persons in the ads whose lives have been touched by AIDS. "Even preachers' kids" can acquire AIDS. This grim reminder and the general strategy of the repetition of the messages serve to make it more difficult for the audience to reduce dissonance by trivializing or ignoring the source of the dissonance. But is this enough? The fundamental nature of the change called for by the CDC suggests that these attitudes, even with an artful mix of emotional, logical and ethical appeals, will be very resistant to quick change. The CDC, after all, seeks change in audience views about sexuality, about the powers of the medical field and perhaps about the role of marginalized groups in our society.

The form of the messages themselves also places certain limits on their potential persuasive success. As most regular viewers of commercial television know, public service announcements are rarely featured at the times when most viewers are watching. Thus the ability of these messages to reach the audience they most desire is lessened somewhat. The problem of incremental change, as well as the problem of media politics and economics, exposes one of the limitations of the Classical Perspective growing out of its emphasis on the single persuasive episode as its frame of reference. Both the unique problems of persuasive *campaigns*, unfolding over time with multiple messages in multiple media, and the role of media institutions in mass persuasion are more appropriately studied within the Institutional Perspective, discussed in Part III of this book.

Despite these limitations placed upon the persuasive potential of the CDC AIDS spots themselves, they are noteworthy for the high ethical standards to which they adhere in their use of motivational appeals. The Classical Perspective places great importance on appealing to the *whole* person through our persuasion. Appeals should address the person's intellect and reasoning as well as his or her emotional state and respect for authority and credibility. As Johannesen observes:

> Assuming that the appeal is ethical in light of other *relevant* perspectives, the "emotional" technique is ethical if it is under girded by a substructure of sound evidence and reasoning to support it. Presentation of this substructure could accompany the appeal in the message, or the substructure could exist apart from the message and be produced upon the request of the critic. When a *sound* proposal is linked to satisfaction of *relevant* audience emotions, values, and motives, then the appeal is probably ethical.[41]

By comparison, appeal to emotions becomes unethical from the Classical Perspective when it leads to conclusions that contradict sound reasoning and evidence or when it is offered *instead of* sound reasoning and evidence.[42] Certainly, "Minneapolis" and "New York City" suggest that the CDC's series of ads respect the rational choice-making capacity of their audience members. As we have seen, the ads are at pains to promote careful, thoughtful, informed decision making and to avoid demagoguery and hatemongering. Therefore, they stand as examples of the principled use of appeals to emotions, even the most potentially volatile emotions.

Notes

1. Reported in Charles F. Turner, Heather G. Miller and Lincoln E. Moses, eds. *AIDS: Sexual Behavior and Intravenous Drug Use* (Washington DC: National Academy Press, 1989), 4.
2. See, for example, the recommendations of the Committee on AIDS Research and the Behavioral, Social, and Statistical Sciences of the National Research Council, in Turner et al., *AIDS*, 1-28.
3. See: Turner, et al., *AIDS*, 264.
4. See: Kenneth M. Ludmerer, "Patients Beyond the Pale: A Historical View," in David E. Rogers and Eli Ginzberg, eds., *Public and Professional Attitudes Towards AIDS Patients: A National Dilemma* (Boulder CO: Westview Press, 1989), 7-18.
5. See: Jeffrey Levi, "Protection of Personal Rights," in Michael D. Witt, ed. *AIDS and Patient Management: Legal, Ethical and Social Issues* (Owings Mills MD: National Health Publishing, 1986), 60-64.
6. Both "Minneapolis" and "New York City," public service announcements on AIDS awareness and prevention produced by the Centers for Disease Control, are available on the videotape.

7. See: Aristotle, *Rhetoric*, trans. W. Rhys Roberts (New York: Modern Library, 1954).
8. Aristotle, *Rhetoric*, 1378a.
9. See: Aristotle, *Rhetoric*, Book II, Chapters 2-11, 1378a-1388b.
10. Malcolm X, "After the Bombing," reprinted in Ray Fabrizio, Edith Karas and Ruth Menmuir, eds., *The Rhetoric of NO* (New York: Holt, Rinehart and Winston, 1970), 31-32.
11. Excerpted from "A Few Minutes with Andy Rooney," *60 Minutes*, Executive Producer Don Hewett, CBS, 4 March 1990; transcriptions by the authors.
12. Ailes' remark was to an interviewer from *Time* magazine; it was quoted in *The New Republic* (14 November 1988):45.
13. For a fuller discussion of the "Yale research" program on fear appeals in persuasion, and subsequent developments, see: Charles A. Kiesler, Barry E. Collins and Norman Miller, *Attitude Change: A Critical Analysis of Theoretical Approaches* (New York: John Wiley & Sons, 1969), 109-112; Marvin Karlins and Herbert I. Abelson, *Persuasion: How Opinions and Attitudes are Changed*, 2nd Ed. (New York: Springer, 1970), 6-10; Daniel J. O'Keefe, *Persuasion: Theory and Research* (Newbury Park: Sage, 1990), 165-169.
14. Fritz Heider, *The Psychology of Interpersonal Relations* (New York: Wiley, 1958). By including Festinger's "cognitive dissonance" research with other "balance" theories, we temporarily ignore the traditional emphasis on distinctions between dissonance and balance theories, as considered in, for example, O'Keefe, *Persuasion*, 7. The grouping together of these two theoretical areas allows us to emphasize their shared differences with "humanistic growth" theories, as discussed later in this chapter.
15. See Leon Festinger, *A Theory of Cognitive Dissonance* (Stanford CA: Stanford University Press 1957); Festinger, *Conflict, Decision, and Dissonance* (Stanford CA: Stanford University Press 1964).
16. Heider's work is developed and advanced in a number of studies and collections by various researchers. For a more detailed discussion, see: Kiesler, et al., *Attitude Change*, 155-178.
17. Heider, quoted in Kiesler, et al., *Attitude Change*, 158.
18. Kiesler, et al., *Attitude Change*, 158.
19. See: Kiesler, et al., *Attitude Change*, 161.
20. See: Kiesler, et al., *Attitude Change*, 165-168; O'Keefe, *Persuasion*, 7.
21. Herbert W. Simons, *Persuasion: Understanding, Practice, and Analysis*, 2nd Ed. (New York: Random House, 1986), 61.
22. Abraham Maslow, *Motivation and Personality* (New York: Harper & Row, 1954); Maslow, *Toward a Psychology of Being*, 2nd Ed. (New York: Van Nostrand, 1968).
23. Maslow, *Motivation.*
24. Maslow, *Toward*, 26.
25. Maslow, *Toward*, 29.
26. Maslow, *Toward*, 30.
27. Maslow, *Toward*, 30.

28. Maslow, *Toward*, 31.
29. Maslow, *Toward*, vi-vii.
30. Aristotle, *Rhetoric*, Book I, 1354a.
31. This worn example, and others, received their first prominent "official" discussion in J. V. McConnell, R. L. Cutler and E. B. McNeil, "Subliminal Stimulation: An Overview," *American Psychologist* 13 (1958): 229-242. For a careful, more complete, discussion, see: N. F. Dixon, *Subliminal Perception: The Nature of a Controversy* (New York: McGraw-Hill, 1971).
32. These and other examples, catalogued for sensational effect, are dwelt upon in Wilson Bryan Key,
Seduction (New York: Signet, 1973); and Vance Packard, *The Hidden Persuaders* (New York: McKay, 1957). More recently, we hear the charge raised that certain music albums contain tracks in which messages—often filled with satanic imagery—have been "back-masked," or recorded backwards and buried within the sound of the music.
33. See: Karl R. Wallace, "An Ethical Basis of Communication," *Speech Teacher* 4 (1955): 1-2.
34. Franklyn Haiman, "Democratic Ethics and the Hidden Persuaders," *Quarterly Journal of Speech* 44 (1958): 387-392.
35. One last observation before leaving the question of subliminal techniques: We *could* argue that the entire approach to persuasion represented by "subliminal perception" theories is outside the scope of the Classical Perspective on persuasion. Recall from Chapter 2 that the Classical Perspective is primarily intended to explain persuasion which is intentional, explicit and episodic in nature. The "subliminal" approach to persuasion does not require that the stimuli be intentionally created, as in the case of split-second facial scowls. Nor, obviously, are subliminal stimuli explicit, since the whole basis of their power is said to rest on the fact that they escape conscious notice by audiences. Finally, the potential of subliminal stimuli in creating or intensifying emotional states seems most clear in cases where the stimuli are repeated and clustered, over time and through many channels, rather than when they are presented in a "one-shot" or episodic fashion. (The tendency to gain meaning only in clusters and in cumulative form is a characteristic of most nonverbal communication behavior, as we will consider further in Chapter 8.)
36. Both "Minneapolis" and "New York City," public service announcements on AIDS awareness and prevention produced by the Centers for Disease Control, are available on the videotape. Transcriptions from both spots are by the authors.
37. Ludmerer, "Patients," 7.
38. Ludmerer, "Patients," 8.
39. Robert J. Blendon and Karen Donelan, "AIDS, the public, and the 'NIMBY' Syndrome," in Rogers and Ginsberg, *Public and Professional Attitudes*, 26.
40. Witt, *AIDS*, 60-61.
41. Richard L. Johannesen, *Ethics in Human Communication*, 3rd Ed. (Prospect Heights IL: Waveland, 1990), 119.
42. Johannesen, *Ethics*, 119.

5

Credibility And Image Management

IN THIS CHAPTER:

Focus on:

KFC and "The Colonel's Way"

1. Theoretical Focus: *Ethos* and the Personal Influece of Persuaders
2. The Classical Foundations: *Ethos*
3. Contemporary Credibility Research
4. Charisma and Image Management
5. *Ethos*, Ethics, and Image
6. Critical Focus: "KFC and The Colonel's Way"

Focus On: KFC and "The Colonel's Way"

Harland Sanders was born in Henryville, Indiana, in 1890.[1] At the age of twelve, he left grammar school and took to the road. For the next 25 years, Sanders worked a variety of odd-jobs, including farm hand, buggy painter, streetcar conductor and ferryboat operator. In 1929, his life took a turn that would influence eating habits in the United States and the rest of the world for at least the next six decades. One biographer summarized this transition as follows:

> In 1929 Sanders opened a filling station in Corbin, Kentucky, and found himself cooking in his back room for an occasional hungry truckdriver. The news of his delectable dishes soon spread, and he eventually opened Sanders' Cafe—a homelike, no-menu restaurant that gradually expanded to accommodate 142 people. It was here that Sanders discovered his method for quickly preparing chicken with the aid of a pressure cooker, yielding a moist and flavorful product. He also perfected his 'secret recipe' chicken coating mix—a blend of eleven common herbs and spices. It was also during this time that he received his honorary military title from Kentucky's governor for contributing to the state's culinary reputation.[2]

The advent of a new interstate highway in 1956 that bypassed Sanders' Cafe forced him to sell the restaurant. Faced with retiring on a modest, social security income at age 66, Colonel Sanders took to the road for the second time in his life. This time he sought to establish a franchise chicken business. By the early 1960's he had franchised more than 600 restaurants in the United States and Canada and had developed a persona as a southern gentleman who was the national symbol for Kentucky Fried Chicken.

In 1964, Sanders sold his expanding company for $2 million to two Kentucky entrepreneurs. When they sold the company in 1971, gross sales stood at $700 million from 3,500 franchises worldwide. Throughout the 1960's and 1970's, Harland Sanders remained with Kentucky Fried Chicken as its official spokesperson, providing leadership in a variety of promotional and public relations campaigns

In 1986, Pepsico added KFC to its growing list of fast food subsidiaries that included Pizza Hut and Taco Bell. Since that time, "fast food has become the largest segment in its portfolio," accounting for nearly 40 percent of its annual revenues.[3] Although prosperous in the late 1980's, Pepsico found its fast food operations leveling off and even losing business in the early 1990's. By 1991, "system-wide sales growth was cut almost in half," and "hardest hit was KFC, with flat average sales, profits off 37 percent for the year, huge layoffs planned and not much luck developing healthier alternatives to fried chicken."[4]

Although KFC still dominated the market for fast chicken in 1992 and its two major competitors—Popeye's and Church's—were in bankruptcy, health-conscious consumers were still rejecting its fried products. Meanwhile new competitors were surfacing as industry leaders in fast food. MacDonald's introduced chicken to their menu, and new franchises such as Boston Chicken and Kenny Rogers Roasters sparked head-on competition for non-fried chicken. By 1993, KFC had dropped from fourth to sixth in the list of top ten market shares for fast food.[5]

Starting in 1992, KFC began a "back to its roots" campaign that included some changes in operation and product development as well as a new advertising assault.[6] By 1994, KFC was prepared to launch a $50 million media blitz that really returned to its roots by resurrecting the Colonel as its spokesman. Their decision to turn to the image of Colonel Sanders for help is illustrative of the faith of KFC's management in the persuasive power of a compelling spokesperson. From the Classical Perspective on persuasion, such faith stems from a recognition of the persuasive power of *ethos*.

THEORETICAL FOCUS: *ETHOS* AND THE PERSONAL INFLUENCE OF PERSUADERS

In the next section of this Chapter we look more closely at the classical understanding of *ethos,* including its relationship to strategies within persuasive messages and to the general values of the community within which persuasion functions. An important area of contemporary development on the classical concept of *ethos* has been a more careful study of the precise nature of credibility appeals and their operation, especially within the context of public speaking. Following a review of this area of study, we turn to two other areas of contemporary study that take a larger, sociological perspective on the attributes of individuals that make them influential and persuasive in our contemporary mass-mediated world. We will discuss charisma, the ability of individuals of exceptional personality to gain great influence over others in special circumstances, and also examine image management, the business of carefully constructing and maintaining an appropriate persuasive persona. After considering the ethical questions that arise when persuasion centers around *ethos*, credibility, charisma and image management, we will return to an analysis of four commercial spots that feature Colonel Sanders.

CLASSICAL FOUNDATIONS: *ETHOS*

In Chapter 2, we note Aristotle's observation that *ethos* was in many ways the most important among the three means of persuasion. If an audience admires and trusts a persuader, the persuader's personal power alone may cause an audience to accept his or her persuasive suggestions. Conversely, if an audience finds a persuader unworthy of admiration or trust, no amount of evidence or careful reasoning offered by the persuader is likely to impress that audience—hence Aristotle's conclusion that "character may almost be called the most effective means of persuasion."[7]

When examining the role of a persuader's own character as an instrument of proof, Aristotle observed that *ethos* seemed to consist of three distinct components:

> There are three things which inspire confidence in the orator's own character—the three namely that induce us to believe a thing apart from any proof of it: good sense, good moral character, and goodwill.[8]

A closer examination of these three elements shows that *ethos* is related both to audience motivation and passions, as considered in the previous chapter, and to reasoned arguments, discussed in Chapter 3. The means by which persuaders demonstrate their good will is by appearing friendly. According to Aristotle, we consider as friends those who wish good things for us and who are pained when bad things happen to us.[9] Persuaders demonstrate their good sense by showing their familiarity with the truth in its various forms—the specific facts and principles of a given case, a ready supply of traditional wisdom, sound reasons and common sense or special experience and expertise.

Because good character is a component of *ethos*, Aristotle reviewed the virtues considered praiseworthy by Athenian society at that time. His list of virtues included:

> **Justice** in one's dealings with others,
> **Courage** in times of danger,
> **Temperance** in enjoyment of physical pleasures,
> **Generosity** and **magnanimity** toward others,
> **Liberality** in making one's wealth available for the good of others,
> **Gentleness** of disposition,
> **Prudence** in practical affairs and
> **Wisdom** in understanding the truth.[10]

According to Aristotle, persuaders demonstrate the excellence of their character to others by letting these virtues be seen within the persuasive situation.

Contemporary social science research reveals a variety of particular techniques that can be used to promote audience perception of one or more of these qualities.[11] These contemporary developments remain consistent with the basic classical premise, that *ethos* is based in perceived qualities of the persuader. However, as we will see later in this chapter, not all contemporary research agrees that character only matters insofar as it is strategically exploited in the persuasive message itself.

CONTEMPORARY CREDIBILITY RESEARCH

Contemporary research in *ethos* blossomed during the 1960's and provided data that largely supported, frequently extended and occasionally contradicted Aristotle's original discussion. Before reviewing the various components of credibility discussed by contemporary researchers, however, it is important to note that contemporary theorists have also provided additional explanations for how a source's *ethos* affects the persuasive process. Congruity theory, developed by Osgood and

Tannenbaum, provides an important explanation for how the attributes of a source assist in persuasion.

Congruity theory could easily be included with equilibrium theories discussed in Chapter 4, because it begins with the assumption that we are driven by discrepancies among our attitudes to restore psychological equilibrium through attitude change.[12] However, unlike either Festinger's cognitive dissonance theory or Heider's cognitive balance theory, which attempt to explain virtually all types of unit relations perceivers might encounter, congruity theory takes as its special focus the discrepancy between a receiver's overall attitude toward a proposition and the receiver's attitude toward the source of that proposition. This more tightly-drawn focus is accompanied by an attempt to consider the *strength* of the liking relation in predicting a perceiver's reaction to disruption of equilibrium, rather than simply the difference between "liking" and "not liking." The result is a model of audience judgment providing several important insights into the formation of attitudes about persuasive sources.

A simple example brings the importance of this difference into theoretical focus. Imagine that Chris likes a certain novel she has just read. Chris also likes Pat, who tells Chris that she also likes the novel. The general model of cognitive balance described in Chapter 4 predicts that Chris will experience balance in this situation and—most importantly—will, therefore, experience no impulse to change any of these liking relations. The congruity model, however, asks a crucial question at this point: how *strongly* do Pat and Chris respectively feel about the novel? As a result of this question, the congruity model suggests that Chris *will* experience some pressure to modify her attitudes, depending on how strongly she feels about each of these liking relations. If Chris likes the novel a great deal but likes Pat only somewhat, congruity theory predicts that Pat's enthusiasm for the novel could "spoil" somewhat Chris' enjoyment of the novel; similarly, we may predict that Pat's enthusiasm for a novel Chris likes a lot may tend to improve Chris' attitude toward her. Conversely, if Chris feels strong liking for Pat and likes the novel only slightly, Pat's praise of the novel may raise Chris' estimation of the novel. Also, it might even tend to lessen Chris' liking for Pat if Pat is extremely enthusiastic about a novel Chris finds only mildly enjoyable at best. Thus the perception of a source *and* of propositions made by the source—the strength of Chris' attitudes about Pat and about the novel—*interact* with one another. In this interaction both attitudes are open to change. Whichever attitude Chris holds more strongly will likely change less than the less strongly held attitude. Note that Osgood and Tannenbaum do not discuss whether the source *genuinely possesses* trustworthiness, competence or expertise, nor are they concerned with the *validity* of a proposition—only the general attitudes of liking/disliking we hold toward sources and propositions.

Cognitive balance theory claims that we experience pressure to reduce the tension caused by unbalanced or conflicting cognitions. Congruity theory lets us add two general principles directly relevant to credibility. First, the attractiveness of the source of a proposition interacts with the attractiveness of the proposition itself, when both are considered from the point of view of a given perceiver. Second, whichever attitude—source or proposition—is initially held more strongly will be more resistant to change in this interaction.

These conclusions suggest interesting implications for the classical concept of *ethos*. First, we might metaphorically say that sources must "expend" or "use" some of their prestige or perceived attractiveness in order to promote a less-attractive proposition. Consider for example, Bill Clinton's proposal soon after his election as President in 1992, that gays be allowed to continue in military service. Compared to other parts of his administration's agenda, this proposal was less attractive to many citizens. However, Clinton's high popularity ratings—common to the "honeymoon period" of a new president—helped to accumulate support for his proposal. Later the unpopularity of the proposal appeared to damage Clinton's popularity. Further, as Simons notes, congruity theory predicts that the wrong source can actually *hurt* the persuasive chances of a proposition, if the one endorsing the proposition is initially perceived as less attractive than the proposition.[13] Knowing whether or not a particular source will hurt the persuasive message can be a thorny problem. For example, while Pizza Hut found Rush Limbaugh a suitable spokesman for their cheese-crust pizza, the Florida Citrus Growers Association were concerned enough about his public persona to drop him as a celebrity endorser in the same year.

Osgood and Tannenbaum's congruity model assumes that this rebalancing of attitudes is largely unconscious and automatic in its operation. Further, the model itself is mathematical in its predictive efforts, based on measurement of attitudes according to a seven-point scale, spanning numerical ratings equivalent to judgments from "like" to "dislike."[14] However, as some persuasion scholars have noted, this aspect of the model becomes something of a drawback to its practical application. The quantified, operational data and clean categories upon which the theory builds are not ordinarily available to us in actual persuasive situations. As Simons observes:

> In looking at examples, it is not always possible to identify who the source is, or what the concept [or proposition] is or whether an assertion is positive, negative, or neutral. When the president of the United States toasts the Russian ambassador at a formal dinner, is either the source or the concept the man, his office, or the country he represents? Is the toast a neutral assertion because of its formality, or is it a genuinely positive assertion?[15]

Despite these drawbacks, however, Osgood and Tannenbaum's general theoretical predictions, as summarized above, remain essentially unchallenged among persuasion researchers. The attractiveness of sources and propositions can interact to influence the formation and rebalancing of our attitudes.

In addition to providing further explanation for how *ethos* contributes to persuasion, contemporary research in this area has also centered on the components of credibility just as Aristotle attempted to describe the components of *ethos*. In general, contemporary scholarship suggests four components of source credibility: competence, good will, moral character and dynamism.

COMPETENCE

In the Classical Perspective, persuaders can display their *ethos* during the act of persuasion by demonstrating their competence (presenting sound arguments that embody common sense and social knowledge). In contemporary investigations, a persuader's expertise and qualifications have been identified as contributing to an audience's perception of good sense. Terry Ostermeier documented that letting an audience know the qualifications, positions and titles held by a speaker enhances his or her status and builds credibility.[16] Thus, political candidates frequently list the various offices they have held and include biographical information that highlights their accomplishments in campaign literature. Similarly, when professional experts are featured in commercial advertisements, they are often dressed in their professional uniforms—a white lab coat or the tailored suit of a banker or lawyer—and situated within a professional setting, whether an elaborate laboratory, a book-lined study or an office with diplomas covering the walls.

Significantly, Wayne Thompson's early review of contemporary research concluded that a persuader's *ethos* may be enhanced through these means. However, an audience's perception of a speaker's competence does *not* seem to be affected by many tactics more traditionally regarded as elements of careful reasoning, such as citing sources of evidence or discussing both sides of an issue.[17] Thompson further notes that the majority of contemporary research on credibility does not support the classical assumption that the soundness of a persuader's arguments and reasoning are perceived by audiences and contribute significantly to successful persuasion.[18] Note carefully that Thompson does *not* say that audiences ignore careful reasoning by persuaders, simply that contemporary research has not established this by its procedures of observation and measurement. Thompson attributes some of this failure not to the irrationality of audiences but to the false assumption, contained in much of the research he reviewed, that reasoning and emotional proofs are not merely separate dimensions but are actually opposites. The popular misconception that reasoning and emotions cannot exist and function simultaneously caused many contemporary researchers to conclude—wrongly, says Thompson—that persuasive messages containing emotional appeals are not examples of sound reasoning. As our discussion in Chapter 2 of the foundations of the Classical Perspective should make clear, *all* audiences respond to *all* explicit persuasion by employing their capacity to make reasoned judgments and their understanding of character and their motivations and frame of mind.

Good Will

Persuaders demonstrate their good will toward audiences by making statements and performing actions that show they have the audience's best interest in mind. Numerous contemporary studies confirm that a persuader's credibility is higher for audiences perceiving that the persuader holds values and opinions similar to their own.[19] Similarly, contemporary research supports the expectation that friendliness on the part of a persuader seems to enhance the audience's perception that a persuader is concerned for their best interests.[20]

Many contemporary studies of *ethos* have concluded that there may be less difference between good will and good character or trustworthiness than the Classical Perspective originally supposed.[21] Research by James McCroskey and others suggests that credibility is primarily determined by perceptions of a persuader's authoritativeness (or competence) and character.[22] This research suggests that those behaviors traditionally grouped by theorists as demonstrations of "good will" are more frequently perceived by audiences as indications of either competence or friendliness.

MORAL CHARACTER

Persuaders demonstrate the content of their character to audiences by showing in their persuasive messages they are persons of integrity and understand and ascribe to the virtues accepted by the community to which both persuader and audience belong. Contemporary research in credibility has reduced the scope of this dimension to a study of "trustworthiness." Although an important attribute, it is clearly less sweeping in its scope than indicated by Aristotle's original discussion of the virtues of an excellent persuader. In this sense, trustworthiness has less to do with excellence of character, as in the traditional sense of "good character," than with reliability or safety, the likelihood that the persuader is not being dishonest.[23] Contemporary research has consistently identified audience perceptions of a persuader's trustworthiness as contributing to successful persuasion.[24] We will return later to the matter of the separation of virtue from trustworthiness in persuasion as we discuss charisma and image management.

DYNAMISM

Contemporary research on oral persuasion has consistently identified another dimension of persuader credibility not mentioned by Aristotle. Audiences tend to form judgments about the persuader based on the persuader's delivery and bearing. These judgments contribute to the audience's overall response to the persuasive attempt. A persuader's perceived dynamism consists of the extent to which that persuader appears interesting, strong, aggressive and active.[25] This finding is also consistent with several studies linking a fluent, conversational delivery to an audience's perception of dynamism and trustworthiness.[26] Even George Bush's decision to consult a speech coach for the 1988 presidential campaign supports the work of David Addington, which demonstrates that thin, nasal voices have a significantly negative effect upon audience ratings of a speaker's competence, dynamism and trustworthiness.[27]

CHARISMA AND IMAGE MANAGEMENT

CHARISMA

Just as contemporary credibility theory has explored the classical concept of *ethos*, contemporary students of persuasion have also attempted to understand how modern audiences perceive virtue or admirable qualities in contemporary persuaders. The modern study of charisma and charismatic leadership theory tries to understand how the right combination of a strong or forceful personality and situational opportunity can produce persuasion, especially in mass movements and organizational contexts.

History is filled with examples of persuaders whose influence was far-reaching, not because of any legally or traditionally defined position they occupied, but because the force of their personal character found unique expression in a special set of circumstances. Such people may emerge in a role of dominance in popular movements, politics, religion, industry or the military. The list includes: Ronald Reagan and Joan of Arc; Adolph Hitler and Franklin Roosevelt; Chrysler Corporation President Lee Iacocca and Jesus of Nazareth; General Douglas MacArthur and the Reverend Martin

Luther King, Jr.; Apple Computers founder Steven Jobs and Indian independence leader Mahatma Gandhi. In all of these cases, the individuals wielded influence far beyond what might have been duly conferred upon them by formal institutions of power. This extraordinary power is *charisma*.[28]

The power of charismatic persuaders may appear beyond normal explanation. Such power is usually reserved for people in special positions of leadership like a president or prime minister of a nation-state or the head of an established religion, for example, the Pope. However, as sociologist Max Weber explained, charismatic leadership goes far beyond traditional and bureaucratic forms of leadership based in tradition, custom or constitutional rules.[29] The presence of a charismatic leader may be taken as a sign of prophetic wisdom, heroic stature, semi-divine nature or heavenly grace.[30] This power may show itself as commanding forcefulness, as in the example of General Douglas MacArthur, or as profound serenity radiating from within, as in the case of Mahatma Gandhi.[31] Not only do charismatic persuaders seem to possess power beyond anything established by formal rules, laws or procedures, but most such figures become instigators of wide-sweeping change in the social or institutional *status quo*. "Historically," writes Conger, "we find that charismatic leaders have always personified the forces of change, unconventionality, vision, and an entrepreneurial spirit."[32]

What, then, accounts for charismatic power? Sometimes charisma is mistakenly considered to be exclusively a matter of the personality of the leader or persuader. Yet, it is not; charisma is only charisma if others perceive it as such. Charisma occurs when there exists an intense, almost-religious relationship between leaders and their followers. Weber notes the importance of an audience's willingness to accept the charismatic power. He writes that the power of charisma "depends on beliefs in revelations and heroism, on emotional convictions about the importance and value of a religious, ethical, artistic, scientific, political, or other manifestation, on heroism, whether ascetic, or military, or judicial wisdom or magical or other favors."[33]

Because charisma depends on an audience's willingness to accept leadership as heroic and inspired, charisma requires the proper time, place and cultural situation for its potency. Thus, the characteristics of charismatic persuaders are like the virtues defining excellence in a persuader, as Aristotle identified them for ancient Athens, in that they are not necessarily universal and may change from one social context to another. Audiences will not treat a would-be leader as charismatic unless they see his or her character as somehow *relevant* to their own situation, needs and perceptions.[34] For example, half a century ago fascist Germany found Adolph Hitler charismatic, while in the United States Franklin Roosevelt wielded charismatic power; both societies found the other's choice of leaders detestable. Thus, because charisma is both dependent on context and likely to result in social or political change, charismatic leaders frequently generate intense controversy.

Although charisma is clearly a power conferred on persuaders by their audiences and highly dependent on the situation, there is, nevertheless, a significant body of research explaining the strategic and behavioral dimensions of charismatic persuasion. Certainly no single behavior can produce the audience reaction associated with charismatic persuaders; such behaviors, if they occur at all, must occur in "constellations."[35] Conger, in his study of corporate charismatic leadership, notes that the number, intensity and relevance of various behaviors can influence the extent to which a leader may be perceived as charismatic.[36]

Conger has identified four general characteristics of charismatic leaders:[37]

1. Charismatic leaders must have *a clear vision for change*, one directly related to the needs of an audience or constituency.
2. Charismatic leaders must *articulate the vision* and the flaws with the *status quo* which justify or demand the envisioned change.
3. Charismatic leaders must *build trust in their audiences*, through a record of success, special expertise, willingness to take risks and willingness to depart from old traditions and norms.
4. Charismatic leaders, to achieve their ends, must resort to *unconventional, audience-centered tactics*, including modeling the desired changes in behavior in their own actions, empowering members of their following to promote change themselves and breaking precedents in behaviors.

As communicators, charismatic leaders frequently employ certain recognizable tactics:[38]

1. *Adapting behavior and language* to both the situation and the audience to a high degree and being extremely sensitive to changes in appropriate style and manner dictated by different settings and audiences.
2. *Employing stylistic devices* in language for maximum effect, including such figures as rhyme, repetition, balance, alliteration; metaphors, analogies and original stories.
3. *Creating involvement* through the use of emotionally-arousing dramas, pageants, ceremonies and so forth.

These principles should call to mind many examples from the careers of charismatic leaders. Martin Luther King, Jr., for example, employed unconventional tactics of passive resistance and peaceful demonstrations and used poetic oratory to inspire the Civil Rights Movement. Ronald Reagan was a master at coining memorable phrases and telling folksy stories during his two terms of office. Mahatma Gandhi's vision of independence and tremendous sense of identification with the people of India helped to liberate that country from British imperialism.

The most conspicuous limit on the power of a charismatic persuader is the absolute necessity of a following, an audience willing and ready to accept that individual as a charismatic leader. The behaviors of charismatic persuaders, described above, can never produce charismatic persuasion by themselves. Only an accepting audience and a situation ripe for fundamental change can enable this kind of persuasive power.

Three other factors can cause charismatic power to dissipate. First, a charismatic leader may be unable to continue producing results, because a charismatic's power depends on the audience's faith that he or she is a true hero or divinely inspired. Any noticeable failures can dislodge that faith. Weber illustrated this point by recalling

Jesus on the cross, who appeared to have been abandoned by God and consequently appeared to be bereft of power; thus prompting many of his followers to abandon him.[39] Second, charismatic leaders may lose their power if they are too successful. Although charismatic leaders tend to work outside of tradition by challenging the bureaucracy, their successes may well become absorbed and "co-opted" by the very system they sought to change. In such structures, traditional and bureaucratic forms of leadership again gain power, and there may be little room or patience left for the charismatic leader. Consider, for example, the reaction of many young women interested in women's rights and equal opportunity who reject the leadership of Gloria Steinem and other pioneers in women's rights from the 1970's. The successes of the women's movement of two decades ago have left those once charismatic leaders with an unstable place in the contemporary movement. Third, charismatic persuaders may succumb to their own exalted image. Operating from a powerful position with high expectations from one's followers can tempt even the most honest persuaders to inflate their own image, exaggerating their successes and drawing attention away from genuine problems. Conger identifies the problems of John DeLorean, an auto maker who became a convicted cocaine dealer, as a case in point.[40]

Despite these potential limits on charismatic power, the enormous persuasive potential of charisma makes it an essential concept in contemporary studies of persuasion that begin with assumptions about the classical concept of *ethos*. A final issue for investigation of contemporary developments regarding *ethos*, image management, is the subject of the next section.

Image Management

Because *ethos* is so important to effective persuasion an entire industry has evolved for the purpose of establishing, maintaining and altering persuaders' images. The task of many public relations firms is primarily image management. These public relations firms attempt to construct and alter the *ethos* of not only individuals, such as Hillary Clinton, Al Gore and Bill Gates, but also of corporate entities like Nike, the tobacco industry and the British Royal Family.

The current importance of image management and public relations in our society rests on a poignant irony. The power of charismatic leaders stems from our longing to believe in heroes, prophets, messiahs and sages; yet, these often seem to be in short supply in the world around us. Consequently, the image management industry is ready to step forward with what social theorist Max Weber called "notables."[41]

The difference between notables and heroes is striking. What do we mean by "hero?" "A man or woman of great deeds," answers historian Daniel Boorstin. "For our purposes it is sufficient to define a hero as a human figure—real or imaginary or both—who has shown greatness in some achievement."[42] Heroes have achieved some outstanding accomplishment in power, wealth, virtue or evil. Examples of each must come readily to mind, from a heroine such as Mother Theresa to a villainous hero such as Adolf Hitler. They are famous because of what they have *achieved*. Those whom Weber calls "notables," however, are famous for an entirely different reason. Instead of achieving fame and prestige because they have performed great deeds or accomplished great feats, "notables" are in the somewhat peculiar sounding position of being well-known *simply because they are well-known*.

"Celebrities" and "notables" fill the gap left by a modern demand for heroes that seems to greatly exceed the supply. The principles of manufactured celebrity apply to groups, institutions and corporations as well as to individuals. Examining these principles will suggest several important conclusions regarding just how contemporary persuaders attempt to secure fame and prestige by building images. Boorstin identifies the most general characteristics of a media image. Boorstin is concerned primarily with corporate persuaders, but his analysis applies more generally to the construction of media images for all persuaders.[43]

First, media images are *synthetic*, the product of planning and strategic creation. The characteristics they build upon may be natural ones, but these natural traits are exploited by calculation rather than left to chance. For example, Ronald Reagan by nature and training possessed a telegenic disposition that would have served any president well. However, this characteristic alone was less important than its careful manipulation by the Reagan image handlers who took care to place Reagan in situations where this aptitude would appear in the best light. Similarly, image makers who market cosmetics or clothing may initially choose a model such as Cindy Crawford for her natural beauty and poise, but they may alter that model's appearance either by an actual physical make-over or by synthetic modifications in photography such as air-brushing.

Media images are *believable* from the audience's point of view. They make sense within a frame of reference determined by the audience's values, knowledge and expectations. Media images create claims about a person or corporation that substitute for reality, or become reality, by retaining some essential plausibility. Consider, for example, the famous MacDonald's commercial that featured Larry Bird and Michael Jordan shooting baskets for a Big Mac. The commercial created images of these two basketball stars making "unbelievable" shots—off the bridge, across the river, through the window, "nothing but net." However, the image makes sense because of the legendary athletic prowess on the court of both Bird and Jordan.

Media images *invite passivity* and a sense of completeness. They present candidates, causes, products and organizations capable of a degree of perfection not found in "everyday," non-media life—reminiscent of the excellence of the heroes for whom they substitute. Such images of candidates and products are portrayed not as the *beginning* of work or effort on our part but as the *end*. The heroes, prophets and charismatic leaders of another age often asked us to join them in great labors and sacrifice. All that media images ask of us is our compliance: accept their descriptions of reality, vote for the candidate, support the cause, buy the product or do business with the corporation. No additional effort is solicited.

Media images are *vivid and concrete*, often appealing to the senses. They are generally *simplified*, compared to the reality they are supposed to represent. Media images are supported by a catchy slogan or phrase. Perhaps most interesting of all, media images are *ambiguous*, capable of reinterpretation in new situations to prevent giving offense and to accommodate changing needs of their creators. Consider the many advertisements for corporate entities, such as Microsoft, Philip Morris, or Nike, that present vivid and concrete images of rugged individualists, or heartwarming community and family connections in order to suggest that the corporation represented embodies these characteristics. The vivid and simplified image appears real, even though it is only representing an ideal.

These characteristics differentiate media images from the ideals they have come to replace in our society, according to Boorstin:

> Images now displace ideals... An ideal, contrasted to an image, is not synthetic. When we think of an ideal we think of something already there. It was created by tradition, by history, or by God. It is perfect, but it is not simplified. It is not ambiguous (or ambiguous only in a very different sense). Its implications are not passive. An ideal is what we actively strive toward, not what we fit into. Credibility is irrelevant. Charity, justice, equality, mercy, are no less ideals because no man or society ever lived up to them. Ideals are needed *because* in their perfect form they are somehow hard to believe.[44]

Thus Boorstin's discussion suggests several important theoretical differences between managed media images and more traditional notions of credibility. Consistent with the general principals of the classical concept of *ethos*, image management centers upon strategic choices by persuaders designed to enhance them *as* persuaders in perceptions of their audiences.

However, this perception, fostered by image management, remains only loosely connected with the relevance, values and truth of any claims made by these persuaders. In addition to the weakening of the connections between the managed image of the persuader and the integrity and competence of the persuader's claims, there are other, more practical differences between image management and the classical concept of credibility. First, image management can apply to products, groups and institutions as well as individual persuaders. Further, image management is more long term in its focus. As we discuss in Chapter 12, image management campaigns are commonly ongoing activities, rather than being focused on a specific situation. However, there may be long-range goals, such as a general election or a marketing target. Third, image management is less dependent upon particular situations or topics. Borrowing from the metaphor in our discussion of congruity theory, image management similarly allows persuaders to "stockpile" or "bankroll" positive perceptions with audiences. These can be "cashed in" in particular situations as they arrive. Finally, image management techniques are more indirect than the traditional classical techniques of credibility in two senses. First, image management creates images and messages associated with abstract values and general themes. The connection of these values and themes to specifically identified proposals or propositions is frequently left unstated. Second, image management does not even require the direct participation of the one whose image is being managed. In this regard, the techniques of image management depart from a general assumption of the classical tradition, which holds that *ethos* is primarily something persuaders establish or demonstrate *by themselves, for themselves*, within a persuasive situation. Certainly endorsements invoking other authorities are important to such a demonstration; but such tactics are always assumed to be employed by the persuader. Image management, however, frequently attempts to bolster the persuasive power of a source without the direct presence of the source.

ETHOS, ETHICS AND IMAGE

The concept of *ethos* as well as modern research about credibility, charisma and image raise several important ethical questions. The most fundamental of these was raised by Plato over two millennia ago. Can a persuasive message be more ethical than the persuader? Plato voiced his concern in the following exchange from the *Phaedrus*:[45]

> **Socrates**: In good speaking should not the mind of the speaker know the truth of the matter about which he is going to speak?
> **Phaedrus**: And yet, Socrates, I have heard that he who would be an orator has nothing to do with true justice, but only with that which is likely to be approved by the many who sit in judgment; nor with the truly good or honourable, but only with opinion about them, and that from opinion comes persuasion, and not from the truth.

Plato's concern revolved around whether or not persuasion dealt with matters of truth or matters of opinion. As we have already discussed, truth is often elusive in matters subject to persuasion. When persuasion concerns conflicting opinions and values, rather than a matter of empirical truth or falsity, audiences must often rely on the judgment of persuaders. Such reliance, however, immediately raises a question about the ethics of those persuaders. What is the proper relationship between the character, knowledge and judgment of a persuader and the *portrayal* of these characteristics within a persuasive message?

Aristotle attempted to answer this question in his discussion of *ethos*. The *ethos* of which Aristotle spoke was assumed to be a genuine and authentic characteristic of persuaders. Persuaders could demonstrate habits of excellence in their speeches by presenting sound arguments and relying on commonly accepted virtues for their persuasive appeals. Audiences who recognized these qualities in a persuader could then feel secure in trusting the persuader's judgment. While Aristotle's discussion of virtue was the foundation for classical approaches to ethical persuasion, later Roman theorists such as Cicero and Quintilian elaborated on his vision by suggesting that the ethical orator was one who was trained in the virtues as well as the art of rhetoric.[46] Contemporary ethicists have developed a similar approach known as "virtue ethics."[47] From this perspective, ethical communication is not simply a matter of communicating in responsible ways in any particular case, but a matter of exercising virtuous conduct repeatedly and habitually.

The concept of virtue, or habits of excellence, goes far in providing ethical guidelines for persuaders and audiences alike. However, another ethical problem arises from this position that is equally troublesome. Is it still possible for persuaders and their audiences to share an idea of excellence in an increasingly diverse, pluralistic and disposable-culture society? In a comprehensive attempt to restructure moral theory, Anthony Cortese points out that ethnicity, culture and gender play important roles in the development of moral judgment and resulting ethical standards.[48] Carol Gilligan makes a similar point in her discussion of the differences in moral development among males and females in our culture.[49] The work of scholars such as Gilligan and Cortese raise questions about what constitutes ethos, credibility and an ethical approach toward the building of such persuasive resources.

Our earlier discussion of the components of credibility and commonly accepted virtues reflects a cultural system that has valued hierarchy, authority and the traditional "masculine voice." Because what is perceived as credible often emerges from an examination of the qualities of those who occupy positions of leadership and high status, much research on credibility, charisma and image may exclude the means by which those new to such positions attain their status. Researchers in the area of political communication, for example, have noted that women face a particularly difficult challenge in asserting their competence and dynamism.[50] Communication techniques that men use effectively frequently result in negative perceptions about women. Perhaps even more important, what is considered virtuous by the dominant culture may not be similarly valued by various subcultures. Missing from Aristotle's list of virtues are items such as compassion, nurturing and egalitarianism. Only recently, have advocates of virtue ethics begun to include virtues traditionally associated with the "feminine voice," such as "caring for self and others, compassion, nurturance of relationships, responsiveness to growth and appreciation of change, resilient good humor and clear-sighted cheerfulness, attentive and realistic love, and a humble sense of the limits of one's actions and the unpredictability of the consequences of one's work."[51] One may ask, then, whether the habits of excellence demonstrated by a persuader or the standards of virtue supplied by an audience are inclusive—a question to which we will return later in our chapter concerning ideology.

Today, as persuaders become increasingly sophisticated in techniques of image building, the classical principle of *ethos* and the contemporary notion of virtue ethics becomes increasingly problematic. Audiences wonder whether political candidates are really as strong, yet as compassionate, as they are portrayed. Receivers become skeptical about whether or not Dow Chemical really does "good things for life," as their advertising slogan maintains. As such examples accumulate in our lives, audiences begin to suspect that the image is *only* an image, an illusion thats relationship to reality is tenuous at best. What if the persuader's ethos is merely an appearance, a technically manufactured illusion at odds with the genuine character of a persuader?

Image management presents us with possibility of persuaders whose shifting personae have no basis in shared community values, but simply in implicit appeals to ambiguous images. The cynicism and distrust that has grown among Americans regarding public figures and public institutions is undoubtedly connected to the increasing pervasiveness of image-managed persuasion in our society. According to Boorstin:

> This can be summed up as the shift in common experience from an emphasis on "truth" to an emphasis on "credibility." All of us—not merely the supposed witch doctors of Madison Avenue, but all American citizen-consumers—are daily less interested in whether something is a fact than in whether it is convenient that it should be believed. Today the master of truth is not the master of facts but the practitioner of the arts of self-fulfilling prophecy. What seems important is not truth but verisimilitude [the appearance of truth].[52]

The problem Boorstin identified need not settle itself on metaphysical discussion of the nature of truth. Image management provides a modern, convenient substitute for the person who tells the truth and also for the hero and the messiah. Our appetite for "celebrities" and "notables" is in part a modern expression of the cult of the individual, an urge to elevate an individual to hero status, which is fundamentally anti-democratic.[53] Political communication expert Kathleen Hall Jamieson goes further to suggest that both the rise of image management and the heterogeneity of contemporary culture may make *ethos* "a less reliable anchor for belief."[54]

Because charismatic leaders so often lead the way in initiating social change, we might expect our discussion of charisma to provide insight for integrating more diverse perspectives into the notion of ethos and image. However, the concept of charisma is no less ethically troubling. While charisma is often enacted through the use of unconventional tactics that are characteristic of diverse cultural subgroups, charismatic individuals can sometimes exert extraordinary persuasive influence by encouraging in their audiences a selfless devotion, an unreasoning support, to the charismatic individual. Such persuasion may well succeed not by empowering its audiences, but by discouraging them from exercising their own judgment.

In such cases, as well as in the general milieu of a heterogeneous and media-saturated culture, the most pragmatic ethical guidelines may hinge more on the role of audiences than on the persuaders attempting to influence them. Ethicist Richard Johannesen has summarized the responsibilities of audiences in persuasion into two principles.[55] First, audiences have the responsibility to exhibit *reasoned skepticism* toward the persuasive messages they see and hear. It serves only the unprincipled persuader if audiences gullibly accept *everything* they see and hear. Yet, it serves no one if audiences become so cynical and suspicious that they refuse to believe that *anything* they see or hear is worthy of their belief and assent. Reasoned skepticism is also *informed* skepticism. It requires us to be prepared to participate knowledgeably as audiences for persuasion. Secondly, audiences have the responsibility to *respond to persuaders* in clear and appropriate ways. Audiences who remain unresponsive, who do not accept the burden of supplying feedback to persuaders, do not improve the quality of persuasive discourse around them. Such feedback may take the form of response or dialogue. It may also mean clear expression of our expectations and standards as an audience. In cases where we must place our faith in the character of persuaders, it is the responsibility of audiences to give careful scrutiny to those persuaders and to make their own ethical standards clear. Especially in the cases of charismatic leaders and image management, the admonition for responsible audience reactions in the form of reasoned skepticism and feedback is significant.

CRITICAL FOCUS: KFC AND "THE COLONEL'S WAY"

From the classical point of view, the most important of the three dimensions of persuasion is the credibility of the persuader. We cannot really understand how persuasion works until we can see how the source of the message, as perceived by the audience, contributes to the persuasive possibilities of the message. The following questions are designed to help you identify the ways in which the image of the source influences the persuasive potential of messages around us.

Critical Questions

1. Does the message depend on ***ethos*, charisma, image management** or some combination of these persuasive strategies?
2. What **persuasive purposes** are served by the *ethos*, charisma or image strategies you have identified?
3. What **specific elements** in the message itself display *ethos*, charisma or image management?
4. How **effective** do these strategies appear to be?
5. To what extent do the strategies revealing *ethos*, charisma or image management conform to **ethical standards** governing persuasion?

Although each of the KFC commercial spots differs slightly, the central message for all is the same: "The Colonel's way is still the best way." From beginning to end, each spot features Colonel Sanders directly addressing his audience about the benefits of buying chicken from the restaurants he founded and made famous. While the appearance and testimony of Colonel Sanders appear to be a straightforward example of *ethos*, the spots also use modern techniques of image management to make their claim. Moreover, the makers of these commercials probably hoped that the Colonel's charisma would also add to the persuasive force of *ethos* in their commercials.

Evidence for the emphasis on *ethos* as a means of persuasion appears early in each spot as each one opens with black-and-white footage of the Colonel addressing the audience and quickly cuts to a graphic that identifies the speaker as "Colonel Harland Sanders, founder." Older audiences recognize the Colonel from his trademark white Palm Beach suit, black string tie, white moustache and goatee and cane. For younger viewers, the graphic identification informs them that the speaker is important—the *founder* of the franchise.

Following Aristotle's conception of *ethos*, we can examine the Colonel's message for how it reveals his good sense, good will and good character, thereby persuading audiences that KFC is the best place to purchase a meal. Following the introduction of Sanders, all of the spots follow a simple formula that reveals something specific about the Colonel's way and ends by first intoning the general principle of the Colonel's way ("If you give someone a good meal at a fair price, they'll come back to you.") and second reiterating the claim that "the Colonel's way is still the best way." Besides sounding sensible, the Colonel's general principle illustrates the good will and good character of Colonel Sanders. He seems to have the audience's best interests in mind when he suggests that his concern is giving them a good meal (quality) at a fair price (fairness). In terms of Aristotle's list of virtues, his comment about a good meal demonstrates generosity, and his notion of a fair price demonstrates justice. By addressing his audience directly, the Colonel conveys a sense of caring, or at least respect, for the customers served by his franchise. Well dressed and neat, even if a bit unusual in appearance, the Colonel conveys a temperate and gentle disposition not unlike a kindly grandfather and very like the quintessential southern gentleman. His obvious age and folksy manners suggest wisdom and prudence (practical common sense).

The specifics of each spot reinforce the *ethos* of Colonel Sanders by providing additional evidence of his good sense, good will and good character. In the first spot viewers learn that the Colonel's original recipe was developed in 1939 as something the Colonel could feed his own family. Knowing that he concocted the recipe adds to the perception that Sanders is competent—after all, people have been following that recipe for 45 years. Knowing that he first devised his method of cooking for his family lends a sense of good will to his message (it must be alright if he would feed his own family that chicken). Sanders also enhances his *ethos* early in the spot by explaining that "people don't always have the time to fix a good meal." That isn't just a sensible statement that takes the needs of his audience into account; it is a statement that takes the blame off parents who aren't making home-cooked meals and allows them to feel alright about picking up a bucket of chicken on the way home from work. It illustrates magnanimity and liberality and, therefore, reinforces Sanders' image as a man of good character.

The second spot features another bit of folk wisdom from the Colonel. He explains that he thinks "the world would be a better place if people could sit down and a enjoy a good meal together." Immediately the spot cuts to the graphic, "The Colonel's Way," alerting the audience that the kernel of wisdom just provided is what the Colonel believes. The audience's reaction is likely to be that the Colonel is a man of good sense. The visuals of people providing a KFC dinner for their new neighbors underscore the common sense approach to building community voiced by the Colonel. Later in the spot, the Colonel lets his audience know that he's prudent as well as wise when he explains that maybe his chicken can't make a better world, but it surely will make a better meal. By backing away from his original claim, the Colonel presents himself as one who has practical wisdom but does not exaggerate.

In the third spot, the specific Colonel's way is elaborated as a respect for difference. Sanders explains that "people are all different, and they like different things." The visuals of different kinds of chicken and side dishes expand on his claim, but the force of his folk wisdom works much the same as in the earlier spots. Not only does the Colonel have common sense about differences, but he is not rigid or judgmental; he is practical and knows that he must adjust to the different needs of his customers.

The specifics of the fourth spot again play on the Colonel's folk wisdom and magnanimous concern for others. His wisdom is illustrated in his opening statement when he remarks that he knows he will have competitors ("I don't imagine I'll always be the only chicken place in town.") and predicts "they'll be poppin' up like dandelions." His solution to the competition, he tells the audience, is to just "keep tryin' to make the best chicken" and to add some side dishes—a practical and fair solution to a practical problem. Later, he again provides some folksy social commentary by reflecting on the fact that "families are separate now." He then hopes aloud that "they need something to bring them together, and my chicken sometimes brings them together." In this case, his practical wisdom appears to generate genuine concern for families, an indication of good will; and his solution is characterized by generosity or magnanimity (his chicken may bring them together).

While both the general features of these advertisements and their specific components build the *ethos* of Colonel Sanders from a classical Aristotelian perspective, there is reason to question whether or not a contemporary audience with diverse views of what is virtuous will perceive these spots as credible. Perhaps more important in determining their effectiveness is the role of image management in the spots. Harland Sanders died in 1980. As a result, when KFC decided to return to their roots in their advertising campaign for the nineties they searched the archives for original footage of Colonel Sanders. Although there was quite a bit of old film, according to KFC's Vice President for advertising Peter Foulds, the Colonel's old interviews were too long-winded to meet the sound-bite needs of today's 30-second spots.[56] Consequently, the direct address by Colonel Sanders in these spots did not come from Sanders himself but from well-known historical impersonator Henderson Forsythe, "who required a four- and-a-half-hour makeup job to achieve the Sanders look."[57] Thus, following standard image management techniques, the producers of the spots filmed Forsythe's acting in black-and-white and edited that with some brief clips of the original Colonel twirling his cane on the lawn and driving his convertible to produce a synthetic image.

The decision of KFC to resort to an impersonator in order to revive the *ethos* of the Colonel in their sales pitch probably was directly related to the other contemporary concept discussed in this chapter—charisma. An innovator in the fast-food business, Harland Sanders' life exemplified that of a charismatic leader. His rags-to-riches story is told in his own book, *Life as I Have Known It Has Been Finger Lickin' Good*, published in 1974. In 1965, soon after he sold the business, but while he still worked as its official spokesperson, Sanders received the Horatio Alger Award, an award given to entrepreneur's who exemplify the American dream. Accounts of how he ran his business as well as his public relations work for the franchise confirm his charismatic style. Shirley Topmiller, curator of the KFC corporate museum in Louisville, Kentucky, worked with Colonel Sanders for nearly a decade before his death in 1980. She recalls:

> 'Inspirational' is sort of a goofy word, but he really was. There were times early on when the company was in trouble and the colonel would get everyone in the lobby and give these stirring speeches and we'd think, 'He's right—if we just get the gravy right, we'll rule the world!'[58]

Thus, apparently Harland Sanders was able to articulate a clear vision to his followers while building trust with his audience through audience-centered tactics. Contemporary executives at KFC were probably anxious to tap into the reservoir of charisma that the Colonel once held as part of their marketing campaign; therefore, they designed spots that would reveal the *ethos* of the person who for so long had personified the company. Advertising executive Foulds, for example, argued that the company was doing America a service by bringing the Colonel back: "He was a character, an icon, as American as apple pie."[59]

Ironically, the same characteristics that probably launched Sanders as a charismatic leader—his incredible life story, innovative yet folksy ways and leadership ability—cause some people to doubt his very existence. Reporting that the advertising critic for *Advertising Age*, Bob Garfield, had doubts, Nancy Kruh explained: "In fact, Garfield is one of apparently many people who have long suspected there was no real Harland Sanders in the first place."[60] Although both KFC and a variety of other sources confirm the founder's existence, the use of an impersonator as part of the image management in this campaign may fuel the fire of disbelief and create further suspicion about just how much of the original Colonel was authentic and how much was manufactured for his role as public relations spokesman for the corporation.

Regardless of their effectiveness, the advertisements featuring an impersonated Colonel Sanders have been questioned on ethical grounds by some media analysts.[61] Forsythe's portrayal of Sanders is clearly identified as Sanders himself in each of the spots, thus blurring the line between reality and fiction. The words spoken were scripted for a time, place and audience that the "real" Harland Sanders never knew. Yet, there is a degree of plausibility to the managed image that can be verified by several reactions to the spots. Shirley Topmiller, for example, reported:[62]

> I had some healthy reservations which quickly went away. I don't mind telling you when I read the storyboards, I got very, very emotional. I thought it was just like the colonel talked.

She later recalled screening the commercials with the colonel's elderly widow:

> I think we looked at them four or five times. She was very quiet at first. Then she said, 'I think they've done a really good job.' It didn't really matter what anybody else thought after that.

But even if the managed image is accepted as sufficiently congruent with reality, reasoned skepticism may still be in order concerning the *ethos* constructed in these advertisements.

Classical approaches and contemporary virtue ethics alike suggest an inquiry into the habits of Colonel Sanders. Did he really and consistently display virtues or did his talk only make him appear to be virtuous? A look at his biography suggests habits of excellence. His competence is confirmed by his life that began as an itinerant worker and ended as a multi-millionaire. His enduring good sense is attested to by his retention for quality control and public relations for the franchise business that he sold. His character, as a prudent entrepreneur and generous philanthroper, is evidenced by his active participation in a number of charities as well as his approach to business for half a century. Hence, his *ethos* appears to meet classical ethical standards for habits of excellence.

NOTES

1. Biographical data on Harland Sanders is provided in several sources, including *Contemporary Authors,* volume 114, 403-404.
2. *Contemporary Authors,* 403
3. E. S. Ely, "Some High Hurdles Loom for Pepsico's Fast-Food Hotshots," *New York Times,* 16 February 1992, F-5.
4. Ely, "Some High Hurdles," F-5.
5. "Shops Shift as Fast-Food Struggles for Answers," *Advertising Age* 65 (September 28, 1994), 32.

6. Stuart Elliott, "Advertising: KFC's Very Real Problems May be Solved in Lake Edna," *New York Times*, 19 May 1992, D-20.
7. Aristotle, *Rhetoric*, trans. W Rhys Roberts (New York: Modern Library, 1954), 1356a.
8. Aristotle, *Rhetoric*, 1378a.
9. Aristotle, *Rhetoric*, 1380b-1381a. This connection, pushed to its logical extreme, prompts McCroskey to assert that *ethos* is an attitude of audiences, like any other attitude, rather than a characteristic of persuaders themselves; see: James C. McCroskey, *An Introduction to Rhetorical Communication*, 3rd Ed. (Englewood Cliffs NJ: Prentice-Hall, 1978), 68.
10. Aristotle, *Rhetoric*, 1366a-1366b.
11. An excellent review of contemporary studies that shows the relationship of their findings to the original work of Aristotle can be found in Wayne N. Thompson, *The Process of Persuasion: Principles and Readings* (New York: Harper & Row, 1975), 57-61.
12. Charles E. Osgood and Percy H. Tannenbaum, "The Principle of Congruity in the Prediction of Attitude Change," *Psychological Review* 62 (1955): 42-55; see also: Charles E. Osgood, G. J. Suci and Percy H. Tannenbaum, *The Measurement of Meaning* (Urbana: University of Illinois Press, 1957).
13. Herbert W. Simons, *Persuasion: Understanding, Practice, and Analysis*, 2nd Ed. (New York: Random House 1986), 60.
14. The quantitative formula, and the seven-point scaling technique, by which the calculation of attitude change is carried out in Osgood and Tannenbaum's model are described in: Simons (1986): 58-59; see also Charles A. Kiesler, Barry E. Collins and Norman Miller, *Attitude Change: A Critical Analysis of Theoretical Approaches* (New York: John Wiley, 1969), 179-181.
15. Simons, *Persuasion*, 60.
16. Terry H. Ostermeier, "Effects of Type and Frequency of Reference Upon Perceived Source Credibility and Attitude Change," *Speech Monographs* 34 (1967): 137-144.
17. Wayne N. Thompson, *Quantitative Research in Public Address and Communication* (New York: Random House, 1967), 54-58. Note that this finding in no way contradicts—and indeed seems to support—the research summarized in Chapter 3 showing that simply *calling* some assertion "a fact" will increase its persuasive clout.
18. Thompson, *Quantitative*, 50-54.
19. Herbert W. Simons, Nancy N. Berkowitz and R. John Moyer, "Similarity, Credibility, and Attitude Change: A Review and a Theory," *Psychology Bulletin* 73 (1970): 1-16; see also, Stephen W. King and Kenneth K. Sereno, "Attitude Change as a Function of Degree and Type of Interpersonal Similarity and Message Type," *Western Speech* 37 (1973): 218-232; Dominic A. Infante, "The Function of Perceptions of Consequences in Attitude Formation and Communicator Image Formation," *Central States Speech Journal* 23 (1972): 174-180.
20. Thompson, *The Process of Persuasion: Principles and Readings* (New York: Harper & Row, 1975), 77-78.

21. McCroskey, *Introduction*, 69.
22. See: James C. McCroskey, "Scales for the Measurement of *Ethos*," *Speech Monographs* 33 (1966): 65-72; McCroskey, *Introduction*, 70.
23. Kenneth E. Andersen, *Persuasion: Theory and Practice* (Boston MA: Allyn and Bacon, 1971), 222-223.
24. Andersen, *Persuasion*; McCroskey, *Introduction*, 69-70.
25. Andersen, *Persuasion*, 221-222.
26. Erwin Bettinghaus, "The Operation of Congruity in an Oral Communication Situation," *Speech Monographs* 28 (1961): 131-142; see also, Gerald R. Miller and Murray A. Hewgill, "The Effect of Variations in Nonfluency on Audience Ratings of Source Credibility," *Quarterly Journal of Speech* 50 (1964): 36-44; John W. Bowers, "The Influence of Delivery on Attitudes Toward Concepts and Speakers," *Speech Monographs* 32 (1965): 154-158; W. Barnett Pearce and Forrest Conklin, "Nonverbal Vocalic Communication and Perceptions of a Speaker," *Speech Monographs* 38 (1971): 235-241.
27. David W. Addington, "The Relationship of Selected Vocal Characteristics to Personality Perception," *Speech Monographs* 35 (1968): 492-503.
28. See Jay A. Conger, *The Charismatic Leader: Behind the Mystique of Exceptional Leadership* (San Francisco: Jossey-Bass, 1989); see also, Max Weber, "The Nature of Charismatic Domination," *Max Weber: Selections in Translation*, ed. W. G. Runciman, trans. E. Matthews (Cambridge: Cambridge University Press, 1978).
29. Weber, "Nature," 227-229.
30. Weber, "Nature," 228; Conger, *Charismatic*, 22-23.
31. Gary C. Woodward and Robert E. Denton, Jr., *Persuasion and Influence in American Life* (Prospect Heights: Waveland, 1988), 171.
32. Conger, *Charismatic*, 17.
33. Weber, "Nature," 231.
34. Conger, *Charismatic*, 23.
35. Conger, *Charismatic*, 35.
36. Conger, *Charismatic*, 36.
37. Conger, *Charismatic*, 25-36.
38. Conger, *Charismatic*, 70-85, 117; Weber, "Nature," 244-245.
39. Weber, "Nature," 236.
40. Conger, *Charismatic*, 149-150.
41. Weber, "Nature," 245.
42. Daniel Boorstin, *The Image: A Guide to Pseudo-Events in America*, 25th Anniversary Edition (New York: Atheneum, 1987), 49.
43. Boorstin, *Image*, 185, 194.
44. Boorstin, *Image*, 197-198
45. Plato, *Phaedrus*, trans. Benjamin Jowett, in *The Dialogues of Plato*, Vol. 1 (New York: Random House, 1937), 263.
46. Donald C. Clark, *Rhetoric in Greco-Roman Education* (New York: Columbia University Press, 1957), 11.

47. Richard L Johannesen, "Virtue Ethics, Character, and Political Communication," *Ethical Dimensions of Political Communication*, ed. Robert E. Denton, Jr. (New York: Praeger, 199-).
48. Anthony Cortese, *Ethnic Ethics: The Restructuring of Moral Theory* (Albany: SUNY Press, 1990).
49. Carol Gilligan, *In a Different Voice: Psycological Theory and Women's Development* (Cambridge: Harvard University Press, 1982).
50. Judith Trent and Robert Freidenberg, *Political Campaign Communication* (New York: Praeger, 1983),.
51. Johannesen, "Virtue Ethics,".
52. Boorstin, *Image*, 212.
53. Boorstin, *Image*, 50.
54. Kathleen Hall Jamieson, *Eloquence in an Electronic Age: The Transformation of Political Speech-Making* (New York: Oxford University Press, 1988), 240.
55. Richard L. Johannesen, *Ethics in Human Communication*, 3rd ed. (Prospect Heights: Waveland, 1990), 135-136.
56. Rptd. by Nancy Kruh, "Original Flavor: A Crusty Col. Sanders Impersonator Spices up New KFC Commercials," *Chicago Tribune* 12 August 1994, 5:2.
57. Kruh, "Original," 5:2.
58. Rptd. by Kruh, "Original," 5:2.
59. Rptd. by Kruh, "Original," 5:2.
60. Kruh, "Original," 5:2.
61. Kruh, "Original," 5:2.
62. Kruh, "Original," 5:2.

6
THE SYMBOLIST PERSPECTIVE

IN THIS CHAPTER:
Focus on:
Finding a "New Generation" of Oldsmobile Buyers
1. Theoretical Focus: Symbols and Identification
2. Symbolist Theory
   The Nature of Symbols
   Codes, Meaning and Form
   Characteristics of the Symbolist Perspective
3. The Process and Functions of Identification Through Symbols
4. Two Realities—Empirical and Symbolic
5. The Problem of Ethics in the Symbolist Perspective
6. Critical Focus: Oldsmobile's "New Generation" of Buyers

FOCUS ON: FINDING A "NEW GENERATION" OF OLDSMOBILE BUYERS

Beginning in the early 1970's, American automobile manufacturers faced a sharply declining share of domestic car sales. The dominance of Chrysler, General Motors and Ford in the American market, once almost complete, had dwindled to a two-thirds share. This gap was most pronounced among younger car buyers, who were much more likely than older age groups to purchase import cars.[1] This represented a sharp change from car buying patterns of previous generations, when children who had been raised in "Chevy families" or "Ford families" tended to buy the same car makes that their parents—usually, their fathers—had purchased.

The change was a small part of the larger gap opening between the generations in the late 1960's. According to Cadillac marketing director James Kornas, "Baby boomers had more money and were better educated.... They also were rejecting their parents' values."[2] This trend, added together with the fuel efficiency, price, reliability and comfort of imports, left Detroit auto makers in a vulnerable position. And, ironically, the same "family" tradition that had once worked in Detroit's favor was now working against it. Import buyers were continuing to buy imports, just as buyers of Detroit products had once stayed loyal to their cars. Detroit manufacturers faced a "lost generation" of car buyers who were unfamiliar with American cars and did not like what little they knew.

The problem American car companies faced extended beyond the perceived quality and economy of imported cars. For American buyers, cars have long been important expressions of self-image and personal values—a connection that car companies have certainly encouraged, if not created, through their advertising. For many younger buyers, American cars had become associated with values and lifestyles of a previous generation from which these younger buyers were eager to distance themselves, if only selectively. According to one independent automotive marketing executive, "A lot of people would have trouble admitting to their peers that they bought an Oldsmobile even if they thought it was every bit as good as a Honda."[3] As a result, Oldsmobile, whose sales volume traditionally exceeded 1 million cars per year, saw sales dip to only 700,000 cars by the 1988 model year. Oldsmobile's problem was a glaring case of a challenge to the rest of the American auto manufacturers, too. How could the loyalty of the younger buyers be won back without sacrificing the "traditional" Oldsmobile buyer, whose average age in 1987 was 51?[4]

Many questions raised by the case of the "lost generation" of Oldsmobile buyers depart from traditional concerns of the Classical Perspective, as discussed in previous chapters. By raising these questions, we mark the transition to a second major perspective on persuasion, the Symbolist Perspective. It will help us to understand the "Oldsmobile problem" as a question not of how we reason together about car purchases, but rather how cars and car buying—like virtually every other area of human activity—can come to symbolize values, motives and shared interests.

THEORETICAL FOCUS: SYMBOLS AND IDENTIFICATION

The Symbolist Perspective has historical roots nearly as deep as the Classical Perspective, but it has seen some of its most important developments in the Twentieth Century. Although it considers persuasion to be central and unique to humans, just as the Classical Perspective does, the Symbolist Perspective reflects another view of what it means to *be* human. The Symbolist Perspective recognizes that humans live in two very different worlds at the same time: an empirical world of sights and sounds and a symbolic world which is equally real, but it is created not from matter and physical forces but from language and other symbols.

From the Symbolist Perspective, persuasion is the process by which we become motivated to act or believe in a particular way through our communication with others, as a product of our own human inclination to interact with symbols together with the form and structure of the symbolic messages to which we are exposed. What is most characteristically human is not that we plan and intend rationally; but rather, we interpret our world and respond to it symbolically. The effects of symbols can be shaped by their creators' intended purposes, of course, but in the end the effect these messages have is determined by how they interact with an audience's values, beliefs and motives. Hence, the process of persuasion, from the Symbolist Perspective, is centered on the audience who interprets and responds, not the person who creates the message or symbolic act. As a consequence, the Symbolist Perspective is able to extend its range to include persuasive events that take place even without the conscious or deliberate intent of a persuader. Central to this perspective is the concept of *identification* as the means by which humans influence others. We identify with others or their actions, when we feel that we see our own interests and motives represented symbolically in the things they say and do.[5] From this perspective, all persuasion is self-persuasion—at least to a certain extent.

In this chapter, we investigate the Symbolist Perspective for what it reveals about such self-persuasion. First, we will describe symbolist theory by looking closely at the nature of symbols, the codes by which audiences make sense of these symbols and the general characteristics of this perspective. Next, we explain and illustrate identification as a fundamental principle of the Symbolist Perspective. Following a discussion of the important philosophical assumptions about our own "humanness" upon which the Symbolist Perspective rests, we consider the problem of ethics from this perspective. The Critical Focus at the end of this chapter explores the symbolic dimension of persuasion by applying the perspective to Oldsmobile's attempt to find a new generation of car buyers.

SYMBOLIST THEORY

The Symbolist Perspective draws attention to the persuasive potential of symbols. Important to this perspective is understanding how audiences determine what symbols represent and how audiences identify with those representations. Part of the explanation for how audiences attribute meaning to symbols comes from the nature of symbols themselves; another part of the explanation comes from the codes that audiences, consciously or subconsciously, apply to patterns of symbols in order to understand their meaning. The distinctive nature of symbols and the coded means by which audience's interpret them suggest several unique conclusions about persuasion from the Symbolist Perspective.

THE NATURE OF SYMBOLS

Symbols are words, objects or actions that come to represent something else. The key to how symbols function is representation—or re-presentation. Symbols make something that is not present become present for us in some way, or they make something present for us in a new way. For example, the American flag is a symbol not because it *is* the millions who have served America throughout its history, or its Constitution, or its principles of law, equality and tolerance for dissenting opinions. Instead it re-presents these things, making them present for us in a way that would not be literally or physically possible otherwise.

All symbols are potentially persuasive. This is because symbolizing, the process of creating and using symbols, is never a purely neutral act. As we will see in Chapter 7, even the seemingly simple act of naming or describing, upon which all symbol-systems such as language are built, always carries within it the power to influence our perceptions of what is being symbolized. For example, consider the number of things in our culture in the past few years that became important to us—that we were persuaded to regard as important—precisely because they were given a name at all, such as "soccer mom," "gen-Xer," "the Web" or AIDS. The demographic groups, the technology infrastructure and the terrible disease existed before they were named, of course; but it was the naming that declared them to be meaningful to us. The act of naming them, alone, urges us to have certain attitudes about them and their importance. Consequently, all symbols contain within them the capacity to influence how we feel about the persons, things, events or ideas the symbols represent. Moreover, symbols allow us to discuss and consider things with which we have no direct experience, thus creating a symbolic world.

Understanding the general nature of two categories of symbols—verbal symbols and nonverbal symbols—is particularly helpful in determining how symbols themselves are persuasive. Verbal symbols—words—tend to operate discursively, meaning that language has the following characteristics:[6]

> **Linearity:** Discursive symbols are structured in a single sequence, like words in a sentence or sentences in a paragraph. The later symbols must wait to be received until after the earlier ones have been received. Only ideas that can be structured in a linear fashion, unfolding sequentially, can be expressed discursively.
>
> **Vocabulary and syntax:** Discursive symbolism begins with a limited lexicon of symbols from which messages are "built up" according to rules of grammar and construction. Commonly, these rules of syntax and grammar reflect the linear character of discursive symbolism: "the dog bit the child" means something quite different from "the child bit the dog," even though both sentences use the same words and have comparable structure.
>
> **Translatability:** Discursive symbols can be defined using other symbols of the same sort, with no loss of meaning. Discursive symbols may thus be defined in terms or other symbols, either within the same language (as in a standard dictionary of American English, for example) or in another language (as in a French/English dictionary).
>
> **Generality of reference:** Discursive symbol systems are built from elements—words whose denotation is commonly general and abstract, such as "cat." More specific reference usually requires combinations of general references, such as "my black-and-white cat asleep over there in the rocking chair."

These characteristics give language its special persuasive powers. In particular, these characteristics are the basis of the persuasive power of naming, as well as of figurative and stylistic uses of language. In Chapter 7 we will examine these two potentials in close detail.

In contrast to language, nonverbal symbols function nondiscursively. They are often presented all at once rather than in linear fashion and in specific images rather than general references. As a result, nonverbal symbols lack most of the defining characteristics of language or words. For example, we may see an actor in a commercial pop the top of a Pepsi can at the same time we hear the perfectly recorded "pop!" and the accompanying music. But our experience of the message is not linear like the description in that last sentence. We do not look first at the character's hand, then hear the sound, then see her face and so on; we take all of these elements in at the same time. Similarly, our physical behaviors in interactions are apprehended as a continuous whole. There are no smallest units into which they can be divided while retaining their meaning. Films and musical or theatrical performances are typically linear in structure, but they are perceived through multiple senses at once. Many of these forms are not reversible or repeatable. Further, much of our nonverbal behavior is highly dependent on context for its meaning because there are no synonyms into which it can be translated equivalently, nor is it often possible to test the "truth" of a particular nonverbal behavior. Finally, the reference by nondiscursive symbolism is often very specific or concrete, rather than general. The written stories of Sherlock Holmes and Dr. Watson, for example, allow the characters and events to be imagined differently by different readers. But, when those characters are represented nondiscursively, such as by the filmed performances of Basil Rathbone and Nigel Bruce, we see them, like it or not, in a very specific way—wearing *this* sort of coat and not *that*, in a Baker Street apartment furnished *this* way and not *that*, and so on.

As these characteristics of nondiscursive symbolism compound, the terms by which we understand how *language* functions, as in Chapter 7, become less and less adequate to explain nonverbal messages. For example, we often explain the persuasiveness of a verbal message by determining how the language presents an argument. However, the concepts of argumentation are difficult to apply to purely nondiscursive message elements. Arguments and the propositions from which they are built require grammar, syntax, general reference and linearity for their operation. Nonverbal symbols ordinarily do not reflect such structure. Instead, nonverbal symbols tend to work by evoking motives, interests and values with which the audience can identify. Media consultant Tony Schwartz's description of the process as it applies to commercial advertising is typical of all nondiscursive persuasion. He explains: "Commercials that attempt to *tell* the listener something are inherently not as effective as those that attach to something that is already in him. We are not concerned with getting things *across* to people as much as *out* of people."[7] Thus, nondiscursive elements of persuasive messages influence their audiences less by "informing" them than by striking the "responsive chord" within them. The sights, sounds and movements of a nonverbal message tap into an audience's reservoir of sensory and imagined experience. Confronted with an opening scene of busy city streets and a close-up of a street sign that says "Wall Street" at the same time we hear honking of automobile horns and other sounds of the city, we "know" we are in New York. No set of claims, supported by data, leads us to that conclusion. We simply know it by reference to our experience, whether direct or second-hand and mediated. Moreover, the nonverbal message evokes that experience regardless of whether or not it advances a claim about that experience. In Chapter 8 we examine the persuasive power of nonverbal symbols in more detail.

CODES, MEANING AND FORM

Symbols depend on systems of *codes* for their meaning. Codes are conventions by which the various elements of messages, verbal and nonverbal, become meaningful and create expectations in audiences. Codes allow us to move from the raw data of words, sentences, sight, sound, touch, taste and smell to the construction of reality and the sharing of this reality with others. Codes are not limited to one type of symbolic element—verbal symbols, nonverbal behaviors, visual images or sound images—but more commonly shape our interpretation of combinations of such elements within messages. Codes are learned, even if they are not always taught formally or explicitly. For example, knowing the "code" of a language, the rules of grammar and syntax, audiences can determine the meaning of a sentence or a paragraph. Similarly, members of a culture understand nonverbal meaning through a system of codes that they may never have studied formally but nonetheless know. For example, people will attribute different meanings to a smile than to a frown as they interact with another person.

Moreover, the same code may not apply from one (sub)culture to the next. For example, a particular gesture, such as the thumb-to-forefinger sign, may be coded to mean "ok" in one culture while it is coded as a rude affront in another culture.

Any particular communication medium—film, television, radio or cyberspace—likely follows its own code or a combination of codes from other media. Especially in our contemporary media age, messages frequently combine language with various nonverbal elements, thereby invoking several codes at once. Film scholar Bill Nichols provides an explanation related to film:

> In film these codes include verbal language (English, French, Chinese, etc.) but also many other codes (color, fashion, lighting, editing, spatial proximity [the science of proxemics], and etiquette, for example). The communications themselves are particular realizations of these codes: They are texts. To be understood they must be read, that is, referred to the codes of which they are a particular manifestation.[8]

Nichols mentions the most obvious codes of language as well as other kinds of codes: color, fashion, lighting, editing and so forth. While we are generally not aware that these elements may have coded meanings, we all use them everyday to make sense of our communicative and persuasive world. For example, we associate low lighting with romance and seduction in one context and with danger in another context, a dark alley at night, for instance. The attire worn by advertising models leads us to make quick—usually appropriate—judgments about the intended market for the products they sell, such as, the young and upwardly mobile, conservative and rural or new-age and health-conscious. Similarly, the conventional codes of editing may lead us to respond with excitement to a series of quick cuts in a film or with serenity and peacefulness as we view a slow, panoramic gaze across a western landscape.

In addition to providing a basis for shared interpretation of texts, codes often lead us to prefer particular meanings for texts.[9] This "preferred reading" can apply to all manner of messages. Television and film rely on their viewers' familiarity with a variety of codes which allow images to be interpreted in the preferred way.[10] For example, in film, we all understand that extreme close-ups, especially at the end of a scene, frequently invite intimacy and empathy with a character, or serve as an indication of villainy. Loyal soap opera fans will recognize that technique as a common way of foreshadowing the evil intentions of the characters shown this way. Other familiar coded elements can be the dissolve between two scenes, the use of multiple images, "overcranked" and "undercranked" film speed to change the apparent speed of the action, and cross-cutting between two scenes to suggest that they are occurring simultaneously.[11] Music can be coded to suggest certain moods, as in the scariest moments of horror films. The codes of horror film sound tracks include a vocabulary of typical instruments used for this effect, such as the bowed string bass (as in the shark's signature theme in *Jaws*), or the high-pitched screech of violins (as in the "shower sequence" of *Psycho*) or the echoing, thundering sound of a pipe organ (as in *The Phantom of the Opera*). What reason, other than tradition and convention, could we give for saying that a bagpipe, a piccolo, a banjo or a kazoo would be inappropriate at such moments? Yet, these instruments would seem inappropriate—they would violate the shared interpretive principles of the code in a way analogous to a grammatical or syntactical error in language or a logical fallacy in an argument. Thus, codes operate persuasively by encouraging "preferred" interpretations of messages.

The pattern of verbal and nonverbal symbols within a message typically alerts audiences to which code is applicable for arriving at its preferred reading. Consequently, the Symbolist Perspective is concerned with the *form* of a message, as well as its content. While we usually understand form as simply the shape or patterning of symbolic content or subject matter, a more specific definintion of form explains the psychological-persuasive effect of such patterning. Kenneth Burke describes form as the ability of a message to arouse a sense of anticipation and in some manner to consummate, gratify or satisfy that anticipation.[12] Audiences have a strong psychological need to see form "played out" or completed. Once we detect a recognizable form or pattern, we feel some sense of expectation; a form is completed when it resolves that sense of expectation. We appreciate a logical argument followed through to its conclusion. We enjoy jokes or stories that involve a familiar image or line recurring again and again in slightly different ways. When we see the hero of a story get into a dangerous situation, we feel some desire to know what happens to the hero. We find comfort in the familiar routines of our work, our family interactions or our religious practice. If the pattern or form is a familiar one, even seeing the pattern "cheated," resolved in an unexpected or surprising way, may be satisfying or enjoyable, when a film has a "surprise" ending, for instance. The resolution may be temporary or permanent, expected or unexpected; what is important is that we continue to see the pattern acknowledged in some recognizable way. "A work has form," says Burke, "in so far as one part of it leads a reader [or, Burke would readily add, a viewer or a participant] to anticipate another part, to be gratified by the sequence."[13] From a purely aesthetic point of view, we judge the artistic merit of a work by how well the outcome resolves the need created by the pattern. From a persuasive point of view, we judge the extent to which the resolution or outcome places the audience in a particular frame of mind or creates in the audience a particular motivation. The persuasive functions of form are examined in detail in Chapter 9.

CHARACTERISTICS OF THE SYMBOLIST PERSPECTIVE

As an approach to understanding persuasion, the Symbolist Perspective has five important characteristics, some of which have already been hinted at by our discussion. First, from the Symbolist Perspective, the term "persuasion" includes both unintentional and intentional persuasion. We may put this another way: Just because A does not intend to influence B (or do so in a particular way) does not mean that B may not find A's actions persuasive anyway. We can find many instances of this aspect of persuasion around us in the course of a day. Sometimes it is fascinating; at other times it may be maddening; and sometimes it can be cause for serious political and ethical concern, as we will consider in later chapters.

Second, the Symbolist Perspective is characterized by concern for the relationship between messages or symbolic acts and those who are exposed to these acts—their intended or unintended audiences. We do not propose to rule out the traditional concern with persuaders themselves in the study of persuasion; and we certainly do not mean that persuasion is something that happens regardless of the conscious plans of a persuader, as if the body of established, prescriptive techniques for effective persuasion were no longer relevant. Instead, we simply draw attention here to the very fundamental relationship between the potential of a message or act to be persuasive and the rhetorical-psychology of the message's audience: The power of any act to influence is always, finally, grounded in its ability to engage the values, motives and interests of the audience.

Third, this perspective draws our attention to the ways in which language and other symbols not only influence our attitudes, beliefs and actions, but also our perceptions themselves. In this way, symbols determine what is *real* for humans just as effectively as do physical forces and phenomena. The persuasive power of language and other forms of symbolic action will be considered at length in Chapters 7 and 8.

Fourth, the Symbolist Perspective emphasizes not only the content of messages, but also their form. Symbols influence and motivate us not merely through their content or subject matter. They are also things that we experience through our senses,things that are (or at least appear to be) located in space and time, with shape and movement. This aspect of symbols, their form, is also important to understanding persuasion from the Symbolist Perspective.

Fifth, the Symbolist Perspective regards effective persuasion as often less bound by the rules of sound reasoning and logic than does the Classical Perspective. As we will see in Chapter 9, while this perspective regards the form and content of a well-crafted argument as potentially persuasive, it also maintains that many messages which are formally invalid from a logical, classical viewpoint are, nevertheless, both potentially persuasive and ethically acceptable. In part, this is because our response to symbols is not only one of understanding and interpretation, but also aesthetic pleasure or gratification. We gain *utility* from symbols as instruments with which to manipulate our environment, and we also get *satisfaction* from using symbols, just as we get satisfaction from eating good food or drawing a deep breath of fresh air, because it quenches an appetite we humans have for symbols. Just as important for persuasion, our response to symbols encourages us to identify with a particular set of motives and values, enabling us to identify with a particular way of viewing the world. This process of *identification* is the topic of the next section.

The Process And Functions Of Identification Through Symbols

Central to the modern Symbolist Perspective is the concept of identification. Earlier, we described identification as the process by which humans influence and cooperate with others through symbols. We *identify* with others or their actions when we feel that we see our own interests and motives represented symbolically in the things that they say and do.[14]

This process of identification rests upon appeals that operate in ways and at levels within us of which we are often not completely aware. Further, the content and the form of messages can reflect our interests and motives and serve as the basis of identification. It is important to remember that our interests and needs are often largely symbolic in nature. Consider, for example, the standard hierarchical description of human needs developed by psychologist Abraham Maslow, as described in Chapter 4. According to Maslow's widely accepted view, once our most fundamental needs—

physiological and instinctual—are met, we are motivated by social needs such as belonging, love and esteem. When these social needs are met, we direct our energies to self-actualization, the ongoing work of fulfilling the potentials of our calling, our talents and our abilities.[15] Clearly, once physiological and physical needs are satisfied, all other needs are met by our interactions with others and are also created or defined through these interactions. The implication for the relationship of motives and symbols to identification is clear and powerful. The most fundamentally human motives, which can be used as the basis of identification through symbols, are already essentially linked to the process of identification through symbols. Successful persuasion can help an audience to fill a variety of needs, but many of these needs have already been brought into being themselves as the result of successful persuasion.

To help clarify the principle of identification, consider an illustrative case.[16] Two bitterly divided groups at the height of domestic opposition to the American involvement in the Vietnam War were brought to see their interests as shared through a symbolic appeal.

The spring of 1970 was a volatile time on American college campuses. Opposition to the Nixon Administration's escalation of the Vietnam War was very strong and vocal on many campuses, and this opposition was merging with and fueled by growing mutual hostility and suspicion between students and President Nixon himself. When, on April 30, 1970, President Nixon revealed to a national television audience that American forces in Vietnam had been conducting secret bombing raids into neighboring Cambodia, claiming that their purpose was to advance American military objectives in Vietnam, the volatile atmosphere on many campuses exploded. The following days saw the protests and demonstrations intensify, culminating shortly after noon four days later, on Monday May 4, 1970, when four students, anti-war demonstrators, were shot to death in a confrontation with National Guardsmen at Kent State University.

On the campus of Southern Oregon College (now Southern Oregon University), an institution of approximately 5,000 students in Ashland, Oregon, the atmosphere was already filled with tension, even before the Kent State shootings. As one observer recalled, "Ashland was an armed camp, with rifle-toting pick-ups cruising Siskiyou Boulevard. Two of our female students had been injured by bricks or rocks thrown from such passing vehicles. The mood on both sides of the issue was very ugly, growing dangerous."[17] In the days following the Kent State incident, anti-war students demanded that the American flag at the center of campus be lowered to half-staff as a response to the Kent State deaths. A numerically smaller group of pro-war students placed themselves at the base of the flagpole, vowing to prevent the lowering of the flag. The anti-war students gradually formed a large crowd encircling both the flagpole and the students positioned at its base. As hours became days, the situation became a standoff—one seeming more likely to erupt into violence with each passing moment.

James K. Sours, president of the college, found himself in what might appear to be a "no-win" position; it fell to him to authorize publicly that the flag either be lowered or left where it was. The two groups were strongly polarized. There were only two ways the flag could be displayed: either the flag would be "up," or it would be "down." If either group believed itself to have "lost" the confrontation—and surely, it seemed, one of them must—violence might be the outcome.

Sours had been attending a professional conference in Iowa City when he learned of these events at Southern Oregon University; he returned immediately to Ashland and met with deans, faculty and student leaders to appraise the situation. He became convinced by Thursday morning that action had to be taken. Sours had originally planned to call a convocation of all students and faculty to discuss the issues involved, but he now believed that taking steps to reduce the potential for violence in the immediate situation was of greater importance than campus-wide deliberation on the larger political and ethical questions raised by the Kent State tragedy. Accordingly, he left his office around noon Thursday and went home to draft a brief statement that he delivered with the aid of a megaphone later that afternoon to the students gathered near the flag.

We invite you to take a moment now and imagine how *you* would respond in such a difficult rhetorical situation? If you were in President Sours' place, what could you say to this audience to prevent a violent reaction when one faction or the other believed its interests had been disregarded or dishonored?

We believe that the key to understanding Sours' response and its effectiveness is to recall that the American flag is a symbol. The same is true of flying the flag at half-staff: It is a symbolic act. Neither the physical pieces of stitched cloth from which the flag was made nor the physical motions used in positioning it on the staff were of primary importance; but what they represented was and is of great importance. Both the flag and the act of lowering it to half-staff or not doing so have meaning for us to the extent that we take them to represent other things, be those actions, ideas, values or beliefs. If Sours could find a way to evoke images of motives or interests shared by both the pro-war and anti-war students, symbolized by the flag, he might create a sense of identification between the polarized groups and provide a means for defusing the potentially violent situation.

Here is a text of the speech that Sours gave at the flagpole to the students:

> We are gathered here beneath the flag of this country. For most of us, this flag is invested with a high degree of symbolism. It symbolizes, for example, the freedom toward which hopefully we are continuing to move. It symbolizes the great and glorious moments of our national history. And it calls to mind the names of the millions of persons, great and small, who have served it and served it well.
>
> But as a symbol of our total national life, it also reminds us of the hard work that remains before us if we are to achieve the freedom and the kind of life for *all* of our people that constituted the dreams of our ancestors. It symbolizes, in other words, both our strengths and our weaknesses. Above all, it symbolizes those who have died as Americans. More than 300,000 Americans have given their lives in Twentieth Century wars. The flag reminds us of their sacrifice. It also reminds us of the tragedy of our national domestic scene which only a few days ago resulted in the deaths of the four students at Kent State University.
>
> By way of commemorating these losses, and to symbolize our determination to build a society that will give our flag its fullest meaning, I am directing that the flag be lowered to half-staff, until 5:00 p.m. Friday.

Following Sours' speech, students gradually disbanded, and the rumors of impending violence abated. The problem of the deep division created by the war, separating the anti-war students and the pro-war students (and Americans of all stripes), did not disappear as a result of this speech, but the immediate threat of explosive confrontation did. And we may assume that the potential for future confrontations of this sort was diminished to some extent because of the way Sours resolved the situation.

In twelve sentences, Sours successfully called up the values and motives represented for the community of students by the flag, then redefined the relationship of these values and motives to one another. By doing so, he moved aside those associations which were the basis of division between the two groups of students and refocused attention on those interests which were shared by both groups as a basis of identification.

In the first paragraph, Sours links the flag to "great moments" in our history and to the honor and remembrance of those who have "served" our country. In that context, the most likely images represented by the flag that Sours' language evoked were images of military triumph and military service. Hence, the pro-war students might have been especially inclined to see Sours' words in the first paragraph as expressing their interests. Yet, notice that both of these terms are left ambiguous. Those "great moments" in America's history might be military triumphs, but they might just as easily be moments of cultural, political, artistic or technological greatness. America was "served" by the men and women in military service, but the reference might just as easily have been to the many other ways, great and small, recognized and unrecognized, by which Americans have demonstrated loyalty to their country. By leaving both terms ambiguous, Sours gave both student groups the opportunity to "fill in the blanks" with particulars from their own experiences, in harmony with their own values and beliefs. Paragraph #1, therefore, does not *alter* the patterns of identifications his audience may experience; it *evokes* them—to call them forward so that they can be influenced by what follows in the speech.

In the second paragraph, Sours moves beyond these original clusters of identifications. He says that the flag represents not only our great moments, but our "weaknesses" and the "hard work before us." Again, these ambiguous references could be interpreted in more than one way, although it seems clear that the anti-war students would have been inclined to hear in this passage an expression of their own interests and values.

By the end of the second paragraph of Sours' speech, something extraordinary happens. The flag, Sours continues, represents values and goals embracing *"all"* Americans and symbolizes our remembrance of "those who died as Americans." Here is an identification perhaps unlikely to have occurred to the Southern Oregon University students in the heat of the stand-off without the influence of Sours' speech. The pro-war students would understandably feel a strong sense of identification with those who died in military service, while the anti-war students would naturally feel strong identification with those who were killed during the Kent State shootings. Yet, Sours shows the two groups—those who died fighting the war and those who died protesting that same war—sharing something common and substantial in that they "died as Americans." By extension, the two student groups are suddenly spurred to view their own interests as shared in an important way. Sours encourages this association by combining these two groups—combat soldiers and anti-war protesters alike—simply as "these losses" in the next paragraph.

By the third paragraph, Sours has created a powerful inducement for both student groups in his audience to recognize a transcending interest shared by both groups. It is altogether fitting and proper, he reminds the audience, to honor those who have died "as Americans." Thus, Sours' speech attempts to transform his audience's perception of their situation, so that this fundamental and shared interest—represented by the flag, the very focus of the present dissention on campus—could become even more motivating to his audience than the terrible and bitter differences spawned by the Vietnam war.

From the Symbolist Perspective, there is much to be learned from this short speech. First, our analysis of the speech is intended to demonstrate the ways in which all persuasion contains at least some element of self-persuasion. Sours' speech relied for its effectiveness upon several potentials within his two audiences; the most important of these potentials is the tendency all audiences have to identify with the values and interests represented by important shared symbols. The students, regardless of their stance on the war and their political affiliation, could be expected to have a large pool of shared images drawn from their experience as Americans. These images were learned in school, through the media and elsewhere—the sum total of concepts about America, American history, Vietnam and the Vietnam war. Probably all but the most politically or socially radical of the students could potentially be motivated by artful reference to these shared images.

Second, notice that the success of Sours' speech has little to do with the principles of formal logic or deductive reasoning. True, we could go back over the speech and impose some kind of syllogistic order on it, translating and rewriting it into more traditional argumentative form. But this would miss the strength of the speech. It does not demonstrate the logic of its conclusion; instead, it evokes images of values shared by otherwise hostile factions in his audience. Moreover, the speech succeeds by skirting some of the common sense patterns of reasoning we identified in Chapter 3: categorization and disjunction. It manages to treat the two groups of demonstrators as if they were alike (belonging to the same category) and different (belonging to different categories) at the same time. The success of the speech is an excellent demonstration that humans are creatures who reason logically to conclusions, as in the Classical Perspective; but they are also creatures who are naturally inclined to cooperate through symbols.

This case also shows that identification can be promoted by both ambiguous reference to images of shared interests and explicit reference to values and motives. Sours' short speech contained several specific references to values and motives, especially in the first two paragraphs. Each of those references was a potential source of identification for at least some parts of the audience. It also mentioned images whose meaning can be interpreted in many different, not necessarily contradictory ways. The most conspicuous example of this is the flag itself. Because the flag is a non-discursive symbol, its meaning in this case is perhaps more easily adaptable to different purposes and interests by persuaders and their audiences. In this way, the effectiveness of Sours' speech demonstrates the extent to which all persuasion involves a component of self-persuasion.

One last important principle governing the function of symbols and the process of identification is shown by Sours' speech on the flag. At its core, the connection between symbols and the things they represent is an arbitrary one. A symbol need not possess a single one of the characteristics of what it represents in order to serve as a symbol. There is nothing wet about the word "water," nor is there anything hot about the word "fire." As language scholar S. I. Hayakawa has written:

> Just as men can wear yachting costumes without ever having been near a yacht, so they can make the noise "I'm hungry" without being hungry. Furthermore, just as a social rank can be symbolized by feathers in the hair, by tattooing on the breast, by gold ornaments on the watch chain, or by a thousand different devices according to the culture we live in, so the fact of being hungry can be symbolized by a thousand different noises according to the culture we live in: *J'ai faim*, or *Es hungert mich*, or *Ho appetito*, or *Hara ga hetta*, and so on.[18]

Furthermore, symbols do not require the presence—or even the existence—of the thing they represent. "The Civil War" maybe discussed and treated as real almost a century and a half after it happened, and the adventures of "Sherlock Holmes" are no less exciting simply because there is no living person to whom the name ever referred. Literature, history, science, politics and everyday conversation all rely on symbols whose reference is not to anything that physically exists, yet these symbols are useful and important to those of us who employ them. The connections between all symbols and what they represent is a matter of conventional agreement and historical circumstance, not physical necessity. While that circumstance and agreement cause a symbol to gain additional power once we have come to use it as such, it is quite different from claiming that the connection between symbol and referent is itself somehow objective and necessary. As a consequence, there is no one, single, "right" meaning or association for a symbol. There are only "approved" and "disapproved" meanings, "agreed-upon" and "disputed" meanings and "obvious" and "obscure" meanings. In a most fundamental way, symbols mean whatever we agree for them to mean.

In the case we are examining, what the flag came to mean for the students as Southern Oregon University was shaped by their experiences with the flag, plus Sours' artful molding of these experiences through yet another symbolic action—his speech. Similarly, notice that his speech forms the basis for a new consensus as to what it means when the flag is lowered to half-staff. The two groups were divided on the meaning of lowering the flag. One group believed it would dishonor those who died in military service; the other group believed it would commemorate the deaths of the student protesters. Sours' speech gave lowering the flag a *new* meaning. It commemorated "these losses" (both the war dead and the anti-war protesters alike), and it symbolized "our determination to build a society that will give our flag its fullest meaning." Such a transformation of a symbol's meaning is possible only because the relationship between symbols and what they represent is arbitrary, not objective. As a corollary to this principle, we should be very skeptical indeed of those persuaders who insist that their interpretation of the meaning of any important symbol—such as the flag—is the one correct or true interpretation. Such persuasive tactics may be a politically convenient way to drum up support for a political agenda, but they totally misunderstand the nature of symbols and the people who use them. They can only be successful by encouraging others to fall victim to similar misunderstanding. The success of Sours' speech demonstrates clearly that the meaning of any symbol is a complex historical and social process and will inevitably change—slightly or radically—from situation to situation and generation to generation.

The Two Realities: Empirical And Symbolic

When identification is moved to center stage as the process by which we influence one another through symbols, we see all the more clearly the ways in which symbols and symbolizing are fundamental to our human nature. Kenneth Burke, in his essay "A Definition of Man," defines the human being as "the symbol-using animal . . . separated from his natural environment by instruments of his own making."[19] Because of our capacity to think, act and interpret symbolically, we have indeed removed ourselves, to a great extent, from both the shocks and the comforts of the purely physical world. The instruments of human technology have made us able to be indifferent to the changes of season, to the passing of day into night, to the barriers to travel and communication once posed by distance, and even in large measure to disease and hunger. It is not only our physical technology which has made this possible; this change is also the product of language, that is pre-eminently human invention. One can argue whether we are better or worse off for having severed our relationship to our natural environment to such an extent, but there is no denying that we have made ourselves unique among the inhabitants of the earth by doing so. Yet, it is only partly true to say that we are removed from our natural environment; it better captures our nature to say that we humans dwell in two environments, two worlds, while other species live in only one.

Both humans and animals live in an *empirical* reality. This empirical reality is shaped by the direct reports of our senses—sight, sound, texture, temperature, hunger, pain and so on—together with instinctive patterns of reaction to these stimuli. In the empirical world, objects move, have texture, make noise and cause pain or ease hunger. Whatever associations exist in this empirical world are direct and pragmatic: pain is to be avoided; predators are to be evaded; nourishment is to be found. But only humans also move in a *symbolic* world—equally real, yet invisible and incomprehensible in purely sensory or empirical terms. Conceptual connections form the associations in the symbolic world, rather than the simple physical and instinctual connections of the empirical world. These conceptual connections shape our human response to situations just as surely as do the physical and empirical connections.

From the Symbolist Perspective, there are many important implications of the fact that humans live in both an empirical world and a symbolic world. This duality can be the source of beauty, greatness and nobility. Our race's triumphs in art, culture, spirituality, technology and diplomacy are all products of this distinctly human side of our nature. It can also be the source of great bewilderment, violence and cruelty. Disagreements over the meaning and use of such symbols as sacred scriptures, treaties and laws have been and continue to be the grounds for misunderstanding, oppression, persecution, murder and holy war among humans.

THE PROBLEM OF ETHICS FROM THE SYMBOLIST PERSPECTIVE

In our generation, it has become fashionable again to disparage "rhetoric," the art of persuasion, as nothing more than bombast, empty public posturing and pandering to audiences. We see political adversaries accusing one another of engaging in "mere rhetoric;" we hear pleas for "action, not rhetoric," as if rhetoric itself had no substance, only outer appearance. This misunderstanding of the art of persuasion has resurfaced from time to time for the last 2000 years. As we noted in Chapter 2, it is Plato, writing from 4th Century B.C. Athens, who remains the most famous and formidable advocate of this view. In his writings, Plato compared the art of persuasion with the "art" of a pastry chef—both produce things which appeal to our senses and our appetites, but which are not "nourishing." Just as a body maintained only on candy and pastries may not feel hunger but will not be healthy, said Plato, persuasion can lead people to form "mere opinions" without giving them any genuine understanding or sense of responsibility.[20] In Plato's version of the ideal society, there would be no practitioners of this corrupt art of persuasion and no poets, since both confuse audiences by distracting them with style and flourishes, rather than improving them by challenging them with the truth.

It is important to consider this ethical objection to certain kinds of persuasion, because from the Symbolist Perspective we will find ourselves challenged to explain the persuasiveness of many of the message characteristics—style, form, appeal to images and the imagination, and the use of persuasive approaches other than logical argumentation and evidence—that Plato (and his later followers on this point) found so ethically dangerous. How should we respond to ethical concerns about messages embodying such elements?

Yes, there is the potential for unethical behavior inherent in the fact that humans respond to symbols in the way that they do. But we do *not* conclude as a result that persuasion whose effectiveness is based on such tendencies in humans, is, *for that reason alone unethical*. First, a small but important reminder: To a large extent, the Symbolist Perspective is simply the messenger of the bad news. Humans have always responded to appeals other than purely and formally logical ones. Given our nature as symbol-using animals, we have no choice in the matter. The simple observation that an audience responds to a persuasive message in ways that defy "pure logic,"—whatever that may be—is not proof that anything unethical has happened, even if the audience is thereby moved to action or belief with which we might strongly disagree. It is a fundamental assumption of the Symbolist Perspective, and of this book as a whole, that audiences interact with and interpret messages in ways that artful persuaders, and even scrupulously ethical persuaders, can guide but cannot completely control. Indeed, remember that audiences can be motivated by the symbolic dimension of actions or events which no one ever intended to be persuasive or, perhaps, even meaningful. So it is inappropriate to question the ethics of a persuader simply by pointing to how the audience responded to the persuader or to what elements of a message the audience responded.

Few would disagree that certain potentially persuasive tactics are ethically intolerable—malicious lying, inciting racial hatred, threatening violence to innocent persons. These are not really the ethically difficult cases. In the passage below, ethicist

Richard Johannesen discusses the choices underlying a persuader's conduct. These choices include decisions about which persuasive tactics to use and whether or not communicating at all is appropriate.

> How thoroughly have *alternatives been explored* before settling on this particular choice? Might this choice be less ethical than some of the workable but hastily rejected or ignored alternatives? If the only avenue to successful achievement of the communicator's goal requires the use of unethical communication techniques, is there a realistic choice (at least temporarily) of *refraining* from communication—of not communicating at all?[21]

The ethical objections to choices about persuasive tactics are clearer and more nearly universally recognized. A persuader, it seems, is much more likely to know when this line has been crossed and, therefore, could be judged accordingly. However, choices about whether to refrain from communication are more difficult for persuaders. More troublesome cases in which such obvious ethical lines may not be drawn so easily arise from the Symbolist Perspective. Consider the following examples:

> commercial advertisements perpetuating sexual stereotypes of women as sexual objects to promote sales of their products;
>
> political candidates whose campaigns focus on negative attacks on the record or character of opponents, rather than upon their own position on important issues;
>
> white supremacist groups distributing literature encouraging hatred for blacks and Jews;
>
> artists whose albums, exhibitions or performances contain material which some find offensive because of its explicit language or imagery;
>
> high government officials who lie or conceal information from the public to protect politically controversial policies; or
>
> advertising campaigns promoting potentially harmful products, such as tobacco and alcohol, by associating them with images of social status, maturity and social popularity.

These cases are more difficult for several reasons. For example, it is not clear in every one of these cases that the persuasion going on is creating or promoting, rather than reflecting, those values we might find offensive or disagreeable. Even this list has omitted some of the most ethically troublesome cases, those in which our communication, drawing as it does on culturally perpetuated images, motives and assumptions, may give aid and comfort to values and motives which we ourselves would find extremely objectionable, but are virtually invisible to us within our own language and actions. Second, while we might find many of these actions or expressions offensive, in the United States it is neither legally nor ethically acceptable to suppress them for that reason alone. Third, especially in the cases of persuasion involving institutions, such as media and corporate advertising, it is very difficult to locate a single responsible individual on whom to place ethical blame when we think it is deserved.

Because the Symbolist Perspective emphasizes the importance of our *human* capacity to *choose* and the unintentional as well as intentional effects of messages, ethical judgments must comprehend both the ends of persuasion and the means by which those ends are reached. Ends come into play because the concept of identification is the theoretical lynch-pin for this perspective. The ethics of a message should be questioned if a message encourages audience identification with values, motives or interests that are morally repugnant.[22] We may apply legal codes, professional guidelines, religious doctrine or utilitarian principles to determine whether or not a particular approach to identification is morally repugnant. Even if the outcome of a persuasive message—the type of identification encouraged—is judged to be ethical, the means by which that outcome is reached may be ethically suspect. Persuasion is unethical if it employs tactics that demean or degrade others, thereby denying their fundamental human capacity to choose. Also, persuasion is unethical if it inhibits choice by the use of tactics such as deception or coercion.

These ethical standards, preliminary as they are, arise directly from the nature of persuasion itself, as viewed from the Symbolist Perspective. They reflect aspects of our definition of persuasion itself from Chapter 1. Because of the way humans interact with symbols, we cannot blame persuaders for the fact that audiences respond to *all* aspects of messages, even those aspects that "purists" like Plato found deplorable; there are, nevertheless, standards, such as those mentioned above, to which persuaders are and should be held accountable. In the chapters to come we will attempt to apply and refine these ethical criteria.

CRITICAL FOCUS: OLDSMOBILE'S "NEW GENERATION" BUYERS

At the beginning of this new section of the book, it seems most important to become practiced at recognizing the extent to which we are immersed in symbols and symbolic actions throughout our daily experience and to be able to recognize the motives and values with which these various symbols invite us to identify. Therefore, in this Critical Focus our objective is to help you to recognize the many symbols and symbolic actions around you and to understand how they can serve as the basis for identification.

To apply this Critical Focus, select a communicative action—whether that message is verbal or nonverbal, public or private. Ask yourself the questions below regarding the communicative action or message. Also, ask yourself *why* you reached the answers you did—to identify the evidence or clues both within the message and external to it upon which you base your conclusions.

CRITICAL QUESTIONS

1. What **types of symbols** (verbal or nonverbal) comprise the message?
2. What do the symbols **represent**?
3. How is the meaning for these symbols **coded**?
4. How is **identification** encouraged by these symbols and their code? What **motives, values or interests** are represented?

5. Do the grounds for identification in the message meet an **ethical standard** that preserves the audience's fundamental humanity?

The "Oldsmobile problem," described at the beginning of this chapter, led the auto company to launch a highly visible series of television commercials, attempting to attract younger car buyers, while retaining the loyalty of older buyers.[23] This campaign, produced by the Leo Burnett ad agency at a cost of $135 million, featured celebrities and their less well-known children embracing "A New Generation of Olds," the campaign's title. The campaign was unveiled in September 1988, during the television coverage of the Olympics. One commercial, featuring Melanie Shatner and her father William Shatner, is typical of the ads produced in the series and will allow us to examine the central concepts of the Symbolist Perspective on persuasion. The "Melanie Shatner" commercial attempts to create identification between younger potential buyers and the Oldsmobile—in this case the Oldsmobile Cutlass Supreme. The commercial does this by artfully representing in its form and content the "union" of the two generations.

The 30-second commercial opens on a field of stars, moving in such a way as to suggest we are traveling forward through it. We hear a brief fanfare of electronic music, replaced by trombones. Next we see Melanie Shatner, who tells us, "My father drove a starship, so it's only natural that I should fly around in something space-age . . . ." Melanie Shatner is standing in a circle of light on a mountain highway at night with a city's lights clearly visible in the valley behind. A Cutlass Supreme materializes in a flash of light beside Melanie, who continues, ". . . My new Oldsmobile Cutlass Supreme, totally redesigned for the future." As she drives the car down the highway, she explains, "Fuel-injected, monitored by an on-board computer"—we see the computer greet her with "good evening," followed by the tachometer reading—"I guess some things were just meant for the next generation." The music quickly swells and becomes the campaign's anthem with the lyrics, "This is not your father's Oldsmobile!" As a shooting star passes overhead, Melanie's father, actor William Shatner, materializes in the passenger seat next to her. The trombones from the beginning of the commercial return for a brief moment. "Ready, Dad?" asks Melanie. "I'm ready—you ready?" retorts her father. "I'm ready," laughs Melanie. "Steady as she goes," nods her father. We look out through the windshield and see a field of stars exploding toward us. As the commercial theme returns—"This is the new generation of Olds!"—the Cutlass supreme speeds away, leaving the highway and disappearing into the stars.

Any viewer even remotely familiar with American popular culture will recognize that this brief message is drenched with references to the classic 1960's television science fiction series *Star Trek* and the subsequent series *Star Trek: The Next Generation*, and the feature films it spawned. These references—both verbal and non-verbal, discursive and non-discursive—are present throughout the message. Some of the references are almost embarrassingly obvious: the presence of Shatner himself, who starred in the films and the original series; the sight of Shatner "beaming down" into his daughter's car; or the mention of "starships" and "the next generation." Other references are more ambiguous, and an audience would probably not connect them to *Star Trek* if the others clues were not there as well. For example, the melody carried by the trombones is similar to the opening notes of the *Star Trek* theme; that, together with the field of stars, becomes strongly reminiscent of the famous opening sequence to the series. References to "space-age," talking computers, "steady as she goes," and the sight of the car flying away are also examples of message elements that might not be associated with *Star Trek* until they are combined with the more obvious references.

But, of course, simply counting up the *Star Trek* references in this commercial is not the point, either of the commercial or this Critical Focus. The question concerning us goes an important step further: how do these images relate to Oldsmobile's problem with younger buyers? For the answer we need to go back to the central questions of the Critical Focus.

The symbolic elements in the "Melanie Shatner" commercial represent a complex set of motives and interests. Some of these have a clearly recognized relationship prior to the commercial; some do not. The representations form several large clusters, centering, respectively, around the relationship between the"real-life" Shatners, the relationship between *Star Trek* and its viewers, the relationship between the commercial's audience of young car buyers and Oldsmobile, and the relationship between the younger buyers and the older buyers.

The play between father and daughter brings to life the ad campaign's identifying slogan: "This is not your father's Oldsmobile." The car—indeed, the whole commercial—is clearly daughter Melanie's; she is the one who calls it "my" car, causes it to materialize, shows us its features and drives it. By comparison, father William's part is limited to that of passenger, a "cameo role," if you will. This is the general pattern followed by every ad in the series; the dominant figure is the less well-known offspring, rather than the well-known parent. Other ads in the campaign feature descendants of illustrator Norman Rockwell and lexicographer Noah Webster, but most use the children of notables from the 1950's and 1960's, such as: Shatner's fellow *Star Trek* star, Leonard Nimoy, (presumably, for those loyal "Trekkies" whose appetites were not satisfied by the Shatner ad), astronaut Scott Carpenter, jazz pianist Dave Brubeck, actors Priscilla Presley and Roger Moore, singer Frankie Avalon and race driver Gary Bettenhausen. Like "Melanie Shatner," each ad plays off of the associations for which the famous parent is known. More important, however, in each case the commercial focuses on the largely unknown son or daughter, rather than the famous elder.[24] In doing so, the creators of the series attempt to center the ads on figures with whom the younger audience can relate, because of their age and their more obvious similarity to the audience members themselves.

This commercial also draws upon *Star Trek's* relationship to its viewers. Certainly the prestige conferred upon a product by association with a popular television series cannot be overlooked, but that prestige, alone, is not the only—or even the most important—element upon which the commercial relies. The ad also uses *Star Trek* symbols to associate the Oldsmobile with the campaign theme, "A New Generation of Olds," by tapping into certain values embodied in the world of *Star Trek*: its high-technology atmosphere and its spirit of adventure and optimism. Identifying Oldsmobiles with *Star Trek* suggests these characteristics as a basis of identification between the values of the younger buyers and Oldsmobiles. Melanie Shatner's reference to "the next generation" embellishes the connection to "a new generation," as well.

The "Oldsmobile problem" is centered on a split between two generations in how they identify or fail to identify with Oldsmobiles. This shows the heart of this particular commercial and the entire series of commercials. The "Melanie Shatner" ad is obviously designed for the generation of baby boomers, sharing along with other characteristics, the experience of growing up on *Star Trek*. Older audiences might very well "get" some of the references, but they would not have the same loyalty to be tapped, the same interests and values to be shared. The most obvious function of this commercial, then, is to create a sense of shared interests between young buyers and Oldsmobiles. However, that was only half of the challenge faced by Olds; the other half of the problem was retaining the older, loyal buyers.

As we discussed earlier in the chapter, these patterns of identification are to some degree ambiguous: they will support multiple interpretations at the same time. The need for this ambiguity is at the heart of the Oldsmobile campaign; the Leo Burnett agency sought to portray its client's product as "a car for both generations."[25] Ambiguity in the patterns of identification within the ads permits Oldsmobile to promote identification with the two distinct audiences it pursues. The *Star Trek* references motivate younger buyers, while the older generation is drawn in a different way. Perhaps most important is the image of parents united with their children by the reaffirming image of the "Oldsmobile family" intact again. The campaign's slogan even exploits this ambiguity. After all, the claim "this is not your father's Oldsmobile" can be interpreted two ways: either as "this is not the same car your father drove" *or* as "it is the same car but it's not your father's anymore—it's yours." Thus, the commercials never really alienate the older generation; this both *is* and *is not* "your father's Oldsmobile." The ads recreate the process of tradition being extended from parent to child, to a new generation.

Formal elements of these commercials also shape their ability to lead audiences to see their interests and values in a new light. They are all fast moving; many, like "Melanie Shatner," begin with something unusual or unexpected. While they contain enough similarity from one commercial to the next, the addition of new celebrities keeps interest over time. Note that the Classical Perspective is unable to contribute much at this point. The Classical Perspective can take into account the background learning that comes from seeing the ads again and again, treating it as shared premises or credibility appeals; but it can not account for *the experience of viewing* these ads, once or several times.

Finally, we may consider whether or not the grounds for identification in this commercial preserve the fundamental humanity of the audience. While the "high-tech" flavor of the references to *Star Trek* technology and the lure of fantasy in this 30-second spot do not explicitly demean or degrade our capacity to choose, the world view with which an audience is asked to identify should be questioned. The commercial appears to promote our humanity if we subscribe to values of progress, material gain and faith in science. However, if our values place our relationship to the environment at the forefront, we might question the ethics of advocating the purchase of new automobiles during a period in which the environmental damage (especially in metropolitan areas) attendant to America's love affair with the automobile is becoming increasingly obvious.

Thus, the Symbolist Perspective, by focusing on how symbols represent motives and values, boldly goes where the Classical Perspective has never gone before. The "Melanie Shatner" commercial successfully sustains a contradiction—sending different messages to two audiences—that the Classical Perspective would be unable to account for.

NOTES

1. Dorin Levin, "Automakers Struggle to Lure 'Lost Generation, '" Eugene OR *Register-Guard*, 9 April 1991: 1B. Leven's article was syndicated by the *New York Times.*
2. Quoted in Levin, "Automakers," 1B.
3. Levin, "Automakers," 2B.
4. Christine Donahue, "New Olds Ads Target Young, "*Adweek's Marketing Week* 29 (12 Sep 1988): 2.
5. Kenneth Burke, *A Rhetoric of Motives* (Berkeley: University of California Press, 1969), 19-23.
6. Suzanne K. Langer, *Philosophy in a New Key: A Study in the Symbolism of Reason, Rite, and Art*, 3rd Ed. (Cambridge: Harvard University Press, 1957), 81-82 and 94-97.
7. Tony Schwartz, The Responsive Chord (Garden City, NY: Anchor Books, 1974), 96.
8. Bill Nichols, *Ideology and Image* (Bloomington: Indiana University Press, 1981), 10.
9. See John Fiske, "Television: Polysemy and Popularity," *Critical Studies in Mass Communication* 3 (1986): 391-408; Celeste Michelle Condit, "The Rhetorical Limits of Polysemy," *Critical Studies in Mass Communication* 6 (1989): 103-122; Bill Nichols *Ideology and the Image* (Indiana University Press 1981).
10. Fiske "Polysemy," 397; also: John Fiske, "Television: A Multilevel Classroom Resource," *Austrialian Journal of Screen Theory* 17/18 (1985): 106-124.
11. See: Fredric Rissover, "Basic Visual elements of the Photograph and the Motion Picture,: in Fredric Rissover and David C. Birch, eds. *Mass media and the Popular Arts* (New York: McGraw-Hill, 1971), 176-184.
12. Kenneth Burke, *Counter-Statement* (Berkeley: University of California Press 1968), 123-149.
13. Burke, *Counter-Statement,* 124.
14. Burke, *Counter-Statement,* 19-29.
15. Abraham Maslow, *Motivation and Personality,* 2nd ed. (New York: Harper & Row, 1970).
16. The authors wish to thank David Sours for bringing the speech to our attention and to express our appreciation to Dr. James Sours for his help and for permission to use the speech in this book.
17. Dr. James K. Sours, former president of Southern Oregon College, in a letter to William Nothstine, 30 September 1990.

18. S. I. Hayakawa, *Language in Thought and Action*, 3rd ed. (New York: Harcourt Brace Jovanovich, 1972), 24-25.
19. Kenneth Burke, "A Definition of Man," in *Language as Symbolic Action: Essays on Life, Literature, and Method* (Berkeley: University of California Press, 1966), 3-22.
20. Plato, *Gorgias*, in The *Dialogues of Plato, Vol. 1*, tr. Benjamin Jowett (New York: Random House, 1937), 521-522.
21. Richard Johannesen, *Ethics in Human Communication*, 3rd Ed. (Prospect Heights: Waveland, 1990), 19.
22. Johannesen, *Ethics*, Chapters 1-3, 6-7, 10.
23. Darcy Eikenberg, "Burnett, Olds Launch a New Spot Generation," *Back Stage* (16 Sep 1988): 1. The commericial from this campaign featuring Melanie Shatner is included in the videotape of case studies accompanying this book.
24. Eikenberg, "Burnett," 16.
25. Eikenberg, "Burnett," 1.

7
Language And Persuasion

IN THIS CHAPTER:
Focus on:
Franklin D. Roosevelt's 1941 "War Message"
1. Theoretical Focus: Language and Persuasion
2. Naming and Creating Reality
   - Denotation and Naming
   - Connotation and Naming
   - "God Terms" and "Devil Terms"
3. Figurative Uses of Language
4. Ethics: Language and Persuasion
5. Critical Focus: Roosevelt's War Message

Focus On: Language And Persuasion: FDR's 1941 "War Message" To Congress

Franklin D. Roosevelt's "war message" to Congress, delivered on December 8, 1941, the day after the Japanese navy attacked the U.S. military base at Pearl Harbor, asking for a formal Congressional declaration of war between the United States and Japan, is generally acknowledged as a significant moment in 20th Century American public address.[1] It is remembered, of course, for its position in a web of historical events. Following Nazi Germany's invasion of Poland over two years earlier, Britain and France had been at war with Germany in Europe, and consequently with Germany's allies, Italy and Japan. A Russo-German nonaggression treaty, negotiated weeks before the invasion, allowed the Soviet Union to remain neutral until June 1941, when Germany violated its own pact with the Soviets and attacked the Soviet Union.

The United States watched the growing militarization of Europe during the 1930's from a stance of isolationism. Vivid memories of the horrors of the World War of 1914-1917, an increasing influx of European immigrants into the United States, economic hardships of the Great Depression, and the geographic isolation of North America from conflicts in Europe and eastern Asia all fuelled the domestic support for American noninvolvement. President Franklin Roosevelt had, since at least 1937, attempted to shift public opinion from this stance, preparing the United States for a war with the Axis powers which he felt was inevitable; but these attempts were not successful and provoked hostility from the leaders of the isolationist cause.

Roosevelt's December 1941, "war message," then, represents a formal moment when the United States would abandon its neutrality and enter the war against Japan, Germany and Italy. The speech, only approximately 500 words in length, is also significant for what it demonstrates about the persuasive power of language.[2] As rhetorical critic Hermann G. Stelzner comments,

> The language of an address by the President of the United States in a time of crisis helps to create and sustain a "climate." It also begins to pattern the perceptions and the behaviors of those who hear it.[3]

In this chapter, we will examine how the choice and pattern of language can have persuasive influence on an audience. The chapter explores the answers to such questions as: How does word choice—particularly naming—shape our perceptions of reality and the values we assign to what we perceive? How does figurative language function to affect audience emotions and perceptions? What ethical guidelines apply to the persuasive use of language? Following discussion of each of these topics, we will return to a closer examination of Roosevelt's "war message" in the Critical Focus of this chapter.

THEORETICAL FOCUS: LANGUAGE AND PERSUASION

In Chapter 6, we offered a definition of humans from Kenneth Burke as a starting point for understanding Symbolist Perspective. Burke characterized humans as symbol-using animals, inclined by their very nature to cooperate through the sharing of symbols, dwellers in two "realities" at once: an empirical world and symbolic world.[4] Of all human symbol systems, language is the most potent and pervasive and the most distinctly human. In this chapter we aim to shed light on the nature of this distinctly human creation and its relationship to persuasion.

At the empirical level, language is a tool, perhaps the most powerful and adaptable tool humans have devised. Like all tools, language lets us manipulate our environment. It provides a "handle" by which we can manage and work with the important aspects of our social and physical world. It is the means by which we can communicate about ambiguous, abstract or unavailable things. We can discuss "hunger" in its absence. We can talk about "cows" without having to specify every single type of cow (or, worse, every single cow) there is. We can write about "Mount Everest" without having to fit it onto the page before us. We can make statements about "quarks" without even being completely certain what one is. We can describe events, give instructions, make predictions and share feelings—all through our manipulation of this tool, language.

This view of language is familiar to us all. Its primary focus is on the strategic and instrumental use of language as a medium of communication and persuasion. This view often assumes that language functions best when it becomes invisible or transparent, like a pane of window glass. The most important attribute of language, when we think of it as a tool, is its potential for *accuracy*—for bringing our attention and understanding to the things or ideas that the language is "about" with the least distortion or error.[5]

It is important for our purposes here to note that such prescriptive theories concerning clarity and precision in language use usually have little to say about *persuasion* itself. Instead, such theories more commonly regard the process of persuasion as little more than the art (if not science) of expressing our point of view with the greatest clarity, trusting this clarity itself to carry the day. Any uses of language beyond this limited prescription tend to be viewed by these theories as "inaccuracy," "imprecision," "error" and "superstition."[6]

Certainly, understanding the deliberate, instrumental use of language is important. But limiting our study or prescriptions only to such uses will not do from the Symbolist Perspective, which begins by assuming that language is much more than its instrumental functions alone. Indeed, as we shall see in this chapter, the seemingly innocent act of naming is already, to an important extent, a persuasive act.

Alongside this image of *language as a tool* in the empirical world, stands a second view of language and a second human world. The Symbolist Perspective also recognizes humans as dwelling in a world whose reality is constituted ultimately by the potency of symbols rather than by the evidence of our direct sensory experience. This second, constitutive, dimension of language reveals that our language is never completely transparent to us in its use. The specific words themselves that we use—their selection, their shape, sound and pattern, their social history—can be potentially persuasive in a way separate from the concepts or objects to which the language refers.

The persuasive power of strategic and artistic language use, whether in poetry, oratory, fiction or journalism, can never be fully explained by assessing the formal and material validity of its reasoning or cataloguing the individual concepts named within the message. The difference we all understand between the words "freedom fighter" and "terrorist" remains despite the truth or falsity of statements made about persons so described. The differences in habitual word choice between professors and their students draw our attention to different social roles and organizational loyalties held by the two groups. In these examples, language becomes not merely a device for referring to things, but also, more significantly, a means by which our socially shared reality is created, displayed and altered by persuaders. This function is not always a matter of intention or strategy, but rather may be an inevitable function of the language itself.

In the following sections of this chapter, we consider two important uses of language and their relation to persuasion from the Symbolist Perspective. The first of these uses is the function of naming: how we indicate, designate and label the objects of our experience. The second concerns stylistic and figurative uses of language. In both cases, we will investigate the ways in which language influences others through the creation and change of patterns of identification.

NAMING AND CREATING REALITY

Our power to name a thing is closely connected to our control over that thing. Perhaps the oldest and most familiar version of this claim is the biblical story of creation, in which humans were given dominion over the world by being allowed to give each kind of animal its name. But our point here is something more concrete. Fundamentally, language gives us the ability to pluck bits from the constant stream of data coming into our senses, pattern them and understand these data patterns as persons and things. To put the focus more sharply, language—naming—is the prerequisite to having any phenomenon become a part of our social, communicative reality. If we have no name for a thing, we would be hard-pressed to claim that the thing is "real," in any usual sense of that term. Moreover, the language which names a thing often carries with it an attitude toward the thing named.

Denotation And Naming

The most fundamental concept necessary to understand the persuasive power of naming is the idea of denotation. Denotation is the referential basis of a word, its conventional or agreed-upon meaning. Denotation is of concern to persuaders insofar as they attempt to select language that accurately reflects their experience and purposes, allowing them to refer audiences to objects and concepts of their shared experience. Theoretical interest in denotative meaning extends at least as far back as the work of Aristotle. The third of the three Books making up his *Rhetoric* is devoted to language as a resource for persuaders.[7] From Aristotle's view, successful persuaders should choose language that is clear and appropriate for the audience's level of understanding. Clarity is necessary for persuaders simply to be understood. Later theorists, such as George Campbell, during the Eighteenth Century, referred to such clarity and appropriateness as "perspicuous language." Campbell explained that in order to present ideas clearly to an audience, a persuader should follow a number of rules, including the avoidance of obscure words, uncertain references, technical terms, ambiguous terms, academese and so on.[8] From another point of view the act of naming itself constitutes or creates these objects, rather than merely pointing to them. The resources of language extend far beyond matters of clarity and appropriateness, even to the point of influencing what is "thinkable"—what is real, in the communicative sense.

In social and political concerns, the power of naming to denote can show itself in two different ways: in how patterns of experience become labeled as "problems" and how the labeling of a problem can shape the search for "solutions." Frequently, a problem must be designated or named as a problem before it is granted enough legitimacy to warrant the search for a solution. The problem of sexual harassment offers a case in point. As feminist critic Sonja Foss notes:

> The term, *sexual harassment*, was created to name an experience woman have for which there previously was no term—women's experience of being fired from or quitting a job because they were made uncomfortable by the behavior of men. In cases like this where there are no terms for women's perspectives, those perspectives tend not to be considered real or acceptable, even by women.[9]

Once an experience is named, previously unthinkable possibilities open up for talking about and acting upon that experience. For example, contemporary marriage and family counselors, who now treat many clients suffering from childhood traumas, explain that such treatment was rare and difficult prior to the naming of families as "dysfunctional" and the naming of those who emerged from such families as "adult children." Lamenting the absence of therapeutic techniques and support groups for victims of child abuse prior to the late 1970's, one writer explains: "The word 'survivor' was not yet in our vocabulary."[10]

The example just described shows that labeling is also a critical aspect of finding solutions for social or political problems and for uniting people around those solutions. Until a solution is named, we may concentrate solely on the problem, but by naming an alternative we allow ourselves to move beyond the problem to a solution. For example, prior to the historic Supreme Court decision that declared segregated schools to be unconstitutional (*Brown v. Board of Education*), numerous essays and articles concerning "segregation" appeared in many popular magazines.[11] The popular focus concerned the problem of segregation. But following the Court's proposals for solutions, a new heading (a new name) appeared in indexes like the *Reader's Guide to Periodical Literature*. That new name was "integration," and suddenly the number of essays dealing with alternative solutions far outnumbered those dealing with the problem.

Perhaps the most widely-recognized theoretical statement about the importance of naming is the *principle of linguistic relativity*, formulated by linguistic anthropologist Benjamin Whorf. The particular language we speak sets limits on our perceptions, thoughts and actions, restricting us to perceptions, thoughts and actions which can easily be conceived or expressed within the language we speak, making all others difficult if not impossible.[12] At its simplest, this principle suggests that the resources of a language—the repertoire of things it allows speakers easily to name and discuss—will change as the general culture changes.[13] Our interest in the principle ignores the "chicken and egg" question of which came first—the new language or the cultural changes—and focuses only on the result. Some shades of meaning or certain experiences are easier to refer to in some languages than in others. For example, the appearance (and, often enough, the disappearance again) of terms, such as "surfing the net," "reverse discrimination," "e-commerce" and "snail mail," are all instances of American English shifting as the experiences available in our culture have changed and expanded. The principle also suggests that we tend to be better at discriminating among our experiences when there are familiar labels for those experiences. For example, painters, designers, printers and fabric workers may be noticeably better than others at easily discerning the differences between seemingly similar shades of color at the same time that they have a richer and more varied vocabulary for describing those differences. Their language and experience together allow them to see and distinguish among "raspberry," "magenta" and "fuchsia," when the rest of us might simply shrug and say, "bright purple." In part, the technical vocabulary of the study of persuasion—"ethos," "warrants," "identification" and so on—serves this same function, allowing students of persuasion to more easily recognize and describe subtle distinctions in their experience.

Moreover, the linguistic relativity principle extends beyond the strict matter of denotation. The principle suggests that the form and structure of a language—its grammar—may structure the possibilities of our thinking and acting. For example, the distinction between "subjective" and "objective" is woven into the fabric of Western intellectual culture; and at the same time it is structurally a part of the grammar of European languages such as English, which divides utterances structurally into subjects and predicates. Yet, other cultures, speaking in other root languages, may find this idea of objectivity either trivial or flatly incomprehensible. Robert Pirsig argues that some differences between Eastern and Western cultures are traceable to differences in how languages and cultures treat the distinction of subject and object:

> [I]n cultures whose ancestry includes ancient Greece, one invariably finds a strong subject-object differentiation because the grammar … presumed

> a sharp natural division of subjects and predicates. In cultures such as the Chinese, where subject-predicate relationships are not rigidly defined by grammar, one finds a corresponding absence of rigid subject-object philosophy. One finds that in the Judeo-Christian culture, in which the Old Testament "Word" had an intrinsic sacredness of its own, men are willing to sacrifice and live by and die for words. In this culture, a court of law can ask a witness to tell "the truth, the whole truth and nothing but the truth, so help me God," and expect the truth to be told. But one can transport this court to India, as did the British, with no real success in the matter of perjury because ... this sacredness of words is not felt the same way.[14]

Thus, while speakers of English may find it easy to speak and think about the idea of objectivity, cultures shaped around different root languages may find this idea (so familiar to English speakers) difficult to imagine, let alone to express or act upon. The linguistic relativity principle thereby leads us also to consider the persuasive consequences of what a language does *not* allow us to easily name or relationships that a language does not easily express. The absence of language to name and discuss a thing restricts our power over it. One well-known illustration of this was created in George Orwell's novel *Nineteen Eighty-Four*. Orwell's novel depicts a grim and oppressive world, ruled by "the Party" and its almost mythic leader "Big Brother," in which Standard English has been replaced as the official language by "Newspeak."[15] The intended political function of "Newspeak" is to make dissent impossible by stripping language of the very capacity to express, even in private thought, a disapproved or unorthodox idea. In the Appendix to the novel, Orwell wrote:

> The purpose of Newspeak was not only to provide a medium of expression for the world-view and mental habits proper to the devotees of Ingsoc [the ideology of the Party], but to make all other modes of thought impossible. It was intended that when Newspeak had been adopted once and for all and Oldspeak [or Standard English] forgotten, a heretical thought—that is, a thought diverging from the principles of Ingsoc—should be literally unthinkable, at least so far as thought is dependent on words. Its vocabulary was so constructed as to give exact and often very subtle expression to every meaning that a Party member could properly wish to express, while excluding all other meanings and also the possibility of arriving at them by indirect methods.[16]

As an example of the power that "Newspeak" represented for those who controlled it, Orwell notes that the familiar language and principles in the opening paragraph of the American Declaration of Independence "would have been quite impossible to render... into Newspeak while keeping to the sense of the original. The nearest one could come to doing so would be to swallow the whole passage up in the single word *crimethink*."[17]

Orwell's example, stark as it is, is nevertheless fictional. But instances can be found around us of the ways in which the structures and absences in our language can limit our social or political power. For example, standard English does not have masculine and feminine nouns, as German or Spanish do; but it also does not have any standardized way of making a third-person reference without introducing gender. This may seem on the surface like a minor technical problem of interest only to grammarians, but the consequences reach much farther. Modern English lacks a generally accepted way to end a sentence, such as "each person should take a copy of the book with ______," without using a pronoun that is either masculine ("him") or feminine ("her"). Moreover, until very recently, convention would have dictated that "him" was appropriate unless the subject of the sentence was specifically known to be female. Many scholars have argued compellingly that this and similar structural features of English tend to tilt the scales of our habitual ways of thinking and acting in favor of a masculine point of view.[18] The principle of linguistic relativity allows us to theorize that changes in the ability of our culture to move easily between (or ignore the difference between) masculine and feminine points of view will be accompanied by changes in the language that will allow such shifts to happen more easily than they do now.

CONNOTATION AND NAMING

Connotation is different from denotation in that it refers to the individual associations we have for a word, rather than its conventional or agreed-upon meaning. Connotative meanings are evaluatively loaded and shaped by personal experiences or cultural norms. While we investigate the denotation of a word by looking for its standardized definition, we investigate the connotation of a word by looking at the additional weights, shadings and connections that people attribute to the word.

Connotation is of concern to persuaders insofar as they attempt to select language that will evoke desired associations in the minds of their audiences. Early theorists of rhetoric often explored this topic by describing figures of speech and thought that would bring the content of a message to life in the eyes of an audience. Later theorists, such as the Eighteenth Century Scottish philosopher George Campbell, referred to this quality of language as "vivacity," the power of language to make an image vivid enough to leave an impression with the audience. That impression would, of course, cause the audience to make associations that a persuader could use to influence their reactions.[19] Although connotation and denotation are very different functions of language, the Symbolist Perspective, regards them as equally important in helping to explain how language can induce an audience to visualize one reality as opposed to another or to take one attitude toward that reality rather than another.

A contemporary illustration of the importance of connotative meaning for the power of language appeared during the 1990 election process. Republican candidates for state office received a pamphlet entitled "Language: A Key Mechanism of Control." This pamphlet was produced by Gopac, a political action caucus whose leader was prominent conservative and then House Republican whip Newt Gingrich of Georgia.[20] Gingrich's political action caucus used extended interviews with focus groups to discover political or quasi-political terms whose connotations had special persuasive power for campaign audiences, leading to some specific advice for fellow Republican candidates. Gingrich's pamphlet, for example, encouraged candidates to fill their own campaign literature, speeches and broadcast ads with "optimistic positive governing words" and supplied a list of about two dozen, including *common sense, courage, crusade, dream, duty, empower(ment), fair, family* and *freedom*. At the same time, the pamphlet recommended that the candidates always describe their opponents and their opponents' positions with "contrasting words" such as *anti-child, anti-flag, betray, bizarre, cheat, collapse, corruption, crisis, decay, destroy, devour* and *disgrace*.

Could any reader miss the enormous difference in connotative, evaluative meanings between the list of "optimistic positive governing words" and the list of "contrasting words?" Of course, when considered out of their intended context of letters, speeches and fliers, the strategy behind these two lists appears crass and obvious, even funny. But putting that aside and reserving comment for now on the ethical implications of Gopac's tactical use of language, we note the fundamental power of connotation: Everything else being equal, the contrast in such language would likely make a tremendous difference in how a reader or listener would feel toward whatever was being discussed in the two vocabularies, one filled with positive connotations and the other with negative connotations.

Connotation is also related to the sounds of words. Even the youngest children understand that the character who "stole Christmas" is the villain of the Dr. Seuss story about him, simply by the grating, pinching sound of his name: "the Grinch." Punning, the playful coining and manipulation of words, exploiting their sounds and the meaning of soundalike words, is often dismissed as silliness; but its persuasive power can be considerable. Certainly its most visible contemporary practitioner is conservative celebrity and talk-show host Rush Limbaugh, who has created a "Limbaugh Lexicon," including such terms as "Feminazi," which Limbaugh "defines" as "a feminist to whom the most important thing in life is ensuring that as many abortions as possible occur," or "Uglo-American," a supposed euphemism for "ugly," which Limbaugh feels "confident will be approved by the arbiters of what is politically correct."[21] The persuasive power of punning comes in the first case from juxtaposition and fusion of two otherwise incompatible terms ("feminist" and "nazi") and in the second case from resemblance to other terms (such as "Asian-American" or "African-American") used by groups whom Limbaugh wants to ridicule for the delight of his fans.

A case from the late 1970's allows us not only to re-emphasize the importance of naming in determining our social reality, but to illustrate the ease with which a struggle to control the language in which a thing is discussed can blur into a contest to determine how we will think and act toward that thing. The case in point is the development by the United States military of a "new" nuclear weapon, the "neutron bomb."[22]

In 1977, Walter Pincus broke the story in the *Washington Post*, revealing that the United States had developed a "new" nuclear device, the neutron bomb, which released an intense but short-lived burst of neutron radiation sufficient to kill people, but with explosive force low enough to leave buildings and infrastructure intact. Pincus's news story attracted much attention and ultimately led to a national debate about the appropriate manufacture and use of the neutron bomb. The debate ranged over the possible political and strategic, as well as military, consequences of such a weapon. The uneasy nuclear peace of the previous three decades had been built in part on the shared assumption that the destruction caused by a nuclear bomb, both by its explosive force and by the concomitant radiation, was so much greater than that of conventional weapons as to be a deterrent to its use. Did the development of this "new" bomb mean that the escalation to nuclear weapons would now become a step that was more easily imaginable—and thus more easily taken?

Significantly, journalistic inquiries subsequently revealed that this "new" weapon had been in existence for several years, but probably as a result of the names given this weapon it had been largely overlooked by most pacifists, many politicians and ordinary citizens alike. As early as 1974, the *London Times* had called the weapon a "mini-nuke." In response, a U.S. Ambassador to the United Nations objected, arguing that this name implied that it was a radically new weapon that could be used on the battlefield in much the same manner as conventional, nonnuclear weapons. The ambassador's response suggested that the problem at hand was one of proper labeling, rather than of military tactics or diplomatic strategy. Certainly, the progression of names by which the weapon had been called was varied. Military officials had referred to the weapon as a "clean bomb" for years. President Jimmy Carter had called it a "tactical weapon." Meanwhile, some scientists were referring to it as an "enhanced radiation weapon."

The various names each implied something different, although taken together they seemed to describe something alarmingly close to what the Ambassador specifically said it was not. For a public familiar with images of the heavy bombs that had wreaked so much destruction on European cities during World War II, the oxymoron "clean bomb" suggested a weapon so different from their experience that it might indeed deserve description as a radically new weapon. The phrase "tactical weapon" made it sound like another type of conventional weapon, something different from those atomic bombs that everyone seemed to worry about. And the term "enhanced radiation weapon" simply defied concrete understanding for many readers and listeners. The controversy about what to call the weapon finally eventuated in a plea from *The Bulletin of the Atomic Scientists* for clarification, "if not to assist the bureaucrats at least as a reference for scholars in the field of political-military science."[23] Some critics of American nuclear policy, making a pun from Orwell's book, gave the name "nukespeak" to the discourse of military, scientific and political experts surrounding the neutron bomb.[24]

Consistent again with the linguistic relativity principle, these various ways of describing the neutron bomb probably allowed the various participants in the debate to understand the phenomenon in terms of their own interests and frame of reference. Hence, the military experts' use of "clean bomb" spoke to their interest in the weapon as one that would allow military forces to enter a bombed area shortly after detonation without risk of contamination. By contrast, the Carter Administration's use of the term "tactical weapon" revealed their interest in the weapon as a part of the calculus of nuclear diplomacy. And the weapons scientists' coining of "enhanced radiation weapon" nicely captured the scientific properties of the device, without special concern for its political or military context. At one level of analysis, the case of "nukespeak" is an unfortunate example of the power of naming to conceal and confuse rather than to enlighten and disclose the reality of our lived experience. Yet, at another more revealing level, it shows the extent to which the problem is more than simply the accuracy of our language: our choice of words begins to reveal the cultures and world views with which we identify.

"God Terms" and "Devil Terms"

At its simplest, connotation involves either a positive or negative association for audiences who encounter language. Rhetorical theorist Richard Weaver argues that all language contains some degree of bias because of the connotative meaning that we attribute to language. Weaver notes, however, that some language is particularly charged with associations of historical, emotional and ideological significance. When these terms are used to describe persons, institutions, policies and so on, audiences may be inclined toward assent simply because of the highly positive (or negative) associations of the term itself. Such terms tend to be linked in hierarchical fashion, so that many terms will gain their power from their association with other, still higher, terms. At the top of the hierarchy, the ultimate term which lends its power downward to those other terms, is a "god term," a term whose power to command our assent is so great that virtually *anything* may be justified or recommended if one can find a way to use this term to describe it.[25]

Note that to call something a "god term" is a matter of degree. We might say that terms become "more godly" as they gain power to command our acceptance simply by their use, until we reach the point where we find *the* "god term" of a culture or society, the term which has the broadest reach and the greatest power. In a culture where there is a single ideology or a single religion, widely and consistently accepted, Weaver argued, we would expect a single "god term" to emerge and dominate in communication. But a culture having several ideologies and cultural values overlapping and competing, such as Twentieth Century America, may well have several clusters of such terms, competing for influence over us or apportioning a part of our lives to their control.[26] The terms including and surrounding "progress" and "science" are an example of such terms. Consider the importance of calling something a "fact." How often do we hear that term used in a manner implying that the speaker expects no further discussion on the immediate matter, simply because it *is* (or has now been called) "a fact?" This word "fact" has the power to command our assent in large part because of its connection ("upward," as it were) to another, "more godly" term in our culture: "science." For the same reason, labeling a person, a statement or a position "biased" is to link it with "devil terms," such as "prejudice" and "irrationality." To call something "science" or "scientific" or to justify something as being "in the name of science," is to go a long way toward gaining public acceptance of that thing *simply because* of the use of that term to describe it. If one group wants to show that a certain industrial policy will be harmful to the environment or to public health, for example, it will assemble "scientists," who then issue a "scientific report," based on "scientific study" and "scientific data," making the group's point. Of course, at the same time, the industries involved will probably marshal their own "facts" and "studies," all clearly "scientific" and all clearly showing that their opponents' claims are "unscientific" and, therefore, not worthy of our acceptance. The public may be unable to assess the actual validity of these facts, reports and claims, but it, nevertheless, feels the strong pull to accept them simply because the term "science" has such power to command assent in our culture. "Science," in turn, gains much of its power from its association with yet another term, one which Weaver suggested in the 1950's might indeed be the true "god term" of American culture: "progress."

We might add other terms from a slightly different hierarchy which might rival "progress" as a "god term" in our society, such as "liberty." A very wide range of actions and institutions can be justified with little further discussion by linking them with "liberty," as in "securing liberty" or "protecting liberty." Liberty, in turn, lends some of its power "downward" to terms like "rights," "freedoms," "democracy," "property" and so on. These terms, in turn, convey persuasive power to still other terms such as "regulation," "deregulation," "anti-crime," "diversity" and "affirmative action." In fact, many of the words on Gopac's list of "optimistic governing words," mentioned above, are words that gain their power by being grouped under the "god term" of "liberty." In a similar way, terms on Gopac's list of "negative words" tend to cluster under more increasingly negative words leading upward (or downward, perhaps) to an ultimate, if unnamed, "devil term" with almost unlimited power to command our *opposition* to anything tagged with the term. In the United States of the mid-1950's, the "devil term" was well known: "un-American," with "backward" and "communist" ranking slightly behind and drawing power from it. Today, historical events have weakened somewhat the ability of that term to express the ultimate disapproval and damnation. Readers are invited to consider what terms might now be in line to succeed as the next "devil term" of our culture.

Weaver's discussion of "god terms" and "devil terms" allows us to draw several conclusions about the persuasive dimension of naming. First, a "god term" is the product of a culture at a particular point in its history. For example, the power of the term "anti-communism" to justify a wide range of actions in America was far greater in 1953 than it was 40 years before or than it is now, almost 50 years later. Different cultures at different times give their assent to different "god terms."

Further, as Weaver's discussion and Gingrich's example show, "god terms" and "devil terms" give legitimacy (or deny it) to people, ideas and policies in ways that can be quite persuasive, even if they seem difficult to explain. In Chapter 13, we will examine more closely the relationship between language and ideology, noting how terms can allow us to persuade in the name of our ideological "world view" even when the very use of these terms makes it harder and harder to explain what we really mean by them.[27]

FIGURATIVE USES OF LANGUAGE

Another aspect of the persuasive power of language is found in the stylistic or figurative use of language. Like naming or labeling, this aspect of language involves word choice and sentence construction. Figurative language serves three particular persuasive functions. First, figurative language may provide aesthetic pleasure for readers or listeners, by interesting, intriguing, surprising or amusing them. Second, figurative language can affect readers' or listeners' perceptions of their relationship with the persuader. Finally, figurative language can be used to modify or completely change the meanings of words for persuasive purposes. Over the centuries, scholars have described nearly 200 different types of figurative language. In this section, we describe a sampling of 10 that seem most useful for understanding the persuasive force of language. Among these, metaphor is arguably the most studied and durable type of figurative language. Hence, we begin with a discussion of metaphor.

Metaphor is the use of language leading an audience to experience one kind of thing in terms of, or in names and descriptions appropriate to, a different kind of thing.[29] Metaphors surprise and delight an audience by suggesting similarities between two things otherwise considered unlike. More important, metaphors shape our perceptions of reality. An extended example will help to explain how metaphors work persuasively.

Consider a famous use of metaphor in American political discourse. In his famous "I Have a Dream" speech at the 1963 Civil Rights Rally in Washington D.C., Martin Luther King, Jr. described the plight of the American Negro in 1963 in the language of slavery, a language ordinarily associated with the plight of the Negro a century before:

> But one hundred years later, the Negro is still *not free*. One hundred years later, the life of the Negro is still *sadly crippled by the manacles* of segregation *and the chains* of discrimination.[30]

King's description of the state of the American Negro in 1962 uses language—"not free," "crippled," "manacles," "chains"—usually found in a discussion of slavery, an institution supposedly abolished in America a century before. Hence, King is using metaphor in this description.

Parts of King's remarks are meant to be taken literally and are not metaphorical: "one hundred years later," "the Negro," "segregation" and "discrimination"—all words and phrases that we have *not* italicized in the passage above—are clearly meant to be understood in their ordinary denotative sense. This part of a metaphorical utterance, the part that is being used literally, is the *frame* of the metaphor. However, the italicized phrases—"not free," and especially "manacles" and "chains"— seem obviously to be used in a non-literal, metaphorical sense. This part of a metaphorical utterance is the *focus* of the metaphor.[31] As the terms suggest, the focus is the new, persuasive way of looking at the object of interest, the frame. Every metaphor juxtaposes literal language of the thing being discussed (the frame) with metaphorical language drawn from the idea to which it is being compared (the focus).

The use of metaphor assumes and requires that we have some familiarity or background knowledge, however limited, with the frame and focus. An imaginary person who did not know that black slavery had been a legal institution in the United States until the 1860's would not "get" the point King was making by using the language of slavery to describe the state of American blacks a century later, in the example quoted above. But familiarity with context, in this sense, is only part of what is required for a metaphor to have persuasive effect. Metaphor evokes the commonplaces associated with the focus and allows them to migrate to the frame. These ideas or associations which the metaphorical focus calls to mind most easily are *associated commonplaces*.[32] The terms "chains" and "manacles," used by King, evoke concepts, ideas or associations which we would commonly associate with them. "Chains" and "manacles" suggest *imprisonment or slavery*, surely. They also can suggest *dehumanization, degradation* or *humiliation*. Chains and manacles are the tools of captors or masters; so these terms might also suggest harm brought to someone *by someone else*, a conqueror or an oppressor. Chains and manacles can also hint at the *potential strength or power of the ones chained*, since a weak or powerless captive hardly needs to be chained and manacled.

Yet, readers familiar with King's speech, the political agenda of the Civil Rights March and with King's own purposes might object that not *all* of these associated commonplaces would apply equally, if at all, to the interpretation of this metaphor. How do we understand *which* of all possible associated commonplaces, suggested by the metaphorical focus, are to be applied to the metaphorical frame? The answer has been given indirectly already. We understand by applying our knowledge of the circumstances, perhaps including the persuader's intentions, to the process of interpreting metaphors. We know by his references to freedom and to the Emancipation Proclamation that King wants us to recall the association of chains and manacles with slavery. His later references to the political, economic and social plight of the American Negro suggest that he also wants to remind us of the association of chains and manacles with degradation and humiliation. The associations of chains and manacles with restrained power and the acts of oppressors seem less appropriate in the particular context of this occasion, however. In a speech designed, as King's was, to rally support among whites as well as blacks for the Civil Rights Movement, such associations—with their overtones of confrontation and strife—are *filtered out* from among all possible associated commonplaces and are less likely to influence our interpretation of the metaphor.

Every metaphor resists, at least to some degree, the translation back into strictly literal language. In some cases, of course—such as "she waded through the paperwork" or "his actions cast a shadow over the rest of the party"—the degree of resistance is extremely small. Although we are considering them out of any context, the metaphor in such expressions would probably contribute little to the meaning or persuasive potency of either expression. If we were to rewrite the phrases with a more obviously literal substitution for the focus—"struggled" in the first case and "somber mood" in the second—very little nuance or meaning would likely be lost. In the case of such cliches and trite expressions, the metaphors have little *force* and can be regarded as not much more than a case of substitution or simple comparison.

As a metaphor gains force, however, it becomes increasingly difficult to translate it into a literal expression without seeming to loose important shades and overtones. The more difficult it is to translate a metaphor into literal language without loss of meaning, nuance or potency, the more forceful the metaphor. A forceful metaphor functions to create a new and persuasively powerful way of seeing or understanding the frame and focus that would not be possible by other means. Thus, the workings of forceful metaphors demonstrate the contemporary Symbolist understanding that language can constitute reality, letting us say that the metaphor *itself* "creates the similarity" between frame and focus, constituting a new "way of seeing" the subject of the metaphor, in addition to providing the formal pleasure of artistic language use.[33] Metaphors can gain force when they invoke associated commonplaces in an unexpected or striking way, as in King's example above. The same example and the remainder of King's speech show that metaphors can also gain force when the system of associated commonplaces is used and developed in an extended manner, gaining subtlety and shadings with each new use.

The range of metaphor in our thinking and acting is almost limitless. There are those that artistic creators, such as King, create for special purposes. There are also metaphors that we come to understand almost as a part of learning our language and our culture. "Up" and "down" and their associated commonplaces are woven into our language, art and culture as metaphors for good and evil or desirable and undesirable.[34] Similarly, "light" and "dark" and their associated commonplaces as metaphors for good and evil are typical in our culture.[35] The variety of metaphorical uses of "the sea," such as "high tides," "stormy weather" and "staying the course," serve similar persuasive purposes.[36] Such a quick list can do no more than hint at the scope of metaphor in our language use.

Although metaphor is in many ways the preeminent figurative use of language in persuasion, it is by no means the only one. Three others rank with metaphor as both figures of speech and figures of thought: metonymy, synechdoche and irony.[37]

Metonymy is the substitution of the name of something concrete for the name of something that is abstract or intangible, but with which it is logically associated. For example, we may refer to "the heart" instead of "the emotions" or "the soul;" to "the White House" instead of "the Clinton Administration policies;" to "a diploma" instead of "an education;" to "a golden ring" instead of "the vows and state of marriage;" and so on. In such cases, metonymy allows a persuader to give vividness and realism to something which might otherwise seem elusive and theoretical.

Synechdoche is similar to metonymy in that it is the interchanging of the name of the whole of something with the name of one of its parts or aspects, but in synechdoche the parts and whole have a direct, often physical, relationship, rather than an abstract one. So, for example, we may refer to "buying wheels" instead of "buying a car" and "car trouble" instead of "engine (or ignition) trouble." Or we may name causes to refer to effects and vice-versa, as when we say "this weather has kept me home from work all week" instead of "this head cold, caused by the weather, has kept me home." Synechdoche allows persuaders to stress for their audiences the interconnectedness of part and whole. Accordingly, most synechdochic substitutions will work "in either direction," compared to metonymy, where the substitution is more often "one way:" We would ordinarily not think of referring to the heart as "the soul" or to the White House as "the Clinton Administration policies."

Irony is an expression that appears to say the opposite of its "real" meaning, although constructed in a way that the audience will be able to recognize the correct meaning. Essential to irony's persuasive power is that there must be both an audience who will "get" the irony and another group (real or imagined) who will not and who are, therefore, in some way the victims or butt of an inside joke between audience and persuader. For example, in Jane Austen's *Pride and Prejudice*, Mr. Bennet, the father of several daughters at or approaching marriageable age, is a curmudgeon who is most pleased when he has something to complain about. Thus, when his daughter Lydia becomes engaged to the somewhat foolish Mr. Wickham, Mr. Bennet observes, ironically, "He is as fine a fellow… as ever I saw. He simpers, and smirks, and makes love to us all. I am prodigiously proud of him." And later, when daughter Elizabeth becomes engaged to the proud and difficult-to-get-along-with Mr. Darcy (after her sister Jane has married the equally unpromising Mr. Bingley), Austen writes:

> Elizabeth had the satisfaction of seeing her father taking pains to get acquainted with [Darcy]; and Mr. Bennet soon assured her that he was rising every hour in his esteem.
>
> I admire all my three sons-in-law highly," said he. "Wickham, perhaps, is my favourite; but I think I shall like your husband quite as well as Jane's.[38]

In this example as in all cases, irony functions at two levels: it provides pleasure for the audience as they are first surprised, then pleased, with the unexpected statement; and it builds a bond of identification between persuader and audience as two parties who are "in on" the same joke.

All four of the figurative devices described thus far alter the meaning of words from their ordinary denotative sense. Metaphor *analogizes* the meaning of the critical words; metonymy *condenses* the intangible into the tangible; synechdoche *represents* the whole with the part, or vice-versa; and irony *reverses* the meaning of the critical words.[39] In all cases, the figures serve persuaders' ends to various degrees by pleasing or amusing an audience and by altering the meanings associated with words. A variety of other figures, many that were developed during the Classical and Renaissance periods, do not alter the meaning of words but shape audience perceptions by aesthetically pleasing readers or listeners. Some of those depend on inflections and grammatical constructions found in Latin and Greek, but not in modern English; more have fallen somewhat out of fashion in much of contemporary public discourse or are reserved mainly for particular formal occasions of speaking or writing. Nevertheless, many remain as useful and potentially persuasive figures of language. The following list, adapted from a compilation by Roderick P. Hart, is only a brief sampling.[40]

Anaphora is the exact repetition or phrase at the beginnings of successive clauses. Anaphora highlights the persuader's mental grasp of a concept by displaying the completeness of his or her thinking. For example, Abraham Lincoln displayed why his "Gettysburg Address" was a fitting but inadequate tribute to fallen soldiers during the Civil War when he used this repetitive sequence: "But, in a larger sense, *we cannot dedicate, we cannot consecrate, we cannot hallow this ground."*

Antithesis is the juxtaposing of contrasting ideas in balanced or parallel phrases. The antithetical structure sharpens significantly the audience's sense of difference between ideas. This figure was almost a persuasive "signature" of John F. Kennedy whose most famous statement of antithesis was probably: "And so, my fellow Americans, *ask not what your country can do for you: Ask what you can do for your country.*"[41]

Hyperbole is an extravagant or exaggerated statement, used to describe something that would otherwise be beyond description. Hyperbole is a favorite figure for bumper stickers, buttons and other persuasive messages that trade on slogans, "catchy phrases" or exaggerated analogies. Consider for example: the feminist tee-shirt that reads, "A woman without a man is like a fish without a bicycle;" the button for a new graduate, that reads, "There is intelligent life on the planet and I'm it."

Oxymoron is a phrase that seems to express an internal contradiction. Oxymoron develops a sense of contrast by first confusing and then intriguing an audience. Descriptive phrases such as "*jumbo shrimp*," "*pretty ugly*" and a "*little large*" are illustrative.

Parallelism is the grouping of similarly phrased ideas presented in rapid succession. Parallelism creates the sensation of quickened pace and a feeling of momentum for an audience. Jesse Jackson provides a clear example of parallelism in a speech delivered to the 1984 Democratic National Convention: "America is not like a blanket—one piece of unbroken cloth, *the same color, the same texture, the same size*. America is like a quilt—*many patches, many pieces, many colors, and many sizes*, all woven together and held together by a common thread."[42]

Rhetorical question is a declarative statement cast in an interrogative form. Despite its question form, it *asserts* rather than *asks*; the "answer" to the question the figure pretends to ask is already known to the audience or made obvious by the question itself. By suggesting the form of an imagined dialogue, rhetorical questions create a sense of involvement and interaction between persuader and audience. This figure is used extensively by salespeople; for example, those on the various home-shopping channels who ask: "Wouldn't a member of your family appreciate a gift like this?" or "Where else could you buy this food processor for this price?"

Ethics: Language And Persuasion

From the Symbolist Perspective, the ethics of the use of language in persuasion is sometimes less clear-cut than we might wish. Among these difficulties is the general problem of intention. Since the Symbolist Perspective regards meaning as primarily audience-centered, it can sometimes be problematic to place ethical blame on a persuader for the interpretation of that persuader's language by an audience. It can be equally difficult to reconcile the relationship between the ethics of persuasion, which calls on persuaders to disavow certain strategies of language use, and the tradition of the First Amendment, which has historically been interpreted to place the fewest restrictions on expression possible.[43]

Consider, for example, the recent trend on many U.S. college campuses to create restrictions on "hate speech." In response to our growing understanding of the power of language to shape and define our social reality, many academics have suggested that "inclusive language," non-sexist and non-racist in nature, become the norm on college campuses. Further, some campuses have implemented policies that make the use of offensive language (e.g., sexist and racist comments) a punishable offense. Both the American Civil Liberties Union and many conservative groups, normally not allies, have raised strong objections to such policies. These groups argue that the Constitution guarantees everyone the right to use whatever language they desire to reflect their view of the world, no matter how offensive that view might be to others; and they castigate campus reformers as bowing to fashion by concerning themselves with what is "politically correct."[44]

Viewed from a different direction, "hate speech" restrictions, as a matter of practice if not of policy makers' intention, present still another problem. Such policies have frequently had the effect of obscuring ethical objections to such speech by diverting attention to its legal status. As Henry Louis Gates, Jr., writes:

> The problem with speech codes is that they make it impossible to challenge bigotry without it turning into a debate over the right to speak.... If someone

> calls me a nigger, I don't want to have to spend the next five hours debating the fine points of John Stuart Mill. Speech codes kill critique.[45]

Gates' suggestion is that ethical critique is superior to legal code as a means for discussing appropriate use of language. To make such critique viable, however, some ethical guidelines are necessary.

Three general ethical principles regarding the use of language can be deduced from the Symbolist Perspective. These principles apply to the accuracy of language, to demeaning or degrading language and to language which restricts choice or discussion. In many cases, the ethical problems involved grow from our ability, as the Symbolist Perspective emphasizes, to respond to both the referents of words and to the associations we have for the words themselves.

The most obvious function of language is its ability to refer or represent; the most important misuse of language is misrepresentation and inaccuracy. *Persuaders have an ethical responsibility to use language accurately*. The most obvious violation of this principle is the case of a persuader who lies, who asserts as factually true something that the persuader knows is not true. Even a persuader whose language is "technically" accurate is ethically responsible if he or she knows that an audience has not grasped the "technicality" and, hence, has been misled, and if that persuader allows this misunderstanding to continue.[46]

However, many cases that might seem to fall under the principle of misrepresentation are not so easily resolved. The persuasive power of connotation and "loaded language" in general, or "god" and "devil" terms, is not resolvable as a matter of accuracy or "fact." Accuracy is an unproductive test to apply to the use of "fetus" versus "unborn child," for example, in evaluating the persuasive messages created by the "pro-choice" and "right-to-life" movements. The vocabulary that we use to discuss a variety of social problems directly influences whether we will recognize a problem, how we will view it and how we may attempt to solve it.[47] As a consequence, we generally hold to the principle that every persuader has the right to put his or her own position in the best light possible. But this right is counterbalanced by two other ethical principles, to which we turn now.

Language that demeans or degrades others by its very use is ethically irresponsible. At a preliminary level, it is irresponsible for the same reason that all misrepresenting language is unethical. As ethicist Richard Johannesen writes:

> At the least, racist/sexist terms place people in artificial and irrelevant categories... . Within a particular political perspective, we might value access to relevant and accurate information needed to make reasonable decisions on public issues. But racist/sexist language, by reinforcing stereotypes, conveys inaccurate depictions of people, dismisses taking serious account of people, or even makes them invisible for purposes of the decision. Such language denies us access to necessary accurate information and thus is ethically suspect.[48]

Racist and sexist language is unethical for another reason, however, quite apart from the question of accuracy. Such language, together with hate speech, can humiliate its targets, blinding others to their dignity and value as humans. "What are the ethical implications," Johannesen asks rhetorically, ... of calling a Jewish person a "kike," a black person a "nigger" or "boy," an Italian person a "wop," an Asiatic person a "gook" or a "slant eye," or a thirty year old woman "girl" or "chick?" One answer to his question, Johannesen notes, is that it makes it just that much easier for speaker and hearer alike to view such people as a threat, ignore them in their need, despise them for their successes or fear them in their differences.[49]

The question of sexist and racist language also exemplifies another ethical principle of language use: *Language that restricts the ability of an audience to discuss an issue sensibly or undermines their ability to exercise free choice is ethically irresponsible.* As Johannesen noted, above, such language may work to exclude certain people or groups from full participation in public discussion, rendering them "invisible." When such language works to silence unpopular points of view, it warps and distorts the very system of public discussion by which it attempts to advance its own aims. Rhetorical critic Philip Wander points out that when our language does not reflect the experience of certain members of our society we run the risk of excluding those people from consideration in our development of community norms and policies.[50] At its worst, language that symbolically nullifies a certain sector of humanity may eventuate in their actual death, as was the case in Hitler's Germany where Jews, Communists, homosexuals and Gypsies were called "parasites," and policies that would exterminate these "inhuman pests" were subsequently implemented.[51]

A related problem involves "loaded language" in general. Sometimes, persuaders are accused of using language that is so emotionally or ideologically charged that it unnecessarily obstructs discussion. For example, pro-choice advocates frequently object to their opponents referring to the "fetus" as an "unborn child" on the grounds that the phrase "unborn child" is so connotatively loaded that a fair and reasonable discussion cannot proceed. At other times, persuaders are accused of using euphemistic language that substitutes words and phrases with pleasant connotations for language that is denotatively more appropriate but connotatively more unpleasant. Abortion opponents, to return to that example, attack the pro-choice advocates' use of "fetus" as an attempt to sanitize and neutralize our perceptions of what the object of discussion really is. Other examples of language that is so loaded that its presence can distort discussion include the word "tax," a label that has almost paralyzed U.S. elected officials for a decade. Federal, state and local governments need revenues, and citizens want services, but no one dare utter the dreaded "T-word." Because anything labeled, for any reason, a "tax" is going to be treated as political poison, elected officials often find themselves devoting as much time to the search for euphemisms ("revenue enhancement," "surcharge") as for new policies. Conversely, quite apart from the specific legal measures that a piece of legislation might propose, if that legislative package is tagged as a "crime bill," representatives vote against it at their political peril. At reelection time, they can expect to have their opponents remind voters that they voted against a "crime bill." Perhaps the bill in question contained many provisions that would have been unpopular with voters, perhaps not; but the power of the phrase "crime bill" can dismiss such substantive considerations—for who wants it to be said that they voted "*for* crime?"

For these reasons, we find Gopac's advice to candidates regarding "optimistic governing words" and "contrasting words," described above, to be ethically offensive. Nothing in the instructions in the Gopac pamphlet suggests that the fairness, appropriateness or relevance of such application is a matter for concern—only that the words themselves tend to produce a desired effect in an audience. True, when these words are placed together in a list such as this one, the ethical problem is more obvious. But imagine the power of these words and those others that cluster around them to influence their audiences when they are scattered throughout a variety of messages, used again and again; their persuasive potential might easily go unnoticed, let alone unquestioned.[52]

Ambiguous language—whose structure is vague and whose denotative references are unclear—can be equally harmful to our ability to discuss issues and make free choices. For example, Reagan administration Secretary of State Alexander Haig was notorious for vague, ambiguous, jargon-laden and convoluted public statements that the "impenetrable fog" of his public comments was labeled "Haigspeak."[53] An all-too-typical example of his language is this excerpt from Haig's public statement that the United States had no plans to use military force in El Salvador. Haig warned his audience that "the sterility of drawing lines around America's potential options constitutes the promulgation of roadways for those who are seeking to move against America's vital interests."[54] Now *perhaps* the Secretary simply meant, "we don't want to reveal our plans to our adversaries," perhaps not. The point is that, so long as the meaning is couched in the language of "Haigspeak," we will never know. Johannesen notes that Haig was quite aware of how impenetrable his language could be, and he once justified it with the uncharacteristically lucid rhetorical question: "Did you ever think about the cost of making a mistake?" Haig's point—for which Johannesen rightly takes him to ethical task—appears to be that it is better to frustrate public discussion of foreign policy by resorting to "Haigspeak" than to explain choices and options clearly and intelligibly, since the latter course would open the door to public question and even disagreement.[55]

Language use may also thwart discussion and choice when it invokes "god" and "devil" terms to name and justify actions or policies. "God" and "devil" terms tend to reduce uncertainty by placing the thing named in a clear, familiar hierarchy of values. But at the same time, such terms have the potential to close off further discussion, deliberation or reflection, since the simple *appearance* of the word tends to command assent. The persuasive power of such terms and their lesser associates may be largely independent of what the term is used to name. We are thus reminded that we often react to the words that people use, rather than to what the *words* are presumably *referring*. "God terms" are specifically *expressions*, for example, the *words* "liberty" and "progress," whose connections to referents the words might conventionally denote is not always clear. Moreover, to the extent that "god terms" express the highest (or most fundamental) value of a culture, their presence in discussion makes it difficult to analyze further the things discussed, to look at them from new directions or find fresh vantage points from which bases of identification might be located. Such discussion may then begin to resemble declarations of faith, not public debate. Consider again the case of the two political movements in the United States mentioned above: the "right to life" forces and the "pro-choice" forces. "Rights" and "choice" are obviously two extraordinarily powerful "god terms" in the American political vocabulary. To call any aim or cause a "right" or to claim that any opposition to an action will restrict "choice" is to grant tremendous presumption to that thing, whether we are talking about consumer products, artistic expressions, educational programs or political positions. Thus, the very names these two causes have taken for themselves—"choice" and "rights"—create a formidable obstacle to identification, pitting an irresistible force against an immovable object. Compromise or concession become almost unimaginable for many, because it would appear to mean either compromising a right or interfering with a choice—two very "un-American" options.

Ethical principles concerning language, like legal ones, can come into conflict in their application. For example, in the case of hate speech discussed earlier, there may be a conflict between the rejection of demeaning language and the need to keep discussion unobstructed to the greatest degree possible. The problem of "hate speech" and policies designed to control it raises another ethical question of particular interest to college students. Is the college campus a site where different ethical standards regarding language use apply than those in society at large; and if so, should campus standards be more or less restrictive than elsewhere? Ethical difficulties run parallel to similar, but not precisely identical, legal dilemmas. On the one hand, freedom of inquiry and expression are the foundation of American educational philosophy and undergird the principles of tenure and professionalism in higher education in the U.S. Yet many legal scholars and educators argue that the special character of a college campus requires restraints on language use. Some of these proponents, notes university president Robert O'Neil, "insist on civility within the academic community ...[because the campus is] an environment that demands tolerance and understanding."[56] Others, such as legal scholar Mari J. Matsuda, argue that the campus deserves special restrictions because:

> Universities are special places, charged with pedagogy, and duty-bound to a constituency with special vulnerabilities. Many of the new adults who come to live and study at the major universities are away from home for the first time, and at a vulnerable stage of psychological development. Students are particularly dependent on the university for community, for intellectual development, and for self-definition.[57]

Although we are not completely satisfied with any solution currently available to these ethical dilemmas, we, nevertheless, generally hold that the most desirable remedy to unethical use of language, including "hate speech," is more free speech—matching persuasion with persuasion, whether as counterdemonstration, social sanction, protests or other like means—rather than restrictive codes.

CRITICAL FOCUS: ROOSEVELT'S WAR MESSAGE

The persuasive power of language is a mainstay for persuasion explained from the Symbolist Perspective. By examining the nature of language in a message, we can uncover the grounds for identification with a particular cause, idea or world view which the message creates or emphasizes. We may also assess the ethics of a persuader's use of language. The following questions can guide such an examination.

CRITICAL QUESTIONS

1. How does **naming** (in its denotative and connotative dimensions) shape the perceptions of the message's audience?

2. How do "**god terms**" or "**devil terms**" incline an audience to **identify** with values and motives?
3. How does **figurative language** create new meanings, please the audience or influence the audience's perceptions of reality?
4. How well does the persuader's language conform to **ethical principles**?

In the case selected for this Critical Focus, Roosevelt draws upon many of the persuasive resources of language to rally congressional and, ultimately, public support for war with the Axis powers. In this section, we apply the critical questions identified above to the understanding of Roosevelt's speech. We will find that word choice, sentence construction and figurative imagery all play a part in the effectiveness of this speech, designed to create a shared sense of the importance of the decision to enter the war and to overcome once and for all the decade-long effort by many Americans to promote United States neutrality. Unfortunately, the speech also raises some troublesome questions about the ethics of such an appeal to war. Roosevelt's speech begins with the sentence which is probably the most memorable line for audiences today:

> Yesterday, December 7, 1941—a date which will live in infamy—the United States of America was suddenly and deliberately attacked by naval and air forces of the Empire of Japan.

Stelzner points out that Roosevelt's strategies of word choice are already at work to create a number of important associations in this passage. He notes that, by saying "yesterday," actually giving the full date and following that with the word "date," Roosevelt impresses on the audience the historical significance of the moment. This is so because we ordinarily associate "dates" with history, with significance as the clear transition point from one era in history to another. If Roosevelt had said simply, "Yesterday, the U.S….," Roosevelt would have downplayed the significance of the event because listeners would have made more casual associations with "yesterday." Similarly, by telling his audience that this date would "live in infamy," Roosevelt invites his listeners to experience Japan as a villainous enemy. We associate infamy with villains, darkness and "bad" dates, dates known for terrible events. Furthermore, Roosevelt tells his audience that they were attacked by "the Empire of Japan." He could have referred to the denotative equivalent, "Japan," but by referring to "the Empire," he connotatively associates Japan with the various monarchies over time that have marched the world over to conquer and oppress. An "empire" sounds more formidable and dangerous than a mere country. An "empire" connotes a worthy enemy; as when, three decades later, Ronald Reagan characterized the Soviet Union as an "evil empire"—the alliterative presence of "empire" here connotes a far more significant enemy, one whose very presence demands more of Americans than would, for example an "evil union of republics." And a legitimate enemy is needed when a President asks for a declaration of war.

Stelzner further notes that positively and negatively loaded words are structured in important ways over the length of the speech. Specifically, everything that is connotatively positive for this audience—such as, references to God, to the government, the military, the people of the United States, to the absence of danger and the presence of peace—is carefully associated with references to future time. By contrast, all that is connotatively negative for the audience—references to "infamy," "dastardly attack," the government, the military, the people of Japan, the presence of danger and the absence of peace—is typically associated with past time. These clusters of contraries are played off one another throughout the speech, moving from balance-point to balance-point of contrasting images. As the movement from past to future becomes a movement from negative images and names to positive, so it also becomes a movement from the national position of isolation and neutrality to one of international involvement.[58]

A striking portion of the speech comes at the point where, having described the devastation following the bombing of Pearl Harbor the previous morning, Roosevelt enumerates the subsequent attacks by the Japanese forces throughout the day on other targets in the Pacific. Notice how anaphora and parallelism, relieved only slightly by the differences in the last two sentences, highlights the *systematic* nature of Japan's actions and seems to emphasize the *scope* of the attack in a way that would be lacking if all the targets were simply listed in a single sentence:

> Yesterday, the Japanese Government also launched an attack against Malaya.
>
> Last night Japanese forces attacked Hong Kong.
>
> Last night Japanese forces attacked Guam.
>
> Last night Japanese forces attacked the Philippine Islands.
>
> Last night the Japanese attacked Wake Island.
>
> And this morning the Japanese attacked Midway Island.

As Stelzner observes, regarding this passage of Roosevelt's speech,

> The "last night" series supports the pace and quality of the attacks. . . . The compressed "last nights," figuratively ticking off the clock, bring yesterday to a climactic end. The three "yesterdays" [which appear earlier in the speech] spanned time and space; the night and the events in the night move faster.... The syntax is itself symbolic of the fast moving military operations.[59]

Finally, at the close of the speech, some of the most powerful "god terms" for Roosevelt's audience are placed in close proximity with some of the most negative characterizations of the Japanese Empire:

> As Commander-In-Chief of the Army and Navy I have directed that all measures be taken for our defense. But always will our whole nation remember the character of the onslaught against us.

> No matter how long it may take us to overcome this premeditated invasion, the American people in their righteous might will win through to absolute victory.
>
> I believe that I interpret the will of the Congress and of the people when I assert that we will not only defend ourselves to the uttermost but will make it very certain that this form of treachery shall never again endanger us.
>
> Hostilities exist. There is no blinking at the fact that our people, our territory and our interests are in grave danger.
>
> With confidence in our armed forces, with the unbounding determination of our people, we will gain the inevitable triumph—so help us God.
>
> I ask that the Congress declare that since the unprovoked and dastardly attack by Japan on Sunday, December 7, 1941, a state of war has existed between the United States and the Japanese Empire.

These short paragraphs display a pattern of movement in the direction of less-to-more positive values or connotations: from the practical duty of "defense to the moral duty of "remembrance;" from "overcoming" the "invasion" to "absolute victory;" and so on. The culmination of this is the final juxtaposition of the "god terms" "confidence" and "determination of our people," who act in "God's" name with "devil terms" describing the "unprovoked and dastardly" actions of the Japanese. Stelzner even argues that very subtle punning word play is at work at this point:

> The generic negation, the Devil term, is "dastardly". Its appearance is surprising; its choice, apt… . As the Devil term, it stands in antithesis to "righteous might," "Sunday," and "God". It has another function. It is as close as the President, speaking to the country in a public chamber, could come to profanity. The movement from "dastardly" to "bastardly" is slight and swift; the latter epitomizes one dimension of the public mood on December 8, 1941. Infamous duplicity has become bastardly duplicity.[60]

In reviewing Roosevelt's speech, with the help of Stelzner's close analysis, we have concentrated on exposing the subtle and blatant associations that particular language choices likely evoke in audiences. Such associations suggest that Roosevelt's language was not intended merely to enumerate the objective grounds for war, but to create a positive feeling of support for the war effort and to encourage a hostile view of Japan, its government and its people.

Here we face an ethical question of great seriousness. Roosevelt's speech is, for the most part, a scrupulously objective-sounding description of a chain of events and an inevitable, though unfortunate, conclusion that he and his audience must draw from it. It is in many places almost painfully literal and direct. And although his tone seems to brook little disagreement with his call for war, there is little indication that on the morning of December 8, 1941, many Americans felt that the question needed further discussion, that Roosevelt's call to arms was somehow preventing. On these scores, then, the speech seems to be ethically acceptable.

However Roosevelt's description of our new military and political enemy, the Japanese Empire and its people, resonated with a strain of anti- Japanese (indeed, anti-Asian) sentiment that was and is never far below the surface in American culture. As Stelzner notes:

> The emphasis which Roosevelt gave to topics in his address provided his listeners an orientation to the Japanese and to the nature of the conflict; these had immediate and long-range consequences. He emphasized the infamous duplicity behind the Japanese attacks; they carefully and deliberately prepared their military onslaught, masking their preparations behind neutral and formal diplomatic negotiations. American political folklore and the folklore of the people generally hold such behavior in low esteem.... Roosevelt's portrayal of the Japanese and their activities fits the sense of such widely known and well-understood commonplaces.[61]

Roosevelt's choice of descriptions and imagery for the Japanese Empire and the actions of its representatives could not fail to merge with long-held stereotypes and long-associated commonplaces. It thus contributed to a tendency which needed little enough encourage-ment as it was: the persecution of Japanese people, including American citizens of Japanese descent in the United States. On the west coast, whole populations of Nisei—American citizens of Japanese-American descent—were forcibly moved to relocation centers, often forced to abandon their homes and property. Their other civil rights were curtailed in many instances as well. As Stelzner observes, the characterization of this new enemy was by no means created by Roosevelt's speech, but the speech certainly gave new comfort and encouragement to "professional patriots, witch hunters, alien haters, and others with private aims, who used the cover of wartime patriotism to achieve what they wanted to do in peace time—rid the west Coast of the Japanese."[62] Note that we do not accuse Roosevelt of such racist ambitions, but we do assert that his words could hardly avoid producing such an effect in portions of his audience.

Wartime persuasion—the use of the term "propaganda" is also appropriate[63]—constantly faces this ethical risk. Contemporary readers may find the recent counterpart of "Roosevelt's doctrine of demonology," as Stelzner calls it, in the transformation by the U.S. government and press of Iraq's Saddam Hussein from political adversary to object of hatred and loathing in the months before and during the 1991 Gulf War. War and the anticipation of war is a time when it becomes all too easy to sacrifice concern with "means" for the sake of "ends." We encourage our readers to remain alert and sensitive to the ethical character of the language in which our leaders address us regarding war and peace.

Notes

1. See, as an example among many accounts of this period, Sean Dennis Cashman, *America, Roosevelt, and World War II* (New York: NYUP, 1989). The following brief historical gloss relies on Cashman's book, principally pp. 1-80.
2. See: Hermann G. Stelzner, "'War Message,' December 9, 1941: An Approach to Language," *Speech Monographs* 33 (November 1966), 419-37; reprinted in *Methods of Rhetorical Criticism*, Eds. Bernard L. Brock and Robert L.

Scott (Detroit: Wayne State University Press, 1980). Our discussion in the Critical Focus is indebted to Stelzner's analysis.

3. Stelzner, "'War Message,'" 318.
4. "A Definition of Man," in Kenneth Burke, *Language as Symbolic Action*: Essays on Life, Literature, and Method (Berkeley: University of California Press, 1969), 3-22.
5. The view of language which has most thoroughly developed this "tool" approach falls under the general label General Semantics. See: Alfred Korzybski, *Science and Sanity: An Introduction to Non-Aristotelian Systems and General Semantics* (Lancaster PA: Science Press, 1933); S. I. Hayakawa, *Language in Thought and Action*, 3rd ed. (New York: Harcourt, Brace, and Jovanovich, 1972); William V. Haney, *Communication and Interpersonal Relations: Text and Cases*, 5th ed. (Homewood IL: Irwin, 1986). See also: Richard L. Weaver, *The Ethics of Rhetoric* (1953; reprinted Davis CA: Hermagoras Press, 1985), 6-10.
6. S. I. Hayakawa, *Language*, uses all these descriptions and throws in hints of "foolishness" for good measure. See, for example, page 49.
7. Aristotle, *Rhetoric*, tr. W. Rhys Roberts (New York: Ransom House, 1954), Book III.
8. George Campbell, *Philosophy of Rhetoric* ed. Lloyd Bitzer (Carbondale: SIU P, 1988), Book 2, Ch 6.
9. Sonja K. Foss, *Rhetorical Criticism: Exploration and Practice* (Prospect Heights: Waveland, 1989), 153.
10. Ellen Bass and Laura Davis, *The Courage to Heal* (New York: Harper and Row, 1988), 13.
11. For a description of the shift in language from "segregation" to "integration," see Nancy Dunbar and Martha Cooper, "A Situational Perspective for the Study of Legal Argument: A Case Study of Brown v Board of Education," *Dimensions of Argument: Proceedings of the Second Summer Conference on Argumentation*, eds. George Ziegelmueller and Jack Rhodes (Annandale, VA: Speech Communication Association, 1981), 213-241.
12. See: John B. Carroll, ed. *Language, Thought, and Reality: Selected Writings of Benjamin Lee Whorf* (New York: Wiley, 1956); Joshua Fishman, "A Systematization of the Whorfian Hypothesis," *Behavioral Science* Vol. 5 (1960): 323-329.
13. See: Fishman, "Systematization."
14. Robert M. Pirsig, *Zen and the Art of Motorcycle Maintenance: An Inquiry into Values* (New York: Bantam new Age Edition, 1981), 315-16.
15. George Orwell, *1984* (San Diego CA: Harcourt, Brace and Jovanovich, 1984). Although Orwell's story, written in 1949, dwells at some length on the role newspeak played in the power of the Party to control society, the most explicit and theoretically-developed statement of these possibilities is found in "The Principals of Newspeak," the often-overlooked appendix to the novel itself. In 1953, during the height of Cold War McCarthyism, theorist Richard Weaver invoked Orwell's discussion of Newspeak to show how a government can manipulate language to confer charismatic authority upon

itself; Weaver's discussion is republished in *The Ethics of Rhetoric* (Davis CA: Hermagoras Press, 1985) 228-230. See also our discussion of Weaver's theories of language later in this chapter.

16. Orwell, *1984*, 303, 312.
17. Orwell, *1984*, 313.
18. For our example, alternative means of expression exist, of course, but none is yet completely satisfactory: "Them," although used quite commonly for similar constructions in casual speech, is grammatically incorrect unless the subject is pluralized too; "it," although gender-neutral, carries nuances of meaning that would make the sentence almost incomprehensible; recasting the sentence as "one should take a copy of the book with one" would seem needlessly formal and cumbersome; "her/him," a solution we have frequently resorted to in this book, is not easy to use in spoken conversation. Each of these problems represents a way in which the structure of our language limits our ability to easily express certain experiences, and thereby hinders our ability to see those experiences as either "ordinary" or " important."
19. George Campbell, *The Philosophy of Rhetoric*, ed. Lloyd F. Bitzer (Carbondale: Southern Illinois UP, 1963), 285-384.
20. This excerpt was reprinted in "Accentuate the Negative," *Harper's* (November 1990), 17-18.
21. Rush Limbaugh, The Way Things Ought To Be (New York: Pocket Books, 1992), 296, 299.
22. For an extended analysis of the language used to describe the neutron bomb, see Martha Cooper, "A Foucaultian Critique: The Neutron Bomb Issue,: Speech Communication Association Convention, Anaheim, CA, 15 Nov 1981, 11-18.
23. Harold M. Agnew, "Primer on Enhanced Radiation Weapons," *Bulletin of the Atomic Scientists* (Dec. 1977), 6.
24. For numerous other examples of this type, see Stephen Hilgartner, Richard C. Bell, and Rory O'Connor, *Nukespeak: The Selling the Nuclear Technology in America* (San Francisco: Sierra Club Books, 1982).
25. Richard M. Weaver, *The Ethics of Rhetoric* (Davis CA: Hermagoras Press, 1985), 212.
26. Weaver, Ethics, 212. The following discussion is adapted from Weaver, Ethics, 212-24.
27. Michael Calvin McGee has labeled these important terms by which we express the fundamental ideas of our ideology "ideographs.: See: Michael Calvin McGee, "The Ideograph: A Link Between Rhetoric and Ideology," *Quarterly Journal of Speech* 66 (February 1980), 1-16. We will return to McGee's analysis in greater detail in Chapter 13.
28. Historically, scholars have divided figurative language into two categories: figures of speech and figure of thought. Figures of speech use the resources of grammar and syntax to produce language that is both aesthetically pleasing and persuasively clear and forceful. In this type words are used literally, but their effect is primarily aesthetic. By comparison, figures of thought are

persuasive uses of language that alter the literal meaning of words to something analogous, proportionate or opposite to the original.

29. This definition is a synthesis on our part, derived from several standard contemporary treatments, most importantly, Max Black, *Models and Metaphors* (Ithaca: Cornell University Press, 1962); see also, George Lakoff and Mark Johnson, *Metaphors We Live By* (Chicago: University of Chicago Press, 1980).
30. Martin Luther King, Jr. "I Have a Dream,: reprinted in Lloyd Rohler and Roger Cook, eds., *Great Speeches for Criticism and Analysis* (Greenwood IN: Alistair Press, 1988), 325. Italics added.
31. Black, *Models*, 27-29.
32. Black, *Models*, 39-41.
33. See Black, *Models*, 37.
34. Lakoff and Johnson, *Metaphors*, 14-21.
35. Michael Osborn, "Archetypal Metaphor in Rhetoric: The Light-Dark Family," *Quarterly Journal of Speech* 53 (April 1967), 115-126.
36. Michael Osborn, "The Evolution of the Archetypal Sea in Rhetoric and Poetic," *Quarterly Journal of Speech* 63 (December 1977), 347-363.
37. This section relies on Kenneth Burke, "Four Master Tropes," in *A Grammar of Motives* (Berkeley: University of California Press, 1969), 503-517.
38. Jane Austen, *Pride and Prejudice* (New York: Bantam Classic Edition, 1981), 246, 284.
39. Black, *Models and Metaphors*, 35.
40. The following section is adapted from Roderick P. Hart, *Modern Rhetorical Criticism* (Glenview: Scott, Foresman, 1990), 226-227.
41. John F. Kennedy, "Inaugural Address," in *Inaugural Addresses of the Presidents of the United States from George Washington 1789 to John F. Kennedy 1961* (Washington DC: United States Government Printing Office, 1961), 267-270, emphasis added.
42. Jesse L. Jackson, "The Candidate's Challenge: The Call of Conscience, The Courage of Conviction," Democratic National Convention, San Francisco, 17 July 1984, transcribed from a videotape recording by Martha Cooper and John J. MaKay.
43. Richard L. Johannesen *Ethics in Human Communication*, 3rd ed. (Prospect Heights: Waveland Press, 1990), 7-9.
44. See, for example, the viewpoints expressed in Kathryn Abrams, W. B. Carnochan, Henry Louis Gates, Jr., and Robert M. O'Neil, *Limits of Expression in American Intellectual Life* (American Council of Learned Societies: Occasional Paper #22, 1993).
45. Henry Louis Gates, Jr., "Truth or Consequences: Putting Limits on Limits," in Abrams, *et al.*, *Limits*, 18-9.
46. Johannesen, *Ethics*, 10.
47. Celeste Michelle Condit, "Crafting Virtue: The Rhetorical Construction of Public Morality," *Quarterly Journal of Speech* 73 (1987): 82-87,
48. Johannesen, *Ethics*, 131-32.
49. Johannesen, *Ethics*, 129.

50. Philip Wander, "The Third Persona: An Ideological Turn in Rhetorical Theory," *Central States Speech Journal* 35 (1984): 197-216.
51. Two sources provide excellent analyses of the relationship between language and action inside Nazi Germany. See, Kenneth Burke, "The Rhetoric of Hitler's Battle," *Philosophy of Literary Form* (Berkeley: U Cal P, 1973), 191-220; see also, Steven Perry, "Rhetorical Functions of the Infestation Metaphor in Hitler's Rhetoric," *Central States Speech Journal* 34 (1983), 229-235.
52. The capacity of language to inhibit discussion of the very thing it describes is also discussed at length in Chapter 14, Ideology and Persuasion.
53. Richard L. Johannesen, "Haigspeak, Secretary of State Haig, and Communication Ethics," in *The Orwellian Moment,* ed. Robert L. Savage, James Combs, and Dan Nimmo (Fayetteville: University of Arkansas Press, 1989); reprinted in Johannesen, *Ethics,* 225-33.
54. Quoted in Johannesen, *Ethics,* 225-33.
55. Johannesen, *Ethics,* 231.
56. Robert O'Neil, "The Pitfalls of Stifling Campus Speech," *AGB Reports* (January/February 1990): 13.
57. Mari J. Matsuda, "Public Response to Racist Speech: Considering the Victim's Story," *Michigan Law Review* 87 (August 1989), 2370-71.
58. Stelzner, "'War Message,'" 302.
59. Stelzner, "'War Message,'" 311.
60. Stelzner, "'War Message,'" 317.
61. Stelzner, "'War Message,'" 318.
62. Stelzner, "'War Message,'" 319.
63. See Chapter 14, "Propaganda and Persuasion."

8

NONVERBAL SYMBOLS AND PERSUASION

IN THIS CHAPTER:

Focus on:

The "Daisy" Political Ad

1. Theoretical Focus: The Power and Range of Nonverbal Symbols
2. Conventionalized Nonverbal Symbols: Emblems and Icons
3. Delivery and Nonverbal Behavior
4. Constructed Images and Persuasive Potency
    - Constructed Images and Reality
    - Constructed Images and The Responsive Chord
    - Constructed Images and Persuasive Effects
5. Ethics Of Nonverbal Symbolism and Reality-fictions
6. Critical Focus: The 1964 Johnson Campaign "Daisy Spot"

FOCUS ON: THE "DAISY" POLITICAL AD

As we hear songbirds chirping nearby, a little girl plucks petals from a daisy on a hillside meadow set against a summer sky. The voice of the child, counting petals, is abruptly replaced by a man's voice, harsh and echoing, beginning an ominous countdown offscreen. The camera closes in quickly on the child's eye, and as the voice reaches "zero" we see "reflected" in the child's eye the mushroom cloud of an atomic explosion. We hear the roar of a distant explosion, followed by the voice of then President Lyndon Johnson, saying, "These are the stakes: to make a world in which all of God's children can live, or to go into the dark. We must either love each other, or we must die." Some readers may already recognize this as a description of the infamous "Daisy" televised political spot, aired once by the Johnson presidential campaign, on September 7, 1964.[1] The ad, deemed by many as "the most controversial political ad ever in America," was produced by media expert Tony Schwartz.[2] Active in advertising and political use of the media for a quarter of a century, Schwartz argues that the sights and sounds conveyed by the electronic media work like music. In contrast to print media, rather than imparting information these media evoke what audiences already feel or know, striking a "responsive chord" within them.[3]

The well-documented controversy surrounding the "Daisy" spot reflected the themes of the 1964 political scene.[4] America witnessed increasing domestic unrest and escalating military involvement in Vietnam. The U.S. and U.S.S.R. were taking the first, controversial steps toward control of atomic weaponry. Johnson's opponent in the 1964 general election, Arizona Senator Barry Goldwater, captured the

Republican nomination only after a particularly bitter and hard-fought primary left his party weakened and divided. Clearly no moderate, Goldwater found his hard-core conservative views unattractive even to many within his own party. Goldwater's several public statements which seemed sympathetic to the possible use of atomic weapons disturbed members of both parties. When the "Daisy" spot aired on national television, a firestorm of controversy began almost immediately. Republicans roared that the ad, which never mentions Goldwater or refers to any of Goldwater's proposals, was a cheap, emotionally poisonous attack on their candidate. Democrats retorted that the spot merely highlighted a well-known difference between the two candidates. Unlike Johnson, Goldwater visibly and pointedly supported both the first strike use of atomic weapons and continued weapons testing.[5] Although stunned by the force of the response to the "Daisy" spot, Johnson campaign leaders concluded that it had accomplished its persuasive purpose. As Bill Moyers, then Johnson's press secretary later, recalled:

> The president called me and said 'Holy shit. I'm getting calls from all over the country.' Most of them said that it was an effective ad. Others said they didn't like it. The White House switchboard lighted up. The president went on for a few minutes in an excited state and then said: 'But I guess it did what we Goddamned set out to do, didn't it.' I said 'I would think so.'[6]

The "Daisy" spot is one of a wide variety of persuasive messages trading on a persuasive approach that illustrates Kenneth Burke's concept of identification as outlined in Chapter 6. Moreover, the "Daisy" ad reminds us of the potency of message elements other than the language used. Many readers may be familiar with the images of that notorious ad, including those who weren't even born until after the original broadcast of the spot. Yet how many would immediately recall the words spoken at the end of the spot by Lyndon Johnson? How many would even remember that there was a spoken and written "tag" at the end of the message? (After Johnson's voice, the words "Vote for President Johnson on November 3" appear on the screen, and a male announcer's voice repeats the same sentence, adding, "The stakes are too high for you to stay home.") The powerful image of the innocent child juxtaposed with the atomic explosion remains in the memory after all else is forgotten. So dominant are the nonverbal elements of this spot that a reporter for the *New York Times*, known for its accuracy in reporting, later quoted the line, "Whose finger do you want on the trigger?" in the mistaken belief that it had been a part of the "Daisy" spot.[7]

THEORETICAL FOCUS: THE POWER AND RANGE OF NONVERBAL SYMBOLS

By presenting symbols whose form and content evoke an audience's storehouse of experience and by encouraging audience identification with the interests and motives represented in those symbols, whether verbal, nonverbal or both, messages such as the "Daisy" ad accomplish persuasion that is best analyzed from a Symbolist Perspective. In Chapter 7, we discussed how verbal symbols produce persuasive effects. In this chapter, we concentrate on nonverbal symbols.

We will quickly discover how differently nonverbal symbols show their persuasive power. One important difference resides in the scope of our nonverbal world compared to the verbal world. For example, in the simple case of persuasion during face-to-face conversation, scholar Ray Birdwhistell estimates that the verbal elements of the conversation account for less than 35 percent of the total shared meaning; the remaining 65 percent or more is the product of the nonverbal elements of the conversation.[8] Later researchers estimate as much as 93 percent of a message's impact depends on nonverbal elements.[9] These rough estimates include only those nonverbal elements common to oral conversation, such as body movement, facial expression, vocal cues and the spatial characteristics of the encounter. How much might that 65 percent figure be increased if we take into account the impact of all other forms of visual images beyond body movements, all other sounds beyond the human voice and all other forms of persuasive communication besides oral conversation?

Other differences stem from the nondiscursive, presentational quality of nonverbal communication, as we discussed in Chapter 6. The meaning of all symbols, whether verbal or nonverbal, discursive or nondiscursive, is governed by codes—culturally shared conventions about meanings. Their presentational or nondiscursive character frequently tends to make nonverbal symbols seem more direct and less arbitrary than verbal language and frequently results in coded meaning that is more experiential and less conceptual.

In this chapter we investigate three aspects of nonverbal communication: emblematic nonverbal symbols, nonverbal behaviors and constructed images. Following a discussion of emblematic nonverbal symbols and their relation to identification that emphasizes the importance of resemblance, we examine two other approaches to the persuasive effects of nonverbal communication. The first of these is nonverbal behaviors, traditionally referred to as delivery, which has interested students of persuasion for centuries. The second, constructed images, arises from more contemporary concerns about the nonverbal elements in media messages. Then we turn our attention to ethical concerns. The chapter concludes with a critical focus that returns to an analysis of the "Daisy" spot mentioned at the beginning.

Conventionalized Nonverbal Symbols: Emblems and Icons

In Chapter 6, we identified the characteristics of discursive symbol systems: They are linear in structure; they have vocabulary and syntax; they are translatable into other symbols; and they are general in reference. Since these are the characteristics of language, which we discussed in the previous chapter, we will begin our discussion here with those nonverbal symbols which are most like language and have the most discursive characteristics.

Among those language-like nonverbal symbols are those which compose a translatable vocabulary, a fairly conventionalized meaning which is agreed upon within or across cultures. Such nonverbal symbols can be used in much the same way we use written or spoken words or phrases. The most common of these symbols are kinesic body or facial movements which scholars traditionally group as *emblems*. Emblems include body movements which have a meaning shared throughout a culture:

the thumb and forefinger touched together with fingers extended, to signal "O.K."; the up-and-down nodding of the head to indicate assent; the fingertips and thumb touched together and drawn toward the mouth to indicate "eating" or "food." In this chapter we are going to expand this narrow sense of emblem to include all *emblematic nonverbal symbols* with strongly conventionalized meaning analogous to the denotative meaning of words. It is characteristic of emblematic nonverbal symbols that they have fairly stable shared meanings, just as most words have generally accepted, denotative meanings. Emblematic nonverbal symbols operate on principles quite similar to language in that they convey somewhat conventional and easily interpreted meanings with both denotative and connotative dimensions.

However, many emblematic nonverbal symbols differ from most words in that they often represent their referents through a process of resemblance, while still being an arbitrary choice for representation. For example, the international symbols for "baggage," "telephone," "restaurant" and so forth, by which we find our way around airports are nonverbal symbols whose meaning is based on resemblance. These symbols are somewhat arbitrary in that other nonverbal symbols could have just as easily been chosen. For example, instead of a knife and fork, a plate of food could be used to signal the existence of a restaurant. However, they are distinctly different from most words in that a primary link between them and their referent is their resemblance to the referent.

Like verbal language, emblematic nonverbal symbols allow us to conceptualize an experience without actually having to experience it. The familiar skull and cross bones is illustrative; it resembles the dead and signals something which is deadly without subjecting its receiver to death itself. A common nonverbal symbol for nuclear war, for example, is the visual image of a mushroom cloud. The image works conceptually as we can use the mushroom cloud image to refer to atomic explosions without having such an explosion take place. The image of the mushroom cloud is emblematic in that the actual cloud itself is a sign of an atomic detonation. However, the connection between symbol and referent is also somewhat arbitrary. True, mushroom clouds accompany atomic explosions, but there is no necessary reason why we must use that image as opposed to some other to refer to atomic explosions.

Many emblematic nonverbal symbols, such as the knife-and-fork sign for "restaurant," function instrumentally. Their usefulness comes from our expectation that we would never find these signs anywhere except in the vicinity of a restaurant. Thus, they serve an instrumental function equivalent to the instrumental function of language we describe in Chapter 7. On the surface, there is little about such emblematic symbols we would consider persuasive; they seem only to denote something that they resemble. However, many nonverbal symbols that are selected for their resemblance to the referent function persuasively because they also evoke powerful connotative meanings. Consider the case of a war memorial. Many communities honor fallen soldiers with nonverbal symbols such as statuary depicting a soldier in uniform or a cavalryman, a preserved tank or even an old bomber. In such cases, the resemblance between the symbol and the event or persons honored is clear. Such memorials also evoke emotional reactions and associations from those who view them. A similar nonverbal symbol that honors the dead is the AIDS Quilt. Again, the symbol denotes in ways that are heavily influenced by resemblance. Frequently, the individual panels include actual photographs of people who have died from AIDS or other memorabilia from their lives such as an embroidered representation of a tennis racket or a theatrical mask. Again, the nonverbal symbol evokes a variety of associations about the persons who have died, their lives and the disease that caused their death. Such connotative associations may begin the process of identification described in Chapter 6.

Connotative meaning and the resulting identification is particularly important for some emblematic symbols. Perhaps the most famous and controversial war memorial in this country is the Vietnam Veterans' Memorial. Like the denotation of a word, the black, granite wall engraved with the names of those who died and the statuary of three soldiers accompanying it suggest a large tombstone, bearing the names of the soldiers who fought in Vietnam. Like the connotation of a word, however, the memorial evokes a variety of sometimes contradictory associations and emotional responses from those who view it. A number of critics have attempted to explain how it strikes various emotional and ideological chords among visitors.[10] These critics agree that the memorial invites—indeed, even demands—multiple and contradictory interpretations by encouraging visitors to reflect on their own experiences regarding Vietnam as they view the memorial. For some, the memorial connotes all that was wrong with the U.S. policy in Vietnam and underscores the tragic loss of life that accompanied a failed foreign policy. For others, the memorial honors the dead, legitimizing and accepting the efforts of those who fought, who prior to its construction had felt disaffected and abandoned by a war-weary nation. Others may find both of these otherwise incompatible experiences summoned up at the same time. In any case, including these and the multiplicity of other interpretations not mentioned here, the connotative meaning evoked by the symbol encourages people to identify with various ways of viewing the world.

A special case of emblematic symbols that hold powerful potential for identification is the *icon*. Icons are nonverbal symbols that evoke powerful motives and interests, frequently of a religious or ideological nature, that often bear some resemblance to their referent and are treated as sacred by the culture in which they are used. Thus, while some emblems which gain meaning from resemblance, like the airport knife-and-fork, are persuasively trivial, icons can and do contribute powerfully to persuasion. Examples of icons include religious symbols, such as the crucifix and the Star of David, and political symbols, such as the American flag, the Liberty Bell and the Statue of Liberty. Some icons, like the crucifix, depend heavily on resemblance for their meaning. A crucifix must at least vaguely resemble the cross upon which Jesus was crucified. Other icons, like the Statue of Liberty, are much more arbitrary. Although there was never a robed woman with a torch greeting immigrants at the shores of North America, which the Statue of Liberty must resemble, the statue does resemble the Roman Goddess of Liberty; and various aspects of the statue were intended to represent aspects of the new democracy, such as the broken chains at the base that represent democracy breaking the shackles of tyranny.[11] Icons are emblematic in that they rely on a particular culture's conventions of meaning and identification. While the crucifix stands for Christianity, the Star of David stands for Judaism, each signifying a distinct religious group, with its attendant world view. Icons tend to evoke strong connotative meaning because of their relationship to important cultural values and experiences. That cultural connection, compounded by its resemblance to some sacred image, is what gives the icon a sacred value. The way in which people respond to an icon defaced is proof of its sacred quality. Flag burning, for example, may be cause for great alarm among patriotic citizens who view such burning as an insult to the whole way of life for which the flag stands. Similarly, graffiti sprayed on the Star of David may signal anti-Semitic attitudes that are intolerable to those identifying with the Jewish faith.

Kenneth Burke wrote in 1935 that "symbols are verbal parallels of experience."[12] Given our discussion of nonverbal symbols so far, it is fair to add that symbols can also be nonverbal parallels of experience, both denoting and connoting meanings that serve as the basis for identification. Importantly and unlike most verbal symbols, emblematic nonverbal symbols frequently work because of their resemblance to what they represent. Often a particular nonverbal symbol is accepted as a particularly good representation because of its intense resemblance to the experience represented and its repeated use. Consider, for example the well-known photograph of the fireman in Oklahoma City holding the burned infant who died in the explosion of the federal building there in 1995. This picture was reproduced in news reports throughout the world and quickly assumed emblematic status as a primary representation of the Oklahoma City bombing. Similarly, the videotaped image of the Challenger space shuttle explosion came to symbolize that tragedy. Pictures such as these are the nonverbal parallels of experience and consequently hold considerable potential for evoking a sense of identification. Indeed, many people may identify themselves as belonging to a particular generation, reference group or culture by their familiarity with such nonverbal symbols. Because they can recognize the picture, the monument or image and call up the denotative and connotative meanings associated with it, they can define themselves as an American in the late Twentieth Century, an aging war protestor from the sixties or an international traveler. We will examine how some persuaders construct images that trade on these identifications later in the chapter. But now we turn our attention to less emblematic and sometimes more ambiguous forms of nonverbal communication—nonverbal behaviors.

Delivery And Nonverbal Behaviors

The study of nonverbal elements of persuasion began with discussions about the role of voice and body movement in public speaking by the classical theorists and orators of ancient Greece, such as Demosthenes. As Edward P. J. Corbett records the incident, "When Demosthenes, the greatest of the Greek orators, was asked what he considered to be the most important part of rhetoric, he replied, 'Delivery, delivery, delivery.'"[13] Scholars credit Aristotle with first raising the possibility of a theory of delivery within a larger theory of rhetoric or persuasion, but his discussion of delivery was far less systematic than his discussion of other aspects of his theory.[14] Aristotle singled out the pitch, volume and rhythm of the speaking voice as aids to the expression of various emotions. Aristotle deliberately limited the scope of his approach to nonverbal elements in public speaking. He asserted only that delivery in public speaking should avoid diverting attention away from artistic proofs within the speech itself. His approval for the study of delivery is grudging at best:[15]

> Still, the whole business of rhetoric being concerned with appearances, we must pay attention to delivery, unworthy though it is, because we cannot do without it. The right thing in speaking really is that we should be satisfied not to annoy our hearers, without trying to delight them: we ought in fairness to fight our case with no help beyond the bare facts: nothing therefore, should matter except the proof of those facts. Still, as has been already said, other things affect the result considerably, owing to the defects of our hearers.

Aristotle's successors elaborated on his rough sketch of the principles of delivery. Some three centuries later, Cicero offered advice on the types of gestures orators should use in order to reinforce particular points in their speeches. In the Eighteenth and Nineteenth Centuries, many British scholars of rhetoric took renewed interest in the study of delivery, under the banner of "elocution."[16] The main interest of the elocutionary movement was developing prescriptive principles for improving the delivery of practicing orators. Consider the following advice, drawn from an 1871 handbook on elocution, regarding the proper use of hand gestures:[17]

> We stretch forth and clasp the hands when we importunately entreat, sue, beseech, supplicate, or ask mercy. To put forth the right hand spread open is the gesture of bounty, liberality, and a free heart; and thus we reward and bestow gifts. Placing with vehemence the right fist in the left palm is a gesture commonly used to mock, chide, insult, reproach, and rebuke. To beckon with the raised hand is a universal sign of craving audience and entreating a favorable silence. To wave the hand from us, the palm outward, is the gesture of repulsion, aversion, dismissal. To shake the fist at one signifies anger and defiance and threatening. The hands are clasped or wrung in deep sorrow, and outstretched with the palms inward to indicate welcoming, approval, and receiving. In shame, the hand is placed before the eyes; in earnestness and ardor, the hands reach forward; in joy they are thrown up, widely apart; in exultation and triumph, the right hand is waved above the head.

The stilted and formal delivery style advocated by elocutionists contrasts sharply to the more extemporaneous and conversational delivery in fashion today. Moreover, contemporary scholars recognize that the interpretation of nonverbal behaviors is shaped by cultural factors to an extent ignored by the elocutionists. However, the very prescriptive tone of the now abandoned elocutionary movement—its preoccupation with precise and detailed rules for the voice, posture and movement—is illustrative of a prescriptive approach to rules for nonverbal behavior that survives to this day. Contemporary self-improvement books often show concern for the same practical problems of delivery as the elocutionists, updated and ranging over topics such as how to dress, sit or interact with others at informal gatherings in order to increase one's credibility at work. While many such books often have little theoretical basis other than the experiences and observations of their authors, there is a body of research that attempts to categorize and explain the persuasive effects of nonverbal behaviors.

According to one recent synthesis of research on the classification of nonverbal behaviors, the most frequently identified classes are: paralanguage or vocal cues;

kinesics, including facial expression, body movements, gestures and eye movement; proxemics, including distance and spacing; and touch.[18] Thus, nonverbal behaviors can be as simple as a hand gesture, like the movements that often punctuate our conversation, or as complicated as the arrangement of a professor's office designed to keep students at an intimidating distance when they come to ask a question.

Much of the research on nonverbal behaviors explains how such behaviors relate to the verbal content of communication. Mark Knapp, for example, asserts that nonverbal behaviors may substitute, repeat, contradict, complement, accent or regulate the verbal message.[19] For example, the familiar thumbs up gesture may substitute for a verbal statement like, "that's a good job." A nervous smile from a speaker discussing child abuse may contradict the message, or a severe gaze and a fist pounded on the podium may complement and accent a stern warning by a speaker about the need for stricter gun control laws. Similarly, speakers may regulate an audience's responses through their nonverbal behaviors. Max Atkinson studied the ways in which speakers induce audiences to applaud during speeches.[20] He labeled these nonverbal devices, such as nodding, repetition in patterns of three and using a chanting tone, as claptraps.[21]

Other research on nonverbal behaviors has followed theories that such behaviors help to establish relationships between speakers and their audiences. Psychologist Albert Mehrabian identifies three relationship dimensions that are carried on chiefly through nonverbal behaviors: immediacy, power and responsiveness.[22] The immediacy or attraction dimension is based on a fundamental principle: "People are drawn toward persons and things they like, evaluate highly and prefer; and they avoid or move away from things they dislike, evaluate negatively, or do not prefer."[23] This approach may be literal and physical. We may actually move toward persons, things or events we find attractive or draw them toward us. More often, however, the approach or avoidance is indirect, symbolic or abbreviated. In face-to-face interaction we may increase or decrease eye contact, lean toward or away from the other person, make interested remarks or remain silent, and so on. Part of Ronald Reagan's power as an orator was his skillful use of the TelePrompTer. This device, which projects the text of a speech directly in front of a television camera and is visible only to the speaker, allowed Reagan to maintain steady eye contact with his audience while reading his speech, rather than continually looking down at a speech manuscript on a desk or podium. The appearance of a steady, unbroken gaze projected a greater sense of immediacy, which Reagan's audiences easily recognized and to which they responded.[24]

The power dimension of messages indicates the relative status and authority of communicators.[25] Significantly, one aspect of power in a communicative relationship is the ability to control the degree of immediacy in interactions with others. Persons in higher status positions, such as presidents, managers or professors, frequently have the prerogative of increasing immediacy and access with those in lower status positions—voters, employees or students. This prerogative is usually not enjoyed by the one in the lower status position. Power is also displayed by controlling larger territory, such as interaction space or office size, and by demonstrating an attitude of physical relaxation around others. Lower status persons, by comparison, are accorded less interaction space and are commonly more physically tense in interaction with those of higher status.

Table 8.1
Nonverbal Behaviors and Persuasive Functions

Nonverbal Behavior	Persuasive Function(s)	Positive Behaviors	Negative Behaviors
Eye behavior	credibility, confidence	+ sustained eye contact + direct eye contact with receivers	- shifty eyes - looking down - excessive blinking or fluttering
Gestures	credibility, confidence	+ appear spontaneous, relaxed, unrehearsed + keep hands and arms away from the body + add emphasis to content of message + communicate intensity of feelings	- hand-to-face gesture - fidgeting, extraneous movements - out-of-context smiling, grimacing, or laughing
Posture	status, power, warmth	+ expansive movement + relaxed posture and walk + leaning forward to show interest	- constricted (crossed arms and legs) - bodily tension
Vocal Cues	credibility, power	+ conversational tone + sufficient volume	- monotone - excessive rate - frequent pauses

The responsiveness dimension concerns the sheer amount or intensity of emotional involvement in a situation or interaction, whether good, bad or mixed.[26] Responsiveness is signaled in general by changes in activity matched to the behavior of the other person. In interpersonal interaction this includes such behaviors as nodding, laughing, changing facial expression and so forth. Responsiveness directly relates to face-to-face interaction or "real-time" equivalents such as telephone or live television; it is not a factor in mediated persuasion which is static, recorded or non-interactive, such as audiotape, videotape or still photography.

Mehrabian's theory of how nonverbal behaviors influence human relationships is consistent with other research that concentrates specifically on the persuasive effects of some types of nonverbal communication. Traditionally, communication research on persuasive effects has focused on the voice and body. A typical approach is provided by Dale Leathers, a communication researcher who reports on his experience as a political consultant and trainer of corporate salespeople. Leathers is convinced that "successful communicators must master the art of selling themselves nonverbally."[27] To that end, he synthesizes a variety of contemporary research on nonverbal behaviors. Table 8.1 is our summary of Leathers' findings. As the chart suggests, nonverbal behaviors may hold a direct relationship to persuasion that occurs on the basis of credibility, power or personal rapport.[28]

Information about the persuasive effects of nonverbal behaviors, like that supplied by Leathers, is exemplary of contemporary efforts to determine the codes of nonverbal communication. While helpful, it is important to remember that such efforts are necessarily limited by an inherent ambiguity of nonverbal behaviors. Differences in culture, gender and personal style have repeatedly foiled the efforts of nonverbal researchers to make all but the most highly generalized statements about the meaning of specific nonverbal behaviors. Scholars in this area consistently note the importance of contextual and individual differences regarding the meaning and effect of nonverbal behaviors.[29] For example, while sustained eye contact in white Western culture generally conveys confidence and credibility, the Navajo understand such eye behavior to signal aggressiveness and, therefore, avoid it in normal interactions.[30] Moreover, many of the positive behaviors described in Table 8.1 are more applicable for men than for women. Mark Knapp observes that women gaze at their conversational partners more, gesture closer to their bodies, maintain less relaxed postures and smile on more occasions than men and notes that these nonverbal behaviors can be used to persuasive advantage by women.[31] Hence, the astute analyst of persuasion may use research like that summarized by Leathers for guidelines about what is fashionable for the dominant culture at any given time, but is wise to bear in mind the importance of other factors, especially cultural and gender differences, in persuasive encounters.

Constructed Images And Persuasive Potency

In some ways it is a small step to move from the sort of nonverbal behaviors relevant to delivery to the notion of constructed images. Practically any salesperson will recognize the benefit of showing a potential buyer a picture of a product rather than simply talking and gesturing about it. Public speakers frequently translate complicated statistics into bar graphs or pie charts in order to make their arguments easier to understand. As president, Ronald Reagan once brought a copy of the several-thousand-page federal budget into Congress to show them and the viewing public just how huge it was—the physically unwieldy printed document suggesting the political unworkability of the actual budget. And 1992 presidential candidate H. Ross Perot helped create a new cross-fertilization of political and consumer advertising, by using infomercial-style charts and graphs about the deficit in his one-half hour, paid advertisements during an unsuccessful bid for national office. In each of these cases, persuaders constructed images to enhance their messages much the same way that individuals learn to modulate their voices or gesture more purposefully in order to increase the likelihood of effective persuasion. Such constructed images create persuasive meaning in much the same way as language that names or describes figuratively creates realities.

Especially with the advent of electronic media, the range of constructed images is awesome. They can be as simple as a line drawing or as complicated as an expansive cinematic scene. They can be a singular nonverbal symbol that comes to function as an emblem, such as the Golden Arches that identify McDonald's Restaurants, or a complicated mix of nonverbal elements like we see in a 30-second commercial television spot or the collages of pictures, sounds and text delivered to our computer screen over the Internet. Often multiple constructed images—computer graphics, filmed scenes, mixed audio tracks, animation, altered "real-time" video images and the like—are artfully overlaid or mixed together to produce a holistic product containing a number of constructed images. Messages that appeal to several senses simultaneously by providing an artful complex of sight and sound are called *polyvocal*, suggesting the existence of several voices or nonverbal images, rather than only one. Moreover, just as many voices together may not all be "saying the same thing," the different images or voices in polyvocal messages may also work together synergistically: The meaning of the whole is typically greater than the sum of its parts. So expansive is the scope of constructed images in our multi-media world, that researchers in this area are even hard pressed to compile a generally accepted catalogue of the types of constructed images or their persuasive effects. The following discussion is intended as an overview; the range of specific examples is obviously far broader than our selection of illustrative examples.

Parallel to the traditional interest in body (appearance) and voice (sound) for those who studied delivery, contemporary research regarding constructed images has centered on visual and auditory images. A recent synthesis of research on nonverbal effects in advertising defined the nonverbal elements of advertisements as including colors and pictures (visual images) and music and sound effects (auditory images).[32] While our discussion of constructed images emphasizes visual and auditory images, we recognize that other types of images can be and are constructed by persuaders. What is central to this discussion is that the image is constructed or manufactured.

CONSTRUCTED IMAGES AND REALITY

The relationship between constructed images and reality is important in understanding their persuasive effects. Such images may be fairly realistic—for example, actual sound tracks of a busy city street—or provide us with fantastic experiences only attainable in the virtual reality of cyberspace, such as the image of balancing a luxury automobile on the slender point of a steel needle. Regardless of how authentic the images are, constructed images usually provide receivers a sense of reality. In our discussion of image management in Chapter 5, we introduced Daniel Boorstin's list of the characteristics of manufactured images. Boorstin notes that images are both synthetic, yet believable, and sensory, yet conceptually ambiguous. Consider what happens to an audience's sense of reality with each of these paradoxical characteristics.

Images are synthetic because they are manufactured, but they are believable because they seem realistic. Consider, for example, some familiar images from food advertisements. The image of a bowl of corn flakes with plump strawberries floating in milk is familiar. Is this image real? Sort of. There is that moment when we prepare breakfast that our bowl of cereal may look very like the image. But, as any of us who eat cereal in the morning know, within minutes the flakes in a bowl of milk get soggy and appear much less appetizing than their crisp counterparts on television. The image has been constructed by a food artist, a little-known employee of the advertiser, who uses white glue as a substitute for milk so that the cereal never looks soggy. The steaming cup of coffee that we see in other commercials undergoes a similar synthetic operation; dishwashing detergent is added so that when it is stirred it has that frothy, just-brewed look. If you've ever wondered why those pictures of the food on the covers of the packages are always carefully labeled as a "serving suggestion," now you know. Though manufactured, the look is realistic because it is believable; consumers have seen the perfect food or drink even if they experience it only infrequently.

Visual images are frequently manufactured to look realistic, while at the same time defying reality. For example, television pictures of guests on a talk show generally look realistic, like an ordinary living-room chat. Yet, anyone who has ever seen the set of a television studio knows better. In "real" life two people may chat comfortably in chairs that are three to four feet apart. If a television camera recorded such a conversation, those conversational partners would appear to be very far apart. So, on the set the chairs are moved much closer together, often as little as a foot apart, for the visual image necessary to capture the appearance of a "friendly conversation." The potential for misrepresentation, if not outright deception, and other ethical implications of the paradox will be discussed later in this chapter. For now, the reality-creating function of the constructed image is our concern.

The paradox of constructed images being sensory and concrete at the same time they are conceptual and ambiguous highlights further the complicated relationship between constructed images and reality by focusing our attention on how constructed images elicit meaning. Constructed images engage the senses—sight, sound, touch, taste and smell. They can engage a single sense, like illustrated billboard advertisements or radio broadcasts; or they may appeal to multiple senses, such as the combination of visual images and scent in "scratch and sniff" cologne advertisements in magazines or sight and sound in a Hollywood film. The sensory appeal of constructed images results in an experiential approach to meaning construction that gives the realities created by these images persuasive potential.

CONSTRUCTED IMAGES AND "THE RESPONSIVE CHORD"

As early as the Eighteenth Century, psychologists and rhetoricians observed that sensory data make an impression on people that is experiential.[33] In other words, when our senses are engaged, we experience it first and think about it only afterward. When we hear an up-beat piece of music, for example, we may experience feelings of confidence and optimism. Similarly, if we smell fresh bread baking, we may experience hunger; or if we have a near-miss auto accident, we may not begin to feel the symptoms of fear until after we have reflected on what almost happened. Following some initial experiences, if a sense is engaged in a similar way, a person may recall or at least associate an entire previous experience. For example, if a child experienced the warmth and love of her mother in the context of smelling freshly baked cookies and hearing traditional Christmas carols playing on the radio, then smelling the cookies baking in a shopping mall or just hearing part of a carol years later may evoke memories of that early experience.

Media consultant Tony Schwartz claims that our experiences with electronic media are coded and stored in a similar way.[34] He explains that if viewers or listeners see or hear an image that *resonates* with their experience, then all the associations that accompany that experience can be invoked. Consider, for example, a recent television commercial for Lee Jeans ("jeans that fit"), showing multiple dressing rooms of young women jumping up and down in order to squeeze into a pair of jeans. The visual image provides sensory data for an experience that is probably familiar to many viewers. The experience includes much more than trying on jeans; it may encompass fears about gaining weight, frustrations with shopping, relief when a garment that fits is finally found, and so on. Hence, the visual image in the commercial can evoke a complex experience. Those aspects of the evoked experience which are "contributed" by the viewer, in turn, may help incline that person to buy the product in question.

Furthermore, because media images constitute experiences themselves (i.e., they provide new sensory experiences), persuaders may elicit experiences connected to other constructed images with which an audience is familiar. Thus, constructed images can be about other constructed images. During the 1995 Superbowl, for example, Budweiser introduced its commercial featuring the three croaking frogs in a pond. In lush, detailed animation, the frogs emit croaking sounds that gradually sound more like "bu-u-ud," "wei-i-is" and "errrr." No explanation is given, but as the commercial closes, viewers see the reflection of a neon Budweiser sign in the dark pond where the frogs sit staring toward the light. Viewers probably were amused by this clever repetition of the brand name and may have even experienced some attraction to the frogs. Within weeks, Budweiser began airing a second frog commercial in which the humor is much broader compared to the subtlety of the first spot. One of the frogs attempts to use its tongue to catch a speeding Budweiser truck like a big fly. The tongue sticks to the truck with a wet smack; the big truck continues unbothered, and we see the frog's tongue stretched to an impossible length. Abruptly, like a slingshot, the frog is snapped through the air behind the speeding truck. With a lusty "Yee-haw!" like a rodeo rider or a bungee-cord jumper, the frog sails tongue-first down the road behind the speeding truck. Doubtless, the attraction for viewers to watch the second ad is the amusing experience of watching the first in the series.

Certainly, the meaning of it depends to some extent on one's knowledge of the earlier commercial. In this case, as well as countless others—such as the several year-long series of Tasters' Choice coffee commercials following the romance of "sophisticated neighbors" who share instant coffee at intimate moments—constructed images begin to take on a life of their own, as if they are "real" experiences.

Constructed Images and Persuasive Effects

Both their reality-creating function and their potential to evoke resonance with experiences help to explain some common persuasive outcomes of constructed images. Julie Edell's synthesis of research on the persuasive effects of nonverbal elements in advertising is illustrative.[35] She observes five persuasive effects that are of particular interest. First, nonverbal elements *convey information effectively*. The old adage that "a picture is worth a thousand words" is often true. A time-lapsed picture of a weed dying, a graph showing a statistical trend and the sound of a car door closing may simply be more effective than words alone in conveying the benefits of a particular weed-killer, the increase of heart disease or the solid-build of a new automobile. Second, nonverbal elements *induce moods*. The soft, pastel colors of a field in spring or the dark, rainy appearance of a lonely road can cause viewers to feel warm and calm or fearful and anxious. Similarly, auditory images can induce moods, such as the scary music in horror films or the upbeat, nostalgic music common in commercial advertisements. Some research has revealed that merely adding musical accompaniment increases an audience's acceptance of the spoken word.[36]

Closely related to mood induction, a third effect is that nonverbal elements appear to *transfer the affect of the nonverbal element to the product or idea being discussed*. If an audience likes a picture, a logo or a musical jingle that appears in an advertisement for a product, they also tend to like the product. Folk wisdom in advertising is that babies, puppies and kittens are guaranteed to transfer positive feelings toward a product; think of the number of commercials that show adorable infants playing inside a shiny, black tire or amazingly talented dogs opening a beer. Conversely, sound or sight can be used to transfer negative affects or feelings toward a situation. Studies show that a negative mood, perhaps evoked through discordant music or frightening images, increases people's estimates of the frequency of negative events (e.g., street crime, chronic depression, stroke) regardless of how similar the image was to the event.[37] Advertisements for better locks, healthier lifestyles or even a new car with better brakes frequently trade on the ability of nonverbal elements to transfer feelings of fear, anxiety or general gloom to the issue at hand.

A fourth effect of nonverbal elements is that they can *attract particular target audiences*. Neither the music nor the visual elements of most commercial advertisements are accidents. Typically, the "look" and "sound" of the constructed image is carefully selected to fit the tastes and preferences of the target audience. When Raisin Bran cereal decided to appeal to the Baby Boom generation, the choice of music ("I Heard it through the Grapevine") was designed to elicit identification with that group of viewers. The black-and-white, MTV-type visuals of Calvin Klein advertisments were likely more appealing to members of Generation X. Setting a Jeep Cherokee in front of a dramatic waterfall or displaying a luxury Lexis maneuvering the tight curves of European highways similarly attracts different types of viewers.

Finally, nonverbal elements appear to *distract audiences* from the claims and product information of persuaders. Large, unframed pictures, as well as music, tend to involve an audience emotionally more than cognitively. Consequently, studies show that viewers are less likely to remember or respond evaluatively to product information or other verbal messages when confronted with engaging visual and auditory images.[38] The pictures and the sounds seem to distract the audience from more conceptual mental operations. This effect may be even more important if we consider the typical circumstances in which persuaders use constructed images. Ordinarily, nonverbal elements are clustered, embedded in larger, more complex messages perhaps containing many verbal and nonverbal elements. The meaning of an individual message element, such as a particular image, behavior or sound must be understood in the context of the larger message, just as the meaning of a word depends upon its context. Thus the redundancy of nonverbal cues within a persuasive message may enhance their distraction effect.

The first two effects just discussed, conveying information and inducing moods, resemble the denotative and connotative effects of verbal symbols as a means of persuasion. The next two effects, transferring affects and attracting a target audience, more clearly explain how constructed images contribute to the process of identification discussed earlier. Audiences may identify themselves or the products and ideas of others with the nonverbal elements of messages. The last effect, distraction, leads naturally to a discussion of ethics.

ETHICS OF NONVERBAL SYMBOLISM AND REALITY-FICTIONS

Insofar as nonverbal symbols act like verbal symbols, we may apply the ethical principles discussed in Chapter 7. We may ask, do the nonverbal symbols used in a message reflect reality as we know it and enhance rather than detract from our human ability to choose?[39] If a product doesn't really look like it is depicted in an advertisement or a pie chart doesn't accurately reflect a bit of statistical data, the unethical nature of a nonverbal symbol may be easy to ascertain. Or, if the nonverbal elements of a presentation so distract an audience that people are unable to make an informed choice, the nonverbal aspects of communication may be judged unethical. But frequently nonverbal symbols, whether emblematic or constructed merely resemble reality rather than directly depicting it. In these cases, ethical judgment may be more problematic.

For example, we can question whether or not the careful staging and choreographing of a political convention accurately reflects the nature of the party that designs it. Such a question brings to mind the 1988 controversy in which the Democratic convention chose to use pastel colors instead of the traditional red, white and blue in their background sets, balloons, etc., because the pastels would show up better on television. Was the party being deceptive and manipulative in their persuasive choices about nonverbal symbols or merely adapting to the visual requirements of television? Similarly, if a candidate like George Bush hires a speech coach to help lower the pitch of his voice so that he will sound more "presidential," is that ethical?

Probably both instances are ethical in that the nonverbal symbols both reflect a reasonable interpretation of reality and provide a clearer basis for choice.

Questions about veracity, resemblance to reality, become more difficult when we take into account the manufactured or synthetic nature of many constructed images. The concoctions of food artists clearly manipulate reality to make consumable items appear more appealing. Yet, few would question the fundamental truth of the image. In other cases, however, the truth of the image, and thereby its ethicality, is less clear. For example, the plastic models of a fetus used by Pro-Life advocates are synthetic products used to advance a cause. Because they are manufactured, synthetic images can show us "realities" that are otherwise unseeable. Features of an infant can be inscribed on those plastic, nonverbal symbols that may not exist or may be indistinguishable on the living being that these models are meant to represent. For Pro-Life advocates, the reality-producing function of their image may be powerfully persuasive; for their opponents, that reality creation may be deemed inappropriate.

Many scholars recognize that constructed images in particular alter reality to present more appealing effects.[40] The careful construction of sound, sight and action scripts in most television programming and Hollywood films and the scrupulous attention to layout, design and photos in persuasive print media suggest that choices are being made about how to depict subjects that possess persuasive potential. Because we know that these images are not reality, ethical considerations based on their accurate reflection of reality may not always apply. Tony Schwartz goes so far as to suggest that a "truth" standard is simply irrelevant to visual and auditory media.[41] Neil Postman, a scholar of contemporary media culture, observes that viewers make their decisions on aesthetic standards concerning whether or not they like an image rather than on truth standards.[42] Consequently, a standard other than the nonverbal symbol's fidelity to reality is needed to judge the ethics of nonverbal communication.

Rhetorical theorist Walter R. Fisher suggests a useful means for understanding the problem just described when he calls the images produced in persuasion "real-fictions."[43] These images are real, says Fisher, because they are finally about the "real world," the practical world of our everyday experience and the ethical choices we make in it. The images are also fictions, however, because as symbolic constructions they always stand for a reality that they refer to or represent. In the case of nondiscursive symbolism, we cannot test these images for truth in the same way that we do discursive propositions and arguments. This ambiguity and multiple levels of meaning in such images provide the basis for identification. We either identify or fail to identify with others when we believe we see or fail to see our interests, motives and values re-presented in their symbolic acts.[44] Fisher argues that these images are "value-oriented interpretations," functioning as signs of shared motives and interests between persuader and audience. "Most important," Fisher adds, "images always reflect how one ought to behave in regard to their [the symbols'] subject matter."[45]

Because of their connection to the persuasive process of identification, these "real-fictions" should be subject to ethical questions about their impact on our fundamental humanity. Do the "real-fictions" promote a world that enhances or detracts from our humanity? In an effort to produce pleasing images, persuaders often present us with pictures of perfection. Airbrushed photographs in countless magazines show us a fictitious reality in which humans are scarcely human at all, probably creating considerable guilt on the part of mere human beings who do not measure up to the idealized images. For example, the cosmopolitan visage of models in Victoria Secret's Catalogue is a manufactured "look." Because they are synthetic, constructed images can be perfect in a way that reality often is not. Numerous other close-up shots of models displaying make-up, jewelry or clothes that appear in many magazine advertisements have usually been airbrushed to eliminate any sign of wrinkles, blemishes or even skin pores. They look "real;" yet, no "real" people enjoy such an appearance. The ethical concern with such images is not so much that they lie to us about appearances as that they set an unattainable standard that causes us to question our fundamental worth as human beings.

Similarly, nonverbal symbols may be vulnerable to negative ethical judgments on the grounds that they induce moods that limit our ability to exercise human choice. In an effort to produce attention-grabbing and riveting nonverbal sequences, commercial advertisers and filmmakers alike resort to complex sound tracks and graphic and sensational images that subtly manipulate and heighten our emotions. These fictitious realities may magnify our fears about the outside world and create in our minds dangers and threats that contribute to a host of neuroses. Such captivating nonverbal messages may also simply overwhelm us with their appeal, either pleasant or unpleasant, so that we withdraw from reality in favor of engaging only the manufactured reality-fictions. Some social critics have suggested that the real danger of our readily-accessible entertainment media is our inclination to spend so much time consuming it that we have little left for other social and political engagements and the choices that attend those activities. These are the sorts of ethical concerns that arise from the unique quality of nonverbal communication as used in persuasion.

CRITICAL FOCUS: THE 1964 JOHNSON CAMPAIGN "DAISY" SPOT

To use this Critical Focus, select a persuasive message in which nonverbal symbolism is present, with or without accompanying verbal symbols. This nonverbal symbolism may take the form of emblematic nonverbal symbols, nonverbal behaviors or constructed images. As you examine this message, ask the following questions, taking care to consider the reasons you would give for your answers as well as the answers themselves.

CRITICAL QUESTIONS

1. What **nonverbal elements** seem to predominate in this message?
2. What is the importance of any **verbal component** of the message relative to the nonverbal elements?
3. How are the predominating nonverbal elements **clustered or related** to one another?
4. Do the nonverbal elements reflect, resemble or provide a **reasonable interpretation of reality**?
5. How do the nonverbal elements **persuade** an audience?

6. What **types of identifications** do the nonverbal elements encourage?

7. Do the nonverbal symbols ENHANCE CHOICE and respect our fundamental humanity?

The notorious "Daisy" ad from the 1964 Johnson Presidential Campaign can illustrate how these questions uncover the persuasive potential of nonverbal symbols in persuasion.

Taken as a whole, two "movements" predominate in the "Daisy" ad: the child counting daisy petals and the detonation of an atomic bomb with Lyndon Johnson's voice-over. The third "movement," the final appeal to vote for Johnson, does not predominate and is often scarcely remembered by viewers. The ad relies heavily on both visual images and sound in these two "movements." Verbal symbols are also present in the child counting from one to nine and the "countdown voice" counting from ten to zero.

The elements of the "Daisy" spot are structured in a pattern of contrasting opposition. Various codes with which the 1964 audience would be familiar juxtapose these two sets of images. The first sequence is filled with coded representations of innocence, peace, safety and nature. None of the message elements would convey this interpretation on its own, but all of the nonverbal elements, considered as a structured whole, cement the desired meaning. The little girl is clearly blond. Her age race and physical appearance invite us to view her as the ideal "all-American," child. We see her engaged in play in a meadow filled with songbirds, suggesting, in combination with the other nonverbal elements present, simplicity and naturalness. The little girl counts daisy petals, a familiar signal for innocence, an innocence unaware of an impending danger. The scene may remind some of a similar "Daisy" scene in the classic film version of Frankenstein. The child doesn't even count in order; she recites her numbers haltingly and in imperfect order:"one, two, three, four, five, seven, six, six, eight, nine." As Jamieson observes, "The authenticity of the child derives in large part from the fact that she counts as children do—with numbers out of proper order. She sounds like a child because she counts like a child…"[46] Finally, the first "movement" ends with the image of the child's eye frozen in an extreme close-up. This technique, as mentioned earlier, can create either a signal of evil intentions on the part of the subject or, as is obviously the case here, a sense of intimacy with the subject. Significantly, the close-up centers on the child's eye—a powerful visual symbol, suggestive of "the window of the soul" and intense rapport and intimacy.

As the image is frozen, the child's gaze has lifted up from the daisy, perhaps toward what we see next: the image of an atomic explosion. While the images in the spot do not insist on this interpretation, they certainly do nothing to discourage such an impression. Jamieson describes the second voice, whose countdown from "ten" to "zero" precedes the atomic explosion, as "a Cape Canaveral voice."[47] Her point is clear. We associate the sound of a male voice counting backwards from ten to zero with missile launches. The audience of 1964 could be motivated by this association, since during this era launches for the Mercury space program were common and were covered with much more fanfare and ritual than today's shuttle launches. Even the voice's drawl invites association with a missile launch; as journalist Tom Wolfe noted, many of the early astronauts were former test pilots who had learned to imitate the West Virginia twang of the premier test pilot, Col. Chuck Yeager. Thus, that drawl is commonly associated with the space program.[48] Yet, we quickly realize that it is not a "Cape Canaveral voice" at all. "Cape Canaveral voices" launch missiles—this voice is detonating an atomic bomb.

From the moment we hear the "countdown voice," new opposing nonverbal symbols begin to undermine every association created during the first "movement" of the ad. The counting itself sets the stage for this reversal. The first voice counts up from one to nine; the second voice counts down from ten to zero. The first is an unself-conscious female child's voice; the second is an adult male's voice, measured and menacing. The child's voice sounds natural and spontaneously captured; the adult's voice is harsh, metallic and echoing. The first "movement" is visually pleasing, with various degrees of light and shadow; the second "movement" is visually harsh, contrasting the blinding white of the explosion with the darkness of the surroundings. The ambient sound in the first "movement" is a songbird; the ambient sound in the second "movement" is the roar of an explosion. When juxtaposed so harshly with the almost lyric visual and acoustical images denoting peace, nature, safety and innocence, the second set of images quickly comes to represent the opposite: war, technology, danger and guilt.

For many viewers of the "Daisy" spot today, these coded associations might be less clear or powerful, but for the 1964 voters these images evoked vivid recent memories of the Cuban Missile Crisis, the widespread building of fallout shelters, and Goldwater's own casual talk about atomic weaponry. "Let's lob one into the men's room of the Kremlin," he had once suggested.[49]

Thus, the first two "movements" of this brief ad work both to affirm an image of peace, safety and tranquility and to contrast that image with one of war, danger and disquiet. This accomplished, the spot seeks one final connection by the viewer which can reaffirm one image and subvert the other. The reaffirmation of the first image followed quickly and forcefully. Johnson's voice rises over the roar of the explosion, "stating," in Jamieson's words, "a lesson that could be drawn from the Sermon on the Mount:"[50]

> These are the stakes: to make a world in which all of God's children can live, or to go into the dark. We must either love each other, or we must die.

Johnson's words affirm the identification between himself and the values represented in the first "movement"—peace, safety and nature.

Yet the ad is scarcely remembered today because of what it did for Johnson's campaign; instead, it is notorious for what it did to the Goldwater campaign. Following the Republican protests the night of the ad's first broadcast, the Johnson campaign abandoned its plan to show the ad twice more on the other two broadcast networks. This hardly mattered since the ad, replayed and discussed several times in the next few days, secured for the Johnson campaign even more exposure for free than it was originally prepared to pay for![51] Certainly, the ad damaged Goldwater's campaign. Yet, in the context of a crippled Republican party waging a divided campaign against an incumbent Democratic candidate, the "Daisy" ad cannot take more than a small measure of responsibility for Goldwater's landslide defeat in November 1964.

More interesting and important now is why this spot so damaged Goldwater, who is never even mentioned throughout the message. Schwartz, the ad's creator, is clear about the answer:

> Well, Senator Goldwater had stated previously that he supported the use of tactical atomic weapons. The commercial evoked a deep feeling in many people that Goldwater might actually use nuclear weapons. This mistrust was not in the Daisy spot. It was in the people who viewed the commercial. The stimuli of the film and sound evoked these feelings and allowed people to express what they inherently believed. Even today, when people try to remember the Daisy spot, they recall their feelings, not the actual content of the commercial.[52]

Thus, Schwartz would deny that the ad represents any breach of persuasive ethics. Certainly, Goldwater made his position on the use of atomic weapons sufficiently public and sufficiently detailed that reference to it could hardly be called unfair.[53] There is, nevertheless, some question about whether persuasive messages like the "Daisy" ad promote or inhibit further discussion of the issues. After all, how can one refute a charge against oneself that has never *explicitly* been made? When one has never even been mentioned by name? The Democrats realized that a strategy linking Goldwater explicitly to atomic war was politically risky, but that to do so *implicitly* and indirectly might be less risky, as Jamieson notes:

> The oblique fashion in which the Democrats argued that Goldwater was more likely than Johnson to start a nuclear war or use nuclear weapons in an existing war whispered their fear that such a claim might be dismissed out of hand as unbelievable or worse as believable but so disquieting that the audience is moved to shoot the messenger who carried it.[54]

Schwartz has since argued repeatedly that by crying "foul!" the Goldwater campaign allowed the "Daisy" ad to do more damage than it might otherwise have done, in effect reaffirming the very same images that the Johnson campaign was seeking to establish: identifying Goldwater with the use of atomic weapons and Johnson with the avoidance of such weapons.[55]

We can pursue the question of ethics by examining the Johnson campaign's decisions regarding similar ads. Although it is not widely remembered, the "Daisy" ad was the first in a series of three ads structured similarly and evoking similar themes.[56] The second, broadcast once on September 12, 1964, juxtaposed images of a young girl eating an ice cream cone with the "soothing, maternal voice" of a female narrator, noting that Senator Goldwater had opposed the atomic test ban treaty that curtailed atmospheric fallout of Strontium 90, a radioactive isotope that accumulates in calcium in dairy products like ice cream.

The third ad, which featured a pregnant woman and her daughter walking through a park linked the fallout from atomic testing, which Goldwater favored, with danger to human fetuses. It was never broadcast. Lloyd Wright, liaison between the Johnson campaign and the advertising agency producing the ads, recalled:

> I remember telling them "no," we would never do it.... The agency personnel felt so strongly that they went out and did it anyway. I saw it in New York and said "I don't presume to speak for the whole campaign but

> that will never see the light of day." Bill [Moyers] and the others agreed. There was no body of evidence indicating that fallout would damage a fetus. Bombs do blow up people so the daisy ad was based in reality but this ad was going beyond the realm of accepted reality. It was straining for scare tactics.[57]

Wright's explanation for the suppression of the third ad suggests that the Johnson campaign attempted to avoid unethical tactics, as they saw it. Certainly their concern for some minimal level of factual accountability and their desire to avoid "scare tactics," suggest some concern for ethical standards.

In any case, this example only hints at the arsenal of weapons available to the contemporary persuader who employs today's media to manipulate nonverbal symbols. The concerns expressed by Aristotle and the Classical Perspective about a persuader's misuse of delivery seems naive when contrasted to these potential abuses.

NOTES

1. The "Daisy" spot is available on the accompanying tape.
2. Jonathan Rowe, "From Political Ad Man to Nightclub Comic," *The Christian Science Monitor* (21 August 1989): 10.
3. See: Tony Schwartz, *The Responsive Chord* (Garden City, NY: Anchor Books, 1974).
4. See: Kathleen Hall Jamieson, *Packaging the Presidency: A History and Criticism of Presidential Campaign Advertising* (New York: Oxford University Press, 1984), 169-220.
5. Schwartz, *Responsive*, 93; see also, Jamieson, *Packaging*, 177-180.
6. Jamieson, *Packaging*, 200.
7. Reported in Schwartz, *Responsive*, 96.
8. Reported in Mark L. Knapp, *Essentials of Nonverbal Communication* (New York: Holt, Rinehart and Winston, 1980), 15.
9. For a summary of such research, see Timothy G. Hegstrom, "Message Impact: What Percentage is Nonverbal?" *Western Journal of Speech Communication* 43 (1979): 134-142.
10. Harry W. Haines, "'What Kind of War?': An Analysis of the Vietnam Veterans Memorial," *Critical Studies in Mass Communication* 3 (1986): 1-20; see also, Carole Blair, Marsha S. Jeppeson, and Enrico Pucci, Jr., "Public Memorializing in Postmodernity: The Vietnam Veterans Memorial as Prototype," *Quarterly Journal of Speech* 77 (1991): 263-288.
11. Marvin Trachtenberg, *The Statue of Liberty* (New York: Penguin, 1986), 63; Mary J. Shapiro, *Gateway to Liberty: The Story of the Statue of Liberty and Ellis Island* (New York: Vintage Books, 1986), 15.
12. Kenneth Burke, *CounterStatement* (Berkeley: University of Southern California Press, 1968), 152.
13. Edward P. J. Corbett, *Classical Rhetoric for the Modern Student*, 2nd Ed. (Oxford: Oxford University Press, 1971), 38-39.
14. Aristotle, *Rhetoric*, tr. W. Rhys Roberts (New York: Modern Library, 1954), 1403b-1404a; 1413b.
15. Aristotle, *Rhetoric* 1404a.

16. See: James L. Golden, Goodwin F. Berquist, and William E. Coleman, *The Rhetoric of Western Thought*, 3rd Ed. (Dubuque: Kendall-Hunt, 1983), 174-187.
17. John D. Philbrick, *The American Union Speaker; Containing Standard and Recent Selections in Prose and Poetry, for Recitation and Declamation, in Schools, Academies, and Colleges, With Introductory Remarks on Elocution, and Explanatory Notes*, (Boston: Thompson, Bigelow, and Brown, 1871), xxvii-xxix.
18. David W. Stewart and Sidney Hecker, "The Future of Research on Nonverbal Communication in Advertising," *Nonverbal Communication in Advertising*, Eds. David W. Stewart and Sidney Hecker (Lexington, MA: D.C. Heath, 1988), 257-258.
19. Knapp, *Essentials*, 11-14. Note that, while Knapp's discussion is intended to apply to nonverbal behavior only, we are extending it in a more general way to include visual and aural images, as well.
20. Max Atkinson, *Our Masters' Voices: The Language and Body Language of Politics* (London: Methuen, 1984).
21. Atkinson, *Our Masters'*, 32-40.
22. Albert Mehrabian, *Silent Messages* (Belmont CA: Wadsworth, 1971), 111-118.
23. Mehrabian, *Silent*, 1.
24. See Atkinson, *Our Masters'*, 66-70.
25. Mehrabian, *Silent*, 24-39.
26. Mehrabian, *Silent*, 116-118.
27. Dale G. Leathers, *Successful Nonverbal Communication* (New York: Macmillan, 1986), 148.
28. Leathers, *Successful*, 147-168.
29. Hecker and Stewart.
30. Nobleza C. Asuncion-Lande, "Intercultural Communication," *Human Communication: Theory and Research*, Eds. Gordon L. Dahnke, Carlos Fernandez-Collado, and Glen W. Clatterbuck (Belmont: Wadsworth, 1990), 214.
31. Mark Knapp, "Nonverbal Communication," *Human Communication: Theory and Research*, Eds. Gordon L. Dahnke,Carlos Fernandez-Collado, and Glen W. Clatterbuck (Belmont: Wadsworth, 1990), 60, 62-63.
32. Julie Edell, "Nonverbal Effects in Advertisements: A Review and Synthesis," Hecker and Stewart, 11.
33. Lloyd F. Bitzer, ed., *The Philosophy of Rhetoric by George Campbell* (Carbondale: Southern Illinois University Press, 1963), xxix-xxxv.
34. Schwartz, *Responsive*, 24-30.
35. Edell, "Nonverbal," 11-27.
36. Reported by Edell, "Nonverbal," 20.
37. Reported by Edell, "Nonverbal," 20.
38. Reported by Edell, "Nonverbal," 17-19.
39. For examples of this concern, see Richard L. Johannesen, *Ethics in Human Communication*, 3rd ed. (Prospect Heights: Waveland, 1990), 126-128.

40. For a discussion of such views, see Johannesen, *Ethics*, 121-122; see also, Scott Ewen, *All Consuming Images* (New York: Basic Books, 1988).
41. Schwartz, *Responsive*, 22.
42. Neil Postman, *Amusing Ourselves to Death* (New York: Penguin, 1984), 126.
43. Walter R. Fisher, "A Motive View of Communication," *Quarterly Journal of Speech* (1970): 131-132.
44. Kenneth Burke, *A Rhetoric of Motives* (Berkeley: University of California Press, 1969), 19-29.
45. Fisher, "A Motive View," 132.
46. Jamieson, *Packaging*, 198.
47. Jamieson, *Packaging*, 198.
48. Tom Wolfe, *The Right Stuff* (New York: Farrar, Straus, and Giroux), 44-46.
49. Jamieson, *Packaging*, 178-179.
50. Jamieson, *Packaging*, 198.
51. Jamieson, *Packaging*, 200.
52. Schwartz, *Responsive*, 93.
53. Jamieson, *Packaging*, 177-188 and 197-208.
54. Jamieson, *Packaging*, 198.
55. Schwartz, *Responsive*, 93-96; see also, Jamieson, *Packaging*, 200.
56. Jamieson, *Packaging*, 201-202.
57. Jamieson, *Packaging*, 201-202.

9

Form And Structure

IN THIS CHAPTER:
Focus on:
Electronic Data Systems—Herding Cats Commercial

1. Theoretical Focus: Form
2. Psychology of Form
3. Message Structures
   Exposition
   Narrative
4. Compliance-Gaining
5. Ethics of Form and Structure
6. Critical Focus: Herding Cats Commercial

Focus On: EDS–Herding Cats Commercial

For many viewers of the Super Bowl, commercials have become as significant to the game as the play. Even non-sports fans tune in to watch the commercials. Sports commentators, media critics and news reporters provide analyses of Super Bowl advertisements in anticipation of and following the game. These ads are the most expensive of any commercials aired during the year. In fact, commercial time for Super Bowl XXXIV in January 2000, cost a record \$2.2-\$3 million for a 30-second spot.[1] With such a staggering price tag, it's not surprising that viewers expect innovative, entertaining commercials, whereas advertisers anticipate the rewards they will reap for their investment in this highly competitive time slot.

The Super Bowl game traditionally is a time for advertisers to introduce new slogans and campaigns, and Super Bowl XXXIV was no exception. What was notable about Super Bowl XXXIV's advertisers, however, was that one-half of them were dot-coms—that is, Web sites and electronic commerce entrepreneurs. The previous year, this sector accounted for only three advertisements. One of the more memorable commercials of Super Bowl XXXIV was for Electronic Data Systems (EDS), titled Herding Cats.[2]

The Herding Cats commercial was EDS' first Super Bowl advertisement. Produced by Minneapolis-based ad agency, Fallon McElligott, the commercial parodied a western cattle drive. It combined the characteristics of the genre—cowboys on horses, herding, whistling, roping and halting a stampede—with domestic cats and their commonly identifiable behaviors, such as darting and running in unpredictable directions, climbing (and then getting stuck in) trees and trying to avoid water. For instance, in one scene, a few cowboys set up camp around a herder who was winding a large ball of yarn. In another scene, cowboys illustrated the 'dangers' of herding cats as one described how the other was clawed by an uncooperative feline. Whether viewers were fans of westerns or cats, the unlikely pairing of the two created a novel and amusing advertisement.

The success of Herding Cats, in terms of its persuasive appeal, was strong, at least initially. EDS reported that within the first 24 hours after the commercial aired, "eds.com registered more than one million hits."[3] Ratings of the commercial generally were strong. Prior to the game, for instance, a *San Francisco Chronicle* writer claimed, "Several million people tune in each year solely for the commercials, and the spot that will make them chuckle best is for Electronic Data Systems, in the high tech category."[4] After the game, *The Times-Picayune* described it as "Very cool, very creative, very funny," and scored it 9th on a scale of 10-high.[5] *USA Today's* 'Ad Meter' showed the commercial as ranking 10th in its top-10 category.[6]

A less-scientific poll taken of our students and colleagues suggested that although the commercial was quite memorable, what it advertised was not so easily recalled. The common response to the question, "What company or product did the ad promote?" was, "I don't know—some dot-com." This response was not wholly unexpected by some, such as *The New York Times* reporter, Stuart Elliot. Prior to the game, Elliot wrote, "The biggest threat is that consumers will be unable to distinguish one dot-com from another, turning what was intended as a shrewd strategy to be noticed into a market blunder."[7] Our students' and Elliot's comments suggest that the form of the dot-com commercials holds an important key to their persuasive ability. We return to the Herding Cats advertisement later in the chapter and explain just how its form creates and satisfies expectations within those who view it.

THEORETICAL FOCUS: FORM

A classical approach to persuasion like that discussed in the earlier section of this book separates persuasive messages into several components, the two most important of which are substance and form. Early Greek philosophers acknowledged that converting material substances to nonmaterial forms is an inherently human trait. As contemporary rhetorical scholar Dominic LaRusso states:

> They realized that, in order to survive, all individuals must engage in acts of transforming chaos into order and existing order into new forms of order. And in doing so, they must go beyond the data of the senses; they must be able to perceive internal qualities as well as external shapes. They must be able to envision with the mind's eye what they cannot see with the eye of the body.[8]

Form, then, is constituted of a message's internal qualities—its essence, the intangible, psychological meanings an individual assigns to it. In contrast, the substance of a message is contained in the presentation of and actual arguments or informational content within, as perceived by the senses.

One implication of this traditional distinction between form and substance is that much of a meaning of a message arises from the forms that we ascribe to it. The familiar statement, "A house is not a home," illustrates this point. Cement, wood, nails, electrical wiring, plumbing and other building materials are arranged to make a house within which people can reside sheltered from one another and the natural elements. The house becomes a home by virtue of the patterns of meaning we ascribe to the structure. Such notions as safety, privacy, stability, history, love and memories are relatively intangible features that transform a house into a home.

Because form is a psychological process evoked by the presented elements of a message—the social context in which the message occurs—and the receiver's frame of reference, the same substance can evoke different forms. The abortion controversy serves as an excellent example of how humans ascribe quite divergent forms to the same content. All the materials of a human being are contained in a fertilized egg, yet the form ascribed to a fetus marks a fundamental difference between anti-abortion and pro-choice advocates' arguments. Anti-abortion advocates ascribe human form to the fetus; that is, the fetus embodies the essence of what it means to be human—action, thought, emotion and shape—despite its undeveloped state. From this premise, they argue that abortion constitutes murder, and contains all of the moral implications of such an act. Conversely, pro-choice advocates ascribe the potential of human form to the fetus, thus denying its status as a fully human form. From this premise, pro-choice advocates argue that the rights of the mother—who is a fully formed human being—should supersede those of the fetus. As we see from this example, form is a significant aspect of the persuasion process.

From the Symbolist Perspective, form is just as important as words or nonverbal elements in producing effects. As explained in Chapter 6, form frequently signals to the audience an appropriate code by which to read the meaning of a message. Sometimes persuaders strategically structure their messages to obtain a particular persuasive result. Other times, sources structure their messages with nonpersuasive purposes in mind, but the audience interacts with the structure of messages in such a way as to produce persuasive effects.

Kenneth Burke explained that identification can sometimes result from the audience's sharing an understanding of the form of symbolic action. Hence, even when the substance of a communicative act might be complex or even antithetical to a person's beliefs and attitudes, if the form of a message is familiar, that audience member can identify to some degree with a message regardless of its content. A ceremony that follows a ritual pattern with which an observer is familiar might cause that observer to feel a sense of community even if he does not really believe in the doctrine or substance that underlies the ceremony. An ability to identify with the form of a traditional marriage ceremony, for example, might allow an atheist to enjoy the ceremony despite his rejection of the religious content.

In this chapter, we investigate how form contributes to persuasion, especially as explained by the Symbolist Perspective. Following a discussion of the psychology of form that includes Burke's typology of forms, we consider the persuasive effects of two general methods of structuring messages: exposition and narrative. Next, we discuss compliance-gaining techniques as unique forms of persuasion. Following a discussion of ethical concerns about form, we return to Electronic Data Systems' Herding Cats commercial, paying particular attention to its formal properties.

Psychology Of Form

Kenneth Burke contrasts the "psychology of form" with what he calls the "psychology of information."[9] He explains that the allegiance to scientific thinking and rational processes characteristic of modern times has led many to believe that information is intrinsically interesting and that information alone informs, persuades, consoles or is meaningful in some other way. We often act as if raw data alone—all those sensory inputs that we receive as sound waves, light waves, smells and so forth—provides meaning in our lives. However, Burke points out that raw data only becomes meaningful when we process it and allow it to take form around and inside of us. He equates form with psychology itself, noting that information alone works on the principles of surprise and suspense. We anxiously await incoming data and are surprised when it arrives, but what we make of that incoming data is inherently linked to the form that the data takes or that we impose upon it. Imagine, for example, that you wake up from a sound sleep. In your initial seconds of consciousness you move from the suspended state of sleep to the anticipatory state of wakefulness. Your waking confronts you with various sounds, smells, sights and other sensations of the world around you. The first time you experienced wakefulness all these sensations were doubtless a surprise. As you've grown accustomed to waking up, these sensations have begun to take on familiar forms. Hence, you understand the light particles filtering through your window as the sun signaling the beginning of a new day. You hear familiar sounds such as birds singing, signaling the season. The morning weather report issuing from your radio alarm lets you know that it's seven o'clock in the morning, and you form expectations for the remainder of the day and so on. Only occasionally, such as when awakened by a loud thunderclap in the middle of the night, do you feel the surprise and suspense of pure information. Even then, you likely pattern that information quite rapidly in order to make sense of it. The patterning of incoming information such as this is psychology, according to Burke. That form, or patterning, that is essential to human perception and understanding is a familiar theme among contemporary theorists.[10] Understanding the nature of such forming lays the groundwork for understanding how persuasion occurs through form.

Fundamental to the human power to perceive is our ability to select from the constant stream of sensory data that bombards us and to emphasize some of those sensations while ignoring or down playing the importance of others. This process is similar to obtaining a perspective on any scene that we view. For example, as we look out our front door, we have many options from which to select and emphasize in our sight line. We could focus on the sky, the ground, the house across the street, the car parked in front, the tree in the yard, the bird in that tree, the flowering bush at the edge of the lawn, the recycling bin at the curb side or innumerable other objects or vistas. Although we may be aware of all these sights, we tend to focus on some, bringing them into the foreground of our vision, while placing less emphasis on others, letting them act merely as the background for what we have placed in the foreground. This process approximates the process of sight itself, in which our eye registers light and shadow to distinguish the form of any particular object that we zoom in on visually. This process of "foregrounding" and "backgrounding" is essential for us to make meaning of what we see. Otherwise, we would be so overwhelmed with all of the possibilities and so busy coping with all of the alternatives that we would be unable to describe to ourselves or anyone else what it was that we were seeing.

Our other senses work similarly. We are able to hear a variety of sounds all at once. Some of those sounds we relegate to "background noise," while others become the focus of our attention. The sounds that we place in the foreground dominate because those sounds become the basis for how we understand the world around us. When the form we give that world through our selective focus distresses us, we may change our focus. Consequently, many stress reduction techniques intentionally orient the listener to those sounds that are commonly relegated to the background in order to induce more peaceful feelings. For example, relaxation tapes may encourage the listener to focus on the sounds of his or her own breathing or may provide the sounds of the ocean lapping against the shore in gentle waves or may furnish white noise—a sound similar to a television set that has remained on after the network has stopped broadcasting. Once placed in the foreground, these "background noises" encourage a perceptual shift in the person hearing them and, thereby, can alter that person's mood. Smell, touch and taste work similarly, as we constantly select from an infinite variety of sensations those that will be placed in the foreground and those that will be relegated to the background.

Perhaps most interesting about the selectivity with which we perceive and thereby form our world is the way in which the foreground and background work together. If either part were missing, it would be impossible for us to focus. In other words, with no background, we can not determine what belongs in the foreground and vice versa. Moreover, the two reinforce one another. What we choose to be in the foreground depends in large part on what is in the background. If something in the background doesn't seem to fit with what we have in the foreground, we may shift our focus to that incongruous element of the background. Consider, for example, a scene in your home where you are focusing on a conversation with your sister. In the background are all the normal sights, sounds, smells and so on that you associate with the hour before dinner. The dog is lying in the corner. The radio is playing. The rest of your family is moving around in the house. The aroma of a casserole in the oven is intermingling with that smell that you associate with "home." You're vaguely aware of the feel of the upholstery on the chair in which you are sitting. Your eyes wander occasionally to the now familiar pictures hanging on the wall, but you focus your attention on your sister, what she looks like and what she's telling you. The background is appropriate for your conversation. Suddenly the background changes. You hear a sizzling and popping sound at about the same time that your nose detects the unmistakable odor of burning food. The green beans are burning! Something in the background has suddenly grabbed your attention, and it moves to the foreground.

Perceptual shifts that reorient us generally occur because we recognize something out of sync with an otherwise complete and coherent form. The human drive to form the world around us as complete and coherent is often referred to as a principle of perception called *closure*. This principle explains that humans feel uncomfortable with the uncertainty that accompanies gaps, omissions, incongruities or contradictions in our perception. Consequently, we either supply the missing elements or selectively ignore those elements that disrupt our understanding in order to close or complete our understanding. For example, when we see a dotted outline of a figure like a triangle, we may supply the missing ink between the dots so that we can close the picture and see a triangle. Similarly, if we hear the first few bars of a familiar piece of music we may add the remaining musical phrases in our heads, thereby completing the song. On the other hand, we sometimes ignore incongruousor superfluous elements within an incoming message in order to understand it as a coherent whole. For example, we are able to read the misspelled and under punctuated messages of a young child learning to write because we are able to overlook the mistakes as we strive toward closure. When we walk along the beach expecting to smell the salt of the sea, we may ignore or overlook the odor of a nearby garbage can because we want closure for our perception that we are communing with nature.

As the previous examples suggest, the principle of closure implies that we strive to make sense of our environment (both real and symbolic) by finding a coherent message. That coherent message is often influenced by what we expect to find. Burke defines form as "the creation of an appetite in the mind of the auditor, and the adequate satisfying of that appetite."[11] Psychologically, the first few bits of incoming data—sensations, symbols, information—create an expectation in us that we fulfill by patterning the remainder of the data to fit into a form. Thus, what we choose to place in the foreground, what we decide to relegate to the background, what details we fill in and what details we overlook are all influenced by our initial expectations. For example, as we watch a videotape that we've been told is a good comedy, we may focus on the humor, search for the funny parts, overlook the tragic episodes that underlie the humor and reflect on our own similar experiences that made us laugh, all in an effort to satisfy our expectations for humor.

Burke and others list a number of common expectations among human beings that seem to guide their forming of messages into patterns. A list of some common expectations is discussed by rhetorical theorist Richard Gregg. Gregg argues that there are six fundamental patterns of human perception in our processing of symbolic data: edging or formulating boundaries, rhythm, association, classification, abstraction and hierarchy.[12]

Edging occurs when we pattern things by contrast, for example, looking for polar opposites by noting the difference between light and dark. Rhythm patterns according to pulses, for example, the meter and rhyme of poetic prose or the beat of music. Association patterns according to similarities that arise from our recognition that two or more phenomena are alike or close in time or space. Classification is an outgrowth of the contrasting that occurs with edging and the comparison that occurs with association, allowing us to understand something as part of a group or class. Abstraction occurs as the result of classification so that we can symbolize about the group or class without imagining particular instances. Hierarchy patterns by placing various phenomena on scales of best to worst, highest to lowest, first to last and so on as we look for the relationship among phenomena.

These fundamental patterns for perception may sound familiar as they echo the types of common reasoning discussed in Chapter 3 and various figurative devices discussed in Chapter 7. For our purposes in this chapter, they are important because they catalogue common expectations regarding form. Receivers of persuasive messages are inclined to find contrasts, comparisons, rhythms, hierarchies and the like. Those inclinations help explain why and how an audience identifies with any particular message.

Building on his notion of the psychology of form, Kenneth Burke provides a useful list of the types of form that many different messages embody.[13] He lists five major forms that messages may reflect and audiences may follow as they strive to identify with a text. Any particular message may reflect one or more of these five forms, and any particular audience member may impose or recognize one or several of the forms as the pattern of an incoming message.

Syllogistic progressions are patterns that advance step by step so that a particular ending is required. Anytime that we move systematically from accepted premises to a conclusion that may be inferred from those premises, we are following a syllogistic progression. A clear example is the case of a proof in geometry that begins with axioms that are accepted as true, proceeds through corollaries that are implied by the axioms and ends with a new geometric principle. But syllogistic progressions are not limited to formal, mathematical proofs. Burke likens this type of form to a mystery story in which all the clues are revealed in an orderly fashion so that the reader will inevitably solve the mystery. Thus, whenever we attend to a set of symbols by searching for the " logical" conclusion or inference that would emerge once we accept the "givens," we are following the pattern of a syllogistic progression.

Burke's second type of form, a *qualitative progression*, follows a pattern in which the presence of a particular quality, mood or feeling prepares us to accept another quality, mood or feeling. Unlike the syllogistic progression in which we anticipate the next step in the argument or the next event in the plot, a qualitative progression moves us through a series of psychological states almost unconsciously. For example, the tension created by a plot that establishes conflict subtly prepares us to feel relief when that conflict is solved. We may not anticipate that relief, but we welcome it as we experience it. Similarly, as we feel urgency and outrage listening to a description of the effects of poverty on the millions of children who live without adequate food, shelter and care, we may naturally adopt an investigative frame of mind, searching for the causes of these deplorable conditions. We might just as easily move into a state of relief as we contemplate solutions, so a discussion of effects doesn't cause us to anticipate a particular course for the argument to follow so much as it prepares us for the psychological state that we experience next. We more easily recognize the appropriateness of a qualitative progression as we reflect on how we reacted to a message rather than as we anticipate what will come next. This characteristic helps to distinguish a qualitative from a syllogistic progression. Just examining a message alone may not uncover a qualitative progression. Equally important is discovering the audience reaction to that message. If it is clear that a person attending to that message moves through a series of moods or feelings that seem to follow one another appropriately, then the message will likely reflect that same pattern.

Repetitive form, according to Burke, "is the consistent maintaining of a principle under new guises."[14] Unlike the two previous progressions that move an audience from one intellectual or feeling place to another, repetitive forms deepen or enrich an audience's understanding or appreciation of the phenomenon they are apprehending. Seeing a character exhibit the same character traits in diverse situations establishes and reinforces a complex identity of that character in the audience's mind. The rhythm of speech or prose that is repetitive in its structure may intensify the feelings or beliefs that are introduced in that message, as in the case of Franklin Roosevelt's repetitive phrases describing the Japanese attacks throughout the Pacific in his "War Address" discussed in Chapter 7. Similarly, a repetitive form, such as rhyming, may help an audience anticipate what will happen, be said or be meaningful next, as is the case with many advertising slogans and jingles. As Burke explains, repetitive forms help an audience stay focused by keeping the audience's attention centered on the main idea. A message may exhibit such repetitiveness or audience members themselves may impose repetitiveness on a message by hearing or seeing each new part of a message as an elaboration or repetition of an earlier theme. This second option may be familiar as it is commonly used by students confronted by difficult material. Once we get the gist of an essay or book, especially if the reading is difficult, we may return to that main idea as a way of centering our understanding as we move through additional material that is unfamiliar to us.

Burke's fourth category of form is *conventional form*. While progressive and repetitive forms operate at a subconscious level, with the audience being unaware that they are responding to or imposing them, conventional forms almost announce their presence. We are aware of the form because it is so familiar to us that it has become conventional. Most rituals follow conventional form. We immediately recognize the pattern of a marriage ceremony, or a funeral dirge or a Christian confessional, for example. Depending on our cultural and educational experience, we may just as easily recognize the form of a sonnet, a problem-solution speech, a burlesque show, a pep rally or the opening of the Olympics. Sometimes the situation itself guides our expectations toward a particular form. Other times the beginning of the message itself dictates such expectations. Early in our confrontation with a conventional form, our expectations for what will come next are set, and we derive pleasure from watching the symbolic activity unfold according to those expectations. If the form is interrupted or changed in some way, we may experience real frustration. For example, many churchgoers object when familiar religious rituals are changed to accommodate new ideas or procedures, such as the introduction of folk masses in Catholic churches in the late 1960's and early 1970's. Those objections can be explained by the appeal of conventional form. Conventional forms are easily described because they are familiar, and we simply know the steps in the pattern either because of our repeated experience with such forms or because we have intentionally learned these forms.

Finally, Burke discusses *minor or incidental forms*. This category refers primarily to figures of speech and thought like those discussed in Chapter 7. Unlike the other four, these forms appear episodically within a message, acting almost like small, independent units of form. Because of our earlier discussion of such forms, we will not elaborate on them again here. However, later in the chapter, we examine a relatively new line of contemporary persuasion research, compliance-gaining strategies, as exemplary of minor forms.

Now that the psychology of form is clearer, we turn our attention to the relationship between the form and structure of messages. We refer to form as evoked by the structure of a message. The structure, however, might or might not reflect the form that an audience ascribes to that message.

MESSAGE STRUCTURES

Because formal patterns are essential to human perception, it is not surprising that those interested in the effects of various messages have exhibited an interest in the influence that message structures have on form. A common principle of rhetoric from at least the time of Plato states that any public message should have a structure that resembles an animal—a head, a body and a foot.[15] Other classical theorists, such as Aristotle, argued that any single argument should consist of two parts: statement and proof.[16] Roman theorists, such as Cicero and Quintilian, expanded concerns regarding the structure of messages by investigating the strategic importance of the arrangement of arguments within a persuasive speech. The unknown author of a Roman text, *Rhetorica ad Herennium*, for example, likened the arrangement of arguments within a message to a military commander's arraying of soldiers on the battlefield.[17] Later theorists built upon these classical foundations in prescribing appropriate organizational tools for the persuader.

Contemporary social scientific investigations of the persuasive effects of organization within messages typically confirm the importance of organization.[18] In one study, subjects were tested for the persuasive effects of organization. The subjects were new recruits to the armed forces. They were divided into four groups, each of which was presented reasons justifying the United States' involvement in the Korean conflict. One group heard a poorly organized presentation with an explicit conclusion. One heard a poorly organized presentation with no conclusion drawn. A third group heard a well-organized speech with a conclusion, and a fourth heard a well-organized speech without a conclusion. The well-organized presentations were better understood than the poorly organized ones. In addition, the researchers found that stating the conclusion was helpful for less intelligent people.[19]

Just what constitutes a well organized presentation has been the subject of much writing. Contemporary treatments of the structure of messages typically divide the subject into two major categories: expository patterns and narrative patterns. *Exposition* reveals a persuader's reasons in a manner similar to Burke's syllogistic progression, while *narration* tells a story that follows a form similar to Burke's qualitative progression.

Exposition

Although exposition is usually associated with nonpersuasive or informative discourse, most early treatments of persuasion, such as Aristotle's, emphasize exposition as the preferred structure for persuasive messages. Aristotle defined two basic parts to any persuasive appeal—statement and proof.[20] The statement was the conclusion to which the speaker hoped to gain the audience's assent, while the proof included any and all elaborative material that a persuader offered in support of his conclusion. Straightforward sales talks, many editorials and a number of documentaries that expose social problems by intercutting interviews with statistics and visualized examples follow an expository pattern. Such patterns present the audience with information that arouses their curiosity and sense of urgency and then satisfies both by elaborating on the various issues that are raised. In a discussion of the persuasive impact of documentary films that follow an expository form, film theorist Bill Nichols explains that documentaries make "a tacit proposal to the viewer" by invoking and promising to gratify "a desire to know."[21]

Those interested in exposition have addressed a number of practical concerns. First, some researchers have investigated how often the main ideas or arguments within an exposition should be repeated. Advertisers argue that the number three is magical and advocate repeating the name of a product or an advertising slogan three to four times within any particular commercial spot.[22] Most public speaking texts offer similar advice leading to the familiar dictum that a public speaker should tell the audience what she will tell them, tell them, and then tell them what she told them.

Second, some researchers focus on how the exposition should be arranged. Most public speaking textbooks that include a chapter on persuasion, as well as writing manuals, advertising copy books and others include lists of typical patterns of arrangement that persuasive messages may follow. Among the most commonly suggested patterns are the problem-solution pattern and the motivated sequence. Borrowing from the work on reflective thinking by John Dewey, communication scholars consistently propose a two-part arrangement called problem-solution in which the persuader first discusses the problem by defining it, showing its causes and describing its effects, and proceeds by describing a solution to that problem. Psychologically, the pattern arouses urgency within an audience as the problem is developed and then satisfies that urgency by offering a solution. A similar, but alternative pattern was developed with the aid of contemporary motivation theories by Alan Monroe, another professor of communication.[23] Called the motivated sequence, this pattern has been particularly useful for sales personnel. The motivated sequence begins by capturing attention, then creates needs in the audience by describing problems or unmet desires, follows with a simple statement of how those needs may be met, then visualizes the results of satisfying the needs by vividly describing the results of meeting those needs and concludes with a call to action. The widespread teaching of problem-solution patterns and the motivated sequence makes them useful as guides for describing the structure of many explicitly persuasive messages.

One feature common to exposition is that within this type of message structure, the persuader's conclusions tend to be explicit. In other words, the audience is not left to their own devices for making sense of the message. Early social scientific research regarding the organization of persuasive messages suggests that this characteristic of exposition makes the structure quite effective. Such research found that generally more explicitly stated conclusions are more persuasive. A variety of social scientific studies seem to confirm the idea that it is better to draw conclusions for the audience and thus increase the likelihood that they will understand what a persuader wants them to do.[24] Exceptions to this generalization include situations in which the persuasive message is very simple or when the audience is likely to be hostile toward the persuader's goals.[25]

Another topic that intrigued social science researchers involves the order in which one presents arguments or reasons for a persuasive case. In particular, researchers were interested in primacy and recency—which order of appearance, first or last in a message, contributes more to its persuasiveness. A host of research indicates that arguments or appeals presented at the beginning or at the end of a communication will be remembered better than arguments presented in the middle.[26] This phenomenon is often referred to as the loss of the middle message. More interesting to researchers and practitioners of persuasion is whether first or last is a better position for the strongest arguments. As Karlins and Abelson note in their review of persuasion research, "early experimental evidence pointed to a primacy effect in persuasive appeals: the message presented first seemed to be the more powerful in changing behavior."[27] However, later experiments suggest that the last message, argument or persuasive appeal heard by the audience was most effective.[28] The conflict in studies led Rosnow and Robinson to conclude:

> Instead of a general 'law' of primacy, or recency, we have today an assortment of miscellaneous variables, some of which tend to produce primacy, others of which, to produce recency. Still others produce either order effect, depending on their utilization or temporal placement in a two-sided communication. Nonsalient, controversial topics, interesting subject matter, and highly familiar issues tend toward primacy. Salient topics, uninteresting subject matter, and moderately unfamiliar issues tend to yield recency. If arguments for one side are perceived more strongly than arguments for the other, then the side with the stronger arguments has the advantage—'strength' being a free variable. Another free variable is 'reinforcement.' When incidents that are perceived as rewarding or satisfying are initiated close in time to a persuasive communication, opinions tend to change in the direction of the arguments closer to the rewarding incident. When an incident is dissatisfying or punishing, opinions tend to change in the direction of the arguments farther in time from it.[29]

Much of the evidence about primacy and recency was gathered in the context of studies concerned with one-sided or two-sided presentations. Researchers were concerned about whether or not the order of presenting reasons for and against some proposition affects the audience's reaction. Others wondered if it is simply more effective not to mention the other side at all. Wayne Thompson provides an apt summary of the research concerning one-sided versus two-sided presentations:

1. The two-sided speech is more effective when the listeners have at least a high school education and when the weight of the evidence clearly is on one side.
2. The one-sided presentation is more effective when the listeners have not completed high school.
3. The one-sided presentation is more effective when the listeners already favor the thesis.
4. The two-sided presentation is more effective when the listeners are opposed to the speaker's position.
5. The two-sided message has an immunizing effect against a succeeding speech that is opposed to the thesis.[30]

NARRATIVE

A second common structure for messages is narrative. Narrative generally refers to the pattern of a story. As religion scholar William Doty observes: "Narrative provides a mode of ordering significant events, that is, a plot, of experienced or ideal existence."[31] A number of contemporary rhetorical theorists have pointed out the importance of such story-telling for persuasion. Walter Fisher argues that narrative forms provide the most important structure for messages to inform or persuade us about important moral and public policy questions.[32] W. Lance Bennett, a student of legal communication, asserts that most attorneys and the juries to whom they speak engage more in story-telling than in presenting carefully structured arguments.[33] Joseph Campbell believes in the importance of those master stories, called myths, for the self-persuasion that we all do as we struggle to find meaning in our own lives.[34]

Unlike exposition that follows a form of statement and proof, narrative form follows a dramatic sequence in which characters take actions within carefully constructed scenes. Narratives provide the concrete details of a dramatic sequence that begins by setting a scene and introducing one or more characters and then follows the character's actions. Typically, narrative form follows a rising and falling pattern in which the action rises, or increases in frequency and intensity, to a point of climax and then falls, or decreases in frequency and intensity to a point of anticlimax. Narrative action usually involves a struggle between one character and another, between a character and himself or herself or between a character and the scene. Depending on the complexity of the story, we may find multiple characters, multiple scenes and multiple actions. Any narrative has at least one plot line, a sequence of rising and falling action. More complex narratives include a variety of subplots, additional sequences of rising and falling action that augment and complicate the main story.

The expectations aroused by narrative differ from the desire to know commonly provoked by exposition. Narratives do not announce their conclusions and follow with support but, rather, announce the beginning of a dramatic sequence and then follow with action and resolution that reveals a conclusion. Film theorist Bill Nichols supplies a useful description of this process:

> "Two men set out across a valley." This single sentence, even in isolation, announces itself as the harbinger of narrative. The trace of narrative can probably be best isolated in the sentence's evocation of a promise, namely, the promise to continue or develop its premise....
>
> "Two men set out across the valley, had many adventures, and returned safely." This single sentence announces itself as an embryonic narrative, too stunted to be considered artful yet somehow registering as a member of the genus *Narrative*. The premise (of departure, quest) has been developed and clothed with a conclusion, however scantily.[35]

While the expository form satisfies an audience's expectations by gratifying their desire to know and understand the steps by which a conclusion was reached, the narrative form satisfies an audience's expectations to know what happened, to find the conclusion. As Nichols points out, some narratives make the conclusion explicit, but an audience can follow a narrative form without being teased by the conclusion ahead of time. The audience experiences a sort of intrinsic pleasure following the action without knowing how things will turn out, so long as eventually some resolution is reached. Yet, even the resolution of a narrative may not be it's ultimate point. Audiences may be left to determine the moral of the story themselves. The form may be complete without ever announcing the moral of the story.

Just as some writers have discussed a number of common expository patterns so have others described a number of common narrative patterns.[36] Three common narrative patterns are myth, folk tale and fable. Mythical stories typically deal with the big questions of life such as who am I, why am I here or where am I going. Within myths, actions usually occur outside of everyday time and space. Mythical stories contain scenes in a distant past, a projected future, a faraway land or a completely different dimension. In addition, mythical characters are frequently larger than life. Heroes and heroines and villains and villainesses may possess supernatural powers that give them superhuman qualities and allow them to engage in fantastic actions. The pattern of the plot within a classic myth usually involves three episodes: separation, initiation and return.[37] Movement through these episodes within a myth tells a story that is universally applicable, a story that deals with human life generally.

Because myths often provide the great master stories from which other stories and many rituals are derived, we should consider the structure of the classic myth in some detail. Probably the most extensive work in this area comes from Joseph Campbell.[38] According to Campbell, mythical stories begin with episodes of separation or departure. The hero or heroine is summoned to adventure by another character or some element in the scene. The heroic figure may refuse the call, but eventually embarks on a journey or quest into uncharted territory facing unknown dangers. First the heroic figure encounters a protective figure, often an old man or woman, who arms the main character with some token(s) of supernatural power to assist him or her on the journey. Shortly thereafter, our heroic figure crosses the first threshold by entering a new and alien scene. The main character may cross a river, scale a wall, walk through a gate, open a door or enter a new dimension of time and space by crossing the threshold. Once across the threshold, the heroic figure finds a whole new world that operates according to rules and principles typically unfamiliar to the scene left behind. Campbell explains that "instead of conquering or conciliating the power of the threshold," the heroic figure "is swallowed into the unknown, and would appear to have died."[39] This sequence of events thus separates the main character from his or her former existence and sets the stage for the next part of the plot.

Another series of events initiates the heroic figure in a myth into the newly entered world. A heroic character generally follows a "road of trials" and endures all manner of ordeals with the aid of those supernatural objects furnished by the helpers during the separation part of the story. According to Campbell, "the ultimate adventure, when all the barriers and ogres have been overcome, is commonly represented as a mystical marriage of the triumphant hero-soul with the Queen Goddess of the World" or a similar union of the heroine with the "King of Kings." [40] But the bliss of that union is soon broken by the hero or heroine's recognition of all that fails to measure up to the ultimate purity of the God or Goddess with whom he or she has united. Consequently, the heroic figure feels unworthy in the eyes of the Father or Mother character whose wrath the main character fears and on whose mercy the heroic character depends. At this point the heroic character must accomplish "atonement" according to Campbell. Then the heroic figure comes to realize that the Mother and Father are one, that wrath and mercy go together and that what seemed to be contradictions are merely paradoxes and within them peace exists. Such recognition leads the heroic character to "the ultimate boon," in which he or she experiences true inner peace and outer satisfaction, filled with contentment and joy. To phrase the experience in terms of the typical Judeo-Christian story, the heroic figure is "in heaven."

It might seem as if we have reached the end of the story, but instead the return remains as the final chapter in the classic myth. Not surprisingly, the return begins with a refusal on the part of the heroic figure. As Campbell explains, "when the hero-quest has been accomplished, through penetration to the source, or through the grace of some male or female, human or animal, personification, the adventurer still must return with his life-transmuting trophy."[41] Something within the magical world of the journey may frustrate the return, or the simple bliss of being there may inhibit the heroic figure's destiny to return. Eventually, however, the main character embarks on a magic flight home aided by his or her supernatural powers or by some supernatural force from the outside world. Regardless of how the heroic figure makes the journey home, a crucial point is the crossing of the return threshold. For the heroic character has been immersed in an unknown land that the reality from which he or she came usually treats as darkness. Yet, in that darkness the heroic figure found the light of transcendental bliss. Once returned, the problem for the heroic figure is how to communicate his or her experience to assist those who have not crossed the threshold recently or ever. In the face of human pettiness, wickedness or even ridicule and humiliation, the heroic character, must confront reality. If the heroic figure survives the return, then he or she becomes "the master of two worlds," with the freedom to pass back and forth across the great divide, carrying the mysteries of peace and fulfillment from the unknown world in which the heroic character journeyed to the everyday world from which he or she came. The hero's or heroine's access to the miracles of the fantastic world in which he or she journeyed provides him or her the "freedom to live," both humbly and confidently and to assist the lives of others.

Examples of the classic myth just described abound. The story of Buddha, Jesus of Nazareth and a number of other heroes of the major religions of the world illustrate this pattern. Similarly, the plot lines of novels from J. R. Tolkein's *The Hobbit* to Janet Auel's *Clan of the Cave Bear* follow a mythical structure. Likewise many popular Hollywood movies, from *Star Wars* to *Raiders of the Lost Ark*, reflect this story line. As Campbell and others have pointed out, so too does the inward journey of psychotherapy and healing from emotional trauma require patients to tell their stories in forms that mirror the stages of classic mythology.[42]

The structure of myths provides a pattern that is emulated in part or as a whole in many other narratives. Folk tales tend to be tied to a particular locale or subculture but include many of the same episodes as myths.[43] While folk tales may include mythic dimensions in terms of characters, scenes or actions, they may just as easily entail more ordinary actions by characters who are more like everyday people. Formally, however, folk tales usually follow plot lines similar to myths, indirectly exposing the values and morals of a culture and thus providing guidelines by which that culture can live. Hence, the story of "Hansel and Gretel" or the tale of *Rip Van Winkle* or even the popular *Wizard of Oz* exhibit parts of the story line of a classic myth, adapted to more ordinary people and events than our sacred and universal stories but still embodying a similar pattern.

Like folk tales, fables are tied to particular cultures for their stories but frequently derive their plot lines from myth. Fables differ from folk tales in that they make the moral of the story explicit.[44] Usually we see the moral of the story exposed directly at the end of the story, thus adding a dimension to the familiar form followed by any story and especially by folk tales. Aesop's fables and the parables of the New Testament provide numerous examples of fables. We return to the subject of folk tales and fables in our discussion of myth in Chapter 13, where we explain the mythic foundations for our cultural ideology. For now it is enough to recognize the structure of these stories.

Narrative patterns can provide the structure for all or a part of any message. Most instances of implicit persuasion such as films, especially Hollywood films, television shows and many novels structure their persuasive potential within an overall narrative pattern. However, even more explicit types of persuasion such as traditional public speeches, editorials or documentaries aimed at raising an audience's social conscience may include narrative patterns within an otherwise expository structure. For example, anecdotes, relatively brief stories that illustrate a point, are a common staple for public speakers. As we mentioned at the beginning of Chapter 3, former President Ronald Reagan was well known for his clever use of anecdotes in his addresses to the nation.[45] Similarly, short dramatic vignettes are common means of illustration for news broadcasts and journalistic exposes that deal with social problems.

Less obvious, but equally important, narrative forms, especially the pattern of a classic myth, provide the structure for many rituals as well. While some theorists equate ritual with formality, others note that rituals reflect the structure of society.[46] Either way, it is clear that rituals are structured. Thus, it is not surprising that Campbell and others would observe that entering a temple or sanctuary mirrors crossing the threshold. Engaging in communion or participating in confession echoes the episodes of uniting with the Goddess or God and finding atonement. Thus, some of the persuasive potential of rituals—our sense of identification when we participate in these rituals—is attributable to the pleasure we derive from following what happens in the narrative structure of a classic myth.

As theorists have investigated narrative forms, two fundamental criteria for a "good" narrative have evolved. The leading narrative theorist in communication, Walter Fisher, refers to these criteria as "narrative probability" and "narrative fidelity."[47] A story has narrative probability if it is coherent or hangs together, if the sequence of events sounds like a story and if there is harmony between character and action. If an audience notices that a character in a story acts peculiarly and can find no clues earlier in the story for the character's behavior, then they may dismiss it as being improbable. Many bad movies suffer from this sort of problem. If the scene has not been appropriately set ahead of time, viewers may be unable to figure out the motivation for a particular character's actions and consequently dismiss the whole plot as improbable. If the psychological state created in the mind of the witness to the story is followed by another that just doesn't seem to fit, then the story may lack narrative probability. Consider, for example, an old joke which begins by describing a papa bear and mama bear sitting in their living room. The mama bear says, "I think I'll go take a bath." Papa bear says "OK" and putters around the house. Meanwhile, he hears splashing and gurgling and mama bear singing in the bathroom. Hours later he enters the bathroom to see what's going on. Mama bear is sitting in a tub of water without any suds. She catches papa bear's eye and asks him to hand her the soap. He replies, "No soap, radio." Most audience's for this joke stare at the teller who laughs and asks, "Don't you get it, no soap, radio?" What is there to get? Actually the joke is on the receiver for expecting a punch line and not getting it. As a joke, this can sometimes work, but as a story it fails dismally because the audience has been prepared, is full of anticipation and receives only nonsense. The "story" lacks narrative probability.

A story has narrative fidelity if it reflects or mirrors real life. This does not restrict the story from including magic or being set in a fantastic place that does not or has not ever existed. Narrative fidelity refers more to whether or not the story is faithful to life as we understand it (past, present or future) than to whether the details of the story are exactly what happened. Consider, for example, a story that has been retold like a folk tale for years in the family of one of the authors of this book.

> When my younger sister was about three, she was learning how to eat at the dinner table. One evening we had hamburgers and everyone was pouring ketchup on their burgers. At some point, we noticed that my younger sister had poured nearly the whole bottle of ketchup onto her plate. My father asked: "Doris, why did you do that?!" Her answer was simple: "I said 'whoa,' but it just kept coming."

Apart from the obvious connection that Doris had made to the Westerns we watched on television where the cowboys said "whoa" and their horses halted, this story can help to explain narrative fidelity. Is the story accurate? Maybe not. Doris may have been two or four or even five when the incident occurred. The family might have been eating lunch rather than dinner. Doris' father might have said something else besides what the family remembers. So the story may not be entirely accurate. Yet the story does seem true to life. Something like that actually did happen. Young children do struggle with understanding what phenomena they have symbolic power over versus which phenomena they must try to physically control. The story is probably close enough to the truth, therefore, to meet the standard of narrative fidelity.

Both narrative probability and narrative fidelity are formal characteristics. Narrative probability is established when the form of the story itself seems complete—when the story provides us a coherent picture and a fitting sequence of events, thus satisfying our need for closure. Narrative fidelity, on the other hand, is dependent on our recognition that the pattern of the story reflects or is applicable to a pattern of experience in real life. Anthropologists sometimes refer to the pattern of experience in real life as the "deep structure" of society and the pattern in a message as the "surface structure."[48] The concern for congruence between surface and deep structures expressed by the criterion of narrative fidelity thus satisfies our human need to repeat the familiar.

COMPLIANCE-GAINING

Earlier in this chapter we note Burke's suggestion that audiences respond to minor forms as well as to more encompassing progressions that are syllogistic or qualitative and conventional and repetitive forms. These minor forms act like small, independent forms that appear within larger messages that may exhibit some other type of structure. One perspective from which to investigate such minor forms is provided by Burke, who concentrates on minor forms that are figures of speech and thought such as those discussed in Chapter 7. Another perspective for understanding minor forms that we find useful is provided by a number of contemporary communication researchers who study what people say when they are trying to influence others.

When we think about persuasive messages, especially those that are explicit such as arguments with our spouses or interactions with salespeople, we may not find fully developed expositions or narratives. Instead, we encounter short conversations or even single sentences that influence us in one way or another. Yet these short units of discourse follow some sort of pattern that we perceive as familiar. For example, we readily recognize when our parents "lay a guilt trip" on us for not visiting them often enough. Also, we may recognize a familiar sales pitch by an unknown telephone solicitor. Probably we have among our repertoire of persuasive strategies a number of self-contained strategies that take on a form that is familiar to us. "If she says that, I'll respond this way." "If he asks about that, I'll sally back with this response."

Many of the brief, self-contained messages just described work in part because of their formal appeal. In other words, a particular statement elicits a particular response, because we have become socialized to experience certain expectations when a particular kind of statement is made that can only be satisfied by a certain kind of response. Much communication research in the last fifteen years focuses on these types of interactions. That research has labeled those strategies "compliance-gaining behaviors."[49]

A major thrust of contemporary research regarding compliance-gaining behaviors provides a taxonomy of these behaviors. Those who first explored these message strategies as well as many researchers to date depended on a taxonomy developed by two sociologists, Gerald Marwell and David Schmitt.[50] The list of compliance-gaining behaviors identified by Marwell and Schmitt provides a standard illustration of what is included under this heading and thus provides a useful taxonomy of the minor forms that are common to persuasive communication (see Table 9.1). A variety of other lists of compliance-gaining techniques have emerged from such diverse quarters as the study of childhood development and international negotiation and bargaining. What is common to them all, however, is a concern for the form that an attempt to gain compliance takes.

In Table 9.1, compliance-gaining techniques may seem to include more than form. Surely telling someone that they will feel better about themselves if they study more entails a different content than telling someone they can no longer drive the car if they don't study. Researchers in this area point out that taxonomies like the one by Marwell and Schmitt "include both the basis for the appeal (e.g., pride) and the form of the appeal (e.g., altercasting)."[51] Thus, as was the case with figures of thought and figures of speech, compliance-gaining techniques blur the distinction between form and content.

We think that treating these techniques as forms is sensible because people tend to use the techniques almost ritualistically, as familiar patterns for attempting to get what they want. A number of researchers in this area point out that conversational patterns, such as those revealed in a list of compliance-gaining behaviors, reflect the cognitive structures inside the people who use them as well as the social structures common to the situations in which they emerge.[52] Their idea is that as we develop and mature, we try out increasingly sophisticated patterns of influencing others.

Table 9.1

Sixteen Compliance-Gaining Techniques with Examples from Family Situations

From Miller, Boster, Roloff and Siebold, 40; Marwell and Schmitt, 357-358.

Promise	(If you comply, I will reward you.) "You offer to increase Dick's allowance if he increases his studying."
Threat	(If you do not comply, I will punish you.) "You threaten to forbid Dick the use of the car if he does not increase his studying."
Expertise (positive)	(If you comply, you will be rewarded because of "the nature of things.") "You point out to Dick that if he gets good grades he will be able to get into a good college and get a good job."
Expertise (negative)	(If you do not comply, you will be punished because of "the nature of things.") "You point out to Dick that if he does not get good grades he will not be able to get into a good college or get a good job."
Liking	(Actor is friendly and helpful to get target in "good frame of mind" so that he will comply with the request.) "You try to be as friendly and pleasant as possible to get Dick in the 'right frame of mind' before asking him."
Pre-Giving	(Actor rewards target before requesting compliance.) "You raise Dick's allowance and tell him you now expect him to study."
Aversive Stimulation	(Actor continuously punishes the target making cessation contingent on compliance.) "You forbid Dick the use of the car and tell him he will not be allowed to drive until he studies more."
Debt	(You owe me compliance because of past favors.) "You point out that you have sacrificed and saved to pay for Dick's education and that he owes it to you to get good enough grades to get into a good college."
Moral Appeal	(You are immoral if you do not comply.) "You tell Dick that it is morally wrong for anyone not to get as good grades as he can and that he should study more."
Self-Feeling (positive)	(You will feel better about yourself if you comply.) "You tell Dick he will feel proud if he gets himself to study more."
Self-Feeling (negative)	(You will feel worse about yourself if you do not comply.) "You tell Dick he will feel ashamed of himself if he gets bad grades."
Altercasting (positive)	(A person with "good" qualities would comply.) "You tell Dick that since he is a mature and intelligent boy he naturally will want to study more and get good grades."

Altercasting (negative)	(Only a person with "bad" qualities would not comply.) "You tell Dick that only someone very childish does not study as he should."
Altruism	(I need your compliance very badly, so do it for me.) "You tell Dick that you really want very badly for him to get into a good college and that you wish he should study more as a personal favor to you."
Esteem (positive)	(People you value will think better of you if you comply.) "You tell Dick that the whole family will be very proud of him if he gets good grades."
Esteem (negative)	(People you value will think worse of you if you do not comply.) "You tell Dick that the whole family will be very disappointed in him if he gets poor grades."

French psychologist and philosopher Jean Piaget was among the first contemporary theorists to investigate the communicative behaviors of children as they developed. He pointed out that children begin merely imitating communicative patterns and talking only to themselves, but by the time they begin to interact with others in games and social activities (about age seven) they start to use patterns that take another into account.[53] Delia and Clark describe this development process as a matter of a child's increasing ability to take the perspective of the other and to adapt their forming of the compliance-gaining message to that other's perspective.[54] In a study of the compliance-gaining techniques used by children in kindergarten to twelfth grade, Delia, Kline and Burelson arranged strategies in a hierarchy according to the subject's level of sophistication regarding perspective taking. The resulting hierarchy moved from unelaborated requests (e.g., "Could I have a party, please?") through bribes (e.g., "If you let me have a party, I'll make something that my father likes to eat.") to elaboration of specific consequences of accepting the request to one with characteristics of the target (e.g., "You've been saying you wanted to get to know my friends better. If you let me have a party, you can get to know them.").[55] Studies such as this treat compliance-gaining strategies as characteristic forms for a short persuasive message or a unit of a longer persuasive conversation.

Besides the general structural nature of compliance-gaining behaviors, these techniques frequently embody the same content while only changing the form. Clark and Delia provide an excellent example when they review the work of discourse analyst Susan Ervin-Tripp.

> Ervin-Tripp has specified five forms an imperative may take: (1) interrogative ("Gotta match"), (2) imperative ("Gimme a match"), (3) imbedded imperative ("Could you gimme a match"), (4) statement of need or desire ("I need a match"), and (5) statement of external condition ("There aren't any matches here").[56]

Obviously, the content of the message (give me a match) is the same in all five forms. Thus, compliance-gaining strategies are often distinguished from one another solely on the basis of the form that the request, threat, promise or whatever takes.

Much of the research regarding compliance-gaining centers on what types of personalities are prone to use which techniques, whether or not males and females differ in their preferred use of techniques, how different situations influence which technique is used and so on. Consequently, much of the work to date yields rich descriptions of how people attempt to persuade. Relatively little research concerns which techniques are most effective, since it appears that effectiveness is highly dependent on the situation and the people involved. A notable exception to this trend is sustained investigation concerning a very common persuasive form known as the " foot-in-the-door" technique.

Foot-in-the-door (FID) research investigates the persuasive potential of sequencing requests such as the persuader beginning with a small request and following with larger requests until finally she or he secures the target's compliance.[57] The first, minimal request is, of course, like getting one's foot in the door to try to make a sale in a one-on-one persuasive encounter. An early study of this technique began by asking subjects to answer a few questions about household products they had in their home.[58] Subjects were contacted later and asked to allow a team of researchers to visit their homes and classify the household products they found there. The researchers found that those who had complied with the initial request were more likely to comply with the second request than those who had not been contacted with the first request. Subsequent studies confirm the general inclination of people to comply once they have let someone "in the door;" however, the nature of the initial request, the timing and level of sequencing and a number of other factors influence just how often this technique increases compliance. Still, the existence of trial products, telephone sales strategies that begin by asking merely informational questions and a host of other standard sales ploys suggest that everyday persuaders understand and have some confidence in this particular persuasive strategy.

As mentioned earlier, knowledge of compliance-gaining behaviors is particularly useful when we are confronted with messages that do not seem to fall into the other types of patterns we have described. Interpersonal conflicts and conversations and bargaining and negotiation situations are prime areas for investigation. However, even in more public arenas such as sales talks or direct persuasive appeals by public speakers, we can observe compliance-gaining strategies.

ETHICS OF FORM AND STRUCTURE

As with other aspects of persuasion within a Symbolist Perspective, form and structure present a number of ethical questions. Because message structures tend to mirror the forms to which human beings typically respond and which they seek in their general processes of perception and cognition, choices by persuaders about whether or not to use expositive or narrative form are not likely to raise ethical problems related to the preservation of an audience's integrity as human beings. However, choices about the particulars of either an expository or a narrative pattern can raise ethical questions.

Among the choices that persuaders must make about either expository or narrative patterns is how explicit to make the conclusions of a message. Put simply, should the persuader tell the audience what he or she hopes will be concluded from the message? Because so much persuasion from the Symbolist Perspective is implicit and unintentional, it may be too stringent to demand that persuaders always inform their audiences of the conclusions they hope will be drawn. However, when persuasion is the ultimate aim of a message maker, we can reasonably expect persuaders to consider the structure of their messages just as they consider the verbal and nonverbal symbols in terms of the ethical standards we outline in Chapter 6. Unfortunately, just the opposite occurs on many occasions when persuaders use message structures designed to obscure rather than illuminate their purposes.

A good example of such an ethical question arising about the organization of messages occurred with the U.S. Government during World War II. The Office of War Information's propaganda policy directive advised the propagandist to withhold eplicit conclusions when: (1) There was a possibility that the audience might on its own stumble on the conclusion; (2) The validity of an explicit argument might be questioned; (3) The audience was being asked to take risks, and they might resent a forthright request; (4) The consequences of the argument were not known, and the propagandist did not want to take full responsibility for them.[59] This directive avoids, rather than embraces, ethical responsibility.

Another area in which ethical questions arise emerges from the psychology of form discussed earlier in this chapter. Because audiences use the initial part of a message to frame their expectations for what will follow, persuaders should consider how the structure of their messages create and satisfy expectations. Expository patterns arouse a desire to know, but is such a focus on knowledge always appropriate? Consider, for example, a number of popular television shows that are characterized as "infotainment." Structured as expositions, such shows create a desire to know in their viewers. Unfortunately, producers of these shows package the content to entertain rather than to impart sold, widely accepted knowledge. Knowing that consumers of these programs will likely respond to the format of the shows in the same way that they respond to "hard news" programs, we should hold producers accountable for engaging in sensationalism and practicing duplicity when they pretend to be providing important information but in reality are using the structure of news to provide entertainment.

A similar sleight of hand regarding structure occurs with the use of narrative forms. The structure of the classic myth provides a common form for many narratives. However, the function of myths is to tell an audience about transcendental truths that provide answers about universal questions concerning human existence. When a mythic structure is used to narrate a problem less significant, we may criticize a persuader for duping the audience about the reality depicted by his or her story. Janice Hocker Rushing, a rhetorical critic, made just this accusation about former President Ronald Reagan's introduction of the Strategic Defense Initiative.[60] The televised speech in which Reagan introduced this nuclear defense plan to the nation was quickly dubbed by many as his "Star Wars" address, indicating his invocation of a popular Hollywood narrative that mirrored classic myth. However, as many scientists and policy experts explained for years afterwards, the story that Reagan presented was very far from the technological reality that existed at the time. Reagan had made a gratuitous use of a standard narrative form that could be faulted on ethical grounds.

The literature concerning compliance-gaining strategies offers an ethical standard for judging these techniques that falls very much in line with the Symbolist Perspective's concern for preserving human choices. As mentioned earlier, Delia, Clark and others suggest that compliance-gaining techniques be ordered according to how well each particular technique takes into account the perspective of the audience to whom it is addressed. For those concerned with ethics, this makes particularly good sense. A compliance-gaining strategy such as a threat or even a plea may sometimes be effective, but it is ethically suspect insofar as it fails to take into account the needs of the target to whom it is directed, thereby diminishing the essential humanity of that person.

Ethical concerns are not limited to persuaders. Audiences share responsibility for their responses. Viewers of films that follow plot lines in which the audience loudly applauds acts of vengeance that seem to naturally follow from preceding scenes should question whether or not there are less violent alternatives for satisfying the desires they experienced as they viewed the films. Listeners confronted with expository speeches or essays can ask whether or not they are granting a knowledge value to what they hear simply because the structure of the message mirrors their image of a lecture or because there actually exists knowledge within the message. Conversational partners in explicitly persuasive situations should ask whether their responses to promises, bribes, altercasting and the like simply reflect old familiar patterns or honest reactions to the problems, conflicts or issues being discussed. In these ways, audience members can assume some ethical responsibility for their responses to message structures just as persuaders should weigh the ethical dimensions of their structural choices.

CRITICAL FOCUS: HERDING CATS COMMERCIAL

The arrangement of messages often works on the psychology of an audience, causing people to activate particular patterns or forms that arouse and satisfy expectations. By examining messages for their form and structure, we can better understand the persuasive potential within messages. The following questions provide a focus for such an effort.

CRITICAL QUESTIONS

1. What **expectations** are aroused in the beginning of the message, and how are those expectations satisfied?
2. What is the overall **structure** of the message (expository or narrative)?
3. What **structural choices** (patterns) are used within the overall structure of the message?
4. Which of **Burke's forms** is the audience likely to use to make sense of the message?
5. What **characteristics of human perception** are encouraged by the arrangement of the message?

Although the Herding Cats commercial for Electronic Data Systems (EDS) aired only once, it reached millions of viewers. Both sports and non-sports fans have come to anticipate memorable commercials during the Super Bowl games. Their motivation to watch the ads is high in large part because of their expectation that the commercials will be entertaining, artistic and innovative. The manner in which the Herding Cats commercial fulfilled these expectations can be discerned by analyzing the physical components of the message, their order of presentation and the relationship between the order and the psychological forms they evoke. The consequence of the commercial is the presentation of EDS as a clever company that can do innovative things for its customers.

Herding Cats contained a number of nonverbal and verbal elements that fall into three categories. Some presentational elements suggest a documentary film. The commercial had personal testimonies to the dangers, challenges and rewards of herding cats; scenes of cowboys in action; and letter-box framing of the scenes. Other presented elements referenced cowboys and the West. Cowboys on horseback were attired in typical cowboy garb of hat, heavy coat, gloves, bandanna, blue jeans and boots. The scenery included a wide, blue sky with puffy white clouds, distant mountains, sunshine, tumbleweeds, wind, river, campfire and chuckwagon, evoking the landscape of the West. Still other elements featured cats sitting on horses, running through the grass, treading water and stuck in a tree. Cats were carried and stroked, and some rode on horses with the cowboys.

The physical components of the commercial were arranged in a metaphoric pattern of order. The ad compared the activities of herding cats to the service that EDS provides. As cowboys herd the cats toward the Western sunset, a narrator reads the copy that appears on the screen, "In a sense, this is what we do. We bring together information, ideas and technologies, and make them go where you want."

The metaphorical pattern evoked conventional and repetitive forms through which the audience transferred the qualities of herding cats to EDS. The familiar or conventional form of a commercial conjures up several expectations. Sophisticated consumers of commercials expect them to be clever, imaginative, captivating, fast-paced and fragmented in their presentation of message elements. Herding Cats satisfied these expectations through their reference to three other conventional forms with which the audience was familiar: documentary films, the Western cattle drive, and the realm of the domestic cat.

The commercial was presented in the expository style of a documentary film. Typically, documentaries are largely informational, objective presentations. Herding Cats began with a cowboy introducing us to an indiscernible picture of his great grandfather, the first cat herder in the family. This bit of history established the past to create a context for the current state of cat herding. One by one, each herder added a piece of information to create a complete composite of the cat-herding task. "Don't let anybody tell you it's easy," states one herder, while another asserts, "Anybody can herd cattle. Holding together 10,000 half-wild short hairs—that's another thing all together." As evidence for these claims, one herder pointed to his face and described an alleged scratch he received that morning. Then, he motioned toward his partner, sitting astride a horse, calmly stroking a white cat, and said, "And if you look at his face, it's just ripped to shreds." The testimony of the cowboys about the challenges and joys of cat herding was provided in a serious, linear and straightforward manner—a progression that is characteristic of documentary-style films.

Another conventional form upon which the persuasion in this message relied was the Western cattle drive. The awe-inspiring, expansive nature of the landscape of the West was illustrated by picturesque vistas of open range bordered by distant foothills, snow-capped mountains or canyon cliffs. The commercial highlighted these typical geographic depictions of the West through its letterbox format, wide-angle panoramic shots, pans, slow dissolves and momentous music. The extreme weather of the Western frontier gave the region an inhospitable reputation. The relatively flat and rocky, sun-parched terrain with scrub trees and shrubs depicted in the commercial are trademark features of any Western story. The conventional form of the cattle drive became pronounced in the activities depicted in the commercial, suggesting that a cowboy's life on the trail was filled with hard, never-ending work. The animals must be maintained, driven, protected and rescued. In Herding Cats, a cowboy carries cats across the river, two others try to bring a group of cats down from a tree branch and another winds a ball of yarn for his charges.

Just as there were characteristic features of the documentary film and the Western cattle drive in Herding Cats, so, too, were conventional, familiar behaviors between domestic cats and their human fanciers referenced. A cat's tendency is to resist attempts to direct or control it in any way. Its habit of perching in high places, such as trees, from which it cannot always descend, and its natural propensity for shedding fur that covers clothes or causes allergic reactions are common knowledge to all cat owners. The precarious relationship between cat and owner, whereby the owner can lose blood by being clawed by the cat one moment and then find gratification in stroking the purring cat the next, is a regular feature of cat-human cohabitation.

Each of the conventional forms of the documentary film, the Western cattle drive, and the cat world evoked by the metaphor was incomplete. Through the fragments presented, we recognize the three conventional forms and move to complete them. By filling in this information, we acknowledge that we know the form. At the same time, we also recognize that the conventional forms have been violated. The documentary film form is violated in that the subject of the "documentary"—herding cats—is trivial and silly, in contrast to the serious topics with which documentaries deal. Herding cats rather than cattle is a violation of the Western cattle drive form. The fact that cats were shown allowing themselves to be herded represented atypical—in fact, foreign—cat behavior. Our ability to recognize both the conventional forms and their violation establishes us as members of an inside group of knowledgeable people. We find amusement in the form's violation. We all laugh together, feeling gratified that we have gotten the joke, pleased at our own cleverness.

The documentary film, the Western cattle drive and the realm of the domestic cat forms developed the metaphor by which we can identify and remember EDS and its services. This commercial relied on repetitive form as well. Repetitive form, which repeats a message in multiple ways, persuaded the audience that EDS is an inventive, modern, talented company. The commercial proved the cleverness of the company, a cleverness that was repeated through the use of the three other conventional forms. As the forms intertwined and offered both their forms and violations of those forms, the level of complexity that resulted reinforced the company's ingenuity, in turn reinforcing the message that the company could handle our complex information and technology needs.

Notes

1. Stuart Elliot, "The Media Business: Advertising Not X'ers, Not O's. It's the Dot-Coms That Matter," *The New York Times*, 28 January 2000, Late Ed., C:1.
2. John Carman, "The Ad That Scores," *The San Francisco Chronicle*, 28 January 2000, Final Ed., C:1.
3. EDS. "Super Bowl Commercial," retrieved May 11, 2000. http://www.eds.com/about_eds/homepage/superbowl.shtml.
4. Carman, "The Ad," C:1.
5. Mark Lorando, "The Commercial Bowl: $2 Million, 30 Seconds, and Loads of Fun for Super Bowl Viewers," *The Times-Picayune*, 31 Jan 2000, D:1.
6. Greg Farrell and Michael McCarthy, "Beverage Titans Ram Dot-Com Rivals: Christopher Reeve Moves Audience in Nuveen Commercial," *USA Today*, 31 January 2000, Final Ed. B:4.
7. Elliot, "The Media Business," C:1.
8. Dominic LaRusso, The Shadows of Communication (Dubuque: Kendall/Hunt, 1977), 148.
9. Kenneth Burke, *Counter-Statement* (Berkeley: University of Califormia Press, 1968), 29-44.
10. For a broad review of such research, see Richard B. Gregg, *Symbolic Inducement and Knowing: A Study in the Foundations of Rhetoric* (Columbia: University of South Carolina Press, 1984).
11. Kenneth Burke, *Counter-Statement* (Berkeley: U California P, 1968), 31.
12. Gregg, *Rhetoric*, 50.
13. Burke, *Counter-Statement*, 123-183.
14. Burke, *Counter-Statement*, 125.
15. Plato, *Phaedrus* in *Dialogues of Plato*, Volume 1, trans. Benjamin Jowett (New York: Random House, 1937), 264.
16. Aristotle, *Rhetoric*, trans. W. Rhys Roberts (New York: Modern Library, 1954), 1414a.
17. *Rhetorica Ad Herenium*, trans. Harry Caplan (Cambridge: Harvard University Press, 1954), III, ix, 18.
18. See, for example: Howard Gilkinson, Stanley F. Paulson and Donald Sikkink, "Effects of Order and Authority in an Argumentative Speech," *Quarterly Journal of Speech* 40 (1954): 183-192; Harold Sponberg, "The Relative Effectiveness of Climax and Anti-Climax Order in an Argumentative Speech," *Speech Monographs* 13 (1946): 35-44; Raymond G. Smith, "An Experimental Study of the Effects of Speech Organization Upon the Attitudes of College Students," *Speech Monographs* 18 (1951): 292-301; Halbert E. Gulley and David K. Berlo, "Effect of Intercellular and Intracellular Speech Structure on Attitude Change and Listening," *Speech Monographs* 23 (1956): 288-297; Mark Knapp and James C. McCroskey, "The Siamese Twins: Inventio and Dispositio," *Communication Quarterly* 14 (1966): 17-18; Ross Winterowd, "Beyond Style," *Philosophy and Rhetoric* 5 (1972): 88-110.

19. D. Thistlethwaite, H. de Haan and J. Kamenetsky, "The Effects of 'Directive' and 'Non-Directive' Communication Procedures on Attitudes," *Journal of Abnormal and Social Psychology* 51 (1955): 107-113.
20. Aristotle, *Rhetoric*, 1414a.
21. Bill Nichols, *Ideology and Image* (Bloomington: Indiana University Press, 1981), 205.
22. H. E. Krugman, "Processes Underlying Exposure to Advertising," *American Psychologist* 23 (1968): 245-253.
23. See Douglas Ehninger, Bruce E. Gronbeck and Alan H. Monroe, *Principles and Types of Speech Communication* 9th brief Ed. (Glenview: Scott, Foresman, 1984), 247-258.
24. B. Fine, "Conclusion-drawing, Communicator Credibility and Anxiety as Factors in Opinion Change," *Journal of Abnormal and Social Psychology* 67 (1967): 47-58; C. I. Hovland and W. Mandell, "An Experimental Comparison of Conclusion Drawing by the Communicator and by the Audience," *Journal of Abnormal and Social Psychology* 47 (1952): 581-588; W. Weiss and S. Steenbock, "The Influence on Communication Effectiveness of Explicitly Urging Action and Policy Consequences," *Journal of Experimental Social Psychology* 1 (1955): 396-406.
25. Marvin Karlins and Herbert Abelson, *Persuasion: How Opinions and Attitudes are Changed*, 2nd Ed (New York: Springer, 1970), 13-14.
26. Karlins and Abelson, *Persuasion*, 30-32.
27. Marvin Karlins and Herbert I. Abelson, *Persuasion*, 27; F. Lund, "The Psychology of Belief," *Journal of Abnormal and Social Psychology* 20 (1925): 174-196.
28. Hovland and Mandell, "Experimental Comparison."
29. R. Rosnow and E. Robinson, eds., *Experiments in Persuasion* (New York: Academic Press, 1967).
30. Wayne N. Thompson, *The Process of Persuasion: Principles and Readings* (New York: Harper & Row, 1975), 120.
31. William G. Doty, *Mythography: The Study of Myths and Rituals* (Tuscaloosa: University of Alabama Press, 1986), 16.
32. Walter Fisher, *Human Communication as Narration: Toward a Philosophy of Reason, Value, and Action* (Columbia: U South Carolina P, 1987).
33. W. Lance Bennett, "Storytelling in Criminal Trials: A Model of Social Judgment," *Quarterly Journal of Speech* 64 (1978): 1-22.
34. Joseph Campbell, *Myths to Live By* (New York: Viking Press, 1972).
35. Nichols, *Ideology and Image*, 73.
36. Robert C. Rowland, "On Mythic Criticism," *Communication Studies* 41 (1990): 105-107; Janice Hocker Rushing, "On Saving Mythic Criticism—A Reply to Rowland," *Communication Studies* 41(1990): 143.
37. Joseph Campbell, *The Hero With a Thousand Faces* (Princeton: Princeton University Press, 1946).
38. Campbell, *Hero*, 49-243.
39. Campbell, *Hero*, 90.
40. Campbell, *Hero*, 109.

41. Campbell, *Hero,* 193.
42. Campbell, *Myths,* 201-232; see also, Charles L. Whitfield, *Healing the Child Within* (Deerfield Beach: Health Communications, 1989), 59-66.
43. Rushing, "Saving," 142.
44. Rushing, "Saving," 143.
45. William F. Lewis, "Telling America's Story: Narrative Form and the Reagan Presidency," *Quarterly Journal of Speech* 73 (1987): 280-302.
46. Doty, *Mythography,* 73-106.
47. Although we borrow these two terms from Walter Fisher, our explanations of the two requirements differ slightly from his in order to take into account criticisms of his standards for assessing narratives that have been offered by other scholars. See, Walter Fisher, "Narration as a Communication Paradigm," *Communication Monographs* 51 (1984): 8. For critiques of Fisher's explanations, see Barbara Warnick, "The Narrative Paradigm: Another Story," *Quarterly Journal of Speech* 73 (1987): 172-182; see also, Robert C. Rowland, "Narrative: Mode of Discourse or Paradigm?" *Communication Monographs* 54 (1987): 264-275.
48. See Clifford Geertz, *The Interpretation of Cultures* (New York: Basic Books, 1973).
49. For a comprehensive review of this line of research, see David R. Siebold, James G. Cantrill and Renee A. Meyers, "Communication and Interpersonal Influence," *Handbook of Interpersonal Communication,* eds. Mark L. Knapp and Gerald R. Miller (Beverly Hills: Sage, 1985), 551-611.
50. Gerald Miller, Frank Boster, Michael Roloff and David Siebold, "Compliance-Gaining Message Strategies: A Typology and Some Findings Concerning Effects of Situational Differences," *Communication Monographs* 44 (1977): 37-51. Their work draws heavily on Gerald Marwell and David R. Schmitt, "Dimensions of Compliance-Gaining Behavior: An Empirical Analysis," *Sociometry* 30 (1967): 350-364.
51. Ruth Anne Clark and Jesse G. Delia, "Topoi and Rhetorical Competence," *Quarterly Journal of Speech* 65 (1979): 195.
52. See Clark and Delia, "Topoi," 187-206.
53. Jean Piaget, *Language and Thought of the Child,* trans. Marjorie Gabain, 3rd Ed. (London: Routledge and Kegan Paul, 1959), 19-25.
54. Clark and Delia, "Topoi," 191.
55. Jesse G. Delia, Susan L. Kline and Brant R. Burleson, "The Development of Persuasive Communication Strategies in Kindergarteners Through Twelfth-Graders," *Communication Monographs* 46 (1979): 248-249.
56. Reported in Clark and Delia, "Topoi," 204; original citation is Susan Ervin-Tripp, "Wait for me Rollerskate," in *Child Discourse,* ed. Claudia Mitchell-Kernan and Susan Ervin-Tripp (New York: Academic Press, 1977), 165-188.
57. For a lengthy review of this line of research, see Siebold, Cantrill and Meyers, "Communication," 584-588.
58. J. L. Freedman and S. Fraser, "Compliance Without Pressure: The Foot-in-the-Door Technique," *Journal of Personality and Social Psychology* 4 (1966): 195-202.

59. Reported by Karlin and Abelson, 13-14.
60. Janice Hocker Rushing, "Ronald Reagan's 'Star Wars' Address: Mythic Containment of Technical Reasoning," *Quarterly Journal of Speech* 72 (1986): 415-433.

10
THE INSTITUTIONAL PERSPECTIVE

IN THIS CHAPTER:
Focus on:
Political Institutions, the Media and GOPTV

1. Theoretical Focus: Defining the Institutional Perspective
   - Characteristics of Institutions
   - Types of Persuasion from the Institutional Perspective
   - Characteristics of the Institutional Perspective
2. Formal Communication Institutions
   - Tension between Public Service and Private Profit
   - The Gatekeeper Principle
   - Agenda Setting Function
   - Relationship of Media to Persuaders
3. Redefining the Audience—Conformity
4. The Flow of Persuasive Messages
5. Ethical Concerns from an Institutional Perspective
6. Critical Focus: GOPTV's *Rising Tide*

FOCUS ON: POLITICAL INSTITUTIONS, THE MEDIA AND GOPTV

The relationship of the American media to the two main political parties has undergone steady transformation since the first nationally televised broadcast of a political convention in 1952. Little by little, media coverage—most conspicuously by commercial television, but including other media—has caused major parties to lose much of the centralized control they once held over selecting candidates, promoting issues and mobilizing voters. Selection of presidential candidates, once the exclusive function and purpose of the nominating convention, is now influenced decisively by the highly focused, poll-driven, media-saturated primary elections and caucus votes or, as in the case of maverick third-party candidate H. Ross Perot in 1992, by phone-in talk shows such as "Larry King Live," where Perot announced his candidacy and did much of his early campaigning. Clearly, the structure of political institutions in America is under continuing pressure to accommodate changes in the media institutions with which they have an interdependent relationship.

Republicans, who between 1980 and 1992 held the White House but were (with only a brief interruption) the minority party in Congress, faced the institutional problem of decline in organizational influence at local precinct meetings, as well as diminished power of the party itself. "Americans used to talk through their problems with their neighbors over the back yard fence," observed Lamar Alexander, former

Governor of Tennessee, Bush administration Secretary of Education and 1996 GOP presidential candidate. "We don't do that much these days."[1] After the GOP gained control of both houses of Congress in 1994, the basic problem remained the same: how to best use the opportunities provided by existing media structures to secure and extend their power, manage discussion and mobilize support on such issues as health care reform, crime, immigration, welfare reform and balance the federal budget. Surrounding them were many new and emerging media, including the Internet and the World Wide Web to which millions of homes have access, burgeoning cable television channels and the breakout popularity of talk radio.

The Republican Party and conservative organizations both directly and indirectly tied to that organization have pioneered a variety of new media and new techniques for exploiting the "old media" since the early 1980's. Members of the New Right, such as then Indiana Senator Dan Quayle, were launched into national office by the unprecedented use of direct-mail tactics by conservative fundraisers in the late 1970's and early 1980's. Pat Robertson's conservative Republican presidential candidacy in 1988 used the resources of and became visible through Robertson's widely broadcast *700 Club* and CBN (the Christian Broadcast Network). In the 1990's, even as conservatives continued to talk about the so-called "liberal media," they also dominated such emerging areas as talk radio where much of the grassroots support for popular issues like Congressional term limits was originally generated. In 1992, they created the Republican Exchange Satellite Network (RESN) and National Empowerment Television (NET), a full-fledged cable network which described iteslf as a "political news talk network."[2] During the 2000 presidential campaign, the party developed a web site through which their Philadelphia convention was webcast. The site gave users the opportunity to virtually program the convention for themselves, choosing from several camera angles through which to view the proceedings.

The GOP continues to pursue an array of media strategies, running the gamut from the vigorous use of phone-in talk radio, public access television, Internet sites and fax machines. Perhaps none of these various ventures illustrates more clearly the connections between political institutions and media institutions—and their persuasive importance—as one of GOPTV's original weekly news magazine programs, *Rising Tide*.

GOPTV's is a coalition of broadcast stations and cable companies, using satellite transmission to disseminate programming produced by the Republican National Committee. *Rising Tide* was a cornerstone of the network's programming that significantly contributed to GOPTV's early success. The weekly broadcast of *Rising Tide* was carried by many television stations, including "superstation" WWOR in New York. The program also was available via tape to cable community programming and public access channels. The WWOR carriage alone meant that the program had the possibility of reaching an estimated 55 million households.[3] *Rising Tide* was produced by the Republican National Committee at the studio facilities of the Republican Media Center in Washington D.C., and was hosted by Haley Barbour, then chairman of the Republican National Committee. Its format was a mix of features that most viewers found familiar. After a summary of the week's news by Barbour, the program turned to "Page One," an in-depth examination of the week's issue, and from there it moved to phone-in talk format, even bringing in some home shopping style selling of GOP promotional and fund-raising merchandise. Its guest commentators and the persons interviewed were Republican officials, and its politics were unabashedly conservative Republican.

In the Critical Focus at the end of this chapter, we will consider the persuasive strategies underlying the creation of GOPTV and *Rising Tide*, as well as the larger context of politics, profits and power within which those strategies must work. To do this, however, we need to establish a third person perspective on persuasion, one capable of exploring issues beyond those of the Classical or Symbolist Perspectives. As we shall see, in this chapter, the Institutional Perspective on persuasion recognizes the significant differences for theory, ethics and practice when formal institutions are themselves the source, the audience or the target of persuasion.[4]

THEORETICAL FOCUS: DEFINING THE INSTITUTIONAL PERSPECTIVE

We include within the Institutional Perspective all persuasion by institutions, within an institutional context and with institutional effects. *An institution is a large scale, historically enduring social system, dominating one or more aspects of our public, civic or social life, empowered by law, custom or tradition to perform certain important social functions.*[5] The federal government is probably the prime example of a social institution. With its many branches and departments, our federal government has endured for over 200 years. Empowered both by law, in the form of the Constitution, and by custom and tradition, government regulations influence daily activities as diverse as obtaining a student loan, registering for the draft or simply reading the cholesterol content of a bag of potato chips. Other institutions influence us similarly. Established churches are social institutions that, by the force of a tradition of belief, affect the lives of their members. Colleges and universities, as institutions steeped in tradition, are charged with several important social functions, such as certifying education by the awarding of credits and degrees.

CHARACTERISTICS OF INSTITUTIONS

Four characteristics are common among the various institutions with which we are all familiar. Examining these characteristics will demonstrate not only the range of institutional persuasion but also the characteristics of institutions that reflect their power as both sources and contexts of persuasion. First, institutions are often characterized by *exclusivity* in that they ordinarily admit or face no competition within their domain. This exclusivity can function both within and across the various areas of our social and civic life. In America, for example, we have a legal system following a common body of law and precedent, not several acting independently. Each of us ordinarily belongs to *one* faith. We deal with *one* gas company, electric company, water company and cable television company. Within each of these areas of our lives, then, a single institution commonly has jurisdiction. Furthermore, education is assumed to be the province of educational institutions, not of political institutions. Similarly, in our political system, the business of lawmaking is assumed to occur within political institutions, not within religious institutions; this is required by our Constitutional principle of separation of church and state. Of course, frequently, a particular institution will attempt to influence the business of another institution.

Various lobbying groups, for example, try to represent the interests of business and industry in political bodies. Legislatures may attempt to regulate the activities of religious institutions. Communication media may investigate the activities of the banking industry and so on. However, in general, particular institutions are deemed responsible for particular segments of our lives and this balance of power—or division of "turf"—remains largely undisturbed from day to day.

Second, institutions manifest *potency* by exerting wide ranging influence over our behavior, attitudes and/or values within their domain. Religious doctrines may determine behaviors that range from what we eat on particular days of the week to whether or not we practice a particular type of birth control. Similarly, educational institutions may influence not only what we consider to be the "facts," but they may also determine the method by which we will find "facts" in the future. We learn that there are certain sources that are "authoritative" and certain methods of investigation that are more reliable than others.

Third, institutions obtain their influence in large part from *authority*, and they confer that authority upon those who act in their names. In other words, institutions are considered "legitimate" as sources of moral, popular or civic authority. If people do not perceive a particular group as "legitimate," then that group is not only rejected as an authority but also rarely accorded the status of an institution. For example, there are many people in the United States who are herbalists. These people cultivate and use herbs for a variety of purposes, including medicinal purposes. However, few people consider the herbalists part of the "medical institution." It is the American Medical Association that we associate with the "medical institution." Despite the fact that many herbal remedies have a long history of effectiveness, that group is rarely accorded the legitimacy necessary to establish them as "authorities" on the subject of medicine.

Fourth, institutions are normally characterized by *complexity* as a social collective. They are commonly bureaucratic, hierarchical or corporate in their structure. Their size and complexity, together with the authority they grant to individuals to act in their name, often result in our characterizing them simply as "the system," as if they have a life of their own. Scholars of organizational communication have noted and studied the "organizational culture" characteristic of various large institutions. While some institutions may be friendly and forgiving and others may be cold and rigid, institutions appear to us as systems with many parts, rules and procedures. Because individuals may work in an institution, we often think of institutions as places or contexts for interaction. Just as frequently, we may come to regard institutions as being "real, live persons"—we think of our interaction with the parts, people or policies of an institution as an interaction with the institution itself. Consequently, we may personify an institution. Religious institutions, for example, may be referred to as "living churches." Or, we may characterize our interactions with officials in government or educational institutions as dealings with the "bureaucracy." The institution and its actions can thus seem to become interchangeable with its members, agents, representatives and spokespersons and their actions: Bill Clinton can appear interchangeable with the executive branch of the federal government; the parish priest with the Roman Catholic Church; the exchange department clerk with the department store chain and the financial aid director with the entire university.

Types of Persuasion from the Institutional Perspective

Although many of the examples of persuasion presented in earlier sections of this text were institutional persuasion as we have defined it here, our methods for analyzing those examples in earlier chapters did not emphasize the institutional factors that influenced such persuasion. Now, however, our concern is with the type of persuasion that occurs at an institutional level and the impact of institutional forces on persuasion. We will be considering four representative types of institutional persuasion in the chapters that follow: persuasive campaigns, social movements, propaganda and ideology. All four of these types of institutional persuasion include particular persuasive messages that can be understood and evaluated according to the theoretical principles discussed earlier in this book. In a persuasive campaign against smoking, for example, there will be a variety of public service announcements that can be analyzed according to the classical means of persuasion—credibility, argument and evidence and emotional appeals—or the more contemporary findings regarding verbal and nonverbal symbols. Hence, in this section of the text we will from time to time draw on concepts introduced earlier to help explain how persuasion is working. However, our main concern in this and the next four chapters is with the characteristics of persuasion that are unique to the Institutional Perspective.

The nature and scope of this perspective can be made clear by defining the four broad types of institutional persuasion—campaigns, social movements, ideology and propaganda. Forms of institutional persuasion differ in three broad ways. First, institution-level persuasion may be motivated by either *public or private gain*. Second, institution-level persuasion may be *implicit, explicit or both*. The public/private dimension and the implicit/explicit dimension of persuasion are both discussed in Chapter 1. Third, institution-level persuasion may operate *within existing institutional structures (or "within the system") or from outside "the system."* Forms of institutional persuasion are characterized by different combinations of these variables.

Persuasive campaigns involve explicit persuasion for private motive or gain within "the system." For example, advertising campaigns are designed to increase profits for particular firms or industries within a larger system of business and industry. Such campaigns do not challenge the capitalistic system, but they work within its constraints. Similarly, political campaigns are designed to elect particular candidates (allegedly a gain for those candidates themselves as well as their parties) within the prevailing political system. Campaigns operate *within* "the system," sanctioned by and cooperating with other institutions such as federal election laws, FCC regulations and policies of the corporate media. Persuasive campaigns are the topic of Chapter 11.

Social movements, on the other hand, *involve explicit and implicit persuasion for public gain that attempts to change a system*. The women's suffrage movement, for example, used a variety of explicit attempts at persuasion, including letters, speeches and marches. News coverage of the events, sometimes positive and sometimes negative, involved more subtle persuasion. Whether purposeful or not, some biographies, novels and poems also exerted persuasive influence in favor of the movement. While social movements such as the civil rights movement or the environmental movement frequently attempt to work within the prevailing social order, they often work to disrupt and radically change that order as well. Civil disobedience, a common tactic for many social movements, actually violates "the system" in order to change it. Chapter 12 discusses social movements in detail.

Ideology, like propaganda, *functions to preserve "the system,"* but ideology does so *through implicit persuasion sponsored or supported by "the system" itself.* Institutions fostering ideology may not be fully aware of the persuasive implications of their work. Network television entertainment, for example, is produced for the explicit purpose of entertaining viewers sufficiently so that advertisers will buy commercial time during the shows. Many of the producers, directors, writers and performers who participate in the entertainment industries more likely characterize their work as "art" rather than as "persuasion." However, the programs that result often serve a socialization function that assists in maintaining the values, expectations and life styles that dominate our culture. Consequently, these "entertaining" messages can be examined for their persuasive, ideological functions. This type of implicit persuasion helps to maintain the continuity of a predominant culture and is representative of ideological persuasion. Ideology is the topic of Chapter 13.

Propaganda is *explicit, institutionally sponsored persuasion by "the system" aimed at a mass audience.* Ordinarily, propaganda is associated with governmental institutions, but other institutions such as religious organizations may also engage in propaganda. Especially during times of war and during other national emergencies, governments may develop programs of persuasion that are aimed at the masses. As we examine later in this chapter, by "the masses" or "mass audience" we mean not only numerically large audiences but also audiences whose members are conceived of in terms of their conformity, rather than their individuality. Propaganda may serve the purpose of either agitating or pacifying the mass audience, but such persuasion always carries a primary goal of obtaining public support for the actions and policies of those institutions that sponsor them. Thus, propaganda differs from ideology in another important regard: propaganda targets the advancement of specific, identifiable and limited goals of "the system," rather than the more diffuse and general goal of perpetuating "the system" itself. The varieties, techniques and functions of propaganda by which it is distinguished from other forms of persuasion will be examined in Chapter 14.

CHARACTERISTICS OF THE INSTITUTIONAL PERSPECTIVE

Despite differences among the four types of persuasion just described, there exist three characteristics common to the Institutional Perspective toward persuasion. First, from the Institutional Perspective we are typically concerned with *multiple messages from diverse sources*. When an institution undertakes a persuasive campaign or a program of propaganda, that institution generally develops a series of messages rather than a single persuasive appeal. Television spots may combine with radio announcements, magazine advertisements, informational brochures, marketing promotions, public addresses or events that are timed for media coverage and a host of other communication events. Even a campaign limited to a single delivery system, like television, may utilize a series of messages in order to reach a variety of targeted audiences. Multiple messages are common in social movements as well. Within social movements, dramatic events like rallies or marches may be supplemented by a variety of public speeches, the production and distribution of buttons and bumper stickers and less costly one-on-one personal interactions. In the case of ideology, persuasion often occurs in even more diffuse ways. Not only will multiple messages foster and maintain ideology but these messages may originate from sources as diverse as Saturday morning cartoons and American history textbooks.

When considering multiple messages from diverse sources, the Institutional Perspective takes a longer range view of persuasion than perspectives designed to deal with single messages. Consequently, a second characteristic of the Institutional Perspective is a concern for *duration over time*. Campaigns, whether they are commercial advertising campaigns or political campaigns, occur over a period of time. They begin; they end. Likewise, social movements begin, gather strength and either provoke change or disintegrate and fade into the background. Propaganda may last for the duration of a war or the life cycle of a particular political party. Ideology will emerge when needed and remain with a culture for some time until it is replaced by a new ideology.

As a third characteristic, the Institutional Perspective investigates persuasion in terms of larger *social systems* rather than in terms of particular individuals or audiences. From this perspective, we examine relationships between and among institutions. Political campaigns, for example, must work through a variety of institutions, including political parties, business and commercial institutions and communication institutions. Perhaps more important, political campaigns are organized in order to influence not just individual voters but the political system itself. Similarly, social movements, when successful, may change the very nature of our society. Propaganda, too, works through some institutions and affects others. Ideology not only permeates most social institutions, but it serves as the basis of culture. Thus, the Institutional Perspective investigates the impact of institutions on persuasion and the impact of persuasion on institutions.

Formal Communication Institutions

Among the many institutions within our society, our formal communication institutions are fundamental for understanding persuasion from the Institutional Perspective. Through these formal communication institutions, most persuasive messages are channeled from source to receiver. The various media industries do not, however, just act as conduits for the messages of others. The media themselves also function institutionally. The recording, movie, television and publishing industries are often referred to as "culture industries" because they manufacture our cultural artifacts. As a consequence, these formal communication institutions participate in both explicit and implicit persuasion.

The sheer size and range of these institutions, whether considered as individual industries or as a single institution, is awesome. Within the communication industry exist organizations as small as an independent weekly newspaper with a circulation of one thousand and a multinational conglomerate that includes a major television network, a Hollywood movie making enterprise, an international recording firm and an international news service. Attempting to characterize such a large and diverse institution runs the risk of immediately suggesting its own exception. Still, the Institutional Perspective toward persuasion requires some understanding of the workings of the media. We begin by comparing the system of media within the United States with that common to many other countries. From such a comparison, one characteristic emerges as fundamental. In the United States, the media is a regulated private industry. In most other countries, most facets of the media are controlled by the government. This unique feature of the American media accounts for a number of the practices and characteristics of these formal communication systems.

TENSION BETWEEN PUBLIC SERVICE AND PRIVATE PROFIT

From the writing of the First Amendment to the Constitution through the evolution of media law, the conviction persists that communication industries should not be subject to governmental intrusion but should serve a public function. The founding fathers believed that free speech and a free press were essential for the new form of democratic government they designed. This belief held that a free press and the freedom to conduct assemblies in which citizens could exercise their right to free speech would serve a public function by providing the free flow of information and opinions necessary for citizen participation in government. In short, this protection of channels for communication ensured that persuasion would be used as the preferred means for resolving public controversy.

As new communication technologies, such as radio, film and television arose, that notion of protecting the channels for communication persisted and influenced the allocation of licenses and the formulation of other rules for early broadcasters. This governmental posture toward the media has resulted in media that are relatively free from governmental intrusion but are not free from operating expense. Operation of a communication network in the form of a publishing house, a broadcasting station and so on is an expensive endeavor. While serving the public is a guiding principle for most involved in media, making a profit is equally important.

The tension between public service and private profit determines many practices of the media. Taken collectively, the various organizations that constitute the media offer three types of communication that are relevant to the study of persuasion: (1) paid media (e.g., advertising, commercial spots), (2) news coverage and (3) entertainment and human interest coverage (e.g., "soft news," television shows, music by recording artists, etc.). The media provide facilities for explicit persuasion through paid media such as advertising. News coverage, on the other hand, may include explicit persuasion in the form of editorial comment about the news or may involve implicit persuasion in the selection and presentation of news itself. Entertainment programming and human interest stories generally involve some implicit persuasion. By examining the development of these three types of communication by the media, the impact of the tension between public service and private profit becomes clear.

In an extensive study of the history of American newspapers, Bernard Roshco traced the development of the types of content just outlined.[6] Roshco points out that the first American newspaper announced that it would publish once a month or whenever there was a glut of news and promptly went out of business after one issue.[7] The problem confronting this early newspaper is typical of that confronting any media organization; in order to prosper the organization must find content sufficiently appealing to an audience that people will buy the product.

These basic marketing pressures have influenced both the content and the tone of modern newspaper journalism. To attract a wider audience, journalists in the 1830's explored human interest stories ranging from the details of the deeds of common criminals to accounts of the rich and famous, and they reduced the prices of their publications. With larger circulations, these papers solicited larger advertising revenues. As the press began reaching larger numbers of readers, the tone of journalism was also forced to change. Through the middle of the nineteenth century, individual newspapers were usually associated with well-known political causes or parties, and their readers understood that the coverage of news in these papers was openly partisan. However, as the readership of these newspapers swelled beyond the ranks of narrowly partisan readers, the modern idea of "journalistic objectivity" was invented to maintain this larger audience for which a manifestly one-sided approach to issues would no longer be marketable. Roshco notes that in time factuality balanced presentation of opposing views, reliance on outside sources and separation of editorials from actual news became characteristic of the press. As new communication technologies such as radio and television developed, print journalists again found a need to adapt their coverage in order to maintain their audiences. Radio and television could provide the headlines, "the facts," to the public before papers and magazines could roll from the presses. Consequently, the print medium emphasized background stories that treated events, people and issues in more depth. These background stories retained a concern for objectivity but combined that need with "interpretive reporting" that moved beyond the story itself to an explanation of the significance and implications of the story.

The adaptations required of the print medium have been mirrored by similar changes by the electronic media. Television programming, for example, includes news coverage but must rely on other entertaining content to attract a sufficient audience to attract the advertising that keeps the industry profitable. Similarly, in light of the mass audiences targeted by the major television networks, the industry embraces standards of objectivity that mirror those in the print medium. As various sources of televised news and entertainment increase in number and competitiveness, television news programming expands to include more in-depth background coverage.

Despite a wealth of evidence that the media as a whole operates as a private business whose primary concern is making a profit, the notion persists that these formal communication systems should serve the public interest. Newspapers and magazines still receive favorable postal rates on the grounds that free flow of information is fundamental to our republican democracy. The Communications Act of 1934, the Public Broadcasting Act of 1967 and other media law rests on the assumption that the airwaves for radio and television really belong to the public. Therefore, it is not surprising that many contemporary controversies surrounding the media turn on this tension between public service and private profit. For example, the Federal Communications Commission has considered on numerous occasions the boundaries of acceptable advertising. Recent studies regarding the ability of children to discriminate actual television shows from the well-placed commercials for toys and breakfast cereal have stimulated concern for the proper balance between serving the public interest and the legitimate rights of advertisers to enhance their profits through the use of the media.[8]

Similarly, these tensions complicate programming decisions by the industry itself. Recent ratings suggest to many television executives that some news programs do not attract audiences as large as those attracted by movies, sporting events or other programming. Consequently, on occasion some networks have refused to cover even weighty events like Presidential news conferences during prime time. "Gavel-to-gavel" coverage of the national political conventions, once the practice of all commercial broadcast networks, has been dispensed with by most networks in favor of limited coverage of important speeches and votes. As a result, the public debate and deliberation which characterized political conventions before the advent of television coverage in the 1950's has been replaced by pageantry and celebrations of party unity for the TV camera. Important speeches are carefully scheduled for evening, East coast time, and the little debating and deciding that is still done at conventions is handled out of sight of the television crews or at undesirable broadcast times like early morning. Thus, because the standard practices of television journalism were inconvenienced by the traditional structure of the political convention, the conventions have gradually transformed themselves into something more conducive to "good" TV coverage. Similarly, network executives have wrestled with whether or not to broadcast some political debates. Given the need to maintain their large audiences, executives have also been concerned with programming that may offend some members of their audience or may include highly unpopular views. Nine companies, for example, pulled their commercial advertising from a recent "World of Audubon" special concerning deforestation. According to the logging industry, this program was heavily weighted toward the environmentalist point of view. Turner Broadcasting Company aired the program but probably lost at least $250,000 in revenue in the process. In other cases, as with the popular television series, "Married With Children," interest groups have boycotted particular shows and particular networks because of objections to the content of the programming. In situations such as these, the tension between public service and profits heightens.

As the foregoing discussion suggests, the nature of the communications industry and the relationship of this system to other systems—such as government and industry—have impacted the practices of the media. The Institutional Perspective toward persuasion must consider both the nature of the institution under study and the relationship of that system to the larger social system and other institutions. We will refer to both the systemic nature of the media and the relationship of the media to other institutions in later chapters. In the following sections we will focus on two dominant characteristics of the media in relation to society and other institutions: gatekeeping and agenda setting.

THE GATEKEEPER PRINCIPLE

We all know that not every story can be covered in any particular newspaper or magazine. Similarly, not every idea for a dramatic or comedy series is developed into a television show. Because the possibilities of items for inclusion in any particular publication or broadcasting outlet far outrun the space and time available, decisions regarding content are inevitable. Students of the media characterize this decision-making process as "gatekeeping." According to the gatekeeping principle, editors and the media in general primarily function to determine what will enter the gate of media coverage and what will not. Early studies of gatekeeping concerned what news journalists decided to cover and how they made those decisions.[9] Similar studies concerned how decisions regarding what to cover were made in the radio and television industries.[10]

In general, the gatekeeping function of the media operates according to the same economic principles that drive other businesses. That tension between public service and private profit is as much in evidence regarding what is let through the gate as in the development of the industry itself. According to *Washington Post* editor Ben Bagdikian, news is processed according to economic and technological constraints. He notes that the editors who play the role of gatekeepers "may see ten times more words and seven times more stories than the reader ever sees" and estimates the startlingly small time that a gatekeeper spends reading discarded stories at about one to two seconds.[11] The split-second judgments of editors regarding what will be included follow similar judgments on the part of these and other people regarding what reporters and camera crews will be dispatched to cover in the first place.

Since not everything eventually makes the news, it is useful to consider the characteristics of those stories that do reach the reading, listening and viewing audience. These characteristics of media coverage provide insight into what factors are important in the decisions of the gatekeepers. According to Roshco, "most of the snap judgments that result in publication or rejection of specific news stories are based upon a social frame of reference derived from the social structure within which the press functions."[12] As a consequence, many analysts of the media have noted that most media content exhibits a moderately conservative bias and supports the status quo.[13] Conservative content is less likely to offend the mass audience, and those advertisers who aim their messages toward the masses pay the bills for the media industry. In hard news programming, for example, issues that entail unpopular life styles may experience delays of months or even years in their coverage as was the case with the AIDS crisis in the mid-1980's.

In addition, stories that support the institutions that are covered are probably an outgrowth of the structure of the news industry itself. As mentioned earlier, the need to maintain large audiences fosters a journalistic concern for objectivity. That necessity for objectivity leads to increasing reliance on outside sources for quotations, explanations and interpretations of whatever topic enjoys coverage. The cultivation of regular sources leads directly to "news beats." Just as police may be assigned a "beat," so news personnel are frequently assigned a particular institution to pry for stories. Presumably, the journalists who regularly visit the White House or the local police department will better cultivate relationships with those who work there and thereby develop sources for stories. The strategy of news beats makes good economic sense, and it also responds to the need to serve the public by maintaining the alleged objectivity of the reporter. As Roshco explained: "The nature of news as a form of knowledge makes the reporter dependent upon news sources for most of the knowledge he will transpose into media content."[14] Dependence on these sources may result in the sources filtering the news rather than in the journalist doing so. For example, White House aides are unlikely to reveal information that they think will be unfavorable to the White House. Consequently, the sources developed through news beats may provide little more than on-site conduits for what would otherwise be provided to news gatherers through press releases or publicity kits. Similarly, correspondents and reporters who become familiar with a particular beat may identify with the institution they are assigned to cover to the point that they treat all stories emerging from those institutions sympathetically. The speed with which the American media rushed to accept the Reagan Administration's explanations of the KAL 007 airline disaster in 1983, while press all over the rest of the world were reporting alternative explanations, is a case in point of this characteristic.[15] In cases such as this, we easily see how media coverage can manifest a bias in favor of the institutions covered and the status quo. The selection of institutions that will be on the beat enhances the bias in favor of the status quo. Generally, only high visibility organizations or institutions are assigned regular reporters. Governmental units, civic groups and volunteer organizations whose membership includes the "real players" in a given community comprise the normal beats. As one study of coverage found, usually only those who belong to the highest social stratum in a community receive mention in the news.[16]

However, the profit motivated structure of the media industry also encourages a desire for a competitive edge. In fact, the idea of news beats depends in part on the notion that reporters on the beat have a better opportunity to cultivate "private" sources, special sources who because of their personal friendship with the journalist will reveal details and news items not otherwise available. Hence, many people believe that the media are always interested in a "new" story, a different angle or generally in "scooping" the competition. Although some journalists, particularly investigative reporters, do harbor such interests, the gatekeeping process probably filters out many unique stories. The economic imperative to remain competitive along with the public service dictate to remain objective has encouraged instead a certain level of conformity among those in the industry. Sometimes referred to as "pack journalism," individual papers, networks and the like tend to cover what others cover, rarely going out on a limb to tackle an otherwise unpopular story.[17] Many observers attribute the long delays in exploring both the story of Watergate and the Iran/Contra affair to this tendency on the part of the media to travel in packs.

Herbert Gans, a sociologist whose extensive studies of the gatekeeping function support our description here, notes that some unique or novel stories receive coverage when the story is dramatic.[18] In other words, to depart from the beaten path gatekeepers require an event that includes the elements of a good drama—interesting characters who may be cast into stereotypical roles like heroes and villains, a particularly engaging scene that will provide vivid and dramatic pictures, rising dramatic action like that typical of conflict or intrigue or dramatic motives that can be explored for their significance. These dramatic elements are always present in natural and man-made disasters. Hurricanes, which almost always receive wide coverage, provide vivid pictures of destruction, generally propel local heroes into the national spotlight and during the course of their movement provide rising anticipation concerning where they will come ashore next. Similarly, plane crashes conform to the need for dramatic scenes and in the sorting out of their causes may be plumbed for villainy and heroism. These events are unique in that they happen infrequently but are hardly unique in the media coverage that they attract. However, they illustrate the characteristics needed by an event to attract media coverage if that event is not already a part of the usual beat. When an unusual story emerges from the regular beat, there is an opportunity for the media to play the role of watchdog. For news organizations to depart from the pack and report stories that actually criticize their regular beats, however, generally requires real drama, as was the case with the famous "Watergate" story. Even on the rare occasions when such stories are pursued, Bennett notes that such exposés typically personalize the problem and nearly always explain when the event being covered is abnormal, thereby avoiding severe criticism of existing institutions.[19]

The importance of the gatekeeping function of the media will be explored more in later chapters. In general, the gatekeeping function may have very real consequences for individuals and society. What the media *don't* report may be just as important as what they *do* report. However, because we don't see or hear about what they don't report, our image of the world may be incomplete or distorted. As David Manning White put it in his original study of the gatekeepers, "the way we organize our image of reality can be as easily distorted because we receive incomplete or no information about parts of the environment as because we receive stereotyped or biased information."[20] The consequences of such distortion can be significant. Donald Roberts contends that "had the media covered urban ghettos before they erupted in the late 1960's, public awareness and concern might have been mobilized in order to correct intolerable conditions and head off the riots."[21]

Agenda Setting Function

Recognizing how gatekeeping decisions influence news leads us to a second theory concerning the media that is of importance here. That theory holds that the media serve an agenda setting function. In the terms of Maxwell E. McCombs and Donald L. Shaw, authors of this theory, the media may not tell us what to think but they do tell us what to think about—the presence or absence of media coverage influences how the public's "agenda" is "set."[22] There seems to be a strong presumption among viewers that what print or electronic journalists say is "news" really *is* the news. Combined with the journalistic tendency of various news media to follow one another's leads and to act as a pack, this presumption allows the media to set an agenda of topics that others will discuss, investigate and attempt to act upon.

To say that the media set an agenda is not to say that the media create problems that do not exist. For example, following the great quake of 1989 in San Francisco, many people discussed and worried about implementing safety measures to avoid the destructive powers of earthquakes. The media coverage of the disaster had been nearly as massive as the quake itself. Such discussions reached beyond California. The Governor of Illinois, James Thompson, immediately launched a state program to study how Illinois could deal with the problem of earthquakes. At first glance, such a program might seem out of place in the Midwest where tornadoes and blizzards pose more frequent natural threats. However, for years geologists had warned residents of the Midwest about the New Madrid fault near Memphis that could precipitate a disastrous quake in the Midwest. In this case, news coverage that stimulated attention to a problem reinforced actual circumstances, but this is not always the case.

Particular instances of the agenda setting function of mass media have been studied extensively in the last twenty years. Even before McCombs and Shaw elaborated their theory, others had pointed to the phenomenon. In the 1950's, for example, sociologist F. James Davis investigated the coverage of crime in four Colorado newspapers. He found that although the amount of coverage varied with actual crime rates, the public's perception of criminal activity reflected the amount of news coverage of the problem rather than the actual crime rates.[23] Other similar studies show that public perceptions regarding the relative importance of national and local issues and the vitality of political candidates confirm the hypothesis that *media coverage* propels issues, people and institutions onto the public's agenda.[24]

During the early 1980's, researchers at Yale University conducted extensive experimental studies regarding the agenda setting function of television.[25] Not only did they confirm the agenda setting hypothesis across a wide variety of issues, viewers and time periods, but they also investigated just what type of coverage would most likely set an agenda for which sectors of the public audience. They found that "lead stories" (those stories that opened a news broadcast) influenced agenda setting more than stories that appeared later in the broadcast. Contrary to their expectations, stories with a heavy human interest angle that focused on single dramatic incidents and the effects of those incidents on single individuals were not as influential. They found that the media agenda influenced all viewers, even those who were in a position to evaluate the situation independently. For example, political coverage influenced politically involved viewers as often as other citizens who claimed to have little interest in or knowledge about politics. Often people with a vested interest in an issue, for example the elderly in regard to the issue of Social Security, were more intensely influenced by media coverage initially and less influenced as time passed. Of particular interest, they found that media coverage often influenced the standards by which viewers judged national institutions and elected leaders. Results of the studies indicate that television coverage of events like Watergate promoted a standard of integrity for Presidential contenders, and coverage of issues such as inflation or hostages promoted standards relevant to competence. In general, the researchers at Yale found that television coverage reinforces traditional, often conservative standards for judging issues, institutions and people. In line with the analysis of Herbert Gans, they agree that "[t]elevision news glorifies democracy, especially the romantic town hall variety; condemns demagogues, bureaucracies, political 'machines,' and movements of the extreme left or right; celebrates capitalism and individualism; and reveres the existing social order."[26]

Regardless of whether media coverage accurately depicts problems or inaccurately sensationalizes situations, the message seems clear: Media coverage provokes the attention of people. As a consequence, persuaders who wish public consideration of an issue, institution or person should pursue media coverage. In other words, the agenda setting function of the media is critical to the relationship of the media to other institutions in the larger social system.

RELATIONSHIP OF MEDIA TO PERSUADERS

Recognizing the power of media coverage to influence national and local agendas, persuaders often center their efforts on obtaining publicity or "free media" coverage. Such efforts usually begin with the hiring of a press agent, public relations firm or communications consultant. A press agent or a communications consultant develops press releases and publicity notices for the media—primarily print and radio—to solicit news coverage. Given the proclivity of the media to report ready-made stories and their hesitation to engage in investigative reporting that departs from the pack, such publicity maneuvers can launch a particular program, activity or product onto the public agenda. Private firms that develop new products may release publicity about them prior to an advertising campaign designed to promote their consumption. In 1988, for example, stories in a variety of large city newspapers reported the development of a new, smokeless cigarette. Within days of such stories, smokeless cigarettes went on sale in a variety of areas. Established politicians and citizens groups alike use similar press releases to announce persuasive campaigns that will be launched soon after.

The two major political parties have refined the use of prepackaged news stories. Capitalizing on the media's role as gatekeepers, both the Democratic and Republican parties maintain sophisticated television studios in the basement of the Capitol building. There Congressional representatives and Senators tape interviews and statements clarifying their stands on various items of legislation and issues of the day then offer those tapes via satellite to local television stations in their home districts. Political analysts claim these efforts have helped propel a whole new breed of telegenic politicians onto the national scene.[27]

Those people or institutions that fall within the regular media beat enjoy a special advantage in shaping the public agenda. Instead of relying on press releases that may or may not be deemed newsworthy, people on the beat can help to shape the news by planning particular events that they know will be covered simply because reporters are assigned to their beat. The Office of the President of the United States best exemplifies an institution enjoying guaranteed publicity with a high potential for influencing the agenda. The multitude of people from the media holding press passes to the White House guarantees coverage for the President. By planning events at the right times (mid-afternoon, in time for the evening television news), with the right scenic backgrounds (the Rose Garden, the Oval Office, the White House steps) and with messages bristling with 10-second "sound bites" suitable for the evening news, the President's advisors act as public relations experts for him. Presidential advisors and political analysts alike see the value of what Teddy Roosevelt called the "bully pulpit." By strategically managing its contacts with the media, the White House—or any other public organization or figure—can exploit the media's agenda-setting function for its own purposes.

Institutions and people who are not part of a regular news beat also seek to shape the agenda. They too may plan events that will prove irresistible to the media. By creating dramatic events or providing the background that the media needs to expand their coverage of a developing story, these institutions can exploit free media just as established governmental bodies do. In Chapter 5, we described Daniel Boorstin's 1961 analysis of these widely used techniques.[29] Boorstin argued that the media often succumbs to "news making" rather than "news gathering" because of the prevalence of what he termed "pseudo-events" that appear to be "news" but are only a sham or imitation of news.

Edward L. Bernays, often called the father of public relations, observed that "the counsel on public relations not only know what news value is, but knowing it, he is in a position to *make news happen*. He is a creator of events."[30] These created events, or pseudo-events, are planned or incited events, crafted simply for the media to report and pre-packaged for the convenience of that reporting.[31] A real event, like an earthquake, simply happens. The media scramble to cover such an event and are preoccupied by what happened. Pseudo-events, on the other hand, are planned, and coverage frequently dwells as much upon what the events *mean* as the events themselves. Many sporting events just happen, like the pick-up basketball games or the touch football games that occur everyday in public parks. But professional sporting events are carefully planned and orchestrated. These professional events—the Super Bowl or the various "bowl" and "all-star" games, to take some conspicuous examples—are planned around media coverage. Sports that do not attract regular media coverage, such as professional women's basketball, generally do not survive. Because the primary motive is coverage, the planning of these events revolves around the convenience of the media. While most of the working world operates Monday through Friday, professional football players work on Sunday or late Monday night because it is at those times that the media can cover the games conveniently and expect a large viewing audience. Even the rules of the game have been changed to accommodate the media. To insure commercial time during the most exciting part of the game, officials developed a two-minute warning. Once the two-minute warning and a commercial break at that time became standard, the game itself changed with the advent of the two-minute drill, rehearsed sequences of plays designed to take this rule into account. The "seventh-inning stretch" in baseball, once a sorely-needed break for the stadium audience after six innings of continuous play, now seems as anachronistic as a buggy whip or a hula hoop in an era when the pace of professional baseball is slowed down to allow commercial television to introduce the maximum number of commercial breaks. Of course the media cover what happens in a professional sports match, but if coverage was limited *only* to what happened on the field, sportscasts would be much shorter than they are. In addition sportscasters act as sports commentators, telling their audience about the meaning of what happened. Our concern and interest is drawn toward the implications of a player-coach dispute, the meaning of the antics of a quarterback for society at large, the salary negotiations between a player's agent and the team's owner and so on. A particular play, a particular game and the Super Bowl itself become important because we tell ourselves through the media that it is important. The innumerable statistics of the game act as self-fulfilling prophecies as well; breaking the rushing record is considered important because the rushing record exists.

It would perhaps be comforting to think that pseudo-events were limited to professional sports, but such is not the case. American politics is deluged with such manufactured news. Probably one of the most discussed pseudo-events of the 1988 Presidential campaign was the famous spat on the air between George Bush and CBS anchorman Dan Rather. In the early stages of the campaign, numerous political commentators noted that George Bush rarely employed television advertising because he successfully secured free media time. Included in that free media time was a scheduled live interview with Rather. During the interview, Rather questioned Bush about his role in the Iran/Contra affair and his relationship to the drug-dealing leader of Panama, General Manuel Noriega. Rather's questions quickly triggered a heated exchange. Rather hinted at Bush's culpability in these foreign policy fiascos; Bush reminded Rather of his "unprofessional" behavior during a much publicized incident in which Rather walked off the set for several minutes during the evening news. Many believe Bush's campaign advisors deliberately planned this event. Certainly they planned for the interview itself, but perhaps they also planned the fiery exchange with Rather. After all, Bush advisor Roger Ailes had scribbled the famous Bush comment on a cue card for the Vice President to read. A nasty argument between a presidential candidate and a famous newscaster would be guaranteed replay by all the media, simply because of its dramatic character. Also, as with any good pseudo-event, commentators could speculate at length on the meaning of what had happened. Confrontations such as the one between Bush and Rather occur all the time, but this one proved to be important *because it was covered* and because media pundits would *say* it was important. After Bush had won the election, his own advisors admitted that the heated exchange helped dispel the image of Bush as a "wimp." Thus, a planned event accomplished for the Bush campaign as much as an expensive public relations campaign.

Grass-roots movements also frequently construct pseudo-events to capture free media coverage. Demonstrations, marches and rallies are typically not planned to accomplish anything other than free media coverage. They appear important because they allow the media and viewers to consider what they mean, how they signal a change in public opinion or the intensity of commitment to a particular cause. Such public events occur with forewarning and at times that make media coverage easy. When planned well, they include dramatic actions or statements in scenic surroundings that will guarantee inclusion on the evening news. These events may look spontaneous, but more careful examination often reveals the careful planning with which they were staged. Recall, for example, the massive demonstrations in Tehran when the followers of the Ayatollah Khomeni stormed the U.S. Embassy there. The demonstrations and mass rallies looked like real events, but the signs were lettered in English. Why not Farsi? Did they need signs that the American audience would understand in order to guarantee coverage by American media? With advance warning, such events play on the media's tendency to add background and context to the story, and thus insure extended coverage of the issue as well.

In addition to free media, many persuaders employ paid media in the form of print advertising, radio or television spots, billboards, direct mail and so on. At this point it becomes less convenient for us to continue referring simply to "the media" as if they were a single, homogenous entity. The selection among various types of media is directly related to another crucial persuasive decision: the kind of audience a persuader wishes to reach. The different paid media survive by defining their audience in different ways. *Directional* media target a select audience with particular distinguishing characteristics; *nondirectional* media seek a general audience that is heterogenous rather than presorted. Large circulation magazines such as *Time* or *People* and the major television broadcast networks are characteristically nondirectional. Their audience is conceived in terms of the lowest common denominator of content and style that yields the largest reading or viewing public.

Until a generation ago, American commercial radio might have been included among the nondirectional media too, but following the loss of listenership to television, most radio stations have redefined their strategy as *narrowcasting* to an audience with specific tastes—such as all news, all talk, all sports, all classic rock, all 1970's rock and so on—rather than *broadcasting* to a wide, general audience. The boom in cable television reception during the 1980's brought a similar explosion of highly directional channels such as C-SPAN, ESPN, MTV, VH-1, Nickelodeon, Arts & Entertainment, Lifetime, the Home Shopping Channel, the Family Channel, the Comedy Channel and so forth. Although the Internet is not precisely a paid medium like newspapers, commercial radio or television, it has also undergone a transformation in recent years, from a narrowcast to a broadcast medium. As a link among users of government, commercial and university computer systems around the globe, access to the Internet was for much of its short history sufficiently difficult and restricted that the community of users remained comparatively small and homogenous. In recent years, however, the proliferation of home computers and commercial online access providers, like America On Line, Hotmail, Juno and webtv, has created a tidal wave of new users, a diverse audience eager to share on-line messages on all manner of interests. As a result, the narrow interests of an older, narrower, homogenous audience have sometimes clashed with those of a larger, heterogeneous audience, with predictable calls to regulate and restrict the content of meterial made available on the Net. The Web allows any individual with a computer and a modem to create her or his own home page, essentially becoming a self-publisher of text and graphic images on any topic under the sun to a worldwide audience, giving rise to new arguments about such issues as free speech, libel and copyright infringement.

The existence of different types of audiences—relatively homogeneous and relatively heterogeneous—adds another dimension to institutional uses of the media. For institutions to use the media effectively and for the media to remain viable by maintaining a sufficient audience, they require a clear notion of who comprises the audience. The definition of audience as associated with the Institutional Perspective toward persuasion, therefore, merits some attention.

REDEFINING THE AUDIENCE–CONFORMITY

Most institutional persuasion depends on reaching a large audience to obtain results. The Classical and Symbolist Perspectives offer insight into how either an individual or a group is persuaded, insight based in large measure on understanding the prior attitudes and knowledge of the audience. However, the Institutional Perspective on persuasion also demands consideration of both the size and the diversity of the audience as a collective.

Most persuasive campaigns, particularly commercial product campaigns, conceive the audience as less than the totality of potential consumers. When an advertising firm surveys the market for a product, they may target a particular group who is particularly likely to purchase a particular product. The process of surveying the market and dividing it into a target group is called *market segmentation*. To be successful and make a profit, a company need not persuade everyone to buy a particular soft drink. Instead, they need only persuade a sufficient number to buy the drink so that they will have a market share large enough to maintain profits. Target audiences are often defined demographically, according to characteristics like age, sex, socio-economic status and educational level. Some products are priced so that only the relatively wealthy can afford them. It would be pointless to aim advertising for these products at members of the lower middle class. Similarly, some products may be of great use to women and of no interest to men. Even when a product could be purchased and consumed by anyone, advertisers may concentrate a particular campaign on a target group.

Some product campaigns and most issue or election campaigns require a persuader to reach a much broader section of the population. In these cases, particular messages may target particular groups, but the campaign as a whole may necessarily appeal to a larger audience. For example, a candidate for state governor needs to win the majority of votes cast statewide in the general election, but he or she would probably identify different target audiences for different aspects of the campaign platform. The campaign would aim persuasion about public education toward families with school-age children, persuasion about business incentives toward business and industry leaders, persuasion about property taxes toward land owners and so on.

When the product or issue itself does not suggest a target group and persuasive efforts must appeal to a heterogeneous audience, persuaders need more sophisticated methods than just demographic analysis. One method of breaking a large audience into smaller targets is to identify *reference groups* for various members of the audience. Reference groups are real communities, usually associated with institutions, to which people belong and derive some sense of identity. For instance, a member and regular participant in the Methodist church may refer to herself as a Methodist. Or a newly registered student voter may identify himself as a "Young Republican." Suburbanites in their late teens or early twenties may consider themselves "Generation X-ers." By comparison, if one assumes that certain smaller groups within a population share some ideas, beliefs and preferences in common, it is a small step to assume that larger communities also share commonalities. Hence, audience researchers may also consider audiences as *cultural groups*, based on the assumption that shared values and myths bind people together in a culture.

For example, the value of individualism is a strong bond in American culture, as noted by nineteenth century philosopher Alexis De Tocqueville in his classic *Democracy in America*.[32] Most members of our culture learn at an early age that we will be rewarded for our ability to be "on our own" and "take care of ourselves." As we grow, we learn to value individual achievement, self-reliance and material ownership. Likewise, American culture contains many shared myths, stories whose factual truth is less important than their ability to represent dramatically the culture itself. American myths include the "American Revolution" with its cast of heroic military leaders and renown political geniuses, "taming the American frontier" and the "American dream." However diverse the backgrounds and circumstances of individuals in America, for example, they all probably know what "the American dream" is: the story of a common man or woman who, by hard work and clean living, attains a better life for himself or herself. The story is woven throughout our history books, our literature and our popular culture.

The research of Ernest Bormann demonstrates the importance of myths and values to the cohesiveness of a culture. Bormann argues that groups—even small, task-oriented groups whose members are previously unknown to one another—quickly begin to create a shared history for themselves, spun out of joking and telling stories about their situation which is typical for all such groups.[33] The "fantasy themes" which recur in these stories begin to chain out and form a *rhetorical vision*, a symbolic construction of reality and history that, like myth, organizes and expresses the values of a group and explains the relationship of the individuals of the culture to one another. When new students enroll in a university, for example, they enter a large and complex culture. Some of that culture's values and ideals are expressed in the lofty language of the college catalogue: "citizenship," "service," "knowledge" and so forth. However, these new students may quickly discover quite another view of the "reality" of this new world, expressed in shared stories about "partying" and "all-nighters," horror stories about "bad professors," encouraging stories about "good professors," heroic battles with the parking office, registration, financial aid, the placement service and so on. The names and particulars of these stories will change as they chain out, but certain fantasy themes recur, emerge, accumulate and gradually coalesce to form a rhetorical vision of the world of which the student is now a part. This rhetorical vision may be an optimistic one or a pessimistic or cynical one, and the details of the shared fantasies from which it is woven may be true, false or apocryphal. It is, nevertheless, an important source of common values for those who share it.

Market researchers and communication consultants alike may attempt to understand the characteristics of such reference and cultural groups by conducting extended unstructured interviews with members of a particular group. These focus groups are invited to gather and discuss a particular topic under the researchers' unobtrusive observation. The researchers identify patterns in the participants' conversations, providing clues to their attitudes and opinions, the myths to which they subscribe and the values they share. Armed with a detailed description of what these focus group members find important, funny, attractive or noteworthy, media persuaders can then design media messages fitting the predispositions of the reference or cultural group as a whole.

Finding unique persuasive appeals for very large audiences brings us to a final way in which institutions frequently view their audience; that is as "the masses." The advent of the mass media, particularly when viewed as nondirectional, necessitates a consideration of the audience as a "mass." Individual characteristics such as age, sex, income and so forth are generally unimportant when the audience is viewed as a mass. Instead, persuaders aim their messages toward the famous "lowest common denominator," a gross measure of what the masses seem capable of digesting. Similarly, characteristics common to reference groups or even the shared values and myths of a culture may not influence persuaders as they craft their messages. Instead, the concept of audience as a mass may lead persuaders to aim their messages toward a collectivity that they pretend has no individual preferences or distinguishing characteristics.

French scholar Gustave Le Bon described this idea as a "crowd mentality."[34] He explained that a crowd often assumes a collective mind, causing the disappearance of individual personality characteristics. He believed that when people begin to think of themselves only as part of the group, they may participate in activities that they would never engage in if they were by themselves. Such crowds need not contain large numbers, although such is generally the case. More importantly, according to Le Bon, individuals lose their sense of individuality and personal responsibility by sacrificing their personal interests for the interests of the group. When individuals lose their conscious personalities in the heat of the crowd, the crowd acts like some supra-individual that is very open to suggestion, impulse and even violence.

Le Bon's description of the crowd is supported by much research in social psychology as well as by everyday examples. In the famous Asch experiments of the 1950's, social psychologists found that the strongest pressure to conform arises when individuals find themselves at odds with other members of a group.[35] In these experiments, subjects were asked to determine which of two straight lines on a screen was longer. The task was straightforward, and one line was clearly longer than the other. However, the subjects were asked to give their answer *after* hearing the response of other "subjects." These other subjects were actually confederates of the experimenters and had been secretly instructed to call the obviously shorter line the longer one. The unwitting subjects frequently modified their answers by identifying the shorter line as the longer one to avoid taking a position unsupported by the rest of the group—even if it meant denying the evidence of their own eyes. Muzafer and Carolyn Sherif conducted a number of studies that investigated collective interaction attempting to explain events like lynchings and riots.[36] They, too, found that conformity pressures often caused individuals engaged in a crowd mentality to undertake collective actions at odds with the personalities and training of the individuals involved. A recent study of the mechanisms of war suggests that the very structure of military institutions exploits the characteristics of collective action that emerge when individuals become part of a mass.[37] Many elements of the process of basic training strip away the individual personalities of young recruits, thus transforming them into fighting units who take orders without question and engage in degrees of violence otherwise foreign to their natures.

The concept of audience as a mass is probably most relevant to persuasion that occurs under the headings we have termed propaganda and social movements. However, the pressure on people to conform to mass thinking underlies any concept of the audience as "mass" and is a relatively common characteristic among the other concepts of mass audiences. In a sense, these different concepts of an audience differ only according to the source of that pressure. Audiences targeted because of similar demographic characteristics are assumed to behave similarly because of these similar individual characteristics. When reference groups are emphasized, the pressure to conform to one's identification as a member of such groups is highlighted. In other cases, an individual's culture is the source of conformity pressure.

Flow Of Persuasive Messages

Regardless of how the audience is viewed, the Institutional Perspective toward persuasion often concentrates on the path by which a message reaches an audience. Our earlier discussion of formal communication systems suggested that most institutions rely on some form of the mass media to reach whatever audience they have chosen. However, the flow of persuasive messages is often more complex than a simple path from source to receiver through the media. Several contemporary theories regarding how persuasive messages reach audiences address this issue.

One approach to the flow of persuasive messages concerns how people select which media to use. Among the most durable theories of this type is the *uses and gratifications approach*, which maintains that individuals tend to use particular media because they serve a particular social function for those individuals.[38] Audiences are differentiated not by demographics, but by the social-psychological motivation for their use of the media. For example, people may listen to the radio in the morning in order to hear the weather report for the day to be able to make appropriate plans for lunch hour; they may read the local newspaper over breakfast in order to keep up with community news; they may tune to their favorite radio station for entertainment as they drive to work; they may turn on a television comedy that evening simply as a way of savoring some time alone. They might switch to a sports report later in the evening because sports is a likely topic of conversation tomorrow morning at the office. Media use itself may serve to gratify audience social needs. These needs are similar to those mentioned in our discussion of Maslow's humanistic psychology—socialization, belonging, status or self-worth.[39] Hence institution-level persuasion serves social functions beyond the explicit goals of persuaders. We will return in later chapters to the ways in which the media-use component of institutional persuasion is related both to socialization and alienation.

Another broad perspective on the flow of persuasive messages in the media falls under the heading of *diffusion of innovation*. For any new idea, technique, product or information disseminated by mass media, there are those who will be among the first to try it, the *innovators*. Contrary to what might seem common sense, however, mass media campaigns aimed at innovators are likely to have little success in influencing the population as a whole. This is because innovators are often perceived as being somewhat peculiar and outside the mainstream. Instead, that segment of the overall population regarded as respected and mainstream may not be the first to adopt an innovation, but when they do, their opinion is highly influential for the rest of the population. Ideas adopted by these *opinion leaders* have a greater likelihood of diffusion throughout the population as a whole. Thus, the process of mass persuasion is often not a single-step process in which an idea reaches and influences all parts of the audience at a uniform rate. Paul Lazarsfeld and his associates labeled this principle the *two-step flow* theory of media effects. Their research on political campaigns in the 1940s discovered that most people were more influenced by their interpersonal interaction with opinion leaders than by the messages broadcast by the mass media. However, the mass media were highly influential among the small segment comprising the opinion leaders themselves.[40] Thus, persuasive messages in mass media campaigns tend to move from the media to the opinion leaders, relying upon the opinion leaders to become the mass persuader's workforce, creating support for the new idea or product through interpersonal interaction with the larger audience. Later researchers modified the theory further, advancing a *multi-step flow* model in which many individuals receive information from the media and then seek out opinion leaders for confirmation or additional information. These researchers' observations suggest that a number of intermediary steps may exist between the media, the message receivers and their attitudes.[41]

When institutions attempt to influence individuals via persuasive campaigns and propaganda, the diffusion of innovations approach helps explain the communication flow. But in other instances of institutional persuasion, the audience may not be individuals so much as other institutions. Some social movements, for example, seek to change the operations of particular institutions. Even when the ultimate aim is widespread public support, as with many propaganda campaigns, the opinion leaders may be institutions instead of individuals. For example, a campaign against smoking may target the insurance industry as its audience. As a consequence, an institution like the American Medical Association may devise a persuasive strategy aimed at the insurance industry to supplement its more general appeals directed toward individuals within society.

If we return to the description provided earlier in this chapter of the media as an institution, we see the importance of communication flow. Persuaders must be aware of which media act as relay points for their intended audience. However, to obtain the media coverage necessary to reach that target audience, a persuader may need to consider the media institution itself as an audience. Knowledge about the communication network operative within the media itself is a necessary first step to using the media as a means to reach one audience who, in turn, acts as an intermediary for the target audience. Thus, from the Institutional Perspective, the flow of persuasive messages is critical.

Ethical Concerns From An Institutional Perspective

While many of the ethical principles discussed earlier in this book apply to persuasive messages that flow from institutions, institutional persuasion poses additional ethical challenges. In a penetrating study of the history of persuasion, rhetorical theorist and critic J. Michael Sproule observes: "notwithstanding surface continuities in the forms of American society and persuasion, the shift during the last four generations from oratorical to managerial forms of social control is evident whether one focuses on source, audience, or message."[42] According to Sproule, institutional persuasion enlists the talents of specialized media managers who carefully select professional channels through which to transmit entertaining packages of slogans, images and ideologies to highly segmented parts of the mass audience.[43] If we dissect Sproule's analysis, we encounter a number of ethical concerns.

Consider first the nature of the source from the Institutional Perspective. Who assumes responsibility for a persuasive message that does not seem ethically sound? For example, if an advertisement presents a slogan that diverts our attention away from the quality of the product or promotes an inhumane worldview, who is responsible—the company that paid for the advertisement, the agency that produced it or the network that ran it? Furthermore, exactly who *within* any of those corporate bodies is responsible—the writer, the director or the producer?

From the Institutional Perspective, the diffusion of information so common for communication networks also leads to a diffusion of ethical responsibility for institutional persuasion. Johannesen outlines this problem in his discussion of ethical responsibility within organizations: "The complex, impersonal, hierarchical nature of modern organizations presents some difficulties for communication ethics."[44] Partly to address the problem of assessing responsibility within an organization, many organizations have developed their own ethical codes. As Johannesen points out, "there is a definite trend in various individual print and broadcast news organizations, and in some other types of companies, toward setting up their own more precise and enforceable ethical codes."[45] From the Institutional Perspective, then, we should question whether or not the lines of ethical responsibility are clear.

Second, ethical challenges arise regarding the messages that emanate from various institutions. The nature of formal communication systems place such a premium on entertainment, images and subtlety that the ideas or "facts" within a message become almost secondary. Pseudo-events, highly dramatic situations and catchy slogans dominate in a system facing highly priced media time and the need to break through the clutter of a multiplicity of messages. Thus, many ethical principles we noted from the Symbolist Perspective may be more applicable here than those we observed from the Classical Perspective. However, the sheer numbers of persuasive messages resulting from these complex and interacting institutions may be so fragmented that an audience simply cannot construct a coherent worldview to evaluate the ethics of any one given message. W. Lance Bennett makes a similar point when he explains that traditional news programming is so fragmented that audiences are often left with little understanding of the issues covered:[46]

> It is no wonder that public opinion studies have shown that most people have trouble thinking in abstract, logically integrated ways about political issues. An inventory of findings from public opinion research sounds like a list of the effects of news fragmentation. The average person has trouble stating clear positions on issues; most people tend to remember few facts about important issues; the majority of people see few connections between issues; and many people change their opinions easily about issues. The parallels between news fragmentation and public opinion characteristics suggest that the public's true failing may have been to follow the news and take it seriously.

So, the messages themselves, because they conform to the system in which they are produced, exhibit characteristics that are ethically questionable, even from a Symbolist Perspective on ethics. An alternative ethical standard from the Institutional Perspective questions whether the message contributes to or detracts from an overall understanding of the world that emerges from the "mosaic" of messages surrounding an audience.[47]

Finally, consider the audience as viewed from the Institutional Perspective. The ethical problems begin with the extreme redefinition of the audience as a "mass" exhibiting a "crowd mentality." Segmented markets that cause the targeting of groups according to their demographic characteristics or cherished dreams also create ethical problems. Such segmenting perpetuates cultural divisions, thereby reducing the chances for human cooperation. Targeting trades on worldviews that are necessarily partial, reflecting only one view at the expense of other viewpoints. Formal communication systems severely compound this problem. Various authors note the potential for cultural imperialism that arises when one culture exports its entertainment packages to another. The same observation applies to subcultures. Thus, one ethical concern of those investigating the audience for institutional persuasion should be respect for cultural diversity.

One way to guarantee respect for diverse opinions is to provide some sort of assurance that all interested parties have the opportunity to voice their opinions, the sort of assurance offered by the First Amendment to the United States Constitution. Unfortunately, even within a democratic tradition that guarantees free expression, the complex and bureaucratic nature of our society often silences a variety of viewpoints by simply not granting access to the media or refusing to give legitimacy to sources not affiliated with high status institutions.[48] For example, minor political parties do not receive the same amount of coverage as major parties, or ordinary people may not be consulted for their views as frequently as experts in day-to-day news coverage. The impact of silencing some members of the audience is most often apathy, an encouraged retreat from participation in real decision making. From an ethical standpoint, therefore, we must ask what impact institutional persuasion has on the audience. Does institutional persuasion render audience members passive consumers or promote their active participation? As Sproule advises, critics should ask whether the new managerial rhetoric is merely self-serving or whether it addresses community interests.[49]

A related issue of ethics returns our attention to the inexorable blurring of categories such as news, public affairs and entertainment which the commercial mass media have brought about. With this blurring of messages and purposes has come a gradual decline of all audiences into consumers, rather than citizens. This problem has been explored in some detail by media critic Neil Postman, who argues that our politics, religion, news, athletics, education and commerce have been transformed into show business, resulting in a society of people "who are on the verge of amusing ourselves to death."[50] According to Postman, our preoccupation with entertainment and the aesthetic standards by which entertainment is judged inhibits our capacity to make informed and significant decisions by any other standards. We see this problem everywhere—from the gradual merging of politics into the entertainment arenas of talk radio and MTV to the obsession of professors and their students that the college classroom be, above all else, fun. Media critic Stewart Ewen notes a related problem: When everything and anything becomes a saleable commodity, and when the value of an idea is reduced to its commercial marketability, then an ideology of consuming and consumerism interferes with our ability to live in community oriented and environmentally sound ways.[51] Unbridled consumerism causes us to demand the production of unneeded products, to throw away perfectly usable goods in favor of new models and to further injure the environment in the process.

Finally, we should note that institutions themselves often call into play very specific, formalized codes of ethics, such as those applying to elected officials and to various professions like advertising, marketing, journalism or law.[52] Although such codes are by no means a guarantee that all institution-level persuasion is ethical, they nevertheless provide a standard of judgment for the conduct of many persuaders in the institutional context.

These questions merely scratch the surface of ethical concerns from the Institutional Perspective. However, they do reveal the flavor of ethical analysis that considers persuasion as it occurs through a complex and bureaucratic system. Our observations may lead one to believe that ideology and propaganda are always unethical, while campaigns sometimes are and social movements frequently are not. To some extent, we *do* contend that self-serving persuasion is always unethical. However, ideology and even propaganda does sometimes serve the public interest rather than furthering only a particular institutional goal. We will explore these ethical concerns in more detail throughout the remaining chapters in this section of the book.

CRITICAL FOCUS: GOPTV'S *RISING TIDE*

The Institutional Perspective toward persuasion directs our attention to the importance of the institutional settings in which much contemporary persuasion emerges. Certain theoretical, practical and ethical factors will emerge as particularly important whenever persuasion created by institutions (such as the Republican National Committee) is aimed at an institutional audience (such as many political reform movements which have used the channels of communication created by RNC) or occurs within an institutional context (the use of existing broadcast and cable-access systems to distribute GOPTV's *Rising Tide*). Indeed the sheer scale of potential influence, as well as the volume of messages in a multiplicity of formal and informal media over time, makes persuasion at the institutional level an area of study that neither the Classical or Symbolist Perspective can completely encompass on its own. The following questions are oriented toward examining persuasion from an Institutional Perspective.

CRITICAL QUESTIONS

1. What is the **nature of the social institution**(s) engaged in persuasion?
2. What **relationships** exist between this institution and other institutions, especially formal communication systems?
3. What **types of persuasive messages** are typically produced by these institutions?
4. What **definition of audience** is most appropriate for and seems to be used by this particular institution?
5. What **channels or networks of communication** appear to be used and to be most appropriate for this particular institution?
6. How do the **institution's choices about audience**, **formal communication systems** and **networks** influence the content and form of the persuasive messages that are produced?
7. What is the **effect** of such institutional persuasion, especially choices about the use of formal communications systems, on other institutions and persuasive practice, generally?
8. To what **extent** does the institutional dimension of such persuasion call into play certain ethical standards of persuasion, and how does the persuasion in question measure up to these ethical standards?

GOPTV's *Rising Tide* is an example of persuasion designed by one institution—a national political party—and shaped by the constraints of several other institutions, most notably federal government and its regulatory power and the goals and practices of the cable industry and local cable companies.

The connections among these institutions are many. The cable industry seeks to maximize its profits; therefore, it works to produce programming that will be widely viewed. GOPTV, in order to earn its space on cable channels, must produce programming that attracts viewers, so that cable companies can attract subscribers. On another track, the profitability of the cable and broadcasting industry is influenced by the regulations placed upon it by the federal government, such as the limits on content and manner of programming. And the industry, in turn, spends a great deal of time and money lobbying lawmakers to shape legislation to the industry's liking. Since GOPTV is the cable station of the party—at this writing the majority party in both houses of Congress—the connection is obvious. The activities of the Republican National Committee are limited by its tax-exempt status as a nonprofit organization; those of the broadcast industries are limited by the presumption that the airwaves are a public trust which they are licensed to use. This simple sketch shows that these institutions influence and are influenced by one another even as they work to reach us, as their primary audience.

The Republican Party, like the Democratic Party, has always had access to broadcast, print and cable media, since these media covered as "news" their activities including press conferences, conventions, conferences, speeches and public statements. The Republican Party and American conservatives in general have recently been more aggressive and innovative in their persuasive uses of television. In 1993, conservative activist Paul Weyrich, president of the populist/conservative Free Congress Foundation, launched National Empowerment Television, now America's Voice, a 24-hour commercial network supported by the tax-deductible support of well-heeled conservative sponsors and think tanks.[54] The Free Congress Foundation's populist conservatism and its founder's media savvy are both reflected in the network's heavy emphasis on live, phone-in talk shows, which average eight hours a day.[55] These programs include *The Progress Report*, hosted by Newt Gingrich, and *Endangered Liberties*, with Paul Weyrich.

The emphasis is on politics and public affairs, but the approach is to address the audience primarily in terms of the conformity principle, as a mass audience rather than as a political public. "In this post-Cold War era, we think the last major battle is Washington versus the rest of the country," says NET president Weyrich. "We've turned the megaphone around."[56] The spirit may be populist, but the image of conservative TV's viewers as being on the receiving end of a megaphone hardly suggests a high regard for individual differences in the audience. One could argue that, in this regard, GOPTV and NET are in the grip of the same logic that has captured all for-profit mass media: the need to operate on a mass scale, drawing mass audiences for advertisers.

This is not to say that there is no attempt to segment audiences on GOPTV's part, however. The audience strategy behind *Rising Tide* is explicitly two-step. Although it welcomes all viewers, the program is especially concerned with using its resources to reach two primary audiences. The first audience consists of local GOP groups gathering regularly on Thursday nights at neighborhood meeting locations with satellite hook-up. These groups view the show and discuss its content, aided by a program guide, not unlike those received by contributors to PBS, A&E and so on. The second audience consists of other politically like-minded organizations who do not have direct access to the live broadcasts but watch, discuss, and further disseminate the programs on videotape. Thus, the active members of these organizations become the opinion leaders who in turn redistribute the party's information and positions to others in the broader population. By organizing their persuasion in this way, Republicans concede the disappearance of precinct-level participation by voters that was the strength of the parties until television became a more direct means for candidates to talk with voters and voters to talk with each other.[57] Satellite broadcast, Internet web sites and chat rooms, and phone-in talk programming have all overtaken the ward captain, walking door-to-door to keep in touch with voters and learn their interests.

The choice of media and the conception of the audience clearly influenced the persuasion found in GOPTV's *Rising Tide*. These influences include explicit choices of tactics and more subtle matters of form and structure. Perhaps the most obvious persuasive characteristic of *Rising Tide* was its imitation of the conventions of standard "nonpartisan" news coverage in its programming. Whether or not one takes the hard-line, Classical Perspective on the importance of logic, evidence and reasoning, certainly the "myth of objectivity" remains woven throughout our culture, as we discussed in Chapter 1. Thus, appeals to "facts" and "the truth," to "objectivity" and even-handedness, are likely to help persuaders in their efforts to influence. *Rising Tide* capitalized on this characteristic of audiences by casting itself in the form of a news or public affairs program that might be found on any network. The graphics, the bright competence of the reporters, the high-tech look of the main set, the folksy and avuncular style of host Barbour, even the occasional commentaries by non-conservatives are all tokens that signal the kind of balance and disinterestedness associated with objectivity. More explicitly, promotional spots for the show include former President Ronald Reagan assuring viewers: "I know I can count on Haley to set the record straight."[58]

And yet, even by the standards of broadcast television, whose claim to objectivity already seems more often like a fig leaf, *Rising Tide* undercut this surface appearance of non-partisanship with an approach that was enthusiastically—even gleefully—partisan. One commentator observed about an episode aired in 1994:

> It takes a moment to realize that this particular installment of *Rising Tide* is not typical television news. The topic is familiar (crime), the image mundane (a blighted inner city neighborhood). Yet the reporter's spiel...is hardly the stuff of conventional journalism. "Soft-headed approaches won't solve America's crime crisis," he concludes. "Tough Republican solutions will."[59]

As the excerpts from *Rising Tide* included on the video for this text show, this tendency is the rule rather than the exception. Barbour leads off this episode by declaring the evening's main topic: "the badly flawed Clinton plan that threatens to transform the world's best health care system into a bureaucratic mess that will mean higher taxes, fewer jobs, and worse care." The partisan pounding continues in the "GOP News Update," in which the anchorperson announces, "We begin tonight with the latest setback to the president's troubled health care bill..." Not all of the loading is this obvious. For example, Clinton and his spokespersons are usually described, ambivalently, as having "promised" or "claimed" with respect to the health care debate, while Republicans are portrayed as more objective and fact-oriented, often described as "pointing out" rather than "claiming" or "promising."

And for those subscribers who received the glossy 32-page program guide, also called *Rising Tide*, the gloves came off entirely, and the bashing of Democrats, liberals and occasionally even moderates continued with gusto. In the regular feature "Them Dems," for example, a page of brief items directed not merely opposition but enthusiastic ridicule at liberalism, Democrats, multiculturalism, political correctness and especially Bill and Hillary Clinton. A similar feature, called "Bill Busters," collected brief quotes and statements by Clinton and his staff suggestive of legal or ethical shenanigans. GOPTV, *Rising Tide*, NET and their followers and imitators may signal a return to the openly partisan politics of the nineteenth century news media.

The effect of the commercial television/mass market medium upon *Rising Tide* was further demonstrated in another, more covert, manner. Like much of televised politics and nearly all of our mass media culture, *Rising Tide* packaged itself in a form that blurred the line between entertainment and public affairs. Many of the persuasive message characteristics we have mentioned are relevant here, such as the attractive anchors and reporters, the catchy music, the slick graphics and the fast-paced editing. Although *Rising Tide* prided itself on its in-depth treatment of issues characteristic of a C-SPAN, that treatment is still covered with the frosting of CNN-style busy visuals and talk show chat.

The potential for persuasive influence of GOPTV's *Rising Tide* was significant, but varied. *Rising Tide* was in a somewhat ironic position that forced it to send strongly mixed messages, adopting many elements of the visual and linguistic codes of nonpartisan television journalism to advance a strictly partisan agenda. Likewise, GOPTV is in the unusual position of using a sophisticated satellite-based television network to proclaim their distance from the "media elites," to use their power and influence to portray themselves as political outsiders rather than insiders. As a Republican National Committee spokesperson explained, "The President has the bully pulpit, and the Republican message doesn't get out there. Our aim is to bypass the media elite with our message." Clearly, the Republican National Committee is counting on the loyalists in its audience to overlook or forgive these contradictions, most notably that group who has their own national cable channel and programming already *is* part of the "media elite."

But the partisanship of *Rising Tide* and of GOPTV in general raises other questions of importance from both a strategic and an ethical point of view. The strongly partisan message of GOPTV and NET is a problem for some cable operators. The analogy with the fate of the *Star Trek* television series during its original broadcast run is an odd but useful example. In both cases, a small but fiercely loyal audience proves to be less economically useful to a network or cable owner if it drives away a less committed, but numerically larger audience of the right demographic makeup for advertisers.[60]

Thus, GOPTV, NET and other networks such as American Political Channel and Conservative Television Network all buck the trend toward lowest-common-denominator programming, at least up to a point.[61] As a result, the persuasion they create is somewhat more tightly focused with respect to its audience than that of other broadcast networks. GOPTV and NET occupy a middle ground between straight narrowcasting and clear broadcasting in defining and reaching their audience.[62] The sheer increase in available cable and broadcast time made possible by the expanded number of cable channels and satellite uplink opportunities makes such programming—comparatively narrowcast and directional—much more viable.

But there is a limit to this expansion of persuasive opportunity, and it is money. For all GOPTV's populist positioning, it still counts on support from sponsors to stay on the air, inevitably including many corporate and industry sponsors. It is not surprising, but almost inevitable, that GOPTV and its fellow conservative networks have been able to tap their corporate sponsors for the funds to get their message out. As Andrew Schwartzman of the nonpartisan Media Access Project observes, the cost of underwriting a television channel will naturally draw corporate sponsors to conservative channels rather than liberal ones. "The business community," says Schwartzman, "has a natural alliance with a channel that's going to promote a flat tax or deregulation."[63] Events seem to bear Schwartzman's prediction out. While National Empowerment Television has a distrubution agreement with cable giant TCI beginning in 1996, NET's liberal counterpart, The 90's Channel, has been unable to strike a deal with TCI for carriage. While TCI claims that The 90's Channel simply hasn't been popular or profitable enough to justify affiliation, The 90's Channel insists that it can't get that kind of cash flow without the exposure that TCI can give.[64] Whichever side we choose in this chicken-or-the-egg problem, however, the moral is clear: The key to "getting your message out" is money, the conservative channels have it, and the liberal ones don't.

Although conservatives claim that all this is nothing more than redressing the imbalance created by years of the dominant "liberal media," there is more at stake here. First, we should note that the claim that the media are biased toward liberalism is a popular exaggeration. True, many individual media figures, in journalism, entertainment and elsewhere, subscribe to liberal politics while a comparable number lean in a more conservative direction. But "the media" taken as a whole—as individual, local, corporate entities or the large international conglomerates of which the local publishers and broadcasters are often subsidiaries—are profoundly conservative entities which respond to the same pressures of profit-making and the marketplace as any other business, whether it be General Motors or AT&T. What originated the charge of "liberal bias" against the American media, especially television, is the traditional "adversarial" or "conscience" role that the news media take for themselves, most conspicuously in their coverage of the Vietnam war and the Watergate investigation.[65] At a time when the American public regards television news with almost as much cynicism as its elected officials, the value of quasi-news programming such as *Rising Tide* that proudly displays its bias rather than concealing it is questionable at best.

More to the point, however, we should be extremely skeptical of the simplistic division between "conservative" and "liberal" that such a charge perpetuates. We are in an era when winning presidential candidates attract less than 40 percent of registered voters, when survey after survey indicates that Americans are cynical and disenchanted with the two major parties, and serious discussions of third party and independent candidates have begun to fill the air to an extent unheard of since the days of Theodore Roosevelt. What this should remind us, as students of persuasion, is that the range of political viewpoints available across our cable dials, from conservative to liberal, is really only a small slice of the spectrum of political thought available in America. Thus, while we congratulate the conservatives for finding a means to advance their agendas in the public sphere, we worry that the existing connections among corporate, political and media institutions in America make it more impossible, as a practical matter, for other groups to advance their viewpoints in any equitable way.

Of course, non-establishment groups have always had their opportunities to reach larger persuasive audiences, such as the pamphlet, the penny newspaper and at one time even radio stations (how many of our readers know that Chicago station WCFL's call letters come from its original owner, the Chicago Federation of Labor?). Occasionally, events continue to remind us of this, as when the 1995 Oklahoma City bombing drew our attention to the use of the Internet as an alternative means of communication and organizing by many right-wing groups. Nevertheless, media scholar Ben Bagdikian warned in 1990:

> In 1981 twenty corporations controlled most of the business of the country's 11,000 magazines, but only seven years later that number had shrunk to three corporations. Today, despite more than 25,000 outlets in the United States, twenty-three corporations control most of the business in daily newspapers, magazines, television, books, and motion pictures.[66]

Bagdikian's tally is far behind the times; corporate mergers and acquisitions have continued apace since then, with almost daily announcements of one media conglomerate acquiring parts of or whole others. Thus, whatever one thinks of the politics of GOPTV, it is representative of an interpenetration of politics, entertainment and corporate profits which should be of concern to all citizens.

Notes

1. Quoted in Rex Nelson, "Live! It's Political TV," [Arkansas] *Democrat-Gazette,* March 19, 1995: J8.
2. Frank Rich, "Tin Cans and String," the *New York Times,* April 13, 1995: A25.
3. Rich, "Tin Cans," A25. A videotape of a 1994 broadcast of *Rising Tide* is included on the videotape of case studies for this book.
4. For a succinct historical review of the rise of institutional persuasion that includes discussion of advertising, public relations, propaganda and ideology, see J. Michael Sproule, "The New Managerial Rhetoric and the Old Criticism," *Quarterly Journal of Speech* 74 (1988): 468-486.
5. Herbert Simons, *Persuasion: Understanding, Practice, and Analysis,* 2nd Ed. (New York: Random House, 1986), 228, n 1.
6. Bernard Roschco, *Newsmaking* (Chicago: University of Chicago Press, 1975); for an excerpt of this work that supports the examples cited here, see *Media Power in Politics,* ed. Doris Graber (Washington: Congressional Quarterly Inc., 1984), 7-22.
7. Daniel J. Boorstin, *The Image: A Guide to Pseudo-Events in America* (New York: Athenium, 25th Anniversary Edition, 1987), 7.

8. Ellen Wartella, "Cognitive and Affective Factors of TV Advertising's Influence on Children," *Western Journal of Speech Communication* 48 (1984): 171-183.
9. David Manning White, "The 'Gatekeeper:' A Case Study in the Selection of News," *Journalism Quarterly* 27 (1950): 383-390.
10. Edward J. Epstein, *News From Nowhere: Television and the News* (New York: Random House, 1973).
11. Ben Bagdikian, *The Information Machines: Their Impact on Men and the Media* (New York: Harper & Row, 1971), 90-103.
12. Roshco, *Newsmaking,* 113.
13. Gaye Tuchman, *Making News: A Study in the Construction of Reality* (New York: Free Press, 1978); see also, Herbert J. Gans, *Deciding What's News* (New York: Vintage, 1980). For a summary of surveys of public attitudes regarding conservative or liberal bias in news coverage that sees such research as inconclusive, see W. Lance Bennett, *News: The Politics of Illusion,* 2nd Ed. (New York: Longman, 1988), 21-22.
14. Roshco, *Newsmaking,* 63.
15. For details of this news story and its coverage, see Farrel Corcoran, "KAL 007 and the Evil Empire: Mediated Disaster and Forms of Rationalization," *Critical Studies in Mass Communication* 3 (1986): 297-316.
16. Leo Rosten, *The Washington Correspondents* (New York: Harcourt, Brace, 1937), 78.
17. For a case study of this tendency, see Timothy Crouse, *The Boys on the Bus* (New York: Random House, 1973).
18. Gans, *Deciding,* 167-171.
19. Bennett, *News,* 53-54.
20. White, "Gatekeeper," 384.
21. Donald Roberts, "The Nature of Communication Effects," in Wilbur Schramm and Donald F. Roberts, *The Process and Effects of Mass Communication,* 3rd Ed. (Urbana: U Chicago P, 1971), 378.
22. Maxwell E. McCombs and Donald L. Shaw, "The Agenda-Setting Function of Mass Media," *Public Opinion Quarterly* 36 (1972): 176-187.
23. F. James Davis, "Crime News in Colorado Newspapers," *American Journal of Sociology* 57 (1952): 325-330.
24. See, for example, A. Mazur, "Media Coverage and Public Opinion in Scientific Controversies," *Journal of Communication* 31 (1981): 106-119; David H. Weaver, "Media Agenda-Setting and Media Manipulation," *Mass Communication Yearbook 3,* eds. D. Charles Whitney and Ellen Wartella (Beverly Hills: Sage, 1982), 680-691.
25. Shanto Iyengar and Donald R. Kinder, *News That Matters* (Chicago: University of Chicago Press, 1987).
26. Iyengar and Kinder, *News,* 132. See also, Gans, *Deciding.*
27. See Hedrick Smith, *The Power Game: How Washington Works* (New York: Ballantine Books, 1989), 35-40.
28. Smith, *Power,* 331-444.
29. Boorstin, *Image.*

30. Boorstin, *Image*, 9-11.
31. Boorstin, *Image*, 11-12.
32. Alexis De Tocqueville, *Democracy in America*, trans. George Lawrence, ed. J. P. Mayer (New York: Doubleday Anchor Books, 1969).
33. Ernest Bormann, "Fantasy and Rhetorical Vision: The Rhetorical Criticism of Social Reality," *Quarterly Journal of Speech* 58 (1972): 396-407.
34. Gustave Le Bon, *The Crowd* (London: Benn, 1947).
35. Solomon Asch, "Effects of Group Pressure upon the Modification and Distortion of Judgment," in *Groups, Leadership, and Men*, ed. Harold S. Guetzkow (Pittsburgh: Carnegie Press, 1951), 177-190.
36. Muzafer Sherif and Carolyn Sherif, *An Outline of Social Psychology* (New York: Harper & Row, 1956).
37. Robert B. Smith, "Why Soldiers Fight," *Quality and Quantity* 18 (1983): 1-32; see also, William Arkin and Lynne R. Dobrofsky, "Military Socialization and Masculinity," *Journal of Social Issues* 34 (1978): 151-168.
38. D. McQuail, J. G. Blumler and J. R. Brown, "The Television Audience: A Revised Perspective," in D. McQuail, ed., *Sociology of Mass Communication* (Harmondsworth: Penguin, 1972); Elihu Katz, Jay G. Blumler and Michael Gurevitch, "Uses of Mass Communication by the Individual," in W. Phillips Davison and Frederick T. C. Yu, eds., *Mass Communication Research* (New York: Praeger, 1974), 11- 35.
39. Katz, et al., "Uses by the Individual," 21; Abraham Maslow, *Motivation and Personality* (New York: Harper, 1954).
40. P. L. Lazarsfeld, P. Berelson and H. Gaudet, *The People's Choice: How the Voter Makes Up His Mind in a Presidential Campaign* (New York: Duell, Sloan, and Pearce, 1948).
41. E. M. Rogers and F. F. Shoemaker, *Communication of Innovations: A Cross Cultural Approach* (New York: Free Press, 1971).
42. Sproule, "New Managerial," 468.
43. Sproule, "New Managerial," 472-474.
44. Richard L. Johannesen, *Ethics in Human Communication*, 3rd Ed. (Prospect Heights: Waveland, 1990), 152.
45. Johannesen, *Ethics*, 172. For examples of such codes, see 177-191.
46. Bennett, *News*, 49.
47. For a discussion of mediated communication as a mosaic of message fragments, see Samuel L. Becker, "Rhetorical Studies for the Contemporary World," in *The Prospect of Rhetoric*, eds. Lloyd F. Bitzer and Edwin Black (Englewood Cliffs: Prentice Hall, 1971), 33.
48. Martha Cooper, "Ethical Dimensions of Political Communication from a Postmodern Perspective," in *Ethical Dimensions of Political Communication*, ed. Robert Denton, Jr. (New York: Praeger, 1991), 23-47.
49. Sproule, "New Managerial," 483.
50. Neil Postman, *Amusing Ourselves to Death: Public Discourse in the Age of Show Business* (New York: Viking, 1985), 3-4.
51. Stuart Ewen, *All Consuming Images* (New York: Basic Books, 1988), 233-58.

53. See: Johannesen, *Ethics*, Chapter 10: "Formal Codes of Ethics."
54. Nelson, "Political TV," J8.
55. Thomas Goetz, "I'm Not A Reporter: But I Play One on GOPTV," *Columbia Journalism Review*, September/October 1994: 13.
56. Goetz, "I'm Not A Reporter," 13.
57. Nelson, "Political TV," J8.
58. Nelson, "Political TV," J1.
59. Goetz, "I'm Not A Reporter," 13.
60. Nelson, "Political TV," 8J.
61. Thomas Goetz, "Cable: Who's Connected?" *Columbia Journalism Review*, July/August 1995: 15.
62. In fact, Paul Weyrich, head of NET, describes the original show upon which the National Empowerment Television network was based as a "narrowcast."
63. Goetz, "Cable," 15.
64. Goetz, "Cable," 15.
65. Edward S. Herman and Noam Chomsky, *Manufacturing Consent: The Political Economy of the Mass Media* (New York: Pantheon, 1988), 298-99.
66. Ben. H. Badikian, *The Media Monopoly* (Boston: Beacon Press, 1990), 4.

11
PERSUASIVE CAMPAIGNS

IN THIS CHAPTER:
Focus on:
Tourette Syndrome Association Awareness Campaign

1. Theoretical Focus: Persuasive Campaigns
2. Stages of the Campaign Cycle
    Diffusion and Adoption: an Audience-Centered Approach
    Campaign Stages: An Institutional Framework Approach
3. Persuasive Strategies And Tactics in Campaigns
    Audience Segmentation and Analysis
    Determining Channels and Communication Networks
    Measurement of Effects and Adaptation
4. Ethics in Persuasive Campaigns
5. Critical Focus: Tourette Syndrome Association's Awareness Campaign

FOCUS ON: TOURETTE SYNDROME ASSOCIATION AWARENESS CAMPAIGN

Tourette Syndrome is a neurobiological disorder characterized by tics, which are involuntary, rapid, sudden muscle contractions. The disorder is also sometimes accompanied by vocal outbursts. General knowledge of the disorder is superficial and often inaccurate. In fact, according to Tourette Syndrome Association (TSA) spokesperson Sue Levi-Pearl, people who have heard of TS usually only know about extreme cases where patients uncontrollably spew venomous invectives and obscenities. Recent studies show that "Cursing, uttering obscenities, and ethnic slurs are manifested by fewer than 15 percent of people with TS." Too often, laments Levi-Pearl, "the media seize upon this symptom for its sensational effect."[1]

Public ignorance, media distortion, an imperative for early diagnosis and treatment and fund-raising to support medical research toward finding a cure constitute the driving forces behind the Tourette Syndrome Association's ongoing awareness campaign. The association is the sole national, voluntary, non-profit health organization dedicated to identifying the cause of TS, finding its cure and controlling the effects of the disorder. It supports research and professional and public education, as well as provides individual and family services through donor funding.[2] TSA's campaign to raise awareness and money is an excellent model for the study of persuasive campaigns because its success depends on reaching a large number of segmented groups over an extended period. The nature of TS is such that, typically, only when a person is directly affected through his own or a family or friend's diagnosis does he care to learn more about the disorder. Consequently, a mass campaign to reach a mass audience is not a feasible strategy for the TSA. Yet, a mass of donors and mass awareness of a disorder that affects 200,000 people in the U.S. are TSA campaign goals. Appealing to a multitude of smaller audiences, each with their own values and social structure, has led to steady progress toward fulfilling the TSA's objectives. Because it appears likely that a cure for TS remains in the distant future, however, the TSA will need to maintain this campaign indefinitely.

In this chapter, we explain how persuasion works within such a persuasive campaign. The scale, duration and institutional context of this type of campaign raise important questions for both the analysis and practice of persuasion in campaigns. Later, in the Critical Focus, we return to the case of the Tourette Syndrome Association's campaign. In preparation for this, we first look more closely at the unique characteristics of persuasive campaigns as a form of institutional level persuasion. Next, we examine two broad theories of the stages of persuasive campaigns, derived from audience and institutional factors faced by those campaigns. Finally, we examine questions of audience analysis, media use and persuasion ethics unique to persuasive campaigns.

THEORETICAL FOCUS: PERSUASIVE CAMPAIGNS

Persuasive campaigns involve explicit and implicit persuasion through the use of multiple messages over time to promote private gain or motives within an institutional context. The most common types of persuasive campaigns are *product campaigns, public relations campaigns* and *political campaigns*. Product campaigns may use the same slogan over a period of time. During this time they incorporate multiple messages for consumers to increase the market share of a particular product. Similarly, political candidates use both paid and free media time to persuade citizens to cast ballots on their behalf in an election that is itself institutionalized within our political system.

The general characteristics of institutional persuasion discussed in Chapter 10 explain a number of the characteristics of persuasive campaigns; in addition, several other unique features are worthy of mention. As we note in Chapter 10, persuasive campaigns involve explicit persuasion for private gain within "the system." As with other types of persuasion that we study from the Institutional Perspective, persuasive campaigns involve multiple messages, exist over a period of time and are structured around intermediate goals as well as ultimate goals. What makes campaigns unique among forms of institutional persuasion is that a campaign generally involves explicit, intentional persuasion occurring within a social context with the purpose of obtaining private gain.

As with other types of persuasion, whether institutional or interpersonal, campaigns may produce unintended effects, but a defining characteristic of a campaign is that it is both *intentional and explicit*. When a corporation employs the services of an advertising agency or public relations firm, corporate leaders typically have a specific goal in mind—to increase sales of a particular product, increase market share or enhance the corporate image. While the messages produced for the campaign might themselves avoid explicit "hard-sell" techniques, persuaders and audiences alike understand and accept that these are *persuasive* messages. Similarly, in political campaigns, a candidate or party typically has a concrete goal in mind. Everyone, both inside and outside of the campaign organization, understands these goals.

Campaign planners typically direct the corporate or political goals toward *individual benefits*. A company may seek an increase in sales to enhance its own profits. Doing so may also stimulate the economy and thus provide some social benefit, but the motivating force is private interest. Election campaigns work in a similar way. Although particular candidates or political parties may believe that winning an election will benefit the public, the motivating factor for a political campaign is usually the private advancement of a particular person's political career or the political advancement of the agenda of a particular group.

Another distinguishing characteristic of campaigns is that they are *conducted within the existing social institutions*. Unlike social movements that may challenge "the system," campaigns operate within and depend upon existing institutional frameworks. In the case of political campaigns, this framework defines when the campaign takes place as well as the goals of the campaign. Because the law sets the term of office for an American President at four years, for example, our governmental institutions guarantee that a political campaign will take place every four years, and "the system" further specifies the process and the goal of electing a president. Here "the system" includes the requirements of federal law, the convenience of the media who cover the election and our social norms that create certain important expectations about how candidates will present themselves and their case. Similar institutional forces, which again we lump together for convenience's sake as "the system," exert a similar influence for campaigns in commerce. Within the mixed free market system in the United States, companies succeed or fail according to their ability to market successfully, to work within a body of laws regarding trade, taxation and commerce and, thereby, to make a profit. Consequently, the general goal of a campaign is defined within the parameters of the prevailing media, legal and economic systems.

Because campaigns work within established institutional arrangements, *their legitimacy*—and that of the persons, products or causes advanced by the campaign and of those who serve as campaign leaders or spokespersons—*is rarely questioned*. Consumers or citizens accept the appropriateness of a campaign because "that's the way 'the system' works." Even when some question a campaign, others defend it on similar grounds. For example, in the spring of 1990, the American press got wind of a striking story. R. J. Reynolds, following a preliminary marketing analysis, was prepared to launch a campaign for a new brand of cigarette, Uptown, targeted primarily toward blacks.[3] The campaign triggered an angry response from black leaders, especially in urban areas, and from Secretary of Health and Human Services Louis Sullivan, who noted both the shockingly low life expectancy of urban black males in America and the fact that alcohol and tobacco are among the main causes of preventable death.[4] The initial reaction of R. J. Reynolds was not guilt or shame, but indignation. They pointed out that since the manufacture and sale of cigarettes was perfectly legal in this country, the company had the same right to advertise their product as do the makers of bran flakes. R. J. Reynolds argued their actions were quite within accepted institutional norms and, therefore, legitimate and that the only wrong doing involved was the leaking of proprietary marketing information. Many companies target their products in a similar way but retain the air of legitimacy by not allowing their strategy to become public knowledge. As one industry observer remarked: "*Being explicit* in the targeting of any group with a product as controversial as cigarettes was a mistake."[5] Eventually, R. J. Reynolds halted its plans to test market Uptown, largely because of the negative media coverage and the intense hostility within the black community to the persuasive campaign. However, such instances are still relatively rare because of the legitimacy typically conferred on campaigns that work within "the system."

Since campaigns enjoy a general sense of legitimacy because of the connections and support of established institutions, persuasive campaigns typically find *relatively easy access to formal communication systems*, including access to both their resources and their prestige. Access and legitimacy are closely related factors. Political candidates from the major parties, for example, can ordinarily depend on media coverage as reporters will be assigned to follow their campaigns. By comparison, third-party and independent political candidates for state and national office rarely attract media coverage and face a deadly spiral. Their lack of affiliation with a major political party causes them to be perceived as "less legitimate" candidates, which in turn causes the media to devote less coverage to them, confirming the perception that their candidacy is "less legitimate" than the well-reported major party competition.

Candidates and corporate sponsors alike encounter little difficulty obtaining paid media coverage so long as they possess the resources to buy air time. However, such access carries with it constraints as well. One of the most important of these constraints is the tendency of media coverage to view political and product campaigns as legitimate but also as competitive events. Consequently, free media coverage may dwell on the campaign as a "horse-race," emphasizing the tactics being used, the consultants hired, fired or rehired and the daily changes in polling results. The results of such scrutiny affect the nature of the campaign itself. Any candidate for President knows, for example, that the importance of a successful showing in the earliest spring primaries and caucuses has nothing to do with the importance of those states themselves, since neither Iowa nor New Hampshire has many electoral votes or a particularly representative population. Yet early contests in these states mark candidates as "winners" or "dark horses" or "losers." The results of these contests can make or break an individual candidate's ability to continue to attract campaign contributions with which to maintain their organization and purchase media advertising time.[6]

These general characteristics of campaigns—their explicit persuasion, use of multiple messages, existence over time and operation within established social systems and institutions—also imply several more specific characteristics. First, campaigns generally pursue *formalized goals* that result from the interaction between private motives and systemic constraints. These formal goals ordinarily create a "life cycle" for campaigns, giving a clearly identifiable beginning, signalled by the announcement of a new product line or the declaration of candidacy, and a clearly specifiable end, such as a target sales figure or a general election. Second, because campaigns occur over a period of time, their *persuasive strategies and messages will change and develop* over the lifetime of the campaign with different persuasive themes prepared for different stages in the campaign. For example, early in a political campaign, a candidate advertises primarily to create name recognition; as the campaign develops, she advertises to establish her position on certain selected issues and to attack the position of the opponent; in the final days of the campaign, she advertises to reaffirm a positive image but avoids the specifics of issues.[7] Third, to take into account "the system," the complex web of institutional constraints within which they operate, campaigns typically rely on *highly organized and centralized planning*.

Occasionally, of course, we find partial exceptions to these characterizations. While issue-oriented or public awareness-oriented campaigns, such as the AIDS awareness campaign discussed in Chapter 4, are clearly motivated by public good rather than by private gain, the other general principles, discussed above, still apply to the analysis and explanation of the AIDS campaign. However, the characteristics outlined above generally apply to all campaigns, whether public relations, product or political. In the discussion of campaigns that follows, we elaborate by referring to particular theories of persuasion that relate to campaigns.

Stages Of The Campaign Cycle

A central aspect of campaigns which distinguishes them among forms of institution level persuasion is that they unfold over a clearly defined period of time. Persuasion theorists point out that campaigns assume different characteristics at different points in their life-cycles and that persuasive messages serve different functions at different points in the campaign. Consequently, researchers developed several conceptual schemes for describing the stages of persuasive campaigns. Such schemes help explain why a message that is very effective at one point may be less effective at another point. Also, these schemes underscore the importance of multiple persuasive messages within a campaign. In the following sections, we examine two different approaches to describing campaign stages. The first, based on diffusion and adoption theory, focuses on the social structure of the audience itself. The second, drawn from the study of political campaigns, focuses on the interplay between the unfolding campaign and the various institutions with which it relates.

Diffusion and Adoption: An Audience-Centered Approach

Arising from the findings of early research into the stages of product and commercial campaigns, the diffusion of innovation theory continues to help describe the patterns by which new ideas take hold throughout a mass audience. As we explained in Chapter 10, this audience-centered model was developed from research in the 1940's investigating the patterns by which mass scale persuasion could influence audience behavior, such as that promoting the use of hybrid seed corn by Midwestern farmers.[8] Media researcher Elihu Katz summarized the general adoption model as based upon an assumed relationship between media use and interpersonal interaction:

> [Two-step flow theory] suggests that individual decisions are influenced less often by direct exposure to the mass media than to the opinions of other people. The theory holds that the individuals who are influential for others are more likely to be exposed to relevant mass media than are the people whom they influence.[9]

This research indicates that *innovators*—those who are among the first to try a new product or support a new candidacy—are not necessarily *opinion leaders*. Opinion leaders pay closer attention to mass persuasion for information about new products or candidacies, make choices and influenc others who are less decided. Instead, this research indicates that successful persuasion on a large scale exploits both mass and interpersonal communication. Some parts of the audience are most influenced by the media advancing a campaign's "message;" others are most influenced by opinion leaders with whom they are related.[9] We will return to the discussion of opinion leaders in the next section of this chapter; here we will consider the process of diffusion as a whole. The model of diffusion developed by Everett Rogers in the early 1960's describes the five-stage movement of new information among members of a mass audience as they respond to any campaign for new products or services.[10] Common sense tells us that no campaign for a new idea, product or candidacy can succeed until some audience is made aware of it. Thus, the first stage in diffusion is the *information and knowledge stage*. At this stage, the consumer or decision maker is given information about the new product or service. Persuasive campaigns at this point simply inform consumers of the existence of the product and seek some kind of name recognition. For example, when Jolt, a soft drink high in caffeine and sugar, hit the market several years ago, the campaign's first stage involved informing consumers of the soft drink's existence and connecting the name with the product.

The second stage of innovation, *persuasion or attitude formation*, occurs when audience members form attitudes, positive or negative or both, about the product. Obviously, the formation of audience attitudes about a product is not *always* a separate and later process from acquiring information about the product. As explained throughout this book, one can never describe the process of "informing" an audience as a persuasively neutral event in which audiences already know their needs and rationally search for the best solution.[11] For example, some early buyers of compact disc players might actually have felt a need for a particular kind of sonic reproduction which their phonograph or tape player did not provide and after doing some searching discovered that compact disc players met this existing need. More CD buyers, however, probably did not feel the urge to improve the quality of their home music listening until they learned of this new product from media advertising or friends. Nevertheless, it makes some logical and conceptual sense for a campaign to divide the problems of *getting the information to the audience* from the problems of *attitude formation based on that information*. Persuasive messages promote the attitude formation stage of diffusion by emphasizing the benefits of the product and reasons for a purchase.

The third stage of the innovation process is *decision*, the point at which audience members choose to accept or reject the innovation, based on their knowledge and attitudes. Creating positive attitudes about Hondas, for example, does not satisfy a Honda dealer unless his customers actually buy cars. At this phase in the process, persuaders may use "hard-sell" advertising, stressing urgency for an immediate decision. Some familiar examples of advertising elements designed to move the audience to the moment of choice as soon as possible are: "Buy now!" "Offer ends at midnight!" "Don't wait!" and "Call this toll-free number right away!"[12] Special promotions, coupons, discounted prices or even free samples may also encourage consumers to try the product.

The next logical stage of innovation, *implementation*, is closely connected to decision. This stage in innovation occurs when audience members, having decided to adopt, purchase or choose the product or service being promoted, put the innovation to use. Perhaps this sounds obvious. Consider, however, how many owners of videocassette recorders understand and use all the options the machine offers? How many subscribers to basic cable television watch much television or watch all the channels? How many consumers who purchase expensive basketball shoes actually appreciate their high-tech features? If we choose the innovation but never put it to use, it does not have the effect that the creators of the campaign seek. Certainly audience members who choose innovations but never implement them are unlikely to gain full satisfaction from them. This is because the *implementation* stage is not necessarily the final stage in diffusion of innovation.

The final phase of innovation, *confirmation*, occurs when audience members continue to seek out persuasive messages regarding the product even *after* the product has been chosen and used. Obviously this indicates reduction of cognitive dissonance by the customer, as we discussed in Chapter 4. For example, a car buyer who purchases a Honda will be likely to seek out information (which would most likely come from Honda advertising or sources like *Consumer Reports*) that will justify his purchase. Thus, he reduces or avoids a state of dissonance about the decision. The last thing in the world that this car buyer wants to hear about his new car is that it wasn't the best purchase he could have made. The general principle predicting such behavior is *selective exposure*: we tend to seek out messages that are consonant with our needs, beliefs and attitudes and to avoid those messages that will produce dissonance by challenging those cognitions.[13] Thus, as Rogers notes, the confirmation phase represents a critical moment in diffusion:[14]

> In the past, change agents have primarily been interested in achieving adoption decisions, but at the confirmation stage they have the additional responsibility of providing supporting messages to individuals who have previously adopted. Possibly one of the reasons for the relatively high rate of discontinuance of some innovations is that change agents assume that once adoption is secured, it will continue. But without continued effort there is no assurance against discontinuance, because negative messages about an innovation exist in most client systems.

Our hypothetical Honda customer may be seduced by the advertising of another car manufacturer, or he may simply discover that his dealer, once so interested in *selling* him the car, is now much less enthusiastically motivated to provide *service* for it after purchase. Either case obstructs Honda's campaign goals. Persuasive campaigns which address an audience's continued need for persuasion after purchase or adoption more likely maintain a positive relationship with the audience and pave the way for success in future persuasive efforts.

The five stages that arise from the diffusion of innovation theory are particularly useful because they concentrate on the campaign's primary objective, the target audience. By following these stages planners of persuasive campaigns can more effectively sequence their messages and structure their campaigns. These stages help us understand the momentum of a campaign. For example, when McDonald's introduces a new chicken sandwich to their menu, we can follow our initial awareness of the product through a variety of commercial spots that tout the delightful product leading to our anticipation of its arrival at the local Golden Arches, then to our trial of the product at the special introductory price and, finally, to our decision to order it again later at the regular price.

CAMPAIGN STAGES: AN INSTITUTIONAL FRAMEWORK APPROACH

We can also study political campaigns for the stages of their development. Although we could examine a political campaign according to the same stages outlined for commercial campaigns, to do so would ignore those distinctly political elements of campaigns. Judith Trent and Robert Friedenberg produced an elaborated model of the stages in a political campaign. These stages differ by persuasive objectives, by the characteristics of the persuasive messages of each stage and by the persuasive functions that these messages perform.[15] Consistent with our general comments on persuasion at the institutional level, Trent and Friedenberg's descriptive structure takes into account the unique features of American political campaigning and the American institutions shaping it.

The initial phase of a political campaign is *surfacing*. Surfacing, according to Trent and Friedenberg, refers to a series of persuasive acts which are both predictable and specifically timed; they serve several essential campaign functions. First, these acts serve the ritualistic function of signalling the beginning of the campaign—or at least of the candidate's entrance into the campaign. Just as some ceremonies signal the beginning of other important social and institutional activities, such as church services, baseball seasons, marriage, Olympic games, presidential administrations or commissioned military service, political candidates must signal that they are now authentic candidates, that they have "thrown their hats into the ring." Second, persuasive messages at this stage must familiarize the electorate with the candidate, help the electorate assess the candidate's competence and authority, and establish in a preliminary way the themes and issues for the campaign.

Several recognizable and predictable types of persuasive messages characterize the surfacing stage of political campaigns. Surfacing includes organizing efforts in the areas the campaign must reach, speaking to attract attention, using opinion polls to determine candidate and issue viability, and organizing and developing strategy for fund raising.

During the second stage of political campaigns, *primaries*, voters choose their party's candidate for the general election. The political primary system, as currently structured at the national level, has greatly altered the structure of political campaigning. The process reduces the power of "kingmakers" in smoke-filled rooms to determine political candidates, changes the role of the political convention from primarily legislative to primarily ceremonial and, perhaps most important of all, forces candidates into public competition with members of their own party. As Trent and Friedenberg observe:

> Many professional politicians and party leaders hate the primary stage of a campaign, because a genuine primary is a fight within the family of the party—a fight that can turn nasty as different factions within the family compete with each other to secure a place on the November ballot for their candidate. In addition, primaries can exhaust candidates, leaving them physically and emotionally drained just before the most important battle.[16]

Persuasion at the primary stage of a campaign serves several specific functions. Most obviously, during the primary stage campaigns provide added information about their candidate to voters. Research further suggests that the image of a candidate formed by the voters during the primary stage often remains unshaken for many voters throughout the campaign, regardless of subsequent persuasion by the candidate.[17] Second, the primary stage is the first time that voters are involved *interactively* in the campaign process. This interaction may be direct, supporting candidates through donations, attending rallies or doing volunteer work. Or this interaction may be mediated, as diffusion research reminds us, through all forms of communication: informal conversations, group interaction, radio, television and the press. The third function of the political campaign's primary stage relates to the second: allowing voters the first opportunity to give direct feedback to the candidates. Up to this point, primary responsibility for defining the images of the candidates resided with the candidates themselves and the with the media. Now the voters have their first "say." The primary returns define a candidate as "front runner," "dark horse" or "loser," a status which a candidate and media cannot predetermine.

Major parties convene *nominating conventions* after the primaries to officially nominate the party's candidate for the general election. The most important of these nominating conventions are the quadrennial nominating conventions before national presidential elections; states and localities also hold nominating conventions.[18] Traditionally, nominating conventions were deliberative bodies, determining a slate of nominees for the general election and writing a platform to detail the party's stance on major issues. They accomplished this purpose through discussion, debate and vote. Today, however, because new party rules emphasize the primaries and greatly magnify the importance of television coverage, we see not deliberation but drama and pageantry. As Trent and Friedenberg observe:

> ...the presence of [television] networks has... had a profound effect on modern nominating conventions. One reason is that the presence of the networks has restructured convention programming so that the party's "important" events occur during "prime time." To make certain that this happens, the convention chair often ignores the activities of the delegates on the convention floor and rushes through any official party business to make certain that those events planned to give the party the most favorable image (for example, ecumenical prayers, civic greetings, performances by show business personalities, keynote and acceptance speeches, and controlled and planned "spontaneous" demonstrations for candidates) will be seen during the hours in which most people watch television. Whether this strategy fails (as, for example, it did in 1972 when George McGovern's acceptance speech began hours after most people had gone to bed or in 1980 when Congressman Morris Udall's keynote address started as the delegates were leaving Madison Square Garden for the night) or is successful, the convention proceedings become ritual with little or no pragmatic value.[19]

This transformed national convention has its own unique functions within the persuasive campaign. First, the pageantry, formal rituals and patriotic symbolism of conventions reaffirm the legitimacy of the convention and campaign process. Hence, just as the various media, political and social institutions legitimize the campaign and convention process, this process in turn reaffirms the power of "the system" itself. Similarly, by much the same process the pageantry and pomp of a nominating convention functions to announce and legitimize the party nominees. Because the primary stage of the campaign is frequently divisive for the party, the nominating convention permits the party to heal publicly internal rifts and to emphasize the unity of the party behind its candidates and platform.

The *general election* is the aspect of persuasive campaigns that is most familiar to voters. At this stage of the campaign, public persuasion in all of its forms heightens to its most forceful and visible level. "'Electing time,'" note Trent and Friedenberg, "means speeches, parades, debates, bumper sticers, media commercials, band playing, doorbell ringing, posters, billboards, polling, and direct mail fund-raising."20 These various forms of persuasion serve two purposes. First, general election stage persuasion disseminates information about the candidates and positions them with respect to one another and to various established issues, such as taxes or unemployment, or to emergent issues, such as the Iranian Embassy hostages in the 1980 campaign or the Willie Horton attack ads in the 1988 campaign. Second, general election persuasion reinforces the legitimacy of "the system," the process of interlocking institutions which enables campaigns to exist. As Trent and Friedenberg conclude:

> While the previous stages also function to fulfill our "demands," the directness, intensity, and finality of the fourth stage emphasize our pleasure or displeasure with the way in which a particular election has or has not met our pragmatic or ritualistic expectations. If during the general election stage the candidates fail to address those issues of paramount importance to us, fail to debate each other, or even fail to provide for us any of the excitement or drama we normally expect, we may feel cheated. It is, in short, the climax of a political season—a time for decision and participation.[21]

PERSUASIVE STRATEGIES AND TACTICS IN CAMPAIGNS

Within the overall structure of a persuasive campaign, there are a variety of strategies and tactics employed to advance the candidate, issue or product. Many of these strategies and tactics turn on ways of defining or redefining a campaign's target audience. Others involve identifying, creating and exploiting communication channels and networks to reach these audiences. Still others enter on the need to determine the persuasive success of the campaign as it unfolds. In the next section, we will consider each of these in turn.

AUDIENCE SEGMENTATION AND ANALYSIS

It is tempting to view persuasive campaigns as massive attempts at persuasion aimed at the general, undifferentiated public. After all, a manufacturer makes the same profit no matter who buys the product, and the potential vote of one citizen adds just as much for a political candidate as any other citizen's vote; why adopt a more complicated view of the audience if essentially the same response is desired from any potential audience member? The fact is that the formalized goals of campaigns and the nature of the system in which they operate generally result in campaign persuaders segmenting their audiences into smaller, persuasively relevant units. Persuaders define these smaller units in terms of the goals and resources of the campaign. For example, which groupings of audience members would already be likely to adopt the goals of the campaign, support the issue or vote for the candidate? Which members could the campaign, given its available resources, reach most easily? Which members might themselves influence other parts of the general audience? Which constitute numerically large enough groups to meet the goal of the campaign? Armed with such information, persuaders steer their campaign through the various stages of development.

Because the range of available products is so great and the number of candidates initially vying for public office so large, there is vigorous competition for the allegiance of consumers and voters alike within the system. Such competition necessitates audience segmenting. For a candidate to surface, he or she need not capture everyone's support or even a majority, just enough to demonstrate viability. Especially in early primaries, the candidate merely needs a respectable showing in the race for office—respectable enough to keep support alive for later primaries. Indeed, in a general election such as 1984, in which barely 50 percent of the registered voters showed up at the polls, the support of less than 30 percent of all registered voters secured Ronald Reagan's reelection. The situation is similar for commercial campaigns. In product campaigns all consumers need not buy the product, only enough to yield a profit. Concerned with their resources, campaigners limit their target audience to the number needed to satisfy their formal goals or to capture the desired market share.

A second factor that encourages audience segmenting is the realization that what appeals to one consumer or voter may not appeal to another. The more heterogeneous the audience, the more difficult it is to craft a persuasive message that is adapted to that audience. While appealing to one person, the persuader may neglect another and even offend a third. Given the sheer volume of persuasive messages available for the public's attention, consumers and citizens may only tune into those messages that seem particularly salient to their concerns. Persuaders break through the clutter of available messages by targeting a particular audience.

Thus, persuasive campaigns target as the primary audience a particular segment of people who share a number of characteristics. Campaigns discover this target audience through the use of polls and surveys. The pollsters or surveyors locate a group of people with a common concern or need. For example, political pollsters may find that a significant number of voters are sincerely worried about the disintegration of traditional American values and want to see policies that restore the prestige of the American family, patriotism and reward for individual initiative. Market researchers may find that a group of upwardly mobile, young professionals simply do not have time to prepare home-cooked meals and want convenience foods that are tasty but require little effort to prepare. Once such a group is discovered, the campaigner has found a *niche* for the campaign. In general terms, he or she has located a potential target audience by finding an unmet need. Some argue that this process of finding a niche happens prior to the development of a product or the selection of a candidate to run for public office. In such a case, market research determines what a group of consumers or citizens want, and then someone develops a product or elevates a candidate who seems likely to be able to fill that need.

After identifying a target audience, campaigners then must analyze that audience to adapt their persuasive messages to it. Sometimes campaigns rely on demographic data from sources such as the U.S. Census Bureau reports to reveal additional characteristics about the target audience such as average age, educational background, socioeconomic status and so forth. At other times, they use additional polls and surveys to gather more specific data on the attitudes, opinions and habits of the target audience. Frequently they employ more in-depth methods to understand the psychological frame of reference for the target group.

A typical method for more in-depth audience analysis is the focus group interview. A focus group consists of a small sample of the target group and a facilitator. A researcher invites and frequently pays the members of the target group to participate in a free flowing discussion about topics that will illuminate their opinions and values so the persuader can use the information to craft persuasive messages. For example, a group of housewives may be invited to talk about baking. Why do they bake? How do their families react when they bake? Do they include their children in the activity? How do they feel about baking? The facilitator leads the discussion and encourages the group to express opinions about questions such as these. Analysis of the discussion may yield important information about the group's attitudes toward certain activities or products or even fantasies and dreams about an ideal world. Using these attitudes, feelings and fantasies a persuader can later craft an appealing campaign slogan, a magazine advertisement or a 30-second commercial spot. A public relations agency employed by the U.S. Army used this technique for determining attitudes about the Army prior to composing the "Be All You Can Be" campaign in the late 1970's. Similarly, the Republican party conducted focus groups in 1987 in order to determine which issues should be emphasized in George Bush's successful bid for the presidency and again in 1994 prior to the creation of their "Contract with America," which described an agenda for the new Republican-controlled House and Senate in 1995.

DETERMINING CHANNELS AND COMMUNICATION NETWORKS

Just as important as analyzing a target audience and adapting persuasive messages to it is determining the appropriate mens by which to transmit messages to that audience. Campaigns may disseminate their messages through formal communication networks like the media or through less formal means such as everyday interpersonal interactions. Navigating both channels is important for persuasive campaigners.

As we discussed in Chapter 10, formal communication systems consist of both paid and free media. When persuaders use paid media, they need to know where to place their messages to gain maximum benefit from their expenditure of funds. Even when a campaign obtains free media coverage, it must choose the appropriate channel. Because media may be either directional or nondirectional, some outlets will more likely reach a target audience than others. For example, news magazines with large circulations, such as *Time*, *Newsweek* and *U.S. News and World Report,* reach large but diverse adult audiences. Other magazines with smaller circulations, such as *Sports Illustrated*, *Woman's Day* or *Seventeen*, may reach fewer people but may reach the very audience targeted by the campaigner.

The same information used by campaign planners to segment the audience can guide their selection and the use of a variety of media. Just as different magazines have different types of readership, so different radio stations cater to different types of listeners, and different television programs attract different types of viewers and so forth. If a persuader finds a media outlet whose audience possesses the same demographic characteristics as his or her target audience, then that outlet offers the best place to spend advertising money or seek free media coverage. This information further helps campaigners choose their channel of transmission. For example, if the target audience enjoys an active life style and is interested in sports, then advertising during the sports report on the late news or during "Monday Night Football" may be more astute than advertising on local radio even if its listeners fit the demographic profile of the target audience.

Persuasive campaigns include a host of messages and promotional strategies that may not take the form of either paid advertisements or news coverage. Campaigns may include the distribution of buttons, bumper sticers, T-shirts emblazoned with a slogan, coupons with discounts for new products and so on. Here too, determining the appropriate vehicle for distributing the message is critical. Persuaders need to know where the target audience goes, the places that they frequent and the areas in which they spend time. For example, if a persuader knows that the target audience commutes to work every morning, then particular commuter routes may be targeted for the placement of billboards that display a persuasive message. Similarly, if the target audience shops at a particular store, then flyers may be distributed there. If a particular community event such as a county fair or a concert in the city draws the target audience, then that event provides a useful forum for distributing buttons, T-shirts or other promotional items. Such events may have the added benefit of attracting media coverage. Consequently, if the campaign centers on these events, it may obtain free media coverage as well. Many readers may recall the appearance of saxophone-playing Presidential candidate Bill Clinton on MTV during the 1992 campaign as part of that cable network's "Rock the Vote" promotions. The amount of free coverage Clinton's performance received—coverage directed back toward the younger voters who watch MTV—was invaluable.

The idea that certain events attract a target audience leads organizers of persuasive campaigns to stage events to reach that audience. A beer company, for example, organizes an event on the beach at Fort Lauderdale during the spring to attract a target audience of young college students. Or, as is often the case, diverse corporations who market a variety of products sponsor sporting events like golf or tennis tournaments, where their corporate logo is prominently displayed, and corporate officials participate in the activities. Staged events almost always draw free media coverage providing a second avenue to the target audience, especially if those members did not attend the event in person.

Other vehicles for campaign messages are the less formal communication networks. The importance of communication networks for a persuasive campaign emerged clearly in the diffusion of innovation theories and research we discussed earlier. If persuaders successfully promote their product, issue or candidate with opinion leaders, then those opinion leaders may spread the word to other members of the larger target audience. The important characteristic of opinion leaders is that these people are influential. Others may have more status or be more willing to try new ideas or products but, they may be perceived by the surrounding community as too innovative, daring or even downright peculiar. However, opinion leaders perform one critical service: they lead the opinions of others. In the case of the quadrennial New Hampshire primaries, the importance of networking among committed supporters of the various candidates—at the level of town and neighborhood—can not be overestimated. Given that a candidate's showing in the New Hampshire primary can make or break a campaign and that in such a low-population state campaigns can be won or lost on a comparatively small number of votes, the importance of interpersonal communication and opinion leaders becomes clear. In the case of recruiting for the military services, the campaign conducted research concerning who leads the opinions of these young men and women. The results of research for the "Be All You Can Be" campaign indicated that parents, teachers and guidance counselors influenced the career decisions of young people.[22] As a result, persuasive messages were channelled through such opinion leaders. Advertisements and informational items may be distributed directly to these opinion leaders or placed in media outlets frequented by these influential people.

In addition, persuasive messages themselves often mention opinion leaders. In recent years young people in the inner city seem easily influenced in their buying of consumer goods like sports shoes by star professional athletes. Marketing agencies employ these opinion leaders to lend their names to products and provide their endorsements for a variety of commercials and advertising messages for expensive shoes, jackets and other sports equipment. The rising number of violent crimes in which the object of the robbery is an expensive pair of basketball shoes has led to citizen outcry over the use of these potent opinion leaders. This example underscores the importance of the informal communication network.

Political campaigns have long recognized the importance of opinion leaders. For decades, a candidate could feel secure if he or she could obtain the endorsement of party bosses or leaders—those who acted as opinion leaders for the rest of the party regulars. Even in recent years as party influence has waned in many localities, opinion leaders remain an important channel for persuasive messages. Instead of party bosses, hopeful candidates often court influential people in business, civic organizations and other community or religious groups as a means of reaching the larger target audience. For example, during his first bid for the Democratic nomination for president, Jesse Jackson enlisted ministers in African American churches across the country to solicit funds and votes for the Jackson campaign. Their influence strongly contributed to making Jackson a credible candidate in 1984. In a similar way, 1992 presidential candidate H. Ross Perot's campaign relied as much upon grass roots organization and opinion leaders as upon the candidate's ability to command media attention with his flamboyant tactics and enormous personal wealth.

MEASUREMENT OF EFFECTS AND ADAPTATION

Because campaigns exist over a period of time, persuasive strategies and planning need to be adapted as the campaign progresses. The functions that a campaign must perform change as the campaign moves through various stages, necessitating changes in messages and channels of transmission. Many techniques of audience analysis and the determination of communication channels must be used repeatedly as situations change. In addition, because of the duration of a campaign over time, persuaders measure their effectiveness at various points during the campaign and adapt accordingly.

Initial audience segmentation and analysis frequently leads to the development of a campaign slogan. However, before actually broadcasting that slogan to the trget audience, persuaders may sample the target group's reaction. Persuaders measure that reaction with questionnaires and focus groups. Similarly, initial advertisements or commercial spots may be shown to a select group from the target audience which is then questioned about its reactions. Several of the controversial television spots of the Bush presidential campaign that attacked the record of his opponent, Michael Dukakis, were subjected to this kind of testing. The campaign enlisted a sample of voters to view the spots and offer their reactions prior to their release to the media.

Often sophisticated technological methods are used to gauge audience reactions to persuasive messages early in a campaign. Pupillometers, for example, gauge the degree to which a viewer's pupil dilates as he or she views a particular television spot. Because psychological research indicates that our pupils dilate when we are attracted or excited, the results of such tests indicate whether the advertisement is appealing or not. Other physical reactions may be tested as well. Hand-held devices that measure the amount of perspiration a person's skin produces, called galvanic skin response testers, can also measure audience response.

Even after slogans or commercial spots are released, campaigners continue to measure audience reactions. Most important political campaigns employ sophisticated polling methods to track the reactions of potential voters to a candidate following the release of new commercial spots or other events such as debates during a campaign. For example, if polls indicate a certain level of name recognition for a candidate, then campaigners may develop new advertisements that build on that name recognition. Similarly, if polls indicate that an opponent is perceived as weak on a particular issue, then that issue may become the target of a set of negative commercials that attack the opponent on those grounds. Bush's attacks concerning Dukakis' treatment of crime, for example, were the result of focus group interviews and polling data that revealed voters were concerned about Dukakis being too soft on crime. In recent elections, researchers have given audiences hand-held devices that allow individuals to register positive or negative reactions as they view a candidate speaking. Researchers then take the specific phrases or nonverbal behaviors that were associated with positive reactions and attempt to weave those into future campaign presentations. Commercial advertisers use similar methods for tracking product campaigns.

Ethics In Persuasive Campaigns

The analysis of persuasive campaigns and the Institutional Perspective in general represent an approach designed to *complement* the Classical and Symbolist Perspectives on persuasion. Concepts from previous chapters—for example, audience motivations or metaphor—are meant to be *integrated* within the larger framework of analysis and explanation provided by the Institutional Perspective, "recontextualizing" them rather than replacing them. This merging of concepts affects our discussion of the ethics of campaign persuasion. Thus, we view our discussion of ethics in campaigns as a supplement to the ethical principles discussed earlier.

Two unique features of persuasive campaigns prompt a discussion of ethics: the interrelationship of multiple institutions within the typical campaign and the general practice of audience segmentation in campaigns.

Many of the institutions involved in persuasive campaigns are affiliated with or represented by associations which have adopted formal codes of ethics. Lawyers, public relations consultants and broadcast and print journalists are all at least nominally bound by formalized ethical guidelines for the practice of their communication related activities.[23] These formal codes define the practices that are appropriate and inappropriate for members of a profession and ideally provide a basis for determining the appropriateness of actions in a given case *before* such actions might occur.

Members of the American Association of Advertisers are pledged not to intentionally produce advertising that would employ:[24]

> False or misleading statements or exaggerations, visual or verbal.
>
> Testimonials that do not reflect the real choice of a competent witness.
>
> Price claims that are misleading.
>
> Comparisons that unfairly disparage a competitive product or service.
>
> Claims insufficiently supported or that distort the true meaning or practicable application of statements made by professional or scientific authority.
>
> Statements, suggestions, or pictures offensive to public decency.

In a similar way, the code of ethics for the Public Relations Society of America contains the following preliminary pledge in addition to the enumeration of specific ethical guidelines:[25]

> We pledge:
>
> To conduct ourselves professionally, with truth, accuracy, fairness, and responsibility to the public;
>
> To improve our individual competence and advance the knowledge and proficiency of the profession through continuing research and education;
>
> And to adhere to the articles of the Code of Professional Standards for the Practice of Public Relations as adopted by the governing Assembly of the society.

Public lobbying groups such as Common Cause and nonpartisan citizens' interest groups such as the Fair Campaign Practices Committee, have also developed elaborated codes of ethical conduct which they urge candidates to adopt.[26]

The number of similar organizations advancing formal codes of ethics is sufficiently long to prohibit a complete listing here. Many address only the specific practices of one narrowly limited field—only a segment of the persuasive activity in a typical campaign. Furthermore, organizations differ in their ability to compel compliance to their guidelines and to discipline infractions. Nevertheless, formal ethical codes perform important and positive functions: educating new members of a profession about their responsibilities, identifying and preventing the most obvious areas of potential ethical trouble and inducing professionals to reflect on the relationship of means and ends in their own practice.

Our discussion foreshadows one ethically troubling area of persuasive campaigns that we find unique—the practice of audience segmentation. So central to current methods of reaching mass audiences in campaigns, this practice can reduce a *public* audience united by concern for public good until it is little more than a collection of alienated and suspicious self- interest groups.

One of the most glaring examples of this capability in current campaign strategy is direct-mail fund-raising.[27] As journalist Gregg Easterbrook argued in 1988, the notorious Political Action Caucuses (PAC's) were hardly the power-wielding giants they were frequently assumed to be, if their power is measured as a percentage of total campaign contributions:

> In the 1986 election cycle candidates for the House raised 34 percent of their funds through PACs; Senate candidates a mere 21 percent. The rest came from individual contributions. And most of those are not of the $1,000 maximum variety. They are small donations.[28]

Direct-mail persuasion is highly targeted and can still be enormously effective even though it raises only small donations because it identifies the most likely targets and returns to them again and again. A campaign identifies target audiences through zip code analysis, cross-referencing magazine subscription mailing lists and so forth; it then builds more valuable lists from the ranks of proven contributors. Targeting ordinarily encourages heavy emphasis on issues of importance to the target audience in the most polarizing of terms imaginable. A former practitioner of direct-mail fund-raising on a national level told Easterbrook:

> The most important thing to understand about current political direct mail is that it's targeted at seniors... Median age of donors is about 55. This is the age when people start to scare easily, and when they acquire the stewardship effect, the feeling that they are responsible for protecting society against an onslaught of change. Add in that today the biggest pool of discretionary dollars is held by senior citizens, not the young, and there's the basic targeting formula for either conservative or liberal appeals.[29]

Such a mailing list presents a valuable source of funds for a campaign. However, the indirect effect of these highly segmented and targeted appeals is that they contribute to fragmentation of the public audience by promoting a "single-issue" mentality. It is fairly easy to mobilize substantial support for legislation to reduce property taxes, for example, simply by targeting persuasive appeals to property owners. Campaign persuasion based on highly segmented audience strategies can undermine this public sensibility, particularly when it is combined with polarizing and "scare" tactics. The scale of mass-audience campaigns virtually guarantees that such problems will continue to challenge us. Trent and Friedenberg note that the fund raising expert has become one of the first persons hired by the candidate contemplating a run for office.[30]

The ethically troubling practice of audience segmented persuasion corrodes a sense of shared public values, because it allows and encourages campaigners to promote identification by setting different audience segments in conflict with one another. The use of highly directional media in such campaigning also reduces the opportunity to evaluate through comparison the persuasive messages directed at each of these highly segmented audiences. In Chapter 4 we discussed the use of "Willie Horton" ads by the Bush/Quayle presidential campaign in 1988. These ads, whatever else they accomplished (and polling data showed that they were influential), pandered to unspoken racism in middle-class whites by "personalizing" the problem of crime in America as the visual image of one individual black convict, Willie Horton. In the context of the 1992 Presidential campaign, the Bush administration blocked the passage of civil rights legislation directed toward employment practices, calling the bill a "quota" bill even though the proposed legislation explicitly prohibited quotas. Critics argued that the Bush strategy was to employ race-baiting tactics similar to those animating the "Willie Horton" ads, so that the inflammatory term "quotas"—itself a code word among many whites for "reverse discrimination" and unfair preferential treatment of minorities—would be available as a potent weapon during the 1992 Presidential campaign.[31] Democratic Senator Bill Bradley challenged the Bush strategy and tactics, both on the Senate floor and elsewhere, justifying his confrontation with the Bush Administration in terms of the ethical problem we examine here:

> I wanted to put up a big red flag and give him [Bush] a chance not to go down that road (of racial division) in 1992...To do that, I felt I had to lay out the record with all the passion I felt about it and at the same time provide him the option to be able to explain himself and lead the country on this issue and let the healing process take place as opposed to constantly exacerbating it.[32]

CRITICAL FOCUS: TOURETTE SYNDROME ASSOCIATION'S AWARENESS CAMPAIGN

Analyzing campaign persuasion frequently involves consideration of multiple messages or of individual messages within a much more complex context. Both considerations fall outside the scope of either the Classical or Symbolist Perspectives. Individual messages still can be analyzed in terms of concepts and theories developed in those two perspectives, but to capture the uniquely institutional character of campaign persuasion an additional set of analytic questions must be brought to bear.

CRITICAL QUESTIONS

1. What **institutions** are involved in the campaign? How are they involved?
2. Is the campaign a **political campaign**, an **issue campaign** or a **product campaign**? What stages best describe the campaign over the period of its existence?

3. Who is the **target audience**? What are the characteristics of that audience? How do those characteristics affect the content and form of the persuasive messages that comprise the campaign?
4. What is the **range of messages** that comprise the campaign? What slogans do they employ? What form do the messages take? How do the messages work together to move the campaign through its stages?
5. What **channels of communication or informal communication networks** are selected for the campaign? Which media outlets are used? Who are identified as opinion leaders? How does the campaign attempt to reach those opinion leaders?
6. How is the **effectiveness** of the campaign measured? At what stages? Through what means?
7. How is the **campaign adapted** to the results of earlier stages and external events?

Two forms of persuasive messages produced by the Tourette Syndrome Association illustrate the various characteristics and strategies of persuasive campaigns discussed earlier. The national commercial spot distributed by the TSA and the documentary *I'm a Person Too* are best understood as only a small part of the larger campaign.

As we mentioned earlier, the motivation for the TSA's awareness campaign is to stem ignorance surrounding the disorder and raise funds to support the organization's goal of finding a cure for TS. Characteristically, the Institutional Perspective toward persuasion recognizes that persuasion often involves complex relationships among a number of institutions. Such is the case with the TSA's campaign. Philanthropic institutions—such as the Kiwanis, Elks, Moose and Rotary clubs—that raise money for research and educate the public are vital partners in the campaign. The medical establishment receives monies raised by the TSA through its campaign. Also, campaign messages assist medical professionals on the diagnostic and treatment end of the disorder. The federal government, which mandates and funds the special educational needs of TS children, has an indirect impact on the content of campaign messages because those who are diagnosed are informed about how they can take advantage of government programs designed to accommodate children with TS. Broadcast media who provide public service announcements make a significant contribution to the success of the campaign. Finally, educational institutions responsible for serving the special needs of TS students, as well as counselors and nurses in the schools who might be the first to recognize TS symptoms in a student, constitute targets of and participants in the campaign.

The TSA's awareness campaign is most accurately described as an issue campaign; it is designed to educate the public about a relatively obscure disorder and to gain support in combating it. The campaign, which has been in progress for more than 17 years, continuously cycles through the information and knowledge stage, attitude formation, and decision and implementation stages. Each newly diagnosed case of TS propagates another group of potential activists who engage in their own mini-campaigns to raise awareness, support and money for the cause.

Although the TSA directs its persuasion to those most likely to be affected by the disorder, message content is designed with specific audience characteristics in mind. The television commercial, for instance, appeals to a general lay-public that is assumed to have, at best, only cursory knowledge of the disorder. Among this public exist undiagnosed TS children and adults. The commercial introduces the potential of this disorder to the largest number of people and features the association's logo—a stick-figure abstraction of a person—as an animated, cartoon-like character who displays the symptoms of TS. At the same time, the comforting and reassuring voice of narrator Richard Dreyfus asks: "Know anybody like our little friend, here, who tics, twitches, makes strange sounds, who just can't seem to stay still? You may know someone, a kid or a grown-up, with Tourette Syndrome, a neurological disorder that's often misunderstood and a lot more common than you think. People with TS can't help it, but you can by calling the Tourette Association for the facts."

The components of this message impart an informal child-like quality to the message, which helps to open the door of denial and fear that often inhibits people from pursuing diagnosis and treatment. The animated logo is playful in its mimicking of common TS behaviors, providing psychological relief as it minimizes the severity of TS symptoms in the mind of the viewer. Dreyfus' warm, soothing voice sounds more like a father reading a bedtime story than an authority figure providing important information. The brief narrative—comprised mainly of one-or two-syllable words, short sentences and phrases such as "our little friend here," and "a kid or a grown-up"—is easy to comprehend and remember. Also, viewers are not overwhelmed with medical jargon that might dissuade them from seeking further information. The unsophisticated nature of the message functions to alleviate stress associated with conscious awareness of the disorder, and serves as a blanket call for new activists who are vital to the continued growth and success of the campaign.

Whereas the television commercial addresses an uninformed lay-public, message elements of the documentary *I'm a Person Too* are designed for more specific audiences—the newly diagnosed and their families and affiliates of those directly affected, who constitute potential activists. The film combats the fear associated with a TS diagnosis and raises awareness of the disorder as a means of gaining public financial support for research and treatment.

I'm a Person Too profiles five TS individuals, with each mini-biography appealing to a particular age, race and socioeconomic class of viewer. The five individuals also exemplify the range of potential symptoms a TS person might experience. Dana is an eleven-year-old, middle class white girl whose most evident symptoms are stuttering and a learning disability, both of which she is likely to outgrow. Orin, a white adult male, is a medical doctor. He displays the most severe TS symptoms of the group; however, Orin demonstrates that even with his coprolalia-cursing, uttering obscenities and ethnic slurs—he is able to have a successful career. Raymond is a Hispanic youth from a working poor family who tics, twitches and has a learning disability. Treatment and training are available to him through government programs designed to accommodate the needs of children with a variety of developmental and learning disabilities. Twenty-six-year-old Laura is a white, working class woman who has outgrown most of her TS symptoms. The severe twitches and tics the white, upper class Bruce exhibits do not prevent him from being a husband, father and successful businessman.

The five individuals profiled speak for themselves. In telling their own stories of how they cope with TS to live normal, happy lives, the five are vivid proof of TS individuals as fully functioning and capable people. For newly diagnosed TS viewers and their families, the five assuage fears, dispel misconceptions and stereotypes and suggest strategies for how those with TS can manage others' responses to them. Also in the film, family members discuss the feelings of guilt they experience as a result of their initial ignorance in dealing with their TS loved one. In light of these confessions, viewers can understand, accept and forgive their own blindness or hesitancy. To affiliates of those directly affected, the five stories illustrate the additional difficulties presented to the TS person by public ignorance and disaffection. Collectively, the vignettes provide a holistic picture of the disorder—its symptoms, progression and treatment—and the various challenges faced by everyone touched by TS.

Although the *I'm a Person Too* documentary is well used, the TSA produces a number of video documentaries that inform viewers and provide directions for how to cope with one's own or others' TS. A wide range of medical research reports is available according to one's interest or need, and can be purchased for a nominal charge. In addition, the association facilitates the development of groups whose goals are to provide support for the relatives of those with TS, and to develop educational publications for the benefit of future generations. The association also publishes brochures in English, Spanish and French that address the most commonly asked questions about Tourette Syndrome. TSA solicits funding through planned giving and special gifts programs. A yearly national awareness campaign orchestrated through the concerted efforts of the 50 charter state associations includes public displays; presentations; broadcast advertisements; and distribution of buttons, flyers, brochures and bumper sticers. These are all designed to introduce an unwary public to the potential existence of this illness in everyone's life and to alleviate the fear that ignorance breeds.

The TSA campaign relies heavily on informal channels of communication. Although they use broadcast media for some public service announcements, the vast majority of users of these media are not likely to attend the message until the illness directly touches their lives or the lives of family or friends. Levi-Pearl credits the bulk of the association's fund-raising and awareness campaign success to the efforts of individuals whose family members have TS and who want to help their loved ones and others live with TS. These are the individuals who incite their civic clubs to hold awareness and fund-raising events, such as dinners and sports tournaments, to enlighten the public and to help advance the cause of medical research.

Opinion leaders in the campaign fall into two primary categories: those who have TS and members of the professional establishment who are working to treat and cure TS. In the documentary, for instance, individuals speak for themselves in an effort to modify viewers' attitudes about TS. Experts present medical facts about the disorder, and they assure the viewer that TS is manageable and that most TS individuals can lead healthy, normal lives. The prevalent ignorance about this illness is mitigated through first-hand accounts from TS individuals and the medical establishment who treat the disorder.

One way the effectiveness of the TSA's campaign can be measured is through the money that is raised to facilitate research toward a cure. More significant than the monetary measure of success, however, is the decrease in diagnosis and treatment time that is credited to the greater awareness facilitated by the TSA campaign. Levi-Pearl states, "It used to be that the gap between the first sign of symptoms and diagnosis was between 7 and 15 years. Since the mid 80s, this gap has narrowed from almost immediate to two or three years, depending on geographic and socioeconomic factors." Because TS sufferers often require special education and training, the imperative nature of early diagnosis is clear. This increase in early detection suggests that childcare givers in the home and schools as well as those in the medical establishment have a greater awareness of early warning signs.

As long as Tourette Syndrome lacks a cure, the TSA will continue its work. Propelled by family and friends whose lives are directly affected by TS and philanthropic organizations dedicated to supporting causes such as TS research, this campaign will continue with some modifications in the campaign strategy. The advent of the Internet, for instance, has opened another channel for disseminating information about TS. Also, a new informative documentary to supplement and update the *I'm a Person Too* film currently is in production.

A campaign such as that mounted by the TSA is strengthened and propelled by the very people it is organized to help. Each new day brings another diagnosis of TS; with that pronouncement, another family and their associates become aware of TS and commit themselves to the cause of finding a cure. When that cure is found, the Tourette Syndrome Association's campaign will end.

NOTES

1. Telephone interview with Sue Levi-Pearl, Tourette Syndrome Association, 4240 Bell Boulevard, Suite 205, Bayside, NY, December 6, 2000.
2. "Facts About Tourette Syndrome: Answers to Most Commonly Asked Questions." Tourette Syndrome Association, Inc.: NY, 2000.
3. "Fighting Ads in the Inner City," *Newsweek* (5 Feb. 1980): 46; "If It's Legal, Cigarette Makers Are Trying It," *Business Week* (19 February 1990): 52-54.
4. "Fighting Ads," 46.
5. "Fighting Ads," 46, italics added.
6. Judith S. Trent and Robert V. Friedenberg, *Political Campaign Communication: Principles and Practices* (New York: Praeger, 1983), 24-35.
7. Karen S. Johnson-Cartee and Gary A. Copeland, *Negative Political Advertising: Coming of Age* (Hillsdale NJ: Lawrence Earlbaum 1991), 25-30.
8. This research is summarized and evaluated in Elihu Katz, "The Social Itinerary of Technical Change: Two Studies of the Diffusion of Innovation," in Wilbur Schramm and Donald F. Roberts, eds. *The Process and Effects of Mass Communication*, 2nd Ed. (Urbana IL: University of Illinois, 1971), 761-797.

9. Elihu Katz and Paul F. Lazarsfeld, *Personal Influence: The Part Played by People in the Flow of Mass Communications* (Glencoe IL: Free Press, 1955), 32-33.
10. Everett Rogers, *Diffusion of Innovation,* 3rd Ed. (New York: Free Press, 1983), 163-209.
11. Rogers, *Diffusion of Innovations,* 164-167.
12. Herbert W. Simons, *Persuasion: Understanding, Practice, and Analysis,* 2nd Ed. (New York: Random House, 1986), 14.
13. Rogers, *Diffusion of Innovation,* 166.
14. Rogers, *Diffusion of Innovation,* 186.
15. Trent and Friedenberg, *Political Campaign,* 23-67.
16. Trent and Friedenberg, *Political Campaign*, 37.
17. Trent and Friedenberg, *Political Campaign,* 42.
18. Trent and Friedenberg, *Political Campaign,* 48.
19. Trent and Friedenberg, *Political Campaign*, 51.
20. Trent and Friedenberg, *Political Campaign,* 61.
21. Trent and Friedenberg, *Political Campaign,* 64.
22. Robert E. Denton, Jr., "'Be All You Can Be': A Case Study of the Army's Advertising Campaign," paper presented at Eastern Communication Association Convention, April 1983. For other details concerning media planning for "Be All You Can Be," see Denton, "Media Recall and Response Methods to Army Advertising: A Report," paper presented at Central States Speech Association Conference, April 1984.
23. Richard L. Johannesen, *Ethics in Human Communication,* 3rd Ed. (Prospect Heights IL: Waveland, 1990), 169.
24. Johannesen, *Ethics,* 176.
25. Johannesen, *Ethics,* 179.
26. Johannesen, *Ethics,* 184-186.
27. Gregg Easterbrook, "Junk-Mail Politics," *The New Republic* (25 April 1988): 17-21.
28. Easterbrook, "Junk-Mail Politics," 17.
29. Easterbrook, "Junk-Mail Politics," 17-18.
30. Trent and Friedenberg, *Political Campaign,* 13.
31. Jack Germond and Jules Witcover, "Calling Bush's Bluff on Race Issues," Eugene, OR *The Register-Guard* (19 July 1991): 13A.
32. Germond and Witcover, "Calling Bush's Bluff," 13A.

12

PERSUASION AND SOCIAL MOVEMENTS

IN THIS CHAPTER:

Focus on:

The Movement to Combat Pesticide Use in California Grapes

1. Theoretical Focus: Social Movements
   - Social Movements Are Sequential
   - Social Movements Act as Collectivities
   - Social Movements Are Noninstitutional
   - Social Movements Face Legitimation Difficulty
   - Social Movements Are Concerned Both with Means and Ends
   - Social Movements Are Loosely Organized
   - Social Movements Contain Militants and Moderates
   - Social Movements Employ Nontraditional Messages
2. Stages of Social Movements
   - Genesis Phase
   - Social Unrest Phase
   - Enthusiastic Mobilization Phase
   - Maintenance Phase
   - Termination Phase
3. Ethics and Social Movements
4. Critical Focus: Organization and Tactics in the No Grapes Movement

FOCUS ON: THE MOVEMENT TO COMBAT PESTICIDES IN CALIFORNIA GRAPES

The economic boycott—in which pressure to change is brought to bear through an orchestrated refusal to deal or do business with a merchant, an employer, a corporation or even a nation—is a long-standing tactic of social movements. The tactic takes its name from the unfortunate Charles Boycott, the agent for an Irish landlord, whose treatment of tenants was so cruel that in 1880 potential renters organized to leave his property without tenants or profits.

In the last four decades in America, the boycott has gained ground as a tactic of choice for social movements, in combination with demonstrations, marches, rallies, speeches, leafletting and more traditional forms of political pressure. Boycotts were used to force merchants and service providers in the south of the mid-1950's to early 1960's prior to civil rights to end their policies of racial segregation.[1] In the 1960's, the tactic was modified in Boston, Chicago and New York schools to fight de facto segregation by organizing students to stay home from segregated schools or attend alternative educational events on a chosen day.[2] Movements championing causes from marine wildlife to family values, from abortion rights to gay rights, have brought boycotts against a range of products and businesses such as canned tuna, movie theatres, ski resorts and take-out pizza. But perhaps no product is so closely associated in America with the boycott as the humble California grape.

The boycott of California grapes was a crucial tactic in the formation of the United Farm Workers of America (UFW) union in the mid-1960's. The tactic not only focused economic pressure on the anti-union growers, it also drew widespread public and political attention to the organizers' cause.[3] During the late 1980's the UFW launched a second boycott against California table grapes, but this time the same tactic was in service to a different cause. This boycott was aimed at curtailing the California grape growers' heavy reliance on pesticides and other hazardous chemicals, often delivered by crop-dusting aircraft. The UFW organizers and their supporters argued that exposure to these pesticides and their residue posed substantial health risks for the workers themselves, their families, the surrounding communities and the unwitting consumer. The UFW's call for a boycott has been combined with consumer education, rallies and lobbying efforts. Many of these tactics are illustrated in the 14-minute video *No Grapes*, produced by the UFW and its volunteer staff.[4]

Boycotts are a form of "creative disorder" in which movement supporters disrupt the ordinary functioning of institutions to attract attention to their cause and often directly to stop practices they consider intolerable. In almost all cases, "creative disorder" uses the single resource that all movements have: the bodies of its members—to see and be seen, to be present, to be withdrawn, to be an obstruction. "Creative disorder" includes other tactics such as school strikes, rent strikes, sit-ins, blocking building entrances, chaining oneself to trees or buildings, lying in front of construction equipment, forming picket and demonstration lines, fasting or holding prayer vigils. All of these forms of resistance are typically nonviolent, but unlike some forms of creative disorder, boycotts typically involve violating customs rather than laws.[5]

The California grape boycott illustrates some of the classic characteristics and challenges of any social movement. As an attempt to bring about institutional change mainly from without, social movements face problems of gaining access to public and popular attention. They employ creative or unconventional persuasive tactics (often because conventional tactics are unavailable due to the movement's noninstitutional status) and reconcile militant and moderate forces many times dwelling within the same movement. As a tactic, boycotts offer several advantages to social movements. For example, boycotts require little in the way of special resources or expertise, only the withdrawal of commercial support from their target. Boycotts can dramatize issues by reducing abstract issues to concrete actions. They provide an opportunity for many people not directly associated with the movement to participate in and identify with it by supporting the boycott.

THEORETICAL FOCUS: SOCIAL MOVEMENTS

In the next section of this chapter we discuss the distinguishing characteristics of social movements. These characteristics include special considerations of structure, duration, institutional status, leadership and goals. Following this, we examine the stages in the "life cycle" of social movements, showing their complexity and variety. The next section of the chapter looks at the unique role of audience and movement membership in social movements and its implications for persuasion in social movements. We then turn to the question of ethics in social movements, regarding matters of strategy and tactics and the goals of social movements. The chapter concludes with a Critical Focus, applying our discussion of the structure and function of social movements to an analysis of the movement to combat pesticides in California grapes.

CHARACTERISTICS OF SOCIAL MOVEMENTS

By *social movement*, we refer to *explicit and implicit persuasion by noninstitutionalized groups seeking public gain by attempting to change some part of "the system."* Such institutional change may be limited to *reform*, which alters some practices or policies of the institutions being challenged but leaves them essentially intact. For example, the movement to increase controls on the availability of handguns in America, leading to the 1991 introduction and 1992 passage in Congress of the Brady Bill, seeks to reform those laws pertaining to gun control. As important as such a change might be, it nevertheless leaves the general system of legislation, courts and law enforcement unchallenged. Similarly, movements organized by local citizens to create ordinances providing for "no smoking" areas in public places urge specific and limited change in the institutional *status quo*. By comparison, other social movements may be *radical* or revolutionary, demanding fundamental change in the existing social and institutional arrangements. For example, the various political reform movements in the former Soviet Union and Eastern Europe, have transformed political, economic and military institutions thus changing the very structure of their society. Whether radical or reformist, social movements have several identifying characteristics. Some of these individual characteristics are shared with the other forms of institutional persuasion we discuss in this section of the book, but the combination of persuasive characteristics of social movements make them unique as a form of institutional persuasion.

SOCIAL MOVEMENTS ARE SEQUENTIAL

Like persuasive campaigns, social movements are phenomena that unfold over time. However, unlike persuasive campaigns, social movements typically lack clearly specifiable beginning or ending points except, perhaps, with the benefit of considerable hindsight. Beginning a social movement requires no formal documents or official statements, nor does the movement recognize any externally imposed deadline or timetable requiring initial action. What transforms a widespread but tacit sentiment into a basis for collective action? Charles Stewart, Craig Smith and Robert Denton argue for the importance of some event which acts as a trigger, a catalyst, to bring a diffusely recognized cause into explicit public awareness:[6]

> The trigger may be a Supreme Court decision, a nuclear accident, an insensitive reaction or statement by an institutional agent, a new law, an economic downturn, a military action, or the appearance of a movement-oriented book on the best seller list. For instance, the comment by a North Dakota legislator to a farm delegation in 1915, "Go home and slop your

> hogs," infuriated farmers and gave rise to the Nonpartisan League in the Midwest. Betty Freidan's *The Feminine Mystique* helped to launch the women's liberation movement, and Rachel Carson's *The Silent Spring* served as the impetus for the ecology movement. The initial results of triggering events may be the first signs of organization with titles that begin: "Citizens for...," "Concerned Parents Against...," or "Workers United to..."

The coincidence of *The China Syndrome*'s theatrical release within a few weeks of the nuclear reactor accident at Three Mile Island in 1979 offers another example of triggering events, coalescing the largely unfocused opposition to nuclear energy. Obviously, however, such events can only rarely be "scheduled" in any way, in contrast to the start of persuasive campaigns. Nor is there a pre-established deadline by which the social movement must succeed or fail, as we would find with persuasive campaigns. Instead, the goals of a social movement evolve as the social context changes and the movement makes progress or faces reversals. The feminist movement in America, for example, follows a persuasive and political agenda which is open-ended. Individual initiatives supported by the movement, such as the passage of the Equal Rights Amendment, may face an institutionally imposed deadline, but the movement's leadership itself does not think of the movement as having to complete its work by a particular future termination point. Moreover, the unique functions and challenges of a social movement change over time, and the forms of persuasion characteristic of the movement change as well. We return to the analysis of the life cycle of social movements later in this chapter.

Social Movements Act as Collectivities

Social movements exist most fundamentally as a collective movement by a substantial number of people, and its leaders normally can act only in the name of that collectivity or the moral principles that unite it. The power of this collectivity is related to its size. The very term social movement suggests *significant* numbers of people believing in a cause and laboring on its behalf.[7] There are several reasons for this numerical necessity. In the absence of institutional legitimation, sheer numbers can offer a different form of legitimacy to a social movement, providing its leaders with the grounds for claiming they speak for "the people." Further, as Christian fundamentalists demonstrated during the 1980's, a numerically significant movement can bring meaningful pressure to bear on those institutions they want to influence, by organizing boycotts of merchants, advertisers or sponsors or by mobilizing votes based on single issues.

Social Movements are Noninstitutional

As we discuss in Chapter 10, institutions are empowered by custom, law or tradition to perform certain social functions. Social movements operate without benefit of this institutional power. As a result, the primary persuasive challenge faced by any social movement can usually be reduced to the problem of *empowerment*—gaining alternative forms of power to compensate for those forms held and wielded by the institutions they seek to change. Certainly, it is possible for social movements to have some ties to existing organizations with strong institutional status. For example, David Zarefsky has argued that Lyndon Johnson's "War on Poverty," a legislative initiative, was fundamentally the product of a social movement even though the key figures in the movement were themselves members of the Johnson Administration, because the resources and power available to the supporters were not those of the institutions involved.[8] Similarly, in the Mexican-American parishes of San Antonio, the activist community organization Communities Organized for Public Service was founded upon principles developed by radical organizer Saul Alinsky and advanced its grass-roots goals by taking advantage of the organization of parishes and contacts already established by the Catholic Church with the support of the local Archbishop.[9] Nevertheless, in both of these cases what was essential to their persuasive character was that they were outsiders with respect to the institutions they attempted to change and lacked the same legitimacy or power as those institutions.

SOCIAL MOVEMENTS FACE LEGITIMATION DIFFICULTY

Legitimation, the process of establishing credibility, is always a special problem for social movements. For most persuasion in an institutional context—campaigns, propaganda and ideologies—the association with existing institutions provides legitimacy for persuaders. By definition, however, social movements lack the same access to these sources of legitimacy. Therefore, social movements must rely on creative tactics for establishing power; the more radical the movement, the greater the reliance. As with any group attempting to place a topic on the public's agenda, social movements quickly find that media coverage is essential to legitimation, promotion and recruitment. As John Waite Bowers and Donovan Ochs point out, social movements can increase both the quantity and quality of media attention by seeking "individuals within the establishment who endorse some part of the agitators' ideology."[10]

For example, after Vice President Al Gore published his book on the deterioration of the global environment, media coverage of environmental issues and activist and activist environmental groups increased, probably because the media found Gore to be newsworthy. Similarly, the involvement in an issue of nearly any celebrity from entertainment or sports will boost media coverage of a social movement. A second way social movements can bring legitimacy to themselves is by the character of their persuasive tactics and public actions. This leads us to the characteristic consideration of social movements for both means and ends.

SOCIAL MOVEMENTS ARE CONCERNED BOTH WITH MEANS AND ENDS

Both the legitimation issues and the nontraditional forms of persuasion associated with social movements are part of a larger necessity faced by social movements: the challenge of justifying and reconciling both their *ends* and their *means*. The ends of a social movement are the changes, limited or radical, that it seeks to cause in existing institutions. The means by which a social movement pursues those ends encompasses its persuasive tactics, chosen from among the wide range of persuasive tactics available. In most other forms of institution level persuasion, the ends and the means are largely circumscribed by the institutions involved. Social movements, acting largely outside the orbit of these institutional constraints, must think through these issues more carefully. Stewart, Smith and Denton observe that the rhetoric of social movements usually assumes a moral tone; participants in movements "see themselves as having the power to distinguish right from wrong, good from evil, and ethical from unethical choices, actions, behavior, and character."[11]

This moral foundation is in part the legitimizing force behind the movement, since it lacks access to institutionalized forms of legitimacy. Further, when the authority of movement leadership rests upon charisma, the moral tone of the movement's persuasion becomes even more important. As a consequence, a social movement must be self-consciously aware of its actions, for each action serves as a new test of legitimacy for the movement. For example, during the Women's Movement of the late 1970's and early 1980's, many women's groups indicted the decision-making process of organizations for following "masculine" rules of competition and majority rule and proposed cooperative, consensus decision-making as an alternative. However, as groups such as the New York Radical Women or the National Organization of Women (NOW) grew, they frequently found consensus to be inefficient and unwieldy. Consequently, disputes over means for achieving equality between the sexes broke out.

Social Movements are Loosely Organized

Social movements should not be confused with the formalized organizations that form in and around them. A single social movement may spawn or become associated with several different formal organizations. For example, the movement for native Americans' rights has witnessed the birth of such organizations as the Indian Rights Association and the Friends of the Indians in the late nineteenth century, the Indian Defense Association in the first half of the twentieth century and the National Congress of American Indians and the American Indian Movement since World War II.[12] These organizations do not serve precisely the same constituency or embody the same leadership, goals or tactics; some would heatedly deny that other organizations on the list deserved to be included at all. Organizations, unlike social movements, typically have an address, enter into contracts such as office rental, pay salaries and taxes, sport letterhead and boast clearly defined memberships. They may consider themselves as acting in the name of a social movement, but they are not identical with it.[13]

Both the leadership and the membership of social movements are difficult to specify in the same way that we could name the leadership and membership of a product or political campaign team. Charismatic individuals, such as Martin Luther King, Jr. or Malcom X in the Civil Rights movement, may rise to prominent positions within a movement, but this leadership position is always tentative at best, for the reasons we discuss in Chapter 5. As agents of change, charismatic leaders can often command strong loyalty from among their followers. They cling to power only by their ability to continue producing pragmatic results; and if they succeed in formalizing and institutionalizing the desired changes, they may produce the very "establishment" context that they were rebelling against in the first place.

We can observe this irony in struggles between the environmentalist organization the Sierra Club and the ongoing environmentalist movement itself.[14] Initial gains in environmental policy to which the Sierra Club contributed caused the organization itself to acquire a more "establishment" image. One member described the problem caused by this gradual transformation: "I don't think John Muir [founder of the Sierra Club in 1892] would join today."[15]

SOCIAL MOVEMENTS CONTAIN MILITANTS AND MODERATES

The Sierra Club's dilemma reflects another characteristic of social movements. After a social movement shapes its own special identity and gains size, complexity and momentum, it then, almost invariably, faces an internal conflict between moderates and militants.[16] In addition, other factions may emerge within the movement. This internal division is a product of the size of the movement's membership, its noninstitutional status and its characteristic lack of formal organization and central control. Further, as the movement widens the scope of the change it envisions for "the system," it also increases the prospects of the split between revolutionary or radical approaches and limited or conservative approaches. Moderates attempt to keep strong ties with the institutions they seek to change (and with other related institutions) by seeking limited change and adopting institutionally sanctioned means of influence. By doing so they gain access to institutional decision-makers, and they secure a certain legitimacy by appearing to be "quasi-institutional" themselves. This access and legitimacy become tools which the moderate forces then, in principle, apply to promote the movement's cause.

Militants seek wide-spread and deep-cutting changes in institutions. As a result they reject highly institutionalized forms of power and legitimation. Their power base comes from other sources: popular appeal among "the masses;" harassment, intimidation or violence directed toward institutions or institutional figures; and the perceived or avowed "purity" of their devotion to their cause. The problem of legitimation is less bothersome to militants. If "being legitimate" means "being acceptable to the power structure they are trying to change," militants rarely want to be legitimate anyway.

Militants are easier to mobilize but harder to discipline than moderates. Moderates are easier to discipline but harder to mobilize. For example, in a college town, where one of the authors was a faculty member, the papers reported an alleged multiple rape at a fraternity house on the edge of campus. Even before this report, there was growing conviction throughout members of the campus community that the incidence of violent sexual assault in the community was very high, much higher than any institutional spokespersons were admitting. When the latest story hit the papers, it served as a triggering event. A group of local residents scheduled a series of meetings to discuss ways of responding to the situation as a community. Militants and moderates quickly became visible. Some people at the emotionally charged meetings announced their intention to spray-paint "rapists welcome!" in day-glow letters on the front door of the scene of the alleged crime. Others conjectured that the negative publicity created by the alleged incident would at last be enough to force the local police and the university to publicize the issue, and thereby break loose support for safety improvements like increased street lighting and sexual assault awareness programs. The militant and moderate groups soon became impatient with each other and separated. The break prevented the incipient movement from achieving the strength it might otherwise have gathered. The moderates could raise money and organize rallies, but they soon became bogged down in the procedural red tape of the very system they were trying to challenge. The militants, unconcerned with the red tape, preferred tactics of confrontation and counter-assault rather than getting post office boxes and monitoring local court decisions, but they found it difficult to act in a concerted way to keep pressure on the university and the city government. Ironically, the passion and energy necessary to keep the community action group mobilized separated from the organizational continuity needed to keep the community action group disciplined.

As the example of the rape-awareness community action group suggests, militants typically view moderates as having "sold out" to "the system." Moderates typically regard militants as unrealistic or naive. The intensity of these views increases as the movement achieves some persuasive successes. In the case of the Sierra Club, one member of a Texas chapter of the Sierra Club complained to the media that the Sierra Club's national leadership had become secure in its relationship with the very politicians they should be pressuring. "They are losing sight of the fact that their mission is to save ecosystems, not to have lunch with Senator Hatfield [of the Senate Appropriations Committee]," grumbles this member. Retorts a member of the Club's national headquarters, "If you embrace the most radical or visionary proposals, my sense is you are not going to be able to rally sufficient political support in the next five years to pass anything and, as a result, we will lose everything."[17] The initial successes of a movement can immediately bring moderates and militants into conflict with each other. "Purists" in the movement may gradually become more militant, attempting to intensify commitment to the principles that led to early successes and to prevent "backsliding" by continuing to keep persuasive pressure on the target institutions. Moderates within the movement may argue that change can occur too rapidly, that initial changes in "the system" sufficiently demonstrate the movement's accomplishment.

Nevertheless, militants and moderates often "need" each other. Militants can point to the "corruption" of the moderates by "the system" to reinforce their own commitment to "pure" (that is, militant) tactics and goals. Moderates, similarly, can use the extreme positions and tactics of the militants to argue that they themselves are "the system's" best chance for reasonable negotiation, that they are the only alternative to the hostile and perhaps even violent sentiments of the militants. Successes by one faction, thus, may stimulate action by the other faction.

A movement with strong moderate and militant factions can make it difficult for established institutions to react in a consistent way, even if they want to, because the same actions or responses often will not satisfy both wings of the movement. The leaders of the institutions under pressure from a social movement can exploit conflict within the movement by playing these two factions against one another and against the general public. They can point to the militants and use them to characterize the entire movement, turning public opinion against the movement and citing their extremism as reason not to concede to *any* movement demands. Alternatively, institutional leaders can make token concessions to the moderate wing of the movement, then declare publicly that the "conflict" is settled, thereby co-opting both factions within the movement.

Over time, initial successes in producing institutional change tend to strengthen the moderates more than the militants. Moderates gain more institutional power with success and, as a result, may have more interest in preserving the new status quo. Militants may find it increasingly difficult to motivate supporters and to keep pressure on the institution while retaining their "outsider" status. The greater the internal tension between moderate and militant factions, the greater the risk that the movement will stall shortly after a small number of highly publicized successes. In such cases the institutional change, if any, will be limited, not radical.

And while moderates and militants maneuver against one another within the movement, "the established order has time on its side," according to Stewart, Smith and Denton:[18]

> It can wait until social, economic, and political crises pass, until a war ends, until establishment leadership changes occur through normal processes, until the public becomes disenchanted with protest and disorder, until the mass media and their audiences become bored with the issue, until movement leadership changes through graduation, military discharge, power struggles, death, assassination, or until movement leaders and followers tire of the struggle or become disillusioned by lack of real progress toward a goal. If social movement leaders and followers do not tire, they may become desperate and make mistakes, mistakes the establishment can use to discredit or to suppress the movement.

SOCIAL MOVEMENTS EMPLOY NONTRADITIONAL MESSAGES

Another characteristic of social movements is reflected in many of the examples mentioned above: the frequently heavy reliance by movements upon *nontraditional messages* to advance their persuasive purposes. "Nontraditional" can embrace an almost unlimited range of message types. Frequently they involve the exploitation of free media by staging pseudo-events. Other movements, such as the union movement, the anti-war movement and the civil rights movement in America, made potent use of protest music to advance and solidify.[19] The American Civil Rights movement adopted tactics of civil disobedience developed during the movement for independence in India. Earth First!, a radical branch of the environmental movement, employs tactics it calls "monkey-wrenching," such as putting sugar in the gas tanks of bulldozers or driving spikes into the trunks of trees and chaining themselves to those trees to prevent them from being sawed down. Nineteen-sixties radical feminists developed a form of action they called "zaps," turning the non-establishment, non-structured nature of their movement to their advantage. As Ann Popkin, a participant, recalls:

> The over-all loose and decentralized structure helped give rise to the popularity of "zap actions." Zaps were often one-shot deals, in which a group of women would go to some public place to expose the sexism of an institution or activity. Often theatrical, zaps usually featured costumes or skits as well as leaflets. The point was to reach new people, women and men, in new ways, and to give a quick jiggle to spectators' normal ways of seeing things.

> An example is the Bread and Roses "Ogle-In" of July, 1970, where men in a busy shopping area were given women's traditional treatment of stares, whistles, catcalls, and pinches. "Don't hide it all under a suit!" the women urged. "Smile honey. What's the matter, lost your sense of humor?" Female passersby were given leaflets and, according to one participant, "It was beautiful—they understood right away."[20]

Such taunting and mockery is a typical part of the social movement's armory. Among Alinsky's "rules for radicals," therefore, are the following:[21]

> *Ridicule is man's most potent weapon.* It is almost impossible to counterattack ridicule. Also, it infuriates the opposition, who then react to your advantage.... *A good tactic is one that your people enjoy.* If your people are not having a ball doing it, there is something very wrong with the tactic.

To some extent the resort to nontraditional messages directly results from the noninstitutional status of the movement. Lacking the legitimation and financial resources of their institutional counterparts may force social movements to rely upon nontraditional messages as the only means available to spread their persuasive message. Alternatively, social movements may employ nontraditional messages because they regard them as persuasively superior, because the *form* of the nontraditional message is more appropriate to the movement's purposes or because more traditional messages involve collaboration with the very institutions they are challenging.

Stages Of Social Movements

Describing the stages of social movements is a daunting task. The comparative absence of institutional constraints and formal organizational restrictions makes it difficult to develop formalized blueprints or theoretical models. Social movements bloom in our culture like wildflowers, each adapting to its own terrain and sustenance. Thus, it is appropriate for Stewart, Smith and Denton to describe social movements as having a "life cycle," from conception and birth through infancy to maturity and discontinuation.[22] Not all social movements reach successful maturity; some incipient movements never survive their infancy, while others may take root and then lapse dormant for long periods of time only to re-emerge in some new outward form, if at all. Each phase of a movement's life cycle has its unique persuasive features—particular challenges, typical strategies and target audiences.

Genesis Phase

All social movements, say Stewart, Smith and Denton, emerge from a genesis stage. During the genesis stage, the central issue or cause for the movement is held to be important only by a few individuals. The majority of society remains unaware of the problem or regards it as unimportant. The nature of this problem is often itself a largely rhetorical creation, not principally an objective or empirical condition, like an earthquake or disease outbreak, but rather a conflict of values and expectations. Corruption, inequality or exploitation within some aspect of the institutional *status quo* (or, more precisely, the *perception* of these things) is the beginning point for any social movement. Movement-oriented persuasion at this stage is ordinarily the creation of a few individuals who perceive a significant problem with the *status quo* and attempt to draw others to their way of thinking. Saul Alinsky caustically observed that one's political point of view and the passage of time will determine whether these early leaders will be called "prophets," "visionaries," and "freedom fighters," or "cranks," "trouble-makers," and "terrorists."[23] As historian David De Leon points out with respect to the abolitionist movement in the United States:

> The first opponents of slavery were generally ignored or despised. When Samuel Sewall wrote "The Selling of Joseph" in 1701, attempting to prevent blacks from being priced "like horses and hogs," he met with little sympathy. David Walker, a free black man who wrote the famous *Appeal* of 1829, died young and impoverished. William Lloyd Garrison, the editor of *The Liberator* (founded in 1831), was commonly considered a nuisance or a lunatic.[24]

Many would-be movements never make it beyond the genesis stage. Lacking persuasive leaders to call attention to the problem or missing a triggering event to catalyze a widespread public perception, such marginal groups tend to remain ineffectual and are considered as only "fringe" groups or troublemakers.

SOCIAL UNREST PHASE

Those groups that succeed in bringing together broadly shared feelings of dissatisfaction can move their would-be movement to a second stage, a stage of social unrest. The transition to this stage is marked by changes in the nature of persuasive messages being created. First, as Stewart, Smith and Denton note, "the establishment" may begin to take notice of the budding movement and its leaders and to respond by supporting its own varied interests:[25]

> Spokespersons for institutions may openly deny the severity or the existence of the problem (exigence) and, often for the first time, take official notice of the fledgling social movement. They may stigmatize the "movement" as naive, ill-informed, or outside the mainstream of society. Their strategy is to stall the movement by ignoring or discrediting it in hopes that it will succumb to ridicule or inattention. The mass media may note with interest, amusement, or mild foreboding the infant social movement and its pathetic claims or overtures.

At the same time, the persuasion being produced by the movement tends to change in character. In a typical action at this point in its life a social movement, particularly one seeking widespread and fundamental change, develops a formal statement of the goals and ideology of the movement.[26] For example, the 1848 First Women's Rights Convention produced a Declaration of Sentiments; in 1868 the National Labor Union produced its Constitution.

It is useful, as Herbert Simons notes, for us to understand such persuasive messages as serving two functions: influencing those outside the movement and building solidarity among those within.[27] By doing so, we become more aware of the importance of persuasion to establishing identification *within* the ranks of the movement as well as persuasion directed by the movement toward established institutions. Externally directed persuasion can motivate awareness, recruitment, agitation or confrontation.[28] However, particularly with social movements seeking radical rather than modest social change, a significant amount of internally directed persuasion is oriented toward consciousness raising.[29] Chesebro, Cragan and McCullough describe the small group processes involved in consciousness raising:

> Consciousness raising is a personal, face-to-face interaction which appears to create new psychological orientations for those involved in the process. Participants develop new group identities often forming "new minorities" which may focus upon sociocultural divisions such as sex, age, sexual preference, education, wealth, power, or prestige. As a result, members often perceive other group members as "sisters" and "brothers" of a new "cultural family" and "community." However, the personal face-to-face interaction technique is selected because it is consistent with the radical revolutionary's belief that shared personal experience should generate political theory and action.[30]

The techniques of consciousness raising were pioneered in the early stages of radical feminism and the Gay Liberation Movement.[31] Although developed primarily for application in small group sessions, the techniques produce characteristics of discourse significant for the social movement as a whole. Groups, for example, develop increasingly polarized language to discuss not only the movement itself but the world in general; through language, the world becomes sharply divided into women and men, gays and straights and so forth. Moreover, these distinctions become strongly value laden and function as "god terms" and "devil terms," organizing beneath themselves a whole array of lesser terms for persons, actions and ideas.[32] As we see in Chapter 7, this rhetorical organization can constitute and define individual ideologies, each struggling to advance its worldview within a pluralistic society. At the same time, the persuasion typical of social movements during the social unrest stage begins to focus not only on establishing a shared sense of a problem, but also on formulating solutions by describing programs for change, demanding action and visualizing a society with the desired changes in place.

Enthusiastic Mobilization Phase

Budding movements that provoke widespread social unrest, articulating an issue of popular concern and advocating a plan for resolving it, typically enter a stage of enthusiastic mobilization next. This stage is characterized by optimism, visibility and vigorous activity in support of its cause. Stewart, Smith and Denton characterize this stage of a movement as "populated with true believers who have experienced conversion to the cause."[33] Several unique persuasive challenges typify this movement phase. Most stem in some way from the swelling of the movement's ranks both with true movement members and with sympathizers won from the larger public. Many movements at this stage face the question of "diluting" their message to make it more palatable to the wider audiences their size, success and legitimacy enabled them to reach. "Hard-liners" and "purists" within the movement will resist such tactics, while others will argue that the need for continued growth demands that the persuasive message be adapted for new audiences.[34]

"True Believers." The role of the "true believer" in social movements deserves closer examination. Some mass movements are essentially democratic in character, whether conservative or progressive, drawing their strength from the independent judgment and reasoning of the movement members. There are also many movements not characterized by such lofty sounding sentiments in all of their persuasion. Eric Hoffer has offered a classic analysis both of mass movements and of the fanatical devotees, whom Hoffer calls "true believers", who are often among the first to join such movements and who tend to form their core. Hoffer's conclusions specific to movements and the psychology of the "true believer" are relevant to the mobilization phase.[35]

By "true believer," Hoffer means an individual "of fanatical faith who is ready to sacrifice his life for a holy cause."[36] The "holy" cause may be a religious creed, a political doctrine, a spiritual revival or a social crusade. The sacrifice may be literal or symbolic. The "true believer" personality type is characterized by a consistent pattern of motivations: *discontent, desire to be free from individual responsibility and strong need for cohesiveness and belonging*. Discontent in no way implies hopelessness. According to Hoffer, discontent breeds "when misery is bearable; when conditions have so improved that an ideal state seems almost within reach."[37] We find true believers among those who have recently suffered and can imagine being back in their former comfortable state or those who see progress around them but are impatient to experience it for themselves. This discontent may not necessarily be directed outwards only, but it may also be directed toward the self. Particularly among revivalist type movements, whether religious or secular, the greatest appeal is "...not to those intent on bolstering and advancing a cherished self, but to those who crave to be rid of an unwanted self."[38] A striking pattern among the most forceful adherents to a movement is this impulse toward redefining the self, making one in effect a new person. Although the two phenomena seem scarcely comparable otherwise, this impulse is evident both in the motivation of true believers to be rid of an impure or undesired part of the self and in the descriptions of the effects of consciousness raising.

The desire to be free from individual responsibility, which Hoffer also associates with the true believer, ties in with this impulse to self-denial.[39] If one believes oneself to be imperfect, impure, why allow that self further free rein? Phrased positively, it may seem to be a bargain to gain access to the power and legitimation of a mass movement simply by giving up such burdens as obligation, blame and accountability. Hoffer states:

> It was not sheer hypocrisy when the rank-and-file Nazis declared themselves not guilty of all the enormities they had committed. They considered themselves cheated and maligned when made to shoulder responsibility for obeying orders. Had they not joined the Nazi movement in order to be free from responsibility?[40]

The appeal of a social movement for a true believer rests in the possibility that, through assimilation into the movement, the true believer can elevate and magnify this impulse toward self-sacrifice and at the same time downplay individual responsibility and visibility.[41]

Usually, Hoffer argues, "true believers" simply require *some* outlet, perhaps even *any* outlet, for their inclinations. *Which* outlet is chosen, or even *which* movement, may be irrelevant. "In pre-Hitlerian Germany it was often a tossup [sic] whether a restless youth would join the Communists or the Nazis," writes Hoffer, adding, "In the overcrowded pale of Czarist Russia the simmering Jewish population was ripe both for revolution and Zionism."[42]

Maintaining the Purity of the Movement. The analysis of "true believers" shows that persuasion during the stage of enthusiastic mobilization serves to advance the movement's cause and also to satisfy fundamental psychological needs of the movement members. Richard Gregg refers to this as the "ego-function" of protest rhetoric.[43] Similarly, rhetoric produced by social movements creates powerful motives for identification among groups and subcultures. Particularly among more radical and militant social movements, the purity of their motives is of extreme importance. The conviction that they, and they alone, hold the truth and act on behalf of the good is essential to the legitimation of their actions and the authority of their leaders. Yet cleaving to the Truth, moving unwaveringly toward the Good, is a goal all groups, as well as all persons, will eventually fall short of reaching. Thus, our ideas of social order contain a contradiction. They assume an ideal of "perfection"—material, social, hierarchical, intellectual or spiritual; however, because that ideal is a symbolic creation, we can never reach it. Whatever we have, whatever we achieve or whatever we accomplish, we can always *conceive* of something more or something better or something purer. This drive toward perfection, says critic Kenneth Burke, is characteristic of humans and implicit in the symbols they use.[44] As a result, Burke concludes, the depiction of ideal social order in any movement's persuasion predestines its members to guilt, which they must find some way to purge.[45]

At the enthusiastic mobilization stage, social movements frequently confront the prospect of their own "guilt," imperfection or impurity. Cleansing itself of this symbolic imperfection becomes an important persuasive task. The symbolic impurity of a movement, like the religious impurity of an individual, can be cleansed in one of two ways: by mortification or by scapegoating. Both strategies involve letting someone or something come to hold or represent the imperfection, then literally or symbolically making it a victim or bringing death or destruction to it. The polarized language of "god terms" and "devil terms" serves the movement in setting the stage for such absolutist measures. For example, as Stewart, Smith and Denton point out:

> When confrontations between the movement and institutional forces become severe, the movement stresses "we-they" distinctions more sharply and bitterly. Persons who do not join and former members become hated traitors, "scabs," and "Uncle Toms." The social movement may look within and decide that some members (whites, males, non-skilled workers) are incapable of true understanding or involvement in the cause. These members are purged to purify the movement in time of decision.[46]

This represents the response Burke calls mortification: the blame for impurity or imperfection is isolated in a single part of the body, and that part is cut away to leave the whole cleansed.

Alternatively, the polarized language of "god terms" and "devil terms" can locate the blame for impurity or imperfection outside the movement on a scapegoat. In Christian theology, the model for Burke's application to secular movements, this was achieved by the crucifixion of Jesus. For the Nazi movement in Germany, persecution and slaughter of Jews served such a symbolic function. For the anti-war is no vice! Moderation in the pursuit of justice is no virtue!"[53] The Republican nomination process fractured the party, leaving it in disarray. The Democratic campaign hammered away at Goldwater with message after message simply reminding audiences of Goldwater's image as too extreme, too removed from the "mainstream" of American politics. One such message was the notorious "Daisy" television spot analyzed in Chapter 8.

Goldwater's resounding defeat in the 1964 general election might well have consigned the conservative movement to oblivion in modern American politics were it not for a 30-minute campaign film produced for the Goldwater campaign and shown on national television one week before election day.[54] The speech was widely praised by state and national Republican leadership, who sponsored the distribution of the film nationwide and published the text during the next few days. The speaker in the film was Ronald Reagan, movie actor, former host of the popular television program *G.E. Theatre*, and until 1962 a registered Democrat and supporter of Roosevelt and Truman. "With this speech," notes rhetorical critic Kurt Ritter, "Reagan rose out of a disastrous Republican defeat to establish himself as a potential candidate for Governor of California, and the 'hottest new product on the Republican horizon.'"[55] The conservative movement remained dormant for a decade at the national level until Reagan returned in the 1976 Presidential campaign. Following Reagan's election, the conservative movement began to dominate the American political agenda.

ETHICS AND SOCIAL MOVEMENTS

Social movements present a challenge for assessing the ethics of persuasion. Lacking institutional status, formal professional codes of ethics are generally nonexistent in social movements. Lacking a clear organizational structure, ethical responsibility for often anonymous acts can be difficult to establish even where ethical grounds seem clear enough. Nevertheless, both the tactics and goals of persuasion in social movements should be subject to ethical evaluation.

Many of the ethical standards for tactics of persuasion discussed in earlier chapters can be applied to the tactics of social movements. For example, the appeals of charismatic leaders can be judged for their empowering or disempowering effects on audiences. Similarly, the use of god or devil terms so frequent in social movements are subject to questions about their demeaning and degrading effects. However, because social movements often strive to radically change the system without the persuasive resources available to other groups, ethical questions are sometimes difficult to answer. More often, ethical issues arise regarding persuasive tactics that appear to be unique to social movements. Two such tactics are *violence* and *obscenity*.

Many social movements explicitly forswear resorting to violence, adopting instead such nonviolent approaches as civil disobedience, mediation and other conflict resolution tactics. Nevertheless, even when stripped of all other forms of power, a social movement can call on one remaining power, the physical bodies of its collective membership. Stewart, Smith and Denton point out the uneasy relationship between persuasion and violence:

> The role of persuasion distinguishes social movements from civil wars and revolutions. *In social movements, persuasion is pervasive while*

> *violence is incidental and often employed for symbolic purposes. In civil wars and revolutions, violence is pervasive while persuasion is incidental.*[56]

Violence represents a tactical as well as an ethical problem and, given the noninstitutional status of a movement, confronts movement leadership with a difficult dilemma. Stewart, *et al.*, explain that, "a few violent acts may doom years of protest, even if the acts are by a fanatical, splinter group," adding, "The public and institutions do not make fine distinctions: an act *in the name* of the social movement is *an act by the movement.*"[57] Saul Alinsky argued that the more radical the change sought by the movement and the more necessary its members perceive the change and the fewer the means and resources available to the movement, the greater the likelihood that its leaders and members will ignore the fine distinctions regarding the propriety of means.[58] As a consequence, to advance its persuasive goals, the movement may employ tactics of coercion, threats and even selective and symbolic violence.

Obscenity presents a slightly different problem. The wide range of activities available as nontraditional messages and the noninstitutional status of the social movement almost guarantee that sooner or later its members will resort to persuasive messages that will strike some as tasteless. In radical movements, their leader generally hopes that moment will come sooner rather than later; it would be a pitiful revolution that was incapable of offending *someone*. After all, standards of taste relate to institutionally approved values, so those standards might understandably be among the first casualties of confrontation.[59] It seems reasonable to wonder, for example, if the 1990 arrest of rap group 2 Live Crew on obscenity charges (of which they were later acquitted) reflected a genuine concern that the group's lyrics offended community standards of decency or establishment revulsion at the challenge posed by the political and ideological content of their music.[60] Haig Bosmajian, in his discussion of the legal and ethical implications of obscenity and protest in the New Left Movement, notes that obscenity can be an attractive weapon for the movement for several reasons:

> (1) the obscenities appear to the dissenters as evidence of their liberation; (2) the obscenities will not extensively be co-opted by the Establishment, as have been so many other aspects of the Movement, such as clothing styles, music, and various symbols; (3) the obscenities label establishment men and actions for what they are seen as—obscene; (4) the obscenities give the dissenters the power to define their adversaries; (5) the obscenities are provoking, and in effect get for the dissenters some kind of response....[61]

In a situation of extreme power difference between the movement and "the system," then, the use of obscenity can serve to advance the short- and long-term goals of the movement.

Although the unique characteristics of social movements make ethical evaluation of their persuasive tactics difficult, the general goal of movements supplies a useful guidline for ethical judgement. By definition, social movements advocate some public good through institutional change. In the debate over whose vision of the public good should be privileged—for example, the pro-choice movement's or the right-to-life's?—we should not lose sight of the fact that the persuasive social movement itself, regardless of its particular agenda, represents a social good. As Alinsky reminds us:

> From the beginning the weakness as well as the strength of the democratic ideal has been the people. People cannot be free unless they are willing to sacrifice some of their interests to guarantee the freedom of others. The price of democracy is the ongoing pursuit of the common good by *all* the people. One hundred and thirty-five years ago Tocqueville gravely warned that unless individual citizens were regularly involved in the action of governing themselves, self-government would pass from the scene. Citizen participation is the animating spirit and force in a society predicated on voluntarism.[62]

Hence social movements represent a *process* which advances the public good to the extent that it involves us all in the process of controlling our own institutionally enveloped lives, as citizens, worshippers and consumers. Movements that encourage participation in this process are probably ethical; those that discourage participation by inviting passivity are ethically suspect.

CRITICAL FOCUS: ORGANIZATION AND TACTICS IN THE *NO GRAPES* MOVEMENT

Appreciating the distinctiveness of social movements as a form of institution-level persuasion requires understanding how their peculiar structure, goals and institutional status shape the persuasion that occurs within them. Of course, the critical study of social movements from the Institutional Perspective may often incorporate theoretical and ethical insights from the Classical or Symbolist Perspective. But because of its status as institution-level persuasion, there will always be aspects of social movement persuasion—such as its life cycle, its use of media or perhaps its specific tactics—that will be beyond the reach of either of these earlier perspectives. Thus, social movements like the California grapes boycott movement that is the focus of this chapter will often invite a somewhat eclectic approach to their analysis.

This Critical Focus is designed to consider individual persuasive messages or clusters of messages within the overall persuasive context of the social movement. In this case, we will examine the 14-minute film *No Grapes*, produced in 1992 by the UFW and its volunteer staff. The following questions are designed to guide your critical analysis.

CRITICAL QUESTIONS

1. What is the **main goal** of the social movement in question? What institution(s) does it seek to change or reform? What is the nature of the reform the movement seeks?
2. What **general strategy** (or strategies) has the movement formed to accomplish the desired change, and how does the persuasive message under examination contribute to that strategy?
3. To what extent does the message under examination reflect **persuasive challenges** that are unique to social movements, including legitimation, leadership and choice of tactics?
4. What **audiences** are most relevant to the movement's long-term goals? What audiences are most relevant to the persuasive

message under examination? What **elements of the message** seem designed to influence these audiences? How?

5. At what **stage** in the movement's life cycle does the message appear? To what extent does the message appear to advance the unique persuasive challenges characteristic of that stage?
6. What **ethical standards** of persuasion in social movements are most appropriately applied to the message in question? To what extent does this message measure up to these ethical standards?

The No Grapes boycott of California grapes has one central goal and several related ones. Primarily, its purpose is to protect the health of farm workers and their families by inducing commercial grape growers to curtail their heavy use of pesticides and dangerous chemicals and to implement greater safety measures in the use and handling of these substances. According to the video *No Grapes*, California's agriculture industry uses 300 million pounds of pesticides per year, 8 million pounds on grapes alone, one-third of which are known carcinogens. The use of pesticides is particularly heavy in grape farming. *No Grapes* presents a tally of miscarriages, birth defects and clusters of statistically rare forms of cancer among the children of grape farm workers, all of which the UFW asserts to be linked to the massive use of these substances by the commercial grape farms. Thus, the boycott is a tactic intended to help the UFW protect its own members, who currently have the highest incidence of job-related illness in California, according to *No Grapes*.

The No Grapes boycott is a tactic of a larger movement instigated by the UFW, whose goals are to protect and support farm workers and their families and to protect and educate consumers and communities, forcing corporations to be more socially responsible. All of these goals are evident in the *No Grapes* video. Thus, we see farm workers and their families represented in the video as well as angry parents in the surrounding community where runoff from the grape farms has introduced pesticide residues into drinking water and concerned officials from the Food and Drug Administration (FDA), the Environmental Protection Agency (EPA) and the General Accounting Office (GAO)—all of whom are involved in the larger issues toward which this movement is addressed.

Although the No Grapes boycott has the backing and support of the parent organization, the UFW, it operates largely outside of existing institutional channels. It operates out of a post office box in California, and it relies on networking and volunteerism more than official clout and establishment power. As a result, its tactics—and its problems—are typical of those of any social movement. It has no army of paid workers it can assign to the organization and conduct of the boycott and related persuasive endeavors. Instead, it operates with volunteers and is funded by contributions from those sympathetic to the cause. *No Grapes* concludes with a list of ways that viewers can help, beginning with "Don't buy grapes" and "Ask your supermarket not to promote or advertise grapes." It then moves quickly to "Send for a free video" and, most important, "Send a donation."

Similarly, although the name of Cesar Chavez, the UFW's founder and first president, is well-known and the *No Grapes* video features scenes of Chavez, taped before his death, like all social movements it must seek authority from those individuals or organizations who lend their support and endorsement. Celebrities featured in the video include actors and other notables such as Martin Sheen, Lou Diamond Phillips, Emilio Esteves, Mike Farrell, Charles Haid, Robert Blake, Linda Dangcil and Edward James Olmos. The video also shows members of other unions marching on behalf of the boycott, and other organizations such as the American Library Association have formally agreed to support the boycott.[63]

The principal aim of the No Grapes boycott is to pressure California grape growers to change their use of pesticides, by reducing the sheer amount of the substances on which the growers rely and by providing greater safety precautions for their handling and use. *No Grapes* demonstrates the dangers of the status quo in several ways, beginning with the ominous opening shot of a helicopter, dark and menacing, flying unwaveringly toward the viewer, with clouds of spray rolling from spray booms extending out from the frame. A parade of negative and often horrible visual images runs throughout the video: children with congenital deformations, the coffins and graves of workers who died of exposure to these chemicals, and the juxtaposed shots of pesticides raining down from helicopters and planes with shots of children playing in the streets and workers in the field with nothing more than work gloves and a bandanna tied over their noses and mouths to prevent contact with the chemicals clinging to the berries and leaves. In addition to this visual imagery, the video builds an important argument: The representative of the GAO interviewed in *No Grapes* readily admits that, for the 50,000 pesticides currently registered with the EPA, the task of determining which ones may have toxic effects undocumented at the time of their initial approval—a process he calls filling in "gaps in the data"—could easily take 30 years. Chavez dismisses the comfortingly objective talk of "risk-benefit" analysis, observing that the "risk" is taken by exploited workers and unaware consumers, while the "benefit" accrues to the growers and sellers.

The *No Grapes* video reveals other facets of strategy, most conspicuously that of consumer education. Indeed, the purpose of producing *No Grapes* was clearly consumer education as much as promoting the boycott itself. The video shows rallies, picket marches, parades of celebrities, the testimony of parents and the endorsement of other organizations, all lending support and authority to the No Grapes action. Nevertheless, the strategy of the movement rests primarily on the economic leverage of the boycott.

No Grapes also displays the characteristic decentralized nature of most movements. Often through the distinctiveness of their tactics, some movements cause a leader to emerge. For example, the 1956 boycott of Montgomery, Alabama, buses not only led to the end of segregationist practices, but it also elevated Martin Luther King, Jr. to prominence as the leader of the burgeoning civil rights movement.[64] The original grape boycott led to formal recognition of the UFW and likewise caused Chavez himself to emerge as a recognized movement leader. Despite the presence of Chavez in *No Grapes*, everything about the video denies the presence of any centralized, top down structure to the movement. Instead, its images are repeatedly those of a grass-roots collective of workers and parents, doctors and educators, community members and concerned consumers.

This emphasis on participants and participation is typical of a movement which has reached the stage of enthusiastic mobilization. The fundamental issues are already articulated and publicized; the important work now is to extend the range and commitment of participants. The tone of this phase is one of optimism and clarity of purpose. "The boycott is so powerful, everyone has an impact," Chavez tells viewers. "And you really see results. Boycotts really work."

Another important facet of the overall strategy behind the boycott is revealed in images from *No Grapes*. Conspicuously absent from the video is any but the most oblique reference to the growers toward whom the boycott strategy is ultimately directed. Their faces and names are not shown; only their anonymous, symbolic stand-ins such as crop dusters and chemical refinery plants appear. The growers are not mentioned in the video because they are not addressed, directly, by the strategy of the boycott itself. That is, organizing a boycott means communicating with and motivating the would-be consumers who might participate, and it means announcing publicly the existence and aims of the boycott. Boycotts are founded on the assumption that direct persuasion applied to the producers or sellers themselves will not be effective and that only the brute logic of sales and profits will influence them. "These are not family farms we're talking about," says Chavez. "These are major corporations and the only way to get through to them is by not buying grapes." Thus, although the UFW's legal and economic clout had diminished, like that of unionism in general, during the 1980's, by 1992 the No Grapes boycott had made progress, not only widening individual participation in the boycott but also convincing large supermarket chains to honor their boycott.[65]

Among all tactics of "creative disruption," boycotts are typically among the most ethically principled. In part this is because the legality of the tactic has long since been established by the courts. Although it remains illegal to coerce others into participating in a boycott, the courts rejected southern segregationists' argument that a boycott was an illegal restraint of trade.[66] Indeed, the legal and moral success of the boycotts employed during the civil rights movement helped make the boycott the main strategy of movements for a decade thereafter.[67]

The UFW boycotts have rigorously followed the tradition of creative nonviolence made a signature of the civil rights movement by the teaching of King.[68] This tradition and the self-purification—clarifying participants' motives and preparing themselves for nonviolent action—preceding its actions, further attest to the ethical character of the No Grapes boycott.[69]

Ironically, because economic boycotts are now generally regarded as legal and have become a commonly-used tactic, the symbolic power of a boycott attracts attention and dramatizes a cause that has been diluted, leaving mainly its economic leverage. For this reason, notes Waskow, the mainstream acceptability of boycotts as a movement tool often means that the tactic is less attractive to the militant factions of a movement than it would have been a generation ago.[70]

In this regard, the increasing popularity of boycotts—two prominent examples being the California grape boycott and the recent boycott of Colorado businesses organized by opponents to the state's anti-gay Amendment 2—underlines the extent to which money continues to shape public interest and action. The point is not that the individual grape growers are impervious to moral reasoning; it is rather that the increase in boycotting may well be a response to the seemingly ever increasing prominence in political affairs of money and the access and influence it seems to buy. Chavez's characterization of the targets of the *No Grapes* boycott as "major corporations"—nameless, faceless and soulless—highlights the way in which persuasion at the institutional level becomes inexorably shaped by the rhetoric of "the system," rather than of the individual. Rather than pursuing traditional electoral solutions to social problems, many movements pursue their goals by going to the perceived root of all social change as well as resistance to change, which is corporate and lobby money.[71] Thus, a last irony which raises some ethical concern about boycotts no matter the purity of their motives and tactics: In the name of populism and grass-roots organizing, movements more and more may be enlisting our support not as citizens, but as consumers—defining us not by our civic responsibilities and rights, but by our purchasing patterns.

NOTES

1. John W. Bowers, Donovan J. Ochs, and Richard J. Jensen, *The Rhetoric of Agitation and Control*, 3rd Ed. (Prospect Heights IL: Waveland, 1993), 107-9.
2. Arthur I. Waskow, *From Race Riot to Sit-In* (Garden City NJ: Doubleday, 1966), 239.
3. Peter Matthiessen, *Sal Si Puedes: Cesar Chavez and the New American Revolution* (New York: Dell, 1969); John Gregory Dunne. *Delano: The Story of the California Grape Strike* (New York: Farrar, Straus, and Giroux, 1967).
4. *No Grapes*, narrated by Mike Farrell. Deborah Ellman, Lorena Parlee, and Lenny Bourin, producers. United Farm Workers (1992). A copy of *No Grapes* is included in the student videotape.
5. Bowers, Ochs, and Jensen, 37; Waskow, 225.
6. Charles J. Stewart, Craig Allen Smith and Robert E. Denton, Jr., *Persuasion and Social Movements*, 2nd Ed. (Prospect Heights IL: Waveland, 1989), 23.
7. Stewart, Smith and Denton, *Social Movements*, 8.
8. David Zarefsky, "President Johnson's War on Poverty: The Rhetoric of Three 'Establishment' Movements," *Communication Monographs* 45 (1977): 352-373.
9. Peter Skerry, "Neighborhood COPS," *The New Republic* 190 (6 February 1984): 21-23.
10. John Waite Bowers and Donovan Ochs, *The Rhetoric of Agitation and Control* (Reading MA: Addison-Wesley, 1971), 19-20.
11. Stewart, Smith and Denton, *Social Movements*, 11.
12. David De Leon, *Everything is Changing: Contemporary U.S. Movements in Historical Perspective* (New York: Praeger, 1988), 74-75.
13. Stewart, Smith and Denton, *Social Movements*, 5-6.
14. See: Scott Sonner, "Dissidents Say Sierra Club Can't See Forest for Trees," Associated Press story carried by the Eugene OR *Register-Guard* (1 April 1991): 1A.
15. Sonner, "Sierra Club," 1A.
16. Adapted from: Herbert W. Simons, *Persuasion: Understanding, Practice, and Analysis*, 2nd Ed. (New York: Random House, 1986), 266-270; and David

Zarefsky, "President Johnson's War on Poverty: The Rhetoric of Three 'Establishment' Movements," *Communication Monographs* (1977): 352-373.
17. Sonner, "Sierra Club," 1A.
18. Stewart, Smith and Denton, *Social Movements*, 8.
19. James W. Chesebro, Davis A. Foulger, Jay E. Nachman and Andrew Yannelli. "Popular Music as a Model of Communication, 1955-1982." *Critical Studies in Mass Communication* 2 (1985): 115-135.
20. Ann Popkin, "The Personal is Political: The Women's Liberation Movement," in Dick Cluster, ed., *They Should Have Served That Cup of Coffee* (Boston: South End Press, 1979), 302.
21. Saul Alinsky, *Rules for Radicals* (New York: Vintage Books, 1969), 128.
22. Stewart, et al., *Persuasion and Social Movements*, 21-34.
23. Alinsky, *Rules for Radicals*, 34.
24. De Leon, *Everything is Changing*, 96.
25. Stewart, Smith and Denton, *Social Movements*, 24.
26. Stewart, Smith and Denton, *Social Movements*, 24.
27. Herbert W. Simons, *Persuasion: Understanding, Practice, and Analysis*, 2nd Ed. (New York: Harper & Row, 1986), 239.
28. Robert L. Scott and Donald K. Smith, "The Rhetoric of Confrontation," *Quarterly Journal of Speech* 55 (1969):1-8; Bowers and Ochs, *Agitation and Control*, 1-15.
29. James W. Chesebro, John F. Cragan and Patricia McCullough, "The Small Group Technique of the Radical Revolutionary: A Synthetic Study of Consciousness Raising," *Speech Monographs* 40(1973):136-146.
30. Chesebro, Cragan and McCullough, "The Small Group Technique," 136.
31. Ann Popkin, "The Personal Is Political: The Women's Liberation Movement," in Dick Cluster, ed., *They Should Have Served That Cup of Coffee* (Boston MA: South End Press, 1979), 192-196.
32. Richard M. Weaver, *The Ethics of Rhetoric* (Davis CA: Hermagoras Press, 1985), 212; Stewart, Smith and Denton, *Social Movements*, 24-25.
33. Stewart, Smith and Denton, *Social Movements*, 25.
34. Stewart, Smith and Denton, *Social Movements*, 26-27.
35. Eric Hoffer, *The True Believer: Thoughts on the Nature of Mass Movements* (New York: Harper & Row, 1951).
36. Hoffer, *True Believer*, x.
37. Hoffer, *True Believer*, 33.
38. Hoffer, *True Believer*, 31.
39. Hoffer, *True Believer*, 31-32.
40. Hoffer, *True Believer*, 36.
41. Hoffer, *True Believer*, 37-48.
42. Hoffer, *True Believer*, 25.
43. Richard B. Gregg, "The Ego-Function of the Rhetoric of Protest," *Philosophy and Rhetoric* 4 (1971): 71-91.
44. Kenneth Burke, "A Definition of Man," in *Language as Symbolic Action* (Berkeley CA: University of California Press, 1966), 15-20.

45. Barry Brummett, "Burkean Scapegoating, Mortification, and Transcendence in Presidential Campaign Rhetoric," *Central States Speech Journal* 32 (1981): 254-264.
46. Stewart, Smith and Denton, *Social Movements*, 27.
47. Leland M. Griffin, "The Rhetoric of Historical Movements," *Quarterly Journal of Speech* 38 (1952): 186.
48. Griffin, "Historical Movements," 186.
49. Stewart, Smith and Denton, *Social Movements*, 30.
50. William A. Gamson, *The Strategy of Social Protest* (Homewood IL: Dorsey Press, 1975), 30-31.
51. Kathleen Hall Jamieson, *Packaging the Presidency: A History and Criticism of Presidential Campaign Advertising* (New York: Oxford University Press, 1984), 169-220.
52. Jamieson, *Packaging the Presidency*, 169.
53. Jamieson, *Packaging the Presidency*, 181.
54. Kurt W. Ritter, "Ronald Reagan and 'The Speech:' The Rhetoric of Public Relations Politics," in J. Jeffery Auer, ed., *The Rhetoric of Our Times* (New York: Appleton-Century-Crofts, 1969), 400-407.
55. Ritter, "Ronald Reagan and 'The Speech,'" 400-401.
56. Stewart, Smith and Denton, *Social Movements*, 16.
57. Stewart, Smith and Denton, *Social Movements*, 27.
58. Alinsky, *Rules for Radicals* , 24-47.
59. Richard L. Johannesen, *Ethics in Human Communication*, 3rd Ed. (Prospect Heights IL: Waveland, 1990), 132-133.
60. Alan Light, "2 Live Crew Beats the Rap (Acquitted of Obscenity Charges)," *Rolling Stone* (29 November 1990):27.
61. Haig A. Bosmajian, "Obscenity and Protest," in Haig A. Bosmajian, ed., *Dissent: Symbolic Behavior and Rhetorical Strategies* (Boston: Allyn and Bacon, 1972), 295.
62. Alinsky, *Rules for Radicals*, xxiv-xxv.
63. American Library Association, "REFORMA Resolution to Support the California Table Grape Boycott of the United Farm Workers of America, AFL-CIO (Revised)," California Ethnic and Multicultural Archives, University of California Santa Barbara, Salvador Guerena, Director [guerena@library.ucsb.ed]. 29 June 1991.
64. Bowers, Ochs, and Jensen, 107.
65. Ron Karten, "Grape Wars," *The Progressive*, July 1992: 14.
66. Waskow, 239.
67. Bowers, Ochs, and Jensen, 197.
68. Bowers, Ochs, and Jensen, 37; Martin Luther King, Jr., "Letter From Birmingham Jail," *Why We Can't Wait* (New York: Harper & Row, 1963).
69. Bowers, Ochs, and Jensen, 114.
70. Waskow, 238.
71. John Leo, "When In Doubt, Boycott," *U.S. News and World Report* 21 Dec 1992: 35.

13
IDEOLOGY

IN THIS CHAPTER:
Focus on:
Advertising and the Ideology of Masculinity
1. Theoretical Focus: Ideology, Worldview and Persuasion
2. The Building Blocks of Ideology
    Social Values
    Cultural Myths
    Societal Power Structures
3. Stages of Ideology Formation
    Abstraction and Hierarchy
    Social Roles and Practices
    Compensation and Adjustment
    Formal Communication Systems and Ideology Formation
4. Ethical Concerns Regarding Ideology
5. Critical Focus: "The Best a Man Can Get"

FOCUS ON: ADVERTISING AND THE IDEOLOGY OF MASCULINITY

In 1970 Jean Kilbourne, a feminist media critic, organized a lecture entitled "The Naked Truth: Advertising's Image of Women."[1] This lecture launched a now 30-year public speaking career by Kilbourne on the subject of how women are depicted in commercial advertising. In the process, two films—*Killing Us Softly* and *Still Killing Us Softly*—have been produced that illustrate Kilbourne's research findings with numerous visuals from contemporary advertisements. In her films and lectures, Kilbourne points out that in contemporary advertisements "women are sex objects, and men are success objects," that the emphasis for women is "youth, beauty, and thinness," and that "women's bodies are frequently dismembered and disfigured" as attention-grabbing ways to promote the sex appeal of particular products.[2] According to a review of her research:

> The commercial image of women has changed very little in 20 years, [Kilbourne] said. Ads acknowledge that women work outside their homes, but they still show women as the primary caretakers of house and children.
>
> Advertising validates sex roles and offers women who are uncomfortable with their dual-job 'superwoman' roles individual solutions instead of political solutions, Kilbourne said....

> She said her studies show that while people don't admit they are influenced by advertising, Americans are very 'culturally conditioned' by ads, and children are particularly vulnerable to them.[3]

In her films and lectures, Kilbourne links this cultural conditioning to a variety of social problems, including widespread violence against women, sexual abuse of women and a host of eating disorders such as anorexia nervosa.[4]

The type of research conducted by Kilbourne exemplifies a third perspective toward institutional persuasion—studies of ideology. Students of ideology examine messages for their ideological content and for their view of the world in order to expose worldviews that may be damaging to various groups of people. Kilbourne is concerned with the view of women that underlies commercial advertising messages and contributes to the oppression of women in our society. While the ideological content of a message helps to explain its success with certain audiences, studies of ideology depart from the Classical Perspective in that they show little interest in the explicit intentions of the persuader or the effectiveness of the message in reaching the persuader's goals. Instead, these studies share with the Symbolist Perspective an interest in the worldview that an audience is likely to construct when confronted with a particular configuration of verbal and nonverbal symbols. However, such studies go beyond the Symbolist Perspective as well. In their critique of society, ideological critics generally turn their attention to the reciprocal relationship between social institutions and the messages that those institutions present to members of the society. In doing so, ideological critics present a unique angle from which to analyze explicitly and implicitly persuasive messages.

On January 1, 1988, almost 20 years after Kilbourne's first lecture, the North Atlantic Shaving Group launched a $75-$80 million advertising program.[5] They designed a campaign to appeal to all nationalities in North America and Western Europe and, consequently, launched it in 14 languages across 18 countries. The theme line for the campaign was: "Gillette. "The Best a Man Can Get"." A primary persuasive message within this campaign, a 60-second commercial spot, touts the "sharp" image a man can obtain from a Gillette razor. While the obvious purpose of this advertisement was to increase sales of Gillette products, especially razors, the North Atlantic Shaving Group's characterization of their theme and its development signal a concern for the ideological content of their campaign. The Group's written explanation of the campaign included the following:

> "Gillette. "The Best a Man Can Get"." This phrase says it all. It is a credible, confident statement that works on two levels—on the product level, by saying that Gillette products are the best in performance, the best a man can buy…and on the user level, by saying Gillette products allow a man to be his best, to achieve individually and socially to the very best of his ability. It is a simple but strong statement of who we are and how we wish to be viewed.[6]

To sell their products, then, Gillette crafted a campaign and developed persuasive messages to tell the audience what was "the best a man could get." To be sure, such messages were based on careful market research that indicated what men in the target group identified with as "best." However, commercial spots such as the one included on the accompanying videotape visualize those images of "best" in very concrete ways. We notice as we view the spot that the emotion-laden images of masculinity embedded in this commercial marketing device manifest an ideology, or coherent view of what it means to be a successful man in our culture.

Theoretical Focus: Ideology, Worldview And Persuasion

To analyze more fully the spot from an ideological perspective, we must first understand more about the persuasive workings of ideology. In this chapter, we investigate ideology as a type of institutional persuasion. In Chapter 10 we defined *ideology* as *implicit persuasion aimed at preserving those current arrangements of institutional power that we frequently call "the system."* This definition does not exclude messages such as advertisements that are clearly intended to be persuasive. However, our definition diverts our attention from the intended effects of such advertising (i.e., increasing sales or market share) toward the cultural effects of these commercial messages. We begin by examining the characteristics of ideology and then discuss three essential building blocks for ideology—cultural values, cultural myths and societal power structures. A discussion of several concepts essential for understanding the persuasive impact of ideology precedes our brief review of ethical concerns regarding ideology. The chapter concludes with a critical focus that returns to the Gillette commercial mentioned above.

Characteristics Of Ideology

Political and social observers offer various definitions of ideology. The term itself was coined by French philosopher A. Destutt de Tracy in the early nineteenth century to refer to a science of ideas that could be used to ground the educational system in post-revolutionary France.[7] Contemporary scholars typically describe ideology in either neutral terms, as the worldview embodied by a message,[8] or with a negative connotation, as a "false" view of the world that reflects the interests of an elite group or dominant class of people.[9] When described in neutral terms, ideological persuasion shows some striking similarities to a persuasive campaign—an "idea campaign" as opposed to a product or political campaign. Similarly, when described as a "false" view of the world, ideologies, like social movements, generally attempt to expose the false worldviews that underpin "the establishment" and to replace those views with their own, newer and allegedly more comprehensive worldviews.

Despite similarities among ideology, persuasive campaigns and social movements, we have reason to treat ideology as a separate category for discussion. For most scholars of ideology, ideological persuasion presents a worldview that is larger and more sweeping than the ideas that drive a particular campaign or social movement. As an ideology is diffused throughout a society, it may permeate an entire culture and endure for a much longer time than any particular movement or campaign. As communication scholar William Balthrop points out, ideology is tied to culture, making "each culture distinct" and giving "direction to every aspect of cultural life."[10]

Becker compares the process of constructing a worldview with watching a floating opera, a showboat drifting up and down the river on the tide.[11] Sitting on the banks of the river, the audience catches only fragments of sight and sound from which they construct their own versions of what must be happening in the story. In the same way, says Becker, each of us constructs a worldview based on multiple messages that may or may not be intentionally persuasive or inherently connected. These messages may approach us as discrete events like a film, radio broadcast or formal manifesto or as message fragments like a headline, an office memorandum, a bumper sticker or a joke. From these mosaic bits we form our understanding of world events and social issues.[12]

Brummett extends Becker's mosaic model of communication to explain how "the bits and pieces of everyday life, *popular culture*, participate in and influence the management of meaning," so that we can make sense of and order our lives.[13] He argues that the media—literary, cinematic and televised entertainment particularly—provide people with patterns by which to understand their experiences and their place in the world. As Brummett puts it: "The media are a major way in which we all find out how to live with others within the rather small social arrangements of our private lives...we see how Mary Tyler Moore, Bill Cosby or Dan Rather makes sense of chaos, and we learn to employ similar patterns in our everyday lives."[14]

The patterns of meaning emerge from these various media messages, socializing us and providing us with guides for understanding our world. Brummett notes, for example, the "myth of the six-gun," a pattern of dealing with the world derived from the American frontier experience, but shaped and modified by western films and TV shows, the ways in which newscasts cover foreign policy and politicians justify foreign policy, and even children's toys like the Mighty Morphin Power Rangers.[15] The creation and repetition of such patterns, as Hall suggests, create an ideology, broadly understood as an inventory of the ways in which we might imagine understanding and living in the world.[16] This inventory reflects our reality to some extent, but it also influences that reality as well. Thus, as Bonnie Dow notes, the 1970's situation comedy *The Mary Tyler Moore Show* reflects both the emerging feminism of American women and commercial television's discomfort with depictions of strong, independent female characters. The show's heroine, Mary Richards, is an independent, single, professional woman—quite a change from the characters in *Father Knows Best*, *Leave it to Beaver*, or *The Dick Van Dyke Show* a decade earlier, where the patriarchal, male-dominated patterns of living were presented without challenge. Yet Mary Richards is always shown reproducing the stereotypical roles of a woman in a man's society: "daughter" to boss Lou Grant, "sister" to colleague Murray Slaughter and "mother" to bumbling newscaster Ted Baxter.[17]

Such mixed messages are combined in our culture with messages that are far less ambiguous: the overwhelming numerical dominance of men over women in business, government, clergy and many professions; the well-documented wage disparity between men and women for equivalent work; the devaluing of jobs and professions that are traditionally occupied by women; and the popularity of sexually exploitative print and film materials portraying women as sexual objects to be possessed or brutalized; the widespread domestic violence against women often described by the media in the language of love (e.g., "jealousy," "crime of passion," "love triangle") rather than as acts of violence.[18] The result of these multiple messages is an institutional context for those aspects of American culture's ideology regarding the place of women in our society, a context in which ideological messages produced by formal communication systems reinforce and are reinforced by existing institutional arrangements. Our awareness of how ideology mirrors existing arrangements cannot be separated from our awareness of how ideology urges us to adopt a certain view of the world and of ourselves, argues Brummett who adds, "and the awareness is not politically neutral."[20]

If ideological persuasion is not politically neutral, as Brummett asserts, then we may ask what political positions are supported by ideological persuasion. Whose side is ideology on? Our answer is that ideological persuasion tends to support the *status quo*, the dominant culture, things as they are, "the system." Just how this process works becomes clearer if we consider the process by which an ideology is constructed.

The Building Blocks Of Ideology

In his study of southern culture, Balthrop draws on anthropologist Clifford Geertz's description of *culture* as "an historically transmitted pattern of meanings embodied in symbols, a system of inherited conceptions expressed in symbolic forms by means of which men [and women] communicate, perpetuate and develop their knowledge about and attitudes toward life."[20] Readers should recognize that this definition of culture mirrors the description of ideology reviewed in the previous section. Ideology is the symbolic expression of a pattern of meaning that we take for granted as explaining the world and our place in it. Such patterns are given form by three distinct forces which comprise what we refer to as the building blocks of ideology. Those three building blocks are social values, cultural myths and societal power structures. We discuss each of these in the pages that follow.

Social Values

Those who treat ideology in neutral terms usually describe the worldview that an ideology embraces as a set of beliefs and values that define a culture. In his extensive study of beliefs and values, social psychologist Milton Rokeach defines a *belief* as "any simple proposition, conscious or unconscious, inferred from what a person says or does and capable of being preceded by the phrase, 'I believe that….'"[21] Rokeach continues by explaining that *values* are "abstract ideals, positive or negative, not tied to any specific attitude, object, or situation, representing a person's beliefs about ideal modes of conduct and ideal terminal goals."[22] Values thus provide the ideals by which people form their beliefs about how the world does and should work. For example, a person who values equality probably believes that democracy is a form of government superior to autocracy, totalitarianism or authoritarianism. Similarly, someone who values efficiency over group consensus and harmony may believe that a task can be best accomplished by dividing it up and assigning the various parts to members of a work team, while someone else who values the sense of community and sharing that can occur when people work together may believe that the best way for a group to accomplish a task is to get everyone involved in an egalitarian, cooperative sort of way.

Obviously, different individuals may hold different values. One person may value material comforts and possessions; another may value nature and her sense of connection to the earth; yet another may value his relationship to God or the spirit-world. Particular groups of people within a culture typically embrace different values and structure the relationships among various values differently. These different values explain why some groups of people tend to support certain policies and types of social arrangements that other groups of people oppose. Consider, for example, the controversy regarding abortion. Those who oppose abortion under any circumstance express beliefs about the sanctity of human life that embody a high value for life in even embryonic forms. Those who favor allowing pregnant women to choose an abortion, on the other hand, express beliefs about personal choice and tragic pregnancies that embody a value for dignity and quality of life for women and their children alike. Both groups value life, but their definition or view of life differs. Across cultures the differences may widen even further. In his study of ethnic differences in moral development, for example, Anthony Cortese found that many blacks and Chicanos valued family and relationships more highly than most Anglo-Americans.[23] As a result of differences in values, beliefs among blacks about the appropriateness of women working outside the home and the importance among Chicanos of submission to patriarchal authority differed between these ethnic groups and the dominant white culture. However, at a cultural level of analysis, when researchers or others are attempting to describe values, they often overlook such differences. As Cortese explains, "the structures of moral reasoning used by Western middle- to upper-middle-class white males appear to be taken to be everyone's ideal type by many researchers."[24] Consequently, when we examine the values of a culture, we should remember that frequently we are examining the values of the dominant group in that culture—those who get to "tell the story"—rather than the values of each unique individual or even of the various subgroups that make up that culture.

For mass audiences values can provide a key for understanding the ideology of a culture. Numerous social and cultural historians have pointed out that in the United States, for example, people believe in the worth of the individual.[25] The rights of individuals are generally taken to be more important than the welfare of the group. Our judicial system presumes innocence on the grounds that it is better to let a few guilty people go free than to unjustly imprison one innocent person. Members of our culture believe that regardless of one's humble origins, individual initiative and hard work can result in success. The "American Dream" itself is founded on our faith in the resources of the individual. The common concern for the underdog, as we root for the "Davids" in the world to defeat the "Goliaths," is symptomatic of our romantic attraction to the power and possibilities of the individual. Thus, individualism is characteristic of the American ideology, one of the complex webs of beliefs or values that define our culture.

Values that define a culture create a coherent worldview that also provides the basis for a host of beliefs that organize our understanding of ourselves, others and particular events. If we return to the example of individualism, the importance of a cultural value for constructing a coherent worldview becomes clearer. In simple terms, valuing individualism encourages us to give ourselves the credit when things work out well and to blame ourselves when they do not. The individual is responsible for successes as well as failures. If we consider more complicated issues like poverty, this value concerning the individual provides us more elaborate explanations. We assume people have a right to the material possessions and wealth that they accumulate because we also assume that wealth is the product of the individual's hard work and initiative rather than other circumstances such as luck or unfair advantage. Within such a worldview, many believe that those unfortunate people who do not attain wealth and worldly possessions are somehow defective individuals, lacking in ambition, persistence or other valued qualities. In keeping with culture's emphasis on the individual, we may blame the individual for his poverty rather than the community. If wealth is a product of individual effort, we may see little obligation on the part of the wealthy to take care of the less fortunate, and since poverty is the consequence of a lack of individual effort, we may assume the poor are just getting what they deserve. We hear a number of "commonsense" arguments and comments daily confirming that many Americans embrace such a worldview. For example, many people respond to the homeless by pointing out that "they're just drunks or mentally ill." Others offer little sympathy to the unemployed by explaining that they "see plenty of 'help wanted' ads; why don't these people just get a job?" Indeed, the very thought of requiring all those gainfully employed and others with wealth to provide ample financial support for those in poverty often meets with cries of "no new taxes" and at least surprise that anyone could even suggest that "we have a responsibility to take care of others who are less fortunate." Generally, Americans view charity as the domain of churches, the Salvation Army and the organizations who benefit from the United Way campaign, not the obligation of individuals. The "truth" of these beliefs will be examined later in this chapter, but for now it is enough to recognize how the value of individualism contributes to a coherent worldview that undergirds an entire set of ideas about how the world does and should work.

Those who have investigated the nature of American culture and the values that underlay that culture point to a variety of values in addition to individualism. One of the most durable lists of this type was developed by Edward D. Steele and W. Charles Redding, two communication scholars who examined a wide selection of famous American public addresses to discover the recurring values embedded within those messages.[26] Their list includes puritan and pioneer morality, the individual, achievement and success, change and progress, ethical equality and equal opportunity, effort and optimism, efficiency and practicality, rejection of authority, science and secular rationality, sociality, material comfort, quantification, external conformity, humor, generosity and considerateness and patriotism.[27] Members of our culture are predisposed by their ideology to respond to persuasion whose claims reflect such values. Probably most citizens of the United States and many members of Western culture, generally, would still agree with Steele and Redding's list of 16 dominant cultural values. Certainly, no member of that culture could fail to recognize those values as expressions of important beliefs.

More recent investigations of shared social values, while confirming many of Steele and Redding's findings, suggest some additional components. In their discussion of the importance of social values for contemporary public decision-making, argumentation theorists Richard Rieke and Malcolm Sillars reported the results of a Gallup Poll in the early 1980's.[28] According to that poll, over 70 percent of Americans nationally valued a good family life, good physical health, self-respect, happiness or satisfaction, freedom of choice and living up to one's potential. Sociologist Robert Bellah and his associates, in their attempt to update de Tocqueville's study of American culture, point out that individualism, self-reliance, success, justice or fairness, honesty, practicality, a sense of community, generosity, individual fulfillment, freedom and hard work are persistent American values.[29] They note, however, that each of these values may be defined somewhat differently by any particular member of the culture. We all may agree, for example, to the commonsense statement, "Success is good." Yet what happens when we try to discover what we all *mean* by success? Some define success as something attained in the world of work, while others find success at home and within the family. The ambiguity of these terms represents an important dimension in ideology that we will return to shortly. Nonetheless, such lists of values provide a start for understanding how an ideology or a coherent worldview works persuasively.

Values such as those just listed provide the basis for beliefs that, in turn, guide people's thoughts about and behavior in the world. However, these values do not exist in isolation from one another. As suggested earlier, a particular culture may give preeminence to some of these values and cluster the others around them. How we resolve conflict of values, reveals which values we hold most important. Our earlier discussion of individualism is a convenient illustration of this principle. Both de Tocqueville and Bellah found that the value of individualism dominated American culture. Other values may also be embraced; but in the face of a value conflict, the value of the individual will likely win the day. The importance of the value of individualism in the ideology of American culture becomes even clearer when we consider the second building block of ideology—cultural myths.

CULTURAL MYTHS

In Chapter 9 we describe the importance of narratives for constructing a view of the world. As we mention there, myths provide the master stories by which people within a culture understand their place in the world. While lists of values, such as Steele and Redding's, provide a rather abstract way of identifying the ideals of a culture, our myths lend form and substance to those ideals by making them concrete in the dramatic action of a story. Balthrop explains that "myth provides that cultural image of perfection."[30] So, if ideology sets forth a coherent view of how the world does and should work and if cultural values furnish a short-hand way of describing the principles of that worldview, then cultural myths are the dramatic enactment of that worldview.

If we return to the American value regarding the individual, we can explore just how cultural myths elaborate a worldview. Bellah, *et al.*, note that a powerful American myth is that of the "self-reliant, but righteous, individual," steeped in the imagery and values of the small town or farm community.[31]

Probably all of us can bring to mind a variety of mythical American stories of rugged individualism, from Abraham Lincoln's rise to the Presidency following a rail-splitting career in which he studied law by candlelight to the story of Jimmy Carter's rise to power from his peanut farm in Georgia. Individuals, like Lincoln, Carter, Martin Luther King, Jr., Franklin D. Roosevelt, George Washington, Susan B. Anthony, Elizabeth Cady Stanton, Clara Barton, Betsy Ross and others are enshrined in national monuments, on coins and in public school textbooks as the heroic characters of such American myths. We learn that these people achieved and succeeded because they were individualists who valued initiative and hard work, fairness and other standard American values.

Balthrop explains that "the more frequently that the myth can be experienced and the greater its variety of guises, usually in narrative form, the more likely that myth extends its power and hold on us."[32] Consequently, it is helpful to remember from Chapter 9 that cultural myths often take the form of folk tales and fables in which characters frequently assume the roles of real human beings performing ordinary tasks but in which the mythic structure of a heroic journey is preserved. In *Tales of a New America*, Robert Reich catalogues a number of such contemporary American folk tales.[33] He discusses "four basic American morality tales, our cultural parables," specifically: "the mob at the gates, the triumphant individual, the benevolent community, and the rot at the top."[34]

In its various forms, the tale of "the mob at the gate" depicts "America as a beacon light of virtue in a world of darkness."[35] America is portrayed as the "best" country in the world and the most democratic of democracies. Yet, there are evil people and countries out there just waiting to bring the country down. Stories about the dangers of illegal aliens to the economy and tales about the threats posed by "Communists" in such small and economically distraught countries as Cuba or Grenada illustrate this cultural tale. Similarly, during the social upheaval of the 1960's, many who protested U.S. involvement in the Vietnam war were pictured as unruly mobs just waiting to storm the gates and destroy America. The same tale shows up in science fiction films such as *Invasion of the Body Snatchers*, frequently treated as a parable about the McCarthy era in which it was made, when alien and undemocratic creatures are cast as villains who pose a danger to our liberty and freedom.

Common to all versions of "the triumphant individual" is "the story of the little guy who works hard, takes risks, believes in himself, and eventually earns wealth, fame, and honor."[36] The classic 1939 Hollywood film directed by Frank Capra, *Mr. Smith Goes to Washington*, traces the life of just such a character who eventually finds an heroic place in the U.S. Congress. Stories of self-made men and women, like many of the early entrepreneurs and industrialists in this country, follow a similar pattern. Almost all contemporary politicians portray their lives similarly. For example, in his own official biographical materials and in commonly repeated stories about him, Ronald Reagan was depicted as an ordinary sort of boy who grew up in a poor family in Dixon, Illinois, who worked hard and held fast to his ideals, finally arriving in the White House, but who still took (televised) time to ride horses, chop wood and display the qualities of one of our most enduring cultural heroes, the cowboy.

A third cultural parable, "the benevolent community," includes variations of the story of "neighbors and friends rolling up their sleeves and pitching in to help one another, and of self-sacrifice, community pride, and patriotism."[37] The good deeds of the poor from Oklahoma who sought a new life in California in John Steinbeck's novel *The Grapes of Wrath*, the solidarity of the Amish community that protected a Philadelphia police officer and a young boy in the feature film *Witness* and the classical music of Aaron Copeland's "Fanfare for the Common Man" all trade on this story. One of the best known examples of this from popular culture is *It's A Wonderful Life*, the classic film by Frank Capra (who, as we discuss in Chapter 14, later made American propaganda films during World War II). The final scene of *It's A Wonderful Life* orchestrates powerful symbols of faith, family, country and community to drive home the lesson: "Jimmy Stewart learns that he can count on his neighbors' generosity and goodness," says Reich, "just as they had always counted on him."[38]

"The rot at the top," the fourth cultural tale that Reich describes, "is about the malevolence of powerful elites, be they wealthy aristocrats, rapacious business leaders, or imperious government officials."[39] The story of the Watergate break-in that led to former President Richard Nixon's resignation, the explanations of a variety of conspiracy theorists from the Ku Klux Klan to Lyndon LaRouche's followers and even much of our popular entertainment illustrates this parable. Consider, for example, the many action films that follow an honest cop who uncovers corruption at the highest levels. Jack Nicholson's portrayal of Jake Giddes in *Chinatown*, for example, comes to mind, but there are certainly many more. The tale of the "rot at the top" dramatizes a common element of the campaign rhetoric of political candidates challenging incumbent officeholders; commonly these candidates describe themselves as starring in some version of a narrative that might be called "Running against 'the mess in Washington.'"

Stories like those just described abound within popular culture. Hollywood films, from *Aliens* to *Star Wars*, provide a pattern for the values that underlay an ideology about what it means to act heroically. Similarly, popular reading, from romance novels to comic books, teaches young men and women what it means to be masculine or feminine in our society. Likewise, popular music, fiction and television programming tell us what "true love" is all about. Competing stories can provide differing views of the world, just as other value systems exist that differ from those that are dominant. Hence, how particular values and stories come to dominate a culture merits our attention. A partial answer to this question comes from ideological critics who analyze societal power structures—the third of the three building blocks of ideology.

SOCIETAL POWER STRUCTURES

Any particular individual or group of individuals may hold values or tell stories that differ from one another. To be fundamental to an ideology, however, values and stories must be shared by a culture as a whole. Usually the cultural values and myths that reflect the interests and views of the people in power in a culture dominate over the values and stories of members of various subcultures or minority groups. Of course, any subgroup within a culture may have its own ideology—a set of beliefs, values and shared stories with which the members of that community identify. As we suggest earlier in this book, such fantasy themes and shared motives apply more to segments of a potential audience than to a culture as a whole. When critics use the term, "ideology," they are interested in the largest level of analysis possible; they view the audience as a culture rather than some smaller demographic or reference group. Thus, many scholars who study ideology refer to the audience for ideology as the masses or "mass consciousness" rather than as target groups.

Probably the most influential scholar investigating ideology and its effects on the masses in recent times was Karl Marx, whose influential theories emerged from his analysis of the struggle for power within society during the nineteenth century. Marx maintained that oppressed workers could not rise up against the wealthy and advantaged citizens who benefited from exploiting them because those workers were, as summarized by scholar Andrew King, "controlled by the dominant belief system, an ideology which both reflects and propagandizes the existing economic arrangements."[40] Marxist social critiques typically define ideology as "the ruling ideas of the ruling class," stressing "the connection between established economic interests and the spiritual formulations in law, religion, and philosophy" that work in favor of the ruling class.[41] In describing the economic class who held positions of status and power in his society and the formulations of laws, religious doctrines and philosophical ideas, Marx laid the groundwork for understanding the connection between ideology and societal power structures.

Marx argued that those in positions of power had access to the institutions that transmitted ideas and information. In the nineteenth century, such institutions included governments that could issue orders and decrees, churches that produced guidelines for moral behavior and transmitted those guidelines through tracts and sermons to congregations and educational centers such as universities that provided scientific and other explanations of the human and natural world. If members of the higher social class held positions of prestige and power within these institutions, then it would not be surprising to find that the documents, speeches, ceremonies and other communications produced within these institutions reflect the values and myths of that economic class. Andrew King summarizes Marx's explanation accordingly:

> Why does the worker not rise up and take hold of his own destiny? Marx maintains that he could not, because he is controlled by the dominant belief system, an ideology which both reflects and propagandizes the existing economic arrangements. The great weapon of the master class is its ideology, a rhetoric which penetrates every aspect of the society, justifying the authority structure and presenting the dominance of the bourgeoisie as morally correct and universally beneficial. Dominating the newspapers, educational system, and other channels of communication, the master class presents its arbitrary, self-serving, and incomplete view of the world as the only game in town. Its values are presented as universally applicable; its voice is the only voice.[42]

For Marx, the bourgeoisie, the highest economic class, those who had accumulated economic wealth, were the rulers who held the reins of power in society. Contemporary treatments of ideology, however, tend to be more eclectic in their designation of who holds power in society.

Among contemporary ideology critics, a group of mostly European scholars known as the Frankfurt School because of their institutional affiliations in Frankfurt, Germany, contribute much to Marx's original formulation.[43] They point out that economic class and political clout alone may not account for the perpetuation of ideology. They explain that any group capturing enough power to influence the public messages that circulate within a society contributes to ideology. They note that many followers of Marx himself became ideologues by perpetuating a worldview that could be accepted uncritically by their followers. Instead of dwelling exclusively on the connection between the economic structure of society and the power to develop and transmit ideology, many members and followers of the Frankfurt School investigate who controls the channels of communication within a society and who generates the mosaic of messages within a culture to determine what power structures influence the dominant ideology.

As rhetorical critic Phil Wander explains, these critics' concern is that ideology expresses a "party interest," a partial worldview that serves the interests of some members of society while neglecting or subverting the interests of others.[44] These writers describe a long list of societal institutions that perpetuate ideologies. Louis Althusser refers to these institutions as "ideological state apparatuses" and includes among them: the system of different churches; the system of different public and private schools; the family; the political system; trade unions; cultural institutions such as those that produce literature, the arts and sports; and communications systems such as press, radio, television and film.[45] Althusser points out that, unlike the coercive power that a repressive police state can bring to bear in order to repress the behavior of the citizenry, these ideological state apparatuses repeat the cultural ideology so persistently and in so many different forms that citizens cannot easily imagine a world that worked any other way. For example, when explaining how the educational system can perpetuate a capitalist ideology that exalts material success and accumulation of wealth, Althusser writes:

> Of course, many of these contrasting virtues (modesty, resignation, submissiveness on the one hand, cynicism, contempt, arrogance, confidence, self-importance, even smooth talk and cunning on the other) are also taught in the Family, in the Church, in the Army, in Good Books, in films and even in the football stadium. But no other ideological State apparatus has the obligatory (and not least, free) audience of the totality of the children in the capitalist social formation, eight hours a day for five or six days out of seven.[46]

The potential to influence a person's worldview looms large for any institution, like the educational system, that has repeated and regular access to people. The combination of messages emerging from multiple institutions becomes almost overwhelming if the messages repeat the same essential values and cultural stories. When a clear pattern of value and myth permeates diverse messages from diverse institutions, members of a culture tend to take the ideology for granted, not questioning its validity or its relationship to reality. The power of such institutionally backed worldviews to dominate within their culture creates or perpetuates a *hegemony,* the ascendancy of one worldview over others, with its implications for power and reality. Most ideological critics refer to such dominant patterns, messages that repeat the basic values and myths of a culture, as hegemonic.

As this discussion of the role of institutions in the formation of ideology suggests, any investigation of ideology is concerned with power or the potential for social influence, as much as it is with the values or myths that the ideology embodies. Consequently, let us investigate the nature of social power. As we noted, Marx located the source of power in economic class: Those with money had power. A variety of other writers have described other sources of power.[47] One of the most durable lists of social power bases that has been used by scholars interested in persuasion was developed by sociologists J. R. French and B. Raven and subsequently modified by Raven.[48] French and Raven listed six bases for social power: informational power, coercive power, reward power, legitimate power, referent power and expert power.

Information power is exerted when an institution's influence is based on the information it holds. For example, many government agencies have access to information that ordinary citizens do not. So long as those agencies control the information, they have power over others. We often do not recognize such power until someone else acquires access to the information. A case in point occurred in the hometown of one of the authors. A citizen's environmental group discovered an illegally high content of radium in the local drinking water supply. Local government officials and the state Environmental Protection Agency had apparently known this for about ten years but neglected to disclose this information. Meanwhile, many of these same officials had endorsed community brochures and other information indicating the benefits of the area for prospective industry and residents alike. They thus exerted power over everyday life by controlling the flow of information.

Coercive power is based on the ability of an institution to mete out punishment to those it wishes to influence. Sometimes the punishment is blatant and physical such as that advocated by Machiavelli in his description of terrorist tactics that a government could use to keep its citizens in line and similar to those tactics often associated with Stalinist Russia or Nazi Germany. Other institutions, churches for example, exert coercive power which is not directly physical, by threatening to excommunicate or shun members who do not practice the prevailing ideology. Similarly, educational institutions may expel students or deny tenure to professors who violate the worldview that predominates there.

Reward power refers to the ability to deliver rewards or benefits to influence others. Institutions may provide financial, material or psychological rewards as a means for exerting power. Consider, for example, educational institutions. Some people obtain college degrees because they want the credential of a B.A. or a B.S. Others do so because they want the benefit of learning. Still others hope to improve their chances of landing a high-paying job. Probably some go to college as a way of getting away from their parents, striking out on their own and maybe finding a good time. Despite the diversity, all of these reasons suggest the reward power possessed by higher education as an institution.

Legitimate power occurs when those who are influenced simply believe that the agents of influence have a right to influence them. In a representative democracy such as the United States, citizens typically believe that if a person is voted into office that newly elected official has the right to influence or to exert power. Similarly, most citizens grant legitimate power to duly appointed officials such as police or fire personnel. Institutions typically claim their legitimacy by referring to one of the other bases of power, for example by showing that they have access to special information or can deliver punishments. Over time, however, the original basis of power may be replaced by simple legitimacy. For example, early newspapers obtained their power to shape public opinion by their claim of access to information, but over the years people have come to grant the press legitimate power by assuming that if it gets into print it must be true.

Referent power occurs when association with a referent group provides the motive for conformity. Some institutions trade on their status, influencing others by tempting them with the right to identify with the referent group. Some people, for example, may wish to be identified with a particular church or religious belief system.

Others may want to be known as "a college graduate." Others may wish to identify with Wall Street or some other commercial or industrial institution. Such cases are clear examples of referent power at work. To secure these various identities, these people accede to the influence of the target institution.

Expert power works because people believe that the source of influence has special expertise. Similar to information power, expert power is derived from special qualifications that make the source uniquely able to interpret the available data. The medical establishment in our culture, for example, uses expert power to influence society. Special training and credentials qualify some to diagnose and treat illness while disqualifying others. Much of the educational system also functions by means of expert power. Although the information with which educators work is generally available, the research methods and procedures within the academy claim to provide a more expert interpretation of that information than would be gleaned by ordinary people.

These six bases of social power obviously help to explain how a particular persuasive message might carry more weight than another. However, for someone interested in ideology, they also explain why the masses may accord a variety of messages credibility and legitimacy such that when the resulting dominant worldview runs counter to their real-life experiences it is nevertheless accepted as "the way things are." By tapping into one of these bases for social power, institutions can produce messages that perpetuate the dominant ideology within a culture. By examining the basis for social power that seems to be at work, an ideology critic might uncover exactly which interests are served by a particular system of values or cultural myth.

STAGES OF IDEOLOGY FORMATION

Compared to campaigns and social movements, the time period during which an ideology flourishes seems almost eternal. For example, the standard American values and myths that characterize the American ideology have existed with only small modifications for over two centuries. Similarly, the worldviews common to major religions of the world such as Christianity, Buddhism and Islam have endured for many centuries. Overwhelmingly, the institutional task rests in perpetuating an ideology rather than forming one. Still, from time to time, a culture changes its identity and may replace one ideology with another. We see this occur most often when a society undergoes a revolution, such as the Bolshevik Revolution in Czarist Russia or the French Revolution in the late 1700's. In the former case, an aristocratic ideology gave way to a Communist one, while in the latter a more egalitarian, democratic ideology toppled aristocratic France.

However, changes in ideology are not confined to the political sphere. What a culture accepts and takes for granted also changes occasionally with shifts in knowledge, religious belief and life style. For example, in the midst of the Roman Empire, the Christian worldview developed. During the eighteenth century, a scientific ideology arose within the educational system in Great Britain and on the European continent that provided formidable competition for the classical, humanist tradition of scholarly pursuits that had dominated for centuries. During the last century, a number of budding ideologies, such as environmentalism, feminism and multiculturalism, have competed with the more traditional worldviews that govern everyday life, such as progress and efficiency, patriarchy and ethnocentrism. Many of these more recent ideologies spring from particular social movements but draw their values and cultural tales from civilizations in the distant past that embraced ideologies much different from those which are dominant today. For example, the environmental movement remembers societies in which the earth was revered and natural phenomena such as the sun rising were worshipped. Within these ancient cultures, human beings accepted the role of preserving the earth, a process of caretaking for future generations. Drawing on values and myths from these earlier cultures, environmentalists in the contemporary period attempt to replace the dominant ideology that views the earth as a repository of raw materials to be used for the benefit of humankind and nature as a set of unruly forces to be conquered with a worldview that advocates living in harmony with nature and preserving the earth.

Intellectual historians and those who investigate contemporary social movements provide some insight into the stages through which ideology passes over the extremely long periods of time that a particular worldview holds sway within a culture. Drawing on the work of a variety of intellectual historians, communication theorist William Brown suggests that there are three primary steps in the process that produce ideology.[49] First, individuals interpret their experience of the world by using an abstraction process common to symbols that allows people to exercise their natural inclination toward building hierarchies. Second, individuals and groups share their ideas of how the world works and, in the process, establish social roles and practices that mirror that worldview. Third, the resulting communication systems repeatedly compensate for gaps or contradictions within the ideology that appear from time to time. If adequate compensation is made, then the ideology maintains itself. If not, it will likely be replaced by some other competing ideology. A closer look at each of these three steps will help clarify the process that Brown identified.

Abstraction and Hierarchy

The idea that symbols allow people to abstract is not new. In Chapters 6 through 9, we discuss the power of symbols to stand for referents or experiences that are not immediately present and the process of human perception that searches for commonalities in order to make sense out of an otherwise chaotic stream of incoming data. In the process of using symbols to categorize experience, as we explain in Chapter 7 when we examined the rhetoric of House Speaker Newt Gingrich, people tend to draw value distinctions between good and bad, higher and lower, that result in the development of ultimate terms that Richard Weaver referred to as "god terms" and "devil terms." These emotion-packed symbols are often highly abstract, referring to a complex set of experiences like freedom or justice rather than to more concrete things or places. Any particular ideology includes a set of "god terms" and "devil terms" that describe a hierarchy concerning which social roles, experiences and other phenomena are valued most and which are valued least. Rhetorical theorist Michael McGee refers to these ultimate terms as "ideographs," one-term sums of a worldview.[50] McGee explains that *ideographs*, like the characters of the Chinese alphabet, are packed with complex meaning while appearing merely to refer to a very concrete experience.[51] The term "equality," for example, is an ideograph within American culture. What does equality stand for? It seems to represent a lengthy list of interactions, experiences, feelings and relationships. When asked to define "equality," we almost always need to refer to particular examples, but the examples alone do not capture the concept, for it is always broader and more abstract than a single example. Moreover, the term "equality" also carries a moral tone of high value within our culture. Simply put, we value equality highly while other cultures may not. Confronted with new experiences, faced with debate about what policies to implement in the workplace or in public life or simply deciding how to get along in our homes, the ideograph "equality" may provide us guidance. Hence, the first step in the ideological process is the construction of ideographs.

The process by which ideographs come into being is not altogether clear. As we point out in Chapter 7, people find it difficult even to consider an idea, problem or issue unless there is language available for its description. Ideographs provide such language, but those symbols are typically the product of a diversity of individuals creating language and many more individuals responding to and interpreting that language. These symbols thus gain their ideologically powerful meanings through the ways in which we use them.

Social Roles and Practices

Within this process of the coordinated production of meaning for ultimate terms, Brown's second stage of sharing a worldview and socially enacting it comes into play. Brown illustrates this stage of ideology formation by referring to the way new ideologies within the field of science take hold. He describes three communication roles that are necessary at this stage: innovator, practitioner and cumulator.[52] The *innovator* creates the language to describe a new worldview. The *practitioner* ratifies that new worldview by using the new language and implementing new practices that conform to that new worldview. By doing so, the practitioner gives the new ideology legitimacy. *Cumulators* disperse the new ideology by transmitting it to novice practitioners and others outside the scientific community. Brown refers to textbook writers and students being introduced to science as cumulators. With each role, there is a change in language, or whatever communications are typically used and also in real practices.

We can expand Brown's description from a single institutional community such as the scientific community to culture as a whole and obtain a better understanding of this second stage. Becker's and Brummett's description of a mosaic of messages applies here. As multiple message fragments circulate in society, certain terms emerge as best describing complex experiences. These terms then become repeated and recirculated to the point that audiences take their meaning for granted. In part, those involved in formal communication systems help to choose the terms that come to characterize a complex set of experiences. For example, the media dubbed those people concerned with preserving the earth as "environmentalists." In part, particularly eloquent individuals may coin a phrase or term that catches on and becomes the ideograph for a particular worldview. Patrick Henry's apocryphal battle cry when the American colonists declared their independence from British rule, "Give me Liberty or give me Death," stood as a significant episode in the establishment of "liberty" as an ideograph for American culture. The slogan of the French Revolution, "Liberty,

Equality, Fraternity," and the lyrics of a host of patriotic songs including "My country 'tis of thee, sweet land of liberty" repeat the term in contexts that let us know its importance, even if they do little to clarify its actual meaning. Thus, the interaction of many senders and receivers of messages in many different forms finally accounts for a term achieving the status of an ideograph. As an ideograph, a term becomes so sacred to a culture that people are willing to sacrifice, fight or even die for "liberty," "equality" or other "god terms" of their ideology.

The work of critic and theorist Kenneth Burke also sheds light on the process by which symbols are used to express the ideals of a culture. Burke argues that any message may be examined for its "motive," a short-hand term that sums up the worldview expressed in a message.[53] The *motive* of a message is the theme or the motif of the message that emerges from a careful examination of the totality of the message. For example, we view a film and say it is an "action" film. The part of the film that stands out is the action; thus the motive is "action," which usually means a set of familiar images and codes involving conflict, danger, escape, heroes and villains will be present. We read a lengthy book that criticizes American foreign policy. When asked, we summarize the book as a "Marxist analysis." We arrive at this conclusion by noting the ways in which the author presented her arguments and observing that the types of arguments are common to other "Marxist" analyses that we have read. The motive of that book, then, is "Marxian." We walk into a room, look at the furniture, the decorations on the wall and so forth and classify the room as "art-deco." The motif, or motive, for the room is thus revealed by a summary of its decorative style. These short-hand summaries of situations or messages characterize the worldview in operation for those who construct these situations or messages, while simultaneously inviting those of us who encounter such situations and messages to experience them in a particular way. Hence, we may understand the second stage of ideology formation in any particular case by searching not only for ideographs but also for what Burke calls "motives" in messages that are shared.

Burke's choice of the term, "motive," may appear a bit peculiar since he really seems to be describing a theme or motif. However, his description of how one uncovers motives provides a useful context for understanding the link between motive and ideology. Burke maintains that humans have a natural impulse to create hierarchies.[54] As a result of such hierarchies, he argues, people tend to dramatize their lives, creating verbal and visual stories that reflect those hierarchies and their positions within them. To analyze the drama that is characteristic of human symbol-use, Burke suggests that critics determine the five elements of a drama within any message.[55] The five elements are: the *act*, or what is happening; the *agent*, or who is doing it; the *agency*, or means by which the act is accomplished; the *scene*, or context in which the act takes place; and the *purpose* for which the act is done. By systematically examining a message or situation to determine which elements of this dramatic pentad predominate, a critic can uncover the motive. Furthermore, the motive may reveal the ideology that is at work in that situation. Burke suggests, for example, that when the act is featured an ideology of realism is at work, while emphasis on the scene may signal an ideology of materialism.[56] He explains that a realist is concerned with things as they really are and getting things done and consequently will talk in action terms. A materialist, on the other hand, may be concerned with the material conditions of existence, the features of the scene and the environment and may explain what is going on as a product of the scene. A realist ideology, when applied to the problem of crime in our major cities, for example, would orient someone toward focusing on the various criminal acts that take place there. The behavior of someone whose worldview was that of a realist concerning crime might show fear or cynicism but certainly would emphasize realistic attempts to avoid being victimized. A materialist considering crime in the city, on the other hand, might focus on the scenic factors that contribute to crime, observing that the poor economic conditions common in the urban ghetto explain why the crime occurs, or advocate more effective lighting in parks and subways as a means for combatting crime. Hence, the worldview that one embraces accounts for different interpretations of the situation and different prescriptions for personal behaviors.

Burke's dramatistic perspective regarding motive helps reveal ideologies fostered by those cultural myths that tell stories to make the ideals of a culture concrete. As with ideographs, these cultural stories are the product of multiple interactions among sources and receivers. It is through the repetition and recirculation of cultural myths that an ideology becomes established. Perhaps a cultural myth at one time was invented by a single author, like Washington Irving's story of Rip Van Winkle, but often multiple authors produce tales that eventually become more well known than their inventors, such as the stories of Helen of Troy or Robin Hood. At other times, a small group engaged in group fantasizing of the type observed by Ernest Bormann, that we describe in Chapter 10, constructs a story that catches on. That story, if repeated outside the group, can eventually reach a very large audience. Within the swirling mosaic of cultural messages, some stories catch on and capture the attention of the culture, and these tales serve as guideposts for daily living.

Whether through ideographs or motives, symbolic representations of a worldview are constructed and shared with others. As these symbolic representations are shared, actual social relationships mirror the stories or the values that embody an ideology. This process, too, is part of Brown's second stage of ideology formation. If, for example, "science" becomes an ideograph, then scientific practices may be instituted in a variety of places and rewarded more highly than other practices. J. Michael Sproule recounts an interesting story of just such a case regarding the study of propaganda and ideology within academic circles.[57] Sproule points out that early in the twentieth century many academics researching propaganda concentrated on teaching students to uncover propaganda techniques, a topic we pursue in some detail in the next chapter. However, following World War II, government and other agencies that funded such research became enamored with new, social scientific methods that emphasized quantification—survey research and mathematical models of public opinion. As a result, those researchers who wished to develop tools for critical analysis found their projects unfunded, while those who proposed to conduct surveys and quantify how many Americans agreed or disagreed with a particular idea found their projects funded. Before long, most academics who desired funding and publication turned to a social scientific mode of investigation. Real practices mirrored the symbolic worldview of an ideology that valued science over critical investigation. This very book stands as an example of real practices mirroring the shared motive or "god terms" of a culture. The advent of sophisticated communication technologies in the last 30 years has made visual media quite important. The videotape that accompanies this text is a testament to the importance of making pedagogical practice conform to our newly emerging worldview of how people learn—not just by reading, but by viewing and experiencing as well.

Compensation and Adjustment

Brown's third stage of ideology concerns the use of communication systems to compensate for gaps or contradictions that appear within an ideology from time to time. He contends that any worldview occasionally encounters events or phenomena that cannot be accounted for easily or obviously within the prevailing ideology. He calls such unusual events or phenomena "anomalies."[58] Consider, for example, a scientific worldview that explains the world by reference to scientific laws of nature and conceptualizes human beings as the most intelligent beings on earth. Into this worldview come reports of UFOs, people who testify that their cancer miraculously disappeared when they found the Lord or tried some nontraditional form of treatment, and a variety of other phenomena not easily explained by scientific laws. Consider the implications for a political ideology that places the "rule of law" above the ambition of individuals, priding itself on being "a government of laws not of individuals," if circumstantial evidence and widely told tales suggest that a President's assassination was the result of a conspiracy inside the government or that high crimes and misdemeanors within a government administration have gone unpunished. These events contradict existing ideology. These incidents are anomalies. Unless communication systems can somehow adapt to compensate for these anomalies, the prevailing scientific or political ideology will lose much of its power to make our social world seem orderly and understandable.

The prevailing ideology can cope with such anomalies in several ways. It can deny that the events are truly anomalies, claiming or pretending that they really are not unusual at all. So, the scientific medical establishment can assert that the newly converted patient still has cancer, disbelieving their testimony, or the National Aeronautic and Space Administration can declare that UFO sightings are merely hoaxes. Another way to deal with such anomalies is to incorporate them into the prevailing worldview by masking the anomaly and by describing it in terms that do not sound anomalous. Doctors can explain that cancer sometimes goes into remission naturally, arguing that is the case with their patient. Scientists can make elaborate explanations about swamp gas and optical illusions to explain away photographic images of UFOs. Demonstrations that women can hold positions of authority and responsibility in traditionally male-dominated areas of business and politics can be brushed aside by references to exceptional qualities of those women or by innuendo about "sexual politics" and "tokenism." Likewise, governments can hold official hearings and issue official reports to dispense with the possibility of political scandal. Alternatively, anomalies can be accounted for by altering the dominant ideology slightly to account for the unusual occurrence. For example, the medical establishment could incorporate psychological and spiritual techniques of healing into their practice, as it has recently, while preserving a generally scientific approach to medicine. If one of these techniques does not work, Brown points out that the system will eventually collapse because of its inability to continue to provide a coherent explanation of the world as experienced. At that point a new ideology may emerge to replace the now worn and incomplete one that had been dominant. Ideology that endures for a long period surely modifies itself to compensate for exceptions to the worldview that it embodies.

FORMAL COMMUNICATION SYSTEMS AND IDEOLOGY FORMATION

Communication through a mosaic of messages is important within all three stages of ideology formation described by Brown. Individuals and groups, working together to construct and interpret a variety of messages, help to construct and maintain any particular worldview. Of particular interest, however, from our Institutional Perspective toward persuasion is the role of formal communication systems in the dissemination of ideology. Mass communication researchers Strodthoff, Hawkins and Schoenfeld have addressed this issue directly with a case study of the ideology of environmentalism.[59] Their research suggests that the media deal with ideology according to three stages as that ideology becomes dominant within a culture: disambiguation, legitimation and routinization. They describe these stages as follows:

> **Disambiguation** is the process whereby the basic doctrinal tenets of an emerging social cause themselves become defined and distinguished from each other and are first manifest in the content of mass communication channels…
>
> **Legitimation** is a process by which those who regulate the content for a given channel or media organization (gatekeepers) recognize various concerns pertinent to a social cause as valid topics for coverage by their particular channels.
>
> **Routinization** is a process whereby content relative to the movement is incorporated into the channel's operations on a fixed basis, such as through regular space, time, or personnel allocation. The approximate point of beginning is evidenced in changes in formats and/or from published statements indicating that such an administrative decision has been made.[60]

Although the first two stages are essential for the formation of an ideology, only when an ideology reaches the third stage of routinization do we recognize it as dominant. However, once an ideology becomes part of the media's routine, the audience for that media takes the ideology for granted. So, for example, our culture takes news coverage of important people like politicians and celebrities for granted and is not surprised that other people and voices are neglected by the news. Also we could turn to the routines followed by advertisers. Until recently, according to Kilbourne's analysis of advertising, old people rarely appeared in advertisements except when they wandered in looking for pain killers or laxatives.[61] The reason for this was that advertisers followed a routine for casting that searched for youthful and active characters that the audience would find appealing and attention getting. In a culture where we take for granted that youth is superior to old age, it is not surprising that older people rarely show up in advertisements. Of course, repeated exposure to messages that reinforce this ideological commitment to youth helps to maintain that worldview. In both cases of news coverage and advertising, the reason for decisions about the content of messages may have little to do with an ideology, but the routines that are followed have everything to do with the perpetuation of an ideology.

Ethical Concerns Regarding Ideology

Ideologies are powerful because they provide people a basis for constructing a coherent worldview that can be applied to various situations, issues and problems. They help us make sense of an otherwise confusing and complex world. But in doing so, ideologies frequently substitute for critical analysis of the world and our place within it. Because ideologies provide us with a view of the world that tells us what to value, who is heroic and how power should be distributed, ideologies carry a strong moral component. Thus arise ethical concerns about ideology.

"Ideology," like "propaganda," is a term with strong connotations—most of them negative. Both ideology and propaganda are words we often hear people use to describe the values and persuasive tactics of their opponents rather than their own values and tactics. Our discussion of ethics should begin with a clarification of this crucial point. To say that ideology is a characteristic of all modern institutions and societies—both those we prefer and those we abhor—is not to issue a blanket ethical approval to all ideological elements in persuasion or to conclude that all institutions are, therefore, morally equivalent.

Some suggest that all ideology is unethical because it is accepted uncritically. Such a position arises from an understanding that ideologies are comprised of beliefs and values that are taken for granted rather than being subjected to critical inspection. The Greek philosopher Plato referred to such a belief system as *doxa*, the Greek term that is the root of related terms in modern English such as *orthodoxy*. In one of Plato's most famous dialogues, *The Republic*, he pointed out the danger of uncritical acceptance of commonsense understandings.[62] In *The Republic*, Socrates tells the parable of the cave, in which lifelong prisoners chained inside a cave see only the shadows of their captors cast by the firelight upon the cave walls in front of them. In time, the prisoners' efforts to understand and explain their world by reference to the movement of these shadows lead them to form a set of commonsense beliefs about the "reality" of those shadows—erroneous beliefs, from our point of view outside the cave, but commonsense, nevertheless, from the prisoners' point of view. Indeed, added Socrates, if the prisoners somehow escaped the cave, being able for the first time to see their guards and the sunlight, it was far more likely that these prisoners would persist in seeing shadows as real. To deny this would be, for the prisoners, to deny common sense. Inaccurate, distorted and oppressive though they were, those beliefs learned in the cave might well be far less painful for the prisoners than staring into the bright light of day outside the cave.

If our commonsense understanding of the world, our ideology, is accurate, then our lack of critical inspection is probably not too threatening. However, as many of those who define ideology in negative terms point out, ideologies frequently present false interpretations of the world around us. Working from a Marxist perspective, many cultural critics describe ideology as a false consciousness. Further, they point out that such worldviews are usually flawed because they are constructed uncritically. Hence, by passively accepting a worldview that does not represent reality, people engage in false consciousness. Once again let us consider the cultural value of individualism and the worldview that emerges from our commonsense understanding of the role of the individual. Studying our culture's use of this concept can contribute to our understanding of false consciousness.

Critical examinations of the causes of wealth and poverty frequently betray the commonsense understanding of the problem of poverty as a product of false consciousness, the result of ideological rather than critical thinking. Recall that the ideology of individualism encourages people to blame those in poverty for their circumstances, assuming they are lazy, immoral or otherwise defective people who have not taken advantage of the land of opportunity in which we live. Critical examination of the facts reveals a different picture. Nearly 40 percent of the homeless are not mentally ill or alcoholic, but they are single mothers and their children.[63] Sixty to eighty percent of those below the poverty line in this country are women and their children, and projections suggest that by the year 2000 nearly all of those in poverty will fall into that category.[64] Substantial evidence suggests that these people cannot "just go out and get a job." Their geographic locations, the types of jobs available, the need to care for their children and the structure of the social welfare system in this country practically guarantee that they will remain in poverty regardless of their individual ambitions or initiatives. Thus, the "commonsense" understanding of the situation is flawed, perpetuated by a false consciousness or ideology constructed from a wide variety of subtly persuasive messages that espouse the value and promise of the individual at the expense of community obligations.

While our view of poverty demonstrates how ideology allows a society to accept as natural conditions that which might otherwise be changed, it is by no means the only example of ideology at work. Our commonsense understandings about our relationship to our environment, to other people and even about ourselves may be similarly false. The ethical imperative that seems to emerge from the potential of ideologies to present a false worldview asks sources and audiences of messages alike to critically evaluate the ideologies that are present in their messages. This ethical responsibility requires us to inspect our commonsense understandings, our values, and to determine how accurately or inaccurately they reflect our social reality. This attitude of critical inspection demands vigilance on our part; for while Socrates' prisoners could leave the cave and view the sun, it is not so simple for us to move outside of our worldview to inspect it. What makes a worldview false is not merely the availability of empirical evidence that can contradict it. Rather, it is the tendency to present the *status quo* it supports as universal when it is cultural, as inevitable when it is only one possible state of affairs, as fixed when it is changeable, as resting on concrete and empirical distinctions which are actually symbolic and arbitrary, and as ordained by God or destiny when it is the product of the actions of flesh-and-blood individuals.

As we inspect the worldviews that we generally take for granted, we should remain aware of the relationship between ideology and social power. Because ideologies are infused with cultural ideals and hierarchies, we need to determine whose interests these ideals and hierarchies serve. Such a determination tells us who and which institutions wield power in our society. Then we may make ethical judgments about whether or not such power relationships are appropriate. Ideological critic Philip Wander points out that often whole classes of people are excluded from the cultural messages that embody a dominant ideology.[65] He notes that Nazi rhetoric excluded non-Aryans as an audience for public discourse, an exclusion that made the elimination of these people easier. Finding the voices that are silenced, the people that are excluded and the groups that are placed on the low end of the hierarchy is a way for ideology critics to address ethical concerns by pointing out the gaps in an ideology. Critical inspection of our taken-for-granted worldview may produce real insight about the world in which we live and serve a consciousness-raising function, revealing who is exploited and who benefits from the dominant ideology.

In addition, as we take ethical responsibility for ideological persuasion, we should not allow ourselves to be distracted by the intent of the message makers. Often ideology formation and perpetuation is almost an unconscious process. As the numerous examples throughout this chapter suggest, advertisements, films, speeches and so on embody cultural values and myths in order to be effective. The makers of these messages make decisions about content and style according to economic considerations, audience and market analysis and a host of other factors. They rarely intend to either introduce or perpetuate an ideology. Yet within their mosaic of messages that produces our cultural identity, their symbolic constructions may perpetuate an ideology that produces false consciousness or inhibits consciousness-raising by validating exploitative or damaging power relationships. Brummett identifies this consciousness-raising function of ideology critique as a primary outcome of cultural criticism generally.[66]

All ideologies may not be equally ethically troubling, but by their nature they present only a partial picture of reality, endorse a particular system of power relationships that benefit some while disadvantaging others and inhibit the coming to consciousness of those who accept the ideology uncritically. A commitment to ethics demands that ideology be inspected to counter these three difficulties. A clear example of ideological criticism that accomplishes these ends comes from the dispute in 1990 about whether or not women who cover sporting events should be allowed in all-male locker rooms. The controversy centered around an incident in which, following a football game lost by the New England Patriots, a female sportscaster was subjected to sexual harassment by several of the Patriot players, most notably Zeke Mowatt. The ensuing discussion that appeared in print and on television by many sports figures and commentators concerned our ideological beliefs about whether or not it is appropriate for women to show up in a room where a bunch of men are in various states of undress. The typical commonsense approach was to argue "no," this activity was inappropriate. The coach of the Patriots energetically explained that he wouldn't want his wife in the locker room and didn't allow the wives of the players in the locker room, so why should a female reporter be any different? Syndicated columnist Mike Royko furnished an answer to the coach's question by critically examining the ideology at work in this case.[67] Royko pointed out that if a player is injured it is not at all unusual for a female nurse or doctor to see the player's naked body. Why? Because that is the professional role of that nurse or doctor. Similarly, the professional role of the sports reporter is to interview players in the locker room. The "commonsense" assessment of the situation made no sense to Royko as he critically evaluated the situation. If we extend Royko's analysis, we can see that those aspects of the prevailing ideology influencing which places are deemed appropriate for women to go clearly puts male sports reporters in an advantageous position for obtaining a story, since they can enter the locker room while women may be prohibited or subjected to harassment if the dominant ideology prevails. Furthermore, those who accept the commonsense understanding drawn from the dominant ideology are thereby inhibited from looking past the biological sex of the reporter to the role the reporter is asked to perform professionally. This ideological response perpetuates an assumption that women are women first and professionals second, a cultural assumption that has proved problematic in a number of professions that seek equality for the sexes.

Royko's critique and the work of other social critics illustrate how one may ethically question even diffused ideological persuasion. The fundamental ethical responsibility for senders and receivers alike is to critically inspect an ideology as it appears in any message. Robert Reich describes why doing so is important:

> Public problems don't exist "out there." They are not discrete facts or pieces of data awaiting discovery. They are consequences of our shared values. Without a set of common moral assumptions we would have no way of identifying or categorizing problems and their possible solutions. Some questions are rarely asked. What is at the root of our quarrel with the Soviets? Does it make sense to speak of American economic competitiveness? Is a citizen's poverty his own misfortune, his own due, or a social problem? What precisely do we mean by government intervention, or the market? These questions do not enter public discourse because so much of the ground from which they spring is taken for granted. To ask them directly is often to end a conversation, because there is nothing left to say; on such basic questions we have collectively, albeit tacitly, reached either essential agreement or stalemate. And yet it is that which we leave unsaid in our debates, not the words that fill the air and the pages, that says the most about us.[68]

Reich's observations point to the ethical necessity of examining the ideological nature of the persuasion which surrounds us and the inherent difficulties which must be overcome in order to do so. Ideology resists inspection because of its status as "common sense" and also because the language that we have to use is itself often scarcely up to the task. The most obvious language in which to discuss aspects of our ideology are ideographs, the individual terms which sum up key elements of an ideology. Yet, as McGee points out, the very language which allows us to express the values of an ideology inhibits our ability to examine these values critically.[69] Once a system justifies its actions in the name of "peace," "freedom" or "prosperity," what then? After all, when was there ever a war in which *both* sides did not use these ideographs to explain and defend their actions? Therefore, the ethical obligation to be aware of the influences of ideology in persuasion carries with it the responsibility to be sensitive to the language we use and its ability to implicitly further ideological aims.

CRITICAL FOCUS: "THE BEST A MAN CAN GET"

At the beginning of this chapter, we mentioned the work of Jean Kilbourne regarding the worldview of women and femininity that is perpetuated through contemporary advertising messages. Our critical focus for this chapter considers a similar issue by examining the Gillette shaving advertisement for its ideological message concerning men and masculinity. Ideology critique generally requires examination of a mosaic of messages within a culture, tracing the ideographs, motives, values and myths throughout their various incarnations in persuasive messages. However, to illustrate the principles of this chapter we focus on only one message and simply refer to the work of other social critics on this subject. The following critical questions can guide an analysis of any message for its ideological potential.

CRITICAL QUESTIONS

1. What cultural **values** does the message promote?
2. What cultural **myths** does the message incorporate?
3. What **ideographs** or **motives** does the message display?
4. **Who benefits** from the common sense and values that are promoted by the message?
5. What values, ideas, people or actions are suppressed, omitted or otherwise **missing from the message**?
6. How well does the ideology contained within the message **accurately reflect reality** as experienced by everyday people?
7. In what ways are the power relationships suggested by the message **ethically appropriate**?

The Gillette commercial spot on the accompanying videotape provided the centerpiece of an $80 million advertising campaign launched by the North Atlantic Shaving Group in January of 1988.[70] According to one review of the campaign at the time, Gillette faced a troubling marketing situation:

> Gillette's problem is one of image. Among older men the name connotes high quality grooming. But among younger men the brand has few if any values attached to it. Indeed, in market research, one young accountant, when asked what Gillette meant to him replied "hollow, blue, and plastic."[71]

In order to change the perceptions of these young men, Gillette developed an advertisement that intentionally linked their name to the dominant ideology regarding masculinity. As a corporate memo explained:

> ...we concluded it's important to convince men that the business we're really in is understanding men and knowing what it takes to make them look and feel their best—best in those many moments—both very great and very small—when men feel special.[72]

In other words, the advertisers intentionally designed a campaign to depict men at their best. As a consequence, this particular message is especially revealing of the dominant ideology in our culture regarding masculinity.

A systematic examination of the advertisement reveals an audio and video track that includes the elements described in Table 13.1.

Table 13.1

EXCERPTS FROM THE AUDIO AND VIDEO TRACKS OF THE GILLETTE ADVERTISEMENT

Audio	Video
You're looking sharp	Bridegroom with groomsmen
You're looking good	Woman straightening man's tie
You've come so far	Young businessman on the phone receives congratulations; long distance runner running
We know how to make	Man shaving
The most of who you are	Older man hugs younger man at wedding; football team scores a touchdown
Father to son	Father lifts weights while son watches; father and son comb hair together; father gives car keys
It's what we've always done	Father holds baby
Gillette, the best a man can get	Man surfing; woman running to greet and hug man; men dancing at a wedding
On so many faces	Montage of faces; men running on the beach
It's plain to see	Man shaving; man and woman on a porch; men running; man and woman kissing
We give you all we have to give	Man on motorbike flirting with woman; man shaving; baseball batter hitting; football line scrimmage
For all a man can be	Astronauts marching; Wall St. businessmen doing business
Where the race is won	Man rinsing face; stockbrokers working; Edwin Moses hurdling
You're the champion	Discus thrower throwing; boxing match; tennis player kissing trophy
Gillette, the best a man can get	Wedding scene with rice being thrown

From both the lyrics to the music and the visual images, we discover the values and cultural tales that portray masculinity. What is valued, according to the lyrics, is looking good, making the most of who you are, giving all you have to give, winning the race and becoming a champion. The visuals illustrate what each of these value-laden terms means. "Looking good" involves a clean shave and professional, wedding or sports attire. A man "makes the most of who he is" by shaving, getting married, making touchdowns, lifting weights and relating to his son. "Giving all you have" is depicted as picking up women, shaving and participating in sports. A man can "win the race and become a champion" by being successful in sports or business and marrying a beautiful woman. Hence, whatever the explicit purpose of the commercial with respect to the Gillette product campaign, the message promotes competition, success, attractiveness, heterosexuality and family as values.

The many images in the spot remind viewers of a number of cultural tales without ever telling a complete story. The men who populate the spot illustrate the

American fable of the triumphant individual. The shots of men lifting weights and running with sweat dripping from their brows remind us of movie stories like *Rocky* and *Chariots of Fire*, both of which embody and celebrate the cultural myth of the triumphant individual. The heavy reliance on images of competition—in sports and in business—along with the opening line that "you're looking sharp" reinforce the relevance of this cultural myth. Besides confirming values, the spot also paints images common to the cultural tales regarding the family. The touching scenes of fathers and sons reminds viewers of male bonding stories that take on a more homey flavor. And the wedding scene reminds viewers that to be masculine means to love and bond with women as well.

A search for ideographs in this message reveals several terms that seem to summarize ideal masculinity: "sharp," "best" and "champion." "Sharp" includes both the experience of looking good and performing well. "Best" refers to the experience of winning races, scoring touchdowns, wooing beautiful women, making successful business deals and becoming a champion. To be a "champion" means, of course, to win. The patterns of these ideographs and motives indicate an ideology that values competitiveness and success at work, at play and in relationships.

Consider also what is conspicuous by its absence in these images. In all of these images of sports, business and wedding, the emphasis is on *doers* (the men who are featured) and *doing* (running, dancing, hugging, shaving, flirting, hitting a baseball, marching, talking). By comparison, the matters of context, purpose and relationship—why are they competing? in what kind of business are they engaged? what has led them to get married?—are far less dominating. The focus on the doer emphasizes the connection between masculinity and individualism, while the emphasis on actions underscores the importance for men of doing, activity and accomplishment.

An ideology that promotes competitiveness, individual effort and achievement and success certainly benefits a capitalist system like that in the United States, which depends on competition and hard work for economic progress. Such an ideology, however, penalizes those who do not become champions, those who choose more cooperative than competitive approaches to life and those who seek spiritual or intellectual fulfillment through a more passive life style than the active one portrayed in the spot. The ideology within this commercial spot would hardly explain or validate a slow and easy life style in which people worked only as much as they needed to meet their basic needs, lived alone or established homosexual partnerships or relationships with people who were not physically attractive and were satisfied with merely engaging in activities rather than winning the trophy or scoring a touchdown or marrying an attractive spouse. Except for a few quick glimpses of women and black men, the commercial depicts white men almost exclusively. While one older man is shown hugging his son, the images consist almost entirely of younger men. Are we to conclude that age prohibits success and championship? Women are shown only as adjuncts to men—their brides, dates or potential girlfriends. The children who are shown are all male. How are men to relate to their female children? Although family and relationships are depicted, the depictions focus on rituals like weddings and show family members as possessions of the featured men rather than emphasizing everyday activities or illustrating more egalitarian interactions. Hence, the advertisement projects an image of masculinity that is incomplete. However commonsense it may appear, the commercial provides nothing more than a set of technologically dazzling shadows cast on the wall of a cave in which men and women sit chained.

Given this brief description of the ideological content of the Gillette commercial, we can now critically evaluate that commercial by examining how accurately it depicts reality and assessing the ethical appropriateness of the ideology contained within it. Let us begin with the notion that men look good, make the most of themselves and are winners. We find that this ideology does not reflect reality particularly well. In an essay that attempts to analyze the state of masculinity in our society in 1991, Andrew Kimbrell provides the following data:

> While suicide rates for women have been stable over the last 20 years, among men—especially white male teenagers—they have increased rapidly. Currently, male teenagers are five times more likely to take their own lives than females. Overall, men are committing suicide at four times the rate of women. America's young men are also being ravaged by alcohol and drug abuse. Men between the ages of 18 and 29 suffer alcohol dependency at three times the rate of women of the same age group. More than two-thirds of all alcoholics are men, and 50 percent more men are regular users of illicit drugs than women....
>
> Real wages for men under 25 have actually declined over the last 20 years, and 60 percent of all high school dropouts are males....
>
> The stress on men is taking its toll. Men's life expectancy is 10 percent shorter than women's, and the incidence of stress-related illnesses, such as heart disease and cancers remains inordinately high among men.
>
> And the situation for minority men is even worse....
>
> Men are also a large part of the growing crisis in the American family. Studies report that parents today spend 40 percent less time with their children than did parents in 1965, and men are increasingly isolated from their families by the pressures of work and the circumstances of divorce.[73]

Reality seems clearly at odds with the ideological message, but how does the ideological message contribute to the somber reality that Kimbrell's facts describe? Confronted with an idealized masculinity that celebrates economic and sexual success above all, many men feel as if they have failed. Some social critics suggest that confronted with the huge gap between the ideal man and their own realities, many young men vent their frustration and guilt through extreme violence, especially directed toward women.[74] Similarly, some therapists believe that many unsuccessful marriages are the result of unrealistic expectations by both men and women concerning the importance and possibility of success for the "man of the house."[75] Still others contend that the heavy emphasis on success and achievement that characterizes the male mystique makes it very difficult for adult men to take the time and energy to develop real friendships, a problem that leads to a number of personal problems for many men.[76] Perhaps most troubling of all, perpetuation of an ideology that depicts masculinity as achievement-driven takes place at the cost of other approaches to life that are more peaceful, cooperative and caring. Kimbrell notes that the modern industrial society removed men from a community minded agrarian life and placed them in a competitive jungle of the industrial workplace, alienating them from family, spouse, children, and nature.[77] Hence, even the ideal of achievement and success presented in the Gillette spot fosters an approach to life that may be ethically troubling.

At the beginning of this chapter we reviewed research that indicated women were exploited by a pervasive ideology that disempowered femininity. At the end, we see that a similar ideology concerning masculinity inhibits a truthful and humane consciousness for men in our culture. We think that sources and audiences alike have a responsibility to evaluate critically the ideologies that underlie the cultural mosaic of messages. We should seek to raise the consciousness of both genders, such that a host of social tragedies might be avoided. Emancipation from our taken-for-granted worldviews is precisely the goal of those who focus on ideology when they study persuasion from the Institutional Perspective.

Notes

1. Nina Burleigh, "Advertisers Still Lagging Behind the Times," *Chicago Tribune* (7 April 1991): section 6, 8.
2. Jill Kilbourne, *Still Killing Us Softly.*
3. Burleigh, "Advertisers," 8.
4. Kilbourne, *Still Killing Us Softly.*
5. The following discussion draws upon various (unsigned) memoranda and promotional materials made available to us by the North Atlantic Shaving Group, 25 May, 1989.
6. North Atlantic Shaving Group, memorandum.
7. For a review of de Tracy's development of the term, see Michael Billig, Susan Condor, Derek Edwards, Mike Gane, David Middleton and Alan Radley, *Ideological Dilemmas* (Beverly Hills: Sage, 1988), 39-40.
8. For representative treatments of ideology as a worldview, see Barry Brummett, "A Pentadic Analysis of Ideologies in Two Gay Rights Controversies," *Central States Speech Journal* 30 (1979): 250-261; and Robert P. Hawkins and A. Clay Shoenfield, "Media Roles in a Social Movement: A Model of Ideology Diffusion," *Journal of Communication* 35 (1985): 132-153.
9. For representative studies of ideology of this type, see Myles Breen and Farrel Corcoran, "Myth, Drama, Fantasy Theme, and Ideology in Mass Media Studies," *Progress in Communication Sciences*, Volume VII, eds. Brenda Dervin and Melvin J. Voigt (Norwood NJ: Ablex, 1985), 195-224; see also, Philip Wander, "The Rhetoric of American Foreign Policy," *Quarterly Journal of Speech* 70 (1984): 339-361.
10. V. William Balthrop, "Culture, Myth, and Ideology as Public Argument: An Interpretation of the Ascent and Demise of 'Southern Culture,'" *Communication Monographs* 51 (1984): 321.
11. Becker, *Discovering*, 13; for the vision by Barth, see John Barth, *The Floating Opera* (Garden City: Doubleday, 1967), 7-8.

12. Becker, *Discovering*, 13.
13. Brummett, *Rhetorical Dimensions*, 68.
14. Brummett, *Rhetorical Dimensions*, 75-76.
15. Brummett, *Rhetorical Dimensions*, 74, 76.
16. Stuart Hall, "Signification, Representation, Ideology: Althusser and the Post-Structuralist Debates," *Critical Studies in Mass Communication* 2 (1985): 93.
17. Bonnie J. Dow, "Hegemony, Feminist Criticism, and *The Mary Tyler Moore Show*," *Critical Studies in Mass Communication* 7 (1990): 261-274.
18. "On Guard," *Chicago Tribune* (21 April 1991): section 6, 1.
19. Brummett, *Rhetorical Dimensions*, 82. Ann Jones, "Crimes Against Women: Media Part of the Problem for Masking Violence in the Language of Love," *USA Today* March 10, 1994; see also "The Top Ten Censored Stories," *UTNE Reader* 69 (May-June 1995), 33-36.
20. Balthrop, "Ideology," 320.
21. Milton Rokeach, *Beliefs, Attitudes and Values* (San Francisco: Jossey-Bass, 1968), 113.
22. Rokeach, *Beliefs*, 124.
23. Anthony Cortese, *Ethnic Ethics: The Restructuring of Moral Theory* (Albany: State University of New York Press, 1990), 91-98.
24. Cortese, *Ethnic*, 94.
25. Robert N. Bellah, Richard Madsen, William M. Sullivan, Ann Swidler and Steven M. Tipton, *Habits of the Heart: Individualism and Commitment in American Life* (New York: Harper Perennial Library, 1986).
26. Edward D. Steele and W. Charles Redding, "The American Value System: Premises for Persuasion," *Western Journal of Speech* 26 (1962): 83-91.
27. For a discussion of each of these values with illustrations, see Martha Cooper, *Analyzing Public Discourse* (Prospect Heights: Waveland, 1989), 86-91.
28. Richard D. Rieke and Malcolm O. Sillars, *Argumentation and the Decision Making Process*, 2nd Ed (Glenview: Scott, Foresman, 1984), 111-113.
29. Bellah, *et al.*, *Habits*, 3-26.
30. Balthrop, "Ideology," 321.
31. Bellah, *et al.*, *Habits*, 40.
32. Balthrop, "Ideology," 322.
33. Robert B. Reich, *Tales of a New America* (New York: Times Books, 1987).
34. Reich, *Tales*, especially 8-13.
35. Reich, *Tales*, 8.
36. Reich, *Tales*, 9.
37. Reich, *Tales*, 10.
38. Reich, *Tales*, 11.
39. Reich, *Tales*, 11.
40. Andrew King, *Power and Communication* (Prospect Heights: Waveland, 1987), 118; see also, Karl Marx, *Capital* (New York: Modern Library, n.d.).
41. Philip Wander, "The Ideological Turn in Modern Criticism," *Central States Speech Journal* 32 (1983), 1.
42. King, *Power*, 118.

43. See, *The Frankfurt Reader*, eds. Andrew Arato and Eike Gebhardt (New York: Continuum Press, 1988).
44. Wander, "Ideological," 1.
45. Louis Althusser, "Ideology and the State," in *Lenin and Philosophy and Other Essays*, trans. Ben Brewster (New York: Monthly Review Press, 1971), 143.
46. Althusser, "Ideology," 156.
47. King, *Power.*
48. J. R. French and B. Raven, "The Bases of Social Power," in *Studies in Social Power*, ed. D. Cartwright (Ann Arbor: Institute for Social Research, 1959), 150-167; B. E. Collins and B. Raven, "Group Structure: Attraction, Coalitions, Communication, and Power," in *Handbook of Social Psychology*, eds. G. Lindzey and E. Aronson (Reading: Addison-Wesley, 1969), 102-204.
49. William R. Brown, "Ideology as Communication Process," *Quarterly Journal of Speech* 64 (1978): 123-140.
50. Michael Calvin McGee, "The 'Ideograph': A Link Between Rhetoric and Ideology," *Quarterly Journal of Speech* 66 (1980): 1-16.
51. McGee, "Ideograph," 7.
52. Brown, "Ideology," 132.
53. Kenneth Burke, *A Rhetoric of Motives* (Berkeley: University of California Press, 1969), 109-110.
54. Kenneth Burke, *Language As Symbolic Action* (Berkeley: U California P, 1966), 3-24.
55. See, Kenneth Burke, *A Grammar of Motives* (Berkeley: U California P, 1969).
56. Burke, Grammar, 128-131.
57. J. Michael Sproule, "Propaganda Studies in American Social Science: The Rise and Fall of the Critical Paradigm," *Quarterly Journal of Speech* 73 (1987): 60-78.
58. Brown, "Ideology," 132.
59. Glenn G. Strodthoff, Robert P. Hawkins and A. Clay Schoenfeld, "Media Roles in a Social Movement: A Model of Ideology Diffusion," *Journal of Communication* 35 (1985): 132-153.
60. Strodthoff, *et al.*, "Media," 132-135.
61. Kilbourne, *Still Killing.*
62. Plato, *The Republic*, in *The Collected Works of Plato*, Vol. 1, ed. and trans. Benjamin Jowett (New York: Modern Library, 1937).
63. Jonathan Kozol, *Rachel and Her Children: Homeless Families in America* (New York: Crown, 1988).
64. Nancy Fraser, *Unruly Practices: Power, Discourse and Gender in Contemporary Social Theory* (Minneapolis: University of Minnesota Press, 1989), pp. 144-145.
65. Philip Wander, "The Third Persona: An Ideological Turn in Rhetorical Theory," *Central States Speech Journal* 35 (1984): 197-216.
66. Brummett, *Rhetorical Dimensions*, 101-102.

67. Mike Royko, "Change of Heart on Female Reporter," *Chicago Tribune* (28 Nov 1990): sec. 1, 3.
68. Reich, *Tales,* 6-7.
69. McGee, "Ideograph."
70. Sean Whelan, "Gillette Sharpens Image to Attract Younger Men," *Marketing* (19 January 1989): 2.
71. Whelan, "Gillette," 2.
72. Personal correspondence, 2.
73. Andrew Kimbrell, "A Time for Men to Pull Together," *Utne Reader* (May/June 1991): 66-67.
74. Barbara Ehrenreich, "Angry Young Men," *New York Woman* (September 1989), excerpted in *Utne Reader* (May/June 1991): 78-80.
75. Warren Farrell, "Men as Success Objects," *Family Therapy Networker* (Nov/Dec 1988), reprinted in *Utne Reader* (May/June 1991): 81-84.
76. Larry Letich, "Do You Know Who Your Friends Are?" *Utne Reader* (May/June 1991): 85-87.
77. Kimbrell, "A Time," 67-68.

14
Propaganda and Persuasion

IN THIS CHAPTER:
Focus on:
  Nazi Propaganda, *Triumph of the Will*
1. Theoretical Focus: Propaganda
2. Characteristics of Propaganda
3. Classical Analysis of Propaganda
    Stages of Propaganda Campaigns
    Classic Techniques of Propaganda
    Doctrine, Audience and Resistance
4. Propaganda in the Modern Institutional Society
    Ellul's Categories of Propaganda
    The Process of Contemporary Propaganda
5. Ethics and Propaganda
6. Critical Focus: *Triumph of the Will*

Focus on: Nazi Propaganda, *Triumph of the Will*

Among the various propaganda produced during World War II, *Triumph of the Will*, Leni Riefenstahl's film of the 1934 Nazi Party rally at Nuremberg, stands out. Following its 1935 premiere in Berlin, the film "was at once hailed as a masterpiece—inspiring to some, sinister and terrifying to others."[1] Hollywood filmmaker Frank Capra, the young military officer charged with producing American films to counteract the persuasive effects of *Triumph of the Will*, described what he called "the classic powerhouse propaganda film of our times" as follows:

> Shortly after General Marshall ordered me to make the *Why We Fight* films for our servicemen, I saw Leni Riefenstahl's terrifying motion picture, *Triumph of the Will*. The film was the ominous prelude of Hitler's holocaust of hate. Satan couldn't have devised a more blood-chilling super-spectacle.
>
> ...It was at once the glorification of war, the deification of Hitler, and the canonization of his apostles. Though panoplied with all the pomp and mystical trappings of a Wagnerian opera, its message was as blunt and brutal as a lead pipe: We, the Herrenvolk, are the new invincible gods! *Triumph of the Will* fired no gun, dropped no bombs. But as a psychological weapon aimed at destroying the will to resist, it was just as lethal.[2]

Still "widely regarded as the most powerful, influential propaganda film in nonfiction cinema history," *Triumph of the Will* has been described as a masterpiece that "represents the very heart of what propaganda is all about."[3] At the conclusion of this chapter, we investigate *Triumph of the Will* as a classic example of propaganda.

Especially during times of war, modern governments frequently consider it necessary to manipulate public opinion in order to secure the continuing confidence of the public or to motivate their citizens to engage in certain actions, perhaps even actions that would otherwise seem contradictory to their self-interest. During World War II, for example, hundreds of thousands of Americans were willing to put their everyday lives on hold and even risk losing their lives in order to travel to distant parts of the world to fight against Fascism. Meanwhile, many citizens in Germany, Italy, Japan and elsewhere were willing to engage in acts that in peacetime would be nearly unimaginable to further the goals of their own political institutions. For students of the Holocaust, a grave and persistent question is how anyone could have committed the atrocities that occurred. Those who study persuasion answer that the villains and even the victims and those whom we might be tempted to call "onlookers" were strongly influenced by a type of persuasion generally referred to as propaganda.

THEORETICAL FOCUS: PROPAGANDA

Propaganda, however, is not confined to wartime, nor are nation-states the only practitioners. Even during peacetime, propaganda messages often flourish. In his review of the history of propaganda, J. Michael Sproule points out several other approaches to propaganda in the twentieth century.[4] For example, government agencies frequently enlist public relations experts and others to influence what is reported as news, thereby influencing public opinion on a variety of issues. Special interest groups often try to influence the curricula of various educational institutions to promote their particular agendas. Such attempts to influence public opinion about a host of issues in peacetime may seem to bear more resemblance to persuasive campaigns or ideology than to propaganda, which is often so closely associated with the strongly biased and sometimes deceptive messages produced by governments during wartime. However, as our discussion in this chapter reveals, propaganda is a distinct form of institutional persuasion.

As Sproule points out, the existence of propaganda in its various forms has spawned a variety of intellectual responses.[5] Some progressive thinkers, such as Walter Lippman and John Dewey, advocated the teaching of critical thinking and widespread propaganda analysis as an antidote to the one-sided publicity campaigns and other manipulations of news that distort the public's ability to sort out issues and arguments. Others, especially professionals within the advertising and public relations industry who earned their livelihoods from just such campaigns and manipulations, advocated ethical codes and strict standards of professionalism to guard against the threats to democratic decision making that were posed by propaganda messages. Still others, especially social scientific researchers, concentrated on simply explaining the process of social influence that such messages promoted. Many of their findings appear in earlier chapters of this book. Finally, according to Sproule, some suggested that the way to attack such propaganda was to use "propaganda analysis for partisan political purposes," an approach that Sproule termed "the polemical response."[6] The polemical response recognizes that propaganda exists and proposes counter-propaganda as a response, like "fighting fire with fire." By engaging in counter-propaganda, persuaders do not so much analyze the propaganda of others as they use propaganda to promote their own agenda which stands in direct opposition to the agenda of other propagandists.

In this chapter, we first consider the general characteristics of propaganda which make it unique as a form of institutional persuasion. Following this, we examine propaganda theory in two aspects. The first aspect, classic propaganda theory, is drawn from the pragmatic research in the first half of the Twentieth Century. The classic approach to the study of propaganda is largely message centered and investigates techniques by which propagandists manipulate their audience's perception of the truth-value of their claims. The classic approach to propaganda also considers ways to defend against propaganda. Following this, we turn to more recent treatments of propaganda that take a somewhat broader and more "systemic" view of the subject. We address the question of ethics and propaganda before returning to an analysis of *Triumph of the Will* in the Critical Focus.

Characteristics Of Propaganda

As we explained in Chapter 10, *propaganda can be defined as institutionally-sponsored persuasion aimed at the masses.* Like other forms of persuasion studied from the Institutional Perspective, propaganda tends to exist over a period of time, involves the use of multiple messages and operates within an institutional context. Many of the characteristics of propaganda are quite similar to those of ideology as discussed in the previous chapter, and the two are usually closely related in practice. We distinguish propaganda from ideology primarily on the grounds that while ideology may be an unintentional by-product of public communication, propaganda is an intentional form of persuasion. Producers of propaganda messages typically intend to persuade an audience with respect to concrete and specific goals, while ideology may be perpetuated by messages explicitly designed for purposes other than persuasion. The intentional nature of propaganda accounts for several of its unique characteristics.

The first unique characteristic of propaganda is that it is *institutionally-sponsored* persuasion. Although studies of propaganda frequently emphasize the type of persuasive messages that occur during times of war, scholars point out that the term, "propaganda," actually originated in more peaceful circumstances.[7] In 1622 Pope Gregory XV established the Congregation for the Propagation of the Faith, whose mission was to revive and strengthen the Church in Europe and carry the Word to natives of the New World. As a persuasive practice, then, propaganda was originally conceived as a type of educational and missionary work designed to win converts in order to maintain and strengthen the Catholic Church. Hence, in its original form, propaganda showed its most distinguishing feature. Sponsored by a religious institution, Church propaganda served the purpose of furthering the specific goals of the Church.

The study of propaganda has been most vigorous when propaganda is sponsored by government institutions. During World War I, for example, the U.S. government established a group known as the Committee for Public Information (CPI) whose objective was to "sell the war" to America. George Creel, a journalist and head of the CPI, explained after the war that the Committee printed and distributed posters and pamphlets, developed speakers' bureaus in a host of localities, worked with Hollywood film makers and carefully controlled information distributed to the press in order to maintain solid support for American involvement in the war.[8] During World War II, Adolf Hitler appointed Josef Goebbels Minister of Propaganda for the Nazi party in Germany and charged him with responsibility for mobilizing support for Hitler's domestic and foreign policies.

Certainly, political propaganda is not limited exclusively to totalitarian states. Following the entry of the United States into World War II, the Roosevelt Administration engaged numerous scholars, journalists and film makers to maintain American support for the fight against the Fascists. At the same time that Goebbels and his staff were manufacturing propaganda in support of Nazism, the United States recruited such film makers as Frank Capra, best known until then for his sentimental Hollywood films, invariably championing the value of the individual, such as *It Happened One Night*, *Mr. Smith Goes to Washington* and *It's a Wonderful Life*. Capra produced for the United States Army a series of seven widely shown films entitled *Why We Fight*, mobilizing American support for the war against Germany, Italy and Japan.

While a national government or a religious institution such as the Catholic Church are obvious examples of institutions that may sponsor propaganda, less well-known and smaller institutions are also potential sponsors of propagandistic messages. Scholars of propaganda point out that commercial advertising might be considered propaganda insofar as the objective of that advertising is the maintenance of the system of commerce. Similarly, social movements have often been accused of engaging in propaganda to maintain the institutions with which they are affiliated. However, to classify advertising or the messages of social movements as propagandistic, we need more than just the recognition of institutional sponsorship.

The second definitive characteristic of propaganda is its *fundamental concern with effects*. Propaganda, like all forms of persuasion, may have unintended and collateral consequences, but the final measure of propaganda is its ability to implement desired outcomes. From the point of view of the propagandist or the propagandist's audience, no other question is as important as the pragmatic question of effectiveness. As sociologist Jacques Ellul describes this imperative:

> Propaganda is made, first of all, because of a will to action, for the purpose of effectively arming policy and giving irresistible power to its decisions. This is the supreme law, which must never be forgotten when the phenomenon of propaganda is analyzed. Ineffective propaganda is no propaganda.[9]

Thus, other questions—even the question of ethics, to which we shall return later—are secondary to the iron law of efficiency in the practice of propaganda. A tragic example of propaganda's concern with effects comes from the Nazi propaganda during World War II.

Fritz Hippler was a film maker for Hitler and oversaw the making of official newsreels under the authority of propaganda minister Goebbels. Hippler directed *The Eternal Jew*, a propaganda film of almost unbelievable hatred toward Jews, shot in the Warsaw ghettos of 1940.[10] As public affairs commentator Bill Moyers described the film, "Audiences gasped at scenes... sensationalizing the Jewish practice of ritual butchering. The shock of such scenes reinforced a calculated campaign of anti-Semitism aimed at arousing German emotions to accept the coming Nazi slaughter of the Jewish people."[11] The film likened German Jews to swarming rats, carriers of disease and destruction, and added: "Just like the Jews among mankind, rats represent the very essence of malicious and subterranean destruction." The film also attacked such prominent Jews as Charlie Chaplin and Albert Einstein.[12]

In a 1982 interview, Hippler recalled (in imperfect English) the explicit purposes of such films as *The Eternal Jew*:

> The German people was not more anti-Jewish than all other peoples. The French people were much more anti-Jewish than the German people. And this fact didn't please to Hitler and to Goebbels. They both wanted to have the German people to be much more anti-Semitic than it was. All the journals, the press, and also by means of the film, the people was shown pictures to make them anti-Semitic.[13]

As commentator Bill Moyers grimly observed, the purpose of *The Eternal Jew*, like all propaganda, is action, action designed to further institutional goals:

> Looking at Fritz Hippler's film *The Eternal Jew*, we must keep reminding ourselves that the purpose of propaganda is action. The viewers were expected to do something about what they saw. When other human beings are compared to rats and vermin that spread disease, it takes no great leap of imagination to know what you're expected to do with the creatures.[14]

A third unique characteristic of propaganda is that it is *aimed at the masses*. Unlike other forms of institutional persuasion that conceptualize the audience as collections of autonomous, free-choosing individuals who may be targeted or segmented according to their attitudes or values, propaganda defines the audience as a mass in the classic sense explained in Chapter 10. Conceived as a crowd or a mob, the masses lose their individual identities. Propaganda regards its audience as undifferentiated aggregates with no strong sense of shared communal interests, not as individuals acting and deciding for the common good. From this perspective, a member of the masses is not responsible for his or her actions, is easy to incite to action, feels enormous pressure to conform to the behavior of the crowd and, therefore, is easy to manipulate.

It was the awareness of this characteristic of propaganda, the conception of the audience as an easily influenced mob, that launched the first major effort to study propaganda in the United States. Stunned by the demonstrable ability of Fascism to mobilize support for extreme political policies abhorrent to observers in other Western nations, the Institute for Propaganda Analysis (IPA) was chartered in 1937. The IPA channeled the efforts of American scholars from a variety of disciplines toward better understanding propaganda. The historians, political scientists and progressive thinkers who worked with the institute were concerned about new forms of persuasion that seemed to be redefining the public as an uncritical mass.[15] Consequently, they analyzed a variety of persuasive campaigns to expose the propagandistic elements contained there and to provide the public with ways of resisting propaganda. The major findings of the IPA will be discussed later in this chapter.

The fourth characteristic of propaganda is that *mass media are the channel of choice*. For the propagandist who conceives of his or her audience as a mass, the appropriate channel for communication is obvious. To reach the masses, the propagandist uses mass media. Films, books, network television, posters, billboards and the like are used not because they target a particular homogeneous audience but because they reach the largest, most heterogeneous audience. Techniques familiar to social movements, such as consciousness-raising in small groups or individual actions designed to attract publicity to the cause, are rarely a part of the propagandist's storehouse of techniques. Propaganda campaigns characteristically saturate the "marketplace of ideas" with a multitude of messages displayed to the crowd. One result of such mass-media saturation is that it can exert tremendous pressure against the rise of multiple viewpoints on an issue, since expressions of noninstitutional viewpoints are drowned in the flood of institutionally sponsored messages. Propaganda promotes the reduction of public issues to one slogan, one formulation of "the problem," one version of "the solution," one rank-ordering of values and priorities and one list of "god terms" and "devil terms." These become the common currency of discussion about the issues involved, since they are the symbols and ideas with which virtually everyone is familiar. If successful, propagandists expect the masses to act uniformly as a group rather than as autonomous, critically minded individuals.

The objective of producing a uniform response among the masses leads to a fifth unique characteristic of propaganda. *Propaganda relies on ideology* to justify or rationalize the existence of the favored institution and to legitimize the desired actions. As our definition of propaganda implies, the purpose of this type of persuasion is the maintenance of an institution. To accomplish this purpose, the propagandist creates attitudes that motivate behavior. Since the propagandist targets the masses and seeks uniformity of attitudes and behavior, he or she advances ideology to manipulate the audience. As a tool of propaganda, ideology provides a coherent system of beliefs or a worldview that justifies or rationalizes "the system" and "the system's" actions. For example, Nazi propaganda relied on a worldview or ideology of Aryan purity and superiority. Similarly, racism and apartheid practices typically rely on an ideology of White supremacy. Support for Desert Storm, the 1991 attack on Iraq, was justified by the United States in terms of the difference between how each political system was represented. Likewise, a host of institutions, both religious and political that maintain hierarchical structures and ask their members for obedience to authorities, frequently rely on an ideology of patriarchy—a worldview in which "father," usually defined as a powerful male, "knows best."

The sixth characteristic of propaganda, that *propaganda represses dissent*, is a direct result of its reliance on ideology. More than nearly any other form of persuasion, propaganda is notoriously subject to questions of ethics. As we discuss in the previous chapter, one characteristic of ideology is that it often presents only limited explanations of the events in our social world, and through this partiality it inhibits diversity. The ideological character of propaganda squashes dissent by omitting or repressing opposing points of view. Such repression of dissent contributes to the primary outcome of successful propaganda—uniformity in the response of the audience. In addition, this repression often leads to persuasive tactics that conceal something from the audience. Not only opposing points of view, but the source of messages, the reasons motivating persuaders and a host of other factors are concealed from audiences. For example, during August 1991, National Public Radio commentator Daniel Schorr reminded listeners of a scarcely noted historical fact: President George Bush made the decision to commit allied forces in the Persian Gulf to an eventual attack on Iraq in late October 1990, three months before the attack was launched, but gave strict instructions to political and military leaders that this decision was not to be announced before the midterm elections a few days later in early November. Such concealment inevitably raises ethical questions about propaganda. Later in this chapter we examine these ethical issues in greater detail.

Classical Analysis Of Propaganda

Classic propaganda theory arises largely from the work of the CPI and the IPA in the early part of the Twentieth Century. Because the research upon which it is based was driven by the urgent practical needs of wartime mobilization and morale, its scope tends also to be limited to the pragmatic. Classic propaganda theory asks the questions "What works? and why?" Findings of classic propaganda research center on the staging and sequencing of propagandistic messages, on the characteristics of such messages and on the means by which propaganda may be resisted.

Stages of Propaganda Campaigns

Like other forms of persuasion that can be studied from the Institutional Perspective, propaganda exists over a period of time. If, for example, a government is concerned about manipulating public opinion for the support of a war effort, then propaganda messages should begin before troops are actually committed and continue through the end of the conflict. Based on his study of political propaganda, religious conversion and other mass persuasion, psychologist J. A. C. Brown identifies three distinct stages to a propaganda effort.[16] Within each stage, several persuasive strategies are common.

First, is the pre-propaganda stage. During this period, the propagandist must gain and maintain attention. This is usually accomplished by causing the audience to feel emotional tension, usually guilt. Consider the events leading up to the Desert Storm Gulf War. News reports of the invasion of Kuwait by Iraq immediately captured public attention by emphasizing the swiftness with which the attack occurred and the haste with which the Kuwaiti royal family fled the country. Of course, small countries frequently fall prey to their larger, stronger neighbors. Commentators at the time pointed out that the Soviet military was similarly occupying Lithuania and that several African nations were under siege by their hostile neighbors. What maintained public attention during this pre-propaganda stage was the emotional tension created by the elaboration of the story. The media depicted Iraq as a military powerhouse, boasting chemical weapons and perhaps even nuclear capabilities, thereby posing a formidable threat to other countries in the region such as Saudi Arabia and the world as a whole. News stories also emphasized the vast oil reserves of Kuwait, instilling fear about the availability of petroleum for citizens throughout the world. Moreover, Kuwait and its similarly threatened neighbors were depicted as "friends" of the United States. Who among us would not feel guilt as we watched our friend's land overrun and our friend's wealth snatched up by someone else? Never mind that Iraq had been depicted as "our friend" only weeks earlier as the Bush Administration attempted to enlist the consent of Congress for an arms deal with Saddam Hussein, the leader of Iraq.

Once guilt and emotional tension awaken an audience to a problem, a propaganda campaign moves into a second stage. During this stage, the emotional tension is transferred to an "out-group," a separate group of people or institutions that the audience can blame for the emotional tension. The out-group may be identified through a variety of means. First propaganda may characterize the out-group with stereotypes. Second, propaganda may furnish the audience with "new" names for the out-group. Third, these stereotypes and the derogatory names associated with them are repeated until they become part of the storehouse of common knowledge. Finally, propaganda may pinpoint particular individuals or institutions as representatives of the out-group, thereby personifying the object of emotional tension.

If we return to the Gulf War, this second stage becomes clearer. The invaders from Iraq were immediately cast as the out-group. Careful to explain that the U.S. had no quarrel with the people of Iraq, the Bush Administration cast Hussein, his government and his army as formidable villains. Hussein was described as "another Hitler," tagging him with the most derogatory name of the Twentieth Century. His soldiers who occupied Kuwait were described as "baby-killers," who unhooked the life support systems of prematurely delivered infants in Kuwaiti hospitals. Although some of the soldiers in his so-called "Red Guard" were touted as tough and experienced fighters, those who occupied Kuwait were depicted as unsophisticated savages who mistook facial cream for mayonnaise as they plundered the stores and markets of Kuwait. Even the Iraqi citizens, with whom we allegedly had no quarrel, were depicted as helpless dupes of Hussein, the dictator.

In the third stage, propaganda impels the audience to action. The action generally suggests obliterating the out-group, the source of the audience's discomfort. Operation Desert Storm, the massive bombing attack that destroyed the infrastructure of Iraq and decimated its military troops, served this function in the Gulf War. Such obliteration may be actual as in the Gulf War or symbolic, concentrating on a symbolic killing. In Nazi Germany, for example, propaganda caused the actual elimination of millions of people. In the Soviet Union during the 1930's and again during the 1950's and 1960's such action involved purges in which not only actual killing took place, but also symbolic killings which eliminated dissidents by sending them to Siberia or to mental hospitals from which they would not return. Even when allowed to remain physically within the society, such dissidents were barred from speaking on political matters, refused the right to publish their books, and so forth. Regardless of whether the death it describes is real or symbolic, propaganda at this stage maintains its institution by purging that institution's perceived enemies.

CLASSIC TECHNIQUES OF PROPAGANDA

One of the most widely quoted sources for techniques of propaganda is Adolf Hitler's book, *Mein Kampf*. Among the techniques recommended by Hitler, four stand out as exemplary of the famous propaganda campaign pursued during the Third Reich. In addition, these four have often emerged in other propaganda campaigns. They are: (1) Tell the audience what is agreeable. (2) Simplify the message. (3) Repeat the message. (4) Emphasize "big" lies rather than "small" lies. Each one of these rules for propaganda incorporates a number of the assumptions about the audience and the objective of propaganda.

Nazi Germany employed the first tactic, telling the audience what is agreeable, by emphasizing the superiority of the Aryan race and the inevitability of German victory. Propaganda films by Fritz Hippler, one of Hitler's propagandists, emphasized the beauty, strength and discipline of the German people by showing well-dressed, well-groomed, well-drilled German soldiers marching in front of appreciative and adoring throngs of people. Much of Hitler's rhetoric recalled familiar myths and folk stories that glorified the German state. Meanwhile, Hitler propagandists forbade any suggestion of weakness or inferiority of the elite German "race." For example, when the black American athlete, Jesse Owens, won gold medals during the Munich Olympics in 1936, observers noted Hitler's unhappiness that his competitors with Aryan blood had lost to someone from an "inferior" race.

The second and third tactics, keeping the message simple and repeating it, are probably best illustrated by the Nazi propaganda concerning the "problem of the Jews." Prior to Hitler's rise to power, Germany suffered terrible economic conditions. The nation had lost World War I and was reeling from that disaster. The reasons for their troubles were complex, ranging from the heavy cost of the unsuccessful war effort to poor leadership following the war. But Hitler's propagandists provided a simple explanation of the cause and repeated it over and over again. The Jews instigated all of Germany's troubles according to the propaganda. As described earlier in this chapter, by simplifying the nature of a group of people—stereotyping—all were condemned. Films, posters, pamphlets and speeches to large rallies repeated "the problem" in numerous locations and at numerous times. While some citizens resisted such a simple interpretation of events and others dismissed these simplistic blaming techniques as mere political hype, many others came to accept the explanation owing to the sheer force of repetition and the appeal of finding a simple answer to a complex problem.

Hitler's propagandists advanced the "big" lie on a number of occasions. For example, following the invasion of Poland, German propaganda explained that the Poles had asked the Germans to annex their territory. The very idea of a sovereign nation requesting an invasion which killed many of its soldiers and citizens and led to an occupation which subjected it to a variety of brutally repressive measures is, of course, preposterous. Yet, German propaganda films and public announcements purported that the Poles were very happy about the arrival of German soldiers. "Campaign in Poland," a documentary film produced by Hippler's propaganda machine and distributed in the United States and around the world, justified the September 1939 invasion of Poland as a "liberation" of the Germans living within the borders of that country (borders Germany disputed) and a retribution for injustices these German people had suffered at the hands of the Poles. Deluged with reassuring images of grateful, cheering Poles throwing flowers at the lines of German tanks, observes commentator Bill Moyers, "Intelligent citizens within Germany watched and believed."[17] German propaganda lied for years about the existence of death camps which subjected political dissidents and non-Aryans to the most inhumane conditions and finally to murder. Instead, German propaganda hailed "family relocation centers," where "security risks" in a time of war were provided comfortable living quarters in which they might survive the war. The cruel irony displayed in propaganda film releases that showed well-dressed professionals listening to first-class symphonic renditions of classical music in these comfortable "relocation centers," while in fact millions were stripped of all material and spiritual well-being and sent to their death, illustrates the "big lie." The reluctance of people around the world to believe reports of Nazi atrocities that trickled out of German occupied territory throughout the war testifies to the power of the "big lie." One could imagine small discrepancies and deceptions, but the concealment of such a huge extermination operation was so unbelievable that the big lie was accepted by too many for too long.

Of course, Hitler is not the only leader to have used propaganda techniques like those just discussed. Practically every government has engaged in telling the people what they want to hear in a simplified message that is repeated and that often contains big lies. Some even argue that the public's reluctance to believe numerous stories of atrocities, ranging from those during World War II to many contemporary abuses of human rights in the Middle East, Latin America, Africa and even here in the United States, result from our skepticism about messages that seem too incredible to imagine. Following the exposure of U.S. propaganda during World War I and revelations about U.S. sponsored propagada, scholars at centers such as the Institute for Propaganda Analysis began to study propaganda techniques in earnest.

The IPA assembled a list of seven techniques of propaganda that they found to be particularly predominant in the United States in the 1930's.[18] The reader should recognize many of these techniques as obvious consequences of various concepts developed within the Classical or Symbolist Perspective of persuasion.

Name-calling attaches "devil terms" and strongly loaded labels to persons holding opposing views and thereby encourages the audience to respond to the label, not the person. For example, during the autumn of 1990 President George Bush referred to Saddam Hussein as "another Hitler" to help mobilize American support for the planned attack against Iraqi forces in Kuwait and Iraq. Commentators who debated the historical validity of the analogy missed the point completely; simply attaching the name to Hussein under such circumstances inevitably triggered popular sentiments against him.

Glittering generalities attach a "god term" or other label with a strong positive connotation to everything associated with one's cause. For example, during the civil war in Nicaragua in the 1980's, official U.S. sources consistently referred to the rebels there as "freedom fighters," suggesting a patriotic and democratic impulse on the part of all who opposed the Communist regime. Opponents to U.S. aid for those rebels in Nicaragua faced a difficult challenge, even though some of the rebels were known to be Fascists or simply thugs, if the public accepted such a generalization that "glittered" with a revered American term like "freedom."

Transfer uses prestige suggestion by citing, quoting or referring to high status authorities in support of one's own position. Thus Roman Catholic propaganda invokes the authority of the Pope and the church hierarchy as the authority for its claims. Similarly, political movements in America frequently strive to show that their ambitions square with the intentions of the architects of the American Revolution or the Constitution.

Testimonial uses the concrete, personal stories of individuals to dramatize one's position. This tactic was put to extremely effective use by President Ronald Reagan, who frequently used anecdotes and letters from "ordinary citizens" in his televised speeches to evoke support for his administration's policies.

"Plain-Folks" repeatedly stresses images of identification between persuader and audience, downplaying status differences and claiming to be "of them" or to "speak for them." During the months of troop build-up before the Persian Gulf war, Saddam Hussein frequently appeared on Iraqi television moving among his troops, enduring their conditions, wearing similar clothes and eating their food with them. As war closed in, such tactics attempted to downplay the differences in rank and consequence between persuader and audience, mobilizing support for Hussein and preventing the loss of morale that might follow if the Iraqi troops believed that Hussein did not share their commitment and, hence, their risks.

Card-Stacking selects only the most extreme evidence, whether positive or negative, to "stack the deck" in favor of one's position. In Chapter 3 we note how Ronald Reagan's "facts are stubborn things" speech to the 1988 Republican National Convention made highly selective use of economic statistics to represent—and occasionally misrepresent—his administration's domestic record in the most favorable terms possible by comparison to the Carter administration's record. Such card-stacking techniques let the propagandist satisfy the conventional expectations that persuasive claims be "supported" with "evidence," yet the evidence is so selected and manipulated that it will allow no other possible conclusion to be drawn.

Band-Wagon encourages the audience to adopt a belief or action because "everyone else is doing it." American opponents to the Persian Gulf War faced the full brunt of this technique in 1991, following the declared end of the war and the return of American troops. During that spring and summer, Americans were deluged with images of enormous homecoming parades in Washington, D.C. and elsewhere, filled with displays of weaponry and cheering; flag-waving throngs welcomed the service personnel home. Nearly every town in America displayed yellow ribbons, symbols commemorating the homecoming of the military personnel. In the face of these images, seemingly everywhere, many Americans found it increasingly difficult not to "join the parade" and express support for the war.

Significantly these various techniques are frequently employed in messages that take on the form and appearance of logical argumentation, such as we discuss in Chapter 3. Propaganda frequently refers to itself as "informative" rather than "persuasive" in nature. In film it often appears in the form of the newsreel and the documentary. It frequently stresses its reliance upon "facts" and the apparent logical necessity of its conclusions. At this point, the tests for evaluating reasoning found in Chapter 3 serve as a means of judging these conclusions. However, there is a fundamental difference here, consequently, the classical analysis of reasoning cannot completely evaluate these classic propaganda techniques. The Classical Perspective on persuasion assumes that argumentation, evidence-use and reasoning, no matter how partisan and dedicated they may be, are bound by a disinterested idea of the truth. In practice, we assume that the process of reasoning leading to a conclusion justifies that conclusion. In propaganda, however, because of its primary emphasis on effectiveness, this is not the case. Instead, the appearance of a reasonable argument is merely one technique of the propagandist, designed to achieve an effect quite apart from the reasonable content of the argument. Because audiences usually respond positively when they believe they are being "reasoned with," this technique is often persuasively effective. Yet, at the first indication that such techniques are not effective the propagandist drops these appearances and resorts to other, more effective tactics such as the torch-light rally or the television spot filled with "feel-good" images.[19]

Although propaganda may choose to call its motives "informational" rather than "persuasive"—as in the case of the Office of War Information for whom Frank Capra worked in World War II—it makes no secret that its purposes are to influence our behaviors and attitudes in specific ways. However, the propagandist sometimes avoids drawing specific conclusions in an explicit manner. The techniques by which propagandists avoid drawing conclusions include many that the reader may recognize from classical and symbolist persuasion theories. For example, the message may build its argument so that the omitted elements are familiar or obvious to an audience, explained by the Classical Perspective's theory of enthymemes. Alternatively such messages may evoke identification through nonverbal or nondiscursive means, as explained within the Symbolist Perspective. The Office of War Information summarized very well the general principle in a policy directive during World War II, advising propagandists to avoid drawing conclusions explicitly in persuasive messages in these four general cases:

> If the conclusion seems to be one the audience could likely arrive at on its own.
>
> If an argument is weak enough that it might attract attention to itself if it was spelled out explicitly.
>
> If the conclusion asks the audience to take risks or make sacrifices that they might resent or refuse if asked outright.
>
> If one's argument might have consequences one cannot predict, and one would prefer to avoid full responsibility for them later, should something go wrong.[20]

Remember that propaganda advances institutional goals through mass persuasion. As a consequence, not every instance employing "band-wagon" techniques, suppressed conclusions and so forth is an instance of propaganda. Neither is every instance of persuasion on a controversial topic propaganda.

DOCTRINE, AUDIENCE AND RESISTANCE

While all propaganda relies on ideology to promote its purposes, classic propaganda tends to rely on ideology that is formalized as doctrine. Classic propaganda is *doctrinaire*, meaning that the institutions being promoted have a doctrine which defines the fundamental principles that brought the institution into existence and has been formalized and publicly proclaimed. For example, persuaders from the American Communist Party, the John Birch Society and the First Baptist Church speak for institutions with formalized doctrines, while representatives of the National

Organization for Women or Democratic and Republican political campaigns do not. The latter may endorse or oppose statements of policies, lists that may change with the public agenda, but these statements do not define the institutions themselves. Analyst of persuasion Roderick P. Hart identifies four general characteristics of persuasion by doctrinaire speakers supported by such proclaimed principles.[21] First, such persuasion relies heavily on the assumptions and axioms of the formal doctrine and is limited only to those arguments, images and forms which can be derived consistently from the doctrine itself. Doctrine defines the ultimate justification for actions and events: for the Marxist, the material forces of history; for the Christian, God's will expressed through Jesus and the prophets and so on. Doctrine similarly defines the "god terms" and "devil terms" in which actions are to be explained, defended or attacked.

Second, doctrinal persuasion relies broadly on assumptions and beliefs shared with the audience and formalized in doctrine to complete the logic of its arguments. When addressing a largely sympathetic audience, the same general principles—drawn from doctrine—can be found again and again, acting as warrants to legitimate the proper conclusions to be drawn from a wide variety of data. Similarly, as we typically find in propaganda and in persuasion to sympathetic audiences, persuaders frequently leave these warrants unstated, allowing the audience to complete the logic of the argument themselves. Conversely, propagandists who attempt to convert or demobilize a hostile audience will be much more careful to select as warrants generalizations which are more specific to their argument, that are less general and sweeping, and to stress these principles explicitly.

Third, the individuals who are the nominal sources for propaganda—the speaker, the author, the film maker and so on—typically present themselves as agents who speak for the institution's doctrines. The persuader's own opinions and positions receive little attention, while institutional and doctrinal authorities are frequently quoted and referred to. Thus, consistent with earlier findings in this chapter, the rhetoric of propaganda de-emphasizes the role of the individual, even the individual persuader.

Finally, highly doctrinaire propaganda stresses the certainty and stability of the relationship between the persuader or the institution on whose behalf he or she acts and the audience or masses. This emphasis can be recognized in the importance given to venerated individuals and images in such persuasion. For example, notes Hart:

> In supporting their assertions, the Mormons refer to the scripture, the prophets, and Christ; the Catholics mention former church tribunals and bishops' decrees; the John Birch Society speakers find support in the words of the founding fathers and the experiences of the ancient republics, and cite many historical instances of governmental corruption. All of these rhetorical choices are, apparently, attempts to bring the weight of precedent to bear on current situations.[22]

Such tactics reinforce the dominance of the doctrine and its history. Further, by elevating the principles of doctrine to the status of history, the persuader is more easily able to portray the audience itself as fundamentally connected to the institution's goals: not "the institution must struggle forward" or "the institution is in danger," but rather "*we* must struggle" and "*we* are in danger." By uniting an audience with the institution whose goals propaganda is designed to support, classic propaganda makes resistance to its persuasion much more difficult.

Classic research in propaganda characterizes it primarily as a collection of techniques by which institutional persuaders can achieve desired effects in their audiences. Given its urgently pragmatic motives, this research also investigated the conditions which made audiences resistant to propaganda and the techniques by which this resistance might be created or reinforced. Such researchers found that the greater the education and intelligence of the audience the less persuasible the audience would be and the less likely were classic propaganda techniques to be effective.[23]

Ironically, many of the techniques identified for inducing resistance to propaganda are themselves strongly propagandistic in nature, frequently grouped under the Orwellian heading "counter-propaganda." For example, if an individual can be induced to make a public declaration of opinion on a topic, that person will probably later be less susceptible to propaganda directed against that opinion than if she had kept her opinion private.[24] This phenomenon can be readily explained by the balance theories covered in Chapter 4. The individual who makes such a public commitment will feel pressure to remain consistent with her own public actions and declarations.

More to the point, the classic approach to propaganda analysis considers free and open flow of information in a democratic society to be the guarantee of its citizens' ability to resist propaganda. As we see later in this chapter, this leads to a practical and ethical dilemma: what happens when it is the democratic society itself that is the source of the propaganda?

PROPAGANDA IN THE MODERN INSTITUTIONAL SOCIETY

In the years following World War II, both the practice and study of propaganda moved into a new era. The modern industrialized states moved from a period of extreme wartime mobilization to the uneasy and often broken peace of the Cold War. At the same time, the pervasiveness and sophistication of the media of mass communication increased. As a result, additional theories about propaganda emerged that offered additional guides for analyzing institutionally sponsored persuasion. No longer does propaganda analysis limit itself to the message-centered interests of the classic approach. Instead, expanded theories of propaganda have merged classic analysis with the analysis of techniques of institutional organization. As a consequence, propaganda's importance in preserving institutional dominance becomes clearer.

ELLUL'S CATEGORIES FOR PROPAGANDA

One of the most influential contemporary scholars of propaganda is French sociologist Jacques Ellul.[25] Among the first contemporary theorists to systematically explain forms of propaganda common in times other than war, Ellul defines propaganda as "a set of methods employed by an organized group that wants to bring about the active or passive participation in its actions of a mass of individuals, psychologically unified through psychological manipulations and incorporated in an organization."[26] In his elaboration of this definition, Ellul draws a number of distinctions between the type of propaganda as explained by classical theories of propaganda and more contemporary types of propaganda. As rhetorical critic Randall

Bytwerk points out, Ellul's distinctions are particularly helpful in understanding the differences among propaganda that emerge from various parts of the world, for example differences between American and Chinese propaganda.[27]

Ellul distinguishes the types of propaganda according to four characteristics. First, he distinguishes between *political propaganda and sociological propaganda*.[28] Classic propaganda theory concentrates on political propaganda where political institutions pursue clearly ideological goals through deliberate and calculated methods. Sociological propaganda, on the other hand, uses the sociological context to spread an ideology, often without any deliberate intentions guiding the process. Like the process of socialization itself, a variety of communication systems reiterate a similar worldview, thereby conditioning the masses to accept a particular ideology. Ellul observes:

> Sociological propaganda expresses itself in many different ways—in advertising, in the movies (commercial and non-political films), in technology in general, in education, in the *Reader's Digest*; and in social service, case work, and settlement houses. All these influences are in basic accord with each other and lead spontaneously in the same direction; one hesitates to call all this propaganda.
>
> ...We have not grouped these activities together arbitrarily—they express the same basic notions and interact to make man adopt this particular way of life.[29]

As this description suggests, Ellul is describing as propaganda what we describe in the previous chapter as ideological persuasion. Still, insofar as such a diffuse network of messages is institutionally sponsored and promotes the objectives of those institutions, it might be considered propagandistic as well.

The second distinction Ellul draws is between *agitative and integrative propaganda*.[30] He points out that traditionally only agitative propaganda, the type of propaganda used to motivate a mass public to act, is studied. Agitative propaganda spurs revolutions, wars or even religious movements such as the Crusades. In contrast, integrative propaganda pacifies the mass audience, rendering people passive and often apathetic about public affairs. Integrative propaganda promotes the very conformity that is so necessary to redefining the audience as a mass. Until the recent changes of Glasnost, Perestroika and the break-up of the Soviet Union or the unsuccessful student demonstrations in the People's Republic of China, both of these regimes concentrated on integrative propaganda designed to keep their citizenry from suggesting modifications or changes within the system. In Western democracies integrative propaganda seems in evidence as well. Ideologies such as individualism or consumerism make sense of the world for citizens who follow the teachings of these ideologies and, therefore, pursue individual goals and material success rather than channeling their energies into political action and reform. As Bytwerk explains, the individualistic emphasis of our mass society makes "the individual, removed from the moorings of family and faith, likelier to accept the perceived attitudes of 'everybody else,' or to accept peculiar ideas restoring him to lost certainty."[31]

Thirdly, Ellul explains that while classic propaganda is *vertical*, contemporary propaganda is *horizontal*.[32] Vertical propaganda works from the top down. A government agency, for example, conceives an ideology and implements persuasive strategies to disseminate that ideology to the general public, as was the case with Hitler's Ministry of Propaganda directed by Goebbels. Horizontal propaganda works from the ground up. Small groups of ordinary people may chain out ideas that quickly develop into full-blown ideologies that then spread throughout a culture. Ellul notes that vertical propaganda conceptualizes the audience as a passive loner within a crowd:

> One trait of vertical propaganda is that the propagandee remains alone even though he is part of a crowd. His shouts of enthusiasm or hatred, though part of the shouts of the crowd, do not put him in communication with others; his shouts are only a response to the leader....[T]his kind of propaganda requires a passive attitude from those subjected to it. They are seized, they are manipulated, they are committed; they experience what they are asked to experience; they are transformed into objects.[33]

Horizontal propaganda, on the other hand, creates at least the illusion of choice for an audience by working through audience participation. Ellul cites Chinese propaganda, in which people are required to attend group discussions about the teaching of Mao and carefully watched to make sure that they verbalize only the accepted doctrine, and cites group dynamics in human relationships, a technique used widely in our culture in which "group facilitators" guide discussants toward expressing "appropriate" ideas, as illustrative of horizontal propaganda.[34] Because participation in horizontal propaganda appears to be voluntary, it exerts powerful influence over the beliefs and attitudes of those who participate. Because horizontal propaganda seeks conformity and is based in group interactions, it frequently leaves individuals feeling altogether committed to their "group," thereby reinforcing sociological and integrative propaganda.

Finally, Ellul draws a distinction between *rational and irrational propaganda*.[35] Classic propaganda tends to rely on irrational messages. As Bytwerk points out, "a key principle of Nazi propaganda was emotional appeal."[36] However, contemporary audiences have embraced a more scientific and technological worldview. As Ellul explains, "modern man needs a relation to facts, a self-justification to convince himself that by acting in a certain way he is obeying reason and proved experience."[37] Consequently, much modern propaganda concentrates on information, facts, scientific explanation and other tactics designed to make propaganda messages sound reasonable and factual. In addition, the modern propagandist develops elaborate systems to provide appropriate credentials for sources that confer legitimacy on the ideas that are presented to the mass audience. Commercial advertising, for example, emphasizes statistics and scientific sounding qualities of goods and services for the consumer. In politics, government officials frequently resort to complicated jargon and claims of special access to information as they attempt to manipulate public opinion. In more diffuse, integrative propaganda, news organizations may follow a variety of norms regarding objectivity and attribution of sources, like those discussed in Chapter 10, that announce their messages as rational and factual. Such trends in contemporary propaganda make intellectuals and others who are immersed in a worldview that values facts and rationality more susceptible to propagandistic messages.

Ellul's four dimensions of contemporary propaganda—sociological, integrative, horizontal and rational—set the stage for several other contemporary theoretical developments in this area. The first three characteristics provide a basis for scholars who have attempted to describe the communication process at work within contemporary propaganda. The last characteristic helps to explain one of the most important and relatively new propaganda techniques, disinformation campaigns. We will consider each in turn.

The Process of Contemporary Propaganda

In their extensive study of propaganda, communication scholars Garth Jowett and Victoria O'Donnell developed a model of the process of propaganda that they describe as follows:

> The process of propaganda takes the form of a message flow through a network system that includes propaganda agents, the media, and a social network, originating with an institution and ending with the possibility of response from the public or a target audience within the public. The message flow is contained within a cultural rim that is itself placed within a social-historical context.[38]

Jowett and O'Donnell's process view of propaganda contrasts with the stage-model of propaganda presented earlier in this chapter in that it looks directly at the systemic features of propaganda. Their position begins with the idea that successful propaganda must take into account the social-historical context. That means taking into account that the propagandist is influenced by past propaganda and by current events. They cite the following examples of past influences:

> For example, the idea that freedom is worth dying for was the basis for Patrick Henry's "Give Me Liberty or Give Me Death" speech in the time of the American Revolution. The same idea provided the impulse for the anti-Communist slogan, "Better Dead Than Red" almost 200 years later. In another culture, the Middle East, present day propaganda can be traced back to the social-historical context of the origins of Mohammedanism in the seventh century and the subsequent spread of the Islamic religion. Thirteen centuries later, Mohammed's charge to his disciples to convert the infidels and be willing to die fighting for the faith still shapes the content that takes form through modern technologies. When the Palestinians commit what Americans may think are "suicidal" acts, they do so believing that a death for the cause will assure them a place on the right hand of God.[39]

Of course, present context also influences propaganda. The communication technologies and general life circumstances common to the times influence the types of messages that a propagandist may use. For example, the terrible economic conditions in Germany during Hitler's rise to power made his extremist arguments about an international banking conspiracy more believable. And, as Jowett and O'Donnell explain, "Martin Luther's ability to reach his audience" when he led a break from the Catholic Church in the sixteenth century, "was made possible by the development of the printing press."[40]

Within this social-historical context, Jowett and O'Donnell note the importance of a "*cultural rim*," a cultural system composed of events, economy, government, ideology and societal myths that in various ways shape the communication systems available to propagandists and the relationships between those communication systems and various other institutions. This network of institutions, events, ideas and myths constrain propagandistic choices. But within those constraints, propaganda is developed and implemented according to the following process:

1. An institution generally initiates and fosters propaganda due to its organizational and financial powers.
2. Propaganda agents facilitate messages directly and through the media for an institution; often there is a hierarchy of agents with a chain of command to ensure that the message will be homogenous.
3. Propaganda agents select and use the media to send their messages, often concealing the original source of the message through the use of public relations or other agencies.
4. A social network composed of opinion leaders, small groups of propaganda agents, and/or others facilitate rumors relevant to the propaganda innocently or deliberately throughout a social network.
5. Public responses to propaganda, such as ignoring it, arguing against it, or producing the desired behavior are measured by the propagandists at the same time that these responses feed back into the cultural rim, thereby altering the social-historical context.[41]

The process of propaganda described by Jowett and O'Donnell suggest several interesting explanations of contemporary propaganda. They note:

> Propaganda creates and is created by strange and powerful bedfellows. Special interests cause groups that are normally diverse to unite in a common cause. The abortion controversy has brought the far right and the Roman Catholics together. The antipornography movement has united the Moral Majority and feminists.[42]

Why do such coalitions occur? The answer seems to lie within the social networks that are used to spread propaganda and the interactive nature of propaganda as the public responds to propaganda messages and influences the social-historical context. By examining the process of propaganda as a communication system, as Jowett and O'Donnell do, we can thus explain events that sometimes seem inexplicable.

Another interesting feature of contemporary propaganda that emerges from Jowett and O'Donnell's model is the use of propaganda agents, people or institutions that design and transmit propaganda messages for others. Sometimes these agents are readily identifiable, as is the case with public relations firms contracted by an institution to spread an ideology. For example, R. J. Reynolds Tobacco Company for many years enlisted the assistance of professionals in public relations to design and provide non-product advertisements that present seemingly factual information about the lack of health risks and the importance of personal freedom that are attendant to smoking in our culture.[43] At other times the agents of propaganda may be carefully concealed, as is frequently the case with propaganda campaigns initiated by governmental bodies such as the Central Intelligence Agency in the United States or the KGB in the former Soviet Union.[44] The use of "backchannels," unofficial sources of news within an organization; "leaks," purposefully released information that masquerades as an "inside scoop;" "fronts," organizations established solely to provide a cover story for the person providing the information and so on are all tactics that deflect attention from an original source and conceal the sponsors of propaganda. This use of agents of propaganda lends an organizational flavor to the process that is important but frequently overlooked by students of classical propaganda.

Ethics And Propaganda

Given our discussion so far, mentioning "ethics" and "propaganda" together may strike many readers as a contradiction in terms. Propaganda analyst Ted Smith declares that "[t]he penultimate characteristic of propaganda is its use of techniques that are *often unethical*."[45] Certainly, propaganda has ethically troubling aspects that stem from its disregard for the judgment of the individual and a preoccupation with effectiveness. However, those who would simply reject all propaganda on ethical grounds may find themselves excluding as unethical a number of techniques and principles of persuasion that are just as common to campaigns or social movements as to propaganda. Moreover, those who reject all propaganda as unethical may find themselves hard pressed to justify not using counter-propaganda techniques, such as those initiated by Frank Capra in response to the Nazi propaganda machine during World War II. Therefore, a closer examination of the ethical dimensions of propaganda is needed.

One typology of the forms of propaganda that addresses ethical concerns divides propaganda into three categories: white, gray and black.[46] According to O'Donnell and Jowett:

> *White* propaganda comes from a source which is identified correctly and communicates accurate information....
>
> *Gray* propaganda is when the source may or may not be correctly identified and when the accuracy of information is uncertain....
>
> *Black* propaganda is when a false source is given and lies, fabrications, and deceptions are spread by the propagandist.[47]

Black propaganda is obviously unethical. Hitler's "big lies" or *disinformation campaigns* which use false sources to confer legitimacy on one point of view or destroy the legitimacy of another point of view are obvious examples. A recent example of such a disinformation campaign involves a propagandistic message designed by the former Soviet KGB to discredit the United States within Third World countries.[48] In 1985 a Soviet magazine published a story that claimed the American military genetically engineered the AIDS virus in a laboratory while researching biological weapons. The story was attributed to an Indian news source. By April of 1987, the story had been reported in more than 60 countries around the world, including by Dan Rather on the CBS Evening News. Unfortunately, such tactics are not limited to the former Soviet KGB. It is now well known that the United States conducted a disinformation campaign aimed at the Libyan leader Muammar Kaddafi prior to bombing his headquarters, and many suspect that news reports about Saddam Hussein's military strength and access to nuclear weapons during the Gulf War were the product of similar black propaganda.

Gray propaganda is less clear in its ethical implications. Often less deliberate in its deceptiveness than black propaganda, gray propaganda may include information that is inaccurate and may or may not correctly identify the correct source. Sometimes, such propaganda may be judged ethical and other times not. White propaganda, on the other hand, is almost always accepted as ethical because of its accuracy and forthrightness concerning sources.

The ethical standards that emerge from O'Donnell and Jowett's typology clearly concentrate on truth and truthfulness—accuracy of information and clarity of intention through the identification of sources. These standards are useful, but may not be sufficient for assessing the ethics of propaganda within the institutional context discussed in this chapter. One event that illustrates the problem involves Frank Capra's recollections of his work as a counter-propagandist during World War II. In an interview with Bill Moyers, Capra displayed his discomfort with even white propaganda and raised a question that sets the tone for the remainder of our discussion on ethics.[49]

Frank Capra described his mission in producing his *Why We Fight* propaganda films in simple terms: "Give the boys a reason to fight *and don't lie*." It was important to the conscience of Capra and the American propagandists that they could defend these messages as based on "the facts" and "the truth," and what could be more truthful than letting the enemy describe in his own words and images his own villainy? The footage used in *Why We Fight* was largely taken from captured German, Italian and Japanese propaganda documentary films, a strategy that the propagandists found rhetorically effective but only somewhat ethically comforting. Forty years after the end of World War II, both Hippler and Capra lived quiet lives of retirement, yet Hippler seemed clearly more content than Capra with the parts they had once played in the "war of ideas." As Moyers recalled, Capra came to the studio for a 1982 PBS interview carrying a series of photos documenting Nazi atrocities:

> I was surprised when Frank Capra brought those still photos of the concentration camps with him to our interview. I hadn't expected it. He talked about them in a sad and incredulous voice, as if still stunned by the revelation all those years later. He had made a series of propaganda films because, as he said, "our freedom is at stake."...And yet, Capra was uncomfortable, enough so to bring the photos as an additional justification for having himself been a propagandist, even a propagandist on democracy's behalf. Propaganda is not a disinterested search for truth, and because it isn't, it defies everything Frank Capra believed in, just as it embodied everything that Hippler's mentality so readily accepted. It's not the least of this century's paradoxes that something so potentially dangerous for truth and freedom became an indispensable weapon in the arsenal of their defense.[50]

Capra's ambivalence about propaganda on behalf of freedom is widely shared. The uneasy truce between propaganda and the ideology of American democracy represents an ongoing dilemma. For example, the film *The Eternal Jew* is now archived at the National Center for Jewish Film at Brandeis University, which has refused to release it for public viewing on the grounds that it will foster anti-Semitism and hatred. Critics argue that First Amendment principles demand that the film, offensive as it is, should be available to those who want to see it and add that the film is available through other purchase and rental sources.[51] The controversy highlights the ethical predicament of propaganda tactics, regardless of how high-minded the institutional cause they serve. Half a century after they were made, these instances of propaganda can corrode the processes of intellectual inquiry and individual freedom, even when—as in the case of *Why We Fight*—they were intended to preserve those values.

The danger to individual integrity and freedom posed by classic propaganda also exists in the more subtle types of contemporary propaganda described by Ellul. Sociological propaganda that integrates a public by spreading horizontally and emphasizing rationality may in some ways pose even greater risks because it presents an illusion of democracy and a free marketplace of ideas. Ellul points to the danger of such an illusion:

> If I am in favor of democracy, I can only regret that propaganda renders the true exercise of it almost impossible. But I think it would be even worse to entertain any illusions about a co-existence of true democracy and propaganda. Nothing is worse in times of danger than to live in a dream world.[52]

In a world which allows such propaganda to flourish, the typical response of concerned citizens is to engage in counter-propaganda and critical analysis of propaganda. However, we should question the ethicality of these responses with as much vigor as we question the ethicality of propaganda. As we note earlier in this chapter, often counter-propaganda and even critical analysis degenerates into a partisan, polemical response that displays most of the characteristics of the propaganda it was designed to counter. The result may be cynicism rather than empowerment. In his discussion of the propaganda common to contemporary democracies, Bytwerk explains that "the critical impulse remains strong," but he observes that "criticism is often now only that, pointing out undeniable evil without giving a convincing view of the world as it ought rightly be."[53] An ethical response to propaganda requires both critical analysis and concern for the ethics of one's analysis, the kind of concern raised by Moyer's interview with Frank Capra.

CRITICAL FOCUS: *TRIUMPH OF THE WILL*

We should be prepared to respond to propaganda. The following questions promote an awareness of the tactics, purposes and consequences of propagandistic persuasion. Answering these questions about a particular propaganda message requires that you already have some knowledge about the source of the propaganda and its purposes, since this information is necessary even to designate persuasive messages as propaganda. These questions can help us understand the propagandistic tactics of *Triumph of the Will.*

CRITICAL QUESTIONS

1. Which of the **general characteristics** of propaganda does the message display?

2. According to Ellul's categories, does the propaganda more closely resemble **classic propaganda** or **modern institutional propaganda**?
3. How do the specific **propaganda techniques** in the message promote **institutional goals**?
4. Which **stage of propaganda** does the message reflect?
5. How do **systemic factors** (according to Jowett and O'Donnell) influence the propaganda process in this message?
6. How **ethical** are the techniques used in the propaganda and what are the **ethical implications** of this propaganda?

Reflecting all of the general characteristics of propaganda, *Triumph of the Will* is an exemplar of classic propaganda theory. Its institutional sponsorship is well documented.[54] The opening credits for *Triumph of the Will* announce its connection to its sponsor and help to define the film as political propaganda that is vertical rather than horizontal: "Produced by Order of the Fuhrer. Directed by Leni Riefenstahl."[55] The film was commissioned by Adolf Hitler himself, who had admired the work of the 32-year-old actress and director Leni Riefenstahl for years. In 1933, just a few months after he had assumed dictatorial power in Germany, Hitler asked Riefenstahl to film the events of a Nazi Party rally scheduled to occur two days later. Following a hurried and stressful production, with which a resentful Minister of Propaganda Goebbels interfered, Riefenstahl completed a short documentary entitled *Victory of Faith*. Soon afterward, Hitler asked her to prepare a feature-length propaganda film of the 1934 Nazi rally in Nuremberg, guaranteeing her plenty of preparation time, an ample budget and all the resources she would need. Riefenstahl then organized a massive production effort that film historian Erik Barnouw describes as follows:

> Never had there been such mobilization and deployment of resources—men and gear. Before long she had assembled a staff of 120 people, including sixteen leading cameramen, their assistants, and supporting technicians. Thirty cameras and four sound trucks would be in operation. Twenty-two automobiles and their drivers were assigned to her, along with uniformed field police. . . . [T]he town of Nuremberg was constructing, to her specifications and on a scale without precedent, special bridges, towers, ramps. A 120-foot flagpole at the Luitpolhain was being equipped with an electric elevator, which was to be able to take a cameraman to the top in seconds.... Camera positions were staked out on city rooftops, on church towers, and in road-side ditches.[56]

Hitler made such resources available because he and Goebbels recognized the power of the mass media, especially newsreel, "to create mass intoxication and to obtain mass approval for the projected deeds of the regime in both domestic and foreign affairs."[57] Their selection of film as the medium of choice for propaganda is given additional weight by Leni Riefenstahl's comments about working for Hitler:

> The Fuhrer has recognized the importance of cinema. Where else in the world have the film's inherent potentialities to act as a chronicler and

interpreter of contemporary events been recognized in so far-sighted a manner?...

That the Fuhrer has raised film-making to a position of such pre-eminence testifies to his prophetic awareness of the unrealized suggestive power of this art form. One is familiar with documentaries. Governments have ordered them and political parties have used them for their ends. But the belief that a true and genuinely powerful national experience can be kindled through the medium of film, this belief originated in Germany.[58]

Riefenstahl's comments underscore the importance of both the suggestive power of film as a medium of propaganda and the institutional goals that film can further. Her concern with "kindling a national experience" testifies to the political and ideological significance of this propaganda film. Film scholars generally agree that *Triumph of the Will* reflected two goals: "the glorification of the Nazi party and the deification of Adolf Hitler."[59] Both of these goals, if realized, function as integrative propaganda, encouraging a passive acceptance of Hitler by the citizenry and a union with the Nazi party. Riefenstahl's recognition of the "suggestive power of this art form" testifies to the emotional and irrational character of the ideological message in *Triumph of the Will*. Film historian Richard Barsam explains:

Nazi propaganda films are marked by an emotional-nationalistic fervor; but they go much further, ignoring rational discourse in favor of an overt appeal to the aroused nationalism. Indeed, unlike the propaganda films produced in democratic countries, Nazi propaganda films make no attempt to appeal to the reason and understanding of their audience. Nazi ideology was built upon the essentially irrational doctrines of Aryan racial superiority, adherence to the will of the Fuhrer, and nationalist expansion, as well as a return to "traditional German values."[60]

The emotional and nationalistic fervor fostered by *Triumph of the Will* indicates its function as agitative propaganda, to mobilize the German population for war.

An examination of specific propaganda techniques within the film helps to explain how *Triumph of the Will* was effective in glorifying the Nazis and deifying Hitler at the same time that it roused a nationalistic fervor among the Germans. Following the credits, the film begins with the following subtitles:

On Septemper 5 1934

20 years after the outbreak of the World War

16 years after the start of German suffering

19 months after the beginning of Germany's rebirth

Adolf Hitler flew again to Nuremberg to review the columns of his faithful followers[61]

These subtitles invoke the social-historical context for the audience by reminding viewers of Germany's struggle and initiate a heroic role for Adolf Hitler as the cultural, political and military leader who reigns over the rebirth of the German nation.

Immediately following the subtitles is a visual sequence that casts Hitler in his god-like role as savior of the German state. The camera follows a lone plane skimming through the clouds, occasionally obscured by mists, and finally landing. Hitler emerges from the plane and descends to a vast crowd. His procession by open military car through the streets of Nuremberg, lined by cheering crowds and waving banners, creates a sense of the savior or returning warrior receiving a hero's welcome. The classic propaganda technique of transfer is thus produced visually as viewers are encouraged to associate Hitler with a savior who descends from the heavens to receive the praises of an adoring public. This technique is repeated throughout the film "in the many shots of Hitler photographed against the sun or sky, in the mists, clouds, and smoke."[62]

The film chronicles the remainder of the first day of the week-long Nuremberg Convention with footage of German folk festivals, torch-light parades, rallies by bonfire and rousing speeches by Hitler and his officers. Except for the official speeches, there is no commentary or direct address in the film. Instead, a musical score that mixes the heavy orchestral tones of Richard Wagner with traditional German folk music and Nazi Party songs backgrounds the visual images. Barnouw writes that "the almost physical impact of the film derives much from [Riefenstahl's] choreography of images and sounds: marching men, cheers, banners, swastikas, eagles, crowds, ancient German streets and towers, folksongs, clouds, oratory, uniforms, women, children—and above all, in a series of apparitions, the Fuhrer."[63] As Barnouw's list of symbols suggests, the film uses god-terms, in the form of sounds and visual images, to associate Hitler and the Nazis with all that is good about German life. Kracauer observes: "Symbols chosen for their stimulative power helped in the total mobilization: the city was a sea of waving swastika banners; the flames of bonfires and torches illuminated the nights; the streets and squares uninterruptedly echoed with the exciting rhythm of march music."[64] Consonant with Hitler's dictum to repeat the propagandistic message, these images and sounds are repeated throughout the film. Absent any negative images or discordant sounds, the effect is to cardstack. Moreover, the relentless repetition of waving banners, cheering crowds and marching troops creates a bandwagon effect that encourages viewers to join in the celebration of Germany's rebirth by donning a uniform, waving a banner or otherwise supporting the cause.

As the film shifts to dawn of the second day, a more subtle elaboration of the heroic story of Germany's rebirth begins. To the tune of inspirational music fitting for the dawn, an array of neatly pitched tents provides a panorama of the encampment of military personnel and Hitler Youth around Nuremberg. As the camera follows their morning routines and general comeraderie, viewers likely associate the military personnel as "plain folks" who, through hard work and clean living, are helping to build a new world. It is, as Hitler suggested, an agreeable story that invokes traditional German values—what Jowett and O'Donnell term the "cultural rim" for propaganda.

The film continues for the next 90 minutes with footage of heroic revelry, crisp marching, crowded rallies and stirring oratory. The speeches by Hitler and others include other classic techniques of propaganda, such as glittering generalities, name-calling and cardstacking. As Barsam observes, however, Riefenstahl's careful camera-work and editing encourages viewers "to look at the speaker rather than listen to his banal oratory."[65] The result is an emotionally charged film that inflames the passions and stirs the soul more than it engages the intellect. As noted above, probably more important than any single episode or speech in the film is the progression and repetition of events that Riefenstahl chronicles. As viewers see march after march, rally after rally, banner after banner—each larger and more ecstatic in its emotional tone—a compelling bandwagon effect is created. By the conclusion of the film, the sweeping, panoramic shots from the sky of columns of troops marching in formation and saluting Hitler prepare viewers to accept both the glory of Nazi Germany and the heroic character of Adolf Hitler.

The strong emotional tone of the film suggests that *Triumph of the Will* is a message well-suited to the pre-propaganda stage. Film historian William K. Everson points out that in 1934, when the film was made, Nazism "was far from being a complete *fait accompli*."[66] Certainly, the emotional tension created by the film seems appropriate for a movement that is first arousing its audience. However, the strong bandwagon effects and relentless sense of movement in the film argue for placing it at a later stage of the propaganda campaign such as mobilization. Also, at least 11 other films advocating the Nazi Party and a host of election films that chronicled political victories of the Nazis preceded *Triumph of the Will*.[67] These films, along with the fictional, mythic romances that Riefenstahl had earlier directed and starred in probably are better examples of the pre-propaganda stage in that they laid the ground for audience identification with a hero who comes from the mountain to restore the dignity and idealism of a struggling community.

While *Triumph of the Will* effectively espoused the glory and pomp of Nazism, like all classic propaganda, it did so on questionable ethical grounds. While the film does not conceal its source or theme, it does provide a fabricated and deceptive view of reality. More subtle than the "big lie" of *The Eternal Jew* and other propaganda that proclaimed the superiority of Aryan purity, Riefenstahl's film both omits important facts about Nazism and provides a deceptive portrait of German life under Nazi rule. Obviously, the terror of the Nazi genocidal program and tyrannical oppression of dissent is absent from the film. In addition, Barsam observes that the film's "narrative continuity does not match the chronological sequence of the actual events of the sixth party rally."[68] Apparently, Riefenstahl's compelling bandwagon effect required a more careful sequencing of events than organizers on the scene were able to provide. Kracauer argues convincingly that the entire film is a historical fabrication:

> Through a very impressive composition of mere newsreel shots, this film represents the complete transformation of reality, its complete absorption into the artificial structure of the Party Convention. The Nazis had painstakingly prepared the ground for such a metamorphosis: grandiose architectural arrangements were made to encompass the mass movements, and, under the personal supervision of Hitler, precise plans of the marches and parades had been drawn up long before the event. Thus the Convention could evolve literally in a space and a time of its own; thanks to perfect manipulation, it became not so much a spontaneous demonstration as a

> gigantic extravaganza with nothing left to improvisation. This staged show, which channeled the psychic energies of hundreds of thousands of people, differed from the average monster spectacle only in that it pretended to be an expression of the people's real existence.[69]

Kracauer's assessment, like that of many classic propaganda theorists concentrates on the truth of the film and finds such truth lacking.

Just as important as the classic concern for truth in propaganda is the contemporary concern for other ethical issues raised by propaganda. Two such issues stand out in regard to *Triumph of the Will*. First, the existence of effective propaganda such as *Triumph of the Will* raises the question of how to ethically respond to it. Earlier in this chapter, we reported Frank Capra's description of *Triumph of the Will* as a lethal weapon of the Nazis. In his autobiography, Capra elaborated on this claim by recalling his own response to viewing the film.

> That film paralyzed the will of Austria, Czechoslovakia, Scandinavia, and France. That film paved the way for the Blitzkrieg. That film practically paralyzed my own will as I walked slowly back to my battered desk to sit alone and unnoticed in a roomful of officers, each engrossed in his own inadequacies to meet the challenge of war.[70]

Capra eventually produced his own counter-propaganda films in order to challenge the power of *Triumph of the Will* and other Nazi propaganda. But as we mentioned earlier, late in his life, Capra continued to question whether his decision to "fight fire with fire" was ethical. We could add to Capra's self-questioning our own concern for how to treat such an effective instance of propaganda. Everson notes that: "Even in retrospect, and fully aware of the horrors and degradations that followed, the film still retains its hypnotic impact."[71] Is the analysis of it here sufficient to blunt that impact? Or is a replaying of the film, even for educational purposes, ethically irresponsible?

A second issue emerges from the first; there is a concern for whether or not a message that furthers a morally reprehensible cause can ever be deemed ethically appropriate. After all, the violations of truth—a narrative out of sequence, omissions and created events—cited for *Triumph of the Will* are illustrative of persuasive techniques common to a variety of non-propagandistic campaigns and movements. These techniques alone seem pale markers by which to condemn a message as unethical. Hence, in recent years, a number of film critics have extolled the beauty and artistic grace of *Triumph of the Will* even as they decry the cause for which it stood; others argue that the effects of the film negate any praise of its artistic merit.[72] Susan Sontag, a contemporary feminist critic, argues convincingly that the real impact of Riefenstahl's film is the ideology that it presents rather than the facts that it omits. She explains that "facism stands for an ideal, and one that is persistent today, under other banners: the ideal of life as art, the cult of beauty, the fetishism of courage, the dissolution of alienation in ecstatic feelings of community; the repudiation of the intellect; the family of man (under the parenthood of leaders)." She concludes that the contemporary impulse to praise Riefenstahl's art even as we condemn her cause ignores these underlying principles of fascism, suggesting an inability among contemporary audiences and critics "to detect the fascist longings in our own midst."[73]

Notes

1. Erik Barnouw, *Documentary: A History of the Non-Fiction Film*, revised edition (Oxford: Oxford University Press, 1983), 103.
2. Frank Capra, *The Name Above the Title* (New York: Bantam Books, 1972), 362-363.
3. Richard M. Barsam, *Nonfiction Film: A Critical History* (Bloomington: Indiana University Press, 1992), 129-130; William K. Everson, "The Triumph of the Will," *The Documentary Tradition: From Nanook to Woodstock*, Ed. Lewis Jacobs (New York: Hopkins and Blake, 1971), 138-140.
4. J. Michael Sproule, "Social Responses to Twentieth-Century Propaganda," in *Propaganda: A Pluralistic Perspective*, ed. Ted J. Smith III (New York: Praeger, 1989), 10-11. See also, Sproule, *Channels of Propaganda* (Bloomington: EDINTO Press, 1994), 1-51.
5. Sproule, "Social Responses," 5-22.
6. Sproule, "Social Responses," 17.
7. Garth S. Jowett and Victoria O'Donnell, *Propaganda and Persuasion* (Beverly Hills: Sage, 1986), 15.
8. George Creel, *How We Advertised America: The First Telling of the Amazing Story of the Committee on Public Information* (New York: Harper & Row, 1920).
9. Jacques Ellul, *Propaganda: The Formation of Men's Attitudes*, trans. Konrad Kellen and Jean Lerner (New York: Vintage, 1966), x.
10. Rebecca Lieb, "Nazi Hate Movies Continue to Ignite Fierce Passions," the *New York Times* (August 4, 1991): 16H.
11. "WWII: The Propaganda Battle," in *A Walk Through the 20th Century With Bill Moyers*, Executive Producers Charles Grinker and Sanford H. Fisher, Public Broadcasting System, 1982. Transcription by the authors.
12. Lieb, "Nazi Hate Movies," 16H.
13. "WWII: The Propaganda Battle."
14. "WWII: The Propaganda Battle."
15. J. Michael Sproule, "Propaganda Studies in American Social Science: The Rise and Fall of the Critical Paradigm," *Quarterly Journal of Speech* 73 (1987): 60-78.
16. J. A. C. Brown, *Techniques of Persuasion: From Propaganda to Brainwashing* (Baltimore MD: Penguin Books, 1963), reported by Charles U. Larson, *Persuasion: Reception and Responsibility*, 5th Ed (Belmont: Wadsworth, 1989), 364-365.
17. "WWII: The Propaganda Battle."
18. Jowett and O'Donnell, *Propaganda and Persuasion*, 136.
19. J. Michael Sproule, "The New Managerial Rhetoric and the Old Criticism," *Quarterly Journal of Speech* 74 1988): 472-474.
20. Marvin Karlins and Herbert I. Abelson, *Persuasion: How Opinions and Attitudes Are Changed*, 2nd Ed. (New York: Springer, 1970), 13-14.
21. Roderick P. Hart, "The Rhetoric of the True Believer," *Speech Monographs* 38 (November 1971): 249-261.
22. Hart, "Rhetoric of the True Believer," 259.

23. Karlins and Abelson, *Persuasion*, 98-99.
24. Carl Hovland, E. Campbell and T. Brock, "The Effects of 'Commitment' on Opinion Change Following Communication," in Carl I. Hovland, E. Campbell and T. Brock, *The Order of Presentation in Persuasion* (New Haven CT: Yale University Press, 1957).
25. See, Jacques Ellul, *Propaganda: The Formation of Men's Attitudes*, trans. Konrad Kellen and Jean Lerner (New York: Vintage Books, 1973).
26. Ellul, *Propaganda*, 61.
27. Randall L. Bytwerk, "Western and Totalitarian Views of Propaganda," in *Propaganda: A Pluralistic Perspective*, 37-48.
28. Ellul, *Propaganda*, 62-70.
29. Ellul, *Propaganda*, 64-65.
30. Ellul, *Propaganda*, 70-79.
31. Bytwerk, "Western and Totalitarian Views," 43.
32. Ellul, *Propaganda*, 79-84.
33. Ellul, *Propaganda*, 80.
34. Ellul, *Propaganda*, 80-81.
35. Ellul, *Propaganda*, 84-87.
36. Bytwerk, "Western and Totalitarian Views," 38.
37. Ellul, *Propaganda*, 85.
38. Jowett and O'Donnell, *Propaganda*, 209-210.
39. Jowett and O'Donnell, *Propaganda*, 210-211.
40. Jowett and O'Donnell, *Propaganda*, 212.
41. Jowett and O'Donnell, *Propaganda*, 215-216.
42. Jowett and O'Donnell, *Propaganda*, 216.
43. For an analysis of this case as a propaganda campaign, see Stanley B. Cunningham, "Smoke and Mirrors: A Confirmation of Jacques Ellul's Theory of Information Use in Propaganda," in *Propaganda: A Pluralistic Perspective*, 151-163.
44. For an analysis of such operations by the KGB, see Roy Godson, "'Active Measures' in Contemporary Soviet Strategy," in *Propaganda: A Pluralistic Perspective*, 99-113.
45. Ted J. Smith III, "Propaganda and the Techniques of Deception," in *Propaganda: A Pluralistic Perspective*, 82.
46. Victoria O'Donnell and Garth S. Jowett, "Propaganda as a Form of Communication," in *Propaganda: A Pluralistic Perspective*, 54-59.
47. O'Donnell and Jowett, 54-56.
48. Details of this campaign are available in O'Donnell and Jowett, 57.
49. "WWII: The Propaganda Battle."
50. "WWII: The Propaganda Battle."
51. Lieb, "Nazi Hate Movies," 15H.
52. Ellul, *Propaganda*, xvi. For an elaboration of Ellul's position, see Richard L. Johannesen, *Ethics in Human Communication*, 3rd Ed (Prospect Heights: Waveland, 1990), 123.
53. Bytwerk, "Western and Totalitarian Views," 44.

54. Historical details of the making of *Triumph of the Will* are based on an account by Barnouw, *Documentary*, 100-104, unless otherwise noted; see also, Siegfried Kracauer, *From Caligari to Hitler: A Psychological History of the German Film* (Princeton: Princeton University Press, 1974), 298-304.
55. Barnouw, *Documentary*, 103. Barnouw notes that various translations of the German credits are possible.
56. Barnouw, *Documentary*, 101-102.
57. Barsam, *Nonfiction*, 129.
58. Quoted in Barnouw, *Documentary*, 103.
59. Barsam, *Nonfiction*, 130.
60. Barsam, *Nonfiction*, 124.
61. English translation of these subtitles is provided by Barnouw, *Documenatary*, 105.
62. Barsam, *Nonfiction*, 130.
63. Barnouw, *Documentary*, 103-104.
64. Kracauer, *From Calgari*, 301.
65. Barsam, *Nonfiction*, 130.
66. Everson, "The Triumph," 138.
67. Barsam, *Nonfiction*, 125-126.
68. Barsam, *Nonfiction*, 130.
69. Kracauer, *From Calgari*, 300.
70. Capra, *The Name*, 364.
71. Everson, "The Triumph," 139.
72. Everson, "The Triumph," 138-140; for a review of other such treatments, see Susan Sontag, "Fascinating Fascism," 31-44.
73. Sontag, "Fascinating Fascism," 43-44.

Index

A

ABC 2
AIDS 7, 62, 63, 77-84, 109, 160-161, 218, 246, 340
Alinsky, Saul 269, 274-275, 282
"America Responds to AIDS" 63, 78, 81
Anaphora 150
Antithesis 143, 151
Aristotle 4, 11, 14, 24-37, 44, 46, 52, 86–92, 97-100, 177, 188
  analysis of the emotions 24, 26, 64, 66-69, 75, 78, 79
  definition of rhetoric 13, 25
  principles of delivery 28, 162–163
  Rhetoric 25–26, 28, 29, 44, 64, 75, 132
Audience
  and modes of proof 24
  as a market 16
  as center of persuasion 8–9
  as public 9
  as source of warrants 48–49
  as the masses 10
  defining 225–228
  segmentation 225–226
  target audience 225–226

B

Backing for warrant 45–46
Bailey, F.G. 12, 21
Balance theory 69-70, 72, 88
Barbour, Haley 235
Behaviorism 31, 32
Belief system 300-302, 310
Benevolent community 298
Black, Max 155
Boorstin, Daniel 94-96, 98, 105, 168, 222, 238
Boycott 265-266, 286
Budweiser television spots 169
Burke, Kenneth 158, 162, 188
  "Definition of Man" 120, 130
  dramatistic pentad 306

psychology of form 113, 182–188
Bush, George 17
Bush, George W. 2, 17, 18, 19, 20

C

Campaigns
and communication networks 253–255
and media 243-259
characteristics 246
defined 243
ethics 256–259
measuring success of 251
types 243
Campbell, George 132, 135
Campbell, Joseph 191-194
Capra, Frank 298, 322-325, 333, 340-342, 347-348
Carter, Jimmy 57-60, 137, 297, 332
CBS 2, 17, 66, 83, 223, 340
Centers for Disease Control (CDC) 62-63, 77-79, 81-82
Charisma
and social movement leadership 93–94, 270, 281
defined 86
Chavez, Cesar 284-287
Cicero 25-35, 41-42, 97, 163, 188
Claim 44–46
Claptrap 164
Classical Perspective
defined 24
Clinton, Bill 3, 27, 89, 142, 211, 235, 236, 254
Closure 184–185, 195
Codes 159, 166, 174
Cognitive dissonance 33, 69-88, 248
Compliance-gaining 197, 206
Connotation 129, 135-138, 145-146, 151
Consciousness-raising 312, 327
Constitutive 131
Constructed Images 159, 166-173
Credibility
and dynamism 89, 91
traditional elements 87, 89–91
Culture
defined 294

D

"Daisy" political spot 157-177, 281
Data 44-60
Delivery 28–29, 91, 159, 162–179
Demosthenes 162
Denotation 129, 132, 135
"Devil Terms" 129, 138-139, 149, 151, 276-278, 281, 304, 327, 331, 334
Dewey, John 189, 323
Dialectic 24, 27, 44
Direct mail 224, 251, 258
Discursive symbolism
  and language 110–111
  and meaning 110, 118
  characteristics 110, 159
Doctrinal persuasion 334
Dreyfus, Richard 261
Dukakis, Michael 67, 256

E

Electronic Data Systems (EDS) 180-181, 203
Ellul, Jacques 318, 321, 331-33, 337-38, 343-45
Elocutionist 163
Emblems 159-161
Emotions 24-40, 62-90, 130, 142, 162, 173, 326
Empowerment 268, 342
Enthymeme 27-28, 38, 46, 333
Equilibrium theories 64, 69, 72, 74-75, 88
Ethics
  and audience segmentation 257–264
  and campaigns 256–264
  and credibility 97–106
  and emotional appeals 75–76
  and empowerment 342
  and ideology 310–313
  and language 144–156
  and message form and structure 199–207
  and nonverbal symbols 171–179
  and obscenity 282
  and professional codes 281
  and propaganda 340–350
  and social movements 281–289
  and tests of evidence and reasoning 51–61
  and the "Willie Horton" political ads 259
  in the Classical Perspective 34–42

in the Institutional Perspective 230–241
in the Symbolist Perspective 121–128
virtue ethics 97
Evidence
tests of validity 30–31
Example 47–48

F

Fantasy theme analysis 227, 299, 318
Figurative language
anaphora 142, 148
antithesis 142,149
figures of speech versus figures of thought 140, 153, 194
hyperbole 142
irony 94, 140-41, 267, 283, 326
metaphor
oxymoron 136, 142
associated commonplaces 139
defined 138
focus 139-40
force 140
frame 139-40
parallelism 142, 148
Film
as implicit persuasion 7–8
Focus groups 135, 227, 253, 256
Folk tale 192, 195
"Foot-in-the-Door" technique 199
Form
psychology of 182–207
types identified by Kenneth Burke 185–187
Frankfurt School 300, 320

G

General Semantics 153
Genre 7
"Gillette: "The Best a Man Can Get"" 291-292, 314-321
Gingrich, Newt 135, 139, 234, 304
"God terms" 139, 147, 149-151, 304-307, 327, 334
Goebbels, Joseph 325-326, 337, 343
Goldwater, Barry 157-158, 175-176, 280-281
GOPTV 208, 233-237, 241

H

Hegemony 301
Heider, Fritz 69-70, 74, 83, 88
"Herding Cats" 180-182, 201-203
Hippler, Franz 325-326, 330, 341
Hitler, Adolph 16, 91-94, 146, 156, 277, 279, 322, 325-326, 329-350
Hoffer, Eric 277-278, 288
Horton, Willie 67-68, 251, 259
Hovland, Carl 32-33, 41, 205, 349
Humanistic growth psychology
  growth defined 74
  hierarchy of needs 73–74
Hussein, Saddam 152, 329-332, 340

I

Icon 102, 136, 157, 159, 161
Identification 11, 16, 93, 100, 108-109, 114-120, 123-126, 131, 133, 143, 147, 148, 158-159, 161-162, 170-172, 174-175, 194, 228, 259, 275, 278, 332-333, 341, 346
Ideographs 154, 304-307, 313-316
Ideology
  and mass audiences 295
  as false consciousness 310–311
  defined 292
  stages of formation 303–321
Image management 86, 91, 94, 96, 99-103
Induction
  logical 28
  rhetorical 28
Institute for Propaganda Analysis 326, 331
Institutional Perspective
  characteristics 213–214
  defined 210
Instrumental 130, 131
Invention 28, 42

J

Jackson, Jesse 144, 255, 279
Jamieson, Kathleen Hall 99, 106, 174-177, 179, 280, 289
Johannesen, Richard 21, 42, 61, 82-84, 99, 106, 122, 128, 145-147, 155-156, 178-179, 230, 240-241, 264, 289, 349
Johnson, Lyndon B.
  1964 presidential campaign 157–158
  reaction to the "Daisy" television spot 158

Jowett, Garth 105, 128, 204, 320, 338-341, 343, 345, 348-349

K

Kennedy , John F. 21, 143, 155
Kent State University 115-117
Kentucky Fried Chicken (KFC) 85-86, 99-106
KGB 339-340, 349
Kilbourn, Jean 290-291, 309, 313, 318, 320
Kimbrell, Andrew 317-318, 321
King, Martin Luther, Jr.
  "I Have A Dream" speech 140
  use of nonviolent tactics 93
Knapp, Mark 164, 166, 177-178, 204, 206
Kracauer, Siegfried 345-347, 350

L

Langer, Suzanne K. 127
Levels of meaning 172
Lincoln, Abraham 82, 143, 297
Logic 6, 9, 22, 26-27, 30-31, 38, 44, 49-52, 54, 60-62, 64, 68-70, 73-75, 77, 81, 86, 88, 104, 106, 113-118, 121, 138-139, 142, 146, 156, 161, 185-186, 189, 194, 213, 231, 234-235, 247, 253, 256, 276, 282, 286, 291-294, 299-302, 305, 308-322, 327, 332, 334-337, 340, 342, 344, 346, 350

M

Malcolm X 66, 83
Market segmentation 225
Marx, Karl 299-301, 306, 310, 319, 334
Masculinity 7, 16, 240, 290, 292, 314-318
Maslow, Abraham 15, 33, 73-75, 81, 83-84, 114, 127, 229, 240
McCarthy , Joseph 153, 298
McCroskey, James 42, 60, 90, 104-105, 204
Media
  Agenda-setting function of 220–221
  as an institution 213–214
  directional 224–225
  free 215
  gatekeeper theory 208
Media Image
  characteristics 95, 95–96
  versus *ethos* 96
Mehrabian, Albert 164, 166, 178
Men

as success objects 290
portrayal in advertising 291, 313–321
Message
defined 5
Militant 266, 271-273, 278-279, 286
Moderates 265, 271-273, 279
Modes of Proof
ethos 8, 26-38, 86-104, 133
logos 26-28, 30, 31-35, 38-39, 44, 64
pathos 26, 28, 30-31, 33, 35, 38
Monroe, Alan H. 189, 205
Motivated sequence 189
Moyers, Bill 158, 177, 325-326, 330, 341, 348
Myth of objectivity 1, 12-13, 192-194, 200, 227, 235, 293, 297-298, 301-303, 307, 316

N

Naming 131–156
Narrative form
narrative fidelity 194, 195
narrative probability 194, 195
National Rifle Association (NRA) 22-23 36, 37, 38, 39, 40, 42
NBC 1-2, 20-21
Neutron bomb 136, 137, 154
News
and pseudo-events 222, 224
and the free media 221–222, 224
news beat 218, 219, 222
"Newspeak" 134, 153
No Grapes 266, 283-287
Nondirectional 224-225, 227
Nondiscursive codes 159
Nondiscursive symbolism, characteristics 111
Nontraditional messages 273, 274, 282
Nonverbal symbols
elements in advertising 173
function 159–160, 160–161
meaning 159, 159–160, 160
structure 111
North Atlantic Shaving Group 291, 314, 318

O

O'Donnell, Victoria 338-341, 343, 345, 348-349
Oldsmobile 107-109, 124-126

Orwell, George 134, 137, 153-156, 335
Osgood, Charles 87-89, 104

P

Pain 28, 64-65, 67-69, 74, 120, 309
Patterns of thinking
  analogical 49
  categorical 49–50
  causal 50–51
  disjunctive 50
Pearl Harbor 129, 150
Perceptual processes
  abstraction 185
  association 185
  classification 185
  edging 185
  hierarchy 185
  rhythm 185
Perelman, Chaim 31
Persuasion
  and coercion 5
  and free speech 3
  and objectivity 12–13
  defined 4–5
  dimensions
    audience-centered/persuader-centered 8–9
    implicit/explicit 7–8
    intentional/unintentional 6
    public/nonpublic 9–10
  from the Classical perspective 6, 11, 23–24
  from the Institutional perspective 11–12, 212–213
  from the Symbolist perspective 8–9, 11, 108–128
Piaget, Jean 198, 206
Plato
  attack on rhetoric 97
  myth of the cave 310, 311
  Phaedrus 97
Pleasure 64-65, 67, 69, 73-74, 87, 114, 139, 141, 143, 187, 191, 194, 251
Polemic response 323, 342
Postman, Neil 172, 179, 232, 240
Propaganda
  and democratic society 335
  and doctrine 337
  and the mass audience 10, 213, 336

characteristics of 324–328
classic techniques of 329–333
defined 213, 324
Ellul's characteristics of 335–338
ethics and 340–342
explicit versus implicit conclusions in 333
resistance to 333–350
Public relations 18, 34, 86, 94, 102-103, 222-224, 238, 243, 246, 253, 257, 289, 323, 339
Pyle, Leroy 36-39

Q

Qualifier 44, 46, 52-53
Quintilian 25, 28, 41, 97, 188

R

Reagan, Ronald
"Facts are stubborn things" speech 43, 55–61
use of TelePrompTer 164
"Real Food" advertising campaign 242–243
"Real-fiction" 172
Rebuttal 44, 46, 47, 52, 54
Reference groups 226, 227, 228
Reflective thinking 189
Republican National Committee (RNC) 233, 234, 236
Rhetoric 13, 21, 24-25, 28-29, 41-42, 44, 64, 75, 83-84, 104-105, 127, 132, 152-155, 177-179, 188, 204-205, 227, 240, 287-289, 319-320
defined 25
Rhetorica ad Herennium 188
Rhetorical question 144, 147
Rhetorical Vision 240
Rhetorical vision 227
Riefenstahl, Leni 322, 343-347
Ritual 120, 174, 187, 192, 194, 196, 205, 249, 250, 251, 277, 300, 308, 316, 325, 331
Rocky 316
Rogers, Everett 82, 84, 86, 240, 247, 248, 264
Rooney, Andy 66, 67, 83
Roosevelt, Franklin
"Declaration of War" speech to Congress 129–156, 148–156
Rushing, Janice H. 200, 205-207

S

Sanders, Col. Harlan 85-86, 100-103, 106
Schwartz, Tony 157, 169, 172, 176-179
Selectivity 184
Shatner, William 124-128
Social movement
  purity of motives 278
  reform versus radical 282
  tactics 282
  types of persusive messages 282
Social values
  defined 294–321
  typical American values 252, 297, 298
Sours, James K. 115-120, 127
Star Trek 236
Subliminal persuasion 64, 75–76
Super Bowl 180, 201, 204, 223
Symbol
  defined 109
  symbolic reality versus empirical reality 120
Symbolic action 21, 48, 114, 119, 123, 128, 153, 288, 320
Symbolist perspective
  assumptions 122

T

Tannenbaum, Percy 88-89, 104
Tension reduction 72-73
The Eternal Jew 325-326, 341, 346
Toulmin Model 31, 43-46, 52, 60
Triumph of the Will 322, 324, 342-344, 346-348, 350
Tropes, Stephen 155
True Believer 276, 288, 348
Tourette Syndrome Association (TSA) 242-243, 260-263

U

United Farm Workers of America (UFW) 266, 283-286

V

Validity
  formal 44
Virtues
  and culture 98
  Athenian 87

feminine 98

W

Watzlawick, Paul 21
Weaver, Richard 138-139, 153-154, 304
Weber, Max 92-94, 105
Whorf/Sapir 133, 153
Why We Fight 322, 325, 341-342
Women
  oppression of 291
  portrayal in advertising 291
World view 6, 14-16, 126, 137, 139, 148, 161, 291-297, 300-318